Only in Oklahoma

Collected columns originally published
in the Tulsa World during
Oklahoma's centennial year

By GENE CURTIS

Dedication

This book is dedicated to the fascinating history of Oklahoma.

– Gene Curtis

Acknowledgments

EDITORS: Debbie Jackson, Rusty Lang

GRAPHICS EDITOR: David Housh

COPY EDITOR: Phil Lamb

GRAPHICS ASSISTANCE: Brad Harvey, Brad Thompson, Sean Rowley

PHOTOGRAPHIC RESEARCH: Rachele Vaughan

ARCHIVAL RESEARCH: Hilary Pittman, Rachele Vaughan

COVER DESIGN: David Carman

PRINTING: Walsworth Publishing Co.

Table of Contents

Table of Contents (cont.)

Table of Contents (cont.)

Table of Contents (cont.)

Fears fizzled over new year of 2000

Oklahomans, along with millions of other Americans, were relieved on Jan. 1, 2000.

Everything still worked. Water flowed, and electricity powered lights and appliances. Computers worked.

The previous midnight had been the most-watched in history, as mankind stood on the threshold of what most considered a new century and a new millennium.

Predictions of dire circumstances had prompted many to stockpile food and to take money out of banks in the year or so leading up to the new year of 2000. They bought portable generators, kerosene heaters and propane stoves in preparation for doomsday.

Tulsa World archives

A bottled-water shelf at Albertson's is nearly empty on Dec. 31, 1999.

But few Oklahomans were that concerned.

And none of the predictions proved true.

Many considered it a new century and a new millennium, but purists insisted that the 21st century and the new millennium really wouldn't begin for another year – on Jan. 1, 2001. Everything also still worked on that date, but such dire events hadn't been forecast in regard to that midnight.

The same issue raged when the 1800s turned into the 1900s – did the new century begin in 1900 or 1901? The Bartlesville Magnet asked editorially, "Was there a year 0?" Pointing out that the debate was continuing, the newspaper said, "We await the results in breathless anxiety."

The issue hadn't been settled 100 years later.

Regardless, it was a unique situation. For the first time, people had to change all four digits when writing the year. Few people alive in 2000 would have been old enough to be concerned about the century change 100 years earlier.

Most Oklahomans weren't greatly concerned about the 1999 doomsday predictions. A Tulsa World poll showed that 71 percent of Sooners considered it just another new year.

Rural area residents were even less excited than residents of Tulsa and Oklahoma City, according to the World-sponsored poll taken by Tulsa Surveys in early December. It was just another year in the opinion of 74 percent of those living outside the two cities; 69 percent in Tulsa and 67 percent in Oklahoma City shared that feeling.

Many Oklahomans partied as usual on New Year's Eve, and while many around the world may have stockpiled jugs of water, the drink of choice in Oklahoma appeared to be champagne.

Others celebrated the new year by attending church services. Many churches offered communion at midnight.

Meanwhile, millions around the world packed streets to welcome 2000, and the drop of a huge crystal ball in New York's Times Square set off an explosion of fireworks and cheering, a celebration watched on television by millions throughout the country.

Although financial institutions in Tulsa and around the country were prepared for large cash withdrawals, they didn't occur. Two large Tulsa banks reported only a 5 percent increase in cash withdrawals. Stocks ended 1999 at record highs.

Seattle canceled a big New Year's Eve celebration for fear of terrorism. The fear stemmed from the arrests a few days earlier in Washington state and Vermont of a man and woman who belonged to a violent Algerian group. FBI agents had fanned out around the country investigating charges of smuggling explosives into the U.S.

Around the world, armies of employees had to forgo parties and stay at work just in case the Y2K bug attacked computers.

In 1900, by contrast, there were several New Year's Eve football games and a turkey shoot were held, and perhaps cowboys fired off their revolvers to welcome in the new year. And there was New Year's Day football, but fans couldn't watch the games on television in the comfort of their homes. One of those games was between a Tulsa team and the Vinita team. Tulsa won 35-0.

A New Year's Day turkey shoot was held at Krebs, young people at Claremore welcomed the new year with a "masque ball," and the Eastern Star held an open house at Vinita for guests to partake of dainty refreshments.

Some may have feared the end of the world as predicted by Elder Hicks of the Methodist Church, but newspapers didn't play up that possibility. Hicks chronologists had placed the time as not later than 1915.

Oklahomans were likely more concerned about the weather than whether things would still function. Weather forecasting at that time was more about looking out a window at the clouds than about studying maps and isobars.

The Claremore Chieftain newspaper called the 1800s the "best century the world ever saw."

"We can all agree upon this proposition for we have all belonged to it. It has given us steam boats, railroad trains, the electric telegraph and telephone, electric lights, dynamite to blow up the people, the new woman and the bicycle, new theology and the Mauser rifle to kill each other with."

If that editor could have seen what came in the 1900s.

Senator's death leads to office swap

The New Year's Day death of Sen. Robert S. Kerr, whose career stretched from a log cabin near Ada to vast wealth and the title of "uncrowned king of the Senate," touched off a political version of musical chairs in 1963:

Gov. J. Howard Edmondson resigned.

Lt. Gov. George Nigh became governor and appointed Edmondson to fill Kerr's Senate seat.

Henry Bellmon was inaugurated as the state's first Republican governor nine days later, and Nigh returned to another term as lieutenant governor.

Nigh, who had lost a bid for governor in the 1962 primary election, said he agreed to make the appointment of Edmondson after conferring with President John F. Kennedy, who was "personally pleased" that Edmondson was to be appointed. Edmondson and Nigh met with Kennedy while the president was in Oklahoma City for the 66-year-old Kerr's funeral.

Associated Press

Honor guards stand at attention beside the casket containing the body of Sen. Robert S. Kerr, D-Okla., at the state Capitol Rotunda in Oklahoma City on Jan. 3, 1963, two days after his death.

Oklahoma's senior senator and former governor died while sitting up in his hospital bed telling his doctor one of the many jokes for which he was famous on the Senate floor. He had been hospitalized for a little over two weeks for a respiratory ailment and had appeared to be improving. Death was attributed to a blockage in an artery to the heart.

Edmondson learned of Kerr's death while in Miami, Fla., watching the Orange Bowl football game between the University of Oklahoma and Alabama, and informed President Kennedy, who also was at the game, at halftime. Speculation about Kerr's successor immediately centered on Edmondson or his brother, 2nd District Rep. Ed Edmondson of Muskogee.

J. Howard Edmondson's position as a U.S. senator turned out to be temporary – he was defeated for the Democratic nomination for a term of his own in May 1964 by state Sen. Fred Harris of Lawton, who was opposed in the general election by Republican Bud Wilkinson, former University of Oklahoma football coach.

Wilkinson's gridiron popularity didn't extend to the political playing field and he was defeated by 21,000 votes, although he drew more votes than any other Republican on the ballot in Oklahoma that year.

Kerr's third term in the Senate would not have expired until Jan. 1, 1967. However, his successor could serve only until the next general election in November 1964, when the office went up for elective grabs for the remaining two years.

Edmondson went into law practice in Oklahoma City and sometimes considered re-entering politics, but didn't. He died in November 1971.

Harris took office immediately after the November 1964 general election and was re-elected in 1966.

What was considered to be a liberal voting record in the Senate caused Harris to lose favor with Oklahoma voters, but it increased his popularity with national liberals. He didn't seek re-election in 1972 but instead became a candidate for the Democratic nomination for president.

He dropped out before the primary election due to lack of finances. He made another bid for president in 1976, but poor showings in early primaries caused him to bow out again and move to New Mexico, where he became a history professor at the University of New Mexico.

Kerr was responsible for the Kerr-McClellan waterway that stretches from the Port of Catoosa to the Mississippi River. He and Dean A. McGee of Oklahoma City, who were partners in the Kerr-McGee Oil Co., began Tulsa radio station KRMG and organized the Farmers and Merchants Bank that later became F&M Bank.

Governor took oath in Tulsa

All except one of Oklahoma's governors have taken the oath of office in the state capital – either Guthrie or Oklahoma City.

That one was George P. Nigh, whose inauguration for his second short term as governor was at Bartlett Square on Tulsa's Main Mall on Jan. 3, 1979.

The swearing-in of Nigh marked several firsts for the 51-year-old lieutenant governor from McAlester. He became the first person to take the oath of governor a second time, the first (and, so far, the only) to take the oath in Tulsa, and the first to be sworn in any place except the capital.

And those weren't Nigh's only firsts; five days later, he became the first person to take the oath a third time, and four years later he became the first person to repeat the oath for a fourth time.

The Tulsa ceremony was almost a spur-of-the-moment event. Nigh had been elected to a full four-year term at the general election in November and was scheduled to take office on Jan. 9 in a ceremony at the Capitol in Oklahoma City.

But Gov. David Boren had been elected to the Senate in the same election to replace ailing Sen. Dewey Bartlett, who was not a candidate for re-election. Boren resigned from the Governor's Office on Jan. 2 to allow him to gain seniority over other freshman senators.

Boren didn't take the oath of office as a senator until Jan. 15. Bartlett kept his pledge to serve his entire term, which ended on Jan. 3.

Nigh recalled recently that his inauguration committee had already made plans for his swearing-in and he didn't want to upset those plans by having a ceremony in Oklahoma City on Jan. 3 and a sequel five days later. "So, I thought, why not move the inauguration someplace else?" he said. He picked Tulsa because the people in Tulsa "have always been good to me."

Nigh also noted that Tulsa would be the base city for that year's celebration of the Will Rogers Centennial, and Nigh had been named by the Legislature to plan the celebration.

He said he chose the exact spot where he took the oath because of a conversation he had with a woman at that spot while campaigning for governor several months earlier.

"She told me, 'It'll be a cold day in Tulsa before you ever become governor,'" Nigh said.

"Well, it is, and I am, and we're here," Nigh told about 300 people.

And he was correct. It was a cold day in Tulsa, although the temperature had climbed to 36 from an early morning low of 10. That temperature had melted much of the snow and ice that fell on the city over the weekend. But the cold returned later that week, schools were closed for four days by ice and snow, and at least three died in weather-related traffic accidents.

Chief U.S. District Court Judge Allen E. Barrow administered the oath of office near the fountain on Main Mall, an area later named Bartlett Square in memory of Bartlett, who died a few weeks later.

The front page of the Tulsa World for Jan. 4, 1979, reported that Nigh as governor was just like Nigh as lieutenant governor – informal, joking, bragging about the state and poking fun at himself.

Lt. Gov. Nigh took his first oath as governor – for a nine-day term – in January 1963 after Sen. Robert S. Kerr died and Gov. J. Howard Edmondson resigned so he could be appointed to the Senate seat by Nigh.

Nigh took the oath as governor a third time on Jan. 9 for the first full four-year term of his own and was sworn in as governor for a fourth time four years later – the first person to serve two consecutive terms.

Nigh joked to the crowd on the mall: "This will break my personal record as the governor who served the shortest time," alluding to his earlier nine-day term.

"Just think," he added, "if you have the seven-day virus, you will miss my whole administration."

Tulsa World archives

George Nigh takes the oath of office for his second short term as governor on Jan. 3, 1979, at the Bartlett Square fountain in downtown Tulsa. He is the only Oklahoma governor to take the oath in Tulsa.

Hunt came from everywhere

Joe B. Hunt "came from near here" – all over Oklahoma.

That's how the popular officeholder became part of the political crowds while campaigning for state insurance commissioner, a post he occupied for 20 years.

"I'm glad to be back," he would tell a political gathering in Idabel in southeastern Oklahoma or in Miami in northeastern Oklahoma or in Guymon in the Panhandle and on and on in other parts of the state.

"I was born near here," he would proclaim before launching into his campaign talk. And his listeners would yell "he's one of us" and "it's good to see you again, Joe."

Someone in his audiences would confide to others "his mother and my mother were in high school together" or "he used to go to my church" or other claims of identification.

It was Hunt's way of endearing himself to the crowd, former Gov. George Nigh recalled recently. And it worked. A Democrat, he was serving his fifth four-year term when he died at 68 of a rare liver ailment in February 1975.

In his obituary voters learned Hunt wasn't born near Idabel or Miami or Guymon or anyplace else in Oklahoma. He was born in Mammoth Spring, Ark.

Hunt won by consistently overwhelming margins at the polls partly because of his likable personality and his flair for getting into the spotlight. And he campaigned the year around – not just in an election year.

A Tulsa World editorial said Hunt would be "remembered not only as a flamboyant public figure but a popular public servant. He was an Oklahoma original."

Flamboyant may have been an understatement. Shortly after taking office for his first term, he threatened the Legislature with an Insurance Commission strike unless the department was given a larger budget. As was often the case, his demands were met.

Several years later, he threatened to set up a tent on the Capitol grounds when the Oklahoma Capitol Improvement Authority ordered his agency to move out of its offices in the Will Rogers Building to make room for the expanding Oklahoma Employment Security Commission. But he

Tulsa World archives

Joe B. Hunt was serving his fifth four-year term as Oklahoma's insurance commissioner when he died in February 1975 of a rare liver ailment.

didn't have to erect the tent; space was found for his agency.

Hunt claimed in 1958 that his life was in peril from the Mafia because of his investigation into state insurance companies. He made a similar claim in 1972 in a press release with the headline "Will the Mafia kill Joe B. Hunt?" after testifying before the House Select Committee on Crime in Washington.

His release said he had "reached the point where he hesitates to step on the starter of his car because it might be connected to a bomb." But no attempt was ever made on his life.

Hunt was criticized in 1960 and 1970 for distributing brochures printed at state expense that bore his name and title and listed facts about Oklahoma and Oklahomans. He said the brochures were given to school children when they visited the Capitol and were mailed to insurance agencies.

"All state agencies do the same thing," he said. "They send out stuff with the governor's name on it and lots of other departments do that, too."

Hunt had a broad background in insurance and insurance regulation. He was an insurance agent before being appointed manager of the rating department of the Oklahoma State Insurance Board in 1942. He served with the department until 1954 when he resigned to file as a candidate for the commissioner's job.

As insurance commissioner, Hunt attacked several large insurance companies. He once ordered an across-the-board 10 percent reduction in automobile rates, but the insurance companies appealed to the state Supreme Court and won a reversal of Hunt's order.

Hunt also advocated for deaf people, claiming they were discriminated against by insurance companies that refused to cover them or overcharged them.

And when he became a candidate for his fifth term in office he issued a letter to friends advising "I don't want your money. I want your votes."

The letter suggested that anyone who wanted to contribute to his campaign should instead send the money to the Jane Brooks School for the Deaf in Chickasha.

Mabelle Kennedy: true pioneer

When Mabelle Kennedy came to Oklahoma in a covered wagon with her parents and three siblings, her grandmother was sure the family would be killed by outlaws or scalped by Indians.

Years later, the woman who became known as "the grand dame of Oklahoma politics" and who served in many political and governmental roles, told a reporter that period's often-rumored Indian Territory dangers remained just rumors. "It was a delightful trip," she said.

The 1891 trip was made in two covered wagons by the family of five from near Kansas City to the Enid area, where they disliked the wind and blowing sand. They eventually settled in Ralston – long before her political career began.

"We bought produce from farmers along the way and camped by streams. It was a picnic to me all the way and I was sorry when it was over," she told a reporter.

While living in Ralston, which she said was "as big as any town in Oklahoma at that time," Kennedy returned to Missouri for schooling. On one of her trips home from Oakland College, she met her future husband, Edmund Kennedy, a young Kansas City banker. He had come to Oklahoma for a visit. After their marriage, they moved to Pawhuska, where he bought the National Bank of Commerce in 1909.

She spent much of her time raising five children until her husband died in 1936, leaving her the bank and five Osage County ranches. "I had never done anything about business in any way, " she said. "I told myself 'I'm not going to let this go down under me' " and enrolled in banking and ranch management courses so she would be more capable of handling business.

She also got more involved in politics. She served as mayor of Pawhuska, delegate to four national Democratic conventions, Democratic national committeewoman from Oklahoma, assistant treasurer of the United States and on a goodwill commission to Brazil – a position that carried the rank of ambassador.

Kennedy had met Harry Truman at one of the political conventions, was impressed by him and joined his "Whistle Stop" campaign when he was a presidential candidate after serving

Tulsa World archives

Mabelle Kennedy and Sen. Thomas Eagleton, D-Mo., arrive for a Democratic appreciation dinner held in her honor at Western Hills State Lodge in 1974.

the unexpired term of President Franklin D. Roosevelt.

She later served on Truman's inaugural committee and he appointed her as assistant secretary of the treasury, the second woman to hold such a position. He later appointed her to the goodwill commission to Brazil, a job she accepted with her usual joking humor:

"If I made a failure of it, I was not well-known enough that it would make a difference."

In 1980, Kennedy was chosen by Gov. George Nigh to receive the fourth annual Pioneer Woman Award. Nigh said she was a person who was "highly deserving and a natural recipient because of her true pioneer heritage and lifelong civic involvement." In 1974, she had been honored with a "Mabelle Kennedy" day in Oklahoma.

Kennedy told a reporter in 1971 that she'd had some heart problems. "It's bound to get out of balance once in a while," she said about her health. She said the first flare-up came 30 years earlier when her doctor told her she should relax. "I told him to relax," she said, adding "you needn't worry about me; they don't have any wings up there to fit me anyway."

She also explained the unusual spelling of her name. She said she was named May Belle after two aunts but when she started to school, she couldn't make the "y" correctly. Her mother told her that a child should have a voice in how he or she is named and added, "From now on, you are Mabelle."

She was "deeply touched" in 1975 when a new highway that replaced a 32-mile stretch of U.S. 60 known as "Lizard Lane" was named the "Mabelle Kennedy Highway." It was the first stretch of highway in Oklahoma to be named for a woman.

The opening of the new highway climaxed a 23-year fight to improve the road between Ponca City and Pawhuska.

"I prayed to live long enough to see this highway finished," Kennedy said at its opening. "But that doesn't mean I'm going to kick off tomorrow. I'm going to live to enjoy it."

She died six years later, at the age of 93.

Many flocked to Tulsa for TV demo

Thousands of eastern Oklahomans were drawn to a downtown department store in 1940 for their first glimpse of a magic box that has become ubiquitous – television.

Including me.

An 11-year-old at the time, I came to Tulsa from Stigler with my family to marvel at the new electronic gadget that would let us see what was going on in another room and on another floor.

Advance stories about the demonstration said Tulsans would be able to "actually see television and how it operates and would have a chance to have their own images sent out over the air."

My image wasn't sent out over the air, but I saw the images of others on the tiny screen.

The demonstration ran continuously from 10 a.m. to 5 p.m. for three days in early October at the Brown-Dunkin store at Fourth and Main streets. For the first time, Tulsans could watch shoppers on another floor, could see people as they were interviewed and see the city's skyline as the camera panned the horizon from a fifth-floor window.

People who appeared on that test broadcast Oct. 1-3, 1940, were given gold lace-edged certificates stating "I've successfully passed a television test."

A reporter wrote the next day that she had yellow spots in her eyes from the bright lights used for the television camera. She said she was told that the makeup she wore would cause her face to appear dirty on the TV screen and she was startled when one of the TV crew held her arms to keep her from swaying while appearing before the camera – a reaction she was told was common for someone unaccustomed to appearing before the camera.

She also wrote that someday television would be in Technicolor.

The equipment used for the demonstration was valued at $110,000 (a large sum in 1940) including the camera that was valued at $12,000, according to B.R. Gamble, manager of the unit. The demonstration required a crew of seven, including engineer Bart Molinari, who had won a trophy in 1924 as the outstanding radio technician in the United States.

The demonstration coincided with publication of a Satur-

Tulsa World archives

An ad from a Tulsa World special section in 1949 includes a set with a "big 12½-inch tube."

day Evening Post article that blamed the failure of television to get under way quickly on the Federal Communication Commission. Author Alva Johnson contended that the FCC had decided it must delay the production to protect prospective customers from buying television equipment that cost more than they could afford.

Molinari told a reporter at the 1940 demonstration that "old flivvers that cruise the streets without proper shielding of their ignition systems" caused problems for television sets. But he predicted that TV would become popular soon.

"Television is not just around the corner – it's here," Molinari said.

It may have been "here" for some parts of the country but not for Tulsa. It was nine years later when station KOTV began broadcasting on Channel 6. And for the first 45 days, the only thing on the tube was a test pattern to help engineers make adjustments to transmitting equipment. But television set owners watched it anyway and discussed the next day how sharp and clear the image was.

The first regular broadcast was Nov. 30, 1949, when Tulsa Mayor Roy Lundy and other civic leaders helped dedicate the station. Gov. Roy J. Turner couldn't attend personally but sent a movie film that was broadcast on the new station. At first, KOTV broadcast only from 6 to 10:30 p.m. and used programs from six networks.

The World published a special 26-page section explaining the basics about the new medium and introducing the officers and broadcasters of the station. There also were numerous ads offering television sets for prices ranging from $200 to nearly $900. Many ads boasted of sets with "large 12 ½-inch screens"; others offered 16-inch screens.

Although plans for KOTV to begin broadcasting had been announced earlier, there were few receivers until it went on the air.

George Cameron Jr., owner of KOTV, must have read the World story quoting engineer Molinari about that 1940 test at Brown-Dunkin. Speaking at the Nov. 30, 1949, dedication of his station, he told his audience:

"Television is not coming or on its way – it is here."

Efforts to make rain eventually dried up

Drought has plagued Oklahomans periodically since statehood in 1907, and many have wanted to make it rain.

Many have tried.

Have they been successful? That remains debatable.

The idea that rain could be produced by dropping dry ice crystals into a cloud was developed in 1946 when a scientist at the General Electric laboratory in New York dropped dry ice into clouds near Albany, N.Y., and produced precipitation.

The ice crystals form a nucleus for water droplets, and when the droplets become large enough, they fall as rain. That scientist, Vincent Schaeffer, was awarded a Nobel Prize for discovering that dry ice forms ice crystals that will produce rain.

A few months later, both the Tulsa World and The Tulsa Tribune tried their own experiments at creating rain over Tulsa.

Tribune editor and publisher Jenk Jones flew into a large cumulus cloud above Tulsa on Aug. 24, 1947, with 100 pounds of crushed dry ice that he dumped into the clouds at 16,000 feet and then at 20,000 feet. Ten minutes later, he wrote, a shower developed over the north end of the city.

Had he made it rain or was it coincidence? Jones didn't draw any conclusion but noted that scattered showers had been predicted and that rain had fallen in Osage County earlier. Additional rain fell later that day.

A World story the next morning said the Tribune's rain-making effort was a "fizzle" but noted that a few drops of rain fell two hours after the experiment.

A World reporter, who had been talking with a government meteorologist about the possibility of a similar experiment, tried a rain-making effort the next day – but the reporter obviously didn't take the effort very seriously.

"For nearly 30 minutes, I flew over Tulsa with a tray of ice from the family ice box," reporter Bob Freeland wrote. "Approximately every two or three minutes we tossed out a cube." When the remaining ice cubes melted, he added, he just threw the water out of the plane.

Freeland said nothing unusual appeared except holes in the cloud where the ice cubes had been thrown, but he couldn't tell what was happening on the ground 2,000 feet below.

He said he had given a Brownie camera to a boy on the

"What, you mean you drank it?!!"

Dave Carman/ Tulsa World

ground with instructions to take pictures of anything unusual that developed – so he was confident there would be a picture of the holes in the clouds. But when the plane landed, the boy and the camera had disappeared.

"After about an hour searching for traces of rain – and our disappearing cameraman we headed for town," he said.

Although that reporter and the Tulsa World may not have taken rain-making seriously in 1947, the city of Tulsa did seven years later when it approved a $12,000 contract with the Weather Corp. of America of St. Louis to seed clouds over the Spavinaw watershed.

Two months later, Water Commissioner John Thomas said the money had been well spent, noting that "drought conditions still prevail but the seeded area has received more than normal rain during the period."

The project engineer told a World reporter that making rain was a simple operation – if you have the right equipment and the proper weather conditions. All it takes, he said, are proper clouds, some dry ice and an airplane to drop the ice pellets into the clouds. Or clouds could be seeded from the ground with silver iodide vapor released from a generator.

The Weather Corp. used both methods. A World reporter rode with the engineer during one of his Spavinaw area seedings from the ground.

Rainmakers were hired during the 1970s by several Oklahoma cities, by Oklahoma State University, by the Bureau of Reclamation and by the Oklahoma Water Resources Board to produce rain in various parts of the state. Some claimed increased precipitation; others said it was a waste of money.

A state program to enhance rainfall and reduce hail began in 1996, and two years later Mike Matthews of the Oklahoma Water Resources Board said the program had shown promising results. But Edwin Kessler, a meteorologist and retired director of the National Severe Storms Laboratory, said the program had not demonstrated any increase in rainfall.

That program ended in 2001 when Gov. Frank Keating vetoed a spending bill.

Feast kicked off Walton's term

Oklahoma Historical Society

Gov. J.C. (Jack) Walton fulfilled a campaign pledge to hold a party for the public after his election. Tens of thousands of people showed up in Oklahoma City in January 1923 for what many considered to be the world's largest barbecue. An aerial view of the barbeque pits set up at the state fair grounds in Oklahoma City was taken from a military aircraft.

It was billed as the country's greatest barbecue – a feast for the masses – and everyone in Oklahoma was invited.

Plans for the big party had caused "almost complete eclipse" of Gov. J.C. (Jack) Walton's Jan. 8, 1923, inauguration, the Tulsa World reported the day before the event.

The feast and party scheduled the next two days were to fulfill a pledge Walton made during his campaign.

"When I am elected governor, there will not be any inaugural ball and there will not be a 'tea dansant.' I am going to give an old-fashioned square dance and barbecue," Walton pledged in each of the 400 speeches he made during his campaign.

"It will be a party for all the people and I want you all to come," he told listeners.

Everyone didn't come, fortunately, but the crowd at the state fairgrounds was called the largest ever in Oklahoma City. Although there was no official record of attendance, one newspaper estimated the crowd at 150,000. The Tulsa World was more conservative with an estimate of between 60,000 and 75,000.

Every hotel room in the city was booked and residents opened their homes for Oklahomans who couldn't find rooms. Huge dance floors for square dancing had been constructed at the fairgrounds. There were fiddling contests, concerts, boxing matches and a football game with one of the teams coached by Jim Thorpe.

Former Oklahoma City Mayor Dan Lackey, who was in charge of the party, was expecting up to 200,000 but made plans to feed as many as 300,000. Six 700-foot long trenches had been dug in preparation for barbecuing the 289 head of cattle that had been slaughtered. Other meat included 65

hogs, 34 sheep, 3,103 rabbits, 134 opossums, 35 squirrels, 1,362 chickens, 2,000 pounds of buffalo, 1,500 pounds of reindeer from Alaska, 15 deer shot in Oklahoma, 100 turkeys, 12 geese and 30 wild ducks.

Three 10,000-gallon coffee urns, heated by a connection to a fire engine, had been built and 100,000 tin cups had been obtained.

The event was covered by newspapers from many parts of the country and the barbecue that had been billed by Oklahoma newspapers as the country's biggest was upgraded to the world's largest by the New York Times, according to a Chronicles of Oklahoma story.

Walton took the oath of office on Jan. 8 before a joint session of the Legislature and promised financial aid for farmers who he said were reeling into bankruptcy. He repeated the oath at the barbecue the next day.

He and retiring Gov. J. B. A. Robertson made peace long enough to walk together into the legislative chamber. Walton had criticized Robertson only two days earlier for last-minute appointments Robertson had made and the Senate had confirmed. Walton demanded that records of all those appointments be on his desk as soon as he took office.

"They will all know who is governor by Monday noon," Walton said.

Walton also was critical of Lt. Gov. Martin Trapp, who was accused of trying to organize the Legislature against the state's new chief executive.

Walton's party was an event to remember, but 10 stormy months later, he was impeached by the House and convicted and removed from office by the Senate.

He was succeeded by Trapp.

Urschel's ears cracked kidnap case

The victim's attention to detail and good memory were the keys to solving the 1933 kidnapping of a wealthy Oklahoma City oilman.

Charles F. Urschel and his wife, Bernice, were playing bridge with Mr. and Mrs. W.R. Jarrett on July 22 on the sun porch of their home when two men pushed open the screen door and came inside. One carried a revolver; the other a machine gun.

"Stick 'em up. We want Urschel," one gunman ordered. "Don't bat an eye, any of you, or we'll blow your heads off. We want Urschel. Which man is Urschel?"

No one identified the oilman, so one of the gunmen said, "We'll take you both." They forced Urschel and Jarrett into a car and sped away after warning the women not to make an outcry.

The kidnappers, later identified as George "Machine Gun" Kelly and Albert Bates, threw Jarrett out of the car a few miles away after they determined which man was Urschel by examining the wallets they found in the victims' pockets. They tied Urschel hand and foot, bandaged his eyes tightly and placed cotton in his ears so he couldn't hear.

Meanwhile, Mrs. Urschel telephoned police, who called FBI Director J. Edgar Hoover in Washington.

The abductors took Urschel to a farm near Paradise, Texas, where he was kept blindfolded through his nine days of captivity except for once when he was told to write a note asking that a ransom be paid and another time when he was allowed to shave.

Although blindfolded, he said later, he could distinguish night from day. The first night he was held in a house where he heard guinea hens. He was moved the next day to a house about a mile away where he heard pigs.

He also heard airplanes fly over about the same times twice a day except for one afternoon during a severe thun-

Charles F. Urschel, an Oklahoma City oilman, was kidnapped by George "Machine Gun" Kelly and another man July 22, 1933. He was released nine days later after a $200,000 ransom was paid, and then helped authorities locate his kidnappers.

derstorm. When he heard the airplanes, he asked casual questions to establish the time.

After a ransom of $200,000 in used $20 bills was paid in Kansas City, Mo., by the Tulsa oilman E.E. Kirkpatrick, Urschel was released July 31 at the north edge of Norman, where he took a cab to Oklahoma City. He immediately began working with the FBI to solve the crime in spite of warnings from his kidnappers.

The FBI found the farm by checking airline schedules and flying on the two flights, using binoculars to find a farm with two houses Urschel had described at the times he had remembered.

Finding guinea hens at one of the houses and pigs at the other, the FBI raided the farm, which was owned by the R.G. Shannon family. Mrs. Shannon's daughter was Kelly's wife. Agents found Urschel's fingerprints, which he had left on as many surfaces as possible to prove that he had been there.

Harvey Bailey, the leader of 11 notorious convicts who broke out of a Kansas prison, was found asleep on a cot in the backyard with a machine gun by his side. His pockets contained some of the ransom money. The remaining members of the kidnap gang, including Kelly, were rounded up within a few weeks.

The Kellys, the Shannons, Bates and Bailey were sentenced to life in prison. Other members of the gang got shorter terms.

The kidnappers probably singled out Urschel because of his estimated $75 million wealth. He had been a protege of Tom B. Slick, who became wealthy as the "king of the wildcatters," and had married Slick's widow about a year before the kidnapping, giving him control of both his own fortune and Slick's.

Slick had died in 1930, and Urschel's first wife, Slick's sister, had died a year later.

OKC job broke 'Machine Gun Kelly'

One of America's most notorious outlaws of the 1930s gangster era was a bootlegger in Tulsa before he began a short-lived big-time criminal career that ended with his conviction for kidnapping an Oklahoma City oilman.

Although his name was George Kelly Barnes, he changed his name to George Kelly early in his criminal career to protect his family, and then became known as "Machine Gun Kelly," a name some say his wife made up to boost his image in the underworld.

His wife, Kathryn, is said to have bought Kelly his first machine gun and to have collected spent shells from his practice shooting to give away as souvenirs.

"He's been on the front page so much that he finally believes he's tough," a federal agent said during the search for Kelly after he kidnapped oilman Charles Urschel from his Oklahoma City home July 22, 1933.

Urschel was freed after a ransom was paid and gave such a good description of the Texas ranch where he had been held that lawmen were able to find it. It was owned by Kathryn's mother and stepfather, R. G. "Boss" Shannon and Mrs. Ora Shannon.

Born in Tennessee, Kelly's first brush with the law was while he was still in high school when he was arrested in a bootlegging investigation.

He later served a couple of prison terms for Prohibition law violations.

A 1933 Tulsa World story published while Kelly was being sought for the Urschel kidnapping said Kelly, while living here for five years, worked for bootlegger R. L. "Little Steve" Stephens, identified as the city's leading bootlegger.

Tulsa businessmen who bought illicit liquor from the affable Kelly joked with him about the risks he took by selling liquor from his briefcase.

Kelly's sleek black hair and pleasant personality also endeared him to Little Steve's wife, Kathryn.

"One day Steve returned home to find that Kelly had taken his wife, expensive automobile and pedigreed bulldog and left Tulsa," the World story reported. Stephens told a World reporter "I don't mind the dirty so-and-so taking my wife and my car but I wish he had left that dog."

Kathryn was identified in subsequent news stories as

Tulsa World archives

George 'Machine Gun' Kelly is led in manacles by W.C. 'Rube' Gears (left), the U.S. marshal from Oklahoma City.

Kelly's wife although there was no mention of a divorce from Stephens or of a wedding to Kelly.

While Kelly and his wife were being sought nationwide, they sent threatening letters to Urschel and to the U.S. district attorney in Oklahoma City who was to prosecute him.

Kelly also was suspected of being the machine gunner who killed four officers and a fugitive in their custody in the Kansas City train station, but he later denied that crime while admitting the Urschel kidnapping.

There are several versions of Kelly's arrest in Memphis, Tenn., on Sept. 25, 1933. Many, including one on the FBI's Internet site, give him credit for adding the term "G-men" to America's vocabulary. According to those versions, Kelly shouted "Don't shoot, G-men; don't shoot" as heavily armed FBI agents made the arrest.

But the Sept. 26, 1933, Tulsa World story about the arrest reported that Kelly was arrested by Memphis Police Sgt. Bill Raney after he knocked on the door of the house where Kelly and Kathryn were staying.

Kelly answered the knock with a .45-caliber pistol in his hand, but Raney had a shotgun that he stuck in Kelly's chest as he ordered, "Drop that gun, Kelly," and Kelly's gun clattered to the floor, according to the World story that day.

Kelly later claimed that he was unarmed, having left his pistol in the bathroom before going to the door.

Some sources also point out that FBI agents were not allowed to carry weapons until nearly nine months later.

The Kellys were returned to Oklahoma City, where they were convicted Oct. 12, 1933, of kidnapping Urschel and sentenced to life in prison. Seven defendants also were convicted in the Urschel kidnapping and sent to prison.

Kelly at first was imprisoned at the federal prison in Leavenworth, Kan., but later became one of the first prisoners to be housed in the new Alcatraz federal prison on an island near San Francisco.

Kelly was transferred back to Leavenworth in 1951 and died of a heart attack July 18, 1954 – his 59th birthday.

Kathryn was released from prison in 1958 and was said to be living somewhere in Oklahoma several years ago.

Ethiopia's emperor paid visit to state

Ethiopian Emperor Haile Selassie flew into Stillwater in 1954 to thank Oklahoma A & M College officials for the school's help in his country's agricultural program.

And to see an American Indian.

It was the first, and probably only, time a king has visited Oklahoma. Veteran reporters could not recall another time when a reigning monarch visited the state.

Selassie, who claimed to be a descendant of King Solomon and the Queen of Sheba, added the Stillwater stop to a 50-day visit to the United States, Canada and Mexico as his personal repayment for the interest taken in his nation by the late Henry G. Bennett, who visited Ethiopia four years earlier.

Bennett, former A & M president, had taken a leave from his duties to head President Harry S. Truman's Point Four program that was designed to teach people in other countries "how to get more per acre through better planting, better seeds or better livestock strains." He, his wife and six other Americans were killed in a Dec. 22, 1951, plane crash that also killed 19 others while flying from Baghdad, Iraq, to Tehran, Iran.

Selassie, known as the Conquering Lion of Judah, Elect of God and King of Kings, had himself declared king in 1928 and built schools, roads and hospitals. He created a constitution and a parliament and abolished slavery.

And he was appreciative of the technical assistance provided by Bennett and others from A & M, now Oklahoma State University, in his efforts to improve the country's agriculture.

"The technical assistance they (Bennett and Selassie) worked out became the guts of the Point Four Program that Bennett headed until his death in the plane crash," Hugh Rouk, former Beggs resident, told a reporter several years ago. Rouk spent 14 years in Ethiopia as director of International Education in the office of International Programs at OSU.

Three hundred Oklahomans were invited to a dinner with Selassie in the Student Union Building, and another 1,600 were invited to a reception that followed.

Tulsa World archives

Ethiopian Emperor Haile Selassie (right) is the only king known to have visited Oklahoma. He visited the Oklahoma A & M campus in 1954 and was greeted by Oliver Willham, president of the school, now Oklahoma State University.

It was understood that Selassie would stand in the receiving line at the reception for only 30 minutes. But he insisted that he didn't want to quit meeting people and shaking hands until all 1,600 at the event had been greeted – a job that required two hours and 20 minutes.

He told A & M President Oliver S. Willham "the people who came here should be greeted."

"I am very glad indeed to be present with you," the emperor said in his speech that he repeated three times to allow everyone in three connecting rooms to hear.

"Indeed I have made an exception to my usual practice on this trip in leaving my itinerary entirely and making this 2,000-mile trip to express to you my deep appreciation for all that Oklahoma A & M has done and is doing in technical assistance to Ethiopia."

An aide said Selassie understood English well – his native tongue was Amharic and he also spoke French – but he had difficulty speaking it.

A few days before his visit, Selassie had sent word that he would like to meet an American Indian. Tulsa artist Acee Blue Eagle was recruited to meet the Ethiopian ruler at the airport.

Wearing full regalia, Blue Eagle presented war bonnets; a piece of pottery with native corn meal inside, representing the sustenance of life; and a branch of evergreen representing eternal life, to the emperor, his son and granddaughter.

Blue Eagle named the emperor Great Buffalo High Chief, named his son Thunder Eagle and his granddaughter Princess Morning Star.

Selassie also bestowed Ethiopian names on Gov. Johnston Murray; Oliver Willham, A & M president; and A.E. Darlow, A & M vice president. He gave Blue Eagle a gold medal.

Selassie was deposed in a military coup 21 years later after he had served as king for 58 years. He was found dead in his bed nearly a year later. Official Ethiopian sources said the 83-year-old former ruler's death was caused by complications from a prostate operation. Many of his followers believed he was murdered.

Cherokee Bill was wild to the end

Crawford Goldsby was big, strong and a "bloodthirsty mad dog who killed for the love of killing."

Before he was hanged at the age of 20 in 1896, he was asked if he had any final words. "I came here to die; not to make a speech," he told the executioner at Fort Smith as a black hood was placed over his head.

A few minutes later, Goldsby dropped through the gallows' trapdoor as 2,500 spectators watched. Goldsby's short but spectacular criminal career was over as he became one of the 83 prisoners hanged by order of U.S. District Judge Isaac Parker, who called him "the wicked man of crime."

You may never have heard of Crawford Goldsby.

But you may have heard of Cherokee Bill, the name given Goldsby after a shootout near Fort Gibson in which a sheriff's deputy was killed. Even his mother used that name for her son during the remainder of his short life.

Goldsby, reported by some to have killed a man when he was 12, became the most feared and best known outlaw in Indian Territory.

Cherokee Bill's criminal career began when he was 18 after he and a brother became involved in a brawl at a dance. A couple of days later, he waited for the man he believed started the brawl and shot him as he arrived for work.

Goldsby fled, incorrectly believing his victim had died. He later teamed up with Jim and Bill Cook, who were wanted for horse theft. The Cooks soon formed a gang that included Goldsby and several others.

Although they were wanted for various crimes, the Cooks and Goldsby wanted their shares – $265.70 each – of the $8.5 million the federal government paid the Cherokee Tribe for the 6-million-acre Cherokee Strip. Because they were apprehensive about going to Tahlequah to collect the money, they persuaded the operator of a lodge to pick up their money.

After she delivered the money to the three bad men, they were met by Sheriff Ellis Rattling Gourd and seven deputies, and a gun battle left Deputy Sequoyah Houston dead and Jim Cook wounded. Cook later recovered.

The sheriff and a posse returned to the house the next

Beryl Ford collection

Crawford Goldsby, better known as Cherokee Bill, was the most feared and best known outlaw in Indian Territory until he was captured. and executed in 1896.

day and asked an employee if Goldsby had been involved in the shootout.

"No, it was Cherokee Bill," she said, and Goldsby had a new name.

Some sources say Goldsby gave himself that name, Bill meaning "wild hand" in the Cherokee country. Others claim the gang leader gave him the name.

The gang roamed around Indian Territory for the next two years, robbing banks, stores and trains. Goldsby, believed to have killed seven to 13 men, including his brother-in-law, became the most feared and wanted criminal in Indian Territory.

Goldsby was not an expert marksman but was a quick shooter. "I shoot so fast I get 'em rattled," he once confided. "They can't hit me and then I take my time and get them."

Cherokee Bill's career neared an end when he was 19 and had the same interests as most other young men: women. He had a special interest in a woman named Maggie Glass, a relative of Isaac Rogers, who served as a deputy at times.

At the request of the sheriff, Rogers invited Cherokee Bill to his home near Nowata for a rendezvous with Maggie. The next morning, Rogers and another man captured Cherokee Bill and took him to Nowata. There a deputy U.S. marshal loaded him into a wagon and headed toward Fort Smith.

At every community they passed through, they were met with an impromptu celebration in honor of his capture. At Wagoner, the group posed for a picture.

Cherokee Bill was convicted and sentenced to hang. He attempted to escape with a pistol that had been smuggled into his cell, killing a deputy during a gun battle in which he fired about 40 rounds.

He was indicted again for murder, and a jury deliberated for only 13 minutes before finding him guilty. Judge Parker sentenced him again to hang and Goldsby was executed on March 17, 1896.

Visiting with his mother and others in his cell, Goldsby asked Deputy Marshal Ed Reed, a son of bandit queen Belle Starr, to "see that nobody runs over my mother."

The execution was postponed until 2 p.m. to allow his sister to arrive and visit briefly with him, and then Goldsby told jailers, "I am ready to go now most any time."

Tulsans filled streets with patriotism

More than 5,000 people showed up at Fourth and Main streets to join in singing "The Star Spangled Banner" and other patriotic songs to support America in World War I.

"Whether you can sing or can't, you are wanted" for the chorus sponsored by the Council of Defense, a Tulsa World story reported on Aug. 29, 1918. "It is guaranteed that, if you can't sing, you'll wish you could before you leave."

Tulsa World archives

Tulsa's War Savings Bank (left) and headquarters of the Tulsa County Council of National Defense were examples of the patriotic movement in Tulsa during World War I.

ings Stamps is unknown but Tulsans went over their goals in several drives. As a result, a gunboat was named Tulsa as the nation's acknowledgment of the city's patriotism. However, the boat wasn't finished in time to participate in the war – it was christened in 1923.

It was a time of high patriotism. The state Council of Defense had formed a speakers bureau to support the war effort and the speaking and teaching of German had been banned. The names of three Oklahoma towns with German-sounding names, Kiel, Korn and Bismark, were changed to Loyal, Corn and Wright.

The victory singing began with the strains of the national anthem followed by such patriotic songs as "Over There," "Keep the Home Fires Burning" and "Pack Up Your Troubles," the latter repeated several times "to put heart in those who can't help worrying." The event closed with the "Battle Hymn of the Republic."

The sing-along was directed by Robert Boice Carson, then head of the music department at Kendall College. Carson later founded Carson Attractions. The singers were accompanied on an organ by Harry Kiskaddon, who later served as Tulsa's police and fire commissioner.

There apparently wasn't much advance notice about the singing – just a story in that morning's Tulsa World and that afternoon's Tulsa Democrat.

"Have you the real spirit of the time?" the World story asked. "Have you the cause of America at heart? Have you done your best? These are the questions that every loyal citizen must ask himself."

It said the government had asked Tulsans to form a chorus, not of trained voices, but of "every man, woman and child who believes in the government – in the boys 'over there' – and most of all in the cause for which they are fighting."

The Democrat told Tulsans that even unpatriotic men, women and children were invited to the singing in front of the War Savings Stamp Bank. It explained that "after they (the unpatriotic) hear the stirring patriotic songs, they may change their viewpoint."

Whether the sing-along boosted the sales of War Sav-

Only 10 days before the victory singing, more than 2,000 men had been detained in a "slacker" dragnet in Tulsa and taken to Convention Hall (now the Brady Theater) until they could show their draft classification cards.

The roundup started at 8 p.m. on a Saturday and concentrated in areas where men were likely to be – in front of movie theaters, in billiard halls and window shopping on downtown streets. Most of the men accosted did not have their draft cards with them in spite of placards warning them to carry their cards at all times that had been posted around the city.

Those without cards were taken to Convention Hall where they were able to call their homes to ask relatives to bring their cards. A number of messenger boys also were on hand to retrieve cards.

"I'm going to string mine around my neck and sleep with it from now on," one man said after being released.

Among the men detained were a former British soldier, a Spanish citizen and two Germans who had documents that allowed them to be released.

The roundup was organized by Tulsa's home guard and representatives of the American Protective League. Tulsa police, sheriff's deputies, a deputy U.S. marshal and representatives of military services also assisted.

Bellmon nurtured two-party system

Oklahomans had always elected Democrats for the state's top job.

But Noble County wheat farmer Henry Bellmon, a World War II Marine, a former state legislator and former head of the Republican Party in Oklahoma, broke that stranglehold in 1962 when he defeated Democrat William P. Atkinson for the governor's office.

He also became known as the father of the Republican Party in Oklahoma.

"I believe it is safe to proclaim Oklahoma has elected her first Republican governor," Bellmon told a Tulsa World reporter as ballots were being tabulated on that Nov. 7, 1962, election night.

It was an understatement. Bellmon had defeated Atkinson of Oklahoma City by more than 72,000 votes. A record 655,000 ballots had been cast in the governor's race. The previous record was set in 1950 when 644,276 voted.

"With a deep feeling of humility and a strong sense of duty, I accept this victory on behalf of Oklahomans, both Republican and Democrats, who have worked in the cause of better government," the then-41-year-old blunt-spoken former Marine said.

The Democrats' stranglehold on the state's top office had been so tight that Oklahomans considered nomination by that party to be election to the office – regardless of the pro forma general election that would follow.

So firmly did Democrats dominate state politics up to that time that there were few Republican primary elections, and people said they had to register as Democrats in order to have real votes.

Many Republicans became "registered" Democrats and voted in the primaries for the weakest candidates so the Republicans would have a chance for victory in the general elections. Bellmon broke the Democrats' chain and was followed as governor by another Republican, Dewey Bartlett, and a few years later by Republican Frank Keating, both of Tulsa.

Most political reporters of that period customarily wrote that the Democrat nominee (in whatever state race) would

Tulsa World archives
Henry Bellmon takes the oath of office as Oklahoma's governor from U.S. District Judge Ross Rizley.

meet the Republican nominee in the general election but that winning the Democrat nomination was tantamount to election.

And it was. Until Henry Bellmon came along and became one of the most popular officials in state history.

During his term, Bellmon served as chairman of the Interstate Oil Compact Commission and on the executive committee of the National Governors Conference.

Oklahoma law at the time prevented Bellmon from running for a second term, so at the end of his four years as governor, he was elected to the U.S. Senate, where he served for two terms and did not seek a third term. He was the first Oklahoma Republican to be re-elected to a second Senate term.

He returned to Oklahoma and was elected governor again in 1986 – in spite of Republicans' fears that controversial votes in the Senate had jeopardized his future in politics.

The 1978 votes were on treaties to maintain the neutrality of the Panama Canal and to turn over control of the canal to Panama – the most controversial ever cast by Bellmon.

Many, including Republicans, predicted his support of the treaties would mean the end of Bellmon's political career and the end of the Republican Party in Oklahoma. Neither proved true.

A Tulsa World editorial in 2005 called Bellmon "more than just a politician; he's a statesman" and pointed out that as a result of his courage and forthright honesty he was respected and admired by both Republicans and Democrats.

That editorial recalled that he had cast votes on busing and the Panama Canal that he believed to be right but that angered many Oklahomans. During his second term as governor, Bellmon championed passage of the historic HB 1017 education reform and revenue law, a measure that was passed despite almost unanimous opposition from legislators of his own party.

Bellmon now lives in retirement in Billings with his second wife, Eloise.

King implored black Tulsans to vote

The largest audience in the history of the church crowded into the North Tulsa First Baptist Church to hear the Rev. Martin Luther King Jr., who gained international fame when he led a 1956 bus protest in Montgomery, Ala.

King, whose Jan. 15 birthday has become a national holiday, came to Tulsa to speak at a freedom rally on July 18, 1960, and to stress the importance of voting.

"The short walk to the voting booth" is the most significant step black people can take toward improving their civil rights, King said. "You are unfair to yourselves when you have only 4,000 voters registered out of a potential 15,000."

King told the Tulsa group that they were living in one of the most momentous periods in history – a period that marked the end of the old order that began in 1619 when the first slave was brought to the New World and the beginning of the new order that dated from the 1954 Supreme Court decision that pronounced segregation dead.

It was more than three years before King made his famous "I Have a Dream" speech, but more than 1,500 blacks and whites – judges, lawyers, business executives, chauffeurs, shoeshine boys – were in the crowd, although Tulsa was still highly segregated.

Among those on the speaker's platform with King were attorney John Rogers; Ohren Smulian, president of Froug's department store; and Donald E. Hayden, dean of the liberal arts college at the University of Tulsa and president of the Tulsa Council of Churches.

King urged his listeners to continue nonviolent but direct action against segregation, pointing out that such action had resulted in 14 cities opening lunch counters within six months. He said it would have required three years and $200,000-$300,000 to achieve that result by court action.

"It may be true that old man segregation is on his death-

Associated Press

The Rev. Martin Luther King Jr. stands with other civil rights leaders on the balcony of the Lorraine Motel in Memphis, Tenn., on April 3, 1968, a day before he was assassinated at approximately the same place. From left are Hosea Williams, Jesse Jackson, King, and Ralph Abernathy.

bed, figuratively speaking, but history has proved that the guardians of status quo are always on hand with oxygen tanks to keep him alive," he said.

"If we go into this new order with bitterness in our hearts, the new order soon will become the same as the old. Someone must have sense enough to know that love is better than hate."

King came to Tulsa from Oklahoma City, where he also made a plea at a freedom rally for blacks to register and vote. He said his Southern Christian Leadership Conference was planning an intensive campaign to double black voter registration in the South. His goal was to increase voter strength from 1,300,000 to 2,600,000.

King was 39 when he was killed by a sniper on April 4, 1968, as he stepped onto the balcony outside the Lorraine Motel in Memphis, Tenn. James Earl Ray, a high school dropout who had escaped from a Missouri prison in 1967, was arrested two months later in London's Heathrow Airport and charged with killing the minister. Witnesses claimed they had seen Ray running from the motel carrying a bundle.

Ray pleaded guilty and was given a 99-year prison sentence but a short while later recanted, claiming he pleaded guilty because he was pressured to do so. He admitted he had bought a rifle but claimed he gave or sold it to a man named "Raoul" in a rooming house where the two stayed. And Ray's father said his son wasn't bright enough to have carried out the assassination.

King's family members said they believed Ray's claim but Ray died of liver failure in 1998 in prison.

Fifteen years after King died, President Ronald Reagan signed a bill making the third Monday of January a national holiday; the first MLK Day holiday was celebrated in 1986.

King's widow, Coretta Scott King, died Jan. 31, 2006, at the age of 78. She spoke in Tulsa in 1991.

Defense attorney had colorful legacy

Temple Houston's closing argument in a murder trial emptied the courtroom, caused a mistrial and gained his client a new trial – and freedom.

"My client was afraid of the man he killed," the attorney told a jury during an impassioned closing argument in a Woodward courtroom in the mid-1890s. "He did what any of you would have done in the same situation:

"This!"

He whipped his two revolvers from their holsters and the startled jurors fled, along with most of the spectators. The judge declared a mistrial. A new jury was empaneled, and the defendant was acquitted.

It was one of the cases that made Temple Houston the best-known lawyer in Oklahoma Territory and Texas in the late 19th century. According to his Aug. 20, 1905, obituary, he had defended more alleged criminals than anyone in the Territory.

Sometimes he preached to juries, as in the 1899 trial of Minnie Stacey on charges of prostitution and running a bawdy house.

He discussed the sordid life of a prostitute, blamed men for women living such lives and related the New Testament account of the prodigal son and the stories involving Jesus and women accused of adultery. "Do as your master did twice under the very circumstances that surround you," he pleaded. "Tell her to go in peace."

The jurors did. She was acquitted in less than 10 minutes.

Sometimes he gave unusual advice, such as when he was appointed to represent a man charged with murder and the judge told Houston to take the defendant into another room and give him the best advice he could.

When Houston returned to court alone a few minutes later, the judge asked where the defendant was.

"You said to give him the best advice I could," Houston replied. "So, after listening to his story, I told him to crawl out the window. And he did."

Tulsa World archives

Temple Houston, the best known attorney in the Oklahoma Territory, was the son of Texas pioneer Sam Houston.

That often-repeated early tale may be apocryphal, but there's no question about the authenticity of a barroom brawl that landed Houston in court on a murder charge.

Houston was accused of killing attorney Ed Jennings in 1899 in a fight that started with a courtroom argument about Houston's legal expertise. Jennings and his brother, John, were on the other side of the lawsuit.

The judge had ruled in Jennings' favor on a point of law, and Ed Jennings retorted, "Houston doesn't know anything about the law."

The Jennings brothers and Houston drew their pistols but didn't exchange gunfire as spectators expected. The dispute resumed later in the bar, turned into a gun battle and Ed Jennings was killed and his brother, Al, was wounded. Brothers John and Al swore they would kill Houston in retribution.

During his trial, Houston, an accomplished artist, did not testify but spent his time drawing pictures of Napoleon and of cowboys firing guns.

Houston died at home in Woodward in 1905, more than a year after a stroke left him partially paralyzed.

Before moving to Woodward, Temple had served in the Texas Senate for eight years and was considering a race for governor. He was wooed by both Democrat and Republican leaders and one assured him of an easy victory.

"Just stand on your father's name and you'll win," he was told.

It was the wrong thing to say to the son of Gen. Sam Houston, who had been president of the Republic of Texas, a congressman and governor of Texas. "I care not to shine in the light of reflected glory," Temple responded. "If my education and record isn't sufficient for Texas, I'll go somewhere else!"

He did just that and moved to Woodward, where the railroad, which he had represented for some time, had extended its tracks into the recently opened Cherokee Strip.

Tinker Field honors general's heroism

An Osage Indian from Pawhuska gave his life for his country during World War II and his name to one of America's largest and best-known military bases.

That Oklahoma hero was Maj. Gen. Clarence L. Tinker, who was officially declared dead five days after his plane disappeared June 7, 1942, as he led a combat flight over the Pacific Ocean to Wake Island.

His name has been perpetuated by his namesake, the sprawling 5,000-acre Tinker Air Force base near Midwest City that has a variety of functions. It employs about 24,000, making it the largest single-site employer in Oklahoma. Home to the Oklahoma Air Logistics Center, it is the largest military repair and overhaul depot in the nation.

Tinker, 54, who had commanded the Army Air Forces in Hawaii since shortly after the Japanese attacked Pearl Harbor Dec. 7, 1941, was leading a combat mission to attack the Japanese east of Wake Island. When last seen by men in other planes, the general's bomber was descending rapidly.

"Because Gen. Tinker would not ask his subordinates to undertake risks he himself would not take, he selected himself as flight leader of an important combat mission," Lt. Gen. Delos C. Emmons, the military governor of Hawaii, was quoted in the June 18, 1942, Tulsa World.

"It may seem strange to some that a man of Tinker's rank would be involved in such violent action, but it was no surprise to those who knew him," a Pawhuska acquaintance told the World.

Other officers in his command said Tinker went just the way he wanted to go. He was bored by peace, one said.

Tinker was the first general to die in action during World War II although two other generals had died in accidents. He had been promoted to two-star rank and named the commander of air forces in Hawaii as part of a shake-up that involved Lt. Gen. Walter C. Short after the Pearl Harbor attack.

Although only one-eighth Osage, Tinker was immersed

Tulsa World archives

Maj. Gen. Clarence L. Tinker, who was raised in Oklahoma, died in action in 1942. Later the military base in Oklahoma County was named in his honor.

in Osage lore as a child. His white grandfather had served as the U.S. government blacksmith to the Osage tribe from 1849 until his death in 1880, and the grandfather's family had moved to Indian Territory with the Osages in the 1870s.

Tinker learned to speak Osage as a child and attended Haskell Institute for Indians in Lawrence. Kan. He became an officer in the Philippine police force when he graduated in 1908 because the U.S. Army was accepting only West Point graduates. He served in the Philippines until the U.S. Army opened its ranks to graduates of other military schools and he became a second lieutenant on June 7, 1912, exactly 30 years before he was killed in action.

The World's story about Tinker's death said he was a striking man about 6 feet tall with a dash about him – that dash possibly stemming from his long and wide sideburns, a small mustache and the riding crop or swagger stick that he had carried, a habit that became his trademark.

Tinker Field is the home of the Oklahoma City Air Force Logistics Center, one of five major aircraft maintenance and supply centers in the Air Force, according to the Tinker Web site. It is the primary maintenance center for the B-1B bomber and more than 25 other types of aircraft. It also is the home of the Air Force combat communications support fleet of AWACS-type aircraft.

Two months after Tinker's death, the Oklahoma City Chamber of Commerce suggested the new Air Force base be named in Tinker's memory – but at that time the Air Force named installations after only geographical locations.

The rationale was that it would take the passage of time to determine which individuals deserved to be memorialized.

But after conferences at the highest levels, Gen. H. H. "Hap" Arnold announced in October that the War Department had made an exception, and the facility was named Tinker Field.

Campaign trail took him on rough road

An eastern Oklahoma politician kept a campaign promise in 1952 by walking barefoot for 7 ½ miles on a gravel highway because it hadn't been paved.

While campaigning for re-election in 1950, state Rep. C. Plowboy Edwards had promised residents of Quinton, in the rocky foothills of the San Bois Mountains, that he would make such a walk if a 24½-mile segment of Oklahoma 31 in Pittsburg County had not been paved by the end of his two-year term.

At the term's end, 17 miles of the highway had been paved, leaving a 7½-mile stretch of gravel-and-rock road. Edwards kept his promise.

Edwards – wearing a sign on his back that said: "Please Governor, remember your promises. My feet bleed for you" – completed the walk in five hours and 15 minutes on June 28, 1952, during a dry spell when the temperature was in the upper 90s.

He had appealed to Gov. Johnston Murray, Oklahoma's congressional delegation and even President Harry S. Truman to save him from his fate. Murray promised help before his term ended but pointed out that he still had 2½ years to go as the chief executive.

After Edwards completed the trek from Featherston to Quinton, civic leaders gave him a 300-pound block of ice.

The barefoot walk generated national publicity for Edwards, who told a Tulsa World reporter that his given name really was Plowboy "because that's what my pappy wanted – after all the girls in the family."

He didn't say how many sisters he had, but his obituary in 1979 listed one sister and one brother as survivors. The "C" stood for Collins.

Whether Edwards' walk had anything to do with it is

"...might re-think those campaign promises."
– Gov. Murray

Dave Carman / Tulsa World

State Rep. C. Plowboy Edwards kept his promise and walked 7½ miles of gravel highway in bare feet after he failed to get the road paved by his self-imposed deadline.

problematic, but the last 7½ miles of Oklahoma 31 were hard-surfaced before Murray completed his term as governor and Edwards completed his next term in 1954.

Edwards never forgot about the highway; he even referred to himself as "Mr. 31" when he ran for a seventh term in office in 1956. The license tag on his car also bore the number 31.

In an ironic twist, it appeared that the controversial Edwards had lost a runoff election for the Democratic nomination for the House seat by 31 votes to Willard Gotcher, a McAlester attorney. A recount, however, showed that Gotcher had won by 191 votes. The candidates had tied in the primary election.

That campaign came a few months after Edwards was exonerated of two extortion counts alleging that he took money from two state prisoners to get a medical leave for one and a parole for another. One charge was dismissed after a preliminary hearing. Edwards was acquitted of the other after a trial in which he testified that the extortion charge was a frame-up by political enemies.

He said the trouble grew out of his returning a favor for a fellow House member from Tulsa County. Edwards admitted receiving $50 from a prisoner but said it was to defray expenses involved in trying to find a job for the convict after he was paroled.

After his defeat, Edwards ran for the vacated seat of state Sen. Kirksey Nix, who had been elected to the Court of Criminal Appeals, but he lost to Gene Stipe.

Edwards later became an agent in the motor fuels division of the Oklahoma Tax Commission and ran for labor commissioner in 1966 and 1970, losing both times.

Edwards died in 1979 at the age of 71.

Albert remained close to his roots

Carl Albert was just a heartbeat away from becoming president twice.

But he never forgot where he came from.

Albert, who served 30 years in Congress from Oklahoma's District 3, became speaker of the House in 1971, putting him next in line after the vice president to succeed to the presidency. It was the highest position ever held by an Oklahoman.

Born in McAlester but reared in nearby Bugtussle, Albert lived a Horatio Alger story. He rose from a poor childhood in rural Oklahoma to become the leader of the U.S. House of Representatives. His father was a coal miner and sometime farmer.

Albert won several speech contests while attending McAlester High School and graduated Phi Beta Kappa in 1931 from the University of Oklahoma, where he had continued his oratorical practice.

Friends recalled that Albert sometimes practiced speaking by addressing mock audiences under the Canadian River bridge near Norman. A companion would mutter rebuttals or sometimes throw sand at him.

When World War II began, Albert enlisted in the Army as a private and rose to the rank of lieutenant colonel by the end of the war. During the war, he saw action in New Guinea, the Philippines and Okinawa. He was also sent to Hiroshima and Tokyo. He resumed his law practice in McAlester after being discharged and entered politics in 1946, where he was elected to Congress by 329 votes, his closest race ever.

"He went on the world stage, but he never left here because he took our values with him," University of Oklahoma

Carl Albert climbs a stepladder to peer down McAlester's Grand Avenue on May 14, 1964. The street was renamed Carl Albert Parkway in honor of Albert, who rose from the poverty of Oklahoma's coal country to become speaker of the U.S. House of Representatives.

President David Boren, a former governor and former U.S. senator, told more than 2,000 who attended Albert's funeral in McAlester. "When it was all over (his congressional career), he came back home. He came back to the people who, in his heart, he never left."

Albert died in 2000 at the age of 91.

His funeral was attended by local residents and a contingent of dignitaries.

Under federal law, the speaker of the House is behind the vice president in presidential succession.

Thus, when Vice President Spiro Agnew resigned in 1973, Albert would have become president had anything happened to President Richard Nixon until Gerald Ford was sworn in as vice president. And when Nixon resigned from the White House in August 1974 because of the Watergate scandal, Albert again was a heartbeat away from the presidency until Ford chose Nelson Rockefeller as his vice president.

Albert once said he felt Nixon was "overly ambitious." But when he was called to the White House on Aug. 7, 1974, to hear President Nixon say he would resign, Albert had only positive things to say about the president.

"It was a very touching thing," Albert told reporters. "He put his arm around me and said, 'We've always been friends. We came to Congress at the same time.'"

Albert maintained an office in McAlester after leaving Congress and occasionally became involved in politics. In 1992 he was honored at the Democratic National Convention as a superdelegate.

State was home to Boy Scout Troop 1

When a new Episcopal minister arrived in Pawhuska from England in 1909, he brought with him a bag full of Boy Scout literature along with his Bible, derby hat and umbrella.

Believing that all boys were the same regardless of nationality, the Rev. John Forbes Mitchell set about organizing the first Boy Scout troop in the United States, in addition to taking the reins of his new pulpit.

The residents of the frontier town where blanketed Indians and cowboys were still an everyday sight probably were startled when they heard the strains of "God Save the King" coming from boyish voices inside St. Thomas Church.

Mitchell, a friend of Sir Robert Baden-Powell, the father of scouting, had served as chaplain for the world's first Boy Scout troop, which had been organized in England a year earlier. He organized the Pawhuska troop according to British rules, which included singing the British national anthem, causing consterna tion among some of the parents. But they couldn't find anything wrong with the song in spite of strong patriotic feelings in the new state of Oklahoma.

That first troop included 19 boys, a third of whom were Osage Indians, and Postmaster W.E. McGuire, the father of the two of the boys, serving as assistant scoutmaster. Mitchell ordered uniforms for the boys from England and while awaiting their delivery taught two to play a bugle and two to play drums.

By the time the uniforms arrived, Mitchell thought the troop was ready to be unveiled to residents of Pawhuska. "We paraded down Main Street, led by the Pawhuska band," one of the original Scouts recalled years later. "I will never forget the line of boys marching so much like little soldiers."

Tulsa World archives

Raymond Redcorn (left), an Osage from Pawhuska, became a member of the first scout troop organized in the United States when he joined the Pawhuska troop in 1922. In this 1999 photo, he is standing next to a bronze statue commemorating the Pawhuska troop's unique role in scouting history. Scoutmaster Jim Weigant stands with Redcorn.

To spread the word about Scouting, the troop hiked 24 miles to Bartlesville the first weekend of March 1910, accompanied by a supply wagon. "It was a long trip in those days," one said years later. "There really wasn't any road, just a hard rocky trail uphill and down."

Dog-tired by the time they reached Bartlesville, the boys reformed their lines of march and swung down the main street with a smart, arm-swinging British hiking gait, to the blare of bugles and the cadence of drums. The brims of their campaign hats were flattened against the crowns in snappy fashion.

They aroused the envy of boys in Bartlesville, where a troop was formed shortly thereafter.

The boys began their hike back to Pawhuska but couldn't make it that night and camped out along the way. But they recalled that they didn't have enough food for either supper or breakfast and all they had was divided equally among horses, boys and men.

When the official Boy Scouts of America was organized in Philadelphia in 1910, the Pawhuska troop immediately affiliated with it, casting aside their British handbooks and uniforms.

That changed the troop's designation from Troop 1. When the Cherokee Council of Scouts was organized, Troop 1 became Troop 33, the number that still designates the group today.

A bronze Boy Scout statue stands in the Osage County Historical Museum as a testament to the country's first Scout troop. The museum also has on display a picture of the troop's 19 charter members with their names written under the picture and the certificate identifying Troop 1.

Singers helped sell state song

"Oklahoma, where the wind comes sweeping down the plain . . ."

Oklahomans sing those words by Rodgers and Hammerstein as part of their official state song, thanks to a performance on the House floor by a Tulsa actor and a Chickasha choir staged by a future governor.

But the song didn't go sweeping through the House as Rep. George Nigh had expected in 1953 when he introduced the bill to make "Oklahoma" the official song. Older legislators didn't care much for change; especially Rep. J.W. Huff of Pontotoc County.

The state already had a state song, "Oklahoma (A Toast)," and on the day the bill was scheduled for a vote in the House, Huff took the floor and sang a capella:

"Oklahoma, Oklahoma, Fairest daughter of the west,

"Oklahoma, Oklahoma, 'Tis the land I love the best.

"We have often sung her praises,

"But we have not told the half,

"So I give you Oklahoma,

"Tis a toast we all can quaff."

Huff captured the hearts and minds of the other legislators. "He moved through the crowd, he sang, he cried and the crowd cried with him. Everyone was in awe," Nigh recalled recently.

Huff's singing of the old state song convinced Nigh that his bill was in trouble, he said, admitting that Huff at that time was much younger than Nigh is now, and he moved that the vote be delayed a day.

Then Nigh recruited Tulsan Ridge Bond, a McAlester native who had played Curly on Broadway and in a touring company, a girls choir from the Oklahoma College for Women at Chickasha and had a piano moved onto the House floor.

When the House went back into session the next day, Bond and the choir sang a medley of songs from "Oklahoma!" They closed their performance with the title song:

"Oklahoma, where the wind comes sweepin' down the plain,

"And the wavin' wheat can sure smell sweet

"When the wind comes right behind the rain.

"Oklahoma, ev'ry night my honey lamb and I

"OKLAHOMA"
"The Nation's Musical Sensation"

〜〜〜〜〜

APRIL 7-13, 1947
CONVENTION HALL

〜〜〜〜〜

Carson Attractions

Tulsa World archives

This is a program for the Tulsa debut performance of "Oklahoma!"

"Sit alone and talk and watch a hawk makin' lazy circles in the sky.

"We know we belong to the land – and the land we belong to is grand!

"And when we say – Yeeow! A-yip-i-o-ee ay!

"We're only sayin'

"You're doin' fine, Oklahoma! Oklahoma – O.K."

And there was an overwhelming vote to make "Oklahoma" the state's official song, replacing the one written by Harriet Parker Camden in 1905. Gov. Johnston Murray signed the bill into law on May 11, 1953.

Nigh said he fell in love with the song in 1943 while he was in high school in McAlester. "I was upstairs at home and I became aware that the radio was playing a song about my state -- a good song," he recalled.

"Oklahoma!" was a smash hit on Broadway that ran 2,202 performances and was seen by an estimated 4.5 million before closing five years later. It is still performed nightly during the summer on an open-air stage at Discoveryland west of Sand Springs.

Incidentally, the name of the play is "Oklahoma!" with an exclamation point; the name of the song is "Oklahoma" without the punctuation. And there is no exclamation point in the song except in the phrase "You're doin' fine, Oklahoma! Oklahoma O.K."

The musical is based on an earlier Broadway play, "Green Grow the Lilacs," by Lynn Riggs of Claremore.

There was a concern that, because the song was copyrighted, the state would have to pay royalties for its performance. But Oscar Hammerstein eased those fears in a letter to The Tulsa Tribune on June 1, 1953, that said, in part:

"Tell your readers and all the people of Oklahoma that not only may they play it and sing it anywhere and everywhere to their hearts' content but we want them and urge them to do so. Mr. (Richard) Rodgers and I are very proud that our song has been adopted by your state. Play it and sing it loud and long and often."

"You're doin fine, Oklahoma! Oklahoma – O.K."

Colorful Kerr was a polarizing figure

There was no middle ground when it came to Sen. Robert S. Kerr.

Everyone loved him.

Or hated him.

But people in both camps agreed that Bob Kerr was powerful in Washington, where he was known as the "Uncrowned King of the Senate" because of his enormous prestige and his committee assignments. When he died, he was the chairman of the Space Committee, the No. 2 man on the Finance Committee and the acting chairman of the Public Works Committee.

Kerr often said he had been crowned many times by his colleagues but "with a crown of thorns."

Former House Speaker Sam Rayburn, D-Texas, called Kerr the kind of man who "would charge hell with a bucket of water and believe he could put it out."

Kerr's philosophy was that what was good for the state of Oklahoma was good for the nation and Bob Kerr. Detractors rearranged that statement to "what was good for Bob Kerr was good for the state and the nation."

Kerr, who died Jan. 1, 1963, did not live to see the completion of the biggest project of his career, navigation on the Arkansas River. But his work on the program assured its completion, and river navigation from the Gulf of Mexico to Tulsa's Port of Catoosa became a reality.

Known as "Mr. Oklahoma," Kerr was an American success story – he was born in 1896 in a log cabin near Ada, at one time was so poor that he had to milk a neighbor's cow – for half the milk – to feed his family; he then became the richest person in the Senate, with a wealth estimated at $40 million to $55 million.

Kerr's family moved to Ada while he was still a baby, and he attended Ada schools. He went to Oklahoma Baptist University in Shawnee and East Central State College at Ada. Kerr also became active in the Baptist church, an affiliation that, along with his backing of Prohibition, proved to be a powerful force in his Oklahoma political fortunes.

He served in World War I as an Army field artillery 2nd lieutenant and studied law after the war. He was admitted

Tulsa World archives

Oklahoma Gov. Robert S. Kerr waits for a taxi at Union Station while visiting Washington, D.C., in 1946. Kerr served as governor from 1943 to 1947, and as U.S. senator from 1949 to 1963.

to the bar in 1922 and began a practice in Ada.

Kerr made a fortune after he and a brother-in-law organized an oil drilling firm in Oklahoma City in 1925, fulfilling part of his early goals of having a family, making $1 million and becoming governor. When his partner, James Anderson, retired in 1935, Dean McGee joined Kerr, and they built Kerr-McGee Corp.

The last part of that goal was accomplished in 1942 in his first political campaign when Kerr became the first native Oklahoman to be elected governor. He had been involved in politics earlier and had helped elect Leon C. Phillips as governor in 1938.

Kerr and Phillips split two years later over President Franklin D. Roosevelt's campaign for a third term. Kerr supported a third term; Phillips opposed it.

During his 1943-47 term as governor, Kerr developed national recognition by making the keynote speech at the Democratic National Convention – the convention that nominated Missouri Sen. Harry S. Truman to be Roosevelt's fourth-term running mate.

Kerr won a Senate seat in 1948. From the start of his service his slogan was "Land, Wood and Water," which became the title of a book he wrote.

Kerr's only major political defeat came in 1952 when he was a candidate for the Democratic nomination for president. He had gained national attention for his support of Truman in the firing of Gen. Douglas MacArthur during the Korean War and thought he could win the presidency, but Adlai Stevenson became the Democratic nominee and the election was won by Gen. Dwight Eisenhower.

He told a reporter shortly before his death that it was easy to get over that virus.

Wearing galluses was Kerr's trademark, and he shunned formal dress. He once told a reporter that he had worn tails only once – to a National Gridiron show in Washington.

"And there's another chapter to that," he added.

"The next time I wear 'em, I'll be all stretched out and folks will be coming by, saying, 'Don't he look natural.' "

Broadcast pioneer once picked cotton

"I've had one of the most interesting lives any human being ever had," Jimmy Leake told an interviewer in 1979.

"And I've enjoyed myself," he added.

The man who picked cotton as a child in the 1920s became a millionaire, a broadcasting pioneer and an automobile enthusiast. Along the way, James Chowning Leake worked at a variety of part-time jobs – in restaurants, a laundry, service stations and as a truck driver.

And he shared his time with a wide array of public service commissions, organizations, associations and civic clubs. The obituary after his July 3, 2001, death at the age of 85 said he "had been involved in every possible civic organization within Oklahoma, Tulsa and Muskogee."

He also had served on many national boards, including serving as chairman of the Affiliates Group of ABC Television.

But Leake probably was best known, at least outside the Tulsa and Muskogee areas, as one of the foremost experts on Rolls-Royce automobiles. His Antique Car Museum in Muskogee and his auctions that have sold more than 30,000 collector cars.

Leake developed a passion for old junkers when old cars were considered junk, the Leake Auction's Web site says.

He traveled to many parts of the world collecting old cars. An auction in 1964 in Muskogee set the stage for annual June auctions in Tulsa and later in Oklahoma City in February and in Dallas in November.

Leake also had a touch of showmanship in him. While he owned Tulsa television station KTUL-TV, he encouraged on-air employees to participate in parades in small towns. And he usually showed up to drive them in the parades in one of his antique automobiles.

Leake's first car was a 1929 Austin roadster that cost $84 and took him two years to pay for – a car he still owned when he was interviewed in 1979. In 1965 he paid $29,000 for a 1911 Rolls-Royce that had belonged to an Indian maharaja. He estimated its worth at $250,000 in 1983.

Born in Chandler in 1915, Leake told a Tulsa Business Chronicle interviewer that he had picked "maybe 50,000 miles of cotton" while growing up in Chandler near the 160-acre farm his grandfather homesteaded. He had staked the plot in the 1891 land run into surplus lands the government had bought from the Sac and Fox Indians.

Leake attended the one-room Stone School that housed the first through eighth grades taught by Leake's mother. He graduated from Chandler High School in 1935 and went to the University of Oklahoma because "my mother started talking to me about getting an education from the day I was born."

Leake worked his way through pre-med but couldn't finance the remaining years of study and instead went to work driving a truck for John Griffin's wholesale grocery company in Muskogee for $15 a week.

"Fifteen dollars wasn't bad in those days, especially when Mr. Griffin (his future father-in-law) paid my expenses; and I got acquainted with all of Oklahoma, Arkansas, Missouri, Texas and Kansas," he said.

After Leake and Marjory Griffin were married in 1940, they moved to Dallas to manage the Griffin interests there.

The Leakes returned to Muskogee when Griffin became ill, and Leake became head of the company when Griffin died.

In addition to grocery interests, the Griffin Co. had started Tulsa radio station KTUL in 1934 and by the end of World War II, the company had two additional stations. When the television industry was developing, Leake obtained licenses for stations in Muskogee, Oklahoma City and Little Rock, which went on the air within a nine-month period.

He later moved his Muskogee station, channel 8, to Tulsa and after 1966 devoted all his time to his television properties. He and his brother-in-law, John Griffin Jr., split those properties later, and Leake eventually sold channel 8 to Albritton Co. of Dallas.

But the family returned to Tulsa television in 2001 when Griffin Communications, based in Oklahoma City, purchased KOTV, channel 6.

Nancy Sevenoaks.

James Leake was best known for his Leake Auto Auction, but also was a broadcast pioneer in northeastern Oklahoma.

Outlaw terrorized Oklahoma bankers

Many Oklahoma bankers, especially in smaller communities, lived in fear of seeing a handsome man with a machine gun nestled in the crook of his left arm walking into their businesses in the early 1930s.

"Kick in the jack," the gunman would announce, and the bankers would fork over thousands of dollars.

The gunman was Charles Arthur Floyd, better known as "Pretty Boy," who had been reared in Sequoyah County and became a criminal after leaving high school and going to Missouri looking for work. He usually had a couple of other men with him.

Insurance rates soared. Many banks installed bulletproof glass at their tellers' windows. Others began keeping only a few hundred dollars on hand.

Floyd and his companions always used the same mode of operation. They struck during daylight hours. After robbing a bank and everyone in it, they kidnapped two or three bank officials, put them on the running boards of their stolen cars for protection, and sped away. A few miles out, the bank officials were released.

They never wore masks, and Floyd was always identified by the victims.

Born in Georgia but reared at Akins, near Sallisaw, Floyd was the fifth of eight children of hard-working farmer Walter Floyd and his God-fearing wife. The elder Floyd usually had at least one other job to support his family.

Among the Floyd siblings were a future longtime sheriff of Sequoyah County, an oil company worker, housewives and Charley – who became known as "Pretty Boy." He was identified as Public Enemy No. 1 when he died in a hail of gunfire on Oct. 22, 1934, in an Ohio cornfield.

Floyd's childhood was described as ordinary. But that changed after he left high school, got married and, looking for work, went to Missouri, where he began his criminal career and got the nickname he detested.

He was working in a bakery in St. Louis when he joined some older men in a payroll robbery that netted $12,000.

According to one story, a witness told police that one of the robbers was a "pretty boy." An officer thought that description fit a boy who worked in a nearby bakery and arrested Floyd, who was sent to prison, where he served four years. It was the only time he served, although he was sentenced to 15 years for another robbery; that time, he

CHARLES ARTHUR "PRETTY BOY" FLOYD

Tulsa World archives

Charles Arthur Floyd, Public Enemy No. 1 at his death, hated his nickname "Pretty Boy."

jumped from a train taking him to prison and fled.

Another explanation for his nickname was that he got it from a prostitute.

Whatever the source, Floyd hated it. There were reports that he killed two men for calling him "Pretty Boy."

When he returned to Oklahoma in 1931, Floyd teamed up with George Birdwell, who was killed in a bank robbery in Boley, and Fred Barker, later to die with his mother after a flaming gun duel with FBI agents in Florida.

Between robberies, Floyd lived with his wife, Ruby, and son, Jack Dempsey Floyd, at 513 E. Young St. in Tulsa. After Ruby divorced Floyd, she still met him for rendezvous, including one that resulted in the death of former McIntosh County Sheriff E. A. Kelley of Eufaula. Kelley, who had been trailing Floyd for three months, learned that Floyd planned to meet Ruby at her father's farmhouse near Bixby on April 9, 1932, and went there with several officers.

When Floyd arrived, Kelley was alone; the other officers had gone to town to eat. Kelley tried to stop the trio, but was killed by gunfire from Floyd and/or Birdwell and Barker.

The notorious Oklahoma outlaw was killed by officers as he tried to flee through a cornfield on a farm near East Liverpool, Ohio, on Oct. 22, 1934. Fourteen bullets hit him in the back and another struck his side. He was 29.

The nation's Public Enemy No. 1 was believed to have committed at least seven murders and possibly as many as five more. The FBI believed he was one of the machine-gunners who had killed five in June 1933 in what was known as the Kansas City massacre. He denied that – even as he lay dying and was questioned by FBI agent Melvin Purvis.

Eight officers, led by Purvis, converged on the Ohio farm after receiving a tip that Floyd was there.

Floyd at first tried to hide under a corn crib as the officers arrived. Then he tried to run, and an estimated 50 bullets were fired at him by officers armed with two machine guns, pistols and rifles, the FBI said. Floyd had an automatic pistol in his hand and another in a shoulder holster, but neither was fired.

When Purvis asked him whether he was Pretty Boy Floyd, he responded with a curse and said, "I am Charles Arthur Floyd," his final repudiation of the nickname he hated.

World's richest bachelor left big legacy

Lew Wentz, one of America's richest men, also had a secret identity as Daddy Long Legs, a year-around Santa who bought gifts and shoes for needy Ponca City children. But few knew it until he died.

It was a role he started long before he had enough money to finance such generosity; when he had to borrow money to meet the needs of those children. But he saw the need and wanted to help.

Among his generosities was to finance treatment for a crippled boy, an act that led Wentz to become one of the founders of and the largest contributor to the Oklahoma Society for Crippled Children, an agency that helped thousands.

His generosity wasn't confined to children or to Ponca City residents. He gave millions to a myriad of charities.

Wentz had a fortune estimated at more than $25 million – a tremendous sum in those days – when he died of coronary thrombosis on June 10, 1949. And even after his death, his fortune grew because of oil discoveries on land he had bought or leased. Only a few years earlier he had been identified as one of seven Americans with annual incomes exceeding $5 million.

He was 68, although his age had always been a closely guarded secret.

Sometimes called the world's richest bachelor, Wentz once said he regretted that he had never married. "Every girl should marry by the time she's 25," he said. "And every man by 30 if he's financially able."

Thousands of Oklahomans owe their educations to Wentz, who was too poor as a boy to go to college but who set up loan programs for students after he became fabulously wealthy.

Hundreds of others were able to start businesses because of loans from Wentz.

Wentz got into the oil business by chance – and on a shoestring. Sometimes he was too broke to pay his room and board bill.

Louis Haines Wentz was one of seven children of a Pittsburgh blacksmith and toolmaker. When he graduated from high school, college was out of the question. He played on and managed semi-pro baseball teams and became the coach of all the high school teams in Pittsburgh.

His job as coach left Wentz time for Republican ward work, and by chance he called on John McCaskey, who had made a fortune selling bulk sauerkraut and who had invested in E. W. Marland's wildcat oil venture on the 101 Ranch near Ponca City but McCaskey couldn't go to Oklahoma because of his kraut business.

Tulsa World archives

Lew Wentz, known as the world's richest bachelor, left a legacy of philanthropy that has helped thousands.

McCaskey hired Wentz to go to Ponca as his personal representative, and the two became partners with Marland. Wentz soon split off from Marland and began cornering leases in the Peckham-Braman region. At one time, Wentz turned down a $400,000 offer for his leases although he had only $39 in his pocket.

Wentz had made his first million dollars by the time of World War I and by 1927 the Wentz Oil Corp. was making a million dollars a month. McCaskey had died and Wentz had bought McCaskey's interest from his heirs. Wentz sold out before the stock market crash of 1929 and invested in government bonds.

He later invested in auto agencies, a string of newspapers, agriculture and many other businesses, even a mortuary. But he retained an interest in the oil business and his fortune continued to grow.

When Wentz arrived in Oklahoma in 1911, he rented a room at the Arcade Hotel, a rooming house a block from the Santa Fe Railroad depot where owner Annie Rhodes treated him like a son. When he couldn't pay his room and board bill, she told him to "pay me when you can."

Wentz never forgot her generosity and paid her with high interest after his wells came in. Many others who stayed there under the same arrangement didn't remember their debts.

Wentz once built a mansion outside of Ponca City but returned to the rooming house to be close to his friends and lived there the rest of his life.

Although Wentz was probably the biggest guiding influence of the Republican Party in Oklahoma, he resisted efforts of party leaders who wanted him to run for governor in 1934 and for U.S. senator in 1944. His only experience in public office was a few years as chairman of the state Highway Commission.

Gov. Leon C. Phillips appointed Wentz to the Will Rogers Commission and he was reappointed by Govs. Robert S. Kerr and Roy J. Turner. He was among a handful of prominent citizens who had furnished the funds to build the garden and crypt at the memorial in Claremore where the bodies of Rogers, his wife and infant son are buried.

Among Wentz's philanthropies was a loan program for students at the University of Oklahoma and Oklahoma State University that had helped more than 2,000 students before his death and is still functioning.

He also lent money freely to young people who wanted to start businesses. A number of his businesses at his death were those he took back after his proteges failed.

Prohibition survived until enforcement

"Oklahomans will vote dry as long as they can stagger to the polls," humorist Will Rogers once said.

It was a pretty accurate commentary long after Rogers' 1935 death, but it changed in 1959 when Oklahomans voted overwhelmingly to repeal prohibition.

Oklahoma had been officially dry since statehood in 1907.

But that hadn't kept anyone from having a cocktail. Liquor was available by free delivery 24 hours a day from bootleggers; cocktails and wine were served at banquets and in clubs, restaurants and hotels.

Bootleggers freely distributed business cards bearing their telephone numbers. Many, on their reverse sides, had current price lists for half-pints, pints, fifths and jugs of various brands of liquor. Private clubs that required membership cards flourished – but memberships were available free or for a minimal one-time fee of $1 to anyone.

Liquor was available, convenient and illegal.

That changed when Tulsa County Attorney J. Howard Edmondson became governor in 1959 and set about to keep his pledge to repeal prohibition – by enforcing prohibition.

One of Edmondson's first acts as governor was to appoint Muskogee County Attorney Joe Cannon as state safety commissioner with instructions to dry up the state. Edmondson also pushed a bill through the Legislature that set an election on the repeal issue for April 8.

During his anti-liquor campaign, Cannon received much criticism and was the target of attack by several senators. At one point, he was reprimanded officially by the entire Senate. But he enforced prohibition.

A bit of humor sometimes cropped into Cannon's raids – such as a sign inside a Tulsa restaurant when the raiders arrived that said "Welcome Cannonball. Vote wet. (signed) The Gang."

At one point, dry forces proposed having schoolchildren picket polling places with placards urging votes against

Tula World archives

Before Oklahoma prohibition was repealed in 1959, bootleggers handed out business cards with price lists on the back, and private clubs, where booze flowed for a price, were all the rage.

repeal, but the idea was dropped because of possible adverse reaction to keeping the children out of school.

Both sides quoted the Bible; Will Rogers and Abraham Lincoln were quoted by the wets. "Prohibition makes a crime out of things that are not crimes," the wets quoted Lincoln.

Rogers was quoted as saying that wine had such an effect on Noah's health "it was all he could do to live 950 years."

"He was the first to discover a use for water, and that was to float a boat on. But as a beverage, he knew it was a total failure."

More than 700,000 voters cast ballots, and the state's growing urban centers flexed their political muscle. Tulsa County provided the largest margin for the wets' victory – 86,600 to 23,700. Oklahoma County voters approved repeal by a vote of 81,000 to 48,000.

It was the sixth time since statehood that Oklahoma voters had voted on the question of prohibition or repealing prohibition.

Subsequent legislation banned public drinking, prohibited price fixing and permitted brand name advertising.

Supposedly "private" bottle clubs with "membership" cards continued until April 1985, when voters approved a law that allowed liquor by the drink.

The repeal of prohibition may have created a drastic change in the drinking tastes of many. It was a new experience for Oklahoma tipplers to visit a liquor store where hundreds of brands of liquor were available – unlike the days of bootlegger-supplied bottles.

While Oklahoma wets celebrated the repeal of prohibition, the bootleggers were less happy.

A Dallas bootlegger told a Tulsa World reporter: "Just like that. It happens just like that. After building up my business for years, those damn Oklahomans go to the polls and vote to make me a bankrupt.

"I tell you, it just ain't right."

Coal-mine disaster killed 73

It was an "awful disaster."

That Page 1 headline in the March 21, 1912, Tulsa World was an apt description of an explosion that trapped 98 men in a McCurtain coal mine, taking the lives of 73. It still ranks as one of the worst coal-mine disasters in state history.

The blast in the Sans Bois Coal Co. Mine No. 2 was heard by most, if not all, of the 3,000 residents of the Haskell County town where nearly everyone was either involved in mining or was related to a miner.

Twenty-five miners were rescued – 14 thanks to the efforts of two miners who were able to break open an air valve, gulp fresh air into their lungs and set about finding unconscious miners who still had pulses and drag them to the air pipe. The wife of one of the mine victims died of grief, boosting the toll to 74.

Shortly after the explosion, a special train carrying doctors and nurses was sent to McCurtain from Fort Smith but returned because there were few injuries – everyone was either dead or was alive with minor injuries. Five doctors were left at the mine to care for injured victims, if any should be rescued.

Hundreds of relatives and friends of the miners huddled near small fires at the mine's mouth to keep warm from a biting north wind as rain and sleet fell while rescue efforts continued. But they were not allowed to view the bodies as they were brought out of the mine because of their mangled and swollen conditions.

Because there was no way of preserving bodies, funerals began at 9 a.m. the next day with a farm wagon used as an improvised hearse. Most were buried without ceremony. Five victims' bodies were never recovered.

Identification of the bodies was difficult, but metal tags that each miner carried to put on the coal cars after they were filled were helpful in that regard.

Two of the rescued miners told about crawling into a pump room where they knew an air pipe existed, but they got into an argument and almost came to blows about who

Coal mining in southeastern Oklahoma was a dangerous but lucrative business in early statehood years. The 1912 disaster at the McCurtain coal mine killed 73. This undated picture from the Oklahoma Historical Society shows workers at a McAlester coal mine.

could better break off a valve to release the air into the small room. After breaking the valve with a metal bar, they began checking other nearby miners and dragging those who were still alive into the pump room, where they were revived with air.

As each was dragged in, he was placed with his face close to the broken air pipe until he regained consciousness. They were rescued the next day.

The father of one miner had started making a coffin for his son as soon as he heard the explosion, but the son was one of the 14 who escaped. He said he had prayed for the first time – and resolved to quit selling whiskey, clean up his life and to pray every day for the rest of his life.

The crude coffin his father had made was to be kept as a memento of his son's brush with death.

Miner Joe Miller had told his wife a few days before the explosion that he was afraid of the mine. "Now if that thing ever happens, all of us fellows will be caught like rats in a trap," he had said.

Miller died in the disaster.

President Carter kept promise to city

It's seldom that a church can't accommodate all the people who want to worship there at a Sunday service.

But that was the case March 25, 1979, when President Jimmy Carter worshipped at the First Baptist Church in Elk City after spending the night at the home of Larry Wade, publisher of the Elk City News and, at that time, the city's mayor.

Additional chairs were set up around the perimeter and in the aisles of the sanctuary and people were allowed in by lot.

Wade doesn't recall the exact number of people the church could seat but said it would have been several hundred. That building has since been torn down and replaced by a larger building.

It was Carter's second time to visit Elk City, and he was keeping a campaign promise. He first visited there in November 1975 when he was the Democratic nominee campaigning for president against Republican President Gerald Ford, who had assumed the office after President Richard Nixon resigned in August 1974. Most observers gave Carter little chance of winning.

"He was 'Jimmy who?' when he was here in 1975," Wade recalled. Carter had campaigned in several Oklahoma cities – Tulsa, Oklahoma City, Lawton and maybe another city or two – but he drew a larger crowd in Elk City, which had a population of about 8,000, than in the other much larger cities.

"When you are president, I sure want you to come back," Wade said he told Carter, who promised that he would return.

And he did.

Carter's visit to Elk City as president was to hold one of his series of town meetings that were held primarily in small cities and towns – the places one doesn't ordinarily expect a president to visit – at which he discussed human rights, foreign policy and other issues.

The president told the cheering crowd that he had been to many important places recently such as Mexico City, Cairo, Jerusalem "and now Elk City."

"I promised to come back to Elk City. You helped me become president and here I am."

The town meeting in Elk City drew about 2,500 to the high school gymnasium, where Carter received a lengthy, sign-waving, standing ovation while the high school band played "Hail to the Chief." It was the seventh such trip to a small city for a town meeting.

Shortly after assuming office, Carter visited Clinton, Mass., an industrial town of about 15,000 for a town meeting. A few months later he visited Yazoo City, Miss., followed by town meetings in Bangor, Maine; Spokane, Wash.;

Tulsa World archives

John Dugger (left), pastor of First Baptist Church in Elk City, shakes hands with President Jimmy Carter on March 25, 1979. Carter returned to the city to fulfill a campaign promise. He first visited Elk City in November 1975.

Aliquippa, Pa.; and one in Berlin during an overseas trip.

Wade said he believes that Carter could relate to small communities because of his hometown of Plains, Ga., which has a population of about 600.

Air Force One carrying Carter landed at the former Clinton-Sherman Air Force Base 18 miles away, where he was met by Gov. George Nigh, Lt. Gov. Spencer Bernard, Wade and other state and city officials. As the motorcade drove through Elk City, American flags were displayed in front of every downtown business and "Elk City loves Jimmy Carter" signs were displayed throughout the city.

Elk City residents had swept sidewalks, edged lawns, raked leaves and picked up litter.

Wade recalled that he and Carter had a glass of orange juice about 6:30 a.m. Sunday before Carter did sit-ups and went out to run four miles at the city airstrip, riding in an ordinary car rather than his presidential limousine so he wouldn't draw attention.

"When he came back, he showered and dressed and we had breakfast, at which he said grace," Wade told a reporter shortly after the visit. "We discussed some areas such as possible deregulation and decontrol of oil, the possibility of raising target prices on wheat, which are important issues in Oklahoma."

And then they went to church. Carter has taught Sunday school in a Baptist church in Plains for many years.

After church, Wade rode in the presidential limousine with Carter back to the Air Force Base, and the president flew to Dallas for another meeting.

It was the first visit ever of a president to Elk City.

It was an event that won't be forgotten soon.

Reason prevailed in Wewoka witch trial

The middle of Oklahoma is a long way from Salem, Mass., and it had been more than 200 years since the witch trials.

But an elderly Seminole Indian woman was condemned to death as a sorceress in Wewoka in 1880 and came within two hours of facing a firing squad. She had been accused of causing a long-sick woman to choke to death – by blowing on a piece of bread given to the ill victim, who tried to eat it.

The story of the Oklahoma witchcraft case was told in the 1923 memoirs of former mission teacher

Oklahoma Historical Society

Antoinette C. Snow Constant poses with her students at the Wewoka Presbyterian mission school, about 1880. The story of an Oklahoma witchcraft case was told in her memoirs.

Antoinette C. Snow Constant, who saved the condemned woman from death. The story of the "witch" trial was published in the Tulsa World shortly after Constant wrote her memoirs and was recently recounted in the book "Alice and J.F.B." by Pulitzer Prize-winning author Vance Trimble of Wewoka.

The young white teacher watched every morning as the old Indian "witch" was led stumbling on foot to the Council House by a light horseman (an Indian officer riding a pony) for her trial. Her long gray hair falling over her shoulders gave her a weird appearance, Constant recalled in her hand-written memoirs.

The trial lasted several days before the old woman was found guilty and sentenced to death. Members of her "Clan of the Wind" were not allowed to speak in the woman's defense or to attend the trial.

Constant wrote that she appealed to everyone she could think of, including the Rev. William Ramsey, a Presbyterian missionary who founded the mission where she taught 50 students, and John Franklin Brown, a half-white man who was the most formally educated man in the tribe's leadership.

"We can do nothing," the missionary told her. "And besides you will lose your position if you interfere with the Indians' affairs."

Brown condemned the trial and sentence but said he could do nothing. "I fear her fate is settled beyond the reach of any aid I might be able to render."

Chief John Chupco, whom Constant had considered a friend, had visited in her home many times. Though he had

asked her to "never leave my people," he refused to talk with her and didn't respond to a written plea for the woman's life. He had already signed the death warrant and had set the execution for 2 p.m. June 8, 1880.

"There is no such thing as a witch," the teacher had written to the chief, urging him to "stay the hand of the executioner." Chupco ignored the letter.

On the Sunday before the execution was scheduled, Ramsey announced from his pulpit, "For all who wish to watch the execution of the witch, I can tell you that it will take place on the Council House grounds on Tuesday at two in the afternoon."

People began to assemble early Tuesday awaiting the event, Trimble wrote in his book. The "witch" arrived at noon, calm and resigned to dying. She was in her family's wagon sitting on a rough pine coffin lined with muslin – while awaiting her date with the firing squad.

Two young light horse privates had been selected for the firing squad and their rifles had been "purified" by a medicine man.

Meanwhile, the teacher had sent an appeal to Maj. A.W. Tate, the U.S. Indian agent whose headquarters were in Muskogee, whose response arrived barely two hours before the execution was scheduled: a letter to the teacher and an order to Chief Chupco to stay the execution.

The "witch" was sent home and, as was predicted by Brown, Constant was fired from her job as a teacher. In spite of Chief Chupco's earlier plea that the teacher "never leave my people," he now ordered the missionary to "get another teacher."

The old woman whose life was spared was grateful. When the girls in the mission school took her to meet Constant the next day, she threw her arms around the teacher and wept with joy. "I could only point heavenward and say to her (in Seminole) 'God has saved your life.'"

A few months later Constant returned to Kansas with her husband and children. She later moved to Edmond, where she lived until her death.

Never again was a "witch" put on trial in the Seminole nation.

First Legislature full of wild characters

Oklahoma's first Legislature adjourned on May 30, 1908, after creating the state's first laws, including liquor prohibition, the Jim Crow law and one requiring 9-foot sheets in hotels.

It had been a stormy session. At one point legislators stood on their chairs and desks and yelled at each other and at House Speaker William H. "Alfalfa Bill" Murray. On another occasion, three legislators rushed toward the speaker's stand, planning to throw Murray out of the chamber.

At the session's end, the Tulsa World called it the "most turbulent any new state ever experienced" but urged readers to give the new laws a fair and impartial trial and to "thank God they are not worse."

About 200 bills remained in committees or on calendars, and there was talk of a special session. But none was called and the pending bills died.

The Legislature convened in Guthrie, the state's capital, on Dec. 4, 1907, less than a month after Oklahoma became a state.

Murray, who had been president of the constitutional convention, was elected speaker of the House without opposition, but his popularity waned during the nearly six-month session.

The turbulence began on the first day when legislators noticed that Ira N. Terrill, who had been a member of the first Oklahoma Territorial Legislature, was a spectator, and they feared he would cause a problem.

Legislators remembered that, while serving in the earlier House, he caused an exodus stampede by pulling a pistol from his boot while trying to get recognition from the speaker and announcing he would use it if necessary to get the floor.

This time, however, he apparently left the chamber without causing a problem. Terrill had served a prison term for killing a man in Guthrie and, after his release from prison, had filed lawsuits against sheriffs, judges and the state

Tulsa World archives

The first Oklahoma Legislature was a raucous group. Future Gov. William H. "Alfalfa Bill" Murray (center) was the first House speaker.

claiming he had been deprived of his liberty by a conspiracy.

The session was anything but peaceful. Once, Speaker Murray attempted to have Rep. "Gristmill" Jones of Oklahoma City put in his seat but Jones dared the sergeants-at-arms to touch him. Other representatives stood on their chairs and desks yelling until Murray finally gained order by rapping hard on his desk with his gavel, and Jones returned to his seat.

Two months later, Rep. Woodson Norvell of Tulsa and several others charged toward Murray, declaring their intention of throwing him out of the chamber. They were stopped by other legislators, but a short while later, Norvell disagreed with one of Murray's rulings, ran down the aisle toward the speaker and shook his fist in Murray's face.

A Jim Crow bill that required separate compartments in train stations and other public places for blacks and whites was the first bill introduced. It sailed through the process and was signed by Gov. C.N. Haskell.

Other laws provided for liquor prohibition, a depositors' guaranty fund, a banking commission, transferred funds from the U.S. Treasury to the state, invested school funds and transferred court cases from Indian Territory to the state.

And there was that 9-foot sheet law.

Many believed that it was prompted by Speaker Murray's dislike of short sheets on hotel beds because of his tall height. But its passage probably had more to do with hygiene. The long sheets allowed a 3-foot overlap of quilts or blankets, which probably weren't washed very often while sheets were washed frequently.

The long-sheet rule was included in a hotel law that also required fire extinguishers, fire escapes in taller buildings and manila ropes in second-story rooms and prohibited the use of dishes with cracks visible to the naked eye for food.

'Summer Santa' made quite a splash

A Tulsa philanthropist's memory of being forced to cool off in water from open fire hydrants when he was a poor, barefoot newsboy in Chicago benefited thousands of children for several generations.

Until state law got in the way.

The benefactor's name was Frank H. Reed, oilman, attorney and philanthropist, who began building wading pools in 1921 for children in Oklahoma, Kansas and Missouri. He died in 1931, but his pool-building was continued by his wife, Isabelle, until her death in 1951 and by a trust fund beyond that.

The trust fund was part of the Tulsa Foundation that Reed and E. W. Sinclair, chairman of the Exchange National Bank, set up in 1919 with Reed as the first donor – using proceeds from a life insurance policy and cash. Many other generous Tulsans have contributed to the foundation that has grown to about $22 million, according to attorney Henry Will.

All of the Reed wading pools in Tulsa have been converted to spray pools because of state law. Mary Ann Summerfield of the Tulsa Park and Recreation Department said state law now requires wading pools to have recirculating chlorinated water.

Reed's first wading pool, built in 1921 in Locust Park at 14th Street and Cincinnati Avenue, was followed by more than 50 before his death. Locust Park disappeared when the land was needed for part of Tulsa's expressway system.

The pool-building started after Reed heard Tulsa World Editor and Park Department President N. G. Henthorne speak at the Kiwanis Club in 1920 about a trip to California where, he said, the park facilities included wading pools for children.

"I think it would be a fine idea for the Tulsa park system to have a wading pool," Henthorne told the Kiwanians.

"How much do they cost?" Reed asked.

And from that question, Reed began building wading pools in Tulsa and other communities. His only stipulation was that they be for children younger than 12 and that they be maintained.

The wealthy oilman set up a $100,000 trust fund, a large

Tulsa World archives

Frank H. Reed was inspired by a Kiwanis Club speech to build wading pools throughout the area.

sum in those days, and within 10 years had built wading pools in many areas of Tulsa and in Oklahoma City, Ardmore, Durant, Ada, Shawnee, Okmulgee, Grandfield, Lawton, McAlester, Eufaula, Muskogee, Sapulpa, Claremore, Hugo and also in Kansas and Missouri.

Reed didn't just build the pools. He participated in dedication ceremonies, too, by providing ice cream cones for all the children who showed up.

Some years later, he recalled that when the pool in Parsons, Kan., was dedicated, he used 400 gallons of ice cream in distributing cones. And the opening of a pool in Muskogee was attended by about 6,000 children who ate 440 gallons of ice cream.

Distributing ice cream cones earned him another title: Summer Santa Claus.

After hearing Henthorne speak at the Kiwanis club, Reed recalled that when he lived in Chicago, where he sold newspapers on the street corners, the best fun of his young life was to find a fire hydrant that was turned on and to lie down in the stream of water or to follow after a sprinkler cart.

His ambition was to learn to swim and dive and to loll in cool water, but he was always too busy working.

Eventually, he became a lawyer, got married and moved to Wewoka in 1905 to practice law. He acquired large tracts of land in Seminole County, and when oil was discovered on his holdings, he became wealthy.

The family moved to Tulsa in 1917 and Reed became active in civic affairs.

He was a member of the Chamber of Commerce, Tulsa Country Club and the Kiwanis Club. The family moved to Neosho, Mo., in 1924 and to California in 1931 a few months before Reed died in San Francisco.

Reed died only a few months after a 29-acre park at 41st Street and Union Avenue was named in his honor. A pool was opened there later. His name had been used earlier for the Reed Playground and Wading Pool at Eighth Street and Delaware Avenue and for the pools in many other communities.

History visible in faded town's statue

A statue at the town's main intersection welcomes visitors to Skedee, a one-time oil boom town in Pawnee County, although there are few visitors or residents to visit.

No stores remain – not even a grocery or a service station – forcing residents to drive five miles to Pawnee for food and gasoline.

The statue is a reminder of an earlier day when two passenger trains a day served Skedee on the line between Arkansas City, Kan., and Shawnee, which was part of the main line to Texas.

The block between the railroad track and the main intersection was lined with businesses – a hotel, a hardware store, a creamery station, a grocery store, a clothing store, a rooming house and a bank. There also were two other hotels, another bank and a few more grocery stores.

Passenger trains stopped overnight at a first-class three-terminal station, and passengers spent the nights in the hotels.

Skedee also had churches, schools and restaurants.

Only boarded-up buildings remain in the Skedee business district. The community still has a church and an old school building that was built in 1924 and is kept in good repair by the community. It is used a few times a year for meetings.

The high school closed in 1949, the elementary school in 1966. The few Skedee children now attend school in Pawnee or Ralston. Its population was estimated at 103 residents in 2003.

Skedee was incorporated in 1903. Its name is an Anglicized version of the Skidi (wolf) band of Indians of the Confederacy who once occupied the area.

The "Bond of Friendship" statue of former Osage Chief

Tulsa World Archives

The "Bond of Friendship" statue, erected by Colonel Ellsworth Walters in 1926, stands at the main intersection in Skedee. The 65-ton statue depicts Walters shaking hands with Osage Chief Baconrind.

Baconrind and Colonel Ellsworth Walters shaking hands was erected in 1926 by Walters, who had been the auctioneer employed by the Department of Interior to sell oil leases for the Osage. Colonel was Walters' given name, not a military rank. He was named in memory of Col. Henry Ellsworth, a Civil War officer admired by Walters' father.

Walters held the lease auctions under an elm tree at the Osage Agency in Pawhuska, and more than $1 million was paid many times for leases – giving the tree the name "Million Dollar Elm."

Incidentally, the original tree no longer is there but has been replaced by another tree. That is where the name for the four Osage casinos in the Tulsa area was derived.

The $20,000 statue in Skedee was dedicated June 19, 1926, at a ceremony attended by about 3,000.

Baconrind, speaking in his native tongue, told the crowd that he wished for eternal peace and understanding between whites and Indians and praised Walters for his efforts to help the Osage get the most for their oil.

"That statue will be here long after I'm dead and gone," Walters said prophetically at the dedication. Baconrind and Walters both died in 1946.

The statue deteriorated over the years but was partially restored in 1972 with state funds, including touching up the lettering of a poem on the base that can be read today. It says, in part:

"Side by side upon the summit,
their good chief and I will stand,
showing to the world our friendship,
by the strong clasp of our hands."

1917 train crash killed 28, injured 50

A passenger train and an empty troop train crashed head-on near Kellyville on Sept. 28, 1917, killing 28 and injuring 50.

It was the worst train crash in Oklahoma history.

Engineer John Ruhl of Sapulpa told reporters the day after the crash that he had been told to stop his westbound passenger train to allow another eastbound passenger train and a troop train behind it to pass.

He said he stopped his loaded westbound train on a siding at the Kellyville station and watched as the eastbound passenger and a following troop train went past. Unaware that the troop train had been split into two segments, he pulled his train back onto the main tracks and was running at top speed when he ran into the second troop train.

The crews of both engines jumped off moments before the crash, saving their lives but causing severe injuries to some.

Fireman W.N. Catterton said his train had just crossed the bridge over Polecat Creek when he saw the other train coming around a curve just ahead. He said Ruhl threw on the train's brakes and whistled for a stop but the train couldn't be stopped in time.

"I jumped as he did," Catterton said. "That's all I remember. I rolled down an embankment 50 or 60 feet and laid there unconscious until picked up." He said Ruhl hit on higher ground and was not badly hurt.

Although injured, Ruhl was found wandering around in a daze miles from the crash. When he talked with report-

Tulsa World archives

On Sept. 28, 1917, the deadliest train crash in Oklahoma history killed 28 people and injured 50.

ers at his home in Sapulpa the next day, he was shaking at times and appeared to be on the verge of collapse.

The passengers weren't that lucky. Many of the passengers with minor injuries joined in a search for survivors.

Most of the 28 dead and 50 injured had been passengers in what was called a combination car – a Jim Crow section for black passengers and a section for smokers. Witnesses said the mail car and the combination car were telescoped together so they looked like one car.

Searchers chopped holes in the sides of these units so they could crawl through looking for survivors.

Some of the rescue crew told reporters later that many severely injured passengers who were pinned in the wreckage begged to be killed to end their severe pain.

Ambulances were sent to the scene from Sapulpa, Kellyville, Bristow and other towns. A special train took doctors and nurses to the scene from Sapulpa, and many of the victims were loaded onto it to be taken to Tulsa hospitals.

Creek County sheriff's deputies rushed to the crash site to guard the contents of the mail and baggage cars. They had orders to shoot any prowlers or looters.

There were reports that an unusually large amount of money was being transported in the mail car.

"It was terrible, the moans of the crushed and dying and the sight of my train torn to pieces," Ruhl said the next day. "I know I'll see it forever."

Bandit had many after-death adventures

Bumbling train robber and bank bandit Elmer McCurdy's body was finally buried in Guthrie in 1977 – 66 years after he was killed in a shootout with Osage County deputies.

In the interim, his body had stood in a corner of a Pawhuska funeral home for several years, toured the country in sideshows, was collateral on a $500 loan and became a featured attraction hanging from a gallows in a California fun house.

The fun house gig ended when owners, who thought the body was wax, discovered

Tulsa World archives
Western re-enactors take part in the burial of Oklahoma outlaw Elmer McCurdy in 1977, 66 years after he was killed in a shootout.

a bone inside when they tried to glue an arm back on after it fell off. The medical examiner's office was called, an autopsy was performed, and the mummy's body was identified as that of McCurdy.

McCurdy's story began about 1880 in Maine, where he was born to an unmarried mother who died when he was about 20. He headed west, tried working as a miner and served a hitch in the Army.

When he was discharged, McCurdy tried a few jobs before deciding to become a bandit. He apparently picked the wrong profession, because he never became an accomplished robber.

In his first attempt at burglary, McCurdy and three companions jumped aboard a train near Lenapah with plans to blow open the train's safe. But McCurdy used too much nitroglycerin and the explosion tore a hole in the side of the express car. It also melted about $4,000 worth of silver and fused it onto a wall. McCurdy was unable to retrieve it with a pick. Train employees later pried it off with a crowbar.

He was equally inept with his next caper. In the middle of the night, McCurdy and a companion broke into a bank in Chautauqua, Kan., with plans to blow the door off the safe. Once again, McCurdy used too much nitroglycerin and the explosion threw the safe door through the lobby – destroying furniture and everything in its path – but an inner door of the safe was still intact.

McCurdy prepared another charge but before he could set it off, the other burglar noticed lights coming on in the town, so they grabbed some coins from the top of the safe, jumped on their horses and fled.

His final foray was on Oct. 4, 1911, when McCurdy and two companions hopped on a train near Okesa (south of Pawhuska) about 1 a.m., expecting to net a large sum of money headed for the Osage Indian tribe. But it was the wrong train: one that carried no money.

Their total loot was about $43 and two gallons of whiskey. The Bartlesville Enterprise reported the haul was "the smallest in the history of train robbing."

A posse of three sheriff's deputies using a bloodhound tracked the incompetent robber to a barn near Pawhuska three days later. An hour-long shoot-out ensued, ending when the would-be robber was shot to death.

McCurdy's body was taken to a Pawhuska funeral home where it was embalmed using arsenic, which acts as a preservative, and the mortician waited for family members to claim the corpse. But no one came; McCurdy was an orphan and apparently had no relatives.

The corpse, still in the clothes McCurdy wore in his fatal fight and with a rifle in his hands, stood in a corner of the funeral home for several years. A few years later, two men claiming to be McCurdy's relatives took the body, and it ended up in a touring sideshow.

That was a common end for desperadoes' bodies in those days, and McCurdy's body drifted around the country for years with such shows until his notoriety was exhausted. At times, his body was displayed along with wax figures of other bandits such as Jesse James.

The corpse was posted as collateral for a $500 loan that went unpaid, and McCurdy changed hands, eventually winding up stored in a warehouse with wax dummies. The body was among several dummies that were sold to an amusement park. McCurdy's body was painted with fluorescent paint and a light was wired to flash on and off to startle visitors to the fun house.

A television crew from the "Six Million Dollar Man" borrowed the set for a TV program and the arm fell off when the body was being moved.

Dr. Clyde Snow of Oklahoma City, a specialist in identifying bodies, was consulted and established McCurdy's identity. The body was sent back to Guthrie, where it was buried beside some of the Dalton gang members in a potter's field with at least 10 other badmen from Oklahoma's early days.

Judge's sentences: good grammar

Juanita Kidd Stout, a native Oklahoman who began her professional career teaching music in Oklahoma schools, became the first black woman to win election to a seat on a state's court of record, which led to service on the Pennsylvania Supreme Court.

But, as pointed out in her obituary in the New York Times, she remained "first and foremost an English teacher."

There was good basis for that observation.

She sometimes stopped lawyers during their arguments to correct their grammar. She told attorneys to learn how to spell before filing motions in her court. She was chagrined when she encountered college professors who misused the language.

And woe to any lawyer who sought to "appraise" her of something.

"I know my value." she would snap. "Now if you want to apprise me, get on with it."

She lectured widely, always stressing the value of education and warning about the danger of declining literacy. Speaking at the annual 4-H Club Congress in Chicago in 1980, she encouraged the 4-H'ers to read more. "Many high school graduates cannot read the diplomas they take home," she said.

Stout was born and grew up poor in Wewoka. "We didn't have indoor plumbing until I was 13," she once said in rejecting a defendant's poverty excuse for crime.

Both her parents were teachers, and she learned to read at 3, entered the third grade at 6 and began college at 16. She first attended a black school in Missouri and graduated with a bachelor's degree in music from the University of Iowa. She received her law degree from the University of Indiana while her husband, Charles Otis Stout, was studying for his doctorate.

After receiving her bachelor's degree, Juanita Stout taught music in Sand Springs and Seminole before going to Washington looking for a job during World War II – and became an attorney by accident, she once said.

The job she found was taking shorthand, which she had learned in high school, with a law firm. That created an interest in the law and she began taking law courses, first in

Tulsa World archives

Juanita Kidd Stout, a native Oklahoman, served on the Pennsylvania Supreme Court, but her obituary in the New York Times pointed out that she remained "first and foremost an English teacher."

Washington and later in Indiana.

She worked in the Philadelphia district attorney's office before being elected to the Common Pleas Court in 1959, the first black woman in America to be elected to a judicial court of record.

Pennsylvania Gov. Robert Casey nominated her during a Martin Luther King Jr. birthday celebration in 1981 to fill the position of a state Supreme Court justice who had died, telling more than 1,500 people at the event "she's a very highly qualified person."

During her years of handling criminal cases in the court, she said, the most common characteristic she found in defendants who engaged in violent behavior was the inability to read. "A child who cannot read cannot succeed," she said.

Judge Stout also maintained a level of decorum in her courtroom. Once she pointed a finger at two defendants. "You and you. Outside. Be back here with respectable haircuts in two hours." And they were.

In 1965, she was threatened several times but sentenced several members of a gang to prison just three days after she received a telephone call from a gang member who warned: "Don't send any of our corner away; we know where you live."

She said she was not afraid or apprehensive, explaining "we can't have Philadelphia run by illiterate gangsters." And while not afraid, she was cautious and her "closest companions" became the police officers who drove her to work every morning and home at night.

Stout also received several death threats in the mail and was outraged. The grammar was atrocious, she said, and the letters were riddled with misspellings.

She was inducted into the Oklahoma Hall of Fame in 1981. She died of leukemia in August 1998 at the age of 79.

A six-page feature on Stout in a 1965 edition of Life magazine noted that the judge "seeks the ultimate approval of only one person – her 82-year-old mother in Oklahoma."

Her mother's admonitions to her daughter were listed as: "Juanita, you study." "Juanita, you be good." "Juanita, be useful."

Oklahoman honored for WWII battle

"This is going to be a fighting ship," Navy Cmdr. Ernest Evans of Oklahoma said at the commissioning of his destroyer, the USS Johnston, which was sunk a year later in the biggest naval battle ever fought.

"I intend to go in harm's way, and anyone who doesn't want to go along had better get off right now," Evans added in his speech to the crew of the new vessel in October 1943 at Seattle. Evans' words were prophetic.

Three months later, the Johnston was shelling the beaches at Kwajalein in the Pacific and saw action in several other battles, but things were relatively quiet until the Battle of Leyte Gulf, also known as the second battle of the Philippine Sea, that began on Oct. 25, 1944. Evans was posthumously awarded the Medal of Honor, the nation's highest tribute, for his part in that battle.

The Johnston was one of three destroyers and four destroyer escorts forming a protective screen around three groups of carriers off Samar when a Japanese task force appeared, apparently headed for the Surigao gulf.

The Japanese task force included four battleships, seven heavy cruisers and nine destroyers – considerably more firepower than that of the American ships. Also in the Japanese task force was an 80,000-ton battleship, the largest ever built up to that time.

Evans suffered shrapnel wounds in the hand, back and face during the fierce battle as his ship was hit by 14-inch shells.

The Johnston was heavily damaged and had used all of its torpedoes but continued making simulated torpedo runs to fool the Japanese sailors, and the crew kept up fire from the ship's five 5-inch guns until it sank.

Because the damage had caused a loss of communication and had destroyed the ship's steering control, Evans shouted steering orders through an open hatch to men who turned the ship's rudder by hand until the Johnston lay dead in the water after three hours of fierce combat, according to the Medal of Honor citation.

Tulsa World archives

Ernest Evans, a native of Pawnee and a Muskogee High School graduate, was posthumously awarded the Medal of Honor, the nation's highest tribute, for his role in the Battle of Leyte Gulf, also known as the second battle of the Philippine Sea, in World War II.

The Johnston was credited with sinking a heavy cruiser and damaging a battleship, two more heavy cruisers and three destroyers.

As the Japanese armada steamed past, the captain of one of the ships saluted the sinking Johnston.

Evans was the last to leave his ship and was seen swimming in the water. He swam and floated for five hours but then disappeared.

It was 50 hours after the battle before the Johnston's survivors were rescued. Half the crew died from wounds, exposure and possibly sharks.

Evans first was awarded the Navy Cross and Bronze Star posthumously and later was awarded the Medal of Honor by President Harry S. Truman who said "his valiant fighting spirit throughout this battle will endure as an inspiration."

Two bronze plaques were presented to Muskogee High School in 1971 in honor of the World War II hero. One plaque bears the text of the Medal of Honor citation describing the battle in which he died. The other has Evans' picture and name.

Evans was one of four officers whose activities during the naval war in the South Pacific are detailed in "Sea of Thunder" by Evan Thomas, which was published in 2006. The others are Adm. William (Bull) Halsey and Japanese Adms. Takeo Kurita and Matome Ugaki. The book's jacket says it is about "four commanders and the last great Naval Campaign 1941-1945."

Evans, a Cherokee Indian, was a native of Pawnee. He graduated from Muskogee High School in 1926 but had attended high school until his sophomore year in Okmulgee. His mother and other relatives lived in Tulsa, where Evans had visited them before taking the Johnston into action.

He graduated from the Anapolis Naval Academy in 1931 and was at Manila when the Japanese bombed Pearl Harbor on Dec. 7, 1941. He was commander of the destroyer Alden before taking over the Johnston.

Tulsa cop invented the 'yield' sign

Drivers throughout the country see – and most observe – a yellow triangular sign every day that was invented by a Tulsa policeman. Variations of it have been adopted in other countries.

The "yield" sign looked a little different when it was invented by police Capt. Clinton Riggs, but the message is the same: "Yield to other traffic."

Riggs first joined the Tulsa Police Department in 1934, and became one of the state's first Highway Patrol troopers in 1937. He later returned to the Tulsa police force in 1945 after serving in the Army Air Corps as an intelligence and plant protection officer during World War II.

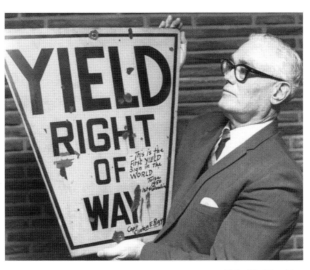

Tulsa World archives

Clinton Riggs, a former Tulsa police officer and Oklahoma Highway Patrol trooper, invented the "yield" traffic sign. In this undated photo, he holds a sign that has been marked "the first yield sign in the world, Tulsa, 1950."

He was the department's administrative assistant chief when he retired in 1970.

The first "yield right of way" signs were installed on a test basis in 1950 at First Street and Columbia Avenue, the most dangerous intersection in Tulsa at that time. Within six months, that intersection had dropped to the seventh most dangerous, and other police departments took notice.

The signs began appearing shortly afterwards throughout the country and eventually spread to foreign countries.

Riggs developed the idea for the signs while attending the Northwestern Traffic Institute in Chicago in 1939 and began experimenting with them while working as a state trooper.

He told a reporter that his idea was not only to control traffic, but to establish civil liability in a collision by showing which driver had failed to yield the right of way.

The first signs, shaped like a keystone, were yellow with black lettering that said "yield right of way." They have evolved into triangle shapes and now say just "yield."

The January 1952 issue of Popular Mechanics magazine reported that the sign had reduced accidents and called it a "shining example of American know-how and inventiveness."

The "yield" sign was just one of the innovations credited to Riggs, but it was the best-known. But Riggs was most proud of the educational and employment requirements he instituted in the department.

"You can't make good rabbit stew unless you have the right kind of rabbit," Riggs said, explaining the need for high standards for police officers, while at the dedication of the Southwest Police Station when it was named for him.

For a police department to operate efficiently, "it must have a good body of knowledge and a way to apply it practically in the field," Riggs said.

One of Riggs' earliest signs is in the Smithsonian Institution in Washington.

He also designed the badges worn by officers from 1952 until they began wearing centennial badges last year and the shoulder patches, shaped like the yield signs but with yellow lettering on a black background. Those patches were worn by officers until they changed to blue uniforms in November 2005.

Riggs was instrumental in creating the Tulsa Police Academy, forming a pension plan, creating a uniform and equipment allowance for officers, and establishing the requirement that officers have university degrees.

Riggs, born in 1910 in Fairview, graduated from Tulsa Central High School in 1929 and earned a law degree from the University of Tulsa in 1954. After retirement, he taught at Tulsa Junior College and the University of Tulsa. He died in 1997 at age 86.

He wrote handbooks for officers, including the "Law of Arrest for Police Officers" and "Police Officer Witness," and was the author of an Oklahoma law that prohibits convicted felons from carrying firearms, a law that bears his name. The Southwest Police Station at 7515 S. Riverside Drive was named in Riggs' honor in 1993.

Convict tried twice to escape life term

It's not always better outside the walls.

Convicted killer Garland Rex Brinlee Jr. escaped twice from the state penitentiary at McAlester but was ready to go back eight days after the second time he broke out.

At least he surrendered peacefully. Prison guards and the Highway Patrol had been searching in the area between McAlester and Eufaula for Brinlee and six other inmates who had escaped on June 19 by crawling through a utility tunnel that runs under the prison. The other prisoners also were captured.

Brinlee gave up June 27, 1976, to an off-duty prison guard in a grocery store in Canadian, a few miles north of the prison.

Brinlee was covered with tick and chigger bites, which may have helped persuade him to surrender to guard C.A. Pierce, who was in the store when Brinlee arrived. He had been wandering through thick underbrush as he tried to evade capture. Brinlee paid for some pop and a sack of potato chips and then met Pierce eye-to-eye.

Store owner Robert Jones said Brinlee started talking to Pierce, then they went outside. Pierce returned inside, made a telephone call and a short while later, Pierce drove Brinlee back to the prison in his pickup truck.

"I didn't want to hurt the man, and knew I'd have to get away, so I just gave up," Brinlee said.

"That's the real image of Rex Brinlee, not the media image everyone's accustomed to. I'm a very fair person. I only get hard if I'm pushed into it. I've always been one to step backwards," he told a World reporter.

Before their escape, all of the men had been on night maintenance assignments and had been working on refitting pipes for a new boiler system. Prison officials said they had sawed some bars at two points in the pipeline utility tunnel.

After his capture, Brinlee insisted the escape was "a spur of the moment thing," but prison officials believed it had been planned for several weeks.

The first time Brinlee escaped was during a July 1973 riot that devastated the prison. He was captured six weeks later in Biloxi, Miss.

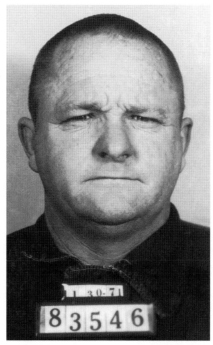

Tulsa World archives

Garland Rex Brinlee Jr. — sentenced to life in prison for the 1971 killing of Bristow teacher Fern Bolding — escaped from the state's maximum security prison, Oklahoma State Penitentiary, in 1973 and again in 1976.

Brinlee, now 74, is serving a life term for the murder of Fern Bolding, a Bristow school teacher, who was killed Feb. 2, 1971, when an explosion ripped apart the family pickup as she started it to go to her school. Her husband, Donald Bolding, had been scheduled to testify against Brinlee in Tulsa County in a pickup theft charge.

Brinlee, a Tahlequah plumber and nightclub owner who had boasted about contracting the bombing, didn't take the news of his conviction calmly.

Although he was stoic at first, he hit KTUL-TV photographer Richard Wilson in the head while in the Okmulgee County courthouse. As he was being returned to the Tulsa County Jail, he attacked Tulsa World photographer Don Hamilton as Hamilton shot a picture.

Bolding's brother, Gene, was the Tahlequah police chief and a bitter enemy of Brinlee.

Brinlee denied from the witness stand that he had arranged the bombing. He said some of the statements attributed to him had been taken out of context and that he made others jokingly, since he was being blamed anyway.

Several appeals for parole by Brinlee have been turned down. He also must serve sentences for escape and larceny and faces federal prison terms if ever paroled in Oklahoma.

Before his second escape, Brinlee had told former Gov. David Hall in a letter that he "owed" Hall and the late Tulsa attorney Patrick Williams about four sticks of dynamite. Hall had signed the extradition request to bring Brinlee back from Mississippi, and Williams represented Brinlee's wife in a divorce suit.

The letter also threatened the late Tulsa attorney Thomas Dee Frasier, who had defended Brinlee in the Bolding murder case, and Sen. Robert Medearis, D-Tahlequah, an officer of a Tahlequah bank that held a mortgage on an apartment owned by Brinlee.

The bank had foreclosed on the apartment to satisfy a $50,000 legal fee for Frasier. The letter also made a threat against an unidentified foreman of Mrs. Brinlee's ranch for becoming too close to Mrs. Brinlee.

Prisoner's art seeks pardon or home

For many years, the only brightness in the drab confines of the Oklahoma State Penitentiary was in the rotunda at the main entrance – four huge paintings by a German nobleman who was a convicted killer.

But those paintings were deteriorating rapidly and were removed about six months ago, leaving no contrast to the bleakness of the prison bars.

The paintings were the work of Conrad Maas, a high-born German who came to America in 1890 with his commoner wife, and tried farming for a while in Blaine County, where he was known as a loner. He was sentenced in 1899 to life in prison for killing his wife.

Tulsa World archives

"The First Thanksgiving in America" is one of four 24-foot paintings that were displayed in the Oklahoma State Penitentiary rotunda until recently. The paintings by Conrad Maas, one of the prison's first inmates, have deteriorated, and prison officials are considering what to do with them.

The paintings were removed because "they were basically rotting away," Linda Morgan, field operations supervisor of the prison, said. "We'd like to find a home for them, but they are part of Oklahoma history, and we don't want them to be moved out of state."

The paintings have seen riots and had bullet holes in them and have faded because of sunlight shining on them. They also are falling out of their frames, Morgan said.

Known as the "Mad Artist," Maas was one of the first 500 inmates at the penitentiary when it opened in 1910 and remained there until he died of a heart ailment in 1936 at the age of 70, leaving the paintings as his only legacy.

He refused paroles in the 1920s and 1930s, but one of his last wishes was that he not be buried inside the prison walls.

A fellow German claimed his body the day after his death and had it buried in Oak Hill Cemetery east of the prison.

Born of Hohenzollern nobility, Maas married a beautiful peasant girl named Martha or Margaret, who was considered beneath his social class. They left Germany in disgrace in 1890 and moved to America, settling in Blaine County, where Maas worked as a stone mason and intended to become a farmer.

Maas knew little of planting and harvesting crops and was slow in adjusting to American customs. He and his wife lived in a dugout beside the Canadian River. They rarely socialized.

His wife disappeared in 1899, causing townfolk to become suspicious. After her body was found in the couple's dugout, Maas was arrested and confessed he had killed her.

After his sentence to life in prison, Maas was confined in Kansas because Oklahoma was not yet a state and had no prison. But when the penitentiary at McAlester opened in 1910, he was among its first prisoners.

Maas taught himself to paint as a diversion from his caged life. He became a trusty and was allowed to occupy a studio in the loft of the prison mule barn.

Using worn mattress ticking for his canvas and brushes smuggled to him, Maas completed more than 50 paintings, most with a religious motif. Many were donated to churches and others were sold to guards and inmates for $5 each.

Many of his paintings were hung in the prison dining room until it was redecorated many years ago. Most were then stored in the basement where they rotted, but four 16-by-24-foot paintings were moved to the rotunda where they were hung 60 feet from the floor until they deteriorated beyond repair.

Three of those paintings were named "Mary and Joseph's Flight to Egypt," "George Washington at Valley Forge" and "The First Thanksgiving in America." The title of the fourth painting is long forgotten.

Morgan said a Houston expert provided a $300,000 estimate to restore the paintings in 1987. But the state couldn't afford that, and nothing was done.

She said the paintings have been featured in Arts and Antiques magazine and have been examined by officials from Tulsa's Gilcrease Museum.

Teague shaped girls' basketball

A first-grade teacher was asked in 1926 by a group of high school girls in the small town of Byng to coach them in basketball.

Bertha Frank Teague had never played the game and didn't know anything about it. She'd never worn a pair of tennis shoes. But she agreed to be the coach, bought a book about basketball for $1, taught herself the fundamentals and retired 43 years later as the winningest high school coach in the history of the game.

Her teams had won 1,157 games, eight state championships and, at one time, had a 98-game winning streak. Her teams competed in 22 state tournaments, won 38 conference titles and went undefeated five times.

Teague, who died in 1991 at the age of 92, had been inducted into the National Basketball Hall of Fame, the Oklahoma Sports Hall of Fame, the Missouri Basketball Hall of Fame and the Oklahoma Women's Hall of Fame. She was named Oklahoma's Coach of the Decade in 1974 and won an OSU Alumni Association Hall of Fame award in 1987.

"My only regret is I never played the game," Teague told a World reporter in 1989 when she became the first woman inducted into the Oklahoma Sports Hall of Fame. Two years earlier, she was the first woman inducted into the Naismith National Basketball Hall of Fame.

Teague recalled that in the 1920s, schools wouldn't hire women as coaches because of a feeling they didn't know anything. "They probably didn't. I didn't," she said. "I got a little book and the first year, my girls won a pennant. I was hooked for the next 43 years."

Generally regarded as the mother of girls' basketball in Oklahoma, Teague founded the Oklahoma Girls Basketball Association in 1962. She was instrumental in getting new rules adopted, which included unlimited dribble instead of

Tulsa World archives

Bertha Frank Teague, shown in 1989 with fellow Oklahoma Sports Hall of Fame inductee and rodeo legend Jim Shoulders, retired as the winningest high school coach in the history of basketball.

the two-dribble limit that was being used nationwide. Those new rules also opened the entire court to play and made contact with opposing players acceptable.

The rules previously divided the court into three divisions and prohibited touching a girl on an opposing team without it being a foul.

Teague wrote what is believed to be the first book on girls' basketball, "Basketball for Girls," a manual that has been used by girls' coaches throughout the country. "When I started coaching 25 years ago, I bought her book," Stigler coach David Sanders told a World reporter in 1991.

He said he followed Teague's ideas precisely and won three state titles. "She's the foundation of what girls basketball is all about in the state," he added.

Born in Carthage, Mo., Teague and her husband, James, moved to Byng in 1926, and she taught first grade for 40 years – in addition to coaching the high school girls' teams. James Teague, who died in 1981, served as superintendent for 39 years.

When she announced her retirement from coaching in 1969, Gov. Dewey Bartlett proclaimed "Bertha Frank Teague Day" on the Saturday her Byng team was to meet the Elk City team in the Class A state finals at Oklahoma City's State Fairgrounds, a game that attracted more than 8,000.

Elk City was leading 39-38 and Byng missed three shots in the final 10 seconds, but Byng sophomore Judy Corvin rebounded, fired a shot at the basket and scored, the final buzzer sounding while the ball was in the air. That basket gave the legendary Byng coach a state championship in her final game and helped make Judy Corvin an All-Stater.

State housed German POWs

Oklahoma was half a continent and an ocean away from the front lines, but thousands of German soldiers spent much of World War II in Oklahoma.

They were prisoners of war captured by American forces during campaigns in North Africa, Italy, France and other places where American troops fought Adolf Hitler's Nazis.

During their internment in Oklahoma, many of the POWs worked on farms, plowing, planting, harvesting crops and doing other chores that normally would have been done by the thousands of Oklahoma farmers who were in Europe fighting the Germans.

And many brought family members back after the war to show them where they had been in prison.

The first German POWs arrived in the state in the spring of 1943 and were housed at Fort Sill, McAlester, Stringtown, Fort Reno, Alva and Camp Gruber. At least two dozen sub-camps were established, and temporary camps were set up in many farming areas.

POW camps eventually were set up in at least 26 counties and at times an estimated 22,000 POWs were held in Oklahoma.

The POW camps at Fort Sill, McAlester and Stringtown had been set up a year earlier as internment camps for Japanese-Americans, who were shipped elsewhere when the need to house POWs arose.

The German prisoners were paid 10 to 80 cents per day for working, the amount depending on rank.

They didn't receive cash, but they could use the coupons to buy toiletries and beer at PX-type stores at their prisons.

Most of the prison camps had bands, orchestras and vocal groups.

Soccer was a popular pastime, and many POW teams were near-professional quality.

A World reporter said the first prisoners who arrived at Stringtown were sun worshippers and ardent practitioners of physical culture.

"They exercise and play games on every provocation

Tulsa World archives
German prisoners of war built replicas of German landmarks during their time at Camp Gruber.

and wear nothing but shorts and sandals and are browned like Indians.

"They are a hardy type and certainly don't resemble the bedraggled appearing prisoners of the once-vaunted Afrika Korps," referring to Gen. Erwin Rommel's command in North Africa.

Some of the prisoners were amazed that they could ride a train for four days and still be in the same country, and at the quality of life they saw from their train windows. They had boarded trains in New York, where they arrived by boat.

Many prisoners tried to escape but were captured within a few miles of where they had walked away from a work gang. Many returned to the camps on their own.

There was a rumor that one prisoner had made it back to Europe after escaping from an Oklahoma camp, but that was never confirmed.

A few of the POWs died while in Oklahoma camps, including Johannes Kunze, who was beaten to death at the Tonkawa camp where hard-core Nazis were held. A kangaroo court had convicted Kunze of treason.

Five Nazi POWs were arrested for the murder and were tried in secret at Camp Gruber. They were sentenced to hang but were not told of their punishment until three months later when they were taken to Fort Leavenworth, Kan., and hanged.

During a 1989 visit to the Alva camp site, Manfred Vieweg, 68, who was held in the camp in 1944 after his capture in Tunisia, recalled the death of a German prisoner who was shot by American guards as he tried to cut through a fence.

He said that incident, only a day or two after his arrival, discouraged him from trying to escape.

Former camp guard Millard Curtis said he seldom worried about his own safety, but recalled that there were times when he walked unarmed into the German prisoner compounds to take roll call and felt uneasy.

Army's Rock promoted education

One of the first 300 Tulsa County men drafted for military service in World War II rose through the ranks to become the second black Army officer to receive a general's star.

That draftee was Roscoe C. Cartwright, a graduate of Tulsa's Booker T. Washington High School, who was killed along with his wife and 90 others in a Virginia plane crash in 1974.

Cartwright had no interest in a military life after graduating from high school in 1936, preferring to attend college, earn a degree and begin a civilian life as a teacher. He attended Kansas State Teachers College at Pittsburg but couldn't complete his degree because of tight finances during the Depression years.

"I recall seeing very few blacks in uniform before World War II," he once told a reporter. "Therefore, being or becoming a soldier did not interest me."

And then came the Dec. 7, 1941, attack on Pearl Harbor by the Japanese. Cartwright was drafted a month later and was sent to Fort Sill as an Army private for training in the Artillery Corps. It may not have changed his attitude about military vs. civilian life, but his military career had begun.

When he entered military life, Cartwright was assigned to a field artillery regiment, an all-black unit except for the officers, who were white. He went to officers candidate school, received a commission as a second lieutenant and led his troops through combat in Italy. He also served in Germany and Japan.

His ambition had been to get through the war, return to his wife in Hope, Ark., and resume his college career. That idea changed when the war ended.

"All the schools were full so I decided to remain in the Army another year." And then his aim became to finish 20 years so he could retire.

But throughout his military career, he maintained an interest in education and established libraries and college courses for his troops.

Cartwright served in Korea and later in Vietnam, where he was a full colonel and was known as a maverick with the nickname of Rock.

During that service, Cartwright had a habit of showing up unannounced for visits to the five battalions he command-

Tulsa World archives

Then-Col. Roscoe C. Cartwright, who was en route to Vietnam, stopped in Tulsa to visit relatives in July 1969.

ed – a habit that he claimed fostered informality rather than pomp.

"When I go out to the firing batteries, I don't want the men to suddenly snap to attention and be rigid," he explained to a reporter in 1970. "I'd rather have them feel relaxed and free to talk over any problems or complaints."

His habit was to move into an artillery battery's area and attract little notice. Sometimes he shook hands with soldiers of two or three gun crews before an officer would catch up to him and welcome him to the area.

"I like to have direct contact with the men to determine their needs," he explained. "They need education and information programs so they won't look at their military tours as one of intellectual deprivation."

Cartwright, who had a bachelor of arts degree from San Francisco State College and a master of business administration from the University of Missouri, opened an education and information office when he assumed command of his 108th Artillery Group of XXIV Corps in Vietnam. He established a library with 2,500 volumes and arranged for college courses taught by accredited teachers serving their military tours.

Cartwright was promoted to brigadier general in 1971, becoming the second black Army officer to receive a star. The first was Benjamin O. Davis who received his star in 1940. Davis' son, Benjamin O. Davis Jr., also became a general, but he was in the Air Force.

Cartwright, 55, and his wife, Gloria, 49, were killed in the crash of a Trans World Airlines plane in Virginia in December 1974. The Cartwrights were returning to their home in Oxon Hill, Md., after a Thanksgiving family gathering at the home of a daughter.

The general had retired four months earlier after serving in the Pentagon. At his retirement, he was awarded the Distinguished Service Medal for his leadership and analytical ability, particularly in connection with development of a supply system to link civilian support units with combat units and Army Engineers.

During his career, the general also earned many other awards and medals, and after his death a scholarship fund was named in his honor.

Noted pianist came from musical family

As the longtime piano player for the sing-along segment of the melodrama "The Drunkard" and a performer at parties, Marna Graham McKinney could play almost any song written.

"If I've forgotten a tune and the person can hum it, I will remember it and be able to play it," she told a reporter in 1971. "I think it's a God-given talent."

The Tulsa elementary school teacher had a huge piano repertoire but never bought sheet music. "If I want to learn a new tune, I just listen to it a time or two and then begin to play it," she said.

She needed that large repertoire during the 15 years she played the piano every Saturday night for "The Drunkard" – accompanying the melodrama's action as well as the sing-alongs before the show and during its intermission and for acts in the olio, a time when amateurs had a chance to display their talent.

Edna Graham

This photograph of the Mill Creek Cornet Band was taken about 1900. Those pictured include Naomi Graham Frost (back row, far left), Ernest Graham (back row, far right), Cecil Graham (front row, second from left), T.C. Graham (front row, fifth from left) and Leota Graham Swinford (front row, far right). Marna Graham McKinney, a Tulsa pianist and elementary schoolteacher, was a daughter of Ernest Graham's.

McKinney, who died in 2000 at age 87, also played the piano for the Tulsa Press Club's Gridiron show for more than 20 years. She appeared on the initial program of Tulsa's first television station, KOTV, channel 6, where she was the music director. And she played at hundreds of parties.

She and her sister, Janice Graham Street, appeared together as "Two Maids of Music" in a piano duet on that first KOTV broadcast. They received so much favorable response from viewers that they were featured on KOTV programs for several months.

McKinney's talent wouldn't have been a surprise to anyone who knew her background.

"My whole family was musical – my parents, sisters and brothers," she said. "Family gatherings always have been fun because we all sat down and sang and played for our own enjoyment."

That family talent is displayed in a photograph of the Mill Creek Cornet Band that was taken about 1900 and was found recently by Edna Graham of Tulsa, McKinney's sister-in-law. Five of the band's 12 players were members of the John Thomas Graham family of Mill Creek, and many of his children, grandchildren and great-grandchildren inherited the musical talent.

Marna McKinney and Janice Street were the daughters of Ernest Graham, who is in the picture.

Their brother Harold directed high school bands in southern Oklahoma for several years and played in the Austin Kidwell Dance Band for 50 years. Janice Street's daughter, Marna Street, is the principal violist with the Cincinnati Symphony.

Three children of Harold and Edna Graham became musicians: Larry Graham is a concert pianist and piano teacher in Boulder, Colo.; Phil Graham is the interim choir director at Kirk of the Hills Presbyterian and a board member of the Tulsa Boy Singers; and Steve Graham is a board member of the Civic Music Association in Oklahoma City and a member of the English handbell ringers of St. Luke's United Methodist Church in Oklahoma City.

McKinney was born in Mill Creek and raised in Ada, where she graduated from East Central State Teachers College with a degree in instrumental music. She got her first teaching job in Maud and later moved to Tulsa to teach kindergarten at Franklin, Osage, Houston and Hoover elementaries.

"I used music a lot in the classroom, and the children enjoyed it," she said.

When McKinney retired from providing music for "The Drunkard," members of Spotlighters Inc., which produces the long-running melodrama, threw a surprise "This Is Your Life" party for her and told the story of her life in music – with McKinney once again providing the piano accompaniment.

The life story recounted that she began taking piano lessons at 5 years old but loved music even before that. According to the story, she was 4 when she interrupted an aunt who was playing hymns in church, calling out: "Play ragtime, Auntie!"

Pioneer attorney could spin juries

The most eloquent courtroom speech he ever made was only nine words long, a pioneer Oklahoma lawyer once told a reporter.

"An old man! An old fool! But still human," attorney Moman Pruiett told the court. And sat down.

Pruiett made the speech in the case of a man charged with violating the Mann Act by taking a girl from Oklahoma to Chicago and Kansas City. Pruiett said he had persuaded the defendant to plead guilty and the only issue before the court was sentencing. The prosecution objected that the nine-word argument was nonsense, but the judge accepted the defendant's plea, fined him $100 and freed him.

It was an unusual argument, but being unusual was typical for Pruiett, who was called "the most resourceful criminal lawyer ever to rise out of the Southwest."

He won acquittals for 303 of 343 accused slayers he represented.

Pruiett's philosophy was that "you got to be an actor, and you got to be a hypocrite and you got to be a faker to be a good lawyer."

"If you're not going to be a good lawyer, then you have no business being one at all," he told a reporter in 1944.

The resourceful description came from J.G. Hervey, dean of the University of Oklahoma law school in the 1940s, who said that to Pruiett a jury was "a musical instrument with 12 keys; if you can play it and secure a responsive chord, you win."

And Pruiett was adept at getting that responsive chord from juries, using three favorite methods of defense – self-defense, the unwritten law and an alibi.

In one hard-fought case, he claimed the victim was not actually dead but had substituted another body for his own. Pruiett had the prosecution so busy proving a main defense witness had lied about seeing the purported victim alive, the jury couldn't agree.

In his candid autobiography, "Moman Pruiett, Criminal Lawyer," published a few months before he died at the age of 73 in December 1945, Pruiett told brazenly about the jury tampering and witness bribing that helped gain his acquittal record. None of the murder defendants he represented was executed, although one was sentenced to hang. That sentence was commuted by President William McKinley after Pruiett argued that his client was too ignorant of civilized conduct to know better.

Pruiett always denied one anecdote about a man in a distant state who had wired the Oklahoma lawyer: "I am charged with murder, have $5,000, will you defend me?"

"Am leaving on the next train with three eyewitnesses,"

Tulsa World archives

Moman Pruiett, in this undated photo, was a pioneer Oklahoma lawyer who won acquittals for 303 of 343 accused slayers he represented. Pruiett's philosophy was that "you got to be an actor, and you got to be a hypocrite and you got to be a faker to be a good lawyer."

was Pruiett's reply, according to the often-told story.

Born on a river boat on the Ohio River, Pruiett worked as a shoeshine boy in Fayetteville, Ark., and later as a janitor for a law firm in Sherman, Texas, where he became interested in the law.

His law study was interrupted by his conviction on two larceny charges, one in Arkansas and one in Texas, by jurors who, he said, dozed during his trials before sending him to prison. He said he made up his mind that "no jury would ever go to sleep on me."

After his second conviction by a Texas jury, Pruiett shouted "I'll empty your damned jails, an' I'll turn the murderers and thieves a'loose in your midst – but I'll do it in a legal way."

His mother obtained a pardon for Pruiett two years later and a judge admitted him to the bar. Pruiett opened a law office at Pauls Valley in 1897 – and his colorful career began.

Defending a man charged with murder for slaying a man who had threatened him with a metal-capped pencil, Pruiett tried to prove that a pencil could look like a knife. The prosecution just laughed at his contention.

But no one laughed when Pruiett whirled toward the jury, his hair in his eyes and a wild look on his face. In his right hand, he held a pencil, poised high above his head. With the other hand, he grasped a juror's collar.

The jurors weren't sure whether the lawyer was holding a knife or a pencil and scrambled out of the jury box. When order was restored, they retired to deliberate and quickly acquitted the defendant.

"I never asked a client if he was guilty," Pruiett told reporters in several interviews. "It was none of my business. I was under oath to offer the best defense I could and with the help of God, I did that."

Although Pruiett spent most of his time representing defendants on criminal charges, he also was involved in politics and attended the Oklahoma constitutional convention representing the Democratic Party's executive committee. He almost had a county named for him.

But he opposed Charles N. Haskell's efforts to control the convention, and the Haskell forces changed the county's name from Moman to Creek to punish him. A Sapulpa street still bears his name.

Pruiett amassed a modest fortune and invested in a mansion and other property in Florida that were destroyed by a hurricane. He returned to Oklahoma to live the last few years of his life on a $40 per month pension in a cheap room in Oklahoma City.

Oil gave American Indian richest title

A dirt-poor, legally incompetent Creek Indian known as "Crazy Jack" became fabulously wealthy after oil was discovered on his "arbitrary allotment" of rocky land early in the 20th century.

When he died in 1933 at the age of 92, Jackson Barnett was known as the "world's richest Indian" although he never realized he was wealthy. He left a $20 million estate that was claimed by nearly 800 "heirs," including three women who claimed to have been his wife. The legal battle for his estate lasted for about 15 years.

The Barnett saga sounds more like a soap opera than a real-life situation. It had its beginning in the early 20th century after the Crazy Snake Rebellion, which involved a group of Creeks rebelling at all government contact, including accepting land allotments.

Creeks were allowed to select land allotments for farming; most chose fertile land along streams. Barnett, a full-blood Creek who was not a Snake, was deemed "too ignorant" to select good land and was given an "arbitrary allotment" of rocky land the others didn't want.

His "arbitrary allotment" near Drumright turned out to be in the middle of an oil field that was discovered many years after the allotments had been made. The value of that rock-studded farmland was estimated at $20 million, giving him the wealthiest title.

And then came romance. Anna Laura Lowe, 38 years Barnett's junior, was working as a waitress in west Texas when she saw his picture in an oil trade newspaper.

"That's the man for me," she said to herself, according to her testimony later in federal court, and she headed for Henryetta.

It apparently was love at first sight, at least on her part, after she took a cab to Barnett's log cabin and found the old man playing a card game while dressed only in pants – no shirt, no shoes, no socks, no underwear.

She loaded Barnett into the cab and headed for Okemah to get a marriage license, but the court clerk knew Barnett was a restricted Indian and refused to issue one. Undaunted, Lowe attempted to get a license in Holdenville, with the same result.

From there, she went to Coffeyville, Kan., where she

Tulsa World archives

Jackson Barnett and Anna Laura Lowe Barnett lived in a $200,000 mansion in Los Angeles built with his oil wealth, but after his death a judge annulled the marriage.

obtained a license and the two were married. She had consulted an attorney, U.S. Rep. Harold McGuigan, who had second thoughts about the marriage and told the new Mrs. Barnett to try Missouri. She and the groom headed to Neosho and repeated vows.

The two lived together for 14 years. Government officials allowed them $2,500 a month to live on and built them a $200,000 mansion in Los Angeles. But after Barnett died, a federal judge in Los Angeles annulled the marriage, ruling that Anna had kidnapped Barnett.

Suits seeking part of the estate were filed in McIntosh, Creek and Okmulgee counties and later were consolidated in U.S. District Court in Muskogee. When the court issued notice to unknown heirs, nearly 800 showed up, including the three women, one black, one Indian and one white, who claimed they were Barnett's wives.

Anna Laura, the last of the three women to testify, admitted on the witness stand that she had never spent even one night in the same room with her "husband." She said she hired a man to lock him in his room every night.

She claimed that she had not kidnapped Barnett; that he had gone with her voluntarily, but the court ruled that he had been incompetent from youth and did not have the capacity to enter a nuptial contract.

Several of the would-be heirs claimed to be Barnett's children, but others testified he had been mutilated as a youth and was never capable of fathering a child.

The estate, which had dwindled to only about $1 million, finally was distributed among several nieces and nephews, and their heirs.

Anna Laura did well for herself. Court testimony showed she drew about $700,000 while living with Barnett. The government tried to recover about $320,000 of the money without success.

Anna Laura said she "spent it." She died in poverty in 1952 and was buried by the Creek Nation.

The Barnett saga reads like a soap opera – except soap opera writers probably wouldn't have enough imagination to dream up all the melodramatic events of his life.

'Mad Dog' couldn't outrun police

Wilbur Underhill, ranked by many as Oklahoma's toughest badman during the 1930s gangster era, was known as the "mad dog of the underworld" and was feared even by some of his partners.

He had killed at least three people and robbed at least nine banks in Oklahoma, Kansas and Missouri. He probably would have killed more but was prevented from doing so by a partner.

Underhill escaped from the Oklahoma penitentiary in July 1931 and the Kansas penitentiary nearly two years later and managed to elude officers of both states and the Department of Justice for more than six months while robbing seven banks.

His downfall was triggered by his marriage to an old sweetheart, the sister of another bank robber.

When he and Hazel Jarrett Hudson obtained a marriage license at the courthouse in Coalgate, the fugitive used his real name on the document. And he gave the preacher who married them an address in Oklahoma City for the license to be mailed to him.

From that time on, Department of Justice and state agents watched the Oklahoma City address until Underhill showed up there on Dec. 30, 1933, and an agent watching the house sounded the alarm.

A posse of federal and state officers arrived too late to capture the fugitive but learned that he and his bride had gone to Shawnee. Armed with machine guns and sawed-off shotguns, the officers headed there – where they caught Underhill literally with his pants down.

Underhill, clad only in his shorts and socks, and his bride were preparing for bed in a house at 606 W. Dewey in Shawnee when the posse arrived and federal operative F.H. Colvin ordered Underhill to surrender. The command was answered by a fusillade from two automatic pistols fired through a window.

Colvin estimated that at least 200 shots were fired in the gunbattle, including about 80 fired by Underhill, who was hit by 13 slugs. None of the officers was hit, but the woman who owned the house was fatally wounded in the crossfire.

Still wearing just his shorts and socks, Underhill managed to walk and crawl 16 blocks in the bitterly cold night, leaving a trail of blood, to a downtown furniture store where officers found him on a bed four hours later.

Underhill's bride, who was arrested after the gun battle, visited him in a Shawnee hospital for 15 minutes; the next day before she was taken back to jail. No information could be found about whether she was charged with a crime.

Dave Carman / Tulsa World

"Our happiness didn't last long," she told reporters. "I love him in spite of what he was or has done."

Although Underhill wasn't expected to live through the night, his excellent physique made hard by his running and hiding and long days working in the Kansas prison coal mine kept him alive, and five days later he was transferred by ambulance back to the prison at McAlester, where he told Warden Sam Brown, "I'm ready to come back home."

Three hours later he died.

The secret transfer back to McAlester was scheduled because of reports that Underhill's cohorts were planning an assault on the hospital to free the gunman.

Underhill had a minor criminal record that turned major on Christmas night 1926 when the 25-year-old gunman and a companion robbed a drug store in Okmulgee. A young clerk yelled for help and Underhill shot him dead. While awaiting trial, he escaped from the Okmulgee County Jail and killed an Ottawa County sheriff's deputy while free.

He was sentenced to life in prison for the Okmulgee murder but escaped in July 1931. Less than a month later he killed a Wichita police officer and drew another life sentence in the Kansas penitentiary.

Less than two weeks after entering the prison at Lansing, he was believed to be the leader in planning an escape, but that didn't occur until May 1933, when Underhill teamed up with 10 other prisoners, including Oklahoma badman Harvey Bailey, who had been public enemy No. 1 for a time.

The convicts kidnapped Kansas Warden Kirk Prather and forced guards to open the prison gate. Within minutes, Bailey told officers later, Underhill said, "I'll kill the warden and that'll be less people in the car. I don't like him anyway," but Bailey slapped Underhill's gun arm as he started to pull the trigger on his gun.

Bailey separated from Underhill later because, he told officers, he was afraid of Underhill's conduct.

"He always wanted to kill someone. We'd drive through some town and every time he saw a cop he wanted to kill him. When he bought gasoline, he'd get mad and want to kill the man instead of paying him," Bailey said.

Other one-time associates also shunned him.

"Mad dog of the underworld" was an appropriate nickname.

A 'strange and disgusting' case

A payoff protection scheme involving Tulsa police and bootleggers was "a strange and disgusting story," the late U. S. District Attorney B. Hayden Crawford told a 1957 federal court jury.

Twenty men, including Police Commissioner Jay Jones, Police Chief Paul Livingston and Tulsa Tribune reporter Nolen Bulloch, were on trial in the scheme that also involved gambling and prostitution. Sixteen were convicted.

It was the most important criminal case spawned by Oklahoma's prohibition laws as well as the most important prosecuted by Crawford, who died Jan. 18, 2007, at the age of 84.

The trial resulted in a reorganized police department that increased its enforcement of liquor laws and may have been a force in the approval by voters two years later of a constitutional amendment that repealed Oklahoma's prohibition laws.

Crawford compared the conspiracy to Tennessee Williams' stage play and motion picture, "A Streetcar Named Desire." Instead of a streetcar, he told the jury in his opening statement, "we have a conspiracy named desire and the desire is for money."

The government alleged that Jones, Livingston, other police and Bulloch shared in payoffs to prevent the arrests of bootleggers and to block bad publicity in the Tribune.

He told the jury that "passengers will board and take part in this conspiracy; some will depart; some will stay on; some will get on later" but that the "conductor of this streetcar is a newspaper reporter – Nolen Bulloch – who is always on the streetcar."

Bulloch and two other defendants were acquitted by Judge Royce H. Savage before the jury began its deliberations. The jury convicted Jones, Livingston, six vice squad detectives, five bootleggers, a Missouri liquor dealer, a bookmaker and a pool hall operator. One person was acquitted by the jury. Some received one-year prison terms, some fines and some both.

Crawford received commendation letters from President Dwight Eisenhower and Attorney General William P. Rogers for his handling of the conspiracy case, which Judge

Tulsa World archives

U.S. District Attorney B. Hayden Crawford handled the prosecution of a payoff protection case involving Tulsa police and bootleggers in 1957. The case, which also involved gambling and prostitution, was the most important criminal case spawned by Oklahoma's prohibition laws. Crawford died Jan. 18 at the age of 84.

Savage called an "outstanding performance by a district attorney."

A year after the payoff trial, Crawford was confirmed by the Senate for another four-year term as DA, but he resigned to become chief of the executive office of U.S. Attorneys, a job that put him in charge of all federal DAs.

Born in Tulsa, "Bunny" Crawford was educated at the University of Michigan, where he worked in a kitchen peeling potatoes and frying eggs to help pay his expenses. He also joined the Naval Reserve Officers Training Corps and developed a life-long love of the Navy.

Crawford was called to active duty during World War II as a gunnery officer on a submarine named USS Spot. He was awarded the Purple Heart for wounds received in a gunbattle with a Japanese ship. After the end of the war, he became legal officer for the Pacific submarine fleet.

He returned to the university to earn his law degree, this time working as a laborer during summers. After establishing a practice in Tulsa, Crawford was appointed as the district attorney by President Eisenhower in 1954 and joined the attorney general's office after the payoff trials.

Crawford resigned from his job as a deputy assistant attorney general in Washington to become the Republican nominee for the U.S. Senate seat held by Robert S. Kerr in 1960, but he lost in the general election. He tried again two years later but lost to incumbent A.S. (Mike) Monroney.

Meanwhile, Crawford continued his service as a Naval Reserve officer and had risen to the two-star rank of rear admiral, the highest rank for a reserve Navy officer, before retiring in 1978.

Crawford also was active in civic affairs and was a 2002 Oklahoma Military Hall of Fame inductee. He had served as president of the Tulsa Kiwanis Club, the Navy League and of various military, university and professional organizations.

He was a member of the Army and Navy Club in Washington, D.C.; Garden of the Gods in Colorado Springs, Colo.; the Beach and Tennis Club in Pebble Beach, Calif.; Southern Hills Country Club; and the Summit Club.

Misguided bomb rattled Boise City

Bombs fell on Boise City in the middle of a July night in 1943, making it one of the few American cities to be bombed during World War II.

The explosions weren't extremely loud, but they awakened most, if not all, of the 1,200 people in the small Oklahoma Panhandle town, caused slight damage to a garage and a church, and triggered a blackout.

No one was injured.

The 30-minute air raid was all a mistake.

The bombs were 100-pound practice explosive devices, each filled with four pounds of dynamite and 90 pounds of sand each.

They were dropped by one of OUR airplanes.

Most of the lights of the small town had been turned out, except for four lights around the courthouse square, when the bombing foray began shortly after midnight.

A cafe was still open and several truck drivers were inside.

A few young couples wandered past the square, walking toward homes after leaving the local movie theater.

The first bomb crashed through the roof of a private garage and exploded, digging a 4-foot-deep hole in the floor. The B-17 made another pass and dropped a second bomb that nicked the white frame Baptist church, exploding beside the building and breaking several windows.

The plane made three more passes, dropping a bomb each time, all hitting within 93 feet of the courthouse.

It dropped a sixth bomb far from any buildings.

When the bombs began falling, the town's air warning officer, John Adkins, wired the adjutant general's office at the nearby Dalhart, Texas, Army Air Corps base: "Boise City bombed 1 a.m. Baptist church, garage hit."

The driver of a munitions truck parked on the square ran from the cafe and quickly drove his rig away.

Another trucker, at the wheel of a gasoline tanker, came within feet of being hit when the third bomb landed.

Frank Garrett, an electric company employee, immediately pulled the master switch that blacked out the town, including the four lights marking the courthouse square.

Either the blackout or a radio message to the pilot in response to Adkins' wire to the Air Corps base caused the pilot or navigator of the plane to realize the mistake – and the sixth bomb fell as the B-17 flew away.

The B-17 got off course while on a training flight with

Boise City News

Boise City marked the 50th anniversary of the July 5, 1943, accidental bombing by an American plane with a party and an unveiling of a 10-foot statue of a bomb buried in a crater. The crew members declined invitations to attend the party.

other planes from the Dalhart base to drop bombs in a range near Conlen, Texas, about 30 miles south of Boise City.

The lights of Boise City's courthouse square had the general pattern of the bombing range.

Lt. Max Siegel, public relations officer at the Army base, said he had determined no one had been hurt and that property damage was less than $25.

Maj. C.E. Lancaster, commanding officer of the base, said the fliers believed the lights were those of the bombing range.

The Boise City News called the event "mortifying" and "horrifying" in its next weekly issue.

The same bomber crew led an 800-plane daylight raid on Berlin a year after the misguided bombing of Boise City and became one of most decorated of World War II.

All of the crew members survived the war and one even married a Boise City girl.

Boise City marked the 50th anniversary of the July 5, 1943, bombing with a party at which a 10-foot statue of a bomb buried nose first in a crater was unveiled.

The crew members of the B-17 all declined invitations to attend the party.

Attorney Stan Manske, who hadn't been born in 1943, said at the statue's dedication "the memorial is really a reminder of the power of motivation."

The Jan. 5, 1943, Emporia Gazette reported that 10 practice bombs had been dropped on Reading, Kan., in an almost identical circumstance. They were practice bombs dropped by planes from Topeka Bomber Base.

Several communities on the West Coast – in California, Oregon and British Columbia – were hit by Japanese bombs that killed a woman and five children near Lakeview, Ore., and caused some damage, mostly minor, elsewhere.

Japan didn't have any airplanes that could fly far enough to drop bombs, so balloons were launched to carry the incendiary devices across the Pacific Ocean. Only about 1,000 of the 9,000 balloon bombs ever reached the U.S. and none started the hoped-for forest fires. Some may not have been found and could still be dangerous if found today.

Of course Honolulu was bombed by the Japanese on Dec. 7, 1941. But Honolulu was not an American city then because Hawaii had not yet become a state.

First OU black student faced hurdles

A retired Oklahoma City professor became the first black student at the University of Oklahoma in 1948, but he had to sit in an alcove separated from other students by a wooden railing.

His admission to the OU graduate school came after a three-judge federal court ruled he must be given equal educational opportunities. He took advantage of that and enrolled.

But George W. McLaurin, who was seeking a doctorate in school administration, was forced to eat at a special table in the cafeteria and was assigned a small table for studying on the fourth floor of the library amid stacks of newspapers for the first semester.

"Naturally I was under a handicap, and the pressure was terrific," McLaurin said of his first semester. "But I feel it was an accomplishment."

That didn't end the fight against segregation for McLaurin, 61, who had retired after 33 years of teaching. He quietly continued his studies and appealed to the U.S. Supreme Court, claiming the restrictions impaired and inhibited his ability to study, engage in discussion and exchange views with other students and, in general, learn his profession.

The high court agreed in a 1950 ruling that annulled segregation at the graduate level and followed that with a 1954 ruling forbidding segregation in public schools.

McLaurin finished his course work, but in spite of the ruling opening Oklahoma's colleges to blacks, he did not receive a degree. Tulsa attorney Amos Hall announced he planned to start an investigation of why McLaurin didn't pass his doctorate examination, but apparently that investigation wasn't pursued.

McLaurin's admission to OU was preceded by the case of Ada Lois Sipuel Fisher, a black woman who applied to the OU law school in January 1946. She was rejected at that time under terms of Oklahoma's segregation statutes. Her case was still in the courts when McLaurin was admitted.

When McLaurin applied for admission to OU, he was rebuffed by a state law dating back to the first Oklahoma

Associated Press

George W. McLaurin listens to Dr. Frank Balyeat's educational sociology lecture on Oct. 14, 1948, while sitting at a desk separated from the rest of the students at the University of Oklahoma.

Legislature in 1907 that provided a heavy fine for any administrator or teacher who operated or taught classes where white and black races were mixed.

Langston University was established for blacks seeking a bachelor's degree. Those seeking professional training in medicine, law, pharmacy, engineering, nursing and other graduate courses had to go out of state. Oklahoma followed the traditional Southern practice of providing grants for black students to go out of state for advanced degrees.

An article in Ebony magazine called the McLaurin family the "most educated family in Oklahoma." McLaurin, who died in 1968, had received a bachelor's degree from Langston and a master's of science in education from the University of Kansas. One son had a doctorate in economics. Another son and a daughter both held master's degrees, and all three had taught at Langston University, as had McLaurin.

His wife, Peninah, who died at the age of 74 in 1966, had more than 300 college hours and bachelor's degrees in economics and English.

The McLaurins had moved to Oklahoma in 1910, and Peninah McLaurin had begun the segregation fight in 1923 when she tried to enter OU. They sent their children out of state when they were 13 years old to complete their educations.

"I wrote the University of Oklahoma asking if I could enroll," she said. "They wrote back and said my credits were acceptable but state law prohibited my attending the white school. I wrote back and asked if I could take extension courses. They gave me the same answer."

When the Fisher case developed, the McLaurins decided to do something to help the situation if they could.

"I told Mr. McLaurin he was the right person," Peninah McLaurin said. "But it wasn't until the last day of enrollment that he decided to go ahead."

McLaurin wrote his doctoral dissertation on "Growth of the Separate Schools Since 1910 in Oklahoma." The dissertation included his own case.

Preacher urged new-time religion

The Rev. William H. "Bill" Alexander was as flamboyant as an Oklahoma City minister as he had been as a nightclub master of ceremonies before switching to preaching.

Almost from the day in 1942 that he became the pastor of the First Christian Church, he struck out for change and drew criticism from other ministers and members of other churches.

He added bowling lanes, pool tables and a dance floor in the church for teenagers. He preached against the Jim Crow law as un-Christian, led a conga line through his church and traded jokes with the comedian Red Skelton. He crusaded for better mental health institutions and criticized the "old-time" religion of the "Bible Belt."

He was criticized for dressing up in a claw-hammer coat and cowboy boots to marry Roy Rogers and the movie actress Dale Evans.

"Why must a good Christian look like an ad for a coffin factory?" he once asked. "If we practice Christianity the way Christ would want us to, we will concentrate on happy living and forget the heavy-hearted ritual."

Alexander became a popular lecturer and speaker throughout the country, ran for the U.S. Senate in 1950, was mentioned several times as a possible candidate for governor and supported the repeal of prohibition.

The Shelbyville, Mo., native wanted "to study anything but theology" when he enrolled at the University of Missouri. He stayed there for a year before taking a $250-per-week job as the master of ceremonies at a floor show at a St. Louis country club. But he changed his mind, decided to follow his father into the ministry and enrolled at Phillips University in Enid. He later switched to the University of Tulsa, where he graduated in 1939.

While attending Phillips, he took a $7.50-per-week job as the pastor of the Christian Church at Stroud, a community of 3,000, but he soon had a radio congregation of thousands through his "Oklahoma's Little Church Around the Corner" program over Tulsa station KVOO.

He outraged other ministers when he introduced billiard tables and Sunday night dances in his church recreation hall. In reply, Alexander simply said, "I'd rather have the boys and girls of my church dancing and having wholesome fun in our church youth center than hanging around the honky-tonks and beer taverns."

Tulsa World archives

The Rev. William H. "Bill" Alexander was the driving force behind the construction of an ultramodern church building that became known as "The Church of Tomorrow" in Oklahoma City.

Alexander endorsed the repeal of prohibition in 1949 when he appeared before a state Senate committee in Oklahoma City. He said he was as much against intemperate use of alcohol as any other minister but that he did not approve of a situation in which his 10-year-old son could dial 100 numbers in Oklahoma City and get whiskey delivered.

Alexander ran into trouble with his draft board in Stroud, which labeled him a conscientious objector. He appealed to Gen. Lewis B. Hershey, the national draft director, after the board refused him permission to go overseas as a war correspondent. He said he was not a conscientious objector.

Hershey finally gave him the permission he sought and he became a war correspondent for The Daily Oklahoman and a religious publication. He flew on bombing missions over northern Italy.

His wife, Charlsie, divorced Alexander in 1951, claiming he treated her like a servant, and she married Dr. Frederick Hulett the next year. Hulett had been Alexander's campaign manager when he ran for the Senate against Mike Monroney in 1950. Alexander married Hulett's ex-wife, Maryloise, in 1954.

Alexander was the driving force behind the construction of an ultramodern church building that became known as "The Church of Tomorrow." It was the building that was used as the survivor center after the bombing of the Murrah Federal Building in 1999.

The congregation spent $2 million in 1956 (a large sum then) for the 40-acre tract and buildings that included a shell-shaped sanctuary, fountains, a large torch and special lights. The center also had a large amphitheater where the Miss Oklahoma pageants were held for several years.

Alexander, 45, and his wife, 36, were killed in a plane crash in Harrisburg, Pa., on April 3, 1960, while headed to a speaking engagement in Hershey, Pa.

Alexander had told his congregation after their marriage in 1954: "She's a wonderful woman. I could spend the rest of my life with her."

Alexander was perhaps best described by Time magazine in 1950: "What Florenz Ziegfeld brought to Broadway and Tabasco sauce to the raw oyster, the Rev. William H. Alexander brought to religion in Oklahoma City.

"He put zing into church going."

Lawman known for toughness

When James F. "Bud" Ledbetter was elected sheriff of Muskogee County at the age of 70, some of the county's most notorious bootleggers closed their businesses.

They knew Ledbetter's reputation, established during more than 40 years as a lawman, including 30 years as a deputy U.S. marshal. He had announced plans to wage warfare against moonshiners and bootleggers.

"I hope they'll quit before I have to arrest them," Ledbetter said when he took the oath of office in 1923, adding that bootlegging and moonshining seemed to be the chief violations of laws in Muskogee County.

Many of the moonshiners and bootleggers took the hint and quit.

They understood the commonly expressed sentiment that "when Uncle Bud comes after you, you better go."

A 1923 newspaper article about Ledbetter's swearing-in said he was expected to be as successful in cleaning up Muskogee County as he had been in other fights during his 30 years as a deputy marshal when he had earned a reputation as a man "who didn't know the meaning of fear."

Early in his law career, Ledbetter became part of a "traveling court" that worked out of Muskogee, according to "The Fourth Guardsman," a book by Glenn Shirley. Working in that capacity, he rounded up suspects so they could be tried on the spot.

Born in Arkansas, Ledbetter's law enforcement career began by accident.

Ledbetter and his wife were farming near Coal Hill, Ark., when he went into town for supplies. Wearing a white linen suit, he walked through a saloon where a group of town bullies gathered around him. They fingered the fabric of the suit "to test the material" and one jerked his shirttail out.

Without a word, Ledbetter walked out, went to a hardware store where he bought an ax handle and returned to the saloon. Passers-by heard a commotion in the saloon and called the town marshal, who forced open the door and found nine men unconscious on the floor.

The town council insisted that Ledbetter take the job of

Tulsa World archives
James F. "Bud" Ledbetter established a reputation for toughness and dogged determination as an early Oklahoma lawman.

town marshal. Before long, the sheriff at nearby Clarksville, Ark., heard about Ledbetter and said a man who could tame Coal Hill belonged on his law force.

Ledbetter became a deputy sheriff of Johnson County, Ark., in 1880 and served 14 years. During that period that he established his fame for dogged pursuit. He trailed a murderer 1,000 miles for 30 days on horseback.

U.S. Marshal S. Morton Rutherford hired Ledbetter as a deputy in 1895. Among the criminals Ledbetter captured was train robber Al Jennings.

Ledbetter also provided security for Creek allotment transfers, quieted some race riots, busted up gambling dens and whiskey joints, arrested infamous criminals and kept a tense peace as statehood approached – for 10 cents per mile and $2 per diem, according to Shirley's book.

The lawman's reputation as a fearless officer was well-known, as shown shortly after he became a deputy marshal. Rutherford was trying to defuse a mob of Creeks who were threatening to storm the jail at Muskogee. Five members of an outlaw group known as the Buck gang were being held there. The gang had killed a deputy marshal and had attacked settlers and Creeks.

The mob wanted to see justice done immediately by hanging the outlaws, and Rutherford had only two deputies to guard the jail. He tried to persuade the mob to disband, but most didn't speak English.

Finally, Creek leader Pleasant Porter stood on a box and shouted: "Men, don't you see who is guarding those jail doors?

"You can rush that jail and you may succeed in getting that gang out, but rest assured many of you will be killed in the attempt."

The group saw Ledbetter and dispersed. Justice was served later – the five Buck gang members were hanged after trials before Judge Isaac Parker in Fort Smith.

Ledbetter retired as sheriff in 1928 and died nine years later.

Key wore many hats while in state

It's known as the Key Gate on maps and on highway signs in the area – a gate that leads into Fort Sill from Interstate 44.

It's appropriately named because it really is the key or main gate to the sprawling Army post in Comanche County – the training ground for all field artillery soldiers, Marines and many international students from allied nations.

Although it is the key gate, it's named in honor of Maj. Gen. William S. Key, former post commander, former 45th Division commander, former provost marshal for all U.S. forces in Europe, former American representative on the four-power Allied Control Commission for Hungary, former warden of the Oklahoma penitentiary, former state WPA head and former candidate for governor.

Born in Alabama and reared on a tenant farm, Key came to Oklahoma at the age of 21 and got a job that paid $12.50 a week. It wasn't long before he started a hardware and undertaking business in Wewoka.

To drum up business, Key waged a campaign throughout Seminole County that would do any political campaign proud. He visited all parts of the county, shaking hands with as many people as possible to inform them that Key's Hardware was about the best hardware store this side of Kansas City.

Key, who had served in an Alabama National Guard unit for a couple of years before coming to Oklahoma, joined a Wewoka Guard unit in 1912 as a private. Two years later he was a second lieutenant and served on the Mexican border campaign against Pancho Villa.

He led the Wewoka Guard unit to France in World War I as a captain, returning 17 months later as a lieutenant colonel.

Cartoonist Bill Mauldin, a member of the 45th Division when Key was the commanding general before and during World War II, once called Key "one of those rare commanders who refuse to order a subordinate to do anything they themselves wouldn't do."

Tulsa World archives

A part of Fort Sill and a state prison are named after William S. Key, who led soldiers, convicts and Depression-recovery efforts in the state.

As an example, Mauldin cited the time that an order was issued for every man in the division to take a series of conditioning hikes, starting at six miles and ending with 25. Gen. Key took the "every man" order literally and made all the hikes.

"Gen. Key has trained this outfit to the peak of perfection," Mauldin wrote after Key was assigned to Gen. Dwight D. Eisenhower's staff as provost marshal for U.S. Army forces in Europe. "And you can bet that every one of us when going into action will automatically think 'is this the way Bill would do it?' "

For five days during World War II, Key was the commanding general of all American forces in Europe. The commanding general was killed in a plane crash, and Key held that position until a successor was appointed.

Between wars, Key served twice as warden at the state penitentiary, the first time in 1924-27 and again in 1933-34. After his first stint as warden, The Daily Oklahoman noted that the penitentiary operation had cost taxpayers $340,000 a year during the four years before Key became warden. At the end of his first two years in the job, the cost had been wiped out and the prison was self-supporting.

The state's minimum-security prison in Fort Supply is named in honor of Key. Key had started an industrial program among the improvements he made at the prison.

In 1935, President Franklin Roosevelt appointed Key as state administrator of the Works Progress Administration. Under his administration, 550 new school buildings were built and additions were made to 478. The WPA under Key also built 129 other public buildings and 52 community buildings that were used for National Guard armories.

Key's only political venture came in 1938 when he sought the Democratic nomination for governor. He lost to Leon C. Phillips, a rabid opponent of Roosevelt's New Deal, by 3,000 votes, which was the closest race for governor up to that time.

C.V. Cessna traded wheels for wings

Clyde Cessna crashed his aircraft several times in 1911 as he experimented with flying at the salt plains near Jet. This is believed to be a photo of one of those crashes.

A car dealer from Enid who grew up on a farm and had no formal training saw an airplane in Oklahoma City in 1910, recognized it as the transportation of the future and returned home, where he built one of his own.

That car dealer was Clyde V. Cessna, whose name became synonymous with monoplanes and who later started the Cessna Aircraft Co.

A speaker at a 1953 testimonial banquet in Wichita related that Cessna, who had been an Overland automobile dealer in Enid for several years, watched two Frenchmen unload from a freight car and assemble a French Bleriot XI monoplane, the first flying machine in the state, in that 1910 visit.

"He was so impressed that he returned to his home at Enid and, from memory, made an 'aeroplane' of his own out of bamboo, wire and linen," George Haddaway, editor of Flight magazine, told those attending the banquet on the 50th anniversary of powered flight.

Haddaway said Cessna used a water-cooled outboard engine for power and trucked the monoplane to the Great Salt Plains near Jet in northwest Oklahoma to test it.

But there was a problem, Haddaway added. "He didn't know how to fly."

Undaunted, Cessna spent several days taxiing the aeroplane around the salt flats and finally pulled its nose off the ground and was airborne, only eight years after the Wright brothers' first flight.

Some sources report that Cessna bought his first aeroplane in New York and had it shipped to Enid where he assembled it. The engine failed to arrive with the plane, however, so he had displays of the plane until the engine arrived.

Regardless of how Cessna obtained his first plane, all sources agree that he taught himself to fly, suffering many accidents in the process, and finally made a five-mile flight in December 1911.

Cessna abandoned the automobile business and became an exhibition flyer at county fairs and other events. He also continued building monoplanes but returned to farming in 1917 to harvest wheat to help feed American soldiers fighting in France in World War I.

He returned to flying after the war, using a Laird "Swallow" biplane and in 1924 formed Travel Air Manufacturing Co. with Walter Beech and Lloyd Stearman, who had been employees of the Laird company.

The company built what it called the "Model A" airplane that first flew in 1925 and was followed by a "Model B." The partners split up later because of a disagreement on design and Beech and Stearman each formed an aircraft company.

All three developed designs that were highly successful.

Cessna and his son, Eldon, founded the Cessna Aircraft Co. and built several models of monoplanes until the stock market crash of 1929 when the demand for airplanes plummeted. Two years later, the board of directors fired Cessna as president and voted to close the company.

Two of Cessna's nephews, Dwane and Dwight Wallace, later wrested control of the defunct company from the stockholders and introduced a new model airplane. Cessna Aircraft again became a major manufacturer of airplanes, with Clyde Cessna participating only in a ceremonial capacity.

Cessna returned to the farm near Rago, Kan., where he farmed and ran a dirt construction business until he died in November 1954 at the age of 74.

President Dwight Eisenhower sent Cessna a congratulatory message at that 1953 banquet because of the prominent part Cessna had played in the development of aviation.

It was a fitting tribute to a man who had only a rudimentary education and never had a pilot's license but made a tremendous contribution to aviation.

Tulsan near famous WWII photo

One of the most famous photographs of World War II , an American flag being raised on Iwo Jima's Mount Suribachi, was shot after a suggestion by a Tulsa Marine.

The picture that emphasized the determination of Marines who participated in the fight was made possible by thousands of other Marines, including many Oklahomans, in the bloodiest battle of the Pacific war.

The hill had been captured two days earlier in a battle so fierce that Americans could advance only about 1,000 yards in two hours because of Japanese snipers hiding in holes in the porous rock of the island, a Marine Corps photographer from Tulsa recalled.

Pockets of resistance remained, and it wasn't safe to walk up the hill.

The late Meyers Cornelius told a World reporter 10 years later that he and another Marine Corps photographer had crawled up the hill, officially identified as No. 556, on Feb. 24, 1945, and both men shot several photographs of a small flag with Marines posed around it.

Suddenly, the Japanese began lobbing grenades at the flag, and all but two of the flag raisers dived for cover. The two flag raisers held the flag in place. The other photographer broke his camera.

The Marines planned to replace the small flag with a larger one. As Cornelius started down the hill, they met other photographers, including Associated Press photographer Joe Rosenthal, who had started up the hill but stopped when they heard the grenades.

"That photographer, Rosenthal and several others crawled up the hill on their hands and knees to record the flag-raising," Cornelius said.

Rosenthal said 10 years later that he didn't realize that he had shot anything special until congratulations began pouring in several days later.

The photo quickly became the subject of posters, war bond drives and a U.S. postage stamp. It was published throughout the world, won a Pulitzer Prize and, years later,

Joe Rosenthal/ Associated Press
One of the most famous images of World War II, the raising of the U.S. flag on Mount Suribachi during the Battle of Iwo Jima, was suggested by a Tulsan, Meyers Cornelius.

Tulsa World archives
Meyers Cornelius.

was the inspiration for the Marine Corps Memorial near Arlington National Cemetery.

The picture is the centerpiece of the 2006 movie "Flags of our Fathers" and a companion movie, "Letters from Iwo Jima."

Five days before the flag was raised, 70,000 men stormed ashore and were met by 20,000 Japanese hiding in caves and holes. For the Marines, Iwo Jima was their bloodiest triumph. More than 6,800 U.S. servicemen died in the five-week battle for the island; the 20,000 Japanese were virtually wiped out.

Tulsan Rex Calvert, then a Marine sergeant who had already been on three beach invasions in the Pacific, told a World reporter two years ago, "We were in our foxholes some distance from the mountain, and some of us saw an American flag on top of the mountain, and I thought, 'Boy, we have the high ground now.' "

Hundreds of Marines who saw the flag, Calvert said, "began hollering. It sounded like somebody had made a touchdown at the Super Bowl."

Calvert retired in 1984 after 42 years with Sun Oil Refinery.

Dr. James Hal Neal Jr., a corpsman on Iwo Jima who practiced medicine in Tulsa after the war, also recalled the shouting, he told a reporter two years ago. "Everyone was yelling, 'Look at the flag on Mount Suribachi,' " he said. "Ships were honking, and men were shouting that the flag was up."

An Oklahoma City corpsman on Iwo Jima, Dr. Jack Van Doren Hough, told a reporter a few years ago that the experience reminded him of a "big football stadium with people shooting at us from the stands."

Hough became a world-renowned ear surgeon, wrote more than 100 books and lectured throughout the world. He was inducted into the Oklahoma Hall of Fame in 1990.

"I remember seeing the flag-raising on Suribachi through my binoculars. It was a thrilling sight. For me personally, surviving the battle let me know that God had a purpose for me," he said.

Childers' heroics earned high honor

Oklahoma soldier Ernest Childers had a broken ankle and was out of hand grenades, but that didn't stop him from attacking – and wiping out – two enemy machine gun nests in Italy in September 1943.

With his ankle taped by a doctor at an aid station, 2nd Lt. Childers lobbed rocks into a German machine gun nest.

The rocks didn't do any damage, of course, but in the early morning darkness, the Nazi machine gunners couldn't tell what they were and jumped out of their cover for fear they were grenades – right into fire from Childers' rifle.

"They didn't move anymore," Childers told a crowd of Broken Arrow residents who greeted him when he returned to his home.

Childers was in an Army action about 40 miles from Salerno about 4:30 a.m. on Sept. 22, 1943, when he stepped into a hole on a bridge and fell – an accident that probably saved his life. His back was grazed by a German bullet as he was falling.

Other soldiers carried him to an aid station where a doctor taped his ankle and told him to stay off of it.

But after seeing several more seriously wounded soldiers brought in, "I just got madder and madder," he said, and returned to the battle.

He gathered a squad of eight men and headed up a hill searching for the Nazi machine gunners. As he continued up the hill, he saw two machine gun nests and killed all the occupants of the nearest one.

Although out of grenades, he headed toward the other nest and threw a rock that landed in the center of the German nest. As the occupants raised up, he killed one, and a member of his squad killed the other. He later captured an enemy mortar observer, even while out of ammunition.

After recovering from his wounds in North Africa, he was sent back into combat and fought at the Battle of Anzio, where he was wounded again.

The citation accompanying the Medal of Honor that he received in Naples said the award was given him "for conspicuous gallantry and intrepidity at risk of life above and beyond the call of duty."

The citation also cited his leadership, initiative, calm-

Tulsa World archives

Second Lt. Ernest Childers demonstrates the use of a .30-caliber carbine to U.S. Sen. Elmer Thomas of Oklahoma in 1944. Childers won the Medal of Honor for heroism during a 1943 World War II battle against Germans.

ness under fire, and conspicuous gallantry as an inspiration to his men.

He later met with President Franklin D. Roosevelt in Washington before returning to Oklahoma.

Childers, a Creek, became the first American Indian to receive a Medal of Honor during World War II.

Another Oklahoma Indian, Jack Montgomery, a Cherokee from Sequoyah County, received a Medal of Honor in 1945. Both had attended Chilocco Indian School at Arkansas City, Kan., which closed in 1980.

Charles LeClair, a retired Army chaplain and member of Chilocco's class of 1948, said it is rare to have two Medal of Honor winners from the same school. "I would say that there is no other school in the country that has two medal winners that are heroes of the caliber of these men," he said.

Childers was welcomed home to Broken Arrow on April 27, 1944, by a large crowd. He was reluctant to talk about his action. At first, he said only that "the men overseas appreciate your support. God bless you."

But the crowd insisted that he give a first-person account of the action they had already read about in reports about Childers receiving the Medal of Honor. And Childers told about his action.

"If anyone says he's not afraid when he goes into battle, he's just a liar," the modest hero said. "But you see the other fellows moving in and you know you're all in it together and you go ahead."

Childers confessed that talking to his hometown people made him more nervous than fighting the Germans.

The welcome home was a big event. Bands paraded down the city's main street along with people riding horses and driving cars. Boy Scouts, American Legion and military representatives, state and city officials were there and Childers received a key to the city.

Childers, who remained in the Army until retiring as a lieutenant colonel in 1965, died March 17, 2005, at the age of 87. Services were at Broken Arrow's Childers Middle School, which is named in his honor.

Boley's bank was not an easy target

The little bank in the quiet all-black village of Boley probably looked like an easy target to bank robber Charles "Pretty Boy" Floyd's gang.

They were wrong.

Before the end of what a bank employee called "a regular war" on Nov. 23, 1932, two of the bank robbers had been killed, one by a bank bookkeeper and the other by townspeople who grabbed their own weapons and opened fire as the robbers tried to flee. All the money was recovered.

Tulsa World archives

D.J. Turner stands on the steps of the Farmers & Merchants Bank in Boley. Turner, the bank's president, was killed in 1932 by a member of Charles "Pretty Boy" Floyd's gang after he set off an alarm during a robbery.

The heroes of the gunbattle were Farmers & Merchants Bank President D.J. Turner, who was killed after he set off a bank robbery alarm, and bookkeeper H.C. McCormick, who grabbed a rifle in the bank's vault and mortally wounded Turner's killer moments after Turner was shot.

The dead robbers were identified as George Birdwell, Floyd's chief lieutenant who was considered the brains of the gang, and novice robber Charles Glass, the driver of the getaway car. Robber C.C. Patterson suffered multiple bullet wounds but recovered and was sent to prison for his part in the robbery.

Floyd didn't participate in the robbery in the town that was one of 29 all-black communities established before statehood. There were reports that he had his henchmen stage the robbery as a ploy to divert lawmen's attention to allow him to visit his wife in a Tulsa hospital where she had undergone an appendectomy or at her father's house near Bixby.

Other reports were that Floyd had warned his gang members against robbing the Boley bank because not much money was there, the people of Boley all had guns, knew how to shoot them and weren't afraid to use them.

There's no way to determine if the robbery was a diversionary tactic, but there's proof that the Boley residents had guns, knew how to use them and did.

Birdwell, armed with a .45-caliber pistol, and Patterson, armed with a shotgun, burst into the bank early that morning. Birdwell, always the speaker in the gang's bank robberies, announced they were robbing the bank and warned

"don't pull no alarm."

Bookkeeper McCormick saw the robbers enter, slipped into the bank's vault, retrieved the rifle kept there for such events and aimed it at Birdwell as he watched the robbers scoop up cash. Turner hit the robbery alarm and Birdwell demanded, "Did you pull that alarm?"

"Sure I did," Turner admitted. Birdwell responded "I'll kill you for that," and shot the bank president to death. As Turner fell to the floor, McCormick fired a shot at Birdwell, who fell mortally wounded at Turner's feet.

Hearing the gunfire, Glass rushed into the bank, picked up the $600 Birdwell had dropped and ordered two customers to carry Birdwell to the getaway car. He and Patterson also returned fire at McCormick.

The robbers were met by a rain of bullets from a sheriff's deputy and vigilantes as they left the bank. The two customers dropped Birdwell on the sidewalk and took cover inside the bank. Patterson fell wounded, but Glass reached the getaway car and was fatally shot as he tried to drive away.

Police set a trap for Floyd when reports surfaced that he planned to visit an Earlsboro funeral home to view Birdwell's body. Although Floyd didn't appear, his wife was one of about 50 mourners who attended Birdwell's graveside funeral service at Seminole.

More than 50 Okemah and Tulsa police officers, none in uniform, provided security at the funeral for Turner that was attended by more than 3,000. There had been rumors that Floyd would attend the funeral to claim revenge for the killing of his aide.

McCormick received a $500 reward from the state for killing Birdwell and was made an honorary major on Gov. William H. "Alfalfa Bill" Murray's staff. Townspeople who participated in the shootout split another $500 reward.

"We'll get these robbers at the scene," Murray said, "and save money and expense in conducting trials and hunting them down. If they are killed in the act, we'll be sure we have the right men."

Black Sunday duster dimmed sun

The day started out bright and sunny, the kind of day for families with cars to drive into the country after church services.

Drought and dust had plagued residents of the Panhandle and other areas of western Oklahoma for a couple of weeks, but there was no sign of dust on this Palm Sunday, April 14, 1935, when churchgoers had prayed for rain.

Clouds appeared shortly after noon, but they were short-lived and didn't produce rain.

Suddenly a north wind blew huge clouds of dust into the area, turning daylight into night. Motorists couldn't see highway markers or buildings, and their cars' engines died because dust got into the carburetors. People had difficulty breathing. Farmers had to crawl back to their houses from the fields where they had been working. A pilot was injured when his plane crashed while trying to land because he couldn't see a landing strip.

Residents of Hammon and Woodward thought the huge clouds signaled an impending tornado and rushed to cellars.

Many headed for churches to pray – if they could find the buildings.

Old-timers said the black duster was the worst they had seen; it was a nasty end for the Sunday that dawned brightly but is remembered as Black Sunday.

It wasn't the first dust storm to hit the Plains area in West Texas, Oklahoma and Kansas, but it's one that is well-remembered. Dust storms had been noted as early as 1913, but they weren't like those of the 1930s.

In the weeks before Black Sunday, many schools had closed and many farmers had given up, loading their household goods onto pickups, trailers and the roofs of cars to head west. The Okie migration to California was portrayed by John Steinbeck in his novel "The Grapes of Wrath."

Oklahoma's Panhandle was the heart of what became known as the Dust Bowl, but drought had scorched land throughout the Southwest.

Dust had been a way of life in the spring and summer in western Oklahoma for several years in those pre-air conditioning 1930s, when residents stretched damp sheets over doors and windows in futile attempts to keep the dust outside.

It was the legacy of drought and overcultivation of marginal land on thousands of tiny farms, a state conservationist told a Tulsa World reporter in 1983 during a dry spell in western Oklahoma.

Tulsa World archives

A cloud of dust is whipped up by winds in this 1935 photo taken near Boise City. Oklahoma's Panhandle was the heart of what became known as the Dust Bowl.

"Land that should have been left in grass was plowed up. Settlers had to till every acre of their farms to feed their families," he explained when there was concern that the dust could return.

Settlers in the Panhandle before statehood were joined by thousands more after Oklahoma became a state in 1907. Over the decades, they plowed up the soil's protective grass. When the rain stopped, the wind began to lift the fine dirt.

Farmers had little or no knowledge of soil conservation, and most prided themselves on being able to plow a straight furrow. They plowed up and down hills instead of plowing along the contour to reduce wind and water erosion. They planted their rows of crops too close to each other.

Wheat and cotton were favorite crops among those early farmers, but both are hard on the soil because they remove large amounts of nutrients. When the crops were harvested, they left little residue on the land, which allowed the wind to carry away soil.

The use of cover crops and chemical fertilizers to restore the soil's fertility was rare.

President Franklin Roosevelt was ridiculed in 1934 when he proposed his tree-planting program as part of his New Deal. Editorial writers proclaimed that if God had wanted a forest on the prairie he would have put it there; that it was silly, if not blasphemous, for Roosevelt to attempt it.

But it worked.

Today, neat rows of trees on thousands of farms in Oklahoma and other states break high-velocity wind, helping prevent soil from being blown away. The trees not only cut wind, they provide shade, trap snow in drifts and put more moisture into the soil.

Geronimo left colorful legacy

Geronimo!

It was the battle cry shouted by paratroopers as they leaped from airplanes to fight the Nazis during World War II.

It was a name that sent fear into white settlers in the early West as well as in Mexicans along the border.

In both cases, it meant "jump," either out of an airplane or to the safety of a shelter.

Yelling "Geronimo!" as a motivational shout apparently began in 1940 when the Army's airborne branch was new. The practice spread and continues today – although the enemy on the ground wouldn't be able to hear the yell and be frightened by it.

There's reason the word sent chills up the spines of homesteaders. It was the name of a Chiricahua Apache warrior who had become synonymous with warfare and cruelty, who allegedly had killed so many men and women that the U.S. government had spent $1 million trying to capture him and the Mexican government had put a price on the heads of all Apaches.

Geronimo's cruelty stemmed from his seeking revenge for the death of his wife, Alope, who was killed when a hunting party of Apaches was attacked by Mexican soldiers while on an excursion south of the border. His hatred of Mexicans expanded to include white settlers.

Geronimo, who is buried at Fort Sill where he was held captive for the last 15 years of his life, was born in 1829 near where the city of Globe, Ariz., now stands. He spent his childhood in a mountainous area on the Gila River, learning to grow corn, beans and other crops and supported his mother after his father died.

He was peaceful as a boy named Ga-khala-yea and was admitted to the tribal council when he was 17, having killed sufficient game to qualify for membership. After his wife was killed, his name was changed by his tribe to Geronimo.

Apache Chief Cochise made peace with the Army in 1872 and the Apaches were given a 3,000-square-mile reservation in Arizona. But after Cochise died, the reservation was closed and the Chiricahua Apaches were sent to the East Coast. Geronimo and a small band of warriors refused to go and fought the Army for 10 years in an attempt to regain the Arizona land.

Associated Press

Geronimo, who is buried at Fort Sill where he was held captive for the last 15 years of his life, was born in 1829 near where the city of Globe, Ariz., now stands.

Geronimo and his followers finally surrendered and were held captive first in Florida, later in Alabama and finally moved to Fort Sill in 1894. They were much healthier and better satisfied at Fort Sill but still made escape attempts.

Geronimo spent the rest of his life living in a tepee near Medicine Creek just west of Fort Sill Boulevard and continued begging to be allowed to return to Arizona and to be allowed to die as a free man.

When Theodore Roosevelt was inaugurated as president in 1905, he had Geronimo and several of his followers taken to Washington to ride in the inaugural parade "to give the people a good show."

In Washington, Geronimo apologized to Roosevelt for killing so many in defense of his homeland and added, "Great White Chief, the place where I and my people are kept (Fort Sill) is bad for us. Let my people go home. Let me die and be buried in my country (Arizona)."

But Roosevelt refused, telling Geronimo "there would be more war and more bloodshed. It is best you stay where you are."

The remaining 237 Apaches held at Fort Sill were freed in 1913 and were given their choice of land in Oklahoma or in New Mexico. Eighty-seven chose Oklahoma and became successful farmers and businessmen.

In his latter days, Geronimo drank heavily and was placed in the guardhouse to sober up so many times that the building became known as the "Geronimo Guardhouse." The building later became the field artillery museum and continued to bear the Indian's name.

Only a few old women attended Geronimo's funeral when he died Feb. 17, 1909. He had lost all influence with the men of the tribe.

Even after his death there were attempts to move the Indian's body to Arizona. The last attempt was made by Arizona Apache leaders in 1984 but was rebuffed by Oklahoma Apaches. The bones remain at Fort Sill.

Historian Angie Debo noted in her biography of Geronimo that he was buried in an elaborately decorated hearse with his riding whip, blanket and other possessions. A monument of stone topped by a stone eagle was erected over the grave in 1931.

Reporter covers mine blast

The bottom of a Wilburton coal mine where an explosion killed 91 miners was described as a "cold, chilly hell" except in one area where a group of miners sweltered and coughed as they tried to subdue a blaze to prevent another explosion.

The description was provided by Tulsa World reporter Peter H. Dixon, who accompanied six miners who had volunteered to try to extinguish the burning coal 200 feet below the earth's surface.

The Jan. 14, 1926, explosion, apparently caused by gas, had entombed 93 men who were working in mine 21 of the Degnan-McConnell Coal Co. The final toll was set at 91, making that the most deadly mine disaster in Oklahoma history. Before statehood, 100 died in an explosion in a Krebs coal mine on Jan. 7, 1892.

Other miners were able to rescue 10 of the 101 men who were working in the mine when it was rocked by the explosion about midnight. One of the rescued men crawled in the mine passages over dead bodies, including that of his father, for 23 hours before he was found.

"I crawled and crawled after the explosion, into utter blackness," miner Cecil McKinney said. "I do not know where I crawled or how long I crawled but I just squeezed through and finally found a slope and came to the bend where I was found."

Some miners believed the explosion would not have occurred if the miners had worn electric lamps on their helmets instead of the carbide lamps required by the state mine inspector.

The inspector defended the use of the open-flame lamps. He said if electric lamps had been in use, less care would have been taken to prevent gas in the mine, increasing the possibility of death by poison gas.

Ministers from surrounding towns joined Wilburton ministers to hold funeral services for the victims who had to be buried immediately after their bodies were recovered. Forty-five convicts from the state penitentiary at nearby McAlester dug most of the graves for the mine victims.

Reporter Dixon wrote that a crew of six miners had gone into the shaft to check on the fire and returned to the surface with a report that they thought it could be extinguished. Six miners volunteered to go back to fight the fire, and Dixon was allowed to accompany them.

Tulsa World archives

Dixon said there was one other living thing in the party – a tiny yellow canary in a wooden cage. He explained that a canary was much more sensitive to dangerous gas than humans and would die if the gas level became dangerous.

"Passageways were partially blocked with debris, timbers were torn and twisted and huge slabs of rock clung to the roof of the passageway, seemingly held by some mysterious magnetism," he wrote.

"Many times we had to crawl on our hands and knees and it was necessary to wiggle flat on our stomachs between a tiny passage left by the explosion.

"Our coats were soaked with water from the dripping sides of the air shaft, stiffened and became ice coated. From the shattered timbers, icicles glistened in the light beams (from the miners' hat lights)."

Nearby, burning coal could be seen and one man crawled through a narrow slit to aim the chemicals from a fire extinguisher at the blaze. All of the men were carrying heavy brass extinguishers.

"The smoke was choking us so we dropped our extinguishers and retreated 100 yards," stepping over bodies to do so, he said. When the men close to the fire called for more extinguishers, the nearest ones were a half-mile away. "We started back for them and that mile there and back seemed more like 10," he said.

Dixon and the crew he accompanied were in the mine for 3 ½ hours. "The long 200-foot climb up the shaft was torture, but the fresh air and sight of trees and other things of the outside world brought a wave of relief," he said.

Dixon's first-person story was on Page 1 of the next day's Tulsa World. It was dramatized on NBC radio's "Big Story" program in 1948 and he received a $500 award from sponsor Pall Mall Cigarettes. It was again dramatized on NBC-TV in 1952.

But receiving the award may have been bittersweet for Dixon. Ironically, he was fired the day after his "big story" was published in the Tulsa World.

He had made the mistake of giving his story to a wire service in time for it to be used in afternoon newspapers before it appeared in the World.

'Mr. Highway 33' pushed for better road

No one who watched television or listened to the radio in northeastern Oklahoma in the 1970s would have been surprised if that had been the epitaph on Dan P. Holmes' tombstone.

His crusade to improve Oklahoma 33, the highway between Tulsa and Siloam Springs, Ark., including more than a dozen years of pleas on television to remember the highway, earned him the title of "Mr. Highway 33."

Holmes, who died in 1983 at age 80, used television time he bought for his insurance business to promote his favorite project but frequently made it clear that "my wife and I don't own any land over toward Arkansas. We have no ax to grind."

But he admitted that he was obsessed with improving the highway. Holmes explained his philosophy: "The important thing is identifying with something good. What we do here now will be appreciated later. This is the most traveled road between northwest Arkansas and Tulsa. What about all the people living in the Little Kansas area, who work in Tulsa and have to drive it every day?"

His battle paid off, first in 1975 when the Oklahoma Highway Commission approved a new bridge over the Verdigris River and named it the Dan P. Holmes Bridge. Later, the historic Highway 33 was improved, but that designation has now disappeared and the route has become Scenic U.S. 412, which parallels the Cherokee Turnpike for much of the distance between U.S. 69 and the Arkansas border.

Holmes said he began supporting an improved Oklahoma 33 after hearing John Dunkin, the vice president of Brown-Dunkin Co., tell a Chamber of Commerce group that the chamber should back the highway because of the volume of business that came to Tulsa from northwestern Arkansas. Holmes said he also was concerned about football fans going to games in Fayetteville.

"I got to thinking, in my business you pick a community project. You have to pick one that doesn't benefit you, that benefits the public only," Holmes told a reporter. Oklahoma 33 met his specifications.

He said years later that his success in business dated from the time he became involved in civic projects.

Beginning in the late 1960s, Holmes bought advertising time on radio and television stations for his Dan P. Holmes Insurance Co., but promoting his firm was secondary to his

Tulsa World archives

R.E. Bresnahan (right) presents Dan P. Holmes a plaque as an honorary lifetime director for his many years of oustanding service for the Tulsa Area United Way.

obsession. Viewers waited for the traditional "Now let's talk about Highway 33" comment that would introduce his latest staccato barrage of condemnation over the condition of the highway.

In March 1979, KTEW (now KJRH) took Holmes' ads off the air, citing the "fairness doctrine." A station official said the station had a policy against mixing opinions with news and commercials.

Holmes responded, "When I pay for my own time, I thought I could say what I wanted if I didn't malign anyone or put the station in jeopardy," and added "this fairness doctrine is not fair." He switched his ads – and opinions – to KTUL a few months later.

The highway was just one of his projects. He was involved in many civic activities, including youth programs. For at least 30 years, he made the highest bid for the champion lamb at the Tulsa State Fair's annual junior livestock auction. His bid for the lamb in 1979 was $13,550, a U.S. record.

Holmes came to Tulsa with his parents in 1913. His father operated a grocery at Fifth Street and Lewis Avenue, and Holmes began selling newspapers at Third and Main streets when he was 11. He continued through high school.

He said many times that he made a mistake after he graduated from high school: His father offered to send him to college or buy him a car, and he chose the car. Young people should go to college, he said. Holmes later was a member of the University of Tulsa's board of trustees.

He was a strong supporter of the Community Chest, now the United Way, and in 1955 raised more than $1 million for the agency. He was made an honorary life member of the United Way and was honored by the Tulsa Press Club as a "Headliner." He also was involved in many other civic activities.

Holmes did not smoke or drink and was a regular churchgoer. He was a board member of Boston Avenue Methodist Church, where he sat in the same seat every Sunday for years, sometimes arriving early to get that seat. He had met his wife, Alice, at a church camp and they were married in 1929. She died in 1988.

Once asked by one of Tulsa's wealthiest men whether all the money the millionaire was giving was going to get him into heaven, Holmes replied: "Only the Lord can do that."

Ex-convict became Creek tribal leader

A Tulsa Muscogee (Creek) Indian who went to prison for killing a deputy U.S. marshal learned the three R's while incarcerated and developed a friendship with a future American president who freed him a few years later.

That Indian was William G. "Billy" Bruner, who later was elected to the tribe's House of Kings (similar to Oklahoma's Senate), where he served for 18 years, and who helped bring order to the frontier by serving as a member of a volunteer posse that, among other actions, killed two members of a notorious gang.

Bruner's name was put on a stop on the now-defunct Sand Springs line between Tulsa and Sand Springs, and by a nearby housing addition known as Bruner addition. Both are on land he received in 1902 as his allotment, near where he was born.

Bruner's body is buried in a neglected Indian cemetery named Tiger Bone, after an old Euchee scout, near Discoveryland west of Sand Springs. Most of the headstones, including the one that marked Bruner's grave, have been broken, toppled or stolen.

When Bruner died in April 1952, his age was listed in his obituary as about 98 or 100. But there is a question about the accuracy of that.

His age was reported as 98 in a 1950 news story about a lawsuit filed by relatives in an attempt to prevent his marriage to a woman they feared was after his fortune. And a 1946 news story in the Tulsa World listed his age as 110, based on Creek records.

Whatever his age, Bruner first got into trouble when his parents sent him to an Indian mission school. He was expelled three months later for beating up his teacher, who tried to punish him for speaking Creek instead of English.

His first serious trouble was in 1889, when he was arrested for selling liquor. As he told a Tulsa World writer years later, it was too late for officers to take him to Fort Smith for trial that night. Some of Tulsa's leading residents vouched for his honesty, so Bruner was allowed to return home after promising he would return to begin the trip to Fort Smith early the next morning.

Meanwhile, the officers who had arrested him bought a bottle of liquor and began a poker game. Shortly before daylight, one became worried that Bruner hadn't shown up and told the others, "Let's go out and get him." The group started firing bullets at Bruner's house as they rode up.

Bruner returned fire, thinking the shots might have

"Billy" Bruner was married either six or eight times and was sent to prison.

come from Indians he'd had trouble with. The first shot from his Winchester rifle killed Deputy Marshal Bill Moody, according to legend. The second grazed a deputy. Bruner finally surrendered and was taken to Fort Smith, where he waited in jail for eight months for a trial before Judge Isaac Parker.

Those details differ slightly from testimony in his trial before Judge Parker. According to testimony as reported in a 1952 Chronicles of Oklahoma article, he was allowed to remain free for several weeks until his case was called for trial. And testimony set the site of the killing as the home of Jeff Berryhill, a young Creek who the officers were seeking to arrest for a larceny charge and who Bruner was visiting.

Both versions agree Moody was killed by Bruner's first shot at the officers. Among those deputies who were trying to arrest Bruner was Grat Dalton, who was killed along with three of his brothers while robbing a bank in Coffeyville in 1892.

Sentenced to 20 years in prison for killing the marshal, Bruner was taken to a prison in Ohio where he became a trusty. During his term, he got acquainted with the Ohio governor who made an inspection of the prison. That governor promised to help him get out of prison.

One of the first actions of that governor, William McKinley, when he became president on March 4, 1897, was to sign a pardon that released Bruner after he had served six years.

Bruner returned to Tulsa, obtained his allotment of 160 acres and became a tribal leader.

The old Indian was alert and witty when he was called to the witness stand in the 1950 County Court trial of the guardianship action against him. On several occasions, he laughed heartily when spectators laughed at something he said.

At one point, he was asked if he knew how many people lived at his nephew's house. "I don't know. I haven't been there for two or three days," he answered.

A guardian was appointed but Bruner appealed to the District Court, which vacated the guardianship and held that Bruner, who had been married either six or eight times previously, was competent and had the right to get married if he wanted to.

Asked after the trial if he planned to get married, Bruner answered "No. I'm too old."

'Cimarron' author found ideas in Oklahoma

When she was doing research for the book "Cimarron" about early Oklahoma, author Edna Ferber spent several days in Oklahoma. Two pioneer Sooners became recognizable characters in the book – although one is a composite of several men.

The book is set in Oklahoma beginning with the 1893 land rush into the Cherokee Outlet and continues through Indian disputes, outlaws and the discovery of oil.

Ferber, one of the most popular authors of the early 20th century, had never been to Oklahoma but developed an interest in the state after talking to William Allen White, the prize-winning publisher of the Emporia, Kan., Gazette, who told her about seeing Indians driving around in Pierce-Arrow automobiles when he visited the state.

It wasn't long before she came here and began writing "Cimarron." She said she wrote the book after spending only 10 days listening to anecdotes about Oklahoma Territory and early Oklahoma while visiting Mr. and Mrs. Walter Ferguson in Tulsa and Walter's mother, the widow of former Territorial Gov. T.B. Ferguson, in Watonga.

Ferguson's wife, Lucia, is clearly recognizable as Sabra Cravat, the leading character in Ferber's book. Sabra's husband, Yancey Cravat, was a composite character fashioned from the lives of T.B. Ferguson, former U.S. Marshal Bill Tilghman and other early-day figures.

The widow of T.B. Ferguson, Oklahoma's fifth territorial governor, was still publishing the family's newspaper, the Watonga Republican, in 1930 when Ferber visited Tulsa and Watonga. She sold the newspaper a short while later. She was named as "State Mother" by the American Mothers Committee of the Golden Rule Foundation in 1946, a year before she died.

Walter Ferguson was a former owner and editor of the Cherokee Republican newspaper who had become a vice president of the National Bank of Tulsa before he died in 1936. He often was referred to as the "Mark Twain of Oklahoma." His wife, Lucia, was a nationally syndicated

Edna Ferber, one of the most popular authors of the early 20th century, had never been to Oklahoma before she wrote "Cimarron."

columnist for Scripps-Howard who also wrote a column called "A Woman's View" and a lovelorn column called "Lucia Loomis" for the Tulsa Tribune. In the Ferber story, the Cravats befriend a Jewish family setting up a newspaper, and Yancey goes to work on the newspaper. The Cravats and other settlers try their luck in the 1893 run. Eventually the Cravats take over the newspaper and build a fortune among Indian disputes, outlaws and the discovery of oil.

The book, Ferber's third novel, was made into a movie starring Richard Dix and Irene Dunn in 1931 by RKO Pictures and again in 1960 by MGM, the latter starring Glenn Ford, Maria Schell, Anne Baxter, Arthur O'Connell and Russ Tamblyn.

When Ferber died in 1968 at the age of 85, the New York Times said she had an uncanny ability to project herself into any environment. If a character, an emotion or a situation captured her fancy, she once told a reporter, she need never have experienced, seen or read about it to write of it.

That was the situation with her book "Show Boat." "I have never been on the Mississippi or in the Deep South," she said.

She also wrote "So Big," a book about farm life that won a Pulitzer Prize, but she said she knew nothing about farming or farms.

Ferber populated her work with men and women of the lower-middle and middle class because, she said, they interested her more than any other American stratum, according to the Times obituary. She always said she found the conversation of a truck driver more vigorous and stimulating than the conversation of a Cadillac owner.

Ferber wrote her first novel while she was a reporter at the Milwaukee Journal. She gained national fame with a series of stories about a character named Emma McChesney, a traveling saleswoman who sold underskirts.

In later years, she wrote more than 1,000 words a day 350 days a year.

WWII hero's service didn't stop with combat

Few of the passengers on the shuttle from the parking lot to the door of the Veterans Administration Hospital in Muskogee recognized their driver.

But veterans seeking medical treatment would have been impressed had they known their driver was Jack C. Montgomery, who was awarded the Medal of Honor, the nation's highest military honor, for action in Italy during World War II.

Montgomery drove that shuttle for several decades beginning in 1972 at the medical facility now named the Jack C. Montgomery VA Medical Center in his honor. And the federal agency he served for so many years as an employee and as a volunteer has been renamed the Department of Veterans Affairs.

Montgomery, a Cherokee who died at age 84 in 2002, was one of five American Indians who received the Medal of Honor during World War II.

The citation accompanying the medal that was awarded by President Franklin D. Roosevelt said Montgomery killed 11 Nazi soldiers, captured 32 and wounded an unknown number of the enemy.

The action started two hours before dawn on Feb. 22, 1944, when a strong force of German soldiers established a position in front of Montgomery's platoon and threatened its position on Anzio Beach.

"Cover me, I'm going forward," he told soldiers as he grabbed his rifle and several grenades and started crawling through the ditch toward where the German soldiers had been reported. He was a 1st lieutenant commanding a platoon in Oklahoma's 45th Infantry Division.

He fired his rifle and threw his grenades so accurately that he killed eight of the enemy and captured four before returning to his platoon for another rifle and more grenades. At that point he also called for artillery fire on a house where the enemy was firing machine guns. As enemy soldiers fled from the house, he captured more Nazis and sent them back to the rear. Three dead Nazis were found there later.

"I didn't look back," he told a reporter later. "I knew I was going to be covered. We had that kind of confidence in each other."

Tulsa World

Jack C. Montgomery, a Medal of Honor recipient, looks at the monument erected in his honor at Bacone College in Muskogee.

"I'd been training for it all those months and years," Montgomery said. "I can't tell you what I was thinking about at the time. I wasn't conscious of thinking about anything."

Montgomery, a native of Long in Sequoyah County, attended elementary school in Cushing and high school at Chilocco Indian School. He attended Bacone Junior College for two years and graduated with a degree in education from the University of Redlands, Calif., in 1940.

He joined the National Guard in 1937 and was mobilized when the Guard was called to active duty in 1940 in anticipation of World War II. He received a battlefield commission as a 2nd lieutenant in 1943 when he was cited for bravery.

By the time of his Anzio Beach action, he had been promoted to 1st lieutenant and had received the Silver Star, the Bronze Star, the Purple Heart with Cluster and the Military Cross of Valor from the Italian government. He was sent back to the U.S. for treatment of serious wounds he suffered when hit by mortar fragments later that day while helping another platoon.

After his discharge from the Army in 1945, Montgomery went to work for the Veterans Administration in Muskogee, Durant and Bartlesville before re-enlisting in the Army in December 1950, a few months after the beginning of the Korean War. He volunteered for combat but because Medal of Honor recipients are not allowed to return to combat, he was assigned as an infantry instructor at Fort Benning, Ga.

Montgomery returned to the VA in Bartlesville in 1953 but retired in 1972 and began his volunteer job as a shuttle driver for the hospital in Muskogee – a job he held for several decades.

The hospital was renamed in Montgomery's honor last summer by legislation introduced in Congress by Sen. Tom Coburn, R-Okla., and Rep. Dan Boren, D-Okla. They said they had consulted with veterans across the state before introducing the bill.

"Jack Montgomery was a true Oklahoma hero and embodied the American spirit of service, honor and sacrifice," Coburn said.

Morris bank's third heist attempt foiled

Bandits picked the wrong bank to rob in May 1932, when one walked into the First State Bank of Morris with a drawn pistol, while another guarded the door and a third waited in a stolen getaway car.

It probably looked like an easy heist. The bank had been robbed twice during the previous year of more than $2,000. And Claire Aggas, 25-year-old bookkeeper, was alone in the bank about 11:15 a.m.

Although she was frightened, Aggas was calm enough to step on the switch of a newly installed alarm. Forrest Bradley, a merchant who heard the alarm, grabbed a rifle and a shotgun and opened fire from the window of his store across the street. Bradley fatally wounded the getaway driver and wounded the man guarding the bank's door.

The gunman in the bank grabbed about $800 and forced the bookkeeper to accompany him to the getaway car. He pushed the dead driver into the rear seat, put the wounded gunman into the rear seat and forced the woman to sit close to him as he exchanged gunfire with Bradley and Marshal I.Z. Thompson as he drove out of town.

Aggas was shot in the face during the exchange of gunfire, but she said later she didn't know who shot her. Bradley said he couldn't shoot at the gunman who had kidnapped the bookkeeper for fear of hitting her.

The robber stopped the car in the woods a few miles out of town, dumped the bookkeeper and abandoned the car with the dead gunman inside. The two remaining bandits, one critically wounded, fled, one possibly in another car and the other through the woods.

Meanwhile, Baron Skinner, Aggas' fiance, and a friend had followed the bandits' car. They found Aggas on the side of a road and started toward the Okmulgee hospital with her. They saw an ambulance driving along the highway that turned out to be a new one being delivered to Okmulgee. The ambulance escorted Skinner and his wounded fiancee to the hospital.

The dead robber who was shot by Bradley was identified as Roscoe Ernest of Drumright, who was wanted in connection with several robberies in Creek County and who had been suspected of stealing a car in Okmulgee the night

Andrea Gillman

Claire Aggas, bookkeeper for the First State Bank of Morris when it was robbed in 1932, was shot in the face, but survived.

before.

Troy Kittrell was arrested a few months later in Detroit and confessed that he was one of the three robbers. He was sentenced to life in prison, according to the family of Skinner and Aggas, and later was killed in a prison brawl.

Aggas believed the other robber died of his gunshot wounds because he was bleeding profusely. Aggas underwent 19 plastic surgeries.

The Morris bank had been robbed the previous September, when Aggas and one other employee were there, and again in December, both times by Charles F. "Pretty Boy" Floyd and his gang. She had told friends that she had a premonition that she would be alone and injured if the institution were robbed again.

During the second robbery, the two gunmen told bank employees they were getting funds to give to widows and needy children for Christmas.

Carrying a submachinegun under his coat, the gunman identified as Floyd laughed and joked with two customers who were in the bank, asking one, "How's business since we were here last, old man?"

It may have been the first time townspeople fought back against bank robbers, but a few months later, two of Floyd's gang were killed along with a banker when they tried to rob the bank at Boley.

Robbers hit 34 banks during the first eight months of that year compared with 30 during the same period the previous year. Many banks had installed alarm systems, but the Jenks Bank of Commerce, robbed twice during the previous four years, went even further, turning the institution into a veritable fortress.

It removed the typical counter running the length of the lobby and replaced it with an 11-foot tall, foot-thick brick wall topped by a heavy mesh screen up to the ceiling. The cashiers' windows were protected with heavy steel bars in front of 2-inch thick glass.

Slots just large enough to slide checks and/or cash through were at each window. Tear gas pipes extended into the lobby from the top of the wall at each cashier's window. The Jenks bank was not robbed again.

But bank officials once forgot to release the door locks when the bank closed for lunch one day. When employees returned, they couldn't get into the bank until a locksmith and a carpenter were called to remove one of the doors.

World's story sparks uproar in state

The Oklahoma House was "stirred" by an article in the Tulsa World, according to a big headline in the Feb. 15, 1913, newspaper, and legislators were accused of trying to shut off freedom of the press.

A subhead resorted to the colorful language of the day: "Tulsa World Curls the Hair on the Oklahoma Legislature."

The headlines were on a story reporting that an attack on newspapers and the Tulsa World in particular by Rep. R.I. Bond of Pittsburg County resulted in the appointment of a committee to investigate the World in reference to a story on its front page the previous day.

Reps. J.B. Griggs and Harry B. Cordell complained that newspapers had published stories about what the House did in executive session and demanded that reporters be brought before the House and forced to tell where they got their information.

The previous day's Page 1 story dealt with an investigation of state officials and appeared under a headline that read: "A Story of Corruption that in History Is Not Surpassed" and a subhead that said "Appears Now That Oklahoma State Legislature Is Going to Uncover Rankest Graft Ever Perpetrated by Administration of a State."

That story said corruption out of the Auditor's Office had invaded the major portion of the offices of the state going back into the Gov. Charles Haskell administration.

"There is a verified rumor that somebody has peached and that as soon as he peached, the whole brazen fabric of corruption began to crumble," the story continued.

(According to the Merriam-Webster Online Dictionary, "peached" as a transitive verb means to inform against; as an intransitive verb it means to turn informer.)

"That the entire state administration is honeycombed with a system of graft which has been going on for many years can be stated with certainty," the story had reported.

TULSA WORLD CURLS THE HAIR ON THE OKLAHOMA LEGISLATURE

THE ARTICLE IN FRIDAY'S ISSUE RESULTS IN SOLONS APPOINTING INVESTIGATING COMMITTEE OF FIVE MEMBERS.

WOULD TRAMPLE FREEDOM OF THE PRESS

MANY REPRESENTATIVES SPEAK COURAGEOUSLY IN BEHALF OF THE FEARLESS NEWSPAPER AND THE TRUTH

STORMY SCENES ARE ENACTED IN THE HOUSE

World Correspondent at Capital Would Be Barred from Sessions By Resolution That Is Introduced in House.

Tulsa World

The Feb. 15, 1913, Tulsa World showed a big headline accusing legislators of trying to shut off freedom of the press.

"The House started out ostensibly to whitewash and has wound up in so much mire that in order to save the party, they are bound to go on and the solemnity of the executive session indicates clearly that the investigating will go on."

Calling that article an insult to several members of the House, Bond moved that the World's Capitol correspondent be denied privileges on the House floor. The motion caused an uproar. Several members tried to speak at once as Rep. H.H. Smith of Shawnee took the side of the World and defended freedom of the press, as did Rep. J. Roy Williams of Comanche.

Another legislator pointed out that the article that caused the furor didn't bear a byline and said it was not fair to charge that World Correspondent J.A. McKeever wrote it.

Williams maintained that the House had no authority to investigate any newspaper and told members they should confine their probe to their own members.

The motion was finally approved, and a committee of five was named to investigate the World.

An inside story reported there were hourly developments in the exposure of graft and corruption that now included claims that Dr. J.H. Stolper, the public defender, had accepted money to obtain pardons for two men accused of crimes. The two were pardoned when Lt. Gov. J.J. McAlester was acting as chief executive in the absence of Gov. Lee Cruce.

The House backed down on Feb. 15 and adopted a resolution holding that "the greatest boon to every American citizen is the freedom of speech and the press" and that "every member of this House is more than willing that his acts and doings as a legislator be given all the publicity which the press of the nation can give."

And little, if anything, came of the World's revelation of unsurpassed corruption in state government.

Killing sprees of '78 sent Stafford to doom

Roger Dale Stafford, one of Oklahoma's most notorious killers, died of a lethal injection at the state penitentiary, proclaiming his innocence and his love for the wife he married while in prison.

Stafford, 43, was executed July 2, 1995, for gunning down a San Antonio family of three that stopped on Interstate 35 near Purcell while headed to a funeral. Stafford also was sentenced to die for the execution-type killings of six employees of a Sirloin Stockade restaurant in Oklahoma City three weeks after the Purcell murders.

It had been more than 17 years since the killing sprees had horrified the state. Stafford's execution had been delayed often by defense maneuvering in attempts to save his life.

"Tell the world you are seeing an innocent man murdered," Stafford said before he began to lose consciousness from the lethal injection. "I've got nothing to lose by telling a lie. Someone, somewhere, somehow, please exonerate me. . . .

"Mickey, I love you. Mickey, you meet me at heaven's gate," were among his last words before he took his final breath.

Mickey Stafford, the killer's third wife, whom he married in 1988 while on death row, prayed aloud in the witness room and repeatedly told Stafford that she loved him during the eight minutes it took for the drugs to end his life. "Hallelujah, you are going to meet the Lord today," she said as the drugs left him motionless.

The crime spree, described by an Oklahoma City judge as the worst in state history, began the night of June 22, 1978, when Melvin Lorenz, 38, and his wife, Linda, 31, both sergeants in the Air Force, and their son, Richard, 12, were headed to North Dakota for the funeral of Melvin Lorenz's mother. They stopped on I-35 near Purcell to help a woman who appeared to have car trouble.

The woman was Verna Stafford, then the wife of Roger Stafford, who admitted later that she had planned what was to have been a robbery. Roger Stafford and his brother, Harold, were lurking out of sight. When Lorenz stopped, they came out of the shadows and demanded that Lorenz surrender his wallet.

When Lorenz refused, Roger Stafford shot him in the face, killing him, Verna Stafford later testified. Linda Lorenz ran from the family pickup toward her husband, screaming "Oh, my God!" and was shot twice. The killers then heard a child's voice from a camper on the pickup, broke out a window and killed him.

The Staffords netted about $600 in the crime.

They dumped the bodies in a field and took the pickup, which they drove until after the July 16, 1978, killings at the

Associated Press

Roger Dale Stafford (foreground) – convicted in two 1978 mass murders – proclaimed innocence to the day of his execution in 1995.

Oklahoma City steakhouse in what Oklahoma Crime Bureau Agent Arthur Linville called a "joy killing."

"They could have gotten more from selling drugs or stealing cars," Linville testified about the steakhouse murders, adding that the victims were doing exactly as they were told before the robbers herded them into a freezer and shot them to death. The robbers got away with about $1,200.

At Stafford's trial in the steakhouse murders, Verna Stafford testified that her husband became upset when the restaurant manager told the gunmen that he couldn't understand why people couldn't work for a living.

Verna said Roger Stafford first killed a janitor, Isaac Freeman, and then he and his brother began shooting the others.

Finally, she claimed, Roger Stafford gave her a gun and insisted that she shoot one of the victims, which she said she did with his help. The other victims were the manager, Louis Zacarias, and four teenage employees – Terri Horst, David Salsman, Anthony Tew and David Lindsey.

The Staffords fled in the Lorenzes' pickup, but a teenager waiting to pick up his girlfriend, Horst, at the steakhouse gave police a description of the vehicle.

The killers then went to Stillwater, where a man was able to identify the pickup and give police descriptions of the occupants.

Ironically, Roger Stafford was responsible for identifying the sketches that were drawn from the Stillwater man's descriptions. After they were published, he called police to say that he had partied with Verna and Harold Stafford at a Tulsa motel. He gave their names.

Harold Stafford was killed in a motorcycle accident near Tulsa six days after the steakhouse murders. A woman who visited the funeral home to see his body was traced to Arkansas, and she provided information that led investigators to Chicago, where Verna was arrested. Stafford was arrested later in Chicago.

At her trial in Oklahoma City, Verna received two consecutive life terms from District Judge Richard Freeman.

In a bizarre twist to Roger Stafford's execution, Assistant Attorney General Sandy Howard, who handled opposition to Stafford's appeals, received a $5 gift certificate to a Sirloin Stockade restaurant from the mass murderer in the mail two days after his execution.

Written on its back was: "Hey, you got away with it. I am murder (sic) and you help (sic) do it! I am innocent and you know it." It was signed Roger Dale Stafford 103767.

The signature appeared to be that of Stafford, based on a comparison with his signature on legal documents. The certificate had been bought at a Sirloin Stockade restaurant in El Reno a year earlier.

Land run reporter jumped at chance

Hundreds of single women made the runs to claim land in Oklahoma.

But none did it with the flair of Annetta Daisey, who became a participant although she went to the Unassigned Lands to report on the April 22, 1889, land run for the Dallas Morning News and Fort Worth Gazette.

That flair was memorialized as part of Edmond's centennial celebration by a statue showing Daisey leaping from the cowcatcher of a train, with her petticoat and skirt flying.

According to legend, she boarded a slow northbound train packed with Boomers at Purcell. The train traveled slowly to allow men to jump from it to stake claims.

When the train left Edmond Station, Daisey persuaded the engineer to let her ride on the cowcatcher.

Two miles north of Edmond, as the train neared the homestead she had selected earlier, she jumped off and planted her stake on the 160-acre site.

She fired a gun into the air, yelled "I salute Kentucky Daisey's claim," and raced back to the train to be pulled aboard the caboose by other reporters.

That tale has other versions, however. A 1990 article by Glenda Carlile in "Buckskin, Calico and Lace," reported that Daisey dropped her stake in the jump, so she ripped off her petticoat and threw it over a bush to mark her claim.

An article by Debbie Kindt Michalke in the spring 1997 Chronicles of Oklahoma doesn't that Daisey was on the cowcatcher but reports that she narrowly escaped a gunshot fired at her while she staked her claim.

Maria DeLong, a Tulsa freelance writer who has done extensive research on Daisey, reported that she jumped from a platform on the reporters' coach at the head of the train, not the cowcatcher.

Edmond Parks Foundation

A statue, "Leaping into History" sculpted by Mary Lou Gresham, commemorates Nanette R. H Kentucky Daisey's exploits. It was commissioned by the Edmond Centennial Commission and now stands in the Festival Market Place in Centennial Park in Edmond.

DeLong wrote that Daisey drove two stakes into the ground, threw her cloak over one and raced to the last car to get back on the train.

Riding the cowcatcher would have been dangerous, DeLong wrote.

Regardless of where Daisey was riding or how she staked her claim, she sent her stories to her newspapers when the train reached Guthrie.

Fellow reporters, who gave her the nickname "Kentucky Daisey," found her good material for their own columns – some dramatically embellished.

Daisey "proved up" her claim, obtained title to the 160 acres and built a small house on it. However, she worked as a reporter and taught school at Guthrie, the capital of Oklahoma Territory.

Daisey joined the run into the opening of the Sac and Fox land on Sept. 22, 1891, and staked a claim in Chandler, leaving her ineligible to get more land in subsequent land runs.

She led a group of 11 women into the Cheyenne and Arapaho lands and set up a camp in advance of the scheduled April 1892 run but was arrested as she headed to El Reno to pick up provisions. Soldiers escorted her out of the area. Undaunted, she returned to the area, but was again captured and escorted out. She led another group of women into the opening of the Cherokee Outlet on Sept. 22, 1893.

While living at Guthrie, Daisey married a Swedish-born soldier stationed there. But their marriage wasn't happy. A short time later, he was sent to Fort Reno and later to the Philippines.

She tracked him down several years later in Chicago and went there to reclaim the marriage. He divorced her instead and married another woman.

Former slave laid down law as deputy marshal

Shortly before Bass Reeves died in 1910, the Muskogee Phoenix said he was "honest, fearless and a terror to the bootleggers."

That description could have gone further to include that he also was a terror to all kinds of criminals -- bootleggers, murderers, robbers, horse thieves. During the 32 years he served as a deputy U.S. marshal, he helped clean up Indian Territory.

But his most recent service had been as a police officer in Muskogee under Chief Bud Ledbetter, also a former deputy marshal, who had declared war on bootleggers.

A former slave, Reeves was believed to be the first black deputy marshal commissioned west of the Mississippi. He was among 200 deputies hired in 1875 by U.S. District Judge Isaac C. Parker and sent into the 75,000 square miles of Indian Territory in search of outlaws.

Reeves boasted he knew Indian Territory "like a cook knows her kitchen" – a boast borne out by his arrest of more than 3,000 wanted men. He also understood several Indian languages.

According to the Nov. 19, 1909, Muskogee Times-Democrat, some of his trips into Indian Territory would last for months, ending with Reeves coming back to Fort Smith with "bands of men charged with crimes from bootlegging to murder."

His philosophy was that there were three principal classes of outlaws – murderers, horse thieves and bootleggers – in the territory.

During his years as a deputy marshal, Reeves killed 14 men, but he always said he never shot a man when it was not necessary. Once he was charged with murder but was acquitted. He spent most of the money he had made from rewards and fees defending himself.

"Everything about Bass Reeves seemed to invite legend," Art Burton of the South Suburban College history department in South Holland, Ill., wrote in his book "Black, Red and Deadly."

According to Burton, Reeves always rode a large red stallion with a white blazed face. But he kept two good rid-

Tulsa World archives

Former slave Bass Reeves, who became a deputy marshal in 1875, was made famous by his exploits capturing outlaws in the Oklahoma Territory.

ing horses for pursuit, as well as a run-of-the-mill horse for undercover work. To outlaws, the sign of a superior pony was a tip-off that the rider was a deputy marshal, Burton explained.

Reeves was known as a natty dresser, usually wearing a large black hat and polished boots, but he sometimes resorted to disguises – sometimes as a drover or a cowboy, or as a farmer, a gunslinger or even as an outlaw.

He once disguised himself as a tramp, wore an old floppy hat that he had fired three bullets through, and carried a cane while searching for outlaw brothers.

According to Burton, Reeves knocked at the door of the outlaws' mother, asked for a bite to eat and explained it was the first chance he had to rest after being pursued by a posse that had put three bullet holes in his hat.

She invited him into the house and later told him that he should join up with her sons. The sons showed up and agreed to the plan, but after everyone went to bed, Reeves handcuffed them without waking them.

Early the next morning, he kicked the wanted men and told them, "Come on, boys, let's get going from here." Their mother followed them for three miles, cursing Reeves.

Reeves' most difficult assignment was to arrest his own son for killing his wife. After two weeks, Reeves found his son and returned to Muskogee with him. The son was convicted of murder and sentenced to prison, but he later received a pardon.

Reeves was born as a slave either in Texas or Arkansas about 1838 and was owned by a man named George Reeves, whose last name the slave took. After a dispute, Reeves fled into Indian Territory and hid until the Emancipation Proclamation of 1863, when he bought land near Van Buren, Ark.

He was a farmer until Judge Parker hired James F. Fagan as marshal and Fagan hired Reeves as one of his 200 deputies. He retired as a marshal in 1907 and at the age of 69 became a police officer in Muskogee.

Oral vaccine conquered polio in 1960s

A dread disease that left its victims disabled – such as President Franklin D. Roosevelt – or dead was finally conquered in the 1960s.

By a sugar cube.

And by more than 2,000 Tulsa volunteers, including doctors and nurses, pharmacists, Boy Scouts, Kiwanians, school principals, custodians, other employees and Civil Defense patrolmen who staffed 40 clinics in schools and at the Armory.

And thanks to that effort and other similar clinics around the country, most people under 50 today have no knowledge of polio and its crippling effects.

Of course, the sugar didn't have any medicinal quality – the liquid vaccine was dripped onto the cubes to make the medicine go down, especially for children, the primary targets for the vaccine.

The oral vaccine was developed by Dr. Albert Sabin, a University of Cincinnati scientist. Its use followed by about 10 years an injected polio vaccine developed by Dr. Jonas Salk that had cut the incidence of polio dramatically throughout the country, including Oklahoma.

During the 1950s, for instance, there were 651 cases in five years in Tulsa. By 1962, that number had been cut to 10 cases, reflecting the effectiveness of the injected Salk vaccine. The liquid Sabin vaccine promised even greater protection.

Doctors stressed that even people who had received Salk vaccinations should get the oral medicine because the injected vaccine was only 85 percent to 90 percent effective while tests had shown the oral vaccine to be 100 percent effective.

More than 780,000 doses of the Sabin vaccine were distributed to 70 percent of the county's population by the Tulsa County Medical Society, which still looks at that community effort as one of the most successful projects of the now-100-year-old organization.

Records show that 265,710 received the first dose of type I on Jan. 20 and 27,1963, more than 257,000 received the second dose of type II on March 10 and 17 and 253,064 doses of type III were given April 28 and May 5, according to Paul Patton, executive director of the Tulsa County Medical Society.

The Tulsa World helped draw attention to the second

Tulsa World archive

Hillcrest student nurse Ruth Lindquist helps pharmacist Tom Mullen drip the oral polio vaccine onto sugar cubes during Tulsa's "Smash Polio" campaign in January 1963. Each person taking the vaccine was asked to donate 25 cents toward the cost of the project. This photo ran in the Tulsa World on Jan. 17, 1963.

immunization on March 10, 1963, with a Page 1 drawing of a syringe dripping a liquid onto a sugar cube and a message overprinted in red: "Get your Type II oral polio vaccine TODAY!"

Because of the overprinted red message, there was no doubt about the importance of the small story at the bottom announcing that the second of three doses of the Sabin polio vaccine was scheduled to be given at 43 locations around Tulsa County that day.

Each recipient was asked to contribute 25 cents for receiving the vaccine. However, the World made it clear that no one would be turned away, regardless of a person's ability to pay.

The story stressed the importance of taking all three doses of Sabin vaccine about six or eight weeks apart. The oral vaccine was believed to confer a lifetime immunity to the disease.

In spite of the big red message on the front page of that day's Tulsa World, only 162,615 showed up at the clinics for the second doses of vaccine. Rain and sickness – many children were out of school with flu, chicken pox and other illnesses – were blamed for the low turnout, and a make-up clinic was scheduled for the next Sunday, when 95,339 more turned out.

It had been only a few years since two of Tulsa's major hospitals, Hillcrest and St. John, created polio wards by moving iron lungs into hallways for victims because they didn't have enough patient rooms.

During the height of the epidemic in the 1940s and '50s, parents kept their children out of swimming pools in the summer and would not allow them to attend movies or other events where they might be in crowds for fear they would contract the virus. During the epidemic's worst days, the World ran Page 1 boxes showing how many new cases had been diagnosed, how many had died and how many had gone home from the hospitals.

A polio epidemic in 1916 had killed 6,000 and paralyzed 27,000 in the U.S. In 1921, Roosevelt, who had been the Democrat nominee for vice president the previous year, contracted the virus while on vacation. At first he walked with the aid of canes and heavy steel braces on his legs but eventually relied on a wheelchair for mobility.

Mob lynches ex-lawman's reputed killers

A mob of 150-200 men overpowered the jailers at Ada, snatched four prisoners from their cells and hanged them from the rafters in an old livery barn. The prisoners had been accused of killing a popular former police officer.

The April 19, 1909, lynchings followed the confession by one of the men at a kangaroo court. The news caused the mob to become so enraged that all four men were lynched.

The four were in the Ada jail awaiting trial on murder charges for the ambush killing of former Ada Marshal A.A. Bobbitt. He was described in a Tulsa World story as a well-known hunter of bad men and as a man "absolutely without fear"; he was shot as he drove a wagon a few miles south of Ada on Feb. 27, 1909. The assassin escaped on horseback.

The mob took only J.R. Miller from the jail at first, and he confessed to Bobbitt's killing after being promised that he would be given a chance in court if he admitted the killing and named others involved. But after hearing his confession at the end of two hours of questioning, the mob reneged on the promise, went back into the jail and marched Jesse West, Joe Allen and D.B. Burrell to the livery barn, where all four were hanged.

Allen and West were described as wealthy cattlemen of Canadian, Texas, who had hired Miller for $1,700 to kill Bobbitt. A disagreement that stemmed from when Allen and West formerly ranched in Pontotoc County near Bobbitt's ranch. They reportedly gave the money to Burrell, who acted as the go-between and gave it to Miller.

The mob took matters into their own hands because members feared the defendants would be acquitted – they had hired attorney Moman Pruiett to represent them. Pruiett had won 303 acquittals in 343 murder trials and had

Brad Thompson/Tulsa World

This pencil rendering shows A.A. Bobbitt, a former Ada marshal killed by an assassin Feb. 27, 1909. A mob later lynched four men suspected of involvement in his killing.

never had a client executed.

Before the mob appeared at the jail, some of its members had forced employees on duty at the Ada power plant to cut electric wires controlling street lights to give them a chance to conduct their examination of Miller and the subsequent hangings without fear of detection.

Some of the mob members reportedly wore masks to conceal their identities, but many others did not, the World reported.

After he was shot, Bobbitt had managed to drive his wagon back to his house, where he told his wife that he had been shot by Miller. He kept his coat buttoned over his wound, told his wife he had only an hour to live. He asked her not to talk so he could spend the last hour of his life talking to her and giving her instructions on the disposition of his property, according to a story in Ardmore's Daily Ardmoreite.

Bobbitt was reported to have been afraid of assassination for several years and had directed in his will that $1,000 of his estate be used to prosecute his assassins.

"All the men hanged are said to be desperate characters with killing records in other states," the World reported. Attorney General Frank Canton said Miller had killed 13 men in Texas and always escaped punishment. He said Miller was "without doubt the leader of a gang (of badmen) that has roamed over the Choctaw and Chickasaw nations."

Gov. Charles Haskell directed Pontotoc County officials to "make a vigorous investigation" and Supreme Court Chief Justice M.J. Kane ordered a special grand jury to be empaneled to investigate the lynchings.

The mob reportedly consisted of friends and neighbors of Bobbitt, but apparently no one would identify any of them and none was ever prosecuted.

Mayor 'Miss Phenie Lou' played hardball

It took a woman to solve the big municipal problem in Broken Arrow in the early 1930s, a problem that other communities probably faced, too.

Unpaid water bills.

Phenie Lou Ownby, the wife of a doctor, got the bills paid when she served as mayor from 1931 to 1933. Her solution was simple: Turn off the water to the customers who failed to pay their bills.

That policy was considered radical and tough, but Broken Arrow gained national attention from her action. It was the first time that a mayor of any gender in an American city had taken such action to collect past due bills, according to a 1932 Tulsa World story.

Ownby, known in Broken Arrow as Miss Phenie Lou, became mayor almost by accident. She had no political aspirations and was surprised when she saw her name on the ballot in the 1929 city election.

She hadn't filed as a candidate and thought someone might have been playing a practical joke on her. She didn't win but she received enough votes that she decided to be a real candidate two years later – and won by 40 votes, becoming the first woman mayor in Oklahoma and only the sixth in the nation.

She took her job seriously and set about examining the city government and issues facing the town of about 2,000.

Shortly after taking office, she told the City Council that the city was in debt because many residents were not paying their water bills.

"Many of our best citizens are ignoring our water bills. What do you propose to do?" she asked.

In today's vernacular, the eight councilmen didn't have a clue. Mayor Ownby said she dreamed of a solution – cutting off water supplies to those who owed bills – and got up in the middle of the night to write it down.

Broken Arrow Historical Society

Phenie Lou Ownby, the mayor of Broken Arrow from 1931 to 1933, caught the public's eye when she cut off city water to customers who weren't paying their bills.

Because the local newspaper wouldn't publish a news story about her proposed action, the mayor bought an ad in the next edition, telling residents, "Some people seem to think the world owes them something. Maybe it does, but they won't get it from this administration."

And then she gave a list of 50 delinquent water customers to Street and Water Commissioner J.E. Chism with instructions to cut off water to those customers. One delinquent customer objected and began to fight Chism. The city marshal called the mayor and asked what he should do.

"Well, arrest him, of course," she replied. "What did you think we would do? We have the law on our side and in this case, we will show the people that we mean business."

The customer was arrested and was fined $19.75 the next day in municipal court.

Her campaign was effective. Water receipts in March 1931, when she took office, totaled $802.34. The receipts for the same month a year later had risen to $1,624.

The mayor said that some of those whose water was cut off were her best friends, and they remained friends.

"The elite have been frankly told that if they don't pay up, they will find themselves after a party some night with stacks of china and glass and silver and not a drop of water to wash the stains away," a St. Louis newspaper wrote. "And we pause to say that Miss Phenie is right."

She had no further political aspirations, despite the publicity she received from her two-year term.

"No," she said, "I will not run for the office again. I have tried my best to serve my city during this term, and I feel that I have done some good. But it is too much work. My telephone rings constantly and there is always something to worry about."

Wiley Post reveled in daring innovation

Wearing a "space suit" that he had invented, Oklahoma pilot Wiley Post made a forced landing at Cleveland, Ohio – short of his Newark, N.J., goal. He had flown from Los Angeles to Cleveland with a record average speed of 279.36 mph.

He would have passed out in a few minutes from lack of oxygen if he had not turned the nose of his plane, the Winnie Mae, earthward, he told reporters after landing March 15, 1935.

Post used another innovation to land at the Cleveland airport. He had dropped the wheels of his plane after taking off in an attempt to prevent wind drag and increase his speed. But he had fitted his plane with special skids for landing.

It was Post's second attempt to set a speed record in a flight across the continent. His first try had ended with engine trouble; Post blamed steel filings or emery dust placed in his plane's engine.

Post said the highest he flew was 35,000 feet and that his plane seemed to make the best time at about 30,000 feet. He flew the 2,044 miles from Los Angeles to Cleveland in eight hours and four minutes. The "space suit" worked fine, he said.

Post had designed what became the world's first practical pressure suit a year earlier because the Winnie Mae's cabin could not be pressurized. The body of the suit had three layers: long underwear, an inner black rubber air pressure bladder and an outer suit made of rubberized parachute fabric.

The outer suit was glued to a frame with arm and leg joints that allowed him to operate the flight controls and to walk to and from the aircraft. The helmet had a removable faceplate that could be sealed and could accommodate earphones and a throat microphone.

He had tested his suit six months earlier when he flew to an altitude of 40,000 feet above Chicago. Eventually he flew as high as 50,000 feet.

When he landed after testing the suit, he said it had worked well. "I turned the air pressure on at 25,000 feet," he said. Post had been lifted in and out of his plane for the first test of the suit, and attendants removed his headpiece to allow him to be interviewed.

After his forced landing at Cleveland, Post was asked by an interviewer whether he had eaten anything. He replied,

Associated Press

Wiley Post poses in his high-altitude pressure suit near his airplane "Winnie Mae" before a 1934 takeoff in New York in an effort to break the altitude record. Post designed his own "space suit" that he used in his attempts to set air-speed records at high altitudes.

"How the hell do you think I could eat in that suit?" The suit, called "grotesque" by reporters in 1935, resembled those worn by deep-sea divers.

Although those attempts failed to set a record for cross-country flight, Post twice set the record for flying around the world; first in June 1931 when he accomplished the feat in eight days, 16 hours with navigator Harold Gatty and again in July 1933 when he made the trip in seven days, 19 hours by himself.

Post was born Nov. 22, 1898, in Texas. He didn't have much interest in education but was fascinated by mechanical things. He began working in the oil fields in 1919. In 1921, he was sentenced to a 10-year prison term for automobile theft but was paroled after one year.

He lost his left eye in an oil field accident in the mid-1920s, and used the $1,800 settlement to buy his first airplane.

Post and Will Rogers met at a banquet in Tulsa in 1931, brought together by a common interest in aviation, and Post flew the famous humorist to an engagement.

He later became the personal pilot of F.C. Hall, a wealthy Oklahoma oilman, and had use of Hall's personal plane, an open-cockpit biplane.

Hall bought a Lockheed Vega, largely for Post's use, but sold it back to Lockheed because of the Depression. He bought a later version of the Lockheed Vega and again nicknamed it "Winnie Mae," the same as the first Vega. This later aircraft is the one most often seen in photographs of Post.

Rogers and Post were killed Aug. 15, 1935, when their plane crashed on takeoff near Point Barrow, Alaska, as they were on an around-the-world trip. They were flying a Lockheed Orion, which had been refitted with the larger wings of a Lockheed Explorer and with pontoon floats from a third plane. The news didn't reach Oklahoma until the next day.

Betty Rogers told reporters she had tried to keep her husband from accompanying Post on the trip. "Don't go, Will. Please don't go," she begged as Rogers prepared to board an airliner to meet Post in Seattle.

She said she pointed out the dangers of flying over icy water in Alaska and Siberia.

1956 ballot battle left Senate to fill seat

The Oklahoma Senate settled the 1956 race for senator from the Okmulgee-Wagoner County district – the first and only time in state history that the Senate was called upon to decide a race.

It seated Tom W. Payne Jr. in a unanimous 42-0 vote. That number is two shy of the 44 members of the legislative body, but the Okmulgee-Wagoner seat was considered vacant and a tie vote for the Logan County district had not been settled.

The decision fell to the Senate because of a chain of events that left neither candidate listed on the general election ballot.

The main players in the issue were Payne, 41, and John Russell Jr., 33, both Democrats, who had feuded during the four years Russell had been in the Senate and Payne had been in the House as Russell's successor. Although other issues may have played a role, their dispute erupted over an attempt by Russell to remove Oklahoma A & M Tech from the control of the A & M regents.

Russell sought to create a separate board to run the Okmulgee school. The Senate had approved the measure, but the House killed it because of Payne's opposition.

Russell led in the 1956 primary election after one of the most bitterly fought races in Oklahoma history, but a runoff election was necessary because of a third candidate, Roy Cocke of Wagoner County.

Payne carried both counties by 508 votes in the July 24 runoff, but his victory was short-lived: A box of absentee ballots gave the victory to Russell, whose victory was also short-lived. All of the absentee ballots were thrown out by a district court judge and court litigation barred both candidates from the nomination.

Thomas H. Payne

It took a vote of the Oklahoma Senate to decide that Tom W. Payne Jr. had won the hotly contested 1956 state Senate race in one eastern Oklahoma district.

Because neither man's name was on the Nov. 6 general election ballot, Gov. Raymond Gary scheduled a special election for Dec. 22. Only Payne and a Republican filed as candidates for the special election.

Meanwhile, the Oklahoma Supreme Court ruled – after the general election – that Russell had won the Democratic primary. The ruling meant little, however, because the general election had passed with neither Payne nor Russell a candidate in it.

Payne was finally seated Jan. 16, 1957. Legislative bodies are always the final arbiters of their memberships.

Payne, his wife and son watched the Senate voting from the gallery and Payne later took the oath of office.

Russell's name was not mentioned during the proceedings, and he was not present.

After investigations of the election, Russell was indicted on charges of conspiracy to defraud the state, in both Wagoner and Oklahoma counties.

The Wagoner County case ended in a mistrial, and the indictment was dismissed. Russell was acquitted in Oklahoma County.

The investigation led to the passage by the Legislature of the first election reforms since statehood. The new laws changed the method of handling absentee ballots and recounts, among other things.

Payne remained in the Senate until his death April 17, 1974.

Russell, a lawyer, moved to Wagoner County, where he was appointed the county attorney in 1958 following the resignation of Max Findley. Russell later became an assistant district attorney and was elected as the district attorney in 1973 and in 1977 in the district, which includes Adair, Cherokee, Sequoyah and Wagoner counties.

'Pistol Pete' always aimed for the spotlight

Frank Eaton was an Indian scout, a stagecoach driver, a deputy U.S. marshal, a cattle herder on the Chisholm Trail, a participant in the 1889 run into what became Oklahoma and an acquaintance of most of the infamous early-day outlaws.

The grips of his Colt .45 pistols had 11 notches, representing the 11 men he killed during the years he was carving his place in history, folklore and legend.

He spent the last 25 or more years of his life as a fixture at old-timer celebrations, pioneer events and in parades, wearing a 10-gallon hat, fancy vest, frontier pants and his revolvers – the dress expected in the mid-20th century of a pioneer Oklahoma cowboy and law officer.

"I guess I'm just a hound for attention," he told a Tulsa World reporter in 1935. "Danged if I ain't."

You probably know him better as Pistol Pete, the mascot of Oklahoma State University, caricatured today at sports and other events by a student wearing a huge fiberglass head designed to resemble Eaton's craggy face, handlebar mustache and oversize hat. The getup may be a reminder of Eaton's early days, but it doesn't provoke fear in bad guys.

Eaton liked riding in parades and waving his big hat at spectators and, sometimes, firing a round or two into the air from his pistol. He liked applause, publicity and posing for pictures.

He was riding in Stillwater's 1923 Armistice Day parade when students from Oklahoma A&M (now OSU) noticed him. They had been searching for a new mascot to replace the tiger the school had been using. When they saw Eaton in the parade, the search was over.

At his death in 1958 at age 97, Eaton was living in Perkins, in the house he built on the land he staked in the land run of 1898. He had operated a blacksmith shop there and had spent many years as the town's constable.

Francis Beardman Eaton was born in 1860 in Connecticut, the son of an English mother and a Cherokee father. When he was 8, the family moved to Kansas, where his father was killed – an event that shaped his life.

Eaton often told in his later years about the night a group of men came to the family's house and asked to see his father, a Yankee who had run afoul of outlaws who had been Confederate soldiers. He said his father went outside, and Eaton never saw him again. A family friend gave him two old dueling pistols and told him that he should avenge his

Tulsa World archives

Frank Eaton, better known as Pistol Pete, said he enjoyed the attention he earned later in his life as a symbol of Oklahoma's early history. He called himself a "hound for attention."

father's death, he said.

"Frank, you take these guns and learn how to use them," Eaton said the friend told him. "You'll never be a man until you've killed the men who killed your father."

He practiced with the pistols so faithfully that at age 15 he won a shooting match against soldiers at Fort Gibson. The fort commander gave him the name "Pistol Pete," which stuck with him for the rest of his long life.

And, according to a 1952 biography by Eva Gillhouse of Reno, Nev., Eaton did kill five of the men who had killed his father, accounting for five of the 11 notches on his guns. He was on the trail of the sixth when that gunman was killed in a poker game in South West City, Mo. The remaining notches came while Eaton was a deputy U.S. marshal for Judge Isaac Parker of Fort Smith.

But Eaton said the notches on his pistol didn't give him pleasure.

"There's some things I'd like to forget," he said. "Some men are killers, and the notches on their guns don't bother them. But there are other men who kill and still sweat over it years after."

Eaton became a deputy marshal at age 19 when Indian Territory was under the jurisdiction of the federal court at Fort Smith. He also carried the mail through Oklahoma, drove the Guthrie stagecoach to other towns and drove cattle from Texas to South Dakota on the Chisholm Trail for Col. Charles Goodnight.

He was a private in a military group formed to fight Geronimo's Apache warriors, leading him to quip in later years: "Ain't it queer how most old soldiers are captains, or colonels or majors? Seems like all the privates must have died young. I'm about the only private of my age anybody's ever saw."

Known as a fast draw, Eaton was demonstrating that talent to a history class at OSU in 1957, the year before his death, when his loaded pistol accidentally went off in the classroom, shooting a hole in the ceiling. Asked why he hadn't unloaded his pistol, he replied: "I'd rather have a pocket full of rocks than an unloaded gun."

Eaton's biography, "Pistol Pete, Veteran of the Old West," includes an introductory note by Eaton: "My friend and partner, Eva Gillhouse, wrote this book. It was her idea and she did all the work. It's just the way I told it to her – it's all true – and I'll back her with both guns."

Guthrie: This man was our man

"Way down yonder in the Indian nation
tion
"Ridin' my pony on the reservation
"in those Oklahoma hills where I was
born. . . "

"The Oklahoma Hills" by Woody Guthrie, an Okemah native, is the official state folk song.

It was one of at least 1,000 songs written by Guthrie, who died Oct. 3, 1967, of Huntington's disease, which destroys muscle coordination. He was 55.

Guthrie is recognized as Okemah's favorite son. Signs on the highway identify the town as Guthrie's hometown, his name is painted on a water tower, a statue of him stands in a park and an annual Woody Guthrie festival is celebrated there around the time of his July 14 birthday.

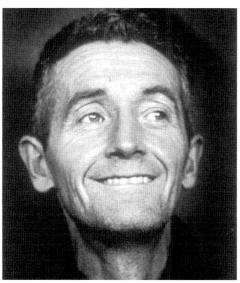

Woody Guthrie is now celebrated as a native Oklahoman.

Guthrie was inducted posthumously into the Oklahoma Hall of Fame in 2006 and into the Okemah Hall of Fame in 2007.

That esteem for Guthrie in his hometown and home state hasn't always been the case.

For years, few people in Okemah, the Okfuskee County seat on Interstate 40, cared to claim Guthrie because of his political leanings during the 1930s and 1940s when he wrote a column, "Woody Sez," for the Daily Worker, the newspaper of the American Communist Party.

As late as 1971, the Okemah City Council refused to proclaim Woody Guthrie Day because of his radical politics. But Guthrie's family went to Okemah anyway to donate a set of Guthrie's books and records to the Okfuskee County Library. They also visited relatives, the house where the folk singer was reared and the family plot at the cemetery.

The Guthries and city officials were worried about possible demonstrations, and some residents feared a possible influx of hippies to see Guthrie's son, Arlo Guthrie, who is also a popular folk song writer and singer. Neither occurred.

The negative feeling about Woody Guthrie eased, possibly because most of the people who remembered him had died, and in 1972 a sign proclaiming "Home of Woody Guthrie" was painted on one of the city's water towers. The Woody Guthrie festival began and a statue of Guthrie was erected in 1998.

The Oklahoma Legislature approved a bill by Rep. Dale Turner, D-Holdenville, in 2001 to make "The Oklahoma Hills" by Guthrie and his cousin, Jack Guthrie, the official state folk song. The governor signed the bill a few days later. Turner said the measure would help promote Okemah's annual Woody Guthrie music festival.

That song became a country western hit in 1945 after Jack Guthrie recorded it for Capitol Records. Woody Guthrie and his cousin, who was his partner on a radio show, decided to share the copyright to the song.

Guthrie was born in Okemah on July 14, 1912, a few months before his namesake, Woodrow Wilson, was elected president. Guthrie's life disintegrated after his older sister died in a house fire and his mother was committed to a mental institution because she was exhibiting early signs of Huntington's disease that were thought then to be insanity.

His brother was sent to live with a sister in Pampa, Texas, but Guthrie remained in Okemah with his father. However, the elder Guthrie was seriously burned in a fire, forcing Woody Guthrie to stay with different families during the school year for two years. During the summers, he hitchhiked or hoboed to south Texas to stay and work with friends. He made money by picking up junk in back alleys, washed and polished spittoons to pay rent on a shoeshine stand, sold newspapers and worked at other odd jobs.

Guthrie sang and strummed his way across the country in the 1930s, appearing in saloons and chili joints, at country dances and in hobo jungles, and began writing and recording songs that made him famous – except in Oklahoma.

He and Jack Guthrie teamed up in the Los Angeles area and eventually landed their radio show, which later featured Maxine "Lefty Lou" Crissman. After Jack Guthrie left the program, it took the name "The Woody and Lefty Show."

About that time, Woody Guthrie began mailing a small mimeographed songbook to listeners who wanted the words to his songs. On the bottom of one page appeared the following:

"This song is Copyrighted in U.S., under Seal of Copyright #154085, for a period of 28 years, and anybody caught singin it without our permission, will be mighty good friends of ourn, cause we dont give a dern. Publish it. Write it. Sing it. Swing to it. Yodel it. We wrote it, thats all we wanted to do."

When World War II began, Guthrie joined the Merchant Marine. He served on three ships, all of which were torpedoed. The Army drafted him in 1945.

Guthrie performed in Madison Square Garden and New York's Town Hall before his disease disabled him. A few months before Guthrie's death, Interior Secretary Stewart Udall gave him a medal and called him a poet of the American landscape.

Guthrie once told a reporter, "I am out to sing the songs that make you take pride in yourself and in your work." Such a song was his most famous – "This Land Is Your Land."

Judge led battle for desegregation

Amos T. Hall, a quiet, peace-loving, humble Tulsan who was a leader in the fight for desegregation and who became Oklahoma's first elected black judge, would have been impressed by the list of people who attended his funeral in 1971.

U.S. Supreme Court Justice Thurgood Marshall, NAACP National Director Roy Wilkins, Oklahoma Gov. David Hall and Mayor Robert LaFortune were among more than 1,500 who crowded into the First Baptist Church to mourn his death, extol his memory and to hear the 75-year-old jurist eulogized.

Oklahoma Historical Society

Amos T. Hall of Tulsa (left), who developed an interest in the law while reading an old set of law books, rose to become the first black elected to a judicial position in Oklahoma. He is seen here with Ada Lois Sipuel Fisher, who reapplied for admission to the University of Oklahoma on Jan. 19, 1948; Thurgood Marshall, attorney from the New York office of the National Association for the Advancement of Colored People; and Dr. H.W. Williamston of Idabel, state president of the NAACP. Hall at that time was resident counsel for the NAACP.

an old set of law books, which he began reading, and developed an interest in the law. He became a justice of the peace (a former judicial position that did not require a law degree) and continued studying his law books at night. He was admitted to the Oklahoma bar in 1925.

A native of Louisiana, Hall had graduated from Gilbert Industrial College in Baldwin, La., before coming to Tulsa in 1921.

He served as the attorney for the Oklahoma NAACP for many years and was president of the Tulsa NAACP. He had been

"I can't think of anything more he could have done," Justice Marshall said in perhaps the most eloquent eulogy during the two-hour service. "He led the fight (for desegregation) here and around the country in the days when it was a little rough – and to say a little rough is putting it mildly.

"It takes strength to stand up quietly, lawfully, peacefully and say 'I will not be moved. I am going down that road and nobody's going to stop me.' Amos Hall did just that and he carried so many with him," Marshall said.

It was an accurate description of Hall, who was found dead of a heart attack Aug. 27, 1971, in his car in the 4300 block of North Frankfort Place. It was about 20 hours after he left his courtroom in the Tulsa County Courthouse after telling his clerk he would return shortly.

Hall failed to return for a trial scheduled for 3 p.m., and police began searching for the missing jurist about 5 p.m. when he missed another appointment. They even checked his car after someone reported it to police, but officers didn't see his body because it was slumped down. The car's quiet-running engine was still running when the body was found the next day.

A testimonial dinner for Hall, with Wilkins as the speaker, had been scheduled for Dec. 10 to honor the attorney for his long years of service to his community and to the Prince Hall Masonic Lodge. The dinner was canceled although organizers at first considered holding it as a memorial service. He had served 31 years as the grand master of Oklahoma Prince Hall Masons.

Hall was working as a church janitor when he acquired

on the board of St. John's Hospital, the YMCA executive committee, the Tulsa NCCJ board and the Tulsa Economic Opportunity Task Force, among others.

Hall became the first black elected to a judicial position in Oklahoma in August 1970 when he drew more than 50 percent of the vote in a four-candidate race for the Democratic nomination for associate district judge, thus avoiding the general election. He had been serving as an appointed special district judge.

Charles Owens, a former Tulsa police officer, who was the first black to serve as a judge when he was appointed in 1969, became the second black elected to a judicial post by winning a seat in the general election in Oklahoma County three months later.

Hall had remained firm in his belief that the battle for equal rights should be fought in the courts and the hearts of men, although he felt that black extremists considered him an "Uncle Tom."

"Even one person is not powerless against those who fight change in this life," Hall said. "Even one person can help to right the wrongs of life and even change the course of history.

"This change, if our nation is to survive and our democracy to continue, will not be effected through violence. It will come only through education and changes in the attitudes and the hearts of men."

Wilkins told those attending Hall's funeral "we should be proud of having known Amos Hall, having shared for a little while in his concern for his fellow man – not white men, not black men, not yellow men, but all men."

First female chief made Seminole history

After Alice Brown Davis took the oath of office as the chief of the Seminole Indian tribe in 1922, a Muskogee Phoenix reporter asked her how it felt to be the first Indian woman chief in history.

"I did feel a little scared at first, but I went through it all right," Davis responded.

Davis, 69, was appointed by President Warren Harding on the recommendation of Maj. Victor Locke Jr., the superintendent of the Five Civilized Tribes, to settle some tribal business. Her brother, John Brown, believing that all tribal business had been completed, had resigned in 1916 after 30 years as the chief.

Locke explained at Davis' inauguration ceremony in the U.S. District Court room at Muskogee that the Dawes Commission had been trying since 1893 to wind up the affairs of Indian tribes and that Indian governments had been abolished when Oklahoma became a state in 1907.

But, he said, some Washington bureaucrat had discovered that some deeds needed the signature of a Seminole chief, qualified by blood, according to the book "Alice & J.F.B." by Vance Trimble of Wewoka.

The appointment of a woman raised some eyebrows among American Indians and whites. A Tulsa World editorial said, "The wise person who declaimed there is nothing new under the sun was only approximately wise.

"Mrs. Alice B. Davis has just proved that there is something new; she is the new chief of the Seminole tribe of Indians."

The editorial pointed out that the traditional business of an Indian chief had been to fight, "but the day of the chase and the war trail has passed."

There was no disputing that Davis was qualified. She had worked on tribal matters in many places, including in Mexico in 1903, 1905 and 1910, acted as an interpreter for the U.S. government in Florida in a celebrated murder trial, and had been a missionary and teacher. She was respected for her knowledge of languages, her intelligence and her willingness to aid her people.

"Alice did not attain the chieftainship through heredi-

Photo courtesy of Oklahoma Historical Society

Alice Brown Davis (front row, center) stands with other women on the steps of the Federal Building in Muskogee on Aug. 16, 1922, the day she was sworn in as the chief of the Seminole Indian tribe. Pictured are (front row, left) Alice Locke, Davis and Joyette Jones; (back row, left) Joyce Davis Jones, Mrs. Ben Locke, Mrs. M.C. Jones, Mrs. H.W. Livinam, Mrs. Vernon Kiker, and Mrs. W.S. Key.

tary privileges but was selected solely upon her ability and qualifications," Locke, a former chief of the Choctaw tribe, told the crowd at Davis' inauguration.

Davis was born in 1852 at Park Hill after her parents arrived there from Florida on the Trail of Tears. Her father, Dr. John F. Brown, was a Scottish-born physician educated at the University of Edinburgh who was assigned to the Seminole tribe, which he accompanied on its move to Indian Territory. He fell in love with a young Indian maiden during the trip.

Alice Brown married George Davis in 1874, and they established a trading post, Arbeka, in the northern part of the Seminole nation. George Davis died when the youngest of their 11 children was 3, leaving Alice Davis to rear all of her children by herself.

Alice Davis' obituary said she remained as the chief until her death in 1935 at age 82. But Trimble said that is incorrect. He said she served only for a month in 1922 and briefly again in 1923 when the government needed a document signed to convey some Seminole property to a white man.

Davis was called to Muskogee and asked to sign some papers, including a deed to Emahaka Mission Academy, where she had been the superintendent, but she refused to sign. The government sent word to the Muskogee office to nominate another chief, and George Jones was appointed.

Jones, however, also refused to sign the deed conveying the property to a white man. The government then appointed a third chief, Harry Tiger, who also refused to sign. The government gave up and let the transaction stand without the signature of a Seminole chief.

Davis did not get rich as the chief. Her only pay was $85 for the first month that she served, Trimble's book says.

Davis was inducted into the Oklahoma Hall of Fame in 1930, and Davis House at the University of Oklahoma was named in her honor in 1951. She was selected for the American Indian Hall of Fame in 1961. A bronze bust of her by Willard Stone was unveiled in 1964 at the World's Fair in New York.

Dust Bowl left its mark on Tulsa

A stiff wind shifted to the north, smashing store windows in downtown Tulsa, snapping telephone poles, ripping signs from their moorings and bringing a grayish-brown cloud from the west into eastern Oklahoma.

Thick clouds of dust had plagued western Oklahoma periodically for several years but had not affected the eastern part of the state much other than to dim the sun and turn the sky a brownish-yellow.

The dust hit the area on March 15, 1935, but a Tulsa World story said it was "not obnoxious." That opinion changed the next day when the worst dust storm to hit here in years caused motorists to use their headlights during the day. Street lights remained on until 10 a.m. because of "tons of silt that drifted through the sky and transformed bright electric lights into dim, red points."

Many Tulsans experienced difficulty in breathing as the dust swirled on the north wind and "gave the city a weird and ghostly appearance."

That was the beginning of 10 days of unusual weather that included several storms of dust that caused airlines to cancel flights on at least two days. Hail had drifted to a depth of 4 feet and thunderstorms with heavy rain that caused flooding and washed out a railroad track.

The heavy dust storm that hit Tulsa on March 16 stretched to Kansas City and portions of Wyoming, Nebraska and central Kansas. It also gave residents of the Eastern Seaboard, including New York and Washington, a taste of grit before disappearing over the Atlantic Ocean.

Commercial flights at Tulsa Municipal Airport were canceled, but some private planes were taking off and landing. A trace of rain fell in part of eastern Oklahoma, creating what forecasters called a "mudfall."

A few days later, flights were canceled again when visibility at Tulsa Municipal Airport was three miles in the middle of the afternoon. Visibility was 50 yards at Guymon, where the dust had been swirling for a week, and was three blocks at Chickasha.

Tulsa World archives

Dust storms, such as this one near Goodwell, rolled across Oklahoma in March 1935.

Undaunted by the week of dust storms, weatherbeaten farmers kept their humor, according to another story in the World, by telling such tales as:

"A horse left tied to a tree overnight was found hanged the next morning, the wind having blown away the sand on which he was standing.

"A traveler reported seeing a prairie dog 100 feet in the air, burrowing.

"Surveyors disclosed the state line had blown a mile and three quarters east."

A March 23 severe thunderstorm brought a few days of relief from the dust but also caused damage to every house in Kiefer and derailed a train pulling 26 cars of gasoline a mile from the Creek County town. The derailment resulted in a fire that could be seen for miles. A witness said he saw a bolt of lightning hit one of the cars, but a Frisco Railway official blamed static electricity.

Thousands of gallons of gasoline spilled from the cars, saturating a large area near the derailment. The train's engineer, William Bayne of Sapulpa, reported that hail was about a foot deep and that a cloudburst had washed out the track, causing the engine and one car after another to overturn, catching fire.

No injuries were reported from either the storm or the fire, which was battled by firefighters from several communities. Traffic was stopped for more than three hours on U.S. 75, which ran parallel to the tracks.

The rain caused flooding in Kiefer and the hail damaged windows and roofs of nearly every house in town. Ditches were brimful of water and hail.

The thunderstorm also struck other areas of the state, causing three deaths – one of a soldier at Fort Sill, who tried to ford a creek on horseback, and two who were struck by lightning at Bristow and Cordell.

Two days later, another dust storm spread over the state, including eastern Oklahoma, but it wasn't bad enough to cause cancellations of airline flights or tie up traffic in Tulsa.

Warden killed in prison gunfight

Warden Jess Dunn was killed in a furious gun battle after four convicts armed with knives and razors took him hostage and broke out of the state penitentiary at McAlester.

Three of the convicts were killed by Deputy Sheriff W.E. Alexander, a former guard. Alexander remembered and followed an instruction from Dunn of several years earlier to not let inmates escape – even if they held the warden hostage. The fourth convict died two years later in the electric chair.

Alexander shot the three convicts a short distance from the prison where they stopped their commandeered car because their path was blocked by a bridge that had washed out. Another former guard, Tab Ford, who was helping Alexander, also was killed before he had a chance to fire a shot.

Alexander was praised by Oklahoma Gov. Leon C. Phillips, who said his "courageous action probably saved many lives."

In addition to Dunn, 49, and Ford, 52, the victims of the battle were convicts Claud Beavers, 39, of Seminole; Roy McGee, 36, of Kay County; and Bill Anderson, 36, of Ada, all serving terms for robbery. Convict Hiram Prather was executed two years later.

The prison break occurred on Aug. 10, 1941, a Sunday, while Dunn and three men from Oklahoma City were in the prison yard planning the installation of a communications device to help prevent prison breaks. Dunn was showing the two men and a boy where he wanted call boxes to be placed.

The four convicts, led by Beavers, who was armed with a razor, accosted the warden's group near the prison hospital. Beavers threatened to kill Dunn by cutting his throat while the other convicts grabbed Hershell Fentress and ordered Poss Murray and his young son back into the building.

With Dunn and Fentress as hostages, the group headed toward the east gate, where Deputy Warden Ben Crider tried to talk the convicts into releasing Dunn and Fentress.

"Boys, you can't get away with it," Crider told them. "If you get through that gate, you'll be killed."

Tulsa World archive

Jess Dunn became warden of the Oklahoma State Penitentiary because of a prison escape and died during another prison escape, as shown on the Tulsa World's front page Aug. 11, 1941.

warden told him.

"You can pass, warden, but these convicts have got to get out of that car," Alexander replied.

Suddenly, the convicts opened fire and the gunbattle was on. Ford was killed by the first shot fired by the convicts. Pollock had grabbed a shotgun when he was recruited by Alexander, but there were no shells for that weapon – leaving Alexander as the only shooter.

Alexander said later he recalled Dunn instructing guards "if there should be a break and the convicts get hostages, even if they get me and march me up with a knife in my back, and I tell you not to shoot, go ahead and shoot."

Alexander followed that instruction.

In an ironic twist, Beavers also had been the leader of, and Alexander was involved in handling, a prison break in 1936 that led to Dunn being named warden.

Dunn was in charge of a posse that spent eight days searching for escapees; they captured Beavers near Pittsburg. Shortly after that break, Warden Wash Kinney was replaced by Dunn.

Known as hard as granite when the need arose but as kindly a man as could be found, Dunn's death saddened even convicts.

Jess Dunn Correctional Center, the state's largest minimum-security prison, is named in the warden's honor.

Dunn ordered two tower guards not to shoot. "My God, we've got an innocent man here," he told Crider. Then, to meet the convicts' demands, he commanded the guards to lower their weapons on ropes. Minutes later, the guards lowered two .38-caliber pistols and two .30-30 rifles that the convicts later used in the gunbattle.

They commandeered a car that belonged to a guard, forced Dunn and Fentress into it. Then they headed north but stopped at the washed-out bridge and headed back south in an attempt to find a way around the bridge.

Meanwhile, Alexander had heard the prison-break alarm, recruited Ford, 52, who was a jailer, and Bob Pollock, a city employee, and headed toward the prison in his car to stop the escape. Alexander saw the convicts' car, blocked its path and jumped out.

"Let them pass, Bill," the

Ruben Rivers is honored at last

Army Staff Sgt. Ruben Rivers was severely wounded in action during World War II but refused medical treatment and continued fighting for three more days until his tank exploded under enemy fire, killing him and wounding the tank crew.

It was an act of valor, and his commanding officer nominated Rivers for a Medal of Honor.

The medal was finally awarded posthumously to Rivers 53 years later. No black servicemen received Medals of Honor during the war, although more than 1 million were in the military.

A special act of Congress was required for the awarding of the nation's highest military honor to Rivers and six other blacks. The deadline for giving the medal to World War II veterans passed in 1952, but Congress waived that deadline to benefit the black heroes.

"No African-American who deserved the Medal of Honor for his service in World War II received it," said President Bill Clinton at an awards ceremony at the White House in 1997. "Today we fill the gap in that picture and give a group of heroes who also loved peace, but adapted themselves to war, the tribute that has always been their due.

"Today we recognize seven men as being among the bravest of the brave. Today, America is profoundly thankful for the patriotism and the nobility of these men for the example they set."

There was precedent for waiving the deadline. A black World War I soldier who served with the 93rd Infantry Division was given the medal 73 years after his death. He had been cited posthumously for leading his squad in an attack against mortar and machine-gun positions in France.

Rivers, a native of Tecumseh, entered the Army in January 1942 and was a member of the all-black 761st Tank Battalion of the 3rd Army led by white Capt. David J. Williams of Miami, who later wrote a book about the all-black unit.

"There is no doubt in my mind that he would have gotten the medal if he had been white," Williams told a Tulsa World

Associated Press

U.S. Army Staff Sgt. Ruben Rivers died heroically during World War II but wasn't recognized with the Medal of Honor until 1997.

reporter in 1979, when black tank veterans of World War II were fighting to have Rivers honored. "White soldiers got the medal for far less than what Rivers did."

The action that resulted in the high honor for Rivers, 25, was typical for him. He was awarded a Silver Star for earlier action near Munster, France.

To clear the way for American troops, he got out of his tank while under fire, attached a cable to a roadblock and pulled it out of the way with his tank.

His final action was Nov. 15-19, 1944, during a battle with the Germans for the town of Guebling, France. On the way into the town, Rivers' tank hit a land mine, destroying the tank and severely wounding Rivers.

Capt. Williams told Rivers that the war was over for him and to get into the medics' Jeep for a trip to the rear of the action. But Rivers refused to leave, telling the captain "the war isn't over for me," according to a battalion history.

"You're going to need me," he told the captain, who insisted that Rivers leave and gave him a direct order to do so.

"This is the only order I'll ever disobey," the soldier responded.

Rivers jumped onto another tank, ordered a sergeant to get off and took command. For three days, Rivers continued to direct his tank's fire at enemy positions. The crew engaged two German tanks, knocked them out of action and got into a battle with two more.

During the final battle on Nov. 19, other tankers heard Rivers' voice over their intercoms:

"Pull up, driver. Pull back, driver. Oh, Lord." And his tank exploded.

According to an article in the July 2006 issue of The NCO Journal, when he died, Rivers had been in combat just 12 days.

He was credited with killing more than 300 Germans and saving the lives of his entire unit and countless infantrymen.

Albert Schwab heroically saved others

A young Tulsa Marine knocked out two enemy machine-gun nests on Okinawa with a flamethrower that he fired until he ran out of fuel. He was fatally wounded in the process.

Pfc. Albert Schwab, 24, a Marine for only a year when he died May 7, 1945, was called Tulsa's outstanding war hero in news stories about his death and later was awarded the Medal of Honor, the nation's highest military award.

Schwab's company of Marines was pinned in a valley and suffering heavy casualties under the fire of Japanese machine-gunners, according to other Marines. Schwab climbed up a ridge with his flamethrower and fired a blast that demolished the first machine-gun nest.

When a second machine gun opened fire, killing and wounding several Marines, Schwab continued his one-man assault despite a low supply of fuel for his flamethrower, the medal citation says.

"Although severely wounded by a final blast from the enemy weapon, Schwab succeeded in destroying two highly strategic Japanese gun positions," the citation continues.

He died of his wounds.

A few days before Schwab's death, he appeared in one of the last columns written by World War II war correspondent Ernie Pyle.

"We are certainly grateful to know where he is and that he is well and finding something to laugh about," Schwab's father, G.A. Schwab, told the World.

Pyle's column appeared on the World's editorial page on April 19, 1945, the day Pyle's death from a sniper's bullet was reported on Page 1.

Rear Adm. J.J. Clark, an Oklahoman, presented the Medal of Honor to Schwab's 4-year-old son, Stephen Albert Schwab, at a Memorial Day ceremony in 1946. Schwab's body was returned to the U.S. in 1949 and was buried with full military honors at Memorial Park.

The Marine Corps named a base on Okinawa in honor of

Tulsa World archives

Pfc. Albert Schwab was called Tulsa's outstanding war hero in news stories about his death and he later was awarded a Medal of Honor.

Schwab in 1958, and a portrait of the hero was unveiled at Oklahoma City's Kirkpatrick Center in 1984. "I would rather have him alive, but I will always value his memory for his sacrifice," Stephen Schwab said at that time.

The Albert E. Schwab detachment of the Marine Corps League was named in the Tulsa hero's honor. It holds an annual ceremony about March 25, designated by Congress as National Medal of Honor Day, in honor of recipients.

Schwab was a 1937 graduate of Central High School and had attended the University of Tulsa. He worked at Barnsdall Oil Co. before joining the Marine Corps in May 1944, when he was sent to boot camp in San Diego.

His 10-day leave after boot camp was the only time his family had seen him in uniform.

Pyle was killed by a bullet on a small island near Okinawa. President Harry Truman said, "No man in this war has so well told the story of the American fighting man as American fighting men wanted it told."

And that probably included Schwab. The small anecdote about Schwab involved a jacket with the word "NAVY" stenciled on its back that Pyle wore.

Schwab told Pyle, "You know, when you first showed up we saw that big NAVY stenciled on your back and after you passed, I said to the others: 'That guy's an admiral. Look at the old gray-haired bastard. He's been in the Navy all his life. He'll get a medal out of this, sure as hell.' "

Pyle explained that "he's a flamethrower and flamethrowers have to be rugged guys, for the apparatus they carry weighs about 75 pounds and also they are very much addicted to getting shot at by the enemy."

"But to see Albert sitting there telling that joke on himself and me, you'd never know that he was a rugged guy at all. I'm not an admiral and I won't get any medal, but you do get a lot of laughs out of this war business when things aren't going too badly."

Pyle was correct. He didn't get a medal. Schwab did.

FDR made 'secret' wartime visit to Tulsa plant

President Franklin D. Roosevelt made a surprise – and, at least officially, secret – visit to Tulsa in 1943 to inspect production of war planes at the Douglas Aircraft Co. plant here.

Because of wartime censorship, newspapers weren't allowed to publish anything until two days after Roosevelt's visit, but editors knew about the trip. And the public could have surmised that a high-ranking official was coming.

Roosevelt came to Tulsa as part of a tour of military bases and war production plants. Before arriving in Tulsa, he had visited Camp Robinson in Arkansas and had spent the night at Camp Gruber near Braggs.

Secret Service agents had been in Tulsa for several days before the April 19 visit to check out safety issues, including Douglas employees likely to come into contact with the president, and to plan every detail. Weekend leaves for soldiers at Camp Gruber had been canceled, and squads of soldiers had been stationed along the railroad route and at highway bridges from there to Tulsa and inside the huge Douglas plant.

Gov. Robert S. Kerr and his wife had arrived on an unannounced visit to Tulsa on Sunday night. Roosevelt's visit was an "open" secret until Gov. Kerr announced it in time for the World's April 21 editions.

The derailment of a Chicago-to-Tulsa Santa Fe passenger train, "The Tulsan," at the Lansing Avenue crossing on Sunday night caused a great deal of concern for the Secret Service. It was decided that the derailment had no connection with the president's impending visit and plans continued.

However, when Roosevelt's seven-car special train left Douglas after his 75-minute tour of the bomber plant, a buffer engine proceeded along the track in front of his train to be sure it was safe.

Accompanied by Kerr, Plant Manager H.O. Williams and Douglas Vice President F.W. Conant, Roosevelt, unable to walk because of polio, rode through the bomber plant in his convertible automobile with the top down. The car moved beneath the wings of four-engine B-24 Liberator bombers and along the wing tips of hundreds of SBD Dauntless dive bombers, the two airplanes assembled at the plant.

He talked with only one worker, Otis Smallwood, who gave Roosevelt a model of a Douglas-built plane and who had been chosen by other employees to represent them. Roosevelt told Smallwood the nation was counting on employees of Douglas for badly needed war planes.

National Archives and Records Administration

President Franklin D. Roosevelt talks with Douglas Aircraft Co. plant worker Otis Smallwood during a presidential visit to Tulsa in 1943.

Kerr's announcement said Roosevelt was happy with what he saw at the plant. Kerr refused to reveal the subject of a 10-minute private visit with Roosevelt and would not comment on whether it concerned the possibility of his seeking a fourth term in office.

It was Roosevelt's second visit to Oklahoma. The first was July 9, 1938, when he came to campaign for the re-election of Sen. Elmer Thomas, but he deviated from his text and also praised Thomas's political foe, Gov. E.W. Marland. In addition, Roosevelt took a potshot at former Gov. William H. "Alfalfa Bill" Murray and snubbed 1st District U.S. Rep. Wesley Disney.

The president's stop in Oklahoma City was his fifth in Oklahoma during that campaign trip. Roosevelt had made platform talks during brief stops at Wister, McAlester, Holdenville and Shawnee before arriving at the fairgrounds.

Gov. Marland, who was running against Thomas for the Senate seat, had called on Oklahomans on the eve of Roosevelt's visit not to "surrender" to the president at the polls. "It's a question whether Oklahoma wants to assert its constitutional right to select its own senator or whether it wants to surrender that right to the chief executive," Marland had said.

Despite Marland's blast, the president included the governor and Sen. Josh Lee in his "few kind words" that had been scheduled for Thomas. He made his praise of Thomas a bit stronger, however, saying "Sen. Thomas has been of enormous help in keeping me informed of the needs of the people of Oklahoma."

Deviating from his text, Roosevelt referred to Democrat Murray as a "nationally known Republican."

Disney, a Tulsa Democrat, was astounded because Roosevelt failed to mention him and credited Thomas and Lee for the Grand River Dam. Disney said that "the only thing Thomas ever did was to oppose the dam."

Disney said he had spent seven years working on funding for the dam and Lee "never knew anything about it." He also pointed out that Thomas had said a few months earlier that Disney deserved all the credit for the dam because he (Thomas) had nothing to do with it.

It was one of the most unusual elections in Oklahoma history. The 1937 Legislature had abolished the runoff primary election, which meant party candidates were chosen by straight pluralities at the July primary.

Church-going boys, the Daltons were

They may have been outlaws during the week, but three of the Dalton brothers liked to attend church on Sundays. And sing.

It would be a frightening experience for members of most churches today to see a bank robber sitting across the aisle in church, but members of the First Methodist in Tulsa learned to "mind their own business."

"When outlaws showed up at church, the members didn't run to the 'law,' " according to "The First Hundred," a history of the First United Methodist Church by the Rev. Wishard Lemons, former associate minister of the church and later industrial chaplain for Parker Drilling Co.

"The 'law' might be in the same service," he said.

Deputy U.S. Marshal Henry "Heck" Thomas, was a member of the Little White Church on North Main that was a favorite place for outlaws Grat, Bob and Emmett Dalton to worship and sing.

Thomas, who later married Maitie Mowbray, daughter of the Rev. and Mrs. George Mowbray, and the outlaws had an agreement: They didn't bother each other within Tulsa.

"They all had beautiful voices," Hannah Mowbray said years later. "They sang in my husband's church on Sundays and ravaged the country during the week."

The Mowbrays had arrived in Tulsa on April 18, 1888, and the new preacher had explained to the congregation that it had been a difficult decision for him to take the job as the third pastor of First Methodist Episcopal Church, North, that was better-known then as the Little White Church and has evolved into the First United Methodist Church.

"After all, we had heard that Tulsey Town was a rendezvous for outlaws. We heard cowboys drove thousands of head of cattle right through the streets and on their paydays terrorized the town with drinking and shooting."

He probably hadn't heard that the Dalton brothers would take a liking to his church after they became outlaws in late 1889 or early 1890 and developed a reputation as train robbers.

The three Dalton brothers, who were among 15 siblings who were raised near Coffeyville, Kan., had worked on the side of the law before becoming outlaws. Their older

Beryl Ford collection

Grat Dalton, age 24 in 1883, was a lawman before he turned outlaw. He also was an occasional worshipper at the church that became Tulsa's First United Methodist Church.

brother, Frank, had been a deputy marshal for U.S. District Judge Isaac Parker but was killed in a gun battle with the Smith-Dixon gang in 1887. Grat had been a deputy out of Muskogee, and Bob had been a deputy for the federal court in Wichita and had been chief of the Osage tribal police.

Emmett had been a member of some of his brothers' posses but primarily was a cowboy.

After being accused of stealing horses, the three had fled to California, where they were accused with their brother Bill of robbing a train. They headed back to Indian Territory – and were accused of several more train robberies.

That's when they planned the big caper – the robbery of two banks simultaneously in Coffeyville, reportedly because they wanted to outdo the Jesse James gang.

It took just 12 minutes to rob the First National and Condon banks. But townspeople became suspicious, grabbed weapons and ambushed the five robbers as they tried to flee with about $25,000. Four of the robbers and four Coffeyville residents were killed in a shootout.

Only Emmett Dalton survived, but he was critically wounded. When he recovered, he pleaded guilty to second-degree murder and was sentenced to life in prison. But he received a pardon after 14½ years.

When he was released, Emmett married Julia Johnson, and the couple moved to Tulsa where, according to Lemons' book, Emmett operated a small grocery store and became a member of the First Methodist Church. The Commercial Club persuaded Dalton to accompany a group of boosters on a trip to the Northeast seeking industrial firms for Tulsa.

Emmett was glad to go as long as he didn't have to talk. Newspapers called him "the silent man of the party," and he attracted attention everyplace the group stopped. The Daltons later moved to California, but Emmett and Julia returned to Coffeyville in 1931 to visit his brothers' graves.

"I challenge the world to produce the history of an outlaw who ever got anything out of it," he said at the cemetery. "The biggest fool on earth is the one who thinks he can beat the law, that crime can be made to pay. It never paid, and it never will."

The 1918 flu hit with a wallop

Public meetings of all kinds – schools, churches, theaters – were closed for most of October 1918 because of a flu epidemic that killed 7,350 Oklahomans and more than 600,000 people nationwide.

Dr. John W. Duke, the state health commissioner at the time, said the epidemic was the worst in a century and directed that no public meeting places were to open without his permission.

Mayor L.H. Hubbard issued an edict, approved by the city commission, that Tulsa was under police rule. The police force immediately began closing businesses, and hundreds were temporarily out of business.

The disease was called Spanish influenza but, according to a Chronicles of Oklahoma article, it originated in the United States. At one point, it had been blamed on the Germans. The first case was reported at Camp Funston near Fort Riley, Kan., where an Army cook reported to the post hospital with flu symptoms: headache, muscle and joint pain, sore throat and fever.

The epidemic had run its course by early December but returned in the spring of 1919, although it wasn't as deadly as the fall outbreak.

An estimated 3,000 to 4,000 cases were reported in Tulsa before an emergency meeting of Red Cross, doctors and city officials was called on Oct. 6.

"Influenza is going to have the fight of its life in Tulsa," an optimistic Tulsa World story reported. "Mobilization of every resource is already under way."

Nurses were going on duty at every school in the city to watch children for symptoms.

That optimism was misplaced.

The next day, the mayor prohibited all public meetings, asked funeral homes to assign their ambulances to the city for use in transporting flu victims and directed garage owners and automobile dealers to provide as many cars and drivers as possible to transport nurses to flu victims. Taxi drivers were directed to provide free transportation

State Health Officer Duke Orders All Schools and Theaters Closed and Stops All Meetings in State

Special to The World

OKLAHOMA CITY, Oct. 18.—Dr. John W. Duke, state health officer, this afternoon issued a state-wide ultimatum, ordering all schools and theaters closed and prohibiting public meetings of any nature.

This order takes out of the hands of local authorities the regulation of the activities of the community and states specifically that no public meeting places are to be allowed open without permission of his office, regardless of any order from city or council of defense officials. Doctor Duke orders that the influenza epidemic be treated the same as smallpox or diphtheria and adds that it is the worst epidemic in a century, 85 per cent of the pneumonia cases proving fatal.

Doctors throughout the state are urged to hold themselves in readiness to be sent to needy towns.

Tulsa World archives

The killer flu of 1918 led to drastic steps by state health officials.

to nurses handling the thousands of flu cases.

The city converted a detention center for women at First Street and Elgin Avenue into an emergency hospital for flu victims after it was fumigated for 18 hours with formaldehyde. Trusties from the county jail carried out old beds (most of which were burned), whitewashed the walls to sanitize them and installed 60 new sanitized cots.

Other cities set up emergency hospitals in various types of facilities.

The City Commission later closed soda fountains, bowling alleys and pool halls. Restaurants were allowed to remain open but were required to be fumigated from midnight until 5 a.m. and to sterilize food utensils after every customer.

The order warned that mercantile stores might be closed later, but that apparently never happened.

The homes of flu victims were quarantined and fumigated with formaldehyde, which appeared to be the chemical of choice for fighting the dread disease. Hotel rooms and the library also were fumigated. According to a Chronicles article, Tulsa streets were washed down twice daily, and formaldehyde was sprinkled on them after they were clean.

A serum compounded in Tulsa from the germs of flu victims was being injected into residents.

Women spent time making masks from washed and sterilized cotton rags, and high school students made sputum cups out of old newspapers.

Many people turned to over-the-counter medications such as Dr. Kilmer's Swamp Root, Dr. Pierce's Pleasant Pellets and Eatonic, but most were not effective. Others used hot mustard foot baths, inhaled salt, wrapped the body in lard and turpentine, wore garlic poultices and ate onions – all folk remedies.

The most popular remedy was whiskey. That was illegal, but it could be dispensed by pharmacists to flu victims with prescriptions. It also was available from bootleggers. Its popularity pushed the price up to $18 a quart, according to a Daily Oklahoman article.

Two cities joined by a toll booth

Oklahoma Turnpike Authority

When the Turner Turnpike opened in 1953, the one-way fare for a car going from Oklahoma City to Tulsa was $1.40.

The beginning of a new era in driving was signaled in 1953 with the opening of the $38 million, 88-mile toll road connecting Tulsa and Oklahoma City – the Turner Turnpike.

The ceremony was at Stroud, about midway between the two big cities, where former Gov. Roy J. Turner, who conceived the toll road idea, addressed 3,000 to 4,000 people who attended the dedication.

It didn't take long for the turnpike to gain favor among drivers because of its 70 mph speed limit, 17-mile shorter distance and the absence of city and town traffic. The route cut at least an hour off the time required to drive between the cities on the narrow, winding U.S. 66.

Speaking at the ceremony on May 16, 1953, Turner and Gov. Johnston Murray, his successor, said toll roads were an answer to the need for better highways. Nine additional turnpikes have been built since then.

People crowded around a speakers' stand to hear Turner, Murray and a few others as clouds threatened rain. After the ceremony, all were allowed to drive home on the toll road without charge. The crowd included the four members of the Turnpike Authority.

Earlier that day, hundreds of cars lined up two abreast in Tulsa and Oklahoma City waiting for the barriers at the toll booths to be removed and a chance to drive on the new four-lane highway. Ray Willhoite of Tulsa was the first motorist at the Tulsa gate to receive a ticket that called for the payment of $1.40 at Oklahoma City.

The Stroud event included a colorful pageant that depicted various modes of travel from the ancient Indian travois to a modern super-powered automobile.

In preliminary ceremonies, Turner spoke at the Oklahoma City end and cut a ribbon while Murray spoke at Tulsa and cut a ribbon. Caravans then proceeded to Stroud for the main event.

Roberta Bushyhead, member of a noted Cherokee Indian family, had been chosen as Tulsa's queen to reign over dedication ceremonies for the Tulsa terminus of the highway the previous day. She and five other queens, representing other cities on the highway, participated in the Stroud event.

Both Govs. Murray and Turner predicted the turnpike would reduce the "useless slaughter" on highways. Both also predicted the toll road would be well received and that the bonds would be liquidated before the 40-year retirement period ended.

Turner also recounted the difficulties in getting the highway financed. He said he required four years to convince the first investment banker that the highway was viable. After that, 40 investment firms submitted bids for the self-retiring bonds.

The Turnpike Authority first borrowed $21 million but had to obtain additional funds before the road could be completed. Construction also was delayed, at first by legislative and legal problems and later by a steel shortage and bad weather.

Oklahomans voted in 1954 to cross-pledge income on turnpike projects, meaning money collected from all the turnpikes helps to pay off the bonds for all turnpikes.

According to the Turnpike Authority's Internet site, the bond debt is now $1.2 billion, set to expire in 2028, assuming no more debt is added.

An Oscar for a saintly performance

There was no question that Tulsans were happy to see Jennifer Jones when she returned home for the Southwestern premiere of a film that was to win her an Oscar.

Hundreds of fans, including Mayor C.H. Veale, met the girl they knew as Phyllis Lee Isley at the Union Depot on Feb. 24, 1944, and others lined the streets to wave and get a glimpse of her as she was driven through downtown to the Mayo Hotel.

No formal ceremony was held at the depot, but Jones took time to sign autographs for fans as they followed her up the stairs from the track level to street level. Her only comment before getting into a car and once more becoming Phyllis Isley was "I'm so glad to be home. I could almost die."

She had been met in Kansas City by her father, Phil, who accompanied her on the rest of the trip to Tulsa. Her mother, Flora Mae Isley, met the train here. The Isleys had moved to Dallas after Isley sold his interest in a theater here.

Huge banners proclaiming "Welcome Jennifer Jones" were stretched across Fourth and Main streets near that intersection, and two giant reproductions of a painting of her by Norman Rockwell were mounted on the First National Bank building, which was then on the northeast corner of the same intersection. One of the reproductions faced west, the other faced south.

Two smaller copies of the same painting of her in her award-winning role were on the marquee of the Ritz Theater in the unit block of West Fourth Street. The Ritz was one of two theaters where the premiere was to be held. The other was the Ritz's sister theater, the Orpheum, a block away in the unit block of East Fourth Street.

The Tulsa actress had been nominated for an Academy Award as best actress for her starring role as Bernadette in the movie "The Song of Bernadette," and Tulsans were sure she would win. She did – eight days later on her 25th birthday. It was the first time an actor had won the award for a screen debut.

At a Tulsa Club dinner given by the theaters' owner Ralph Talbot, she was introduced by Glenn Condon, a Tulsa radio executive who had taken Jones to New York years earlier to audition for stage and movie roles. She was offered contracts by two movie studios but couldn't accept because she was pregnant.

After the dinner, she appeared on the stages of both sold-out theaters before the film started.

Associated Press

Jennifer Jones, known in Tulsa as Phyllis Lee Isley, won an Academy Award for her work in the film "The Song of Bernadette."

The only other appearances she made were at a Chamber of Commerce luncheon and at Monte Cassino School. There she had studied acting and Sister Ursula, her instructor, had persuaded her that she had talent.

While visiting Monte Cassino, where she graduated in 1936, a statue of her in her film role as Bernadette was unveiled.

Sister Ursula said the statue was a tribute to the actress's "greatness of character, her spiritual qualities and the fulfillment of ideals – not to her fame."

The statue was in a grotto that had been constructed four years earlier. It was a replica of the shrine at Lourdes, France. Sister Ursula said other replicas all had statues of Bernadette but the replica at Monte Cassino did not.

"We found that 20th Century Fox's characterization of the simple peasant girl of Lourdes conformed so closely in historical accuracy, that we decided it came nearer to the real Bernadette than any likeness ever before attempted," she said.

Church circles had praised Jones' role as Bernadette but a succession of more worldly roles put her on a more earthly plane. Catholic leaders condemned her a few years later for her torrid role in "Duel in the Sun." The movie had to be cleaned up to get by the Legion of Decency.

Jones married three times. She met her first husband, actor Robert Walker, when both worked for a Tulsa radio station. They saved their earnings until they could get married in 1939.

The newlyweds took a wedding trip to Hollywood but could not find jobs in the movie industry. They then went to New York, where Phyllis found work as a model and Walker got radio roles. Movie producer David O. Selznick hired her in 1942, changed her name to Jennifer Jones and 20th Century Fox chose her for Bernadette later that year.

Jones divorced Walker in 1945 and married Selznick four years later. Walker died in 1951 and Selznick died in 1965. Jones married multimillionaire Norton Simon in 1971. He died in 1993.

Today, she serves as president of the Norton Simon Foundation Board and contributes to mental health and charity organizations. She lives in Malibu near her son, Robert Walker Jr.

Gov. Johnston got the boot

Henry Johnston had been a delegate to the constitutional convention, helped write the state's Constitution and was president pro tem of the first Senate, but he was kicked out of office midway through his term as Oklahoma's seventh governor.

For general incompetence.

It was a stormy period. Jack Walton, the most recently elected governor before Johnston, had been impeached less than a year after his term began and was succeeded by Lt. Gov. M.E. Trapp.

In 1926, the year Johnston was elected,

Trapp tried to run for his own full term as governor. Oklahoma law limited governors to one term, and Trapp claimed, unsuccessfully, that he was not the governor, just an acting governor.

Talk of Johnston's impeachment grew in the summer and fall of 1927, much of it stemming from the alleged domination of the governor by Mrs. O.O. Hammonds, his confidential secretary. It was reported that she dictated appointments and made decisions in the governor's office.

Johnston refused legislators' requests late that year to call a special session so they could investigate him. He told leaders they could meet as private citizens but not as the Legislature, and he called out the National Guard to prevent them from meeting at the Capitol.

The House then met in a secret night session at the Huckins Hotel in Oklahoma City — with some members there in pajamas and robes — and voted impeachment charges alleging general incompetence, conspiracy to defraud, improper appointments and illegal use of state funds.

The state Supreme Court later ruled that the hotel session was illegal and nullified the impeachment action.

The legislators renewed their impeachment attempt when the Legislature met in 1929. The House voted 11 charges of impeachment against Johnston.

A long Senate trial followed. The upper chamber voted

Oklahoma Historical Society

Amid rumors about his staff and allegations of general incompetence, Gov. Henry Johnston was impeached and removed from office in 1929.

35-9 to oust the governor for general incompetency but dismissed 10 other counts.

Johnston was born in 1869 in a log cabin near Evansville, Ind., in the same room where his father had been born 30 years earlier. As a baby, he moved with his parents to Kansas. After graduation from high school, he went to Denver, got a job running errands in a law office and, before long, was preparing briefs and passed the bar exam.

Although he did not make the run into the Cherokee Strip, he went to Perry the day of the strip's opening, Sept. 16, 1893, to open a law office.

He rented office space on the second floor of a downtown building in 1909 and retained the same office until he died in 1965 at the age of 97.

Throughout his career, he used two desks that he had brought to Oklahoma on the day of the run.

Johnston's long political career began when he was elected to the territorial Legislature in 1897. He also served as the Noble County attorney from 1901-05 and was elected as a delegate to the constitutional convention at which he made the opening speech in 1906. He became closely associated with William H. "Alfalfa Bill" Murray, the president of the convention, and helped Murray write the state's Constitution.

After statehood, Johnston was elected to the Senate and was chosen as the president pro tem while Murray was speaker of the House.

Johnston made the nominating speech for Murray when he unsuccessfully sought the Democratic nomination for president at the Democratic National Convention in Chicago in 1932. His last political race was in 1932 when he was elected to the Senate.

In his latter years, he dabbled at his law practice but his main interest centered on reading and maintaining contact with old friends.

Go tell it on the mountain

A Lawton minister led his small congregation 16 miles into the roadless Wichita Mountains on April 4, 1926, to hold Easter Sunday services in what he called the holy city of Jerusalem.

The Rev. Mark Anthony Wallock had told members of the First Congregational Church at midweek services that they should wear warm clothing and comfortable walking shoes for the service on the mountain. And he asked several male members to help him carry an organ up the mountain.

"We are the first, but some day there will be thousands who will return with us," he said as they walked over gullies and hills.

From that prophetic mustard-seed beginning, the annual Lawton Easter Pageant became the longest-running Passion Play in America and in 1939 attracted 225,000 to watch the retelling of the story of Jesus' last hours before his crucifixion.

Holy City of the Wichitas

A letter from the Rev. Mark Anthony Wallock found its way to President Franklin D. Roosevelt, who ordered a $94,000 grant be sent to Wallock to build his holy city on 640 acres. The holy city, 22 miles from Lawton, is the site of the annual Lawton Easter Pageant.

But the crowds have diminished for several years, and only about 10,000 were expected for two performances in 2007. About 1,000 attended the first performance March 31, a much smaller turnout than expected, probably because of heavy rain that started on March 30. About 9,000 were expected at the second performance that started at 6 p.m. Saturday but chilly weather may have cut that number. For several years, the show has ended about 10 p.m. In the early days, it ended at daybreak.

Wallock was born in Austria near Oberammergau, Germany, where a Passion Play has been performed every 10 years for several hundred years. He came to the United States as a small child with his parents in 1892.

During his study at a Bible institute in Chicago, Wallock spent his weekends and holidays exploring by hitchhiking and telling motorists who gave him rides "I'm looking for a mountain." It wasn't until after he accepted the pastorate in Lawton in 1918 that he discovered what he was looking for – a mountain in the Wichitas that looked like the hills of Judea and a valley that created a natural amphitheater large enough to build a city in.

As the cast and the audience for his play grew, Wallock realized that his small congregation and the city of Lawton couldn't finance the setting he needed for his pageant.

Wallock wrote letter after letter to Harry Hopkins, President Franklin D. Roosevelt's adviser, and to Oklahoma congressmen seeking assistance. One of his letters finally found its way to Roosevelt, who directed that a $94,000 grant be sent to Wallock to build his holy city on 640 acres contributed by the federal forest reserve. The entire miniature Jerusalem was built of native stone as a Works Progress Administration project.

It was the first and possibly the only project of a religious nature ever financed by the federal government. The government agreed to build the facility because the pageant is nonsectarian and the facility was available for use by others.

The holy city, 22 miles from Lawton, extends six city blocks and is a half-mile wide.

A 1949 movie called "The Lawton Story" told the story of Wallock and his Passion Play, using the Jerusalem-like structures for the pageant scenes. The movie had its premier in Lawton on April 1 that year, with seats selling for $1,000 each. Proceeds went to the pageant.

The movie climaxed at dawn with the resurrection scene from the pageant and a sky-writing airplane spelling out the words "He is risen" high above the audience.

Wallock, who died the day after Christmas 1948, had been told 30 years earlier that he had less than a year to live because of a heart disease. But he lived long enough to see his dream develop into a play with a cast of 3,000 that attracted several hundred thousand viewers.

He had been named Lawton's outstanding citizen of 1938 and was inducted into Oklahoma's Hall of Fame in 1939.

Although Wallock started the pageant and directed it until his death in 1948, he never took part in the portrayal.

"I'm not good enough," he once explained.

Manion expanded Tulsa park system

When Noble Manion was appointed to the Tulsa Park and Recreation Board in 1958, some doubted that a woman who had no children could help direct the city's recreation programs.

Eleven years later, a 23-acre park at 56th Street and Delaware Avenue was named in honor of the first woman to serve on the board, a period that included serving as chairwoman.

"When I was appointed, I supposed that all we would do would be to plant trees and daisies," Manion told a reporter in 1970. "We did much more."

That "much more" included developing 64 parks during her tenure, bringing the total at that time to 84.

"My husband (P.P. Manion Jr.) and I have no children, so through the recreation program, I have been a mother to many Tulsa children," she told a reporter.

There hadn't been much emphasis on Tulsa's parks until 1958, when the airport authority was separated from the park board after a charter amendment was approved by voters. The Parks and Airport Authority's primary interest had always been on building the air industry and facilities.

Tulsa World archives

Noble Manion is pictured on April 5, 1977, at the park named in her honor. During her 11-year tenure as the city's recreation director, 64 parks were developed.

During his campaign for mayor that year, Jim Maxwell promised he would establish a year-round recreation program. The new board he appointed began by studying parks and recreation programs nationwide. The programs developed here found immediate acceptance among elementary-school children and older people. Teenagers were more difficult to please.

Manion's appointment by Maxwell was for three years, but she was appointed for two additional four-year terms, the maximum allowed. After her retirement, she was named chairman of the new Tulsa Recreation Council, a residents' advisory group.

Manion, who died in 1994 at the age of 87, came to Tulsa in 1937 and got involved in civic affairs when she joined the Tulsa League of Women Voters in 1942 "as a means of 'paying the rent' – the rent she felt she owed for living in this country."

Among the successful projects promoted by the Tulsa league was to separate the park board from the aviation authority. Manion helped draw up membership qualifications for the position to which she later was appointed.

She served as the local league's president twice, as president of the state group and as a member of the league's national nominating and finance committees.

During her tenure as president of the local league, she was credited with pushing through the Legislature the bill that created a juvenile court, the state's first, in Tulsa in 1949. Similar courts were created later in Oklahoma and Comanche counties.

As president of the state league, she was instrumental in securing the passage by the Legislature of a grading and labeling law for milk.

She had also served on the Tulsa Metropolitan Planning Commissions charter change steering committee, the Locomotion Board and the Community Service Council. She was an elder of the First Christian Church and former president of the Tulsa Senior Services Board.

Manion also worked in the Tulsa YWCA Family and Children's Board, the United Way and the Oklahoma Economic Opportunity Task Force Board. In recognition of the 37th year of the United Nations, then-Gov. George Nigh appointed Manion as state U.N. Day Dinner chairwoman in 1983. She was the first woman to hold this position.

She once told a reporter that she got involved with the League of Women Voters because "I felt I needed to do something for this country. I wanted to get involved somehow. I heard a radio spot about the league."

Colcord 'first citizen of Oklahoma'

A pioneer Oklahoman was on a hunting trip with two friends in 1905 when his two Kentucky wolfhounds chased after a wolf and disappeared, leading to the accidental discovery of oil on farmland owned by a Creek Indian named Ida Glenn.

Charles F. Colcord, who died in 1934 at the age of 75, frequently told about that hunting trip and the later search by Frank Chesley and Robert T. Galbreath for the dogs.

While searching for the dogs, which he found, Chesley discovered a spot where oil was seeping from some rocks.

The accidental discovery was in much the same manner as television's Clampett family did some 50 years later in the television sitcom, "Beverly Hillbillies."

Chesley and Galbreath organized the Creek Oil Co. with Colcord and J.O. Mitchell. The group drilled a discovery well, the site protected by armed guards to keep others from getting too close. On Nov. 22, they hit the first oil gusher in what would soon be known as the "Glenn Pool," the richest ever discovered up to that time.

The Glenn Pool discovery well 12 miles south of Tulsa began spewing oil at 5 a.m. Nov. 22, 1905, and triggered the oil boom in Oklahoma.

Within months, the Glenn Pool field was producing more oil than the entire state of Texas. It drew thousands of people to the state, spawned a string of major oil companies and turned Tulsa into the "oil capital of the world."

The discovery set off a boom of growth for the area, bringing in hordes of lease buyers, producers, millionaires, laborers, tool suppliers, drunks, swindlers and newspeople. Daily production soon exceeded 120,000 barrels.

It wasn't Colcord's first venture into the oil business. After Dr. Fred Clinton and Dr. J.C.W. Bland drilled a successful well in 1901 north of Red Fork, 2,500 people were attracted to the area, including Colcord and Galbreath, who had been partners in a real estate business.

Colcord and Galbreath organized the Red Fork Oil and Gas Co. and drilled the first wells in the town limits of Red Fork, Clinton recalled years later. Colcord later drilled in Healdton, Loco and Duncan fields before oil was found in the Glenn Pool.

Colcord used his Glenn Pool profits to build Oklahoma's first skyscraper, a 12-story building in Oklahoma City that he envisioned as a hotel – and that's what it became 96 years

Tulsa World archives

Charles Colcord was involved in many of the most important events in state history — from the discovery of Glenn Pool oil to the moving of the state capital to Oklahoma City.

later.

When he built the building in 1910, it was the first steel-reinforced building in Oklahoma. It was used as an office building until October 2006 when Tulsa developer Paul Coury of Tulsa remodeled it as a boutique hotel similar to his Ambassador Hotel in Tulsa. Colcord wanted the steel reinforcement because he had seen the devastation to buildings in San Francisco during the 1906 earthquake.

Born in Kentucky, Colcord moved to Texas with his parents as a child and later lived in dugouts in the Cherokee Outlet for several years while helping his father in a cattle business.

Colcord later told about helping two men bury two men who had been killed in a fight with Indians. After covering the bodies in a common grave, one of the others said someone should offer a prayer. "All three of us were uneducated cowboys who had had no chance to attend church services, so none of us knew what to say or do."

The others declined to say anything and insisted that Colcord "say something."

"I took off my hat and raised my face to the skies as I said, 'God, take care of these poor boys.' Such was the prayer that I offered."

Colcord bought a team of horses and a wagon for $66 and made the run into Oklahoma Territory April 22, 1889. He traded his horses and wagon for a shack and a lot in Oklahoma City that became Lot 1, Block 1.

Colcord served as Oklahoma City's police chief for several years and later was Oklahoma County's first sheriff. He was appointed as a U.S. marshal by President Grover Cleveland.

Colcord also made the run into the Cherokee Outlet and staked a claim in Perry where he also built a house.

He was involved in the move of the state seal from Guthrie to Oklahoma City in 1910 and served as chairman of the finance committee for building a new Capitol on North Lincoln Boulevard.

Colcord died in 1934 at his ranch in Delaware County near the town of Colcord that was named for him.

A 1935 Chronicles of Oklahoma article called Colcord the "First Citizen of Oklahoma." He had served in many civic organizations, including president of the Oklahoma City Chamber of Commerce, and was president of the Oklahoma Historical Society from 1926 until his death.

Racy rumors only added to her allure

It was typical for entertainer Ruby Darby to speed into an Oklahoma oil town wearing a fur coat while driving a big red car several hours before a scheduled appearance.

After her arrest by a local officer on a speeding charge, the word would get out that she "wasn't wearing nothin' under her coat," and she would be bailed out of jail just in time to open at a packed theater that night.

It happened in Drumright and in several other oil communities where she appeared to entertain the workers. Most of the rumors were started by her press agent.

Ruby and her manager, her first husband, Ed Gardiner, knew the racier the rumors, the bigger the crowd. They made sure the rumors about her attire were spread.

There were other rumors that built her reputation:

"She stripped at the drop of a driller's hat."

"She rode a hoss completely nekkid down the mud-and-oil-splashed streets of Kiefer."

"She danced bare-skinned on a tool shack roof as men tossed silver dollars at her feet."

Some may have been true, but there's no way to separate rumor from fact.

But it was fact that she was popular among Oklahoma's oil-field workers.

Other entertainers didn't want to play an engagement in a town where she was performing. Theater managers were eager to book her, and it didn't make much difference how good her show was. Her name guaranteed a full house.

According to the book "Petticoats, Politics and Pirouettes," she was a beautiful girl and one of the greatest of the blues singers. Her trademark song, "Memphis Blues," always brought the house down.

Ruby knew how to move her eyes, hips and torso until she had every man in the audience under her spell awaiting her grand finale, usually a striptease. She was a pioneer of the striptease, preceding and rivaling the famed Sally Rand.

Frederick B. Graves

Ruby Darby was a legendary entertainer, even if many of the stories about her were legendary.

Most shows of that era had a maximum of eight chorus girls but Ruby's shows had 16, and the girls in her shows had beautiful costumes with several changes each show, and they always wore silk stockings rather than the cotton stockings worn by the girls in other shows.

Oil-field workers were so taken with her shows, they adopted her name to mean something good in their slang, shouting "it's a Ruby Darby" to describe a gusher and later shortening that to just "it's a darby" or "it's a darb."

Ruby was born in 1896 or 1898 in Alva, where her father was a farmer, a railroad detective and a police officer. Her show business career began in a Dallas theater about 1912 when she was either 14 or 16 and married the theater owner's son.

After that marriage broke up, she began entertaining troops in Army camps during World War I and sometime in that period was married again to Oklahoma City banker Luther Jones. That marriage didn't last long.

She hit the big time during the 1920s with an audition at the Palace Theater, where about 200 agents were assembled to pick entertainers for their shows. She was booked for shows at a series of theaters, with her first show to be at Baltimore.

The show date arrived and Ruby didn't. Tulsan Glenn Condon, who had been active in vaudeville in New York, later received a postcard from her that was postmarked El Paso. The card told Condon she was having a good time but gave no hint of an address.

Ruby was married again to a man named Bud Harrison and had two children. After their divorce, the children lived with their father but frequently spent time with their mother.

Her daughter, Ruby McEnery, told a Tulsa Tribune reporter in 1977 that her mother was a free spirit who might go to a store for a loaf of bread and end up in Mexico.

But, the daughter said, her warmth and love of life gave her family wonderful memories. Ruby died in 1936 of pneumonia, probably aggravated by alcoholism.

A day of death, all around

The president was dead.

Minutes after wire services transmitted a flash report on Franklin D. Roosevelt's death to newspapers and radio stations, massive tornadoes hopped and skipped through eastern Oklahoma, killing 86 people, injuring at least 690 and causing millions of dollars worth of property damage.

The greatest damage was at Antlers, where a tornado killed 63, and at Muskogee, where the death toll was 12, including three students at the Oklahoma School for the Blind.

Four other eastern Oklahoma communities were hit by tornadoes spawned by the same system that day. Oklahoma City had been hit earlier that afternoon.

The storm struck on April 12, 1945, only 15 days before the third anniversary of a tornado that destroyed Pryor's business district, killing 77 and injuring 329.

Roosevelt, 63, had died of a cerebral hemorrhage at 3:35 p.m. while sitting in front of a fireplace in his "little White House" at Warm Springs, Ga. Roosevelt, the only president ever elected to more than two terms, had begun his fourth term less than three months earlier. Muskogee's radio station announced the death but was knocked off the air before it could report details.

In addition to the deaths in Antlers and Muskogee, the storms caused four deaths in Oklahoma City, four in Sallisaw, three in Hulbert, one in Boggy and two in Red Oak, the next day's Tulsa World reported. There were reports that the storm had hit other communities, but none was confirmed.

The death toll was raised to 111 the next day when it also was reported that at least 25 had been killed as the storm system moved through Arkansas and Missouri.

The storm struck primarily in eastern Muskogee, where many students at the School for the Blind were injured. Damage to the state-owned school was estimated at more than $1 million.

Power to the city's water plant was knocked out, causing the city to operate on its reserve for more than 24 hours.

The Antlers tornado struck the center of town, destroy-

Tulsa World archives

April 12, 1945, was a big news day. President Franklin Roosevelt died in Warm Springs, Ga., and deadly tornadoes hit Antlers, Muskogee and Oklahoma City.

ing about a third of the town of 3,000, leaving only one telephone functioning. U.S. Rep. Paul Stewart, an Antlers resident, was home when the storm hit. He estimated damage at more than $3 million.

Ambulances from many cities were sent to both Muskogee and Antlers. Tulsa sent police officers to Muskogee to help control looting. The Oklahoma Highway Patrol opened an emergency operations center in the gym of the Antlers high school. Power was knocked out to the water system, leaving the entire town without water.

The Antlers Funeral Home, which lost two of its three employees in the storm, was overwhelmed. The dead were taken to funeral homes in Atoka, Hugo, Durant, Idabel, Talihina and Paris, Texas, for embalming. The bodies were returned a few days later to a temporary morgue in the high school basement for relatives to identify.

Heavy rain fell for several days after the tornadoes, causing flooding on the Arkansas, Verdigris and Neosho rivers, and closing highways in at least 14 places in eastern Oklahoma. Webbers Falls and Salina were evacuated.

The high water killed seven people in the Seminole-Wewoka area and one at Dewar.

The water also washed out the roadbed under the Missouri-Kansas-Texas railroad tracks a mile south of Oktaha, causing a passenger train to plunge into swollen Elk Creek.

When engineer Tom Wilson and fireman J.K. Rosebury saw the washed-out track before the train reached the creek area, they set its brakes and jumped into the water. Swimming underwater, they were able to uncouple the locomotive to keep its weight from pulling the other cars into the water.

The locomotive sank rapidly, but all of the passengers in the passenger car and the train crew members in the baggage car were able to escape uninjured.

The passengers were ferried across the swollen stream, and another train was sent from Muskogee to take them back to the city.

A 'crown jewel' for courting tourists

Thousands of azaleas are in full bloom in Muskogee's Honor Heights Park, ready for about 250,000 visitors expected to drive through to enjoy the beauty of what is considered the "crown jewel of Muskogee's park system."

The azaleas didn't just happen there. They were planted to attract attention to Muskogee and to the park that was bought by the city in 1909.

They succeeded in doing that. The azalea festival has brought national recognition to the city and annually draws the largest crowds of any festival in Oklahoma. It has been listed in Discover America's 20 top attractions and has won many other awards.

The original 40 acres of the park atop Agency Hill was bought by the city for $4,500 in 1909 and was dedicated on Flag Day, June 14, 1920, as a memorial to the Muskogee area veterans of World War I. The Veterans Administration's Jack C. Montgomery Hospital and the Five Civilized Tribes Museum are near the park.

A cornerstone near the hospital explains "This park is laid like a wreath of honor on the highland of this city by the people of Muskogee as a tribute to those of our country who served in the World War 1914-1918 in camp or in field at home or abroad in all the multitude of ways that contributed to the success of America and her Allies."

The park was always beautiful but not as it is today with the many colors of the azaleas. A spokeswoman at the park said the flowers should be in full bloom throughout April.

The annual Azalea Day parade through downtown Muskogee is scheduled at 11 a.m. Saturday. A chili cookoff is scheduled to begin at the same time and will run until 3 or 3:30 p.m. at a new market square in front of the downtown civic center.

Before there was a festival, the idea for planting azaleas in Honor Heights Park had its beginning in 1951 when the city was looking for something to make its park outstanding in some respect.

"We wanted something that would make the park known for something beautiful, something colorful and something that people would travel to see," the late Arthur Johnson, Honor Heights Park director, said in 1969. "With limited funds and competition with larger cities, the 'biggest' of anything was out of the question."

He said roses were rejected because of Tulsa's rose garden (although Honor Heights Park does have a lot of roses). Irises were rejected because they don't have enough color and have too short of a season, and the climate was wrong for lilacs and camellias.

Stephen Pingry / Tulsa World

A horse-drawn trolley lumbers through Muskogee's Honor Heights Park in 2001. The park's azaleas have drawn crowds to the city for years.

So the city settled on azaleas because no other city in Oklahoma or the Southwest had tried mass planting them.

Johnson transplanted 50 small blooming plants into the park in 1957, but within a few days all 50 had been stolen.

The transplanted plants came from thousands of azaleas he had planted in rows in 1951. The thefts showed that larger plants would have to be planted – ones that looked too big to pull up – to prevent their theft. So he let the plants grow for another four years before putting them out in the park for the public to enjoy.

By 1964, the park contained more than 25,000 azaleas of more than 100 varieties, and Muskogee residents reacted with enthusiasm. The Kiwanis Club and Kappa Kappa Gamma alumni underwrote the purchase of 12,000 color postcards that were sold at local and state stores.

Johnson, a native of Massachusetts who died in 1984, came to the Muskogee area when he was in the Army stationed at nearby Camp Gruber during World War II. When he went overseas, his wife, Henrietta, remained in Muskogee.

After the war, the Johnsons decided to remain in Muskogee, and he took a job with the park department.

One of the things that made him want to improve the park was the statement of a woman shortly after he took the job. She told Johnson she hadn't been to Honor Heights for three years.

"If a person doesn't have a reason to go to the park in three years, then the park isn't serving any worthwhile purpose," he said.

His goal was to provide that purpose.

Race car sparked a brief industry

A dark-horse race car called the "Tulsa" did so well in the third annual 500-mile race in Indianapolis in 1913 that Tulsa oilman J.B. Levy decided to open an automobile manufacturing plant here.

The "Tulsa" came in ninth, but Levy and race fans were impressed with its performance. "We were the only car in the race that did not raise the hood," Levy bragged in a Tulsa World story two days after the May 29, 1913, race.

"With the exception of the stops at the pits for oil, gasoline or a change of tires, the car was not halted a moment," Levy said. Some of the famous cars in the race had to drop out because of mechanical problems.

The "Tulsa," built by Carden Green of Broken Arrow, came in ninth in a field of 27 and earned a $1,500 purse. It was the only car in the race that was not built by a well-known factory staffed by automotive engineers with modern equipment.

The win created a demand for the car to compete in other races, but Levy decided to use it to drive to his oil leases. Green began working on "Tulsa No. 2" to enter in other competitions.

A few days after the Indianapolis race, Levy announced that he would build a factory in Tulsa to manufacture the cars, but his ambitious plans were slowed, probably by the gathering war clouds in Europe.

More than four years later, a two-page ad in the Tulsa World of Oct. 14, 1917, announced that the Tulsa Automobile Corp. had been organized by 10 Tulsans, and the production of the "Tulsa Four" would begin immediately.

Neither the ad nor a news story in the same edition mentioned Levy. Green had stock in the corporation but moved to Kentucky before the plant opened. According to that ad, the Tulsa Four would be available in three models – touring, roadster and oil field runabout – for $995 (Model T Fords were being advertised for $500), and buyers could save freight charges by purchasing it, as compared with other brands that would have shipping charges from Detroit or some other location added. The company bragged there was "no sand too deep or oil field going too rough to daunt the 'Tulsa Four.' "

The cars were expected to reach a speed of 52 mph "in a reasonable time" and get 22 miles per gallon on smooth roads and 18 in oil fields. A canvas bag of tools "suitable for maintaining the car" was included with each vehicle.

Production was expected to start about Dec. 1 in a plant, located at Wheeling Avenue and the Frisco tracks, that was

Tulsa World archives

Tulsa's locally produced automobile – the "Tulsa Four" – was designed to be affordable and tough enough for the oil fields.

to produce 100 cars per month and provide employment for about 1,000 men. The corporation also opened a service station at Brady Street and Boulder Avenue that included a repair shop, re-paint shop, supply house and showroom.

The original plan was to build the car completely, using a mold from Green's race car engine. But high costs changed the plans and the "Tulsa Four" plant became an assembly plant, using parts from other manufacturers.

"By buying absolutely proven standard parts in the open markets – shipping them direct to Tulsa in economical knockdown form – assembling them under the eyes of experts and delivering them upon their own wheels in our own market, it is possible to produce a car equal to the Western demands and yet keep the price low," a company brochure said.

The engine was a Lycoming four-cylinder of 37 horsepower with a Carter carburetor. The vacuum system was from Stewart, which also supplied the speedometer. The ignition system came from Delco and the clutch came from Borg and Beck. Artillery-type wheels were made by Stanton and tires were by Goodrich. All the parts came from top-rated manufacturers.

Many Tulsans and the Chamber of Commerce bought "Tulsa Fours," but it never achieved the production expected.

The struggling company never recovered from its loss after a 1919 fire at the plant. It produced a 1923 model in 1922, but the company folded in 1923.

A pioneer of the sagebrush scene

A pioneer Oklahoma woman whose talent for drawing was recognized when she was 5 became known in later years as the "Prairie Painter," the "Sagebrush Artist" and "Oklahoma's Grandma Moses."

Augusta Metcalfe disliked the comparison with Grandma Moses and called herself simply a "memory artist."

Whatever her title, Metcalfe became known as one of the great artists of the Southwest with paintings of Oklahoma scenes hanging in many places throughout the country. She won many awards for her art and was inducted into the Oklahoma Hall of Fame in 1968 at the age of 87.

She was born in Kansas in 1881 and came to the unsettled Oklahoma Panhandle with her parents, Edward and Mary Corson, five years later in a covered wagon. To keep Augusta busy during the long trip, her mother had given her paper and a pen and told her to draw what she saw.

"Everyone was amazed at the five-year-old's remarkable likeness of a horse," according to "Petticoats, Politics and Pirouettes," a collection of stories about Oklahoma women from 1900 to 1910. Her mother, a former school teacher, recognized Augusta's talent and sent samples of her drawings to her brother, a college professor in California. He sent art supplies to his niece for several years.

Metcalfe's mother provided the only schooling for the artist, who never had any formal training in art.

When the Cheyenne-Arapaho country was opened in 1893, the Corsons moved to that area, where each parent claimed a quarter section of land along the Washita River for homesteading. When Augusta was old enough, she also claimed a quarter section next to her parents' land.

About 1900, Edward Corson built the rock house that was featured in many of Metcalfe's drawings and was the artist's home until 1940; she remained on the farm the rest of her life.

Life was rough for pioneers in Roger Mills County, especially for Augusta and her mother after Edward Corson died in 1903, leaving the two women to do the housework, the

The Metcalfe Museum

"Moving to Oklahoma" was painted by Oklahoma artist Augusta Metcalfe in 1962. Metcalfe, who was born in Kansas in 1881, started drawing as a young child while moving to Oklahoma in a covered wagon. She received some praise for her art but didn't earn much money until after a one-woman show in Oklahoma City in 1949.

plowing and planting of crops, and tending to the livestock.

But Augusta continued painting, and her first painting recognition came as a blue ribbon winner at the Oklahoma State Fair in 1911. All of her paintings and drawings recorded life as she saw it, much as other historians did with the written word.

Augusta married James Metcalf when she was 25, but the marriage didn't last long. When Metcalf left, Augusta added an "e" to her last name and became the sole manager of the farm while caring for her young son, Howard Metcalfe, and her invalid mother, according to "Oklahoma Living," published by Electric Cooperatives of Oklahoma.

She continued to receive praise and win blue ribbons at many county fairs, but she didn't earn much money for her art until after a one-woman show in Oklahoma City in 1949. A Life magazine article about the "Sage Brush Artist" a year later brought her national attention and created a demand for her work.

She also developed fans during World War II when she sent letters to her son, Howard, an Air Corps mechanic stationed in the South Seas, that used watercolor and pencil sketches to tell picture stories of life back home. The GIs sometimes spent entire afternoons trying to figure out the meaning of the sketches.

The next best thing to getting their own letters from home was a chance to read Augusta's letters to Howard.

Art critics in Oklahoma really took notice after the Life magazine article about Metcalfe in 1950. She was inducted into the Oklahoma Hall of Fame in 1968 and posthumously into the National Cowgirl Hall of Fame in 1971 in Hereford, Texas.

A special exhibit of her work was on display at the Metcalfe Museum and her Break O'Day Farm as an official Oklahoma Centennial project. The Break O'Day Farm, the historic Metcalfe homestead, consists of a modern art facility and a number of historic and recreated buildings on 640 acres. It is the only Oklahoma farm on the National Register of Historic Places.

Bullets that ended the bloodshed

Gene Paul Norris, an Oklahoma badman who was believed to have killed 40 to 50 people, died in a creek in a gunbattle after a high-speed chase through the suburbs of Fort Worth.

"The most heartless of killers died screaming like a baby," Texas Ranger Capt. Jay Banks said later.

Norris had been struck by 16 bullets during the furious April 29, 1957, gunbattle with Texas Rangers, sheriff's deputies and Fort Worth police on the eve of what was to have been his biggest crime – the robbery of the $225,000 payroll of the Strategic Air Command's headquarters at Carswell Air Force Base.

Norris, 35, and William Carl Humphrey, 32, were making a "dry run" of their planned escape route when they were seen by Banks and other law enforcement authorities who had received a tip about the planned hijacking.

"We started tailing them," Banks said. "They saw us immediately and the race was on. Either Norris or Humphrey fired a shot at us."

Tulsa World archives

Notorious Oklahoma murderer Gene Paul Norris, also known as the "Smiling Killer," is shown in a photo scanned from the Jan. 5, 1957, Tulsa Tribune. Norris was killed by Texas lawmen in 1957.

Other officers joined in the pursuit. Numerous shots were exchanged during the chase, which reached a speed of 120 mph and ended about 25 miles northwest of Fort Worth when the robbers wrecked their car. Still shooting at law enforcers, the two jumped out of the wreckage and ran for a creek. Norris died with his feet dangling in the creek that he was trying to cross.

Humphrey died in a thicket; he had 23 bullets in his head, chest and legs.

Norris, who was called the most feared man in the Southwest, was born in Crescent and reared in Stilwell. As an adult, he lived in Lawton for several years.

Banks said Norris and Humphrey planned to kidnap an employee of the bank at Carswell, hold her son as a hostage and use her car – with a Carswell sticker on its windshield – to get on the base and take the payroll in broad daylight. One of their confederates, however, tipped police about the plan, and officers were looking for the badmen when they made their "dry run."

The magazine Texas Ranger Dispatch said in a 2003 article that Norris took a particular joy in not just killing, but killing in as brutal a way as possible. That trait was shown

in the murders of a Houston gambler, Johnnie Brannan, and his invalid wife on April 16, 1957, only two weeks before the planned Carswell robbery.

Norris and Humphrey apparently killed the Brannans as retaliation for Johnnie Brannan's testimony 20 years earlier against Norris' brother, Pete Norris, who was convicted of killing a bookie. Brannan's testimony was the key evidence against Pete Norris, who was sentenced to 99 years in prison. The Norris brothers swore that Brannan would die.

The Brannans' heads were beaten to pulp. Evidence indicated that after they killed the couple, Gene Norris and Humphrey had washed blood off themselves in the bathroom and calmly drank coffee in the Brannans' kitchen.

Gene Norris smuggled a gun into the prison farm to help his brother shoot his way out. However, Pete Norris was recaptured and was sent back to prison with sentences totaling 256 years.

Gene Norris, sometimes called "the smiling killer," was often referred to by police in Oklahoma and Texas as the Southwest's No. 1 badman. He was often charged but seldom convicted.

He was believed to have been one of three gunmen who robbed Cuban gunrunners of $248,000 in 1952 in a Fort Worth motel. FBI agents said the Cubans had come to the U.S. to buy firearms for a counterrevolution in their island country. The trio posed as firearms salesmen, but instead of delivering guns, they pulled out theirs and took the Cubans' cash.

Norris and one of his alleged partners were acquitted, but one of the bandits was convicted. He is serving a life term in a Texas prison.

Authorities later unearthed $140,000 of the money near Azle, Texas, not far from where Norris died.

Fort Worth Police Chief Cato Hightower said Norris' death closed nine murder investigations. There were reports that his many alleged victims included several bootleggers in Oklahoma City.

Texas Ranger Dispatch said, "There are wells all over Texas that Norris stuffed bodies in."

He turned spent cartridges into cash

A Tulsa banker who was once described as being as "much a part of Oklahoma as her broad, sweeping plains and native hills," got his start in business by selling empty cartridge shells he collected from Temple Houston.

The banker was Walter Ferguson, who had been a vice president of the National Bank of Tulsa until he became executive vice president of the Kansas-Oklahoma division of the Mid-Continent Oil and Gas Association a few months before his death in March 1936.

He died at the age of 49 of a heart attack while on a business trip to Washington.

Ferguson, whose Tulsa home overflowed with Oklahoma historical items, became a well-known political columnist in early Oklahoma before becoming a banker. He always had an eye for history and collected all kinds of memorabilia that he stored in a special room in his house.

He was born in Kansas and made the 1892 run into the Cheyenne and Arapaho lands of Oklahoma Territory with his father, Thompson B. Ferguson, when he was 8. He made the run into the Cherokee Outlet with his father in 1893.

The elder Ferguson moved his family to Watonga in two covered wagons – one containing the family's possessions, the other his primitive Washington printing press and a few fonts of type that he used to start his Blaine County Republican newspaper.

Because Watonga was known as a court town for the western territory, Ferguson became acquainted with most of the attorneys of the time, including Temple Houston, the son of Sam Houston, who probably was the best-known lawyer in the territory and fast with the two guns he wore.

Ferguson sold used shells from Temple Houston's guns as souvenirs for two to five cents each. Before long, he branched out as an agent of the Wichita Eagle newspaper and as a delivery boy, riding often to the nearest railroad station in Fort Reno, carrying mail, telegrams and messages for those at court.

When Thompson Ferguson was appointed territorial governor in 1901, the family moved to Guthrie, the capital, and the 17-year-old Walter Ferguson began writing a political column called "Over the Tea Cup" for the Shawnee Herald that, according to a Chronicles of Oklahoma article, became a sensational news source.

"So much inside information appeared in the column that the governor's advisers complained that the tea pot must be on the family table," the Chronicles article states.

Tulsa World archives

A political columnist and Tulsa banker, Walter Ferguson was better known for his broad knowledge of early state history. His Tulsa home overflowed with Oklahoma historical items.

Walter was barred from future party discussions but his reputation as a political writer had been established.

Young Ferguson covered the constitutional convention for the Guthrie State Capital, the most influential newspaper of the territory, and became acquainted with the convention president, William H. Murray.

His friendship with Murray paid off later when Murray became speaker of the House for Oklahoma's first legislature in 1907. Murray named him the session's reading clerk.

Ferguson bought the Cherokee Republican and married his college sweetheart, Lucia Loomis, who helped her husband with his newspaper and became a nationally syndicated columnist for the Scripps-Howard syndicate.

When Ferguson was elected to the state Senate from Alfalfa County in 1916, he exhibited his philosophy that a legislator should represent the views of his constituents, even if they differed from his own.

He introduced and fought for the passage of a bone-dry liquor bill that provided a fine and imprisonment for the possession of liquor, although he personally enjoyed a social drink.

Ferguson left the newspaper business in 1909 to become vice president of the First National Bank of Oklahoma City and moved to Tulsa in 1927 as a vice president of Exchange National Bank, which later became the National Bank of Tulsa and then evolved into the Bank of Oklahoma.

He turned the third floor of his home here into a mini-museum that contained thousands of historical items. After Mrs. Ferguson died in 1962, the collection was catalogued by the Smithsonian Institution and donated to the University of Oklahoma. It contained more than 75,000 pieces of manuscript.

In addition to thousands of books about early Oklahoma, the room contained a bar from a territorial saloon, a faro dealer's bank that started out in Dodge City, Kan., and later was in a Guthrie gambling house that Belle Starr once robbed of $6,000.

Other items included a large collection of mustache cups, photographs, early maps, framed copies of early Oklahoma newspapers, range branding records and even branding irons – among thousands of other items.

"Here in one room is the history of Oklahoma," an early Tulsa World reporter wrote. "Written history, of course, but dearer still, the materials that go to make up the vast unwritten history of our state."

A columnist in search of suffrage

A young University of Oklahoma graduate from Boggy Depot who had studied pharmacy and taught piano and violin got a newspaper job by necessity and became one of America's best-known syndicated columnists for four decades before she was killed in an automobile crash in 1962.

Writing a newspaper column wasn't what Mrs. Walter Ferguson planned as a career.

Her column, called a Woman's View by Mrs. Walter Ferguson, was distributed by the Scripps-Howard Syndicate and was published in newspapers throughout the country. She also wrote a daily lovelorn column under her maiden name of Lucia Loomis.

She got into the newspaper business when she married Walter Ferguson, who had left the University of Oklahoma in 1907 to work as a reporter covering Oklahoma's constitutional convention. Shortly after he bought the Cherokee Republican newspaper, the two were married.

"We were just out of college, young, broke, blissfully ignorant and rapturously happy when we took over the paper," she told a reporter many years later.

She helped her husband in soliciting advertisments, writing articles, reading proofs and all the other chores associated with publishing a small-town newspaper. Her responsibilities increased as Ferguson continued his interests in politics, duck hunting and fishing.

And when Ferguson was elected to the state Senate in 1916, the entire publishing responsibility fell on her shoulders. It was fortunate that she had studied several writing courses at OU.

She said the newspaper was "solvent only by spurts" until her husband suggested that she should "write a piece every week advocating votes for women, while he would do an editorial opposing the idea." She didn't like the plan, and he wrote her column as well as his editorial the first week.

"The results were breathtaking," she said. "After a few weeks, the community rocked with the controversy. Men said it served Walter Ferguson right for marrying a college graduate. Give a woman an inch and she takes a mile."

Tulsa Historical Society

Mrs. Walter Ferguson gained fame as a newspaper columnist who advocated women's rights.

Many even expected a rift in the Ferguson household, but the newspaper's circulation tripled in three months and was being noticed throughout Oklahoma as well as in Kansas, Missouri and Texas.

Although she had not been greatly concerned about women's rights, Mrs. Ferguson's columns opposing her husband's editorials convinced herself of their rightness, and she became an advocate of women's rights – views that were considered extreme and revolutionary at that time. "I found much evidence that showed we didn't have any rights," she said.

The Fergusons sold their Cherokee newspaper in 1920 and moved to Oklahoma City, where Walter Ferguson took a job with a bank. A year or so later, she was asked by George Parker, a college friend of the Fergusons who now was the editor of Scripps-Howard's Oklahoma News, to write a column. Within a short time, her column was being printed daily by all of the chain's newspapers and was distributed to others.

When Ferguson became a vice president of the Exchange National Bank (later the National Bank of Tulsa and now the Bank of Oklahoma), the Fergusons moved to Tulsa, and Mrs. Ferguson continued writing her column here.

It was in the Fergusons' home in Tulsa where Edna Ferber stayed while she did research to write her novel "Cimarron."

Lucia Loomis was born in Boggy Depot, where her father was a doctor. He later moved his practice to Wapanucka, where he also opened a drugstore. She was educated at a convent in Denison, Texas, and later at Hardin College at Mexico, Mo., before enrolling at OU in 1904.

She became a popular speaker at conventions, meetings and college commencements and received many honors, including being inducted into the Oklahoma Hall of Fame in 1937.

Mrs. Ferguson was killed in 1962 in an automobile accident near Cross City, Fla., that also killed Mrs. C.C. (Audrey) Cole of Tulsa and injured Ida Lambert. The three were returning to Tulsa after a visit with Dr. Tom Ferguson, the Fergusons' son.

Murrah made history before McVeigh

An orphan who did odd jobs while riding freight trains around the country became one of the youngest federal judges and later the chief judge of the 10th U.S. Circuit Court of Appeals in Denver.

The life of Alfred P. Murrah was a true Horatio Alger story.

His name is now remembered not because of his 36-year career on the bench, but because of the horrendous April 19, 1995, bombing of a federal building in Oklahoma City.

The best description of the event was on Page 1 of the next morning's Tulsa World: "Bombing Terror."

It was terrifying. Most Oklahomans are familiar with details of the bombing by Timothy McVeigh that killed 168 and injured hundreds more in the worst domestic terrorist attack in U.S. history.

McVeigh, 27, had served in the Army in Operation Desert Storm and was known to have anti-government leanings because of the Branch Davidian tragedy in Texas. He was arrested as a suspect in the bombing two days after the explosion. He was in jail in Perry, after being stopped for a traffic violation a few hours after the bombing.

McVeigh was convicted of federal murder charges in 1997 and was executed four years later. His co-defendant Terry Nichols, an Army buddy of McVeigh, was convicted in federal and state courts and sentenced to life in prison without parole.

Details of the bombing, its investigation, the trials of McVeigh and Nichols and the building of a memorial and a new federal building in Oklahoma City were widely reported around the world.

But little has been written about the judge whose name became a household term because of the bombing.

Murrah, who believed that law is just common sense, was born in 1904 near Tishomingo. His mother died when he was a child, and his father took him to Alabama. After his father died a few years later, Murrah began hoboing around the country on freight trains, earning a few dollars by selling newspapers and doing odd jobs in various cities.

Kicked off a train in Oklahoma City when he was in his teens, he decided he needed more education. He met a Tuttle farmer who gave him a home in return for his doing chores. Murrah went back to school and graduated at the top of his high school class in Tuttle.

Murrah hitchhiked to Norman, where he worked his way through the University of Oklahoma and graduated with honors from its law school in 1927.

He opened a law practice in Seminole, where he slept

Tulsa World archives

Before his name was linked in history with Timothy McVeigh, the Oklahoma City bomber, U.S. Judge Alfred P. Murrah made history for his part in forcing the Oklahoma Legislature to reapportion its seats for the first time in the 1960s.

in his office because he couldn't afford an apartment or house. He married an Oklahoma City teacher and moved his practice to Oklahoma City.

He was appointed as a U.S. District Court judge by President Franklin D. Roosevelt in 1937 and quickly attracted attention for his forthrightness and common sense. In remarks on and off the bench, he described prisons as schools for crime and honky-tonks and nightclubs as breeding places for crime. He also criticized deals between prosecutors and criminals for recommended sentences.

"Law," he once said, "must be a living thing, guided by the precedents of history, yet flexible enough to meet the changing conditions without straying from the great historic principles of our heritage."

He was appointed to the 10th Circuit in 1940 and became its chief judge in 1959. He took senior judge status in 1970 and became the director of the Federal Judicial Center in Washington.

On the bench, he was a probing, restless questioner and attorneys had to be ready to defend their arguments. "Now, Mr. Lawyer," he would say as he pressed for facts or legal persuasion.

Murrah's best-known case in Oklahoma was in the 1960s, when he presided over a three-judge panel that brought an end to half a century of legislative refusal to properly reapportion the state Legislature. Along with Judges Fred Daugherty and Ross Rizley, he ruled in 1962 that the Legislature must be apportioned on the basis of "one-man, one vote" in both houses.

Murrah and Daugherty decided two months later to give the Legislature one more chance, although Rizley wrote a bristling dissenting opinion. The Legislature proposed a reapportionment formula that the three judges ruled in mid-1963 was inadequate. They ordered their own plan put into use.

The 1964 Legislature was the first since statehood in which urban voters had power equal to that of voters in rural counties.

Murrah spoke frequently in Tulsa. He gave the dedication speech at the opening of the county courthouse in 1955.

Murrah died in 1975, and the Oklahoma City federal building was named in his honor two years later.

"I didn't learn the law," he once told a reporter. "I just found out as well as I could what truth is and followed it. Law is just common sense."

Not so up with trees back then

Oklahoma Territory's first newspaper publisher planted the first trees on the barren, windswept plains where a gentle slope toward the south didn't do much toward protecting the area from the summer sun or blocking the bitter winter wind.

"What this place needs is trees. Lots of trees," Will T. Little said after he staked a claim on a homestead north of Perry in the 1893 run into the Cherokee Outlet.

"Trees would slow down the prairie wind," he told anyone who would listen. He also said over and over that trees would help prevent dust storms and would help hold the moisture, both in the atmosphere and in the soil.

Little finally told the right people – the Noble County commissioners, who agreed to pay for 1,000 American white elm seedlings for the courthouse square – an area later known as Central Park in Perry – if Little would plant and take care of them. But Little ordered 10,000 and started planting the pencil-sized seedlings in 1896 – on the square and in many other places.

Within three years, he was in the tree business. While thinning out the trees, he transplanted them in many places in the town, on rural school grounds, and at churches, and he sold trees to farmers in the Perry area with proceeds going to the county. The sales to farmers brought in enough money to more than pay for the county's original investment.

Thanks to Little's vision, Perry blossomed with shade trees that provided children a place to play and others a place to sit on warm afternoons. And, just as he said, they provided a windbreak from the bitter north winds.

Many of the trees or their replacements lasted for decades, but Fred Beers wrote in a 2002 Northwest Corner column in the Perry Daily Journal that the trees were no match for Mother Nature's knockout punch that winter.

January's ice storm killed many of the remaining trees, and Perry once again appears as a barren, wind-swept plain.

Little also developed a second park, taught soil culture and published Oklahoma, a quarterly magazine with advice for farmers about the planting and care of trees. "If we had a Noble County Pioneers' hall of fame, Will Little should be among its occupants," Beers wrote in a 2001 column in the Journal.

Little may be best remembered in the Perry area for his tree-planting, but he was well-known in Oklahoma Territorial politics before making the Cherokee Outlet run.

Cherokee Strip Museum / Oklahoma Historical Society

Perry's Central Park, as seen circa 1910, still featured many of the elm trees planted by Will T. Little. In addition to his tree-planting, Little was also a pioneer Oklahoma journalist and a legislator.

He moved to Guthrie from Kansas on April 22, 1889, the day of the first run into the unassigned lands of Oklahoma Territory and a week later published the territory's first newspaper, the Guthrie Getup. Frank Greer had distributed the first newspaper in the territory the afternoon of the run, but his newspaper was printed in Kansas a couple of weeks earlier, as had been others that were distributed within a day or two in Guthrie and Oklahoma City.

"The Guthrie Getup prances into the promised land at the head of the procession and issues before one week after the glorious 22d April, 1889," the 26-year-old Little wrote in the flowery language of the day in his first issue.

"It shall be the endeavor of this sheet to give all the news, aye, even more. Should any man even so much as kick his dog, we will give the public an accurate estimate of the motive power used. Each political power will come in for a due amount of praise and other things."

That first issue was a small 10-by-15-inch sheet printed on one side by a job press and contained an apology for not being larger.

The Getup was being published in a tent, the same type of home as for other newspaper offices and printing plants. "There are more than one hundred printers in town and only one newspaper," Little wrote in an early edition – the one newspaper referring to his publication.

Little's newspaper lasted only a few weeks before it was absorbed by the Guthrie Daily News, and Little went to work for Greer's State Capital, considered the most influential newspaper in the territory. Greer campaigned to keep the Oklahoma capital in Guthrie and closed his newspaper shortly after the capital was moved to Oklahoma City in 1910.

While working for the State Capital in 1890, Little covered the territory's first legislature, which he joined as a member of the House from Noble County five years later. He helped write legislation that was adopted by Oklahoma.

Little was the curator of the Oklahoma Historical Society, which was organized in 1893 by the Territorial Press Association, from 1895 until 1899. He resigned to become an appraiser for the Dawes Commission. He was appointed as Perry's postmaster in 1901 and held that position until shortly before he died in 1908.

Little's body is buried in Perry's Grace Hill Cemetery near one of the elms he probably planted.

Sooner ingenuity started the presses

Oklahoma Territory's first newspaper went on sale in Guthrie only hours after the first run into unassigned lands began at noon April 22, 1889.

Frank Greer, a young Kansan who had slipped into Guthrie the night before by hiding in a load of telephone poles on a train, staked a claim to a Guthrie lot, posted a sign on his tent announcing "The Oklahoma State Capital, the first paper published in Oklahoma," and began selling the newspaper at 4 p.m.

Actually the newspaper had been printed in his brother's shop in Winfield, Kan., before he began his clandestine trip into Oklahoma Territory. But the residents of the tent city that sprung up that afternoon didn't care. They wanted to read the news – even if it was old. The newspaper "went like hotcakes," Greer recalled many years later.

Many men who had made the run and had staked claims helped Greer sell that first edition in return for half the money they collected. A few days later, Greer and a friend sold 200 copies in Oklahoma City's tent city where, because of the newspaper's name, many buyers thought it had been printed in Oklahoma City.

For a time, the part of Greer's newspaper containing news from other places was printed in Winfield, and Greer added local news on the other side of the page. But business was good, especially for job printing, and it wasn't long before Greer had bought a new cylinder press and several fonts of type to allow him to print the entire newspaper in Guthrie.

Although Greer was a Sooner who had slipped into Guthrie by hiding on a freight train, he and his newspaper became vigorously anti-Sooner after "the State Capital saw that it must array itself on the side of the law-abiding citizens," Greer wrote years later in an article reprinted in the Chronicles of Oklahoma.

The Sooners – settlers who sneaked into the Unassigned Territory ahead of the April 22, 1889, land run – accused Greer of being a traitor. Greer denied nothing, made no fur-

Tulsa World archives

Frank Greer published Oklahoma Territory's first newspaper and fought efforts to move the state capital from Guthrie to Oklahoma City.

ther effort to claim land or town lots and continued battling away for the law-abiding, non-Sooner element.

Greer wrote that he and two friends had bribed the engineer and brakeman on the freight train to let them hide on the train, expecting the train to slow sufficiently for them to jump off at Guthrie. It didn't, and a few miles farther south, they bribed the brakeman again and the train slowed to about 10 mph, allowing them to jump.

The State Capital newspaper building burned a few years before statehood, causing damage estimated at $200,000. Residents of Guthrie raised $50,000 for him to rebuild, but he refused to accept the money except as a loan.

Meanwhile, businessmen from Oklahoma City attempted to get him to move his newspaper to Oklahoma City. Greer refused.

Greer was vehemently opposed to single statehood for Oklahoma and had pleaded with President Theodore Roosevelt to refuse to sign the enabling act admitting Oklahoma as one state instead of two.

Greer's newspaper remained the state's most prominent newspaper until 1910, when Oklahoma's capital was moved from Guthrie to Oklahoma City in a middle-of-the-night ride orchestrated by Gov. C.N. Haskell. It was not supposed to be moved at least until 1913.

Oklahoma City had been chosen as the capital in an election the previous day.

Greer led a hopeless fight to force the return of the capital to Guthrie, and his newspaper died in 1911. He moved to Tulsa, where he became an active community leader, worked in real estate and oil investments and married Laura Leigh Hanson. His first wife, Blanche, had died in 1906.

In a feature story about Greer after he died in 1933, Tulsa World reporter Marshall Smith, who had worked for Greer in Guthrie, recalled that 14,000 votes had been cast in Oklahoma City in favor of moving the capital there. He said that was the largest number of votes ever cast in Oklahoma City until 1920, when women were allowed to vote.

'As good an American as anyone'

When Rufino Rodrigues discovered the coal mine where he was working was on fire, his first thought was to warn the other miners, most of whom were working on lower levels.

"I'll never see you alive again," a fellow miner told the young Mexican native as he prepared to issue the warning.

The danger didn't stop Rodrigues from running a mile and a half through several levels of the mine at Lehigh in Coal County to sound the alarm and to lead to safety up to 250 other miners who were not aware of the fire.

Rodrigues carried a bucket of water to soak his wool shirt that he used to cover his face to block the fumes from the burning coal. When he finished his run, he was dazed from smoke inhalation and had to be carried out of the mine by a rescue squad. He was taken to a hospital at McAlester for a couple of days.

But he saved at least 150 miners. The number is indistinct because newspaper reports after the fire credited him with saving from 241 to 259. The citation that accompanied a Carnegie Hero medal he was given set the number he saved at 150 but noted other claims were greater.

The trouble started on Feb. 22, 1912, when a workman accidentally dropped a lighted lamp into a barrel of oil in the main shaft of the mine. The oil blazed, and rather than try to put out the fire, the workman dropped the barrel to the bottom of the mine shaft – and fled.

Rodrigues and another miner who were among a group working 250 feet below the surface soon smelled the smoke fumes that began seeping throughout the mine. Rodrigues told his friend that he was going to warn the others. That's when the friend shook Rodrigues' hand and warned that he would die in the attempt.

Tulsa World archives

Rufino Rodrigues received a Carnegie Hero bronze medal for saving the lives of at least 150 coal miners during a 1912 mine fire in Coal County.

"That was at 10:30 in the morning and he did see me alive again, but not until 6:30 that night," Rodrigues told a World reporter in 1943. "There were 18 lifts in the shaft and I went to each one to warn the workers and help them out."

Meanwhile, in the area where Rodrigues was, all the other miners jumped on a hoist and rushed to the surface.

"But I couldn't help nine of them. They smothered to death," he added. Among those he rescued was his 14-year-old brother.

Rodrigues received the bronze Carnegie medal about a year later along with $1,000 from the Carnegie Hero Fund Commission. He used the money to buy a three-room house in Lehigh. The Carnegie fund, established in 1904 by Andrew Carnegie, recognizes acts of heroism but it isn't given often. Only 85 Oklahomans received the medal during the 20th century.

Rodrigues lost the house during the Great Depression because he couldn't pay the taxes on it, moved to Nevada to work in gold mines and returned to Tulsa in 1935 and worked as a mechanical engineer.

When war clouds were forming before World War II, Rodrigues was forced to register as an alien along with other foreign-born residents. He was born in Mexico but had lived in the U.S. since he was a month old.

"I have lived in the United States 50 years," he told a reporter. "I have raised two sons and two daughters. I have educated them in American ways. And in my heart I am just as good an American as anyone in this country."

Rodrigues, who died at the age of 90 in 1980, finally became an American citizen on July 8, 1943 – a milestone he considered his second great honor in this country.

Kate Frank retired, but never quit

A retired Muskogee teacher who was reared on a farm where she "practically taught herself as a child" was named the first National Retired Teacher of the Year in 1972.

Kate Frank, 82, received the honor in Washington from Pat Nixon, a retired teacher herself and the wife of President Richard Nixon. Frank was chosen from among 50 states' retired teachers of the year. She also received a trip for two to Hawaii from the National Retired Teachers Association.

"I enjoyed doing it," Frank said of the accomplishments that brought her the selection by the National Retired Teachers Association and the American Association of Retired Persons. "I didn't do it for money."

Those accomplishments included serving on the Oklahoma Teachers Retirement System's board for 10 years; organizing two Muskogee senior clubs – the Golden Agers and the Non Quitters – serving as a member of the mayor's advisory council, the YWCA board and the Muskogee Community Council; and working in the Meals on Wheels program.

She also was the first woman president of the Oklahoma Education Association. She attended the White House Conferences on Aging in 1961 and 1971 and took advantage of being in Washington to promote an apartment project in Muskogee.

After the 1961 conference ended, she went to the Housing and Home Finance Agency, where she told officials about her plan to build an apartment project for retired teachers and received the necessary funding.

She considered that project her greatest achievement. The 96-unit apartment complex was originally meant for retired teachers, but later was opened to anyone older than

Tulsa World archives

Kate Frank is pictured in this undated photo. Frank, a Muskogee native, retired in 1954 after 47 years of teaching. Having served the community and state in many ways, she was named the first National Retired Teacher of the Year.

62 who was still ambulatory.

It stands as a memorial to her – named "Kate Frank Manor" in her honor.

It angered the retired teacher to have the apartment complex be referred to as a nursing home. "No one wants to go to a nursing home," she said.

"There's never a dull minute around here," she said. "One thing about living in a place like this is that you can be by yourself if you want to, or you can get out and mingle."

Frank, who retired in 1954 after 47 years of teaching, was a native of Muskogee. She began her teaching career in a one-room school in a Missouri mining town, where she was paid $30 a month.

"It was not a picturesque setting," she told a reporter in 1972. "I was 18 years old at the time and served as teacher and janitor for eight grades.

"My parents were farmers. I practically educated myself," she said.

"I can remember picking strawberries for a penny a box to raise money to go to the county seat to get my certificate for teaching."

She later received a bachelor's degree from Southwest Teachers College in Springfield, Mo., and a master's degree from the University of Missouri. She taught business education at Muskogee High School for nearly 40 years.

Marriage never appealed to her, she said: "I said 'no' three times. In those days I had the willpower to say no. Today, no one comes along."

She told a reporter after she won the award at age 82 that "I want to keep on serving, especially the elderly. I don't intend to quit.

"If anything was ever important to me during my life, it remains important. I don't quit on anything."

I-40 collapse led to 14 deaths

Traffic was moving at a normal 70 mph on May 26, 2002, when cars and trucks suddenly began driving off into space and falling into the Arkansas River.

A 600-foot span of the Interstate 40 bridge near Webbers Falls had collapsed after it was hit by twin barges being pushed up the river. Fourteen were killed.

A fisherman at the scene told state investigators that the barges were moving straight and true down the 400-foot-wide navigation channel but suddenly veered west, shearing one of the bridge piers, the Tulsa World reported the next morning.

"It's a sad and sorrowful day for us in Oklahoma," Gov. Frank Keating said.

The victims were in vehicles whose drivers didn't see the collapsed bridge or were unable to stop before driving into the chasm left by the missing bridge sections. At least five survived crashes caused by the collapse that occurred about 7:45 a.m.

The toll would have been higher except for the actions of Harrah fishermen Alton Wilhoit and Kirk Washburn, who alerted authorities and warned drivers of the peril.

As they were speeding in a boat to a fishing spot in a Jimmy Houston Fishing Tournament, they saw the barges hit the span and watched as two trucks flew off the bridge into the water 70 feet below.

Washburn told Game and Fish magazine that he dialed 911 on his cell phone and told an "unbelieving" sheriff what had happened.

"I had to assure him that I wasn't joking. This was a very serious matter. I told him to send emergency help at once."

The two fishermen stood in their boat waving their arms but they couldn't be seen by the drivers they were trying to alert. "We felt helpless. It seemed there was nothing we could do to stop the traffic," Washburn said later.

The two finally backed up their boat, and Wilhoit fired a flare that got a trucker's attention when it hit his truck's windshield. The trucker stopped at the edge of the chasm and blocked traffic in front of the collapsed area.

After the traffic stopped, the two fishermen and several

The Memorial Day weekend 2002 collapse of the Interstate 40 bridge at Webbers Falls killed 14 people.

others used their boats to rescue several survivors from the water. The U.S. Coast Guard later determined that tugboat Capt. William Joe Dedmon violated federal law when he was allowed to pilot the vessel despite a lack of sleep.

I-40 traffic was forced to make long detours – about 12 miles for westbound traffic and about 40 miles for eastbound – creating massive traffic jams until a new bridge was opened in just over two months on July 29.

Department of Transportation spokesman Justin Magee said the speedy construction was an amazing feat; the contractor, Gilbert Central Construction Co. of Fort Worth, earned $1 million in bonuses.

The Coast Guard said the investigation concluded that the company allowed the captain to work more than 12 hours in a 24-hour period, a violation of federal law.

Dedmon voluntarily surrendered his pilot's license and has not worked since the accident, his attorney Joel Wohlgemuth said. Dedmon told the National Transportation Safety Board investigators that he only remembered waking up and suddenly seeing motorists plunge one after another into the Arkansas River.

"I was just screaming, 'Why don't those people stop? Why don't they stop?' " Dedmon said, according to an NTSB transcript.

Medical evidence included in another NTSB report indicated that Dedmon tested negative for drugs. Additional testing revealed he suffered from coronary disease and had a cardioverter defibrillator implanted in his chest, reports show.

Dedmon's physicians believe he passed out due to heart problems just before the vessel entered the bridge area. A medical report by an Indiana cardiologist indicates Dedmon suffered similar attacks later.

Dedmon, Magnolia Marine and Ergon Inc., Magnolia's parent company, settled lawsuits with the victims' families, survivors and the state of Oklahoma. Amounts of the settlements were not disclosed.

State transportation officials estimated the bridge collapse cost Oklahoma taxpayers close to $30 million in repairs and lost revenue.

Hometown proud of Billy Vessels

It was inauguration day for Dwight D. Eisenhower, America's top general of World War II, who had been elected the first Republican president in 20 years and Cleveland, Okla., was a Republican area.

But the 3,000 residents of that Pawnee County town had their own hero, the late Billy Vessels, who took top billing that Jan. 20, 1953. It was Billy Vessels Day in Cleveland, his hometown.

It was the first time in Cleveland's history that the residents had seen fit to pay such a tribute to anyone. Vessels, a high school football hero, went to the University of Oklahoma where he became OU's first winner of the Heisman Trophy.

Vessels, known locally as Curly, arrived by train with OU Coach Bud Wilkinson and line coach Dee Andros, received a big key to the city, rode in a parade that included high school bands from Pawnee, Hominy, Dewey, Drumright and Cleveland and was watched by an estimated 4,000. He made the dedicatory speech at the new Cleveland Memorial Stadium and was honored at a banquet.

The stadium he dedicated was renamed the Billy Vessels Memorial Stadium in 2003 after Vessels died in 2001.

Vessels wasn't just a football hero although there was no question about his being that. He also was an all-around great person, residents of Cleveland remembered.

A canvas banner proclaiming "Home of Billy Vessels" had been stretched across U.S. 64 several weeks before his day because, explained Cleveland native Jack Daugherty, "We're proud to let everybody know Cleveland is Billy's hometown. He's loved by every one of the town's 3,000 residents."

That became evident to a visiting Tulsa World reporter that day as he watched Vessels say "howdy" to everyone he met, most of whom he called by a first name.

Speaking at the banquet attended by more than 500, Vessels showed his humility: "Wow. Can you imagine people doing a thing like this for a kid like me?"

The football hero was given $2,600 in savings bonds that had been bought with contributions from townspeople who had donated from $1 to $100 each. He also was given an engraved silver tray.

All of Vessels' schoolteachers except Geraldine Holroyd were hostesses at the reception. Ms. Holroyd, his first-grade teacher, had died. But others were still telling the anecdote about when she caught Vessels using a pair of scissors to cut his curly black hair because he didn't like that nickname.

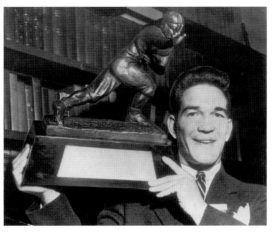

The Oklahoman

The late Billy Vessels holds up the 1952 Heisman Trophy. Vessels later said that when he was told he had won the award, he had never heard of it.

Even without the curls, the nickname stuck.

"He had one consuming desire, even as a youngster of only seven or eight," Superintendent W.R. Young told a reporter at Vessels Day. "That desire was to be a great football player ... to be a fine athlete."

It was a desire he achieved. A World reporter wrote in 1979 that Vessels "was the type of player who could do it all. Run, return kicks, block, throw a pass and make a crucial tackle or interception – he was the best."

Three other OU football players have won the Heisman Trophy since – Steven Owens in 1969, Billy Sims in 1978 and Jason White in 2003. Oklahoma State's Barry Sanders won the honor in 1988.

Vessels told a Miami (Fla.) Herald reporter in 1985 he didn't know anything about the Heisman Trophy when OU sports information director Harold Keith told him he'd won.

"People think I'm making this up, but I had no dreaming idea of what the Heisman Trophy was when Harold told me," Vessels said. When he told his wife that he was going to New York to accept the Heisman, her response was "Congratulations but I've never heard of it."

Vessels also became known as an "all-American" hitchhiker while in elementary and high school at Cleveland. He frequently thumbed his way to Tulsa or Stillwater to see college football games.

The idea for the tribute to Vessels had been brewing for some time but when he was named the Heisman winner, about 500 men held a meeting and set in motion the plans for the big day.

After Vessels' graduation from OU, he had a brief professional career with the Baltimore Colts and the Canadian Football League until he was injured.

Vessels became involved in horse breeding in the late 1970s. He served on the Florida Pari-mutuel Commission from 1976-83 and later became its executive director. He was elected president of the National Association of State Racing Commissions in 1984 and served as director of the Florida division of Pari-Mutuel Wagering from 1987 to 1989.

A Cleveland resident told a World reporter at Vessels Day that residents were proud of the football player because "he represents the kind of person most of our young sons would like to be when they get older.

"And he represents the kind of person that most of us older fellows would like to have been when we were younger."

Pryor tornado of '42 among the worst

A tornado swept along Pryor's main street from the western edge of the business district to the eastern edge of the city, destroying nearly every building and causing extensive damage to the residential section.

The twister was described by a witness as the "most awful looking thing anyone could imagine."

The storm killed 52 people, according to the U.S. Weather Bureau, but The Associated Press set the total at 60 two days after the storm. More than 400 were injured in the April 27, 1942, storm that caused damage estimated at $3 million.

The F4 tornado struck about 5 p.m., an hour and a half after one hit near Talala and mowed a path about five miles long, killing three and injuring 12. Talala, which was not hit, is about 30 miles northwest of Pryor.

Both of Pryor's hospitals were wrecked by the storm, the city's water supply was disrupted and there was no electrical or telephone service. Residential areas also suffered extensive damage.

Gov. Leon C. Phillips put the area under martial law, but because the Oklahoma National Guard had been activated for service during World War II, he sent state troopers to rescue victims, maintain order and prevent looting.

The troopers were assisted by soldiers stationed at the Oklahoma Ordnance Works south of the city and by employees of DuPont Co. , which was to operate the gun powder plant at the OOW. Ambulances were on the scene from Tulsa, Muskogee, Vinita, Claremore, Wagoner and Siloam Springs, Ark.

Water was trucked in from Vinita and from the Oklahoma Ordnance Works. Tulsa doctors interrupted their weekly meeting, and a team of 20 went to Pryor to care for victims. Others went to the Tulsa hospitals to treat any victims sent there.

A shuttle train that usually transported workers between Muskogee and the Ordnance Works site was pressed into service to transport injured victims to Vinita for treatment.

The Pryor tornado ranks as the fifth deadliest in Oklahoma history behind tornadoes at Woodward in 1947, Snyder in 1905, Peggs in 1920 and Antlers in 1945. The May 3, 1999, tornado at Midwest City caused more damage but fewer deaths.

Talala residents said they did not see the typical funnel of

A crane cleans up damage to Pryor's Main Street after a 1942 tornado.

a tornado in the storm. They said what looked like a series of streaks reaching from the clouds to the ground leveled everything in their paths.

But there was a definite funnel at Pryor. Two young Tulsans, George Wolfe and Leonard Wallace, were headed from Pryor toward Claremore when they saw the storm.

"I did what every other motorist did," Wolfe said. "I turned around and stepped on the gas."

They and several other motorists stopped at the top of a hill to watch the tornado, which by that time was purplish black and clearly defined.

"It moved in zig zag fashion and from all sides were spilling cows, calves, whole trees with their roots attached, telephone poles, wire fences and roofs."

When the sky turned black, someone of the group said the storm probably had lifted and everyone got into their cars to leave – a tragic mistake for some of the motorists.

A short distance away, the group ran into the center of the tornado.

Wolfe said he rammed his truck into an earth bank and the two jumped out. "From where I was standing, I could see automobiles picked right off the highway and carried a quarter of a mile. Some that were being dumped looked like twisted steel."

Wolfe and Wallace rescued two other drivers and used their truck to take them to the Claremore hospital, but one died before arriving there.

Pete's Place the product of a mishap

A coal mine accident is responsible for one of southeastern Oklahomans' favorite beverages and one of the state's best-known restaurants.

Italian immigrant Pete Prichard was 8 when he came to this country in 1903 with his mother to settle in the Pittsburg County community of Hartshorne, home of many Italian immigrants. Prichard's father had been working in a coal mine there since arriving in the United States two years earlier.

Mining was about the only work available for the immigrants, and when Pete was 11, he followed his father into the hard, dangerous work. Miners scratched out the coal with hand tools and donkeys pulled the loads up the long shafts to the surface.

Pete Prichard worked in mines at Hartshorne, Carbon and Henryetta until 1925, when his leg was crushed in some machinery. After weeks in a hospital, he knew his days in the mines were over. Mining was the only trade he knew, except for making a brew called Choctaw beer.

That's when he started making the cloudy, unfiltered brew with a slightly fruity flavor and selling it from his home in Krebs. The Choctaw Indians had taught many Italian immigrants how to make the beer, and it was described as one that could be made by any housewife.

Soon he also was selling bread, cheese and sausage.

It was a natural progression to running a cafe that he called simply Pete's Place. That restaurant is still flourishing 82 years later in the same but enlarged house.

Choctaw, or choc, beer is still on the menu with a difference.

It's legal now.

The recipe for brewing choc beer varied – apparently depending on what was available – but the most common used a mixture of barley, hops, tobacco, fishberries and a small

Tulsa World archives

Joe Prichard's grandfather, Pete Prichard, used this crock to brew choc beer in the 1920s. Joe Prichard (pictured) returned the newly legal brew to the menu of the family's Krebs restaurant in 1995.

amount of alcohol, according to an article by Steven Sewell in the Journal of Cultural Geography. Other recipes added oats, corn, malt, sugar and yeast. And some added snuff and flavorings.

The Krebs Banner observed in a 1906 article that "a few swigs of the stuff will make an ordinary cottontail rabbit spit in the face of a bulldog," Sewell's article said.

The first choc beer brewed by Prichard was made in 20-gallon crocks, and each batch was different from the preceding one. The brewing is more uniform and scientific today, involving larger vessels controlled by a brewmaster.

Prichard was arrested for violating Prohibition laws in 1932 and served a prison term, but the sale of choc continued at Pete's Place until 1981, when a newspaper article called attention to the restaurant's violation of the law by brewing beer on-site.

Pete's grandson, Joe Prichard, returned choc to the menu in 1995, after obtaining a license to operate a brew-pub. Pete's choc beer is now available in some liquor stores.

Although the sale of choc had always been illegal, politicians from throughout the state had been served, Pete Prichard told a World reporter in 1967. "We've served every U.S. senator and governor Oklahoma has ever had," he said.

He said his guests have come from every state and include ambassadors, musicians, movie stars and powerful politicians, nearly all of whom drank his brew.

Prichard also recalled that a 16-year-old boy tried to get into the restaurant in the late 1920s, but he refused to allow him in.

"One of these days I'm coming in," the boy told Prichard.

Thirty years later a tall, raw-boned man strode into the restaurant. "I'm Chill Wills," the cowboy movie star said. "You wouldn't serve me the last time I was here. I told you I'd be back."

The teenager and the telephone

A Cherokee teenager's fascination with a new instrument called a telephone became the solution to a communication problem for his tribe several years later.

And it may have led to Oklahoma's first telephone system. Putting his idea into practice wasn't easy.

E.D. Hicks told a Tulsa World reporter in 1935 that he was 16 when he went to the St. Louis World's Fair in 1882 and saw the fascinating new invention. He told a Chronicles of Oklahoma writer the same thing. However, there was no World's Fair in St. Louis in 1882. He probably was referring to the St. Louis Exposition of 1884.

Regardless of when he was in St. Louis, Hicks was intrigued and knew the telephone could be a boon to his tribe. His attempts to interest other members of the tribe were met with suspicion and sometimes bitter opposition.

Hicks believed the telephone would solve the communications problem that was especially acute when the Cherokee council was meeting at Tahlequah, the tribe's headquarters. Council members needed to communicate frequently with the Indian Agency in Muskogee 35 miles away, but there was mail between the two towns only three times a week. A telegraph line was too far away to be of value.

The council used couriers, who were frequently delayed because of congestion at the ferry boat crossing of the Arkansas River, to send messages to the agency and then had to wait for the couriers to return with answers.

Recalling his viewing of the telephone, Hicks and several relatives and friends organized a company to finance the construction of a telephone line from Tahlequah through Fort Gibson to Muskogee in 1886. That was simple compared with getting permission to build a telephone line. Some Cherokees were opposed to anything that might open their country to the outside world.

After the tribal council finally granted a permit, Hicks and his uncle, J.W. Stapler, went to St. Louis to buy the parts for three telephones and have them assembled at a cost of $75 each.

The cumbersome instruments made history when they were brought to Tahlequah, where Hicks and Stapler connected two of them for a demonstration and allowed two full-blood Cherokees to try them out. When the Indians

Tulsa World archives

E.D. Hicks was a telephonic pioneer in Indian Territory. He connected Tahlequah and Muskogee by telephone years before statehood.

learned the telephones could speak Cherokee, opposition waned, a 1935 World story said.

Stringing the telephone line between Tahlequah and Muskogee presented another problem. The permit specified that the line must go through land that was not accessible to railroads and that no surveyors' instruments could be used. The Cherokees believed that a surveyed line was the first step in building a railroad and they were opposed to railroads.

Instead of using poles, Hicks, a teamster and two helpers strung the line through trees whose tops had been cut off to act as poles. And since no surveying instruments were allowed, the line as laid probably didn't represent the shortest distance between two points.

Crossing the Arkansas River presented a special problem. The line was stretched from the top of a cottonwood tree on one side to a sycamore 800 feet on the other side – but not for long. The copper wire wasn't strong enough to support its own weight and $105 worth of wire fell into the river. It was replaced with steel wire.

Five weeks after the project started, the line had been strung from Tahlequah to Muskogee – and telephone communication between the two towns was established.

Hicks became the manager of the telephone company that later became part of Southwestern Bell Telephone Co. He retired from that company in 1934.

A 1933 Chronicles of Oklahoma article challenged Hicks' claim of having the first telephone system in Oklahoma. That article included a reprint of a short story from an August 1884 Cheyenne, Okla., Transporter that reported a telephone line had been set up between Fort Reno and Darlington.

And a 1936 Chronicles article reported that the Army had used telephones between Fort Sill and Fort Reno in 1881. James McGranahan, a farmer who lived near Piedmont in Canadian County, claimed the Army had used the telephone even earlier by connecting the instruments to telegraph lines.

He said he heard the regimental band playing at Fort Reno over a telephone hookup while he was at Fort Sill nearly 100 miles away in 1879 or 1880. It caused much excitement among listeners at Fort Sill, he said.

That pioneer spirit – in bronze

Pioneer women who helped settle Oklahoma and the rest of the West showed courage, faith, determination, self-reliance, fearlessness and bravery.

And those were the qualities Ponca City oilman E.W. Marland wanted displayed in a statue he commissioned in 1927.

Marland frequently said, "If we had not had the type of pioneer women we had, we would not have the America we have today." Because of his desire to preserve the story of the pioneers' struggle to settle and hold their land, he decided on a giant statue of a pioneer woman as a memorial.

Marland, a future congressman and Oklahoma governor, invited 12 of the world's outstanding sculptors to a dinner in New York where he promised each $10,000 for a model of a statue displaying those characteristics.

The models were as varied as their artist creators and Marland liked them all. Because Marland couldn't decide which was best, he took all 12 models on a tour of the country in 1927 in a special railroad car, and nearly a million people cast votes for their favorites. The winner would serve as the model for a heroic-size statue in a park he created in Ponca City.

The statue created by English-born sculptor Bryant Baker, who was the son and grandson of sculptors who came to America at the beginning of World War I, was chosen by 2-to-1. His statue depicts the woman as a young, enthusiastic mother, striding confidently, Bible in hand, bundle under her arm and strongly clutching the hand of her young son, who is clad in rough, homemade clothes.

Four of five proposed designs for Oklahoma's state quarter include likenesses of "The Pioneer Woman" statue, but without her Bible.

The 17-foot-tall, 12,000-pound bronze statue was erected on a 5½ acre park built on Marland's land after Marland had lost most of his money and had to borrow funds and sell stocks to raise $300,000 for the project.

The statue was unveiled on April 22, 1930.

"The Pioneer Woman's composite character is the character of our nation," Secretary of War Patrick Hurley, who

Tulsa World archives

The statue was created by English-born sculptor Bryant Baker, who was the son and grandson of sculptors who came to America at the beginning of World War I.

was from Tulsa, said in his dedication speech from his home in Washington. "These women who came here at the opening of this country were the bulwark standing between civilization and barbarism."

Hurley couldn't attend because he was ill at his home in Washington. A special radio hookup carried his speech to loud speakers in Ponca City for about 40,000 attending the ceremony and to the nation. Hurley, who later served as a general during World War II, was introduced by President Herbert Hoover on the same radio connection.

Others on the dedication program were there in person, including humorist Will Rogers, Gov. William J. Holloway, Marland, sculptor Baker and musician Bob Wills.

"Others can tell you all the historic facts," Baker told the crowd. "My work was to immortalize for you this character; her determination, her invincible will to succeed, her bravery, her spirit of adventure."

Baker said he had tried to interpret into the mother's figure neither the right nor left but straight ahead, her goal and future.

After Baker finished the sculpture in New York, he put burlap sacks over the heads of the woman and boy and nestled them into a railroad coal car for the statue's trip to Ponca City. Once in Ponca City, the statue was covered by canvas until it was unveiled by Mrs. John H. Hull of Washington, who was a native of Oklahoma.

Rogers put everyone at ease by beginning his talk with "now that the applesauce and baloney are all over" and kidding everyone from the pioneers to President Hoover. Looking at Gov. Holloway, he told the crowd: "I'm here to pinch hit for the governor in case he is impeached before the thing is over. The large crowd here came hoping to see an unveiling and an impeachment all at once.

"Stick around," he added. "You may be right."

Holloway had become governor after Gov. Henry Johnston was impeached. Johnston's elected predecessor, J.C. Walton, also had been impeached.

Marland, who became governor in 1935, gave the deed to the statue and the land it was on to Holloway as a gift to the state.

Deadly '99 tornadoes horrified

A storm that began near Chickasha tore through Moore and Midwest City, where the tornado it spawned reached F5 status – the strongest on the Fujita scale – and destroyed nearly 2,000 buildings. The same system produced other tornadoes that razed much of Stroud and continued on to Tulsa.

National Weather Service records set the fatality toll at 36 and estimated damage at $1.1 billion, making the Moore-Midwest City tornado the fourth costliest in American history.

The storm was first reported about 5:50 p.m. on May 3, 1999, near Chickasha, and it moved through mostly rural areas until nearing the Oklahoma City metro area.

"This is the worst storm devastation I have ever heard of," Gov. Frank Keating said the next day.

"As far as the eye could see, there was debris, just debris," a reporter wrote after visiting Moore. " 'Oh, my God! Oh, my God!' a woman wailed. Others just wandered, stunned."

As the storm moved northeast, another tornado destroyed a large section of Stroud, including the Tanger Outlet Center, the town's largest employer, which was never rebuilt. It caused extensive damage to the city's only hospital and left the city without power, for as long as a week in some areas.

When the storm reached Sapulpa, its winds were estimated at 100 mph. A mobile home park was destroyed, scores of buildings were damaged and trees were uprooted. The most heavily damaged building in Tulsa was the Carbondale Assembly of God Church, 2135 W. 51st St., with an estimated $1 million in damage. The church was rebuilt.

About 150 miles north of Oklahoma City, a tornado spawned by the same system tossed mobile homes like tin cans, damaged houses and killed at least five people in Wichita, and its suburb of Haysville, Kan. Hospitals treated more than 100 people.

There was plenty of warning about the storm, but it was unusually large and powerful. Much of the state had been under a tornado watch, and at least 10 tornado warnings had been issued.

"It looks like the Murrah Building, but instead of nine stories tall, it's spread out over a large area," said Jon Hansen, Oklahoma City assistant fire chief, comparing the damage to that of the federal building that was bombed on April 19, 1995, killing 168 people.

The tornado formed a dark funnel as it sucked up debris along its path. Tornadoes often are masked by rain and can't be seen, but not this one.

Mike Simons / Tulsa World

A school bus sits among the wreckage in Midwest City off Will Rogers Road on May 6, 1999. The damage was caused by a tornado on May 3, 1999.

"It sucked our hair straight up," said Kathy Martin. "I'm here to tell you, whoever did that movie 'Twister' has got it down."

Some witnesses said the entire sky appeared to be spinning.

It may have been impossible to avoid casualties, Dennis McCarthy, chief meteorologist for the National Weather Service in Norman, said. Entire subdivisions were flattened, leaving no protection for people without underground shelter.

"With a storm of this intensity and this magnitude, sometimes even if you do the right things, sometimes you just don't have enough shelter," McCarthy said. "We've seen that before. It's sometimes impossible to avoid injuries."

Fred Carr, director of the University of Oklahoma School of Meteorology, said the tornado was a super funnel, of sorts, with a path said to be one mile wide and touching the ground for up to 60 miles.

He said most tornadoes measure only 500 to 600 feet wide and reach the ground only briefly. That Oklahoma City-area storm caused the most damage of any in Oklahoma history, but an F5 tornado that hit Woodward in 1947 killed 107, making it the deadliest.

The OKC storm hit a day after the anniversary of a storm that killed 13 in an Okfuskee County farming area, three in Pawhuska, three in Turley and one each in Dewey, Fisher (west of Sand Springs) and Childsville (Okfuskee County). The May 2, 1942, storm lashed at towns in an area 100 miles long and 50 miles wide.

The Turley victims were children who were at home with their mother when the house was blown away. The woman and her five children were dumped into swollen Bird Creek, from which neighbors rescued the mother and her two older daughters but could not save the three younger children, who were swept away.

A May 2, 1920, storm at Peggs killed 71, according to Weather Service records, making it the third deadliest in state history.

Sixteen were killed and 58 were injured in LeFlore County on May 5, 1961, by an F4 tornado that hit the hamlet of Reichert, roared through the Potts Mountain area of nearby Lake Wister and chewed a path through Howe, badly damaging the town of fewer than 500.

The tornado destroyed the Howe Methodist Church as well as a new Baptist church that was to have been dedicated the next day.

Town names can be a bit bizarre

A small community that grew up around a general store in Creek County around the turn of the 20th century was supposedly named after land owner John Weaver's daughter, Helen.

But store owner Jepay Color got into a financial dispute with Weaver and Color reneged on his promise.

Instead, he named the community Pumpkin Center.

Oklahoma Historical Society

There's more than one version of how the town of Hominy got its name.

An American Indian warrior grabbed an Army officer by the hair during a 1791 battle near Fort Wayne, Ind., known as "St. Clair's Defeat," but the soldier was wearing a wig, which came off in the warrior's hands. The soldier escaped.

Thereafter the other American Indians called the warrior "Pawhuska," which means "white hair," a name he retained after he became a chief of the Osage Tribe. According to a 1924 Chronicles of Oklahoma article by Grant Foreman, Pawhuska wore the white wig from then on for good luck.

When the Osages moved to Oklahoma, the main town of their reservation was named Pawhuska after the old chief; after statehood in 1907, that town became the county seat of Osage County.

Those anecdotes were included in a 1940 thesis by Raymond G. Wilson, then a principal at Garfield School in Sand Springs, who was seeking a master's degree at the University of Tulsa. The thesis was published as a book called "Place Names of Six Northeast Counties of Oklahoma" that was placed in TU's McFarlin Library.

George Shirk's book "Oklahoma Place Names" doesn't mention Pumpkin Center, but it agrees that a post office was established at Pawhuska in 1876 and was named for Chief Paw-Hiu-Skah which means white hair.

But Oklahoma road maps show a Pumpkin Center on Oklahoma 65 in Comanche County. No explanation could be found for its name.

Many post office names were chosen by postal officials in Washington, Shirk says. He also points out that many communities' names were chosen by the townsite developers or post office applicants to honor family members, which could explain the great number of female names.

Hominy, Wilson said, could just as well have been called Harmony. He and Shirk agree that the name of that Osage County town could be traced to the Harmony Mission of Missouri. Shirk believes it became Hominy because of a corruption of the word Harmony, but Wilson disagrees.

According to a story told by George Tinker, an Osage, 15 or 20 American Indian girls were stranded at the Harmony

Mission when it was abandoned. When they were rescued, they had only hominy to eat, so the mission became known as Hominy Mission, and the name was used for the Oklahoma community when the Osages came to Indian Territory in 1872.

Wilson investigated 1,361 place names in Creek, Mayes, Osage, Rogers, Tulsa and Washington counties, including many that are now ghost towns.

But there's no shortage of interesting city, town and community names and stories of how those names developed.

A post office was established in 1879 for what has become Oklahoma's second-largest city. Its name came from Tulsey Town, an old Creek town in Alabama, according to Shirk's book.

Wilson says Tulsa was named after the clan of Creeks called Tulsa Lochapoka who settled in this area in 1836. He quotes the Handbook of American Indians, which says that the word comes from Talsi, a contraction of Tallahassee. He quotes Legus Perryman, a Creek who established the first post office in the area, that the word was a Creek word meaning "town" or "group of people."

Several Oklahoma towns were named for Adm. George Dewey, the hero of the Battle of Manila Bay in 1891. The town of Dewey in Washington County and Dewey County in western Oklahoma were named for him, along with the Custer County town that later became Weatherford.

Patriotism determined the names of three Oklahoma communities that had what were considered German names until World War I. The community of Bismark in McCurtain County was renamed Wright; Kiel in Kingfisher County was renamed Loyal to show the community's loyalty to the U.S.; and Korn in Washita County was renamed Corn, which was considered more of an American name.

A Noble County community was an oil boom town that residents wanted to call Mid-Co, but the postal department didn't like that name. "When the oil's all gone, what would it be?" a postal inspector asked.

"It would be a town, that's what it would be," answered the postmaster, and the new post office became known as Wouldbe, sometimes spelled as Would Be.

And, of course, there's Slapout in Beaver County in the Panhandle.

Slapout got its name because the storekeeper was always out of whatever anyone wanted to buy. His answer when asked whether he had an item was always, "I'm slap out of that."

At least that's the legend.

Tulsa's rail facility was a jewel

A crowd estimated at 60,000 jammed into and around Tulsa's new Union Depot to listen to a bunch of speeches and participate in other activities that were part of the formal dedication of the facility in 1931.

It was the first union station or depot in Oklahoma and replaced small depots that were used by the Frisco, Santa Fe and Katy rail lines serving the city.

Was it a station or a depot? That question wasn't answered although a debate had developed. A speaker at the ceremony, an assistant to the president of the Katy Railroad, referred to it as Tulsa's new railway facility to avoid the controversy of whether it should be called a station or depot.

The name on the front of the building identified it as Tulsa Union Depot. News stories in the Tulsa World called the two-story facility a station but in later years, it became known as Union Depot.

"We can all congratulate ourselves upon the securing of such a splendid facility," Harry Rogers, chairman of the union station committee, said. "We now have a station that is both the pride of the participating railroads and Tulsa citizens."

The stone and steel building, equal to a five-story structure, had cost $3.5 million and was hailed as a modern marvel of beauty and construction.

"Details of police were unable to cope with the throngs that surged over the elevated streets – Main Street, Boston and Cincinnati Avenues – which stand out as parapets against the imposing walls of the gigantic structure," a Page 1 story in the May 13, 1931, World said.

The dedication program was relatively brief, but the celebration went on all night and featured displays of ox carts, stage coaches, a new locomotive with nickel and brass trimmings, and "Old 94," which, according to Frisco tradition,

James Gibbard / Tulsa World

Once the city's transportation hub, Union Depot is now the home of the Oklahoma Jazz Hall of Fame.

pulled the first passenger car into Tulsa years earlier.

Visitors from a wide area came to see the splendor of the glistening marble walls and floors and shiny brass rails inside the facility that lay between some of the shiny new tracks.

More than 100 Oklahoma City businessmen paraded through Tulsa's downtown led by the Oklahoma City high school band.

There was shouting, singing and dancing to Jimmie Wilson's Catfish Band; Indians performed stomp dances on the track platforms, special trains jammed with revelers rolled in from Dawson and Broken Arrow. Flags waved everywhere, corner street hawkers were selling souvenirs and all of the day's event were broadcast on radio for those who couldn't attend.

Col. Frank G. Johan, chief engineer of the Frisco, presented Mayor George Watkins with a real railroad ticket five feet long and a foot wide.

"This ticket, Mr. Mayor," Johan said, "will take you anywhere along the Santa Fe's 112,000 miles of road, the Frisco's 6,800 miles of road and the Katy's 3,700 miles of road." There's no record as to whether Watkins ever used that ticket.

Over the years, millions of people passed through the depot – famous people such as Will Rogers, former President Theodore Roosevelt, Mrs. Franklin D. Roosevelt, Enrico Caruso, Josh Cosden, Harry Sinclair, W.G. Skelly and thousands of soldiers, sailors and Marines going off to war or returning home during World War II.

The depot served well until May 13, 1967, when the last train went through Tulsa and the depot closed.

The depot's doors were locked after Frisco's "Oklahoman" left Tulsa for Oklahoma City, ending a service that had started in 1872 when the first passenger train reached Tulsa.

Grover Bishop put crime under the gun

A young World War I veteran used a submachine gun and a pair of matching Luger pistols to enforce law and order in Cherokee County during the late 1920s and 1930s era of gangsters such as Charles "Pretty Boy" Floyd and George "Machine Gun" Kelly.

The submachine gun was the weapon of choice for nearly all the gangsters of that era, and Grover Bishop figured when he became a deputy that he needed the same thing.

"If I hadn't used one (machine gun), I wouldn't have lasted as long as a snowball in you know where," Bishop told a Tulsa World reporter in 1973.

A Bentonville, Ark., native who was part Cherokee, Bishop learned to use a submachine gun in the Army in France during World War I.

He adopted the weapon for law enforcement when he became a deputy under Cherokee County Sheriff Sam Johnson in the early 1920s. He became the undersheriff in 1926.

Bishop was elected the sheriff in 1934 after he promised voters that he would tell outlaws that "you are gonna go in like a man, or else I'm gonna shoot you and drag you in."

He did just that.

"Boy, we had some bad ones here" in the 1920s and '30s, he told a reporter. He remembered 1932 as the roughest year, when "some 30 outlaws and sheriff's folks" were killed.

He recalled that a cousin who had been a deputy marshal many years earlier would bring in outlaws draped over the back of his horse.

"When I brought 'em in," he added, "I just stuck their heads into the trunk of my car and let their feet hang out."

When Bishop retired in 1942, one of his deputies said, "He was one of the all-time greats."

That opinion was shared by many. Bishop was named "Public Hero No. 1" of 1938 by the "Gang Busters" radio program, and he received a plaque for "heroism and valor" from Falstaff Brewing Co., one of the program's sponsors.

Tulsa World archives

Grover Bishop practiced a deadly form of justice as a Cherokee County deputy and later as the sheriff.

The plaque noted that its metal was made from melted-down guns that had been seized from gangsters.

Bishop was a little reluctant to talk about the award, which came after "Gang Busters" had broadcast a re-creation of his handling of a case involving a gang of criminals. Bishop killed three of the gang's members and captured eight more.

"Gang Busters" ran from 1936 until 1957. All of its scripts were based on police records and were approved by the FBI. The segment involving Bishop was broadcast Aug. 15, 1938.

The radio show always opened with the sounds of police sirens, Tommy guns and screeching tires, inspiring the expression "coming on like gang busters." It always ended with descriptions of wanted criminals, which produced tips that led to the arrests of many.

After he retired, Bishop and a neighbor got into an argument that developed into an altercation in which the neighbor was killed.

Bishop was arrested and charged with murder but was acquitted.

Bishop, who died in 1980 at age 89, once told a reporter about coming under shotgun fire when he went to arrest a man. The pellets missed Bishop but knocked a hole in the radiator of his car.

Bishop returned fire but missed, and the fugitive ran into his house to get a pistol, which he stuck out a window.

"I thought I would kill him but then I thought that would be a shame," Bishop said. "He wasn't one who deserved killing, so I shot him in the shoulder."

Bishop also convinced the district attorney that the man shouldn't be sent to prison:

"I thought a fine would be enough. But he also had to pay for my radiator."

Bishop said the man became a law-abiding citizen and later a preacher in Arkansas.

Pryor's leading citizen set off battle

It took more than four years, dozens of lawyers and a special act of the Legislature to settle the estate of William Alexander Graham after Pryor's leading citizen died on March 29, 1952.

Graham, a banker and philanthropist who had helped build Pryor before statehood and helped rebuild it after a tornado destroyed much of the city in 1942, left the bulk of his $3.5 million estate to "Pryor Creek, Mayes County, State of Oklahoma" in a handwritten will that was dated just 18 days before his death at the age of 100.

The will touched off arguments over exactly what Graham meant and how the money should be distributed. Litigation included 25 appeals to the District Court, 19 appeals to the Oklahoma Supreme Court and three appeals to the U.S. District Court – and innumerable hearings in the probate court.

"Perhaps no other case in the history of Oklahoma law has attracted such voluminous litigation," District Court Judge Ralph Hodges said in 1962 when he ruled on an issue that sought reimbursement of some expenditures by C.D. Mitchell, the estate administrator and stepson of Graham.

After specific bequests to seven nieces and nephews, his housekeeper, a longtime employee and a few others, the residue of the estate was appraised at $1,868,968, including a horse, a stepladder and a 1945 copper penny that was found in his wallet.

Trustees Mac Q. Williamson, the Oklahoma attorney general, former Pryor Mayor Earl Ward and Mayes County Treasurer John O. Baker, whose appointment had been approved by the Oklahoma Supreme Court, finally received the money in December 1956. A 1953 legislative act had provided for the trusteeship.

Funds from the estate eventually were used for such things as a library, an auditorium, equipment for city parks, street lights in downtown Pryor, an agricultural center, water systems at Adair and Chouteau and a sewer system at Locust Grove.

Graham, who had saved enough to buy a flour mill in Georgia while working in the mill and teaching school, came to Indian Territory in 1884 at the age of 33 after selling the mill for $15,000. He came to meet a cousin who had told him that "we can make a million dollars."

Graham and his cousin, J.C. Hogan, went into the cattle business. Graham later branched out into other ventures and did make a million dollars. He had been involved in every civic betterment project for the town that was known

Tulsa World archives

Pryor's leading citizen William Alexander Graham, seen here at 100, started a lengthy court battle when he revised his will just 18 days before his death on March 29, 1952.

as Pryor Creek when he arrived. He was a rancher, a merchant and organized the First National Bank in 1900. He also organized the First National Bank of Vinita and helped form banks at Claremore, Miami and Eufaula.

The holographic will that was probated was written by Graham after he tore up an earlier will, which left much of his estate to Mitchell, because the Pryor bank was closed on George Washington's birthday, a federal holiday.

According to testimony at one of the hearings, Graham had his housekeeper drive him to the bank and was angered when he discovered it was closed. Then he had her drive him to the Vinita bank, where he also was chairman of the board, and discovered that institution also was closed.

A few days later, he tore his signature off his will and wrote a new one, leaving the residue to "Pryor Creek, Mayes County, State of Oklahoma." Exactly what Graham meant was an issue early in the probate case. Some attorneys argued that he wanted the residue to go to Pryor and had added Mayes County and State of Oklahoma to identify the city. But the court ruled that the money was to go equally to all three entities with all the funds to be spent in Mayes County.

A bank official testified he heard Graham say after discovering the banks were closed "the boys in the banks don't want to work and took off for a holiday whenever they could."

Graham had complained "the government makes me open my bank at 9 a.m. and close it at 2 p.m. That doesn't give us enough time to transact business. If I had my way, I would open it at 6 a.m. and close it at 7 p.m."

The banker lost the two things he loved most – his wife and his town – on the same day. His wife, Roberta, whom he married in 1906, died on April 27, 1942, two hours before a tornado ripped through Pryor, destroying most of the business district. Graham later helped rebuild the city.

Graham used to tell people he had three doctors – Dr. Work, Dr. Sun and Dr. Walk. His philosophy had always included working long hours and taking long walks, sometimes from Pryor to Salina, and he always planned to live to be 100. At a 1945 bank board meeting he told the other directors:

"I expect to be right here with you fellows every year up to 1952 when I'll be an even hundred. After that . . . well, I don't know."

Chief justice felt calling at early age

Alma Wilson knew when she was 8 years old that she wanted to be a lawyer.

It was an idea she got from her father, William Bell, whom she once described as a talented abstracter and frustrated lawyer.

"Daddy wanted me or my twin sister to be a lawyer," she told a World reporter in 1983, when she was 66. "Since I was supposedly the smarter one, I was to be the lawyer. As it turns out, my sister is the smart one. She's retired and plays golf."

Although she knew at an early age that she wanted to be a lawyer, Wilson probably had no idea she would become the first woman to serve on Oklahoma's Supreme Court and, later, the first woman to serve as chief justice of that court.

When she joined the high court, Wilson said she would bring a new dimension to the tribunal. "I'm a daughter, a wife, a mother – but I'm not a 'female' judge," she said.

"I'm so gratified that the governor gave me the opportunity. You can't be a first until you're given the opportunity. To say I'm not lucky would be dumb."

Her philosophy of law focused on people. "I try to breathe some kind of lifelike perception into each case by treating each individually and staying with it until I get the right result," she told a reporter.

"As the first woman to sit on the Oklahoma Supreme Court, she was a light in the legal profession and a tremendous example for all Oklahomans," Gov. Frank Keating said when Wilson died at age 82 in 1999.

"She was a treasure and a true example of Oklahoma spirit," he added.

Former Gov. George Nigh, who appointed her to the Supreme Court in 1982, said people would always point out that Wilson was the first woman on the court and to serve as chief justice "but in essence that was just a small part. She was a good appointment regardless" of her gender.

Tulsa World archives

Alma Wilson became the first woman to serve on Oklahoma's Supreme Court and, later, the first woman to serve as chief justice of that court.

Her appointment came a year after her good friend Sandra Day O'Connor was appointed to the U.S. Supreme Court.

Wilson was retained on the court by voters four times after her appointment. She served as chief justice in 1995 and 1996.

Born in Pauls Valley, Wilson was valedictorian of her graduating class at Pauls Valley High School. She attended Principia College in Elsah, Ill.; Oklahoma City University; and the University of Oklahoma, from which she received her bachelor's and law degrees.

She and her late husband, Bill, practiced law together in Oklahoma City and Pauls Valley for 25 years, and she also served as Pauls Valley municipal judge. In 1969 she was appointed as a special district judge for Garvin and McClain counties. In 1975, she was appointed as the first female district judge in Cleveland County and was a member of the Court of Tax Review.

During her time on the Supreme Court, Wilson considered thousands of cases, including many that involved significant public issues. She presided over several history-changing decisions, including the Southwestern Bell rate-refund case, cases dealing with school funding and cases that determined the way the Oklahoma Legislature can make its own appropriation legislation.

Through her tenure on the bench, children remained her priority. She championed their causes off the bench as well as on it, her family said in a statement. Wilson also was instrumental in helping make Tulsa's Drug Court a model program for the state.

Among her awards and honors are the 1996 Oklahoma Hall of Fame Award from the Oklahoma Heritage Association; the 1974 Guy Brown Award for Outstanding OU Alumni; the 1983 Oklahoma Women's Hall of Fame Award and the Governor's Advisory Committee on the Status of Women.

Ray Fine championed the little people

Ray Fine considered himself the champion of the "little people" during his 30 years in the Oklahoma Senate and House.

"You take the oil companies," he once told a reporter. "They are well represented. They can afford lobbyists. But take the orphans, the old folks, the deaf, the insane. They don't have anyone. So, I selected myself to represent them."

As part of representing the "little people," Fine led the opposition to reapportionment of the Legislature that, in spite of a constitutional provision calling for reapportionment every 10 years, had not been done since statehood in 1907.

In Oklahoma, he said, a city-controlled legislature would cut back the welfare program and raid the rural road fund. It might even slap another tax on snuff, which he called a necessity of life in eastern Oklahoma.

He said the cities had never suffered because country boys controlled state legislatures, but he insisted rural areas would suffer if the city boys took over.

"I'm in favor of giving Tulsa and Oklahoma counties more representation because our young people from the counties go there to live and find work," he explained to a reporter. "We don't want them to control the Legislature – that wouldn't be good for the state."

Prior to reapportionment and the establishment of the state merit system, state Senate districts were little empires and their senators ruled like feudal barons, deciding who got patronage jobs and other political plums.

Fine was no exception, and it took courage for anyone in his district of Sequoyah, Adair and Cherokee counties to run against him. He didn't have any opposition from 1942 when he won election to the unexpired term of Sen. Paul Carlile until Howard Fink, a teacher, waged an unsuccessful race against him in 1960.

Fink's campaign slogan was "change the letter and make things better," but too many voters failed to change the "e" for a "k."

Fine joined the Army in 1943 during World War II but retained his Senate seat and was re-elected to another term in 1944 although he was serving in Europe. He was cap-

Tulsa World archives

Ray Fine, who served 30 years in the Oklahoma Senate and House, said he appointed himself to represent the "little people."

tured by the Germans in January 1945 and was freed on VE Day, May 8, 1945. He returned to Oklahoma in time to support Gov. Roy J. Turner for governor. His power reached its peak during the 1955-59 administration of Gov. Raymond Gary. Fine served both as president pro tem and as floor majority leader of the Senate and became the unquestioned "king" of the old guard.

Fine led the opposition that defeated a reapportionment proposal by Gov. J. Howard Edmondson, whom Fine considered arrogant and cocky. Fine also became Edmondson's chief antagonist.

But in 1964, a three-judge federal court panel ordered the Legislature reapportioned. The new district put Sequoyah and LeFlore counties into the same district and Fine didn't seek election in the new Senate district, leaving that post to Sen. Clem Hamilton of LeFlore County. That's when he was elected without opposition to the House from Sequoyah County, a position he held until 1972 when he retired.

During his years in the Senate, Fine became a spell-binding orator and frequently used a mythical "Aunt Minnie and Uncle John" to stress an argument about their problems as an elderly welfare couple "from the forks of the creek."

Fine described them as a hard-working couple on a little farm who, after working all their lives, asked for only the simple necessities of life and, perhaps, a pinch of snuff.

One of six children, Fine was born in a one-room log house at Fine Springs, Ark., which was named after his great-grandfather. The family moved to Gore when he was 10. As a youth, Fine skinned rabbits and other animals for Christmas money, picked strawberries and cotton, and served as a hotel porter-custodian. In 1926, he worked as a barber in the oil boom towns of Seminole, Wewoka, Bowlegs, New Lima and Old Lima.

He earned a teaching certificate at Northeastern State College at Tahlequah during the Depression and later taught in the one-room school of Redbird Smith on Blackgum Mountain near Vian.

Fine died in 1975.

Te Ata state's first 'Cultural Treasure'

When Te Ata was named the state's first "Oklahoma Cultural Treasure" in 1987, Oklahoma Arts Council Director Betty Price predicted it would be many years before another such award would be made.

She was correct. It was eight years before the second such award was made. Today, 20 years later, only 11 "Oklahoma Treasures" have been named.

The designation is made by the governor and the Arts Council. The designee must be at least 70, be a bearer of intangible cultural assets and have outstanding artistic or historical worth, according to the council's Internet site.

In addition, a recipient must be an Oklahoman or someone who has practiced his or her skills, talent or knowledge as a resident of Oklahoma, and who has been recognized previously for his or her contribution. Te Ata had all of those qualities.

Te Ata, whose Indian name means "bearer of the morning," was born Mary Thompson in 1895 in Tishomingo, one of nine children of Thomas Benjamin Thompson, a store owner who entertained his children in the evenings by telling Chickasaw stories.

She remembered the stories and repeated many of them, embellishing some, for classmates at Oklahoma College for Women in Chickasha, beginning what became a distinctive career of telling Indian stories throughout the country and in Europe.

"I was shy and the only Indian at OCW," she told an Ardmore reporter in 1980. "The girls would gather at night in one room and gossip as girls do. One night they asked me to tell something about my life, and I repeated some stories that my father had told around the fireplace at home, stories of creation, Indian legends.

"The girls were fascinated, and this was the beginning of my repertoire."

After leaving OCW, she studied drama in Pittsburgh and went to New York to act. In the summers, she traveled the Chautauqua circuit with her Indian program, and New York hostesses frequently called upon her to entertain their guests after dinner.

"I liked the stage work I was doing, but I hated the aggressiveness you had to have to secure a role," she told a reporter in 1976.

When she toured the country doing Indian shows, she was careful about the things she selected for her acts.

"I wanted to do something different from all the scalp-

Tulsa World archives

Te Ata was inducted into the Oklahoma Hall of Fame in 1957. During her career, she appeared in all 48 contiguous states as well as in England, Sweden, Denmark, Scotland and Canada.

ings and wars that people were seeing in movies and show the creative and spiritual side," she said.

Te Ata often performed for children's groups. She always told them that the word Oklahoma comes from two Chickasaw-Choctaw words – Okla meaning people and homa meaning red. "When you say Oklahoma, you are speaking my language," she emphasized.

She also stressed to the children that "we never lived in tepees," but when children sent her pictures they had drawn after her performances, they always put her in a tepee.

Her program was difficult to sell, her booking agent told her, because audiences expected someone to come on stage with a little campfire and do a few dances but not talk. Her program, however, consisted of telling stories.

She performed in the White House for President and Mrs. Franklin D. Roosevelt and presented an Indian folklore program at Hyde Park, N.Y., during the visit of King George and Queen Elizabeth in 1939. That performance resulted in an invitation to present her program in England, which became the first of several tours in Europe.

During her career, Te Ata appeared in all the 48 contiguous states as well as in England, Sweden, Denmark, Scotland and Canada. She was inducted into the Oklahoma Hall of Fame on Statehood Day, Nov. 16, 1957, and also was inducted into the Chickasaw Hall of Fame.

She met her future husband at a 1954 performance at Columbia University in New York City. Clyde Fisher, then the curator of education at the American Museum of Natural History, was in the audience. He thought Te Ata was beautiful and wanted to get acquainted.

They were married at Bacone College in Muskogee. Fisher later became the director of the Hayden Planetarium in New York City. He was a popular lecturer and the author of several books on birds and nature.

Fisher died 15 years later, and Te Ata returned to Oklahoma. She died in 1995, shortly before her 100th birthday.

U.S. Rep. Tom Cole, R-Okla., a nephew of Te Ata's, said his aunt was an integral part of his family's identity. When many people "thought of Indians as a vanishing race, a disappearing civilization," Te Ata proved that that was not the case, Cole said.

He said her statement to the world was "that we're strong, that we're proud of who we are, and we're proud of who we're going to become."

Famed auto worthy of love and money

The only remaining Tulsa Four automobile is on display at Tulsa International Airport.

The Tulsa Four was the subject of a recent "Only in Oklahoma" column about the Tulsa factory that built cars, including one model specifically designed for use in oil fields, from 1916 until it went out of business in 1923.

The car at the airport is owned by the Tulsa Historical Society, thanks to a group of Tulsans who bought it for $37,800 from the Mac McGlumphy Collection in 2004 at the annual James Leake Auto Auction and donated it to the society.

It was recovered in the 1970s from a ravine on an Okmulgee County farm by the late James C. Leake and his son, James C. Leake Jr., according to James Leake III, who said the engine and drive train were there but only part of the body remained. He said his grandfather and father traded a Honda dirt bike and $500 cash to the land owner for the old car.

The Leakes sent the Tulsa Four to London, where a noted Rolls-Royce restorer was commissioned to restore it, using pictures of similar cars to rebuild the body.

"It was pretty rotted out," Felix Graves, who helped recover the car, told a Tulsa World reporter in 1975. "We had to cut the saplings out of the hood and roots had come up through the louvers."

After it was restored, the car was on display at Leake's Muskogee museum for several years and was displayed at his annual auctions in Tulsa. It was sold at a Leake auction several years ago to McGlumphy, who owned a Tulsa electrical supply store and Mac's Antique Car Museum, 1624 E. Fourth St.

The restored 1918 oil-field roadster went on the block at the Leake Collector Car Auction in 2004 with the rest of the late McGlumphy's automobile collection.

Concerned that it would be purchased by an out-of-state collector, the Greater Tulsa Automobile and Truck Show, Florence (Bisser) Barnett and the Walton family anted up $37,800 for the little two-seater.

"We just didn't want to let it go," said Donald Walker, the president of Arvest Bank who put together the group that bought the car and donated it to the historical society.

Mauldin subject: The dispute between Bill Mauldin, who drew the World War II cartoons featuring GIs Willie and Joe, and Lt. Gen. George C. Patton was the subject of an "Only in Oklahoma" column.

Mauldin was from New Mexico but was in the 45th Infantry Division, which was made up of National Guard

Tulsa World archives

Mac McGlumphy shows off the Tulsa Four automobile in his collection. After McGlumphy's death, the car — the last of its kind — was bought by a group of Tulsans who donated it to the Tulsa Historical Society.

members from Oklahoma, Colorado, Arizona and New Mexico. He began drawing his cartoons for the 45th Division News while stationed at Fort Sill and continued after the division was sent to Europe to become part of the 3rd Army commanded by Patton.

The general considered Mauldin's cartoons to be attempts to undermine military discipline, and he summoned Mauldin to a private audience.

Another Mauldin and another Patton – sons of the cartoonist and the general – met during the Vietnam War, but the meeting was congenial.

Bruce Mauldin was a helicopter pilot who was assigned to fly Patton, an Army officer (whose first name was not available).

Bruce Mauldin lives in Bedford, Texas, and his son is in his first year at West Point.

Pryor memories: "I remember it like it was yesterday," Kate Torres said after the April 26 column about a twister that destroyed most of downtown Pryor on April 27, 1942, when she was 9.

"I was holding a teenager's hand while she was dying. I'll never forget her pleas for me to call her parents and then she died," said Torres, now of Fairfax. She said Pryor looked like a war zone. She also remembered hearing pleas of "Where's my baby?"

When the storm hit, she recalled, her mother covered her and her sister with a Navajo rug, sat on top of them and held on to a gas stove. The only injury to anyone in her family was a head bruise her mother suffered when a deer head fell off a wall. They fled from their house after the tornado left it leaning, but they stepped over four dead bodies and went back inside to get bedspreads to cover them.

Her father arrived from work at the DuPont Powder Plant but couldn't find the family house until he recognized the bedspreads over the bodies beside the house – and immediately assumed the worst.

He put his wife and daughters in their car and had them drive to Fairfax while he stayed behind to help the injured.

Art exhibit: The column about Augusta Metcalfe, the pioneer Oklahoma woman who became known as the "Prairie Painter," the "Sagebrush Artist" and "Oklahoma's Grandma Moses," created interest about the Metcalfe Museum and her Break O'Day Farm.

The historic Metcalfe homestead consists of a modern art facility and a number of historic and recreated buildings on 640 acres north of Cheyenne. It is the only Oklahoma farm on the National Register of Historic Places.

Harry Sinclair got rich in oil business

Harry Ford Sinclair studied to become a pharmacist, planning to follow in the footsteps of his father, a druggist in Independence, Kan.

Instead, he began dealing in oil leases, developed an uncanny ability to select profitable leases and became one of the richest men in America as head of the Sinclair Oil Corp.

When Sinclair left the corporation's board in 1953, the firm was worth about $1.2 billion.

Along the way, Sinclair became one of the principal figures in what was called the Teapot Dome oil scandal in the 1920s and 1930s. He was acquitted of a conspiracy charge but later went to prison for contempt of the Senate and contempt of court.

The scandal caused hardly a hitch in his career, and Sinclair continued to be active in the oil business until his death at the age of 80 in 1956 in Pasadena, Calif., where he had lived for several years. He also was known as a big league baseball tycoon and the operator of a highly successful racing stable.

Born in West Virginia in 1876, Sinclair moved with his family to Independence as a child. He studied pharmacy and business administration at the University of Kansas, where he graduated in 1898, two years after his father died.

Young Harry took over his father's store in Independence and later opened a pharmacy in Coffeyville, but both efforts were far from successful. He got involved in oil prospecting, first in Kansas and then in Oklahoma. He knew the area and the people around Independence well and was able to obtain drilling rights on many farms.

With his earnings from his job as a lease broker for Cudahy Oil Co., Sinclair became an independent producer, bringing in his first well in 1905 in what was Indian Territory and is now Washington County.

He expanded his operations with a number of older and wealthier partners, operating in fields that made the Mid-Continent area famous – Nowata, Glenn Pool, Wann, Drumright, Flat Rock, Hominy, Ponca City and Stone Bluff, among many others.

By 1907, Sinclair had become the richest man in Kansas, according to the Kansas Historical Society. In 1916, with $16 million of public financing, he organized Sinclair Oil & Refining Corp. with assets of $51 million. It was followed a year later by the Sinclair Gulf Corp. with a pipeline from Oklahoma to the Gulf of Mexico, marine terminals on the Gulf Coast and the Atlantic seaboard, and a fleet of oil tankers.

Tulsa World archives

Harry Ford Sinclair founded an oil company that shared his name and was a major player in the Teapot Dome scandal.

Those companies were consolidated in 1920 into the Sinclair Consolidated Oil Corp, with assets of about $200 million.

Sinclair had moved to Tulsa in 1912, although he had become a frequent business visitor much earlier. He helped organize the Exchange National Bank that later became the National Bank of Tulsa and today is known as the Bank of Oklahoma.

Although he moved to New York City in 1916, Sinclair maintained an office suite on the top floor of the Sinclair Building, Fifth and Main streets, for many years.

The Teapot Dome scandal, one of the biggest ever to rock the country up to then, actually was three charges that stretched from 1924 until 1929: civil charges of fraud and bribery, criminal charges of fraud and bribery and charges of contempt.

The case began in 1920 when Congress gave the Navy authority to have oil produced from land set aside for the Navy at a 10,000-acre tract of oil-rich land in Wyoming known as Teapot Dome.

When the case finally went to trial, it took a Washington jury an hour and 49 minutes on April 22, 1928, to decide the government had failed to prove the charges that had hung over the former Tulsa oil tycoon for five years.

The investigation that led to the charges began after Wyoming residents learned the land had been leased by the government to a private concern.

Senate investigators learned that Interior Secretary Albert Fall had leased the entire reserve for $25 million to the Mammoth Oil Co., formed by Sinclair. Fall contended it was necessary to lease the land because it was being drained of oil by adjacent fields.

The government charged that Sinclair had given the interior secretary $233,000 in Liberty bonds and $35,000 in cash for the Teapot Dome oil reserves.

Although he was acquitted of the conspiracy charge, Sinclair served six months in jail a year later for contempt of the Senate for refusing to answer questions about the scandal and for contempt of court for having members of the jury that tried him shadowed by private detectives.

Teapot Dome long ago ceased to be anything but a historic site.

Sinclair developed an interest in baseball in 1907 and owned shares in many clubs. He also owned several racehorses that competed in major races.

Pennies a nuisance? Try handling mills

Oklahomans had to learn how to deal with two extra coins in 1935 – in addition to the regular half-dollars, quarters, dimes, nickels and pennies.

Of course, silver dollars also were being minted but few had them in 1935.

That's when the state began issuing mills to make paying sales taxes more accurate. A five-mill coin was worth half a penny; the one-mill coin a 10th of a cent.

Although many people won't pick up a penny today, America was in the middle of the Depression in 1935 and a penny was important. But it was impossible to charge the correct tax on a sale if fractions of cents were involved. Rounding up meant the purchaser had to pay more and rounding down meant the merchant was cheated.

The mills made it possible for merchants to collect the proper amounts more accurately.

A 1 percent sales tax was voted by the Legislature in 1933 and became law on July 8 without Gov. William H. "Bill" Murray's signature. Murray, who had threatened to veto the sales tax bill, said he allowed it to become law because it wasn't effective until July 1, 1935, unless it was re-enacted by the 1935 legislature. The legislature met only every other year during that period.

Proceeds from the new tax that went into effect first in Tulsa and Oklahoma City and spread across the state benefited Oklahoma schools. Half the revenue was earmarked on a per capita basis to reduce property taxes, 30 percent was to retire outstanding school warrants, 17 percent was to bolster the weak school fund and 3 percent was designated for the Oklahoma Tax Commission for administration and enforcement.

The tax on a 25-cent article was a quarter of a cent and the price would either have to be made 26 cents or left at 25 cents, in the latter case the merchant eventually having to pay the tax.

Tom Gilbert / Tulsa World

Oklahoma used one-mill and five-mill coins to facilitate state sales tax payments.

Thousands of Oklahomans protested excessive sales tax collection, according to Tax Commission Chairman H.L. McCracken, who announced in November 1935 that Oklahoma would follow the lead of a dozen other states that had adopted the use of tax tokens.

"We want to make it possible for the vendor to collect exactly 1 percent on sales, and we want to protect the consumer as far as possible to see that he does not have to pay more than 1 percent on his purchases. We believe the token system will accomplish that."

Each mill represented a 10th of a penny so one mill was added to a 10-cent purchase, two mills for a 20-cent purchase, etc.

The sales tax was raised to 2 percent in 1936 when voters approved an initiative petition supported by Gov. E.W. Marland that also earmarked the proceeds for old age pensions. Voters also approved a separate issue at the same election that provided a $15 per month pension for Oklahomans over 65 who could not support themselves. That money was to be matched by the federal government. Needy children and the blind also benefited.

Oklahoma's sales tax tokens were round, made of aluminum and had a hole in the center.

In other states, some mills were square, some were oblong, many were round and they were made out of various materials such as aluminum, copper, brass, zinc and plastic.

Because of a shortage of metal during World War II, Oklahoma used cardboard mills, as did many other states.

The Department of Treasury attempted to halt the use of states' sales tax tokens, and President Franklin Roosevelt sought a national sales tax in 1935, but Congress refused.

The mill system lasted through World War II in Oklahoma but later was replaced by a bracket system that levies sales in pennies for sales in various brackets.

Football star became a war hero

Paul Henry Carr was a hero on the football field during 1940-42 when he played center for the Checotah High School Wildcats – helping his team reach a 10-1 record during his senior year.

Two years later, he became a national hero in the World War II Battle of Leyte Gulf, which has been termed the greatest naval action of all time.

Although he was mortally wounded, Carr didn't want to quit firing his mangled gun that Oct. 24, 1944. He was finally carried away from it and laid on the deck, where he died a few minutes later.

His ship, the USS Samuel B. Roberts, had been crippled by Japanese gunfire and was taking on water through a hole in its side.

Carr, 20, and his crew continued firing their 5-inch gun even after a safety device on the gas-ejection system of the gun failed. They fired six rounds before a final one exploded in the gun, killing or wounding all the sailors in the gunhouse – including Carr, who was torn open from his neck to his thigh.

The sailor, who had never seen an ocean before he enlisted in the Navy in 1943, was posthumously awarded a Silver Star. A guided missile frigate was named the USS Carr in his honor when it was commissioned in 1985. A street in Checotah also was named in his honor.

Carr joined the Navy a year after graduating and married his high school sweetheart, Goldie Lee Jamison, Oct. 21, 1943, slightly more than a year before he was killed.

Carr was a gunner's mate third class and commanded one of the two 5-inch guns on the destroyer escort that was named for a coxswain who was killed in 1942 while rescuing Marines from Guadalcanal. The ship became known as "the destroyer escort that fought like a battleship" in its final engagement.

The Roberts and a few destroyers were the sole line of defense against a large group of Japanese battleships, cruisers and destroyers, whose target was a group of six American carriers providing aircraft support for the U.S. Army forces on the beaches of Leyte Gulf.

Tulsa World archives

Paul Henry Carr was a hero on the football field before he became a hero in World War II.

The battle lasted less than an hour, but it was one of the bloodiest in naval history.

An earlier "Only in Oklahoma" column told the story of another Oklahoman, Navy Cmdr. Ernest Evans, skipper of the USS Johnston, who led his destroyer during the Battle of Leyte Gulf and was awarded a Medal of Honor.

"Throughout the battle, your husband's gun delivered rapid and accurate fire," the Samuel B. Roberts' executive officer wrote to Carr's widow.

He said a lesser man would have abandoned the gun, but Carr led his men in loading, ramming and firing the gun entirely by hand, resulting in several damaging hits on a Japanese cruiser. Navy records report that Carr's gun fired more than 300 rounds of ammunition in 50 minutes.

After Carr's gun exploded, a petty officer found Carr in the gun mount, holding a 54-pound shell and asking the petty officer to help him load the gun that had become an unrecognizable mass of steel.

The petty officer helped remove an injured sailor from the gun mount and when he returned, he discovered that Carr was again trying to load a shell into the gun. Carr was carried to the main deck, where he died a few minutes later while receiving first aid.

The ship's captain ordered his men to abandon ship into shark-infested water. Of the 217 men aboard, 128 survived after spending two days and nights clinging to three life rafts.

Carr's widow, who had since become Mrs. Goldie Bensilhe and lived in Arizona, didn't know he had been awarded the Silver Star until March 1982 when she was called by an official to advise her that the Navy planned to name a ship in Carr's honor.

She and Carr's eight sisters attended the commissioning of the frigate in Seattle in July 1985.

The Carr is stationed in Norfolk, Va., where it is part of Destroyer Squadron TWO that has operated in numerous theaters.

'Ol' Wiley' was colorful legislator

A legislator from Grove who hitchhiked from his home to the Capitol because he didn't own a car became known early in his 30-year career as a champion of the elderly and the poor.

And as feisty and colorful.

His name was Meadum W. Sparkman but he was known more commonly as Wiley, his middle name. Or simply as "Ol' Wiley" to the people in his 5th District.

Except for a two-year break from 1954 to 1956, Sparkman was the representative for Delaware and part of Adair counties from 1951 until 1982 when his resignation was accepted reluctantly by Gov. George Nigh, who won his first term in the Legislature the same year as Sparkman.

"If there ever has been a little man's representative in the state Legislature, it has been Wiley Sparkman," Nigh said of the 76-year-old legislator.

"You could be on the opposite side of an issue with him, but you could never doubt his sincerity or his love for the people he represented."

Sparkman, a native of Springdale, Ark., moved to Grove with his parents when he was 12. He and Norena Brown, a native of Grove, were married four years later and Sparkman never finished high school.

It wasn't that he was raised in poverty; his father was a doctor. Sparkman didn't finish high school because "I didn't want to" and became a day laborer to support his wife and three children.

"I'd go and then drop out when football was over," he told a reporter in 1982. "It was in the House that I got my education," adding, "and that's where you get an education."

When Sparkman was elected to his first term in the House, he hitchhiked between his home and Oklahoma City because he didn't own a car until 14 years later. Legislators were paid only $15 per day for the first 90 days of each biennial session and $3 per day for the remaining 21 months of a two-year period. And many sessions went beyond 90 days. They did not receive travel or daily expense allowances. Because hotel rooms cost $3.50 per day, Sparkman sometimes slept on cots in fire stations.

Tulsa World archives

Except for a two-year break from 1954 to 1956, Meadum W. Sparkman, known to many as "Ol' Wiley," was the representative for Delaware and part of Adair counties from 1951 until 1982.

He was defeated for re-election in 1954 by 39 votes because, he said, he spent most of his time campaigning for Raymond Gary for governor instead of for himself. "I got to be a statesman, argued issues with the people," he said, "and the people retired me."

Sparkman spent most of his career fighting for people unable to fight for themselves, becoming a one-man lobby for the underprivileged and unfortunate. He also was a staunch supporter of bills dealing with education, including teacher retirement funding and was co-author of a constitutional amendment setting up the present court system in which Supreme Court justices run against their records instead of against opponents.

That court system also added new courts to Oklahoma and Tulsa counties. He received plaques from the Delaware County Retired Teachers Association and from the Oklahoma Bar Association – the latter award the first given to a layman in 35 years.

Sparkman considered his most important bill one that transferred crippled children from University Hospital to Crippled Children's Hospital.

Sparkman noted that he was plain-spoken and even cussed a little, but "I always voted for my people and no one ever had to guess where I stood. That might be where the 'colorful' tag originated."

He also had the reputation of a hard-drinking, gun-toting lawmaker, perhaps a throwback to the days when frontiersmen ran the Legislature. He once pulled his pistol in a parking lot near the Capitol and fired slugs at a concrete retaining wall as wide-eyed freshman legislators watched.

Sparkman, who died in 1995 at the age of 89, was noted for his rambling but riveting addresses punctuated by swearing and sobbing until he would break into tears that caused him to be unable to continue – that many observers noticed came on schedule when he was trying to pass a bill.

To suggestions that his unorthodox delivery was carefully designed for effect, Sparkman retorted, "Whatever I've said just comes.

"I couldn't make a speech. Shoot. I wouldn't know how."

Nurse served with 'Angels of Bataan'

"Home. We're really home."

That was the comment Feb. 24, 1945, of one of 68 nurses on an Army Air Corps plane as it came within view of Hamilton Army Air Field near San Francisco. It was their first glimpse of the United States after years as prisoners of the Japanese.

"I never expected to see it again," a nurse commented.

Most of the women, known as the "Angels of Bataan," had been captured on Bataan or Corregidor, including 1st Lt. Rosemary Hogan of Chattanooga, Okla., in Comanche County. Hogan had been seized three years earlier when the plane she was on was forced down on the Japanese-held Mindanao Island.

San Francisco looked like heaven, the nurses said as their airplane landed. It was their first chance in years to have the luxury of baths, shampoos and telephones.

Hogan had been sent to what she considered a tropical paradise in the Philippine Islands in December 1941 – shortly before the Japanese bombed Pearl Harbor on Dec. 7. After the attack, heavy fighting broke out in her tropical paradise.

As a chief nurse, she was sent with 25 other nurses to the Bataan Peninsula on Dec. 24 to set up a 1,000-bed hospital in a large warehouse, where they had to unpack their medical equipment and supplies. A short while later, Hogan and her nurses were ordered to move farther down the peninsula to be closer to the fighting.

She and another nurse were assisting an Army surgeon in the operating room when bombs destroyed the hospital. She was hit in the head, leg and arms by shrapnel. The bombs killed 47 and wounded 67 patients at the hospital.

Another nurse from Oklahoma, Lt. Wilma Hook of Renfrow in Grant County, saw Hogan shortly after the shrapnel hit her. Hook said, "I thought her face had been torn off.

"But she wiped the blood with a sheet, smiled and said, 'It's nothing; don't bother about me. It's just a nosebleed.'"

Her nose probably was bleeding but so were the other wounds on her face, left arm and right leg. She was pushed into a foxhole where she and other wounded nurses lay uncomplaining to allow soldiers to be treated first by the doctors.

Hogan was sent to Corregidor with others who had been wounded, but their plane was forced down on Mindanao, the Philippines southern island, and they were captured by the Japanese. She was imprisoned at Santo Tomas prison in Manila until the prison was liberated by

Tulsa World archives

Army nurse Rosemary Hogan of Comanche County was one of the "Angels of Bataan."

American forces in 1945.

But that didn't end her nursing duty. During her internment, she helped care for the many American and Allied patients who also were prisoners there.

No mail was received by the prisoners during 1942 and 1943, but Hogan received 30 letters during 1944. And Red Cross packages were delivered in 1943.

"They were wonderful," Hogan said after her liberation. They contained blood plasma that she said was "hoarded like so many precious jewels." When the prison was liberated the closely guarded stock still contained 10 bottles that were being saved for emergencies. The Red Cross packages also included vitamins, liver extract, materials for clothing, even clippers for their hair.

The prison had only two bathrooms with five toilets, five showers and three wash basins. At one time, about 4,000 prisoners depended on those facilities, Hogan recalled.

Cheers and shouts rang out around the prison on Feb. 4, 1945, when the prisoners realized they were being liberated by American soldiers. At first they had thought it was the Japanese coming for them.

Among the Americans was Theo Tanner of Hollister, who had been a friend of Hogan's when they were teenagers.

The Japanese didn't go peacefully when the Americans arrived. Sixty-eight barricaded themselves in one wing of the building with American prisoners as hostages. They traded their hostages for being allowed to go free and marched down the road fully armed. Later, many of the Japanese returned as snipers and fired at the prison.

One of the snipers, the officer who had cut the prisoners' food rations earlier, was wounded, and Hogan helped a doctor dress his wounds. He died, however.

Hogan later received Purple Heart and Bronze Star medals. After the war, she transferred to the Air Force and was promoted to full colonel in 1958, one of the first four women who achieved that rank, when she was serving as chief of the nursing division of the Tactical Air Command surgeon at Langley Air Force Base.

The nurses' experiences at Santo Tomas prison were recounted in a book and a movie, both titled "So Proudly We Hail." Hogan's character was played by actress Paulette Goddard in the movie, which also starred Claudette Colbert and Veronica Lake.

Hogan died in 1964.

Smith was a fiery orator

Gerald L.K. Smith, a fiery preacher and political figure, was revered by his followers as a tireless fighter against atheism and communism but denounced by his enemies as a racist demagogue.

Everyone agreed that the former Tulsan was a masterful orator with a gift for moving audiences.

That talent was best described by H.L. Mencken, who wrote in The Baltimore Sun in 1936 that Smith was "the gustiest and goriest, the loudest and lustiest, the deadliest and damnedest orator ever heard on this or any other earth."

Smith's controversial activities spanned four decades and included formation in 1938 of his own organization, the Committee of One Million, that he said didn't stop at 1 million and eventually grew to 3 million members who endorsed his beliefs.

He was a bitter foe of the New Deal and President Franklin D. Roosevelt, whom he called "that cripple in the White House" and "cat's-paw of the Jew bankers." He opposed racial integration of schools, was a rabid anti-Jewish campaigner, joined the American Silver Shirts – inspired by the Italian Black Shirts and Hitler's Brown Shirts – and campaigned against U.S. action in World War II.

But when America became involved in the war, he called it a crusade against "the godless orientals of Japan by the Christian West." His only child, Gerald L.K. Smith Jr., joined the Army and was wounded four times during the war.

Smith supported neighborhood schools, FBI Director J. Edgar Hoover, impeachment of liberal members of the Supreme Court and prayer in public schools. He strongly opposed communism, pornography, recognition of China and fluoridation of water.

He's probably best remembered today as the man who restored the tourist business to Eureka Springs, Ark., after 40 years of decline.

The revival began in 1964 after Smith and his wife, Elna Smith, bought Penn Castle, a Victorian mansion that they remodeled into a lavish summer home. They built a seven-story statue of Jesus, an amphitheater where a Passion play is performed and several other religious attractions, some of which were completed after Smith's death in 1976.

Associated Press

The Rev. Gerald L.K. Smith, a former Tulsan and director of the America First Party, speaks June 25, 1944, in the Grand Ballroom of the Stevens Hotel in Chicago. Smith's controversial activities spanned four decades.

Even the statue was controversial. Smith said it was more beautiful than Michelangelo's art, but an art critic said it looked like a milk carton with a tennis ball on top.

Art or milk carton, the statue marked the beginning of the religious projects that attracted thousands of visitors and helped revitalize the city.

A Wisconsin native, Smith graduated from Valparaiso and Butler universities in Indiana and followed his father, grandfather and great-grandfather into the ministry. He served churches in Wisconsin and Illinois before moving to Shreveport, La. There he learned politics from the master, Huey Long, "the Kingfish," who was just beginning a political career that included terms as a governor and U.S. senator.

Smith said he joined forces with Long because he believed that Long, who was sometimes called the Louisiana dictator, was the most effective weapon against Roosevelt.

During the 1930s and 1940s, Smith was known for his lectures and articles that appeared in his monthly magazine, The Cross and the Flag, and under pseudonyms in more than 200 newspapers. His most widely publicized battles came during his days as a Tulsan in the late 1940s and early 1950s when he was an "America First" speaker and was often kicked out, chased off and hampered in his oratory.

As one of Long's strongest supporters, Smith was present when the Kingfish was assassinated in September 1935 in the Louisiana Capitol, a month after Long announced that he would be a candidate for president.

Conceding that Smith was a masterful orator with a gift for moving audiences, the Tulsa World said after his death: "Like all demagogues, he had the ability to make half-truths sound like the Gospel – which made him all the more dangerous."

The World editorial said his life "was a tragic waste, for he could have done so much good if only his outstanding abilities had been put to positive use in a truly Christian cause."

The Arkansas Gazette concluded its obituary on Smith with these words: "To have the power to touch men's hearts with glory or with bigotry, and to choose the latter, is a saddening thing."

Integration fuss cost librarian her job

A Bartlesville librarian was fired in 1950 after 31 years of service for what the City Commission called insubordination, but her friends claimed that she lost her job because she let black people borrow books.

The librarian, Ruth Brown, sued the city to regain her job but lost.

Now she is back at the library, and will remain there: A sculpture of her was unveiled and put on display this year, 57 years after she was fired and 33 years after her death at age 84.

"Miss Brown lost her job because of her determination to promote equal rights for blacks, not only at the library, but also at churches and businesses," said Joan Dreisker, the chairwoman of the Women's Network Ruth Brown project, at the unveiling. "She was ahead of her time in her quest for truth and justice."

The ruckus that resulted in Brown's discharge started Feb. 16, 1950, when a group of residents complained at a City Commission meeting about three magazines in the library – The Nation, The New Republic and Soviet Russia Today.

The group also raised questions about Brown's support of equal rights for blacks because she had taken blacks to community meetings and church, and even accompanied them to challenge the Jim Crow policy in certain stores.

Mayor E.S. Dunaway said Brown's activities in regard to integration were her business, but he appointed a citizens' committee to work with the library commission to determine whether the magazines were subversive or communistic.

The library commission reported a few months later that The Nation and The New Republic should remain in the library but that Soviet Russia Today, a propaganda organ, should not.

The citizens' committee, however, condemned all three magazines plus Negro Digest as subversive. The committee later added Consumer Reports to its list of magazines

Tulsa World archives

Ruth Brown, a Bartlesville librarian, was fired in 1950 after questions were raised about some magazines in the library collection and her politics.

that should be removed from the library.

Apparently the City Commission disagreed with the library board's report, as it abolished the board by enacting an ordinance that set up a new library board. The new ordinance gave the commission full control over the library and provided that employees could be fired without a statement of cause.

"We got a letter thanking us for our service and stating that we had been replaced," one of the former library board members said.

Brown was summoned to an executive session of the City Commission a few weeks later by Dunaway, who admitted that her support of integration was one reason for the interview.

At her appearance, Brown said she would answer questions about the operation of the library but would not answer questions about her personal life unless they were put in writing, and she added that her answers would be in writing.

She was fired an hour later.

"She, an employee of the city, spoke to us that way," Dunaway said. "We considered that insubordination."

Brown's lawsuit to regain her job failed in district court and on appeal to the Oklahoma Supreme Court. A committee of the Oklahoma Library Association condemned her discharge as "an act of intolerance."

The library committee said, "We can only infer that Miss Brown was unjustly and cavalierly discharged because of her private beliefs and because of her professional belief in free libraries."

Brown's actions were vindicated in a move that began more than a year ago to raise funds for a sculpture of her by the American Indian artist Janice Albro.

More than $25,000 was raised for the Ruth Brown memorial. Any funds left over will be used to endow a scholarship for library employees seeking a master's degree in library and information sciences.

World brought hidden disease into light

It was a word that wasn't used in polite society.

Most referred to it as a social disease. Newspapers used the same term – if they referred to it at all.

It was a major threat to Americans' health. An estimated 200,000 Oklahomans, including 9,000 Tulsa County residents, were believed to have been afflicted with it in December 1936 and January 1937, when the Tulsa World's reporter Walter Biscup broke the taboo against using the word and wrote a series of six articles about:

Syphilis.

"It was the state's biggest health problem, and something had to be done," Biscup said years later.

The series drew praise from ministers, civic clubs, physicians, the U.S. surgeon general and dozens of readers who wrote letters to the editor that filled an entire page in a Sunday edition in January 1937.

The series also brought reform to the state's syphilis laws and was reprinted in many cities around the country. The 1943 Legislature provided for health authorities to require blood tests of anyone suspected of having the disease and strengthened laws against prostitution.

Lawmakers voted two years later to require premarital blood tests for syphilis. The requirement lasted until 2004, when the Legislature removed it.

After the requirement was dropped, William Pierson, the chief of the Oklahoma Health Department's HIV/STD service, said only five new cases of syphilis had been confirmed in 60,000 tests a year in the previous five years.

He credited the drop to better tracking through health agencies as well as identification of those who may have been exposed to the bacteria, which is spread through sexual activity.

Booklets reprinting Biscup's series were offered free to individuals, civic and study clubs and other similar groups. They could be obtained from the World's business office or by sending a 1½-cent stamp to cover postage.

The World was one of the first newspapers in the country, aside from The New York Times, to report on the sexually transmitted disease, or even to use the word. Dr. George Osborn, the president of the Oklahoma Medical Society, commended the newspaper for "removing the mask of secrecy from the hideous features of syphilis."

"While medical science has determined the cause of

A NATION
WARS
on
SYPHILIS

This booklet, reprinting a series of articles on Syphilis published by the Tulsa World, is distributed for the purpose of co-operating with civic organizations, health groups, medical societies and public officials in their widespread campaign to bring the disease under control.

Compliments of
THE TULSA WORLD

Tulsa World archives

Reprints of Tulsa World reporter Walter Biscup's 1936 and 1937 series on syphilis in Oklahoma were offered for the cost of postage.

syphilis and evolved methods of diagnosis and treatment, society must recognize its responsibility and cooperate," he said.

State Sen. H.C. Timmons of Tulsa told the Senate that he had made a survey of Tulsa County and found as conservative a World estimate that one of every 10 persons was infected. He said current laws seemed to cover the situation but that enforcement was dormant because of a lack of funds and cooperation from physicians.

The high rate of venereal disease wasn't something new. After Biscup's series was published, the Rev. Guy Tetirick, the pastor of University Methodist Church, noted that the highest rates of rejection from military service during World War I were in Kansas, Missouri and Oklahoma.

He said the federal government established clinics in the tri-state region after the war to combat the disease. He said huge benefits resulted but that dwindling appropriations finally closed the clinics.

Biscup's series noted that Oklahoma County had the greatest incidence of the disease with 11,370 cases, followed by Tulsa County with 9,378. The fewest number of cases was in Harper County, which had 175. One article said that, with the exception of measles, it was the most prevalent of all communicable diseases in Oklahoma.

The series traced the discovery of the disease to 1493 in the West Indies and said the first known outbreak in the U.S. occurred in 1646 in Boston, 26 years after the landing of the Mayflower.

Some of the information in the series is badly outdated. It blamed prostitution for most cases but said 40 percent of victims acquired the disease innocently from cups, pipes or cigarettes, linens, or in receiving services from servants, barbers or beauty salon operators.

More modern information is that syphilis cannot be spread through casual contact with toilet seats, door knobs, swimming pools, hot tubs, bathtubs, shared clothing or eating utensils.

The series said a patient had a good chance of being cured – "if he does not get discouraged or impatient and stop treatment too soon."

The treatment in those pre-penicillin days required 18 months. Today, a single dose of penicillin is usually all it takes to cure a case.

Logging towns literally on the move

Their names remained the same, but the towns' locations shifted – depending on where a growth of timber was to be cut – in early-day southeastern Oklahoma logging.

Loggers and their families lived in the same houses and did only minimal packing of household goods when they moved. The houses were cut in half, loaded onto wagons, trucks or railroad cars and hauled to their new sites.

It was a way to provide the comfort of home for the loggers who worked in the forests of southeastern Oklahoma. Instead of packing up and moving to new houses in new towns, the lumber company moved the towns, lock, stock, house and even post office.

The traveling timber towns was the idea of J.C. Leeper, the chief engineer for Choctaw Lumber Co. operated by the Dierks family. Choctaw Lumber Co. later became Dierks Forest Inc. Dierks' operation was sold to Weyerhaeuser Co. in 1969.

Four German brothers – Hans, Herman, Peter and Henry Dierks – had organized the Dierks Lumber and Coal Co. in Nebraska in the 1880s. The company expanded into southeastern Oklahoma in 1898, buying lumber from the Choctaw Indians who owned the land and the timber.

The Dierks brothers named their first McCurtain County lumber mill town Bismark in honor of Otto von Bismarck, the Prussian prime minister in the 1860s. But because of anti-German sentiment during World War I, the name was changed in 1918 to Wright and in 1920 to Wright City in honor of William W. Wright, the first McCurtain County soldier killed in the war.

As loggers cut enough timber to keep their mills running efficiently, the new timber available for harvest was farther and farther away from the mills and the lumber camps.

That's when Leeper's idea was born. The company would provide mobile lumber camps so workers could live in the forests – where the trees were. Otherwise, it would have required hours every day for the loggers to reach the harvest areas.

The system is described in a book, "The Traveling Timber Towns" by Fayrene Benson, Jimm Jacobs and Bob Burke. Benson taught school in two of the traveling towns, and her husband, James Benson, grew up in the timber camps. Jacobs is a native of McCurtain County and an author. Burke,

Oklahoma Forest Heritage Center

Loggers gather outside the Clebit post office in 1938. The post office was mobile and followed the loggers as they moved from site to site.

a native of Broken Bow, is an Oklahoma City attorney and the author of many books.

To facilitate the moving towns, the company built small frame houses that cost $12 to $15 each and were constructed so they could be sawed in half and the pieces re-attached at the next site. The company provided its own lumber and had to buy only nails, hardware for the doors, glass for the windows and tar paper for the roofs.

The timber towns also had a company store, a post office and a boarding house for single workers, according to the book. Cooks prepared large breakfasts for the workers who began work in the woods long before dawn.

The company, concerned about children's education, built schools and hired teachers. But in later years it shared the costs with the local school districts. Lumber workers were charged 50 cents per month per child attending school.

The sameness of the houses and their new locations could cause problems. The book tells of one sawyer who came home to his house in a new location, patted the woman inside on the rear and discovered he was in the wrong house.

The two traveling towns were named Alikchi and Clebit, although Alikchi also had a couple of other names – 18-Mile and Asberry Brannon. Clebit was believed to be a corruption of the French "Chalybeate," the French word for describing iron content or taste in water, which referred to the water from a spring at the first Clebit site.

At one location, Clebit was called the Camp in the Hole because it was in a hole in a valley.

The population of the traveling lumber camps varied, sometimes being as large as 800.

"There was no shortage of friends and neighbors," former resident Gladys Damron Brock recalled. "It was a very friendly place to grow up, even though the rest of the world would probably look down on us as backward and poor."

Although the traveling towns are no longer traveling, they can be seen in a People of the Forest Exhibit. Other forest events include the Festival of the Forest and the Beavers Bend Folk Festival and Craft Show. Information is available at the Forest Heritage Center at (580) 494-6497.

135

Crime couple no strangers to state

Bonnie Parker, who died with her partner in a hail of bullets in a police ambush on a Louisiana road, lived in Oklahoma before she met Clyde Barrow and joined him in blazing a path of crime across the Southwest.

And the bandits' last big crime – the killing of a constable – was in Commerce, where Parker lived before she moved to Dallas. There she met Barrow at a restaurant where she was a waitress. During the next four years, they killed at least 13 people – mostly law enforcement officers – and spent time in Oklahoma either robbing or hiding out.

The criminal careers of Barrow, 25, and Parker, 24, who were the most dangerous public enemies of that era, ended May 24, 1934, when they were killed by Texas Rangers and Louisiana law enforcers. They were tipped off by Henry Methvin, the killers' partner in crimes, whom they were supposed to meet at his father's house in Arcadia, La.

Barrow and Parker were each struck by at least 50 bullets, the Tulsa World reported the next day.

When the shooting began, Barrow kicked open the door of the car the two were in and attempted to fire back but died before he could pull the trigger of his gun. Parker, who had been eating a sandwich, had a machine gun on her lap, but she died before she could point it.

The law enforcers had hidden in bug-infested bushes and tall grass for more than seven hours as they waited for Barrow and Parker to drive past in a stolen 1934 Ford V-8. Ivan Methvin, the father of Henry Methvin, pretended to be fixing a flat tire as the killers went by. They offered to help him, but he waved them off and signaled to the officers.

As the killers' car approached, an officer ordered them to halt. When the order was not heeded, all six officers fired, not stopping until their guns were empty. The officers fired at least 167 bullets, a World story said.

"They gave the bandits the same medicine they had meted out to their victims," the story said.

Officers found arms and ammunition in the car along with a saxophone and sheet music. Barrow apparently played the sax when he wasn't tinkering with his guns. Their arsenal had two riot guns, three submachine guns, eight automatic pistols, a .38-caliber revolver and 2,000 rounds of ammunition. Officers also found two magazines, one of detective stories, the other romance stories.

Parker was born in Caney, Kan., north of the Oklahoma-Kansas border, and lived in Commerce in her early teens,

Tulsa World archives

Clyde Barrow and Bonnie Parker were romanticized as "Bonnie and Clyde," but there was little romance in their murderous crime spree through Oklahoma and other states.

according to a World story published after she was killed. She was married at 15 to Roy Thornton, who was sentenced to 60 years in prison for robbery.

When she met Barrow, it was infatuation at first sight, and the two became partners in crime. Shortly after they met, Barrow was sentenced to prison for burglary, but he escaped after Parker smuggled in a gun to him. He was recaptured and sent to prison. Paroled in 1932, he rejoined Parker, and their crime career resumed.

Their last crime, about six weeks before they died, was the killing of Constable Cal Campbell at Commerce, where they apparently planned to rob the bank.

Campbell and Commerce Police Chief Percy Boyd went to investigate "a carload of drunks" stuck in a ditch west of town. Instead they discovered Parker, Barrow and Methvin, who opened fire, killing Campbell.

The trio took the wounded Boyd captive and took him along on a foray into Kansas. They bandaged his wounded hand and released him in Fort Scott, Kan.

After the two were slain, authorities towed their car into Arcadia with Barrow's head hanging out the driver's window and Parker's head between her legs, just as she had died. While headed to town in a 150-car caravan, the wrecker stopped at a school to let the children look.

The bodies were laid out in an embalming parlor in the rear of a furniture store but eventually were rolled out to the sidewalk in front to prevent the store's wares from being scratched by people who wanted to see the bodies.

In return for Methvin's aid in setting the trap for Parker and Barrow, other states agreed to not prosecute him.

Oklahoma, however, wasn't among them.

Methvin stood trial in Miami in Ottawa County for killing Campbell. He was convicted and sentenced to die in the electric chair. The sentence was commuted to life in prison, but Gov. Leon C. Phillips later pardoned and released him. He apparently was never in trouble with the law again.

A movie about the killers won an Academy Award and helped create a legend about them, but it bore little resemblance to the truth.

The ambush ended a crime spree that Parker and Barrow knew could end in only one way: death.

True to that prediction, Barrow and Parker went down together – but their bodies were buried in separate cemeteries in Dallas.

Semi-centennial soggy, but crowded

Oklahoma's semi-centennial was celebrated in Tulsa in June 1957 with a spectacular pageant – a week later than planned but still six months before the state's 50th anniversary.

The event had been planned to begin June 1 but heavy rain forced cancellation of part of the event, a demonstration of aerial acrobatics by Air National Guard pilots, and a week's delay in a production called Tulsarama.

A downtown parade opening the celebration continued as scheduled although some of the floats were pulled out and at least one high school band rode in a school bus, but the majority took part as planned. Parade officials said the thousands who stood through the intermittent downpours "formed one of the largest crowds ever to see a Tulsa parade."

The scheduled Saturday night opening of the seven-day Tulsarama historical pageant at first was postponed until Tuesday night because the track at the fairgrounds grandstand where it was to be performed was ankle-deep in water. But the rain continued and the opening was postponed until June 8.

Air Force Reserve Col. Robert Creamer, chairman of the jubilee's aerial events, said, "We prayed for an end to the drought but we forgot to say 'amen.'"

Meanwhile, 11,000 square feet of steel mats commonly used during World War II to establish emergency air strips were borrowed from Tinker Air Force Base and laid over a covering of chat at the fairgrounds track to provide a solid footing for the performance.

A capacity crowd of 7,000 jammed the grandstand for the June 8 opening of the two-hour performance by about 2,000 actors, who told the story of Oklahoma and Tulsa. But the rain wasn't over. The pageant had to be canceled twice during the next week and was extended for two days after its

OFFICIAL PROGRAM

TULSARAMA

☆

CORONATION CEREMONY

☆

TULSARAMA!

☆

T-TOWN TOM TOM

☆

PATRONS

☆

SPECIAL EVENTS

☆

DAILY PROGRAM

☆

A dramatic historic spectacle by the
TULSA GOLDEN JUBILEE INCORPORATED
AND THE CITIZENS OF TULSA

TULSA FAIRGROUNDS
JUNE 1-8, 1957
Eight-Fifteen Each Evening

Managing Director: James W. Kling   Producer: George S. Elias

Activities Coordinator: Robert Wayne Powers

Technical Director: Harry Graf   Associate Director: Madge Graf

Administrative Secretary: Lucille D. Powers

Original Scenario by Dr. Herb O. Brayer

A J O H N B. R O G E R S P R O D U C T I O N

**TULSARAMA! is based on historical outline and slight changes have been made to meet demands of staging and dramatic effects.*

University of Tulsa McFarlin Library

The official program of Tulsarama was part of the city's celebration of the 50th anniversary of statehood, the semi-centennial.

scheduled closing. Between 5,000 and 7,000 attended most of the shows.

The pageant began with a scene depicting the visit of Washington Irving to this area in 1832 and included episodes about the Civil War, the Trail of Tears when Southeastern American Indians were relocated to what became Oklahoma and the coming of the first railroad.

To add realism, a herd of cattle was driven across the stage and a locomotive pulling one car chugged in on railroad tracks in front of the audience.

The pageant included old wagons, buggies and plenty of horses and featured perhaps 300 square dancers in one scene.

A group of nine narrators provided voices for the actors and told the story of Tulsa and Oklahoma from a control booth behind the scene.

An estimated 15,000 attended the eight-day performances of another semi-centennial production that was called "Dancing Moccasins," which wasn't affected by the weather because it was performed inside the Fairgrounds Pavilion.

Other events during the celebration included queen selections, Faith of Our Fathers Day, Pioneer and Homecoming Day, Industrial Progress Day, Ladies Day, Young America Day, All Sports Day and Greater Oklahoma Day.

Philbrook and Gilcrease museums also had special exhibits.

A 36-page special section filled with pictures and stories about the history of Tulsa and Oklahoma was published in the May 30 Tulsa World to tell readers about plans for celebrating the semi-centennial, which was originally scheduled to begin that day.

Although many aspects of the state's history were featured, none of the stories revealed why the semi-centennial was being celebrated in June. Statehood day was Nov. 16, 1907.

Clothing drive benefited Koreans

When Herman J. Smith of Ponca City was in Korea fighting his third war, winter was colder than a Kansas blizzard and he was concerned about thousands of Koreans, many of them children, with little or no clothing to protect them.

He wrote to his wife, Louise, asking her to go through the stock of the clothing store they owned and to send whatever she didn't want to keep in the store's inventory. He thought it might make life a little brighter for some Koreans.

Before she could send the $500 worth of clothing she selected, the word got out in Ponca City; schools and civic clubs got into the act.

By early January 1952, Smith had received $16,000 worth of clothing – 76 large bundles containing 9,000 items such as winter playsuits for children and warm overcoats for adults. And the packages continued arriving.

Smith's "Operation Warm Clothes" was under way.

Tulsa World archives

Herman J. Smith of Ponca City was hailed as a hero in Seoul, South Korea, where he started "Operation Warm Clothes" while serving in the Korean War.

"You can drain the treasury of the United States and not do democracy as much good as we are doing here," Smith happily told a reporter while sorting a roomful of clothing.

He and friends from Fifth Air Force headquarters, where Smith, then a major, was serving as protocol officer, and Seoul Mayor Kim Tae Sun began distributing the clothes at two of the seven milk stations in Seoul. There refugees waited in line for hours to get their daily rations of rice porridge or thin rice soup – the only nourishment they would receive for 24 hours.

"The waiting line at the milk stations usually has 700 persons at any given time," Smith told a reporter in Seoul. "But at the sight of our friendly gesture, about 2,000 assembled in a few minutes, all ages from babies to old people too feeble to walk.

"In each case we had to turn away hundreds empty-handed."

Smith, who was mayor of Ponca City when he was called to active duty for the Korean War, was amazed at the response to his letter home. It was seen by Joe Goldenstern, an oil tank manufacturer and an old friend, who wanted to help.

Then the schools and the local chapter of the American Business Clubs got into the act. Before long, Smith's group had distributed five tons of clothing that had been collected in Ponca City.

Smith was hailed as a hero in Seoul, where Mayor Kim gave him a key to the city and several medals. His clothing drive didn't end when he left Korea in August 1952 after being promoted to lieutenant colonel. After his return to Ponca City, he led a drive that collected 12 tons of clothing that was shipped to Korea.

It also wasn't the end of Smith's philanthropy. He and his wife made a home for Kitty Kim, 23, who had been Smith's interpreter during his clothing giveaway, and Laura Lee, 19, while they attended college at Northern Oklahoma Junior College at Tonkawa.

The Smiths later arranged scholarships for six other Korean students, four girls and two boys.

The Korean War was the third for Smith. He enlisted in the Army as a private toward the end of World War I. He was in the Army Air Corps in World War II and patented what he called a "Port-a-PX," which he described in civilian terms as a flying department store.

"We could fly in and set it up in about 20 minutes," he explained.

Smith and his wife had operated Smitty's clothing store since 1929, with his wife taking over full management during his military service during World War II and Korea. For 20 years before he was called to active duty in Korea, Smith and his wife had rented a theater for Christmas parties for Ponca City children, sometimes attracting 3,000 youngsters.

One year during the Depression, he charged each child one potato apiece and received enough potatoes for 100 families on Christmas Day.

Smith also coached a girls' basketball team to a 1919 national championship and worked as a referee in state and regional tournaments until retiring in 1938 – "the year I began wearing glasses; that was the time to quit."

After returning from Korea, Smith joined several others in battling to have the Kaw Dam and reservoir built.

"People here and in Washington told us it would never be a reality, but after 98 trips to Washington, we got it," Smith said in 1982.

Smith died in 1989 at the age of 91.

Wounded officer became judge

A former Illinois congressman who studied law and was admitted to the bar while recuperating from a wound suffered in the Civil War became one of the first judges for Indian Territory.

He was John Robert Thomas, who enlisted as a private in the Indiana Volunteer Infantry in 1863, was wounded in November 1864 when he was hit by a bullet that remained in his upper thigh for the rest of his life, causing pain and inconvenience. He had been promoted to captain by the time his company was mustered out of service.

The wound didn't hamper his activities, except to force him to walk with a cane.

While recuperating, he studied law in the office of a family friend and was admitted to practice in 1869. Thomas served three terms in Congress, personally knew every president from James Garfield, who was elected in 1881, to Woodrow Wilson, who was elected in 1913. Thomas appeared to have the inside track to be named secretary of the Navy in 1889 and 1897; was vice chairman of the constitutional committee of the proposed state of Sequoyah in 1905; and would have become its first congressman if Indian Territory had become the state of Sequoyah instead of being combined with Oklahoma Territory into the one state of Oklahoma.

Thomas was elected to the House of Representatives in 1878 from the Illinois 20th district when Rep. John A. Logan was named to the Senate. While serving in the House for 10 years, Thomas became chairman of the Committee of Naval Affairs and was so knowledgeable that he was referred to as the father of the American Navy.

He made many speeches stressing the need for a powerful sea force and even designed a 235-foot monitor with 10-inch armor that was adopted at a cost of $1.5 million, according to a 1974 Chronicles of Oklahoma article.

When President Benjamin Harrison was elected, most political observers predicted that Thomas would become the secretary of the Navy because of his knowledge and interest in naval affairs, and many sent congratulatory letters to him. His picture was even published on the front page of a Washington newspaper along with others who were named to cabinet posts.

But the post went to another person because of machine politics, according to the Chronicles article.

"When I came into power," Harrison explained later, "I found that the party managers had taken it all to themselves. I could not name my own cabinet. They had sold out every place to pay the election expenses."

A similar situation occurred in 1897 when William McKinley became president and was expected to appointed Thomas as secretary of the Navy – an appointment that went to someone else.

It may have been a consolation prize when Thomas was appointed as one of the first U.S. judges in Indian Territory to relieve the heavy caseload of the court in Fort Smith.

Less than a year later, the Muskogee Phoenix reported that Thomas had disposed of more than 700 cases. In two of the cases Thomas had sentenced the defendants to hang; in two he had sentenced the accused to life imprisonment; and "in the opera house the other night in the presence of a large audience, he passed sentence on the entire Spanish navy and condemned it to everlasting defeat."

Judicial appointments at that time were for four years, and Thomas was not reappointed because of the patronage power of Illinois Rep. Joe Cannon.

At the Sequoyah constitutional convention in Muskogee in 1905, Thomas and three other men were nominated to represent the district in Congress – if the state were formed. Thomas received the largest vote in a subsequent territorywide election.

Thomas was killed by escaping prisoners at the penitentiary in McAlester on Jan. 19, 1914, while he was sitting in the warden's office. Six others, including the three armed prisoners who were trying to escape, also were killed.

Thomas' home in Muskogee, later occupied for the rest of their lives by his daughter, Carolyn, and her husband, Grant Foreman, is a tourist attraction today. The Foremans wrote more than 20 books on Oklahoma history and were inducted into the Oklahoma Hall of Fame.

Oklahoma Historical Society

John R. Thomas of Muskogee is pictured in this undated photo. Thomas became one of the first judges for Indian Territory.

'Champion' of old folks controversial

Ora J. Fox considered himself a champion of old people and used radio, newspapers and direct mail of letters to beg for $1 and $5 donations from old age pensioners, telling them that their pensions were in jeopardy unless he could raise money to save them.

Others, such as a House of Representatives committee, had a different opinion of the controversial figure in Oklahoma politics for three decades.

That committee accused Fox in 1949 of perjury, chicanery, demagogy and hypocrisy in his dealing with the elderly.

Those charges were contained in an eight-page report issued by the panel after a six-week investigation that involved questioning of 40 witnesses. But Oklahoma County Attorney Granville Scanland declined to file criminal charges because, he said, no violation of criminal statutes was shown in six volumes of testimony.

The committee also urged that the investigation continue in the next session but that didn't happen. It also urged that a law be enacted prohibiting definite promises in return for money, which the next session did.

It wasn't the first time the organizer and president of the Welfare Federation Inc. had been investigated and accused. He was indicted in 1945 on a charge of embezzlement of $10,000 belonging to associates of the committee but was cleared of that grand jury allegation when the prosecuting attorney said there was no evidence to prove that he kept the money.

The grand jury had alleged that he received the $10,000 to defray expenses on a lobbying trip to Washington for which his expenses were less than $500 and he kept the balance.

Fox organized his Welfare Federation with himself as president in 1936 and began making his appeals for $1, $2 or $5 from old age pensioners, telling them he needed the money to keep their pensions from being stopped or cut. Pension checks at that time ranged from $46 to $50 per month.

Fox, born in Tennessee, came to Oklahoma when he was 18. He became a political power in 1931 when he served as marshal of the Corporation Commission and as vice president of the National League of Senior Citizens.

Practical politicians in the 1940s and '50s considered Fox's support essential until his poor showing in two state-

Tulsa World archives

Ora Fox used small contributions from pensioners to build a political base in Oklahoma, but it turned out his influence was not as powerful as many thought it was.

wide races proved otherwise. He finished fourth in a race for the Democratic nomination for Senate in 1948 and sixth in a 1954 run for the Democratic nomination for governor. Most of his support came from counties where welfare was the leading industry.

When Sand Springs banker H.C. Jones ran for the Democratic nomination for governor in 1946 he was told his first move should be to give Fox $25,000. "I didn't think anyone's support was worth that much," Jones said later.

Fox supported Roy J. Turner, who won the nomination and the election.

During his gubernatorial campaign, Fox told voters that he and his wife would not live in the governor's mansion because she would feel uncomfortable there. The mansion, he said, would be used to house visiting dignitaries.

He also promised he would knock down the gates of the Turner Turnpike with a bulldozer and would make the highway a free road. He didn't explain how the state would pay the turnpike's bonded debt with no revenue coming in from tolls.

Fox continued his campaign for higher pensions for the elderly – and his pleas for money – until a few months before his death in July 1962 at the age of 60. Another time when he appeared before a legislative committee, he took the Fifth Amendment 30 times.

Fox's bookkeeper testified before the 1949 committee that he had taken in $79,200 the previous year but she said she didn't know where the money went. Fox told her it was "a personal matter," she said.

The professional old folks' friend acquired considerable real estate in Oklahoma City and claimed homestead exemption on at least two houses in addition to his personal residence in 1952, although homestead exemption is limited to a taxpayer's personal home.

He later told a reporter that if he filed on more than one house, it was by mistake because he wasn't trying to avoid paying taxes. "They don't amount to very much anyway," he added.

He said he acquired the real estate by trading and buying while he and Mrs. Fox worked at Douglas Aircraft Co. during World War II.

Trio's escape attempt ends with 7 dead

Three prisoners armed at first with one pistol forced their way into the warden's office at the Oklahoma State Penitentiary at McAlester on Jan. 20, 1914, in a desperate attempt to escape.

The convicts – China Reed, Tom Lane and Charles Kuntz – finished their day's work in the prison tailor shop about 4:30 p.m. and went to the administration building, where they told a turnkey they needed to see the parole officer. They beat and shot the turnkey, took his keys and headed for the warden's office.

Oklahoma Historical Society

Oklahoma State Penitentiary in McAlester was the scene of a murderous 1914 escape attempt by three prisoners. Seven people were killed, including the three convicts.

Frank Haikey, another life termer who was in the warden's office with Thomas, his attorney, said the trio shot down Thomas without provocation. He told prison officials that Thomas raised his hands and stood when ordered by the convicts and was shot as he started to sit in response to another order by the three.

Their bid for freedom ended in death about 15 minutes later and a half-mile away as they fled in Warden R.W. Dick's buggy, chased by guards on horseback, one of whom fired the shots that killed them. The guards also had to shoot the warden's horse because, frightened by the gunfire, it kept running as the convicts lay dead in the buggy.

Seven people died in the deadliest prison break in Oklahoma history. Besides the convicts, the dead were John R. Thomas, a Muskogee lawyer who was waiting in the warden's office for a conference with Dick; Assistant Deputy Warden D.C. Oates; Guard Sgt. R.D. Godfrey; and H.H. Drover, an expert in the Bertillon identification system.

The convicts kidnapped Mary Foster, the prison's telephone operator, to use as a shield and to prevent her from calling for help. She was wounded in the thigh by the only shot fired in the prison yard before the trio commandeered the horse and buggy.

"It was the most horrible 15 minutes of my life," she said from her hospital bed.

The fleeing prisoners shouted for other inmates to join them, but none was that desperate for freedom. Some cheered them on, however.

"You'll never take us alive," Reed yelled at the pursuing guards as he stood in the buggy and fired at them. Moments later, shots fired by guard R.J. Ritchie killed the three convicts.

Rather than join the flight, some prisoners helped the guards. A life termer who had just returned from town in the custody of a guard told the guard, "I'm with you; get me a gun," but it was against the rules to let prisoners have guns.

Another convict repaired the telephone switchboard, which the convicts had disabled, and called guards at the prison lake to warn them that the convicts were headed their way. He also called McAlester police, but by the time they arrived, Ritchie, who had been at the lake, had killed the felons.

Some speculated that the convicts killed Thomas because they thought he was the warden.

Early reports said each of the convicts had a gun, but prison officials said later that the three had only one gun until they acquired another from a guard they killed. The trio's gun had been bought in McAlester a few days earlier. Authorities thought at first that a trusty bought the gun and smuggled it into the prison, but the merchant who sold the gun and another customer who was present couldn't identify any of the trusties who had been in town that day.

Prison officials then speculated that the gun had been smuggled into the prison by a friend of one of the convicts. A strange car had been reported near the prison the night before the break.

"As far as we have been able to learn, no blame can be attached to the prison management or any of the prison officials," Dr. A.K. West, the chairman of the prison control board, said. "We find that nobody was connected with the affair except the three men who were killed and some accomplice who furnished the gun."

No record could be found to show whether the person who furnished the gun was ever identified.

The three convicts were known as "bad men." Reed, who had a long criminal record in Indian Territory, was serving a two-year term for horse theft. Lane, of Pauls Valley, had 18 months left on a five-year sentence for forgery, and Kuntz, whose hometown was not reported, was serving 40 years for bank robbery in Roger Mills County.

Thomas had been a former U.S. representative from Illinois and had been one of the first federal judges in Indian Territory. Oates had been a Rough Rider with Teddy Roosevelt in the Spanish-American War.

Drover was a photographer in McAlester who had recently accepted a job as a Bertillon expert at the prison. The Bertillon identification system, devised by a French officer named Alphonse Bertillon, relied on body measurements and other characteristics. It was replaced by fingerprinting.

LBJ grounded female astronauts

Jerrie Cobb had the right stuff but was the wrong sex.

She passed the same physical and psychological tests as the Mercury 7 astronauts – America's original spacemen selected in 1959 – and was expected to become the first woman to fly into space.

Just days before she and a dozen other women in what was called the Mercury 13 program were scheduled to report to the Naval Aviation Center in Pensacola, Fla., for further training, the program was abruptly canceled.

Cobb and another of the potential female astronauts appeared before a subcommittee of the House Committee on Science and Astronautics in July 1962 to plead for women to be allowed to make space flights.

But the panel decided that training women astronauts would hurt the space program. Cobb complained the next year that chimpanzees were treated better than humans after she learned that chimps had flown into space – she even offered to take the place of a chimp on a later flight.

Jerri Truhill, another member of the Mercury 13 program, told National Public Radio recently that then-Vice President Lyndon Johnson, the head of the National Aeronautics and Space Council, ordered the end to the women's training, according to records obtained through the Freedom of Information Act.

"From the beginning, we were walking all over great, giant egos of the men," Truhill said. "They didn't want us; they didn't want women around."

As a consolation, NASA hired Cobb as a consultant. But after going two years without being consulted, she quit that job as well as her job as the chief test pilot for Rockwell International's Aero Commander in Oklahoma City. She then turned her flying skills another direction – as a medical and agricultural missionary in the Amazon jungle, an area she knew from her days as a ferry pilot.

"It's more remote than the moon," the devout Christian pilot told a Tulsa World reporter on a visit home in 1979 to participate in the 50th anniversary commemorative race of the Women's Air Derby.

"I would be interested in going to the moon if the government wanted to send a woman, but I'm very happy with what I'm doing," she said. "I feel I can accomplish more in South America.

"I've got it all," she said, adding, "I'm one of the most for-

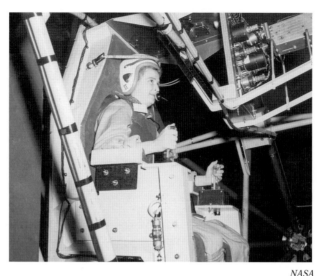

NASA

Jerrie Cobb, shown in a NASA training device, never got her chance to go into space, but created a role for herself as a missionary in South America.

tunate people in the world."

Cobb used her small airplane to deliver supplies to primitive Indian tribes and make surveys for future missionary work. She would fly over the jungle until she found natives waving and calling to the "great bird." She would then land near a neighboring tribe with which she was acquainted and ask someone to introduce her to the new group.

She also spent a lot of time on her hands and knees planting and teaching the natives how to plant beans, squash and okra in the mud near the river.

Cobb was born in 1931 in Norman, and she graduated from Classen High School in Oklahoma City, but she considered Ponca City home – her parents moved there after she graduated from high school. She began learning to fly at age 12 in a biplane, instructed by her father, a retired Air Force lieutenant colonel. She soloed and got her license at 16, the earliest age possible. She skipped college to become a commercial pilot and in 1955 was the only woman in the country working as a ferry pilot, delivering airplanes all over the world.

She was inducted into the Oklahoma Hall of Fame as the most outstanding female pilot in America, the Oklahoma Aviation and Space Hall of Fame and the Women in Aviation International Pioneer Hall of Fame. She also was nominated for the Nobel Peace Prize in 1981.

She established several world records for speed, altitude and distance. She has written several books and has been the subject of others.

Cobb's friends organized a foundation in Texas to provide information about her life and her mission in the Amazon, which has continued for 44 years. It explains that she is a devout Christian who believes in living and sharing her faith in God and uses her ability as a pilot to bring help and hope to isolated people throughout the Amazon basin.

Cobb explains on the foundation's Internet site that "every penny, nickel, dime and dollar from the foundation goes toward buying seeds and medicines for the primitive Indians. I have always believed in supporting myself, and insist The Bird does the same.

Some things cause her to feel distress as she lies in her hammock at night but, she wrote, "the next day the sun does shine, The Bird and I take off on another jungle flight, and, yes, I realize that many are dying, many are suffering, but some are living because we are here."

E.L. Goodwin: champion for blacks

The grandson of a slave, Edward Lawrence Goodwin moved at age 10 to Tulsa, where he operated a clothing store, published a newspaper, practiced law and finally started a catfish farm after he retired from his other occupations.

Throughout those varied careers, he was considered a spokesman and leader of the city's black community. He always found time for civic, church, lodge and other projects to better his community and his people.

A Tulsa World editorial written after Goodwin's death in 1978 called his life a Southern black version of a Horatio Alger story.

Goodwin, who was born in Water Valley, Miss., where his father operated a grocery, came to Tulsa with his family in 1912 and graduated from Booker T. Washington High School. He went to Fisk University in Nashville, Tenn., where he played football and earned a degree in business administration.

Following graduation, Goodwin moved to St. Louis, where he operated a shoe store for three years before he returned to Tulsa to open a haberdashery. He later became Tulsa County's first black case worker for the state welfare department.

Goodwin bought The Oklahoma Eagle – a black newspaper that his wife later said had one Linotype machine and a lot of debts – in 1936, installed modern machinery and for a time published weekly newspapers in Okmulgee and Muskogee as well as Tulsa.

Goodwin became known for writing vigorous editorials and for promoting education for blacks. He once told a reporter that knowing how to manage money is more important than receiving a flood of federal dollars.

He said that the Small Business Administration's program of providing low-interest loans to minorities to help get them started in businesses had shown few successes because the loan recipients had no economic background.

Tulsa World archives

When Edward Lawrence Goodwin bought The Oklahoma Eagle in 1936, it had, in his wife's description, one Linotype machine and a lot of debts. He built it into a successful weekly newspaper.

He said an improved economic picture was needed to better the plight of blacks but stressed the need for education, which he said must be coupled with common sense.

The Eagle has remained in the hands of the Goodwin family. Goodwin's sons, Edward L. Goodwin Jr. and James O. Goodwin, are its co-publishers.

Thirty years after his graduation from Fisk, the elder Goodwin went back to school, this time at the University of Tulsa, where he received a law degree. He opened a law practice with Charles Owens, a one-time police officer who is now a district court judge in Oklahoma City.

Owens became Oklahoma's first black judge when he was appointed in 1969, and he became the state's second black elected judge, winning a November 1970 election in Oklahoma County. Tulsa claims the first black elected judge, the late Amos T. Hall, who won his position in the August 1970 Democratic primary. No Republican had filed for the post.

Goodwin's leadership and participation in various civic functions earned him several honors, including an honorary doctor of laws degree from Oral Roberts University, a citation from Mayor Jim Hewgley in 1966, a citation for organizing the north Tulsa district for the Community Chest (now United Way) campaign in 1949 and induction into the Oklahoma Journalism Hall of Fame and the Tulsa Historical Society Hall of Fame.

After he retired from his newspaper and his law practice, Goodwin started a third career that required more physical labor than the others did – he opened a catfish farm on property in the former Alsuma district, near 51st Street and Mingo Road.

"I found it amusing and fun and at the same time I saw people paying to catch fish," Goodwin recalled. "I was close to retirement, and I thought this might be a way to pick up a little extra money."

Would the buried Belvedere make it?

It's nearly time to claim my new 50-year-old car.

I don't know the exact date I'll receive that 1957 Plymouth Belvedere but it will be sometime during the state's centennial celebration in 2007.

You might remember my car. It's the one that was wrapped in a special coating, placed in a huge plastic bag and buried in a concrete time capsule on June 15, 1957, on the Tulsa County Courthouse lawn. It was part of the city's semicentennial celebration that also included a production called "Tulsarama."

The car belongs to the person (or that person's heir) whose 1957 guess is closest to the population figures of 2007. And, of course, that's me.

The car will be a step up from the car my wife and I owned then. It was a Plymouth Belvedere station wagon.

"It ought to last 1,200 years," a representative of the Orchard Paper Co. of St. Louis said in 1957. "It should be in driving condition" when it is dug up and unwrapped, he added.

E.S. French, the Orchard representative, said heavy kraft wrapping paper coated with a chemical called dicyclohex-ammoniumnitrate and backed with aluminum foil was used to swath the inside and outside of the car before it was slid into the plastic bag and heat sealed in a partial vacuum.

The car was buried along with 10 gallons of gasoline, some motor oil, a case of beer, copies of the Tulsa World and The Tulsa Tribune, statements written by Gov. Raymond Gary and Mayor George Norvell, an outline of that year's Chamber of Commerce projects and movies of the Tulsarama activities, all sealed inside a steel capsule inside the vault.

The car's glove compartment was stocked with what organizers considered the typical contents of a woman's handbag – a bottle of tranquilizer pills, 14 bobby pins, a compact, a package of cigarettes, matches, two combs, an unpaid parking ticket, a tube of lipstick, a package of gum, a plastic rain hat, facial tissues and $2.73.

Life and Look, weekly news magazines of that period, and MovieTone News, which produced news films for movie theaters, covered the event.

I missed the car burial because I was on active duty at Fort Chaffee, Ark., with a Tulsa Army Reserve unit. But my guess should be on the microfilm inside the steel capsule.

I'll also receive the proceeds of a $100 trust fund – maybe. That qualifier is because the trust fund was set up with Sooner Federal Savings and Loan Association, which was liquidated in the 1990s.

My guess no doubt was closest to the 2007 population. What was it?

I can't remember.

Editor's note:
After Tulsa's buried 1957 Plymouth Belvedere was unearthed, officials tried to figure out who had the best claim

Tulsa Historical Society

Whose car is it? In 2007, officials determined the winner the Plymouth Belvedere that was buried in the Tulsa County courthouse lawn in 1957 during the semi-centennial ceremony shown above.

on the car. It was to be the winner of a contest, conducted 50 years ago as part of the state's semicentennial, predicting Tulsa's 2007 population.

The 1957 Plymouth was extricated to much fanfare and thousands of spectators on June 14, 2007, from a vault under the Tulsa County Courthouse.

The closest guess for Tulsa's 2007 population was found to have been made by Raymond Humbertson of Cumberland, Md., who died in 1979.

His wife, Margaret Humbertson, died nine years later. The car went to the heirs of Mrs. Humbertson.

A career Marine, Humbertson apparently was passing through Tulsa on his way from the West Coast to his home in western Maryland when he entered the contest.

The car was in poor condition because of water damage, but still some Tulsans were distressed about the contest, and wanted the car to stay in the city.

Tulsa's worst flood one to remember

Tulsa's worst flood hit on the first day of the 1984 Memorial Day weekend, the holiday that would begin the summer season for many.

No one was concerned early that Saturday night when rain began falling, but four hours later the light rain had become a deluge that eventually measured up to 15 inches in some areas of the city. Flash flooding took 14 lives, drove more than 3,500 families from their homes and caused damage estimated at more than $180 million.

It resulted in the development of Tulsa's flood-plain management and warning system that became a model for other cities and drew praise from the Federal Emergency Management Agency.

The U.S. Weather Service Internet site calls that storm "arguably the most significant urban flash flood in Oklahoma history." It said the rainfall may have been more than the 15 inches it measured "because many gauges overflowed."

Some of the worst flooding was along Mingo Creek in east Tulsa and Dirty Butter Creek in north Tulsa. Most other areas of the city also were affected.

An unoccupied house was washed into the middle of a street in west Tulsa and nearly all low-lying areas were flooded. Helicopters, boats and four-wheel drive vehicles were used in record efforts.

A woman sitting in the dark on her kitchen cabinet with her dog to stay above the rising water in her house saw a man floating through her backyard but was unable to assist him. Cars floated out of driveways, their headlights eerily shining through the water. Many came to rest stacked up on top of each other; others lodged in the limbs of trees. The water rushed through convenience stores, washing away their stocks of canned food and drink. Tulsans were warned not to use the contents of those cans because they would be contaminated, in spite of attempts to sterilize them.

About 28,000 cases of beer stored at a warehouse had to be destroyed because of contamination to the outsides of the cans and bottles.

Dozens of police cars were flooded at the police garage.

Tulsa World archives

Rescuers use a canoe to help a flood victim near 29th Street and Cincinnati Avenue following the 1984 Tulsa flood.

A foot of rain fell in six hours at Skelly Drive and Interstate 44, twice what the storm sewer system could handle, said James Carpenter of the city street department. When the storm drainage system isn't capable of carrying water, it forms ponds, he said.

Water in most areas of the city receded rapidly and by Sunday afternoon, only the destruction caused by swirling water remained.

A National Guard unit from Sapulpa was called to help in search-and-rescue operations because Tulsa guardsmen were at summer camp. Red Cross and Salvation Army workers drove through the damaged areas distributing food, water and cleaning materials to homeowners trying to salvage what they could.

Flooding was a part of Tulsa's history dating back to 1908, a year after statehood, when the Arkansas River went out of its banks and caused $250,000 in damage – a great sum in those days.

Millions of dollars had been spent on flood control projects that had not stopped the rampages over the years, including a Memorial Day 1976 flood that left three dead and caused damage estimated at $40 million to more than 3,000 buildings. That flood came from a 10-inch deluge centered over the headwaters of Mingo, Joe and Haikey creeks.

According to a City of Tulsa Internet site, a new approach to flood response was born within days after the 1984 flood.

A new flood control program included relocation of 300 flooded homes and a 228-pad mobile home park, $10.5 million in flood control works and $2.1 million for master drainage plans. A stormwater utility fee was established by ordinance in 1986 to operate the program.

The program resulted in Tulsa having the lowest flood insurance rates in the country, according to a FEMA announcement in 2000. Among the activities that earned Tulsa the rating were the acquistion of nearly 1,000 flood-prone properties and the preservation of more than a quarter of its floodplain as open space, strong building codes and community outreach to advise residents of flood hazards and mitigation solutions.

Memorial Day 1945 was a special one

The fighting in Europe had ended earlier that month but it was still raging in the Pacific when Tulsans paused for a day to remember their war dead in ceremonies similar to those across the nation.

The main ceremony on that Memorial Day of 1945 was at Boulder Park, 18th Street and Boulder Avenue, where 51 white wooden crosses had been erected to represent the 622 Tulsa County soldiers, sailors and Marines who had been killed in action during World War II. That park now is known as Veterans Park.

There wasn't enough room to plant a cross for each of the dead, but the names of all 622 were displayed in the flower-covered small white memorial building erected by Veterans of Foreign Wars Post 577.

Tulsa World archives

In May 1945, wooden crosses in Boulder Park memorialized the 622 Tulsa County soldiers, sailors and Marines who had died in World War II.

More than 1,200 people filled all the folding chairs that had been set up for the program that featured patriotic music by the American Legion band, the burial ceremony used by the VFW post at the graves of veterans, placing of wreaths and flowers at each cross and speeches by Mayor Olney Flynn and Army Lt. Col. Harry L.S. Halley, a judge who had served in both World War I and World War II. Hundreds more went to the event but left after putting flowers on the crosses.

Thousands had visited Oaklawn, the oldest cemetery, Rose Hill and Memorial cemeteries earlier on that May 30 to put flowers on the graves of relatives and friends. A special service was held at the Catholic cemetery.

It was a Wednesday, long before Congress changed the holiday to the last Monday of May with the National Holiday Act that took effect in 1971, long before Memorial Day became part of a three-day weekend marking the beginning of summer.

Gasoline was still rationed – most car owners got three gallons a week – but many Tulsans used some of their fuel to take advantage of their middle-of-the-week day off to have picnics at Mohawk Park, take dips in the Newblock Park swimming pool and walk through the Woodward Park rose gardens that were blanketed in blooms.

That 1945 ceremony was so special because Germany had surrendered on May 7. Allied forces were gaining the upper hand in the Pacific, where fighting continued until after the U.S. dropped bombs on Japan on Aug. 6 and 9.

Memorial Day of 1919, called Decoration Day here, had a special significance. Units of the 36th Infantry Division made up of Oklahoma and Texas soldiers arrived in New York after service in Europe during World War I. Oklaho-ma Gov. J.B.A. Robertson and a large group of Tulsans greeted the returning doughboys.

Many gathered at Fourth and Main streets and took a trolley to Oaklawn cemetery at 11th Street and Peoria Avenue for a ceremony. Another ceremony was held at Owen Park.

Memorial Day ceremonies in the 1930s typically began at Memorial Hill, Cincinnati Avenue and Easton Street, where a flagpole had been erected in a park, and moved later to Oaklawn Cemetery. The Memorial Hill ceremonies were handled by the Daughters of the American Revolution and cemetery rites were handled by the VFW, American Legion and United Spanish War Veterans.

Fifteen Civil War veterans attended the 1929 ceremonies but their ranks had thinned to fewer than 10 the next year and to two by 1933. That was the last year they were mentioned in news reports about the events.

Memorial Day was first observed May 30, 1868, after Gen. John Logan, national commander of the Grand Army of the Republic, proclaimed it as a time to honor Union and Confederate soldiers by placing flowers on their graves in Arlington Cemetery.

Southern states honored their war dead on a different date until after World War I, when the event was changed to honor all war dead, not just Civil War's. Several Southern states still honor Confederate dead on a different date.

The holiday was called Decoration Day until about 1882, when Memorial Day was first used but the two names were used interchangeably for many years. Memorial Day became the official name by federal law in 1967, although Decoration Day continued in use then and today. In many places in the South, Decoration Day is observed on the Sunday before Memorial Day. It also became common to decorate the graves of all relatives, not just veterans.

Beginning in 1922, veterans' organizations sold paper poppies, symbolizing the flowers that grew in Flanders Field during World War I, for Americans to wear on Memorial Day; the poppies later were made by disabled veterans and worn to commemorate veterans' sacrifice.

Most Americans have now forgotten the meaning and traditions of Memorial Day – it's now just a holiday.

The VFW said in a 2002 Memorial Day message: "Changing the date merely to create three-day weekends has undermined the very meaning of the day. No doubt, this has contributed greatly to the general public's nonchalant observance of Memorial Day."

Killer flood took town by surprise

The Washita River was almost dry at noon but became a raging torrent a few hours later, sweeping away dozens of farm houses, many with their occupants still inside.

An unexpected torrential rain upstream caused the flooding that killed 17 and left 200 to 300 people homeless near Hammon in Roger Mills County on April 4, 1934. Damage was estimated at $625,000.

"We were all asleep in the house, and the wind and rain were so loud we could not hear the floodwater coming," 16-year-old Hurl Adams told a reporter after being rescued.

His mother and six sisters died when their floating house was dashed against a road near a bridge downstream.

Heavy rain started about 2 p.m. in Cheyenne, reached Strong City two hours later and arrived at Hammon about 6 p.m., but a weather observer discounted the possibility of flooding. He said the river's crest would not reach Hammon until the next morning.

But the rain continued, and by 9 p.m. the North Canadian River several miles north of Hammon had risen from a small trickle to 200 feet wide and to flood stage in an hour, with water backing up into Minnehaha, Dead Woman and Wild Horse creeks. The Washita also rose rapidly.

The total rain at Hammon during the thunderstorm was only about 2 inches, but 14 inches had fallen upstream during a six-hour period, swelling the usually lazy, narrow river to two miles wide. Along with houses, the flood washed away miles of railroad tracks and thousands of head of livestock and caused massive crop damage.

Water burst into the Adams farmhouse near Hammon about 11 p.m. The family tried to hold the water out by stuffing up the cracks between boards.

"We couldn't stop it, so we all climbed into the loft," Hurl said.

"Then with a lurch, the house was swept from its foundation and raced down the flood. We rode along for about half a mile in the attic while Dad and the boys (his two older cousins) were trying to get Mother and the girls onto the roof."

U.S. Soil Conservatiion Service

In this aerial view, the Washita River is out of its banks east of Hammon in 1954, 20 years after a more devastating flood that killed 17 and left 200 to 300 people homeless. In 1954, Congress approved the Watershed Protection and Flood Prevention Act that resulted in construction of a series of upstream flood-prevention dams.

The house suddenly hit something and shattered. He, his father, a younger brother and the cousins made it to the bridge, but the mother and girls didn't.

The bodies of the mother and five of the girls were found within a short time. A skull found several miles downstream two years later was identified as that of a 6-year-old Adams girl who had been swept away in the water.

Willy Beene, another farmer, told about his family's riding a mile downstream without knowing it. The 31-year-old farmer said the family was asleep when the flood came, "but I woke up when the house tipped to one side."

Beene figured the foundation had washed out, and, with a foot of water in the house, he put the bed on four chairs to keep it out of the water and put his children on the bed.

"All this time we were floating down the river, but I didn't know it until later," Beene said. The storm was making so much noise, he didn't realize that they were moving.

When the house hit a hill and stopped moving, the family members climbed out and were rescued.

A series of upstream flood-prevention dams was finally built after Congress approved the Watershed Protection and Flood Prevention Act in 1954.

"These watershed dams protect lives and property, yet few even know they exist," U.S. Rep. Frank Lucas, R-Okla., said in 2004. "That's probably because the only time people notice a dam is when it fails. Because they don't fail, the possibility today of a disaster like that of the Hammon flood seems more like a movie storyline than something that could actually happen."

But Lucas warned that many of the 2,000 dams built in Oklahoma have reached the end of their expected 50-year lifespans and that without proper upkeep, a failure could occur.

"We need to ensure that scenes like the Hammon flood are always a part of our collective memory but never a part of our future," he said.

Territorial day scholar nearly forgotten

Alexander Posey had studied English but didn't speak it until he was 12 – and then only to appease his father.

But he became a newspaper editor, a scholar, a teacher, a poet, a historian, a statesman, a humorist, a politician, a linguist and a philosopher. He earned national fame as an English-Indian dialect writer with his Fus Fixico letters.

Few today probably remember his writings. He may best be remembered, at least in the McIntosh County area, because of his death – he drowned in the flood-swollen Canadian River in a pool of water along U.S. 69 north of Eufaula. The area was afterward known as Posey Hole until it was inundated by Lake Eufaula.

Posey was born in 1873 near Eufaula. His mother, a full-blood Creek of the Wind clan, was named Pahas Harjo and used the English name of Nancy Phillips. His father, Lewis H. Posey, claimed to be part Creek, which most doubted. He was Scots-Irish and was reared by a Creek family after his parents died.

The elder Posey insisted that his son speak English, a language the boy had studied and could understand but was afraid to speak. At 17, Alexander Posey was sent to Bacone Indian College in Muskogee, where his passion for writing developed while he worked on the student publication, setting type. He was a commencement speaker at his graduation.

Posey entered tribal politics by being elected to the Creek House of Warriors in 1895 and became well known to members of the Five Civilized Tribes. A year later, he became the superintendent of the Creek orphan asylum in Okmulgee and later the editor of the Indian Journal at Eufaula, where he began writing letters under the pseudonym of Fus Fixico.

Fixico seemed to be an Indian without much education but plenty of savvy who usually fractured English while waxing eloquent:

"Experience neve intends her lessons to be forgotten. Her percepts come like the white man into Indian Country – to stay."

Posey's Fixico writings didn't do much to remedy the situation in which Indians felt helpless as the Dawes Commission was closing the affairs of the Five Civilized Tribes, but they showed his wit.

Posey referred to Indian Commissioner Tams Bixby as "Tams Big Pie." U.S. Sen. Robert Owens was "Col. Robert L.Owes-em" and Interior Secretary Ethan Hitchcock was "Secretary Its-cocked." After statehood in 1907, he referred

Beryl Ford collection

Now barely remembered, Alexander Posey was a pre-statehood newspaper editor, scholar, teacher, poet, historian, statesman, humorist, politician, linguist and philosopher.

to Gov. C.N. Haskell as "Gov. C.N. Has-It."

The letters were designed as conversations among Wolf Warrior, Kono Harjo and Tookpofko Micco, old Creek men, and men prominent in Indian Territory affairs – Bixby, Hitchcock, Owens and Haskell.

The Fus Fixico letters were reprinted in many newspapers throughout the United States and in the London Times.

After Posey became the editor of the Muskogee Times, he began to work with the Dawes Commission to help with the orderly transitation from tribal to state government. He was an asset because he spoke Creek and was trusted by the Indians, many of whom wanted no part of the commission's works.

When a group of Indian leaders called a constitutional convention in 1905 with plans to apply for statehood, Posey was made secretary of the group. He was largely responsible for writing the constitution and suggesting the name "Sequoyah" for the proposed state.

Posey decided later to return to the Eufaula newspaper. He and a friend, R.D. Howe, a lawyer, started for Eufaula on a train that stopped because a bridge was washed out north of Eufaula.

Posey, Howe and two other men borrowed a boat to ford the stream, but they lost their oars and the boat was swept into a whirlpool and smashed into a fence. The men jumped out of the boat and Howe ran two miles to Eufaula for help. When he returned two hours later, Posey, who was afraid of the water, was clinging to a tree limb.

The rescue party threw a rope to him, but he was too weak to hold on. He drowned, as did one of the other men in the boat.

Ironically, one of Posey's last poems, "My Fancy," indicated a premonition of his drowning fate:

Why do trees along the river
lean so far over the tide?
Very wise men tell us why, but
I am never satisfied:
And so I keep my fancy still
That trees lean out to save
The drowning from the clutches of
The cold, remorseless wave.

Posey's body was found downstream two months later. He was buried in Muskogee's Greenhill Cemetery beneath a stone on which is carved the words of another of his poems.

Politico unsurpassed campaigner

Victor Wickersham shook hands with thousands of constituents and invited them to "write, wire or call" if they had problems – not just during campaigns but any time.

He was known to friend and foe alike as being without parallel as a campaigner.

That helped the Mangum Democrat win nine nonconsecutive terms in Congress and four in the Oklahoma House of Representatives, beginning in 1941 and extending to 1988, a month before he died.

Wickersham was never a power figure in Washington or Oklahoma City. He drew criticism from national columnists, faced bogus-check charges, had squabbles with the IRS, became a millionaire from real estate and later filed for bankruptcy.

He was best known as a campaigner. And a handshaker. And a complainer about the pay given to members of Congress.

In addition to shaking hands, Wickersham annually mailed thousands of pieces of literature, including pictures of himself, to constituents. In 1962, he mailed 853,000 pieces of mail using his congressional franking privilege.

He also was known for his campaign promises. In 1960, his Republican opponent said: "If he gets all the roads paved that he says he will get paved, the district will be one slab of concrete. And if he gets all the lakes he has promised, the slab will be under water."

Wickersham made junkets, most at taxpayers' expense and some unauthorized, to places around the world where he thought he might capture headlines. He made slides and movies of his travels and visited schools in his district to speak and show his films to students.

The fact that the children were not old enough to vote did not bother him; his theory was that in time they would be of voting age and would remember him at the polls.

Before he left politics, the same thing could have been said about those children's grandchildren. The span between his first race, for Congress, and his last race, for the state House, was more than 50 years.

During World War II, Wickersham obtained lists of where the servicemen from his district were stationed and tried to visit all of them on junkets – usually to the consternation of

Tulsa World archives

Victor Wickersham, shown with his wife, Lorene, was sworn into the Oklahoma House of Representatives on his 82nd birthday, Feb. 9, 1988. The Mangum Democrat was elected nine times to Congress and four times to the state House.

their commanding officers, who had to find them for the meetings.

Wickersham always insisted on eating lunch with the servicemen rather than with their officers. "We did our best to break down the Army caste system," he told a reporter later.

Wickersham was born on a farm in Arkansas. He became a deputy county clerk in Mangum in 1936 and made his first political races, losing both, in 1938 and 1940 against U.S. Rep. Sam Massingale in the old 7th District. Massingale died, and Wickersham won a special election in 1941 to fill out his term.

He was re-elected in 1942 and 1944, defeated in 1946, returned to office from 1948 through 1954, voted out in 1956, defeated again in 1958 but re-elected again in 1960 and 1962. He lost in 1964 and failed in two comeback attempts, in 1966 and 1968.

His political career was not over, however, as voters sent him to the Legislature in 1971. He held the seat for eight years.

After his first election loss, Wickersham made money in Oklahoma City by buying houses that were in the way of oil operations, moving them and fixing them up for resale. He later sold real estate in Washington and at one time owned a one-quarter share of the Huckins Hotel in Oklahoma City, which he said "turned out to be an unfortunate business venture."

Wickersham, who once listed his wealth at $1.5 million, filed for bankruptcy in 1973, listing liabilities of $2.5 million, for which he blamed the hotel. He said he was burdened with its debts although "I was not the manager and was not in charge of the fiscal affairs of the business."

Wickersham returned to the state House in 1988, winning an election to succeed a legislator who had resigned. He was sworn in on his 82nd birthday; members sang "Happy Birthday" to him after he took the oath as the House's newest and oldest member, slightly more than a month before he died.

He said at the time that he was capable of performing his legislative duties.

"I had a doctor examine me a few months ago, and he said 'You can do anything a 60-year-old man or a 10-year-old mule can do,'" he said.

Outlaw left crime for lecture circuit

Texas Jack, who claimed to be the last of the "47 most notorious outlaws" of Indian Territory days, spent the last years of his life lecturing that crime doesn't pay and selling booklets about his life.

Texas Jack was Nathaniel Reed, who came to Indian Territory as a young man, fell in with border desperadoes and robbed a Santa Fe express train, the beginning of a life of crime that ended when he was shot in a later train robbery.

By then, according to his boasts, he had pulled four train robberies, seven bank jobs, three stagecoach holdups and two gold bullion robberies. When he died in 1950 at the age of 87, his body testified mutely to direct hits by 14 bullets, although he had claimed that he had been shot 27 times.

As with many old-time badmen, Reed's stories probably were enhanced as he aged. For instance, he claimed to have helped the Dalton boys in their dual bank robberies in Coffeyville in 1892 and to have been involved in the infamous gunfight at Ingalls in 1893. No reports of those events indicate he was involved in either.

Although he had been shot many times, it was the wounds he suffered in a train robbery near Muskogee in 1894 that convinced him he was in the wrong business – and he spent the rest of his life telling others that "crime doesn't pay."

Texas Jack claimed to have ridden with the Dalton gang, Bill Doolin, Henry Starr and other members of the Southwest's bandit fraternity. He was believed to have helped "Cherokee Bill" escape from prison in Fort Smith in the 1880s.

He was best known for his part in the robbery of a Katy train at Blackstone station north of Muskogee Nov. 13, 1894, the job that marked the turning point of his life.

He told a Tulsa World reporter in 1936 that he had been an outlaw for eight years when he and a gang of badmen stopped the passenger train at Blackstone – and were met by gunfire from deputy marshals who were on the train. Reed said the gang had received a tip the train was carrying a large shipment of cash but knew nothing about the deputies.

Tulsa World archives

Nathaniel Reed, also known as Texas Jack, reformed from a life of crime after getting shot during a train robbery near Muskogee.

Because both Katy and Missouri-Pacific passenger and express trains had been robbed, Katy officials had placed deputies on all its trains going through the area.

As planned, Reed threw a switch that forced the train onto a siding where the robbers began firing their guns into the air to scare the passengers and train crew. They were preparing to use dynamite to open the express car. But their fire was returned by the four deputies on the train, killing one of Reed's gang and wounding Reed.

The train robber was able to jump onto the train and go through the cars, forcing passengers to put their valuables into a sack before he and his gang fled in a hail of gunfire.

Reed was hit by rifle fire from Deputy Bud Ledbetter. After a few miles, Reed said, the pain was so severe he gave some of the loot to his partners and took refuge on a blanket under a rock ledge until an Indian woman found and cared for him.

After recovering from the wound, Reed went to Arkansas to stay with a brother and decided it was time to quit his life of crime. He wrote to Judge Isaac Parker, known as the hanging judge, who gave him probation in return for his testimony against the man who had planned the robbery but didn't participate.

"I was given strength to lisp the truth," Reed told a World reporter. In his latter years, he said his relief at being freed rather than hanged was immense and he was proud that he outlived his criminal days and "made good on the narrow road."

He also carried around a letter from Ledbetter that declared the famed deputy recognized Reed as a man he shot and his signed parole from Judge Parker.

Reed wrote a small book about his criminal life, "The Life of Texas Jack" that he sold for 25 cents while touring the country with a series of wild West shows and later while sitting on a folding chair on Tulsa streets, where he also lectured anyone who would listen about the folly of a life of crime. A copy of that book is listed on the Internet for $1,500.

Reed, who was not the only early badman known as Texas Jack, had no relatives when he died.

Tulsa native painted Capitol's 'Visions'

"An artist is the only thing a man can claim to be and nobody can prove he ain't."

Artist Wilson Hurley, a native Tulsan who lives in Albuquerque, N.M., recalled those words of the late humorist Will Rogers when Hurley was inducted into the Tulsa Historical Society Hall of Fame in 2001.

He recalled that "Will Rogers was at our supper table and my dad told him 'We have a budding artist at our table.' " And that was Rogers's reply, the artist said.

No one who has seen his work would try to prove Hurley "ain't" an artist. He was called the world's best living landscape artist by Ann Alspaugh of the Oklahoma Arts Council at the Hall of Fame induction ceremony.

With good reason.

Hurley created five mural-size works for the 1,200-seat special events center at the Cowboy and Western Heritage Museum in Oklahoma City – a room he always called "my room." He also created four Oklahoma landscape paintings called "Visions of the Land" for the second floor of the Capitol.

"I am not out after social significance or political statements or anything other than how beautiful the world is," Hurley told a reporter in 2002. "There is enough ugliness we see in the world by accident. I think art is something that should be pleasant, uplifting and joyful to people."

His centennial suite representing the four quadrants of Oklahoma's landscape certainly qualify as something pleasant, uplifting and joyful.

The four paintings are "Spring Morning Along Muddy Boggy," representing southeastern Oklahoma; "Autumn Woods North of Tahlequah," representing the northeast; "Sunset at Roman Nose," from the northwest; and "A Storm Passing Northwest of Anadarko," from the southwest.

Hurley visited many areas of the state for inspiration for his paintings, the first of which came from visiting his grandmother's grave in the Lehigh Cemetery, near where his father was born in the Choctaw Nation.

"There in the spring," Hurley said, "the low clouds were racing northeast and the sun was swinging great shafts of light across the shadowed land. One burst of light washed over a field of yellow flowers like an all-forgiving and comforting blessing, an affirmation of how beautiful Oklahoma is."

He stood on a bridge near Anadarko and painted in light rain to capture what he called a storm's "terrible beauty"

Associated Press

Betty Price, head of the Oklahoma Arts Council, listens as artist Wilson Hurley speaks at an unveiling of his work, "Spring Morning Along Muddy Boggy," at the state Capitol in 2001.

for his storm painting.

In addition to the National Cowboy and Western Heritage Museum, his works are in collections throughout the country, including Gilcrease Museum and the Whitney Gallery of Western Art. His landscapes have been compared to Albert Bierstadt, Thomas Cole and Thomas Moran.

Hurley, who was inducted into the Oklahoma Hall of Fame in 1995, was named the state's 10th Cultural Treasure in 2002 at the 27th Governor's Arts Awards ceremony in Oklahoma City. The Cultural Treasure designation honors native Oklahomans who have made an impact in the arts, achieving national and international acclaim for their work.

Hurley's father, the late Army Maj. Gen. Patrick J. Hurley, was inducted into the Tulsa Hall of Fame at the 2001 same ceremony. Gen. Hurley, a Tulsa attorney, was President Herbert Hoover's secretary of war and later served as President Franklin D. Roosevelt's representative to the Middle East and as ambassador to China.

Born in Tulsa in 1924, Wilson Hurley always had an interest in art, an interest that was stifled by his father but encouraged by his mother, Ruth Wilson Hurley. The family moved to Washington in 1928 when Patrick Hurley joined Hoover's Cabinet. Wilson Hurley attended elementary and high school in New Mexico but always considered Tulsa his hometown.

Wilson Hurley graduated from West Point in 1945 with a degree in military engineering, was a fighter pilot near the end of World War II, got a law degree from George Washington University in 1951 and was a forward air controller in Vietnam.

He wasn't satisfied with life as an attorney and closed his law practice in the mid-1960s to become a professional painter. It was five years before he sold a painting.

He once told an interviewer that he became aware of his mortality while writing a will for a dying client – and decided to become a full-time painter.

When Betty Price asked Hurley in 1999 about painting a series of Oklahoma scenes for the Capitol, he told her, "I'm 75, and I only have 10 good years left. I'm not spending five of them painting the state Capitol."

He eventually agreed to produce the four landscapes at a cost of $125,000 each as a part of a state Capitol master plan.

'Aunt Rachel' offered help to needy

The word "welcome" was painted on a step at the entrance to the home of a pioneer Creek Indian widow known simply as "Aunt Rachel."

That's not unusual. Many houses have door mats that say welcome, but, in this case, it wasn't just a word on a mat or painted on a step. Aunt Rachel was serious about her welcome and became well-known for feeding the hungry, caring for the sick and wounded, and taking in homeless children.

It was said that no one who went hungry to her door was ever turned away unfed, no homeless child who sought lodging was denied and no visitors who stopped in were met with ungraciousness.

Travelers were welcome to stay a few days at her house to rest and eat, not to mention drink from the sofka jug on the back porch.

That even included outlaws such as the Dalton brothers, who may have been killers to the rest of the world but to Aunt Rachel were "just hungry boys."

Aunt Rachel was the widow of prominent Creek Indian George B. Perryman, who at the time of his death in 1899 at the age of 52, owned more land than any other Indian in the Creek Nation. His land covered from what today is about 19th Street and Peoria Avenue south to 51st Street and east to Lynn Lane road, according to an early World story.

Rachel Alexander, whose father was a Confederate soldier who was killed during the Civil War, and George Perryman were married in 1868 and at first lived in a small log house south of Tulsa that soon became too small. In 1870, they built what became known as "the white house" near what today is 41st Street and Troost Avenue.

Tulsa's first post office was located in that 10-room house with George Perryman's brother, J.M. Perryman, as postmaster for $15 per year. George Perryman helped his brother Josiah with the mail.

It also was where the Perrymans first kept open house for the countryside, according to an early reporter. Twenty-three unrelated children lived there along with the Perrymans' own seven children.

She frequently drove in her buggy to help care for the

Beryl Ford collection

Rachel Perryman, known to most as "Aunt Rachel," became well known for feeding the hungry, caring for the sick and wounded and taking in homeless children.

sick and injured. Many sick and wounded men lived to tell how they had been nursed back to health by Aunt Rachel. She could be seen often in the woods or on prairies gathering herbs in her apron with which to brew health-giving tonics.

The Perrymans left that house to move into town to send their children to Tulsa's first public school. They built a large two-story house on the block between Fifth and Sixth streets and Main Street and Boulder Avenue that they called High Hill. Aunt Rachel boarded some of the city's first school teachers and others there.

Aunt Rachel always said she was not educated. By that she meant that she couldn't read or write. She also didn't speak English. One of her daughters always acted as an interpreter when she was communicating with whites.

Although she didn't speak English, she understood it and was known to speak some English under stress. Her longest sentence was believed to have been when her grandson died. She told a friend "George's baby . . . stuck nail in foot. . . bad sick . . . died."

After Perryman died while on a business trip to Muskogee, Aunt Rachel had many offers to buy the land and finally sold it to a man named J.E. Hayward of Danville, Ky. Hayward told her he wanted the property badly and to name the price she wanted for it. She set the price at $65,000.

When payment time came, she told her attorney she wanted the money in cash – she didn't have much faith in checks. Hayward gave her the cash, which she put in her apron pocket and walked across town to her bank as calmly as if carrying that much money was an everyday event.

Hayward sold the southwest corner of that block to the county as the site for the Tulsa County Courthouse that was built in 1910. County offices remained in that building until 1955 when a new courthouse was built two blocks west. The old courthouse building was torn down in 1960.

The High Hill house was moved to 13th Street and Elwood Avenue where it still stands.

Aunt Rachel moved back to the white house and died there in 1933. She and George are buried in the Perryman Cemetery near 32nd Street and Utica Avenue.

Fierce 1974 storm killed 13 in state

Tornadoes and floods left 13 dead June 8, 1974, in several state cities and towns, including in Tulsa, where one person was killed and damage was estimated at $29 million.

Ten residents of a Drumright nursing home were killed.

No estimates were available for damage in other areas, but it was extensive.

The severe weather first struck Oklahoma City, damaging the National Weather Service building at Will Rogers World Airport. A tornado touched down minutes later in a residential area about four miles from the airport.

Tulsa World archives

Residents walk along Peoria Avenue in the Brookside area following a tornado June 8, 1974. The storm killed one Tulsan and destroyed homes and businesses across the city.

Ray Myers, the store's off-duty manager, was at home when he heard a radio report about the storm. He called the store, instructing employees to escort shoppers to the cooler. The storm razed the store, leaving only the meat cooler.

One customer had wanted to go out to the parking lot to get her husband out of a camper, but a store employee convinced her they didn't have time. The storm flipped the camper, injuring the husband, but not seriously.

The funnel at Drumright had touched down about 5 p.m. about two miles southwest of the city and stayed

Two storms tore through Drumright, killing 10 people, destroying 94 homes and damaging 115 more. The storm also knocked out the city's water system.

The Tulsa storm, then called the worst in the city's history, killed one person, damaged more than 1,300 homes and caused at least $29 million in damage, primarily in the city's west, southeast and east. It was the first time in more than 60 years of weather agency records that anyone had been killed by a storm in Tulsa.

Oral Roberts University's administration building and a $2 million aerobics center scheduled to open the next month on campus sustained severe damage, as did Riverside Airport, Don Thornton Ford and a Warehouse Market grocery.

Between 25,000 and 30,000 Tulsans were still without power 24 hours after the storm. Others storms that day hit Prattville, Sperry, Tahlequah, Chelsea, Olive and Westville. A woman was killed in Chelsea when a flash flood washed her car off the highway into a ditch. Floodwaters killed a 2-year-old boy in Tahlequah.

The storm damaged 14 Tulsa school buildings.

About 30 people survived by taking refuge in the meat cooler of the Warehouse Market at 4915 S. Union Ave.

on the ground for 3½ miles. Staff members at the nursing home had moved the patients into a hall shortly before the tornado blew off the roof, causing the rafters of the dining hall to fall onto the tables.

Other storms that day killed five people in Emporia, Kan., and two drowned in a 12-inch deluge at El Dorado, Ark.

An Arkansas State Police trooper said police received a telephone call about a bridge that had washed out, forcing a motorist to turn his car around. The driver came upon another washed-out bridge and then collided with a gravel embankment caused by the heavy rain, killing him.

Many people in the El Dorado area had to be rescued from their flooded cars after fleeing their flooded homes.

The same storm system caused a small plane to crash near Fort Worth, killing the pilot and five passengers. The 60,000-foot-tall thunderheads flipped the plane upside down, then bashed it into the ground with such force that it was nearly buried.

The pilot had told a tower controller that the storm had flipped the plane but that he was trying to bring it upright and find a hole through the storm.

Statue unveiling filled U.S. Capitol

An estimated 2,000 Americans showed their love for Oklahoma humorist Will Rogers by filling the U.S. Capitol Rotunda for the unveiling of a statue of the man "who never met a man I didn't like."

"Never before has there been anything like it in Washington," a reporter wrote for the June 7, 1939, Tulsa World.

The 800 seats in the rotunda were filled more than an hour before the ceremony began. Capitol employees had been dubious that a capacity crowd would be on hand. But the crowd was there.

Top Washington officials who for years were the targets of Rogers' sharpest barbs but who laughed with him mingled with the hundreds who crowded into the building to watch the unveiling of Oklahoma's tribute to her favorite son. The crowd included Vice President John Nance Garner, Oklahoma's first two U.S. senators -- Thomas Pryor Gore and Robert I. Owen – scores of national figures and members of Rogers' family.

Tulsa World archives

A statue of Will Rogers was unveiled in the U.S. Capitol on June 7, 1939.

Senators and representatives from states far from Oklahoma stood against the walls or beside other statues or on the stairs and on a balcony overlooking the statue. They refused to leave until the ceremony was over.

David Lynn, the Capitol architect, said there had never been such a crowd or such a ceremony in the building.

Eyes were filled with tears from the moment Rogers' sister Sally McSpadden of Chelsea pulled the cord that lifted an American flag off the statue until after Luther Harrison, a Daily Oklahoman editorial writer, delivered a eulogy. The bronze statue was created by Jo Davidson, an internationally known sculptor.

Rogers' wife chose Davidson to make the statue because of his talent and because he was a close friend of Rogers, who called him the "headhunter" because he was always looking for heads to sculpt and because of his unruly hair and beard.

Working from an assortment of photographs, Davidson made the sculpture in clay and sent it to Brussels, Belgium, to be cast in bronze. The casting in the rotunda was funded by a state appropriation.

Davidson paid for a second casting of the statue and donated it to the Will Rogers Memorial in Claremore.

Harrison told the crowd that Rogers' statue was added to Statuary Hall with the "unqualified approval of an admiring nation." He said the statue of George Washington was the only other one that had national approval.

The ceremony was preceded by a concert by the Navy band, which played many of Rogers' favorite songs, including "Old Faithful."

Kentucky Sen. Alben Barkley, who later became the vice president in the Truman administration, accepted the statue for the nation, saying that Rogers was one of only 12 private citizens of the 76 men whose statues were in the hall. Oklahoma Gov. Leon C. Phillips presented the statue.

Harrison said: "A man who undertakes to eulogize Will Rogers is subject to considerable handicaps. Will Rogers has been eulogized by some of the most capable orators in America and the world.

"I have a lurking suspicion that the kindly spirit of Will Rogers is behind a curtain poking fun at my feeble attempts to pay him tribute."

Harrison, who collapsed on the speakers' stand after the eulogy, traced the origin of Statuary Hall and pointed out that some of its statues were of men who were not nationally known.

Tulsa World Editor N.G. Henthorne, a member of the state's Will Rogers Commission, told the crowd that the other Oklahoman represented by a statue in the hall also was not an elected official.

"Twenty-two years ago today at this same hour, citizens of Oklahoma came to Washington and gave to the nation a statue of Sequoyah, native American, Cherokee Indian and author of the Cherokee alphabet," Henthorne said.

"Today we come again to present a statue of another great citizen whose character and reputation and record long since reached beyond the confines of our state and who was known throughout the world, wherever the printed word was read or pictures were shown.

"In presenting this statue of Will Rogers, it is with pride of fellow citizenship with such an illustrious son, but in humbleness and in realization of great loss."

Rogers and Wiley Post, the record-setting pilot from Oklahoma, were killed when their plane crashed Aug. 16, 1935, near Point Barrow, Alaska. They were on a flight around the world and had just taken off for what was supposed to be a 10-minute trip to Point Barrow.

Rogers was Oklahoma's favorite son in 1939, and he still retains that ranking in 2007, reaffirmed recently by the Oklahoma Poll, sponsored by the Tulsa World and KOTV, channel 6.

Almost 60 percent of the 752 people surveyed April 27-30 for the poll named Rogers as their "favorite Oklahoman of all time." The star athlete Jim Thorpe was a distant second at 9 percent.

Victims' kin saw McVeigh execution

Timothy McVeigh, who had been sentenced to death for killing 168 people in the April 19, 1995, bombing of the Alfred P. Murrah Federal Building in Oklahoma City, was executed by lethal injection at the federal penitentiary in Terre Haute, Ind.

The 33-year-old McVeigh did not make a last statement before he died on June 11, 2001, but issued a copy of the 1875 poem "Invictus" by William E. Henley. "Invictus," which means undefeated, ends:

I am the master of my fate;
I am the captain of my soul.

Many believed that poem showed McVeigh was arrogant and defiant to the end – typical of the attitude they had witnessed throughout the years of trial and appeals for the killer who drove a rented truck packed with 7,000 pounds of explosives to the front of the federal building, lit a fuse and ran to his getaway car a few blocks away.

The explosion destroyed about a third of the building and damaged more than 300 other nearby buildings.

A state trooper stopped McVeigh on a traffic violation near Perry about 90 minutes later, and the bomber was arrested after the trooper found McVeigh was carrying a concealed weapon.

Authorities did not connect him with the bombing until two days later when, luckily, he was still in the Noble County Jail.

The killer had been linked to the bombing by the vehicle identification number on the axle of the exploded truck. Authorities had traced it to a Kansas City rental agency, where McVeigh had rented it.

Shortly after McVeigh was arrested for the bombing, his Army buddy, Terry Nichols, was identified as the person who helped build the bomb. Nichols surrendered two days later.

McVeigh and Nichols had served in the Army in the Gulf War but developed anti-government leanings. McVeigh said he acted to avenge government conduct at the Branch Davidian event near Waco, Texas, and at Ruby Ridge, Idaho.

McVeigh was convicted and Judge Richard Matsch sentenced him to death. The conviction and sentence were upheld in several appeals.

Tulsa World archives

Timothy McVeigh, convicted of killing 168 people, was executed June 11, 2001. McVeigh's bombing of Oklahoma City's Alfred P. Murrah Federal Building is the deadliest act of domestic violence in U.S. history.

Co-defendant Nichols was convicted in both federal and state courts for his role in the bombing and was sentenced to life in prison without the possibility of parole. A third conspirator, Michael Fortier, testified against McVeigh and Nichols and was sentenced to prison for failing to warn authorities.

Bungling of records by the FBI delayed McVeigh's scheduled execution for five days. A stay was granted after McVeigh's defense team was handed 3,135 documents that the FBI should have provided more than three years earlier during McVeigh's trial.

But McVeigh told his lawyers to stop their appeals. He spent his last day writing letters, phoning farewells to family and friends, and visiting with his attorneys.

The execution was witnessed by about three dozen in viewing rooms at the penitentiary and 232 victims and survivors of victims in a closed-circuit transmission to a federal building in Oklahoma City.

Many of the witnesses at the closed-circuit viewing said they were disappointed that McVeigh was allowed to die peacefully while his 168 victims met violent, agonizing ends. One said "I just wish it had been a little harder on him."

McVeigh's execution was the first of a federal prisoner for 38 years.

A few days before McVeigh's execution, one of his attorneys said, "McVeigh was sorry that 168 people had to lose their lives. He takes no joy in that. But in his view, in his opinion, in pursuing his goal, it was necessary."

In a biography co-written by Buffalo (N.Y.) News reporter Lou Michel, McVeigh referred to the 19 children who were killed in the bombing as "collateral damage."

"Today, every living person who was hurt by the evil done in Oklahoma City can rest in the knowledge that there has been a reckoning," President Bush said in Washington.

One of the witnesses at the closed circuit event was Raymond Washburn, who operated the snack bar in the Murrah building and who is blind. His comment about the bombing probably best summed up the feelings of the other survivors and relatives:

"McVeigh is a coward and a low-down bastard."

Navy sub Batfish lived up to her name

Oklahoma's navy consists of only one vessel – and it's on dry land in Muskogee.

Today, the submarine called Batfish that once sank a ship in Tokyo Harbor and earned a distinguished record during World War II is a tourist attraction.

The killer sub is located in War Memorial Park near the Port of Muskogee and is the focus of periodic reunions of sailors who served on the sub and other submarines.

It wasn't the boat originally intended, and it isn't located at the planned site. And Muskogee isn't the place you would expect to see a submarine – even on dry land.

During the war, it earned a Presidential Unit Citation and nine Battle Stars in addition to honors received by her crew: a Navy Cross, four Silver Stars and 10 Bronze Stars. Those awards came from the Batfish's seven World War II patrols during which she sank three enemy submarines and 11 other enemy vessels – to live up to her namesake batfish, a ferocious West Indies fish.

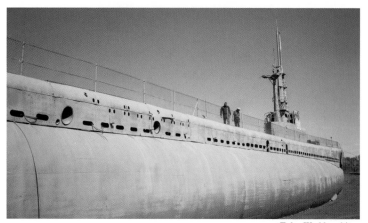

Tulsa World archives

The USS Batfish wasn't meant to end up as a Muskogee tourist attraction, but that's what happened.

The idea of obtaining a submarine as a tourist attraction came from Jim Inhofe, then a state senator, who wanted to create the state's first naval war memorial in Tulsa. He introduced a bill in the Legislature in 1969 that created an 18-member Maritime Advisory Board empowered to obtain a submarine called the USS Piranha and to issue $200,000 in bonds to finance the project.

But when the advisory board went to a naval facility at Port Orange, Texas, it discovered that the Piranha was in bad repair, but the USS Batfish was in good condition and had an attractive wartime record. So, the board chose the Batfish for the tourist attraction.

The state at one time tried to give the ship back to the Navy because of the costs and problems incurred in moving it up the Arkansas River to Oklahoma and its permanent site. But the Navy didn't want it.

The Batfish started up the Mississippi and Arkansas rivers on a flotilla of barges. The Batfish is 312 feet long,

which turned out to be too long to navigate the sharp turns of the Verdigris River from Muskogee to near Tulsa.

That problem was solved when Sen. John Luton of Muskogee signed on as co-author of Inhofe's bill and got the sub's destination changed from Tulsa to Muskogee.

Moored in the river, the submarine was opened to the public on July 4, 1972, and attracted an estimated 16,000 visitors before it was closed six months later because of a 35-degree list to starboard.

The Oklahoma Tourism and Recreation Commission voted in March 1973 to ask the Navy to take back the submarine after Gov. George Nigh warned that the sub could slip its mooring and possibly cause damage to the Port of Muskogee docks or the U.S. 62 bridge. But the Navy didn't want the ship. Nigh also said the U.S. Corps of Engineers pointed out that the liability insurance policy on the Batfish had lapsed.

The original maritime board was abolished and its functions were assumed by the Port of Muskogee Trust Authority.

The port authority donated five acres for the memorial park and a canal was built from the river to the park site. When the submarine had been floated to the park, a dike was built along the river bank, the canal was drained and the submarine settled onto the ground for its final resting place.

The cost of moving the boat from the river to the park was paid for by Oklahoma City philanthropist John Kirkpatrick, a retired rear admiral.

The Batfish was launched in 1943 and went to the Pacific Ocean where it sank a minesweeper and a destroyer on its fourth patrol. It destroyed three submarines in four days on its sixth patrol in the Luzon Strait.

She was retired from duty in 1946 but was reactivated in 1952 as a training ship in the Caribbean. She finally was retired and her name stricken from Naval registration in 1969.

Lawyer helped get race riots under control

A black attorney had been in Tulsa only a few months when the race riot of 1921 erupted, but he was able to convince a surging group of black residents they shouldn't invade white areas to set fires.

The riot, which continued into the next day, had erupted after an angry group of whites became a mob planning to lynch a black man because of a rumor that he had accosted a young white female elevator operator.

Buck Colvert (Ben) Franklin shouted until he was hoarse that May 31, 1921, to bring the mob under control.

"Think," he begged. "Two wrongs don't make a right."

He made such a persuasive speech that the group that had gathered in front of Booker T. Washington High School decided against getting gasoline to set fires in white neighborhoods in retaliation for damage to the Greenwood area. It was believed that his action prevented much greater damage from the riot.

After Franklin's speech to the other blacks, he was rounded up with many others and taken to a detention center where they were held while all their belongings were stolen or burned.

Shortly after the riot, Franklin set up his law practice in a tent and drafted a lawsuit aimed at blocking a new ordinance passed by the city commission. The lawsuit eventually went to the state Supreme Court, which threw out the ordinance.

The ordinance would have required fireproof construction in rebuilding the Greenwood area, which would have made the cost prohibitive for blacks. Franklin believed the real purpose of the ordinance was to force blacks to move out of town rather than rebuilding.

Franklin's best-known criminal case was in 1934 when he convinced a District Court judge that black people should be allowed to serve on juries. The trial of his client, R.C. Foster, was the first time a black person was on a jury in Oklahoma. Foster, charged with murder for killing an underworld character, was acquitted.

Born in the Chickasaw Nation in southern Oklahoma, Franklin was the son of slaves. His father was owned by the brother of a governor of the Chickasaw tribe; his mother by Choctaws who treated her the same as a member of their

Tulsa World archives

Buck Colbert Franklin was a Tulsa leader after the race riot of 1921.

family.

Franklin received his first education at a black school founded by white missionaries of the Baptist Church and later attended Roger Williams University in Nashville and Atlanta Baptist College.

After graduating and getting married, Franklin and his wife moved back to Oklahoma to farm, but his interest in law exceeded his interest in farming and ranching. With his education and sharp mind, he was able to pass the bar examination after completing a correspondence course in law.

He opened law offices in Ardmore and Rentiesville, one of the dozens of all-black towns that developed in the late 19th and early 20th centuries. Franklin also served as postmaster for a time in Rentiesville.

But it was difficult for a black lawyer to make a living, especially in a small community, so he moved to Tulsa months before the riot.

Most blacks hired black lawyers only if the other side had a black lawyer. They preferred to hire white lawyers because they believed a black lawyer could not prevail against a white lawyer with a white judge. In his autobiography, Franklin noted that "white lawyers hired black runners to falsely warn black people that black lawyers could not prevail against them."

Franklin, however, was able to prevail in many of the cases he handled after the race riot. He was credited with knocking down the ordinance that would have prohibited rebuilding of the Greenwood area.

Franklin, who was honored by Greenwood residents at a special ceremony when he retired in 1959, died in 1960.

Speaking in Tulsa at the 2000-01 Presidential Lecture Series at the University of Tulsa, historian John Hope Franklin credited his father for his love of reading. "When I wasn't in school, I was at his law office watching him work," John Hope Franklin said. "I guess that's why I read and write for a living."

The younger Franklin, a past president of the American Historical Association, has received many honors. He has been inducted into the Oklahoma Hall of Fame, has been named one of the state's 11 cultural treasures, was named to Oklahoma Historians Hall of Frame and received the Peggy V. Helmerich Distinguished Author Award.

Governor OKs liquor sales in 1959

Oklahomans could begin buying legal liquor by Sept. 1, 1959, Gov. J. Howard Edmondson assured them nearly three months after they voted to make the state wet.

Oklahomans had voted in record numbers on April 7, 1959, to repeal the 51-year-old prohibition law, but they couldn't buy liquor legally until a control bill was passed and put into effect.

More than 700,000 voters cast ballots, approving the repeal issue by a 3-to-1 ratio. As expected, Tulsa County provided the largest margin for the wet victory – 86,600 to 23,700. Oklahoma County voters approved repeal by a vote of 81,000 to 48,000.

The Senate liquor control bill roared through the House like a Sherman tank on June 22, 1959, and was sent to Edmondson, who signed it the next day. Repeal of prohibition was one of the issues he had promoted in his campaign for governor.

And approval of the bill was one of the key issues that needed to be considered before the Legislature could adjourn.

The only hang-up between the Senate bill and the House approval involved the amount of tax, which ended up being $2.40 per gallon.

The bill that cleared the Legislature after nearly three months of study banned public drinking, prohibited price fixing, permitted brand-name advertising and set a deadline of Sept. 1 for legal package sales.

Rep. Jim Nance of Purcell, chairman of the committee that wrote the bill, called it a "people's bill."

"This is the best liquor control bill that has ever been written by any legislature in any state in the union," Nance said. He said the Senate had refined parts of the bill but did not make any substantial changes.

Many thought they should be allowed to buy liquor or import more than a quart immediately after the Legislature's action, but Edmondson said his interpretation was that dry laws remained in effect until Sept. 1 or an earlier date if he issued an executive order.

Edmondson appointed J.M. Hewgley Jr., later a Tulsa mayor, J.L. Jennings of Bartlesville, W.A. "Gus" Delaney

Tulsa World archives

Supreme Court Justice Denver Davison swears in members of the first Oklahoma Alcoholic Beverage Control Board: (from left) W.A. "Gus" Delaney, Ancel Earp, A.C. Link, J.M. Hewgley Jr., and J.L. Jennings.

of Ada, Ancel Earp of Oklahoma City and A.C. Link of Chickasha to the Alcohol Beverage Control Board to write regulations and set up the operation of the board that would supervise stores and sales.

The board had issued licenses to 459 stores in nearly all of the state's 77 counties by the day before sales began. Eighteen wholesale dealers also had been licensed.

"Tomorrow won't really mark any change insofar as the presence of liquor in Oklahoma is concerned," Edmondson said on the eve of legalization. "It will mark the beginning of an era of taxation of intoxicating liquor.

"Therefore, I trust and am confident the people will approach this new era with a sense of temperance and sobriety and this new industry will operate in a reasonable manner."

Many retailers had worked around the clock for several days to get the shelves stocked and their stores ready to open. Some even opened with their stock still in boxes on the floor.

When the day finally arrived, the actual kickoff of repeal seemed almost anticlimactic. Souvenir hunters and curiosity seekers swarmed the liquor stores rather than panting, thirst-crazed, long-denied drinkers. One state official said there probably was less liquor buying in his town that day than at any time in the previous three months.

There was some elbowing into the liquor stores at the 10 a.m. opening but mostly the eagerness was aimed at being "first to buy it legally."

Some customers had difficulty making a liquor purchase in the daylight when they could be seen by everyone. Some sidled into the stores, made their purchases and carried them out in sacks from dry goods or other stores to prevent onlookers from knowing what they had bought.

Repeal also was expected to create a drastic change in the drinking tastes of many. Instead of indulging in bourbon, scotch, gin and vodka, the prohibition dominants, it was expected that many people would develop tastes for fine wines, either domestic or imported.

They did.

Midnight trip took capital to OKC

A dirty shirt hid Oklahoma's state seal and some state records when they were slipped out of the state Capitol at Guthrie for a dead-of-night trip that moved the capital to Oklahoma City.

The clandestine trip was made June 12, 1910, at the direction of Oklahoma Gov. Charles N. Haskell after returns from a statewide election showed Sooners preferred Oklahoma City over Shawnee and Guthrie as the state capital.

Haskell had been in Muskogee, his official residence, the previous day to vote for Shawnee as his preference and had stopped in Tulsa to spend the night at the Brady Hotel when he received the voting results. He organized a special train to take him and several others to Oklahoma City and called W.B. Anthony, his private secretary, with instructions to take the seal to the Huckins Hotel by the next morning.

Anthony was in Oklahoma City after voting at Marlow when he received Haskell's call. He enlisted Secretary of State Bill Cross, Earl Keys, an employee of Cross, and Paul Nesbit, chief clerk in the Governor's Office, to assist with slipping the seal past sheriff's deputies who were guarding the Guthrie building because of a district court judge's injunction against removing the seal.

Keys, Nesbit and Cross were allowed into the building after they told the deputies that they were going after some laundry Anthony had left there. They emerged a few minutes later with Anthony's dirty shirt hiding the seal and records from the Secretary of State's Office.

Anthony said he didn't go into the building because "to do so would have aroused suspicion."

"We left Guthrie about 4 o'clock and arrived in Oklahoma City at 7 o'clock on Sunday morning in what was altogether a very uneventful trip, as compared to what has since been written and said of it," Anthony said.

Anthony took the seal and records to Oklahoma City where he met Haskell at the Huckins Hotel and hung a "Governor's Office" sign on a hotel door, establishing Oklahoma City as the capital.

Tulsa World archives

Gov. Charles Haskell (left) is shown at his desk on the mezzanine floor of the Huckins Hotel after moving the state capital from Guthrie to Oklahoma City in 1910. With him is Bill Cross, Oklahoma's first secretary of state.

There have been many reports over the years about the event, most claiming that Haskell personally retrieved the seal and made a midnight ride to Oklahoma City.

Some reports were that the seal was stolen by someone who leaped from the third floor of the Guthrie building to a waiting automobile and a wild dash with armed guards in pursuit.

At least a half-dozen men claimed in whispered tones that they accompanied the governor on the ride, but Haskell told the Daily Oklahoman several years later that "it was my secretary, W.B. Anthony, who brought the seal to Oklahoma City. Just who was with him at the time, I do not know. But I am quite positive that I was not."

Anthony made the trip in a car furnished by the Oklahoma City Chamber of Commerce.

Several hours after the seal was moved, Haskell signed a document declaring the capital of the 2-year-old state was now in Oklahoma City. He told the Tulsa World, "I have simply done my duty. The capital is now in Oklahoma City."

He also called a special session of the Legislature for December and pushed through a law designating Oklahoma City as the capital.

That wasn't the end of the capital dispute. Several lawsuits were filed in an attempt to force the state to abide by the Enabling Act that had designated Guthrie as the capital at least until 1913. The U.S. Supreme Court ruled several months later that the state could locate its capital where it pleased. Because there was no Capitol, Irving High School served for that purpose for several years.

Anthony served in the Legislature for the first three sessions, including a 1910 special session when he was speaker of the House. He claimed years later that moving the seal was the proudest moment of his life.

Anthony was on the State Capitol Commission that chose the site for the building at 23rd Street and Lincoln Boulevard and later was city manager of Walters before joining Oklahoma Gas and Electric Co. He was assistant to the president of OG&E when he died of cancer at the age of 63 in 1933, only a few weeks after Haskell died.

Capital location a fight to the finish

The state seal was spirited out of Guthrie in a clandestine late-night ride within hours after a June 11, 1910, election chose Oklahoma City to be the state capital.

But the fight wasn't over.

Opponents of the move filed actions in state and federal courts in Guthrie and in the state Supreme Court, which ruled that the election was invalid because of technical flaws. The Legislature was called into special session and after much wrangling fixed the Capitol site as the center of Lincoln Boulevard at its intersection with the center of 22nd Street in Oklahoma City.

That didn't end the fight, either. The Legislature's action was challenged on the grounds that the 1906 congressional enabling act that created Oklahoma specified that Guthrie would be the capital at least until 1913. The high court ruled, however, that the Legislature was not bound by the enabling act.

Gov. Charles N. Haskell and other state officials had moved their offices to the Huckins Hotel and other buildings in Oklahoma City immediately after the June election, but the Legislature still met in Guthrie, where residents wanted to retain the capital. And until the Supreme Court's ruling, there were efforts to take the capital elsewhere. Even Skiatook made a bid.

After other legal matters were settled, Gov. Lee Cruce broke ground for the new building on July 20, 1914, more than four years after the election, on the site on Lincoln Boulevard, a half section line. The Capitol wasn't occupied until 1915.

Haskell was in Tulsa on that June 11 day when Oklahomans voted on whether to have the capital in Guthrie, Oklahoma City or Shawnee, and he learned of the results shortly after midnight.

He immediately signed a proclamation designating Oklahoma City as the capital and called his secretary, W.B. Anthony, to ask him to notify Secretary of State Bill Cross and for the two of them to take the seal from the Logan County Courthouse to Oklahoma City by 7:30 a.m.

Tulsa World archives

An artist's sketch of the proposed Oklahoma state Capitol building, as envisioned in 1912.

Haskell boarded a special train, financed by Tulsans Tate Brady, Robert Galbraith and Mayor John O. Mitchell, at 3 a.m. to take his party from Tulsa to Oklahoma City, where he met Anthony and Cross with the seal. The seal was stored in a roll-top desk on the hotel's mezzanine for six weeks.

"I have simply done my duty," Haskell was quoted in the June 14, 1910, Tulsa World. "The capital is now in Oklahoma City."

Opponents, including the World, cried foul, claiming the capital was stolen from Guthrie. The World's story about the move said a pledge repeated "in every speech and in its own and hired newspapers" in Oklahoma City was that no attempt would be made to move the government until after 1913 and a suitable Capitol would be ready.

"This is the first repudiation of plighted word," the World said and warned, "Watch for the next."

Tulsans had urged voters to "vote no" on the move, and the World had printed that message in large type on front pages. Tulsans had become irritated at the "big brother" attitude of Oklahoma Citians, who believed there was room for only one big city in the state.

While the Legislature was meeting in special session, it received bids from several cities and towns seeking the capital, including one from Skiatook, which offered 500 acres, $800,000, free gas for five years and free water for 20 years to have the Capitol built in "the Gateway City of the Osage."

But the bid arrived too late for consideration – it was the day the Legislature finally agreed on a site.

KC massacre had Oklahoma ties

Seven law enforcement officers, along with the Oklahoma train robber and killer they were returning to prison, were ambushed in the Kansas City, Mo., train station by gangsters carrying submachine guns .

The attack early on was considered the work of the Oklahoma badman Charles "Pretty Boy" Floyd.

The June 17, 1933, massacre of four officers and their prisoner was staged in an effort to free Frank Nash, who had escaped three years earlier from prison at Leavenworth, Kan. He had been captured at Hot Springs, Ark., the day before the massacre.

A witness identified Floyd as one of the machine-gunners, but Floyd denied any involvement through a postcard sent to a Kansas City detective a few days later.

"Dear Sir: I – Charles Floyd – want it made known that I did not participate in the massacre of officers at Kansas City," the card said.

Authorities didn't believe him. Floyd was one of those blamed for the massacre – along with his partner Adam Richetti and Vernon Miller.

Floyd was killed in an Ohio field by federal agents and Miller's mutilated body was found in Detroit, leaving only Richetti to face trial on murder charges in the deaths of the four officers and their prisoner.

Several others, including Nash's widow, were charged with conspiracy to help a prisoner escape. The charge against Mrs. Nash, who was believed to have tried to free her husband, was dropped and she testified against the others. Each was sentenced to two years in prison and fined $10,000.

Richetti, who also had an Oklahoma criminal record, was convicted of murder and sentenced to die in the Missouri gas chamber. He was executed Oct. 7, 1938.

"I don't believe they intended to kill Nash," R.E. Vetterli, the agent in charge of the Kansas City office of the Justice Department, said. Officers said four men with machine guns had hidden near the law enforcers' cars and patiently waited for the group escorting Nash.

The slain included McAlester Police Chief Otto Reed, a federal agent and two Kansas City detectives. Special Agent F.J. Lackey of Oklahoma City was paralyzed for life and another agent was wounded less seriously.

Nash, described by Tulsa postal inspectors as being "as smart as he was vicious and as vengeful as he was well-

Tulsa World archives

The bloody machine-gun shooting in the Kansas City, Mo., train station was initially pinned on the Oklahoma outlaw Charles "Pretty Boy" Floyd.

read," had a long criminal record. It began in 1915 when he was convicted of murder in Kiowa County for killing a burglary accomplice who had confessed to the crime. Nash was sentenced to life in the state penitentiary but was paroled shortly afterward. He joined the Marine Corps and served overseas during World War I.

An avid reader, Nash displayed his rhetorical skills when he and the Al Spencer gang robbed a train in Osage County in 1923. While other member of the gang were rifling mailbags, Nash was guarding the conductor and some passengers – and making a speech.

Nash insisted to his captive audience that Sam Blythe was the greatest contemporary commentator on politics – an argument with which his audience may not have agreed but nodded approval at because of the two pistols Nash was holding.

The bandits escaped with $20,000. Nash and Spencer were tracked down by postal inspectors, who killed Spencer and captured Nash and other members of the gang. He was convicted in federal court and was serving a 25-year sentence at Leavenworth when he escaped.

Even at his trial, Nash couldn't resist trying to show off his intelligence, including his knowledge of the Bible. When the judge asked whether he had anything to say before sentencing, Nash replied in a ringing voice:

"I know nothing in all history except the crucifixion of Christ, which equals my persecution!"

Three years after he escaped, he was arrested in Hot Springs by Lackey and another federal agent and was returned to Kansas City by train. The agents planned to drive from there to Leavenworth with their prisoner.

Nash was already in the car when the shooting began.

A Tulsa police officer who came to know Nash while a guard at the penitentiary in McAlester believed that Nash was executed by gangsters who feared he would talk about their criminal activities. He said Nash had been known to be a "snitch" in prison.

Floyd, who had used a machine gun in many of his crimes, was the object of another active search south of Kansas City. The search came after he freed a Polk County, Mo., sheriff whom he had forced to accompany him on a 500-mile trip through Missouri a few days earlier. Floyd also was suspected of being the gunman who killed the Boone County sheriff and a state highway patrol trooper in Columbia, Mo., after a bank robbery in Mexico, Mo.

FBI agent's gun skill off mark politically

The fast-draw gunmen of the old West couldn't have come close to beating an Oklahoma FBI agent with the unlikely name of Jelly.

Jelly, whose original name was Delf A. Bryce, could draw his pistol and fire in two-fifths of a second, according to a Life magazine article in 1945.

"Mr. Bryce is so fast that he can hold a silver dollar at forehead level in his shooting hand, drop the coin and have his gun out and shooting before the coin has fallen to waist level," the magazine reported.

Bryce killed three men during the first year he was a police officer, including one on the first night he served on the Oklahoma City Police Department in 1927. All had tried to shoot Bryce, who drew his gun after they had a bead on him.

Bryce was so good with firearms that he had become legendary among lawmen long before he retired from the FBI in 1958 to make an unsuccessful run for governor. He demonstrated his prowess at many meetings of officers and others.

Born in 1906 at Mountain View in Kiowa County, Bryce developed an interest in firearms early in life – and spent his childhood years developing his talent for fast-drawing and shooting.

He became a game ranger after graduating from high school but later that year competed in a shooting contest at Shawnee as part of the annual Sheriffs and Peace Officers Association convention. He did so well, Clarence Hurt, the night police chief of Oklahoma City, hired him as an officer.

In addition to a job, Bryce won the $100 first prize for shooting and helped the Oklahoma City pistol team win, too.

On his first day as an Oklahoma City officer, Bryce saw a man whose picture he had seen on a wanted poster at the police station, walked up to the car he was sitting in and asked the man what he was doing. When Bryce identified himself as a police officer, the wanted man drew a gun and

Tulsa World archives

D.A. Jelly Bryce is believed to have killed 19 men during his career as a police officer and FBI agent.

pointed it at the new officer.

Before the gunman could pull the trigger, Bryce had drawn his gun and fired, killing the gunman.

And then he was arrested because other officers didn't know him and Bryce didn't have a badge yet.

It is believed that he killed 19 men during his career.

When the FBI was given authority to carry guns in 1934, Director J. Edgar Hoover began searching for officers who could shoot, and Bryce was among the first hired. Bryce later became the agent in charge in Oklahoma City, a position he held until retiring to run for governor as an independent.

Bryce based his campaign on what he said was the state's need for a "racket-busting governor." He claimed he could enforce prohibition laws by calling bootleggers and warning them.

"I'd tell them they had better shut down or else," he said. "They'd shut down."

But Bryce never got a chance to test that theory. He ran third in a three-man field in the general election that year, behind winner J. Howard Edmondson, a Democrat, and Phil Ferguson, a Republican.

After the political campaign, Bryce returned to Mountain View where he lived until his death in 1974 at the age of 67. He was attending a gathering of retired FBI agents at Shangri-La when he died in his sleep.

Bryce gained that Jelly nickname early in his career as an Oklahoma City officer when he was called a jellybean, a slang term for a natty dresser, because of his neat dress. After a gun battle with two men, one of the injured criminals crawled into a downtown theater followed by Bryce who had the manager turn on the theater's lights.

He walked up to the wounded man who looked at Bryce, dressed in white slacks, vest and hat, and said "I can't believe I was killed by a jellybean like you."

He liked the nickname and in 1958 had his name legalized as D.A. Jelly Bryce, the way it appeared on the ballots.

Fireworks factory blasts left 21 dead

Tulsa World archives

Smoke rises from the Aerlex Corp. fireworks factory near Hallett, where explosions killed 21 people June 25, 1985.

A series of explosions that leveled the Aerlex Corp. fireworks factory at Hallett between Terlton and Jennings, killing 21 of the 26 people there, could be heard in Tulsa, about 25 miles away.

The June 25, 1985, blasts apparently started just outside the factory, where workers were loading a pickup, Oklahoma Highway Patrol Trooper Jim King said. An explosion at the pickup may have caused a chain reaction, destroying the rest of the factory – a large steel building and seven smaller ones.

The blasts sent a mushroom cloud a half-mile into the sky that was seen by a neighbor who drove toward the fireworks factory to help survivors. He said he met a man on fire running toward him.

"He asked if I had some water and if I would pour it on him," said the neighbor, Yuell Canida. "He was burned all over."

A man in another pickup poured water on the victim and put ice packs on him until an ambulance arrived, Canida said.

A doctor from Drumright said the scene "looked like a napalm bomb had been dropped." Bodies were blown as far as 200 yards from the factory, the doctor said.

Richard O'Bryant, one of the survivors, told a World reporter several days later from his hospital bed that he had been working with Aerlex's founder and owner, Richard Alan Johnson, when he heard a boom.

He said Johnson turned and ran – and he did the same.

"They'd always stressed to just run, get away. So I didn't hesitate," O'Bryant said.

O'Bryant ran a few steps before an explosion knocked him to the ground. He forced himself to get up and keep running until he fell into a pond where he stayed "until it quieted down," he said.

It was the second explosion since the factory opened in 1973, after Johnson returned from the Vietnam war. The first blast, in July 1979, was much smaller, causing about $100,000 in damage, but all the employees escaped without injury because of a few seconds' warning.

Aerlex was cited by the Occupational Safety and Health Administration for 13 safety violations and was fined $58,000. Five of the citations alleged willful violations, those that managers knew about but didn't correct.

The citations alleged the factory had inadequate exits, used careless unloading procedures and trucks that weren't flame-proof and stored explosives in unbarricaded buildings. The citations also alleged that smoking was allowed inside the factory.

A lawsuit filed against Aerlex three years later claimed that the explosions started because two employees mishandled explosives they were unloading from the pickup.

One worker stumbled while unloading a canister of friction-sensitive material and his momentum carried him into an assembly room where an explosion occurred, the lawsuit alleged.

That explosion caused other blasts throughout the plant, it was alleged.

A $3 million default judgment was granted to the survivors of four employees who were killed in the explosions, but their attorney, John Nicks, said he expected it would go uncollected because Aerlex "has no money, that's for sure."

Johnson, who had moved to Fort Worth, did not attend the trial. Nicks said his clients wanted him to establish legal liability, "and we've accomplished that."

Clark known as 'Patton of the Pacific'

Dozens of Navy airplanes were returning to their carriers in the South Pacific short of fuel and after dark after battling Japanese forces in the World War II Battle of the Philippine Sea.

It could have been a disaster; many of the planes' engines were running on fumes, and it was almost impossible for the pilots to see the carriers in the dark. Until Rear Adm. Joseph J. Clark of Oklahoma ordered:

"Damn the submarines; turn on the lights!"

Clark's subordinates had warned him that turning on the lights would make the ships in his task group good targets for Japanese submarines lurking nearby. After his group's lights came on, Clark immediately notified Vice Adm. Marc Mitscher, the task force commander, who ordered all the ships in the task force to turn on their lights. Soon the black night was aglow with lights stretching for miles.

And the returning pilots could identify carriers from other ships.

Mitscher, also an Oklahoman, directed the returning pilots to land on any carrier in the task force – without regard to where they were assigned. All the carriers looked the same from the air at night and the pilots didn't have enough fuel to search for their own carriers.

Clark's order paraphrasing Civil War Adm. David Farragut's command to "damn the torpedoes; full speed ahead" saved the lives of many pilots – and many airplanes. Because they were allowed to land on any carrier, nearly all the pilots landed safely, although some had to ditch in the ocean where they were rescued.

Clark, who died in 1971 at the age of 77, became known during World War II as "Patton of the Pacific," a reference to Gen. George S. Patton who commanded Army troops in Europe, because of his aggressiveness against the Japanese.

When a guided missile frigate ship was named in his honor in 1980, Navy historian Samuel Morrison described the admiral as "part Cherokee, part Southern Methodist, but all fighter."

His career proved that.

Clark earned a reputation as a fearless, aggressive leader and brilliant tactician during his 40-year Navy career. He became a deck officer during World War I shortly after gradu-

Tulsa World archives

Rear Adm. Joseph J. Clark of Oklahoma saved the lives of many pilots because he gave an order to turn on the lights of ships in his battle group during the World War II Battle of the Philippine Sea.

ating from the Naval Academy, was a carrier task group commander during World War II, a task force commander during the Korean War and later became commander of the 7th Fleet.

He served twice as assistant chief of naval operations but it was his daring in battle that distinguished his career. In addition to turning on the lights in an ocean filled with enemy submarines, he also had once ordered his carrier, the USS Hornet, into a dangerous turn to allow the pilots to take off into the wind on a mission to rescue fellow airmen who had been shot down.

Before every mission, Clark told his pilots "get out there and strike a blow for liberty."

He had received many decorations, including the Distinguished Service Medal, Navy Cross, the Silver Star and the Legion of Merit, and retired in 1953 as a full admiral.

Born near Alluwe in Nowata County, Clark attended school at Chelsea and was a junior at Oklahoma A&M College, now Oklahoma State University, when he was appointed to the Naval Academy at Annapolis in 1913. That's where he got the nickname Jocko that stuck with him throughout his life.

Clark became a Navy pilot in 1925 and played a key role in developing naval aviation, directing the outfitting of many early aircraft carriers. He also spent time testing flying boats.

During the 1930s, the Navy brass didn't think flying boats, the PBY Catalina airplanes that could land on water, had much value to the Navy. But after Clark took Vice Admiral Henry Butler on a test ride in a PBY, the brass' attitude changed.

Clark took fellow Oklahoman Will Rogers, whom he had known since they were children, for a flight that started by being catapulted from an aircraft carrier – shortly before Rogers and fellow Oklahoman Wiley Post were killed in a plane crash in Alaska.

Chelsea residents celebrated "Joe Clark day" in 1945 to honor the admiral who called the event "the greatest day of my life" and said it was "a fitting tribute to all the boys who fought – not just me."

Hundreds of farmers and ranchers showed up to say hello and shake hands with Clark who, to them, was just plain Joe. And the admiral enjoyed every minute of it.

Aunt Chick taught many how to cook

When one of the Tulsa World's most popular columns began in 1935, the author didn't tell her husband about it – until after he read her first column in the newspaper.

"That crazy woman will start a run on the bank if people think she has to work!" Sam McBirney shouted as he jumped up from the breakfast table and headed upstairs to confront his wife.

The "World's Kitchen Log" column hadn't used her full name – just Aunt Chick – but most knew Aunt Chick was Nettie McBirney, the banker's wife. It was 1935 and the nation was in the midst of the Depression. McBirney was vice president of the National Bank of Commerce that his family founded about 1908.

Aunt Chick's column taught a lot of people a lot about cooking: how to make good pie crusts, how to keep pie dough from sticking to rolling pins, how to keep the bottom crusts of fruit pies from being soggy and how to keep meringue from weeping.

But McBirney's fears were unfounded – it didn't start a run on the McBirney bank.

Aunt Chick had graduated from Stout Institute in Menomonie, Wis., a school that taught only home economics, and she came to Claremore in 1909 to teach that subject. Two years later, she became supervisor of home economics at Muskogee schools. She came to Tulsa in 1916 as the wife of McBirney, who was coach of the University of Tulsa football team.

While writing her Kitchen Log column for the next 20 years, Aunt Chick also found time to write several cook books, most of which dealt with pies and other desserts. She also invented a pastry canvas and a cookie cutter that is still in demand.

She began demonstrating cooking methods, first at Vandever's Department Store, and later at other stores in Tulsa and in many other parts of the country. She learned a lot about cooking in the process.

The women themselves developed the demonstrations with their questions, and she listened to everyone wherever she went but didn't take anyone's word for their recipes. In a 1973 interview, Aunt Chick recalled meeting a woman at who claimed her recipe for lemon pie was the best there was.

"I took the recipe and tried it and agreed," she said.

Tulsa World archives

When Nettie McBirney, also known as Aunt Chick, began writing one of the Tulsa World's most popular columns in 1935, she didn't let her husband know about her new job until after he read the newspaper. Here, she demonstrates her cookie-cutting techniques at Southern Hills Nursing Center in 1977.

At one of the demonstrations, she mentioned that everyone had trouble with weeping meringues – but a young woman in the audience told her she didn't have any trouble.

Aunt Chick had suggested that the pies should be baked in an oven with a temperature no higher than 325 degrees. But the young woman said she didn't have a thermometer and never knew the temperature of her oven. She added that she couldn't even shut the door on her oven.

That was the answer to the meringue problem.

"I'd stumbled onto the secret – no more weepy meringues – just leave the door open about an inch and it'll work like magic," she said.

Aunt Chick's first inventions were the pastry canvas, treated with a chemical, and a rolling-pin cover that prevented noodles, cookies and pie crusts from sticking. She later developed a heavy steel pie pan and the "Crispy Crust" pie pan that promised perfect bottom crusts on pies.

Although she also developed several other kitchen gadgets, the item for which she was most famous was the device now known as Gramma's Cutter, designed to help the cookie dough slide out of the forms. They are available at grammascutters.com.

Aunt Chick included a recipe and some sage advice in every cookie-cutter box: such as "If you don't follow directions, Heaven help you." or "Don't have a neighbor show you how to do these, because you must follow these instructions."

When Aunt Chick moved into a retirement home in 1973, she donated her collection of about 1,000 cookbooks to the Tulsa City-County Library. She had been collecting the books since 1913.

Moving into a retirement home didn't stop her cooking demonstrations; it just changed the venue. She presented her demonstrations to other residents of the center, where she died in 1982.

Aunt Chick once told a World reporter that when she decided she wanted to begin writing a cooking column, she approached World Editor N.G. Henthorne, who offered to pay her $15 a week for the column that appeared Tuesday through Friday on the newspaper's society page and on Saturday in a food shopping guide. She accepted.

But, she added, "I would have written about good cooking for free."

Blacks' right to vote overcame opposition

Black Americans were allowed to vote beginning in 1869 when the 15th Amendment to the Constitution was passed.

Except in several Southern states – and eventually in Oklahoma – that required literacy tests but exempted certain people from those tests in what was called a "grandfather clause." It had the effect of allowing whites to vote while prohibiting blacks from the same right.

Oklahoma's grandfather clause was ruled unconstitutional by the Supreme Court in 1915, but the Legislature was called into special session in 1916 and enacted another literacy test, with another grandfather clause, leaving the would-be black voters exactly where they had been before.

A constitutional amendment approved in August 1910 fixed a literacy test that required voters to be able to read and write any section of the Oklahoma Constitution. However, it exempted those who could prove either that their grandfathers had been voters under any form of government before Jan. 1, 1866, or had been citizens of some foreign nation.

The exemption's effect was that illiterate whites could vote – their grandfathers had either been voters in 1866 or residents of a foreign country – but illiterate blacks could not because most of their grandfathers had been slaves in 1866 and had no voting rights.

It was similar to grandfather clauses in other Southern states and had effectively disenfranchised all would-be black voters.

The issue came to a head when J.J. Beal and Frank Guinn, election board officials in Kingfisher County, who had followed the law set out in the grandfather clause, were convicted in September 1911 in federal court at Enid of violating the civil rights of would-be black voters at an election Nov. 8, 1910, for refusing to allow them to vote.

No one expected a white jury to convict election officials of violating the civil rights of blacks, especially since the officials had been following the state law. Judge John H. Cotteral had instructed the jury that if the two had made a mistake in how they enforced the election law, they should

RIGHT TO VOTE GIVEN NEGROES OF THIS STATE

Supreme Court Holds the "Grandfather" Clause Unconstitutional.

INVALIDATES MANY LAWS OF THE SOUTH

Decision Reaffirms Conviction of Two State Election Officers.

Tulsa World archives

A headline from the June 22, 1915, Tulsa World front page reports the Supreme Court ruling allowing black people to vote. However, another law passed in 1916 again disenfranchised black voters.

be acquitted.

On the other hand, he said, if they knew or believed their purpose was to deny the right to vote to them on account of their race and color, then they should be convicted.

The law did not include a penalty for violations so Beal and Guinn were neither fined nor sentenced to jail. Their convictions eventually were appealed to the U.S. Supreme Court in a test case. The convictions of two election board officials from Blaine County who were charged after Beal and Guinn were convicted also were appealed.

Many expected the Guinn case to be dropped by the government after Democrat Woodrow Wilson, a Southerner, was elected president in 1912. But the government continued its prosecution of the voting rights case, which was argued before the high court in October 1913.

The high court ruled in 1915 that the Oklahoma law was unconstitutional although literacy tests were not unconstitutional per se. The court held that Oklahoma's grandfather clause clearly had no purpose except to keep black people from voting, making it unconstitutional.

The Tulsa World called the court's ruling "one of the most important race decisions in the history of the court." At the same time, the court held that a Maryland voters' qualification law was unconstitutional and awarded damages to three blacks who were denied the right to vote.

"It doesn't make much difference. There will be no illegal Negro votes in Oklahoma," state election board chairman A.L. Wilker said after the high court ruling, expressing the opinion of many Oklahomans. "We'll enact a law taking its place or submit another amendment to the people that will conform to constitutional requirements."

Gov. Robert L. Williams convened the Legislature in January 1916 to consider the voting rights issue – and a new literacy law with a grandfather clause was enacted.

The new law effectively disenfranchised blacks because it required all potential voters who had not voted in 1914 to register as voters but provided only 12 days -- from April 30 to May 11, 1916 -- as the registration period. But it remained the law in Oklahoma until 1939 when the Supreme Court held that grandfather clause also was unconstitutional.

'King of bank robbers' nabbed by teen

Badman Henry Starr, called the "king of the bank robbers," was captured by a teenage boy who shot the bandit after he and his gang had robbed two banks at Stroud.

"I wouldn't have minded it so much if a man had shot me," Starr reportedly said after being wounded.

The boy, Paul Curry, heard gunfire from the bandits as they marched several hostages from both banks toward the livery stable after the March 26, 1915, robbery. He borrowed a .44-caliber octagon-barreled rifle and ammunition and hid behind his father's grocery store, waiting for a good shot.

As Starr, whose identity Curry didn't know but who appeared to be the leader, approached, the boy shot him in the hip. Starr fell, Curry ran up to him, pointed the rifle at him and ordered, "Drop your gun or I'll kill you." Starr followed the order.

Curry was 19, although some newspapers listed his age as 17 or 18, but looked to be 14. He picked up Starr's gun and turned his attention to Lewis Estes, another bandit, who had mounted his horse and returned to help his fallen leader. Curry shot him in the neck but Estes was able to ride out of town, leaving a trail of blood and silver dollars, which he had stuffed into his pockets during the robbery. He was found leaning against a tree near the town cemetery.

While Starr and Estes were being treated at a doctor's office, Starr said, "I've never killed a woman or a boy and I don't intend to start now," a statement that probably explained why the robber hadn't shot Curry after being wounded.

He freely admitted robbing the banks and both he and Estes were sentenced to prison – but Starr, as in past prison terms, became a model prisoner and was pardoned after serving less than four years of his 25-year term.

After his release, he told a World reporter, "I'm 45 years old and 17 of my years have been spent in prison."

Starr was given the "king of the bank robbers" title by Deputy Marshal Bill Tilghman because of the large number of banks he had robbed. The bandit confirmed his record six years later when he told a doctor as he was dying after being shot in a Harrison, Ark., bank robbery, "I've robbed more banks than any man in the United States."

Born in Fort Gibson, Starr's bandit career was interspersed with periods when he claimed to have gone straight and he frequently advised others that "crime doesn't pay," as he did after the Stroud capers.

He pleaded guilty to a robbery charge and was sentenced

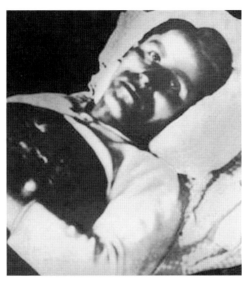

Henry Starr, known as "king of the bank robbers," is pictured after he was shot by Paul Curry on March 27, 1915. Starr survived, but died six years later from gunshot wounds received while robbing the People's National Bank in Harrison, Ark.

to 25 years in the state penitentiary at McAlester but was paroled four years later. He began urging young people to earn their livings instead of turning to a life of crime.

It was the second time he had been released from prison early and the second time he had tried to go straight. His first release came in 1903 after President Theodore Roosevelt cut the length of his prison sentence in gratitude for Starr's help in disarming badman Crawford Goldsby, alias Cherokee Bill, who was trying to break out of jail and was later hanged at Fort Smith.

Starr was in the Fort Smith jail serving a term after his guilty plea of manslaughter for killing a deputy U.S. marshal for which he had twice been convicted and sentenced to hang, both convictions being overturned by the Supreme Court.

After being treated following the Stroud robberies, the two injured bandits were taken to the basement of the county jail at Chandler, where people flocked to see them. Among the curious was John J. Davis, later a Tulsa furniture store co-owner, whose uncle was the Lincoln County attorney.

"Boy, don't ever get in any scrapes like I have. It just doesn't pay. Always be honest and upright," the bandit told Davis, who was allowed to go into the cell with Starr.

Davis, who died in 1993, related that story frequently during his latter days and always said, "I've never forgotten that good advice." But it was advice he probably didn't need, friends say.

After serving about four years, Starr received a pardon but his robbery days weren't over, despite his claim that he was going straight and his new position as a movie actor.

He returned to Stroud to star as himself in a movie about the double bank robbery and became known as the "Evening Starr" for his roles in that and other films. But during the filming, he left Stroud for a day or two, times that corresponded with bank robberies in Chandler and Davenport.

And then he was mortally wounded Feb. 18, 1921, while he and others were robbing the People's National Bank in Harrison, Ark.

An officer of the bank shot Starr from the vault where he and several other bank officials had been forced by the bandits.

The bank robber lingered for four days in a hospital in Harrison and told the doctor treating him that he turned bank robber again because he was in debt.

"I am sorry but the deed is done," Starr said.

Tragedy marred July Fourth in 1912

Three people were killed and 18 were injured when a fun day of celebrating the Fourth of July ended in tragedy in 1912.

The victims were on a Sand Springs Interurban car jammed with about 300 passengers. Some were on outside platforms, some hanging onto the outside of the open car and others on the roof of the car that struck the rear of a stalled, fully loaded car on the same tracks when the interurban car's brakes failed.

The accident occurred about 10:45 p.m., minutes after the car left the Sand Springs Park where thousands had celebrated Independence Day.

Beryl Ford collection

Shortly after a loaded streetcar left the Sand Springs Park station on July 4, 1912, it struck a stalled streetcar on the same tracks. Three people were killed and 18 were injured.

Motorman E.E. Sims, who was new to the job, was in charge of the interurban car when the brakes failed minutes after it left the park headed toward Sand Springs, where it would loop back toward Tulsa. Witnesses said the car was going down grade at "a terrific speed" before it hit the stalled car.

Sims shut off the power and yelled to passengers riding on the rear platform to set the hand brake but they either couldn't hear his shouts because of the screams of the passengers or didn't have time to set the brakes before the crash.

Witnesses said Sims tried crawling over the crowd of passengers in a futile attempt to reach the hand brake.

"The lights went out and a scene beyond description followed," one unnamed passenger told a Tulsa World reporter. "The moans of the injured mingled in the night air with the shrieks of the frightened."

A special car with five doctors and nurses left Tulsa immediately after the crash to help the victims. A long line of automobiles, wagons and buggies waited for more than two hours at the Tulsa station for interurban cars bringing survivors back to the city.

Most of those who were killed or seriously injured were riding on the front platform or in the reversible seats toward the front of the car. The backs of seats in interurban cars were made so they could be pushed one way for a trip if the car was headed in one direction or the opposite way if it was going in reverse. The Sand Springs cars went forward to Tulsa but went in reverse to Sand Springs.

Industrialist Charles Page, who owned the interurban, blamed the crash on two men who were riding on the top of the car and the inexperience of Sims. He also took the blame for the accident.

He said the two men who got onto the roof of the car and refused to get off were knocked off when hit by electric lines about 1,000 feet from the accident scene. Sims saw the men fall, became excited and lost control, Page said.

Page said no damage suits would result from the crash because he "would do the right thing for all those who suffered injury or loss in the wreck.

"I want the people to blame me, and I would not feel right unless they did," he said.

The Sand Springs celebration was the big event of the area that year. Other celebrations were held in Tulsa at Central and Owen parks where shade was available on grassy areas for picnics. Automobile races and baseball games were featured at Collinsville, and boxing, racing and baseball games were on the program at Red Fork.

Sen. Robert L. Owens made a stirring speech at Collinsville about the 136th anniversary of the signing of the Declaration of Independence – a speech that attracted a large contingent of Democrats, including candidates for various political offices.

Dancing was provided at Cain's Pavilion at Orcutt Park.

But they didn't compare with the activities or the crowd at the big event at Sand Springs Park. Thousands rode the interurban cars that left Tulsa every 20 minutes for the park to picnics, relax in the shade of stately trees on the lawn that sloped down to a lake, and watch a fireworks show provided by the Boy Scouts. No mention was made about swimming in the lake, which, in later years, was a favorite swimming area.

It was a pleasant respite from the rising summer temperature – and it ended in tragedy.

Legal beer made a splash in state in 1933

Oklahomans were thirsty.

Especially in Tulsa, where beer had never been sold legally.

They turned out in droves to vote to legalize the sale of 3.2 beer on July 11, 1933. The state's heaviest vote was in Tulsa County, where the issue was approved by a ratio of more than 4-to-1. Oklahoma County voters approved beer by a ratio of nearly 3-to-1.

Statewide, the issue was approved by two-thirds of the voters, and supporters believed the margin would have been even greater if the day had not been so hot. Election Day temperature was 105, the 15th consecutive day it had been more than 100 degrees.

Tulsa World archives

Former Tulsa World Publisher Eugene Lorton (left) and Mayor Herman Newblock pose in front of the the first legal delivery of cased beer in eastern Oklahoma. The delivery in July 1933 was made to the Tulsa World Building because Lorton had been a supporter of the move to legalize beer sales in Oklahoma.

But the lopsided approval didn't mean Oklahomans could buy a brew the next day.

Gov. William H. "Alfalfa Bill" Murray said the sale of beer would have to await his official proclamation, and he called out the Oklahoma National Guard to ensure that 50 rail cars of brew in the Oklahoma City train yard were not opened.

Although Attorney General J. Berry King said the sale of beer became legal with the election, dealers preferred to wait until the governor approved sales.

Murray had given the Frisco Railroad permission to bring the 43 cars of beer into Tulsa on condition that they not be unloaded until he gave his approval. Twenty-seven of those cars were for Tulsa.

Beer companies and dealers anticipated the approval by buying large advertisements in that day's Tulsa World.

Murray issued his proclamation the next day, and the first legal delivery of a case of beer in eastern Oklahoma was made to Tulsa World Publisher Eugene Lorton in front of the World Building at 315 S. Boulder Ave. – delivered on a wagon pulled by Anheuser-Busch's famous six horses.

A large crowd of Tulsans gathered in front of the newspaper building to watch the ceremony, which included Mayor Herman Newblock and World Editor N.G. Henthorne, who was a member of both the state and Tulsa County committees of the Beer for Oklahoma League. Lorton was one of the original advocates of making the sale of beer legal in Oklahoma.

Two days later, a price war had developed as many beer sellers cut their price to 15 cents a bottle from 20 cents. Beer distributors and sellers had agreed a week earlier that beer would be sold for 20 cents a bottle at hotels, coffee shops and restaurants and could be sold at two bottles for 35 cents at grocery stores.

A survey showed that only a few drugstores retained the 20-cent price. Those selling at the agreed on price said they probably would have to cut their prices to meet competition.

Admiral led awe-inspiring task force

A captured Japanese fighter pilot was "convinced Japan had lost the war" after he saw the ships of the Navy's Task Force 58 "scattered over the sea as far as his eyes could peer."

That captured pilot's assessment was pretty accurate, although the Japanese didn't surrender for another 14 months. But the task force commanded by an Oklahoman already had changed the direction of the war in the Pacific when the Navy revealed its existence in June 1944.

Called the "most powerful and destructive naval unit in history," it was organized six months earlier under the command of Vice Adm. Marc Mitscher and included aircraft carriers, battleships, cruisers and destroyers.

"Just where this floating strategic air force will strike next," the Navy said, "is a constant source of conjecture and worry for the enemy."

The huge armada won the battle at Midway; destroyed the Japanese forces at Truk and the Marianas, Japanese strongholds that had been considered invincible; and later launched 600 carrier-based planes that participated in a joint daylight raid on Tokyo with about 200 Army Air Corps B-29 Superfortresses from Guam.

Mitscher's task force included a task group headed by another Oklahoman, Vice Adm. J.J. "Jocko" Clark, who gained fame for ordering the lights of his ships turned on to guide returning Navy pilots to the carriers. That action was supported by Mitscher, who extended the order to the entire task force and directed the pilots to land on any carrier without searching for their own carriers.

Both Mitscher and Clark later received the four stars of a full admiral.

Mitscher, who became one of the Navy's first pilots in 1915, was commander of the carrier Hornet when Army Air Force Lt. Col. Jimmy Doolittle's 16 B-25s took off from it in April 1942 to bomb Tokyo in what was called "the start of offensive warfare directly against the heart of imperial Japan."

Navy / National Archives and Records Administration

Vice Adm. Marc A. Mitscher, who grew up in Oklahoma City, was commander of Task Force 58, one of the most powerful armadas ever assembled, in World War II. He is pictured here on board his flagship, the USS Lexington, during the Marianas campaign in June 1944.

Short and bald, Mitscher endeared himself to his men because of a personality characteristic – he never claimed personal credit for his ship's or task force's activities but always used the pronoun "we," giving his officers and men full credit.

A 1947 Time magazine article said Mitscher directed the mightiest naval unit in history "in a soft, flat monotone that belied the compressed fury with which he fought. He was never known to get excited, even when Kamikaze flyers almost literally blew him off the flagships Bunker Hill and Enterprise." The article called him a master tactician whose battle plans were flexible and were a bewilderment to the Japanese.

A native of Wisconsin, Mitscher made the run of 1889 into Oklahoma with his parents when he was 2. The family settled in Oklahoma City, where his father, Oscar Mitscher, became that city's second mayor. After Mitscher graduated from high school in Oklahoma City, he graduated from the Naval Academy in 1910.

Mitscher was awarded a Navy Cross in 1919 for piloting an NC-1 from Newfoundland to the Azores in the first trans-Atlantic flight. In 1926, he was assigned to the USS Langley, the Navy's first aircraft carrier. He received a Distinguished Service Medal for commanding Task Force 58 and had received many other decorations.

As a full admiral, Mitscher was the commander-in-chief of the Atlantic fleet in 1947 when he suffered a heart attack on his 60th birthday. He died eight days later while in the Norfolk Naval Hospital for a "complete and thorough checkup."

"The nation has lost a great leader," Fleet Adm. Chester Nimitz said. "I always had a sense of security and comfort when Adm. Mitscher was the leader of Task Force 58 against the Japanese.

"I knew that what had to be done would be done in full measure. All he needed was opportunity, and he made the most of every opportunity."

Hat collector had a head for politics

Dorcas Kelly of Bristow served two terms as Republican national committeewoman from Oklahoma.

She probably was better known for her hats than for her eight years as Oklahoma's top Republican woman when she played key roles in electing Republican Govs. Henry Bellmon and Dewey Bartlett.

Although she enjoyed her hats, which she said were a hobby, she took a more serious stance when it came to politics, civic activities and her family. She was known as Oklahoma's Mrs. Republican and campaigned for several candidates, serving as honorary state chairwoman of the Women for Richard Nixon campaign during his campaign for president.

Her hats became part of her political character beginning in 1960, when she wore a beige wide-brimmed straw hat adorned with elephants bearing candidates' names to the Republican National Convention in Chicago, where she was elected to her first term as national committeewoman.

"I wanted something unusual and attention-getting for the convention and whipped up my hat with the elephants on top," she told a Tulsa World reporter later. "What I really wanted was lots of publicity for Oklahoma, and the hat did its share."

She had ordered a hat from a Dallas milliner but when it arrived, she explained, "it was a lovely purple (her favorite color) hat but it wasn't a convention hat." Then while shopping in Okmulgee, she saw the elephants and created her own hat.

Kelly took the purple hat to the convention, too, and wore it to a meeting of the Oklahoma delegation with Vice President Richard Nixon, who told her "that's a good color."

At political meetings during the next four years, when she wore a different hat, she was always asked "where's your elephant hat?" So she made three hats with elephants on them to take to the 1964 convention.

Deciding against seeking a third term in 1968, she told a reporter, "I don't want to sound presumptuous but I feel

Tulsa World archives

Dorcas Kelly was known for her politics and her flamboyant hats.

many good things were accomplished in my terms.

"I thought it would be good for the party for me not to run again. I felt the party was in tip-top shape, and it was time to move and let in the younger people."

She was interested in politics most of her life and had held several positions in the Republican Party before becoming national committeewoman. She served as the state vice chairwoman of the party from 1952-60 and in 1952 was the first female delegate from Oklahoma to attend a national convention.

All of Kelly's hats – estimated at about 200 in 1972 – were of different design and most were her own creation. She sometimes bought basic hats but did her own trimming.

Each hat had its own story. For instance, she sometimes wore a hard hat with red, white and blue trim that she said was for going out among her "enemies." A White House hat had elephants around the building exterior with political names on them.

Four Tulsa Republican women's organizations – Pro America, Republican Women's Precinct Club, Republican Women's Club of Tulsa County and Tulsa County Federation of Republican Women – staged a 1962 pageant called "A Story of 50 Hats" that portrayed Kelly's life – using hats from her collection that they obtained by telling Kelly they were to be used in an event to raise money for the Republican Party.

Born at Skedee in Pawnee County, Kelly became a nurse and moved to Bristow in 1921 to start the city's first hospital. That's where she met Albert Kelly, a banker and cattleman, who became her husband. He died in 1946.

During their five sons' high school years, she was involved in band organizations, PTA and other activities. She also was always active in Presbyterian Church activities.

"I have enjoyed my life," she told a reporter in 1972, 11 years before her death in 1983. "But I wish more Americans would take more interest in what's happening.

'Alfalfa Bill' fought a war with Texas

A delay in opening free bridges across the Red River between Texas and Oklahoma touched off a controversy in 1931 that became known as the Red River bridge war.

Before the issue was settled, Oklahoma Gov. William H. "Alfalfa Bill" Murray had declared martial law, created a military zone extending into Texas, assumed personal command of his troops, defied a court order and dared a federal judge to cite him for contempt.

The controversy developed after a court order delayed the opening of the free spans built by the two states to replace privately owned toll bridges.

There wasn't much controversy over Murray's opening of the new free bridge on U.S. 81 between Terral, Okla., and Ringgold, Texas. And the new bridge on U.S. 77 between Marietta and Gainesville, Texas, remained closed because the approach on the Texas side hadn't been completed.

The war, fought mainly in newspaper stories, involved the new bridge on U.S. 69 and 75 between Durant and Denison, Texas. That span was the object of the injunction against Texas Gov. Ross Sterling and his highway commission obtained by the Red River Bridge Co., which claimed the Texas Highway Commission had promised to buy the span for $60,000.

In response to the injunction, Sterling ordered all three new bridges barricaded on the Texas side, pending settlement of the court action.

Within minutes after Murray ordered the three bridges opened on July 16, an Oklahoma Highway Department crew had gone to the Texas side of the Terral bridge and removed an old truck that barricaded the highway, acting on the theory that Oklahoma owned half the span lengthwise across the stream. Before evening, the action had been duplicated at Denison.

Asked about possible resistance at the Denison span, Murray said, "There is an old watchman there and I have instructed that he not be hurt. I directed highway officials to take his pocketknife and chewing tobacco away from him."

Murray also wired the Texas governor to advise him of his removal of the barricades and plans to have his highway department tear up the approaches to the toll bridges.

Oklahoma Historical Society

Oklahoma Gov. William H. "Alfalfa Bill" Murray assumed personal command of state troops during a 1931 controversy known as the Red River bridge war.

"I feel you have extended your authority beyond all reason," Sterling responded, and he directed Texas Rangers to erect new barricades at the Denison-Durant free bridge, where they stood guard armed with shotguns in front of a sign advising motorists that the bridge had been ordered closed by the U.S. District Court.

But Murray claimed that Oklahoma had jurisdiction over the Texas banks of the river by virtue of old Spanish treaties, claiming the U.S. Supreme Court had upheld that authority. "So I wasn't exceeding my authority," Murray said in response to Sterling's criticism.

Several days later, Murray activated some units of the National Guard, placed the approaches leading up to the toll bridge under martial law – an order he extended into Texas the next day – and set up a military camp near the bridge.

An order obtained by owners of the toll bridge in federal court in Muskogee didn't faze the colorful Murray, who, wearing a large hog-shooter pistol on his belt, assumed personal command of his troops.

When the judge threatened Murray with a contempt citation, Murray responded, "He can't cite me; let him try it." He also threatened to call out the entire Oklahoma National Guard if the federal court interfered.

Guard Lt. Col. John MacDonald told an attorney he would accept service of a federal court order but he would pay no attention to it.

"I am taking orders from only one man and he is the governor of Oklahoma," the colonel, also a state senator from Durant, told the lawyer.

The governor said he would keep the free bridges open despite any order from any court or other authority except President Herbert Hoover.

The controversy ended on Aug. 6 after the Texas Legislature, in special session, passed a law allowing the Red River Bridge Co. to sue the state and the federal court dissolved the injunction that touched off the "war."

That free bridge served the public well until 1995, when it was dynamited and traffic was shifted to a new bridge – also free.

Man bungles Tulsa plane skyjacking

An American Airlines plane headed from St. Louis to Tulsa was commandeered by an armed skyjacker who parachuted from the plane with $502,000 in ransom but never got a chance to spend the money.

The skyjacker, who was armed with a .45-caliber submachine gun, took charge of the Boeing 727 as it neared Tulsa on June 23, 1972.

The drama had all the earmarks of a Keystone Kops movie—an indecisive and inept hijacker, a car that crashed into the taxiing hijacked plane and the loss of the money and his weapon while the gunman was parachuting from the plane.

Officials at first believed the skyjacker might have been killed during his jump but later arrested Martin McNally, 28, of Wyandotte, Mich. He was convicted and sentenced to two life prison terms.

When he took charge of the flight, the gunman at first ordered the pilot to return to St. Louis but changed his mind and directed the flight to Fort Worth. He changed his mind again as the plane neared Fort Worth and ordered a return to St. Louis, where he released all but one of the 92 passengers.

Passengers were informed of the hijacking as the plane began its descent to the Tulsa airport, according to Dean A. McGee, chairman of the Kerr-McGee Corp. who was one of the passengers. The pirate, sitting at the front of the coach section, had produced his submachine gun from a trombone case and then made his demand.

The hijacker ordered all the men to move to the coach section, the women to move to the front and announced that the women would be released but the men would be kept as hostages. But he changed his mind again when the plane landed at St. Louis and the captain reported all the men seated on the right side of the plane could leave with the women and children.

"I'm happy I was sitting on the right side," McGee told a reporter later.

The passengers who were released were forced to slide down an emergency chute from the plane—including a woman in a wheelchair. But no one was injured.

The gunman asked for the money, a parachute and instructions on its use. Two FBI agents posing as airline officials boarded the plane. One showed him how to use the

A spokesman for American Airlines (top, right) at Tulsa International Airport talks to friends and relatives of Tulsa-bound passengers aboard a flight skyjacked from St. Louis on June 23, 1972.

parachute and how to jump from the airplane. Airline attendants later said he had difficulty understanding how to use the parachute.

The agents said they could not stop the skyjacking because the gunman kept his submachine gun aimed at an attendant.

The pilot reported the hijacker was satisfied with the money and parachute and the plane began taxiing down a runway. Then a 1972 Cadillac driven by St. Louis businessman David Hanley, 30, crashed through a wire mesh fence, chased the jet along the runway and caromed off the plane's nose gear and into its landing gear in what appeared to be an attempt to stop the hijacking.

The car, which had been a Mothers' Day present to Hanley's wife, was demolished and Hanley was critically injured in the crash.

He had been sitting in a motel bar near the airport when he told a friend "turn on the radio in a few minutes and you'll hear something that will rock the world" and left.

A few minutes later, Hanley began his chase of the taxiing jet at speeds up to 90 miles per hour. Then his car went to the end of the runway, turned around and headed straight toward the plane.

The hijacker switched to another plane and it took off with three male flight crew members, two female attendants and a male passenger aboard as hostages. The hijacker instructed the pilot to head for Toronto, make a low pass to assure him of the location and then to head for John F. Kennedy Airport in New York City.

But he plunged from the plane near Peru, Ind. The bags containing the money were found in a soybean field on a farm near Peru by farmer Lowell Elliott.

"I thought it was a groundhog in the field," Elliott said. "It didn't move so I took a closer look."

Meanwhile, the gun was found five miles away by another farmer, Ronald Miller, who at first thought the commando-type weapon was a toy when it was turned up by the blades of a liquid fertilizer distributor.

McNally, an unemployed service station attendant, was arrested at his home. He had been questioned and released by Peru police the night after the skyjacking. His partner, Walter J. Petlikowsky, 31, of nearby Detroit, confessed his role and identified McNally for the FBI.

FDR's visit preceded unusual election

President Franklin D. Roosevelt came to Oklahoma in 1938 to "say a few kind words" in support of Sen. Elmer Thomas' bid for re-election. But it didn't go as expected – he also praised Thomas' political foe, Gov. E.W. Marland.

And he had "a few kind words" for U.S. Sen. Josh Lee, although the state's junior senator wasn't a candidate that year.

In addition, Roosevelt took a potshot at former Gov. William H. "Alfalfa Bill" Murray and snubbed U.S. Rep. Wesley Disney, a 1st District Tulsan who was on the speakers platform with the president and several other Oklahoma politicians.

About 20,000 people crowded into Fairgrounds Park in Oklahoma City on July 9, 1938, to hear FDR three days before the primary election. It was his fifth speech in Oklahoma during that campaign trip; he had made platform talks during brief stops at Wister, McAlester, Holdenville and Shawnee before his 10-car train arrived in Oklahoma City.

The speech was broadcast on all of Oklahoma's radio stations.

FDR's visit to Oklahoma was part of a last-minute campaign tour to help defeat Georgia Sen. Walter George, also a Democrat, who had opposed administration issues on several occasions, and to re-elect Thomas, who had supported the president's issues. Roosevelt's entourage included Secretary of State Cordell Hull and Treasury Secretary Henry Morganthau.

Marland, who was running against Thomas for the Democratic nomination for the Senate seat, had called on Oklahomans on the eve of Roosevelt's visit not to "surrender" to the president at the polls. "It's a question whether Oklahoma wants to assert its constitutional right to select its own senator or whether it wants to surrender that right to the chief executive," Marland said.

In spite of Marland's blast, FDR included him in his "few kind words" but he made his praise of Thomas a bit stronger – saying, "Senator Thomas has been of enormous help in keeping me informed of the needs of the people of Oklahoma."

Deviating from his text, Roosevelt referred to Murray, another Democrat, as a "nationally known Republican."

Disney was astounded because Roosevelt did not men-

Oklahoma Historical Society

President Franklin D. Roosevelt visited Oklahoma in 1938 to support U.S. Sen. J. Elmer Thomas, D-Okla. Thomas is pictured in this undated photo.

tion him and gave credit to Thomas and Lee for the Grand River dam. Disney said that "the only thing Thomas ever did was to oppose the dam."

Disney said he had spent seven years working on funding for the dam and Lee "never knew anything about it." He also pointed out that Thomas had said a few months earlier that Disney deserved all the credit for the dam because he (Thomas) had nothing to do with it.

It was one of the most unusual elections in Oklahoma history. The 1937 Legislature had abolished the run-off primary election, which meant that party candidates were chosen by straight pluralities at the July primary.

In those days, winning the Democratic nomination for a state office was tantamount to election although Republicans were running for some offices, including the Senate seat.

And two former governors were candidates for governor – the colorful Murray, who served during 1931-35, and Jack Walton, who was impeached and convicted in 1923 in the first year of his term. Walton was a corporation commissioner when he ran in 1938.

All the major candidates for state offices except Murray and Walton were at the Roosevelt speech, hoping they would receive his famous smile on their campaigns. Murray and Walton continued their regular campaign schedules.

Roosevelt's endorsement may have helped Thomas win re-election. He ran far ahead of his nearest competitor, Gomer Smith of Oklahoma City, who had been endorsed by the Tulsa World in an editorial that appeared on the same front page that reported FDR's visit.

Marland ran a distant third. Thomas had a Republican opponent, but he defeated him in November by a large margin of votes.

Leon C. "Red" Phillips of Okemah won the Democratic nomination (and election) for governor, Murray came in third and Walton ran a distant fourth.

In spite of the snub by Roosevelt during that campaign trip, Disney won the Democratic nomination and re-election. He eventually served seven terms in the House, leaving in 1944 to run as an anti-New Deal candidate against Thomas, who won the nomination again.

Executing criminals just another job

Pulling the switch on the state's electric chair to execute condemned criminals was "just another job" to Rich Owens, who killed more people in Oklahoma than anyone except for Murrah Building bomber Timothy McVeigh.

Owens served as the state's executioner from 1918 until 1947, a period during which he killed 61 in the chair that he built in 1915.

"Someone had to do it," Owens frequently told reporters, adding that he didn't do the executions for the money – $100 per single execution and $50 for each extra execution on days when two or three were electrocuted. His regular job was as a gang boss of inmate work crews at the state penitentiary in McAlester.

"I never give 'em a thought afterwards," he told a reporter for The Daily Oklahoman in 1948 a few weeks before he died of cancer at the age of 67. "When I pull that switch, it don't bother me any more than jerking a chicken's head off. Tomorrow after an electrocution, I can't even recall the name."

Owens also performed the only hanging at the state penitentiary, which didn't go well, and electrocuted three in New Mexico, two in Arkansas and two in Texas. He also killed two with a knife, six by shooting and one with a long-handled shovel, most as they were trying to escape. He was tried and acquitted of murder charges four times.

Joplin native Richard Ernest Owens' first killing was when he was 13 and shot a man who was stealing a horse owned by Owens' father. He killed a man with a knife during a fight in Heavener; fatally shot a disgruntled miner, whom he had fired, during a gunfight; and killed another man while trailing a fugitive who had killed a sheriff's deputy.

Owens was a coal-mine pit boss before going to work for the penitentiary in 1909. He built the electric chair in 1915 when the state's first capital punishment law was enacted and set the method of execution as electrocution. He tested his design by electrocuting a calf.

The electric chair was first used on June 1, 1915, but prison chief engineer S.C. Treadwell pulled the switch that time and the next eight times. Owens assisted Treadwell by strapping in the prisoners and making connections. "I was sort of general handy man," he said.

The prison hired an executioner from Arkansas but he

Tulsa World archives

The electric chair formerly used at Oklahoma State Penitentiary is now on display at a museum next to the prison. Rich Owens designed the chair and was the executioner for 61 condemned inmates.

was so drunk for his first execution at McAlester, he had to have help to pull the switch. Two months later, he was too drunk to pull the switch on a scheduled execution and the warden asked Owens, "Can you pull it?"

"I didn't say a word. I just walked over and slapped it to him like I had been doing it all my life," Owens told an Oklahoman reporter years later. "Someone had to do it as the fellow was already in the chair waiting."

Owens was offered the executioner job the next day and kept it until his health forced him to retire in 1947.

The only hanging at the penitentiary was June 19, 1936, when Arthur Gooch, a federal prisoner convicted under the Lindbergh kidnapping law. He was put to death by Owens on a special gallows built inside the prison walls and dismantled before prisoners awoke the next day. Because the noose around Gooch's neck slipped or the knot was faulty, Gooch choked to death, a process that took 15 minutes, rather than dying of a broken neck.

Owens beat a prisoner to death with a shovel after that prisoner and another tried to use him as a shield in an escape attempt. They had taken Owens hostage, hit him on the head with a hatchet, tied his hands with barbed wire and stuck a knife into his back.

He said later the prisoners twisted the knife in his back to indicate which way to walk. Owens warned the two that their escape attempt would be futile and that they shouldn't ask for mercy because he planned to kill them if they continued. In response to Owens' shouts, a tower guard shot one of the convicts and Owens was able to wrest the knife away, using it to kill that escapee.

The other man jumped through a window of the tool shed where Owens grabbed a shovel and beat him to death as he pleaded, "Please don't kill me, Mr. Rich."

Owens' electric chair was used 15 more times after his retirement, the last in 1966. The Supreme Court ruled in 1972 that the death penalty as then administered was unconstitutional. When executions resumed in 1990, the method of execution was changed to lethal injection, which has been the form of death for 84 prisoners since.

Using the injection method, three drugs are injected by three persons who are not identified as executioners and are not allowed to talk with reporters.

The chair built by Owens now sits in the penitentiary's museum.

Teacher believed in glow of the future

Calling the century nearing its end "the sublimest the world has ever known" and predicting greater things to come, Jessie Thatcher became the first female graduate of Oklahoma A&M College.

It was 1897, and she marveled at the comforts and conveniences of the 19th century in her speech to the other two graduates of that year and the guests at their commencement exercise.

"Look back 50 years and from the dim twilight of the tallow candle, we now stand in the brilliant electric light," she said in her oration. She also pointed to other comforts: "We travel in elegant cars, sleep on luxurious beds, dine better than the kings of old. Our railroads carry us all over this great country, even in midwinter, without the least discomfort."

After she listed many comforts and conveniences that were not available just a few years earlier, she pointed out that the processes that brought them about had not been easy.

She said the progress had come from conservatism, from the persistent efforts of enthusiastic, radical men and women with ideas in their brains and with the courage in their hearts to make them practical.

She predicted that "mental development of the next century will be more complex and will bring versatility on a higher plane than has yet been known."

Thatcher made the oration in keeping with the example set by the previous year's class – the first at the college established by the 1890 Oklahoma Territorial Legislature – that all graduating seniors should deliver an original oration. She would have been a member of that first class, but a bout with typhoid fever caused her to miss a year.

"Education is the one all-important thing, paramount to everything else," she said in the key point in her oration, which she titled "The Dawning of the Twentieth Century."

She supported education for the rest of her life, working

Tulsa World archives

Jessie Thatcher Bost, the first female graduate of Oklahoma A&M College, was a teacher for many years in Stillwater, Alva and Cleveland, Okla. She remained a supporter of her alma mater throughout her life.

as a teacher for many years in Stillwater, Alva and Cleveland, Okla., and always boosting her alma mater.

The college, now Oklahoma State University, honored her in 1925 by naming one of its women's dormitories Jessie Thatcher Hall.

She is a member of the Oklahoma Women's Hall of Fame, inducted posthumously in 1997, and is one of Oklahoma's "100 Notable Women of Style," according to Oklahoma Today magazine.

Her 1897 oration is on file in OSU's special collections and archives.

An Iowa native, Thatcher came to Oklahoma Territory with her parents in a covered wagon. She and her sister, Jennie, were among the 40 or so students enrolled in the college preparatory class when A&M opened in 1891.

After graduation, she taught at Stillwater for nearly 10 years and married Henry Bost, another A&M graduate, in 1902. They homesteaded in western Oklahoma, where they lived in a sod house for a year before moving to Alva in 1907.

She put her teaching career on hold until her four children were grown, but she never lost her interest in education. She organized the Parent-Teachers Association of Alva and later was the organization's district chairwoman.

After her husband died in 1933, Bost taught two years at Alva and then moved to Cleveland to begin a teaching career that lasted nearly 20 years. She never missed an OSU reunion until she had a stroke in 1961, two years before she died.

When she retired, OSU President Dr. Henry G. Bennett praised her for attaching herself "to a great cause – the education of youth" and called her Oklahoma's first woman of education.

"I like to think of her as a symbol of all that womanhood, womanly institutions and womanly courage have brought to our civilization," Bennett said.

Big posse fanned out to find outlaws

More than 1,000 men from Oklahoma, Kansas and Arkansas formed a posse in a driving cold winter rain to search for six notorious outlaws believed hiding in the rugged, sparsely populated Cookson Hills of eastern Oklahoma.

The posse arrested 21 people, including three women, but the searchers were disappointed because they didn't find any of the "big guns" they were seeking, such as Charles A. "Pretty Boy" Floyd. Most of those arrested were released after questioning.

Word of the planned search of the hills that had become known as a bandits' haven leaked out before the posse began its search, forcing it to move up its action by several hours on Feb. 18, 1934.

Still, O.P. Ray, leader of the Oklahoma Bureau of Investigation, was elated at the success of the drive, which he said had shown the state's peace officers what results can be obtained from a concentrated drive on criminals.

"The natives of these hills will think twice in the future before they board and room criminals in their homes or afford them protection of any kind," he said. Authorities had long believed that criminals took refuge there because they would be fed and housed by residents.

Ray said future notices of such raids would be sent in code to prevent the public from knowing of a drive in advance. "In several instances, raiding parties searched known bandit hide-outs, only to find the persons being sought had left just a few hours earlier," he said.

The posse was made up of Oklahoma National Guardsmen; state officers from Oklahoma, Kansas and Missouri; sheriffs and deputies from counties in Oklahoma as far away as Comanche; federal agents; and city police officers from Tulsa and Oklahoma City.

It was called the largest manhunt in the country's history.

Posse members stopped all cars as they traveled on the few highways through the area that generally was bounded by Tahlequah, Fort Gibson, Muskogee, Gore, Vian, Sallisaw, Marble and Stilwell. Some of the posse members walked through the hills to search remote houses.

The National Guard set up roadblocks (that was years before the Oklahoma Highway Patrol was organized) that were manned with machine guns. About 40 of the other officers had submachine guns.

Maj. Wint Smith, commander of the Kansas Highway Pa-

Tulsa World archives

The Tulsa World front page on February 18, 1934, announced a multiagency posse armed with machine guns and bombs converged on the Cookson Hills for what was called the largest manhunt in the country's history.

trol, who brought 25 of his men to join the search, said Kansas officers had an interest in the raid because "every time there is a break at Lansing (the state penitentiary), most of the escapees head for the Cookson Hills."

The Cookson Hills crime offensive was a topic at a state convention of the Oklahoma Peace Officers Association in Tulsa six weeks earlier, and officers later gathered information from informants that Floyd and the other five men were hiding out there.

The time for the raid was moved up after Police Chief Tom Brumley, officer C.P. Lloyd and three robbers were killed in a Sapulpa shootout Feb. 4, and a sheriff's deputy and robber were killed in a shootout at Chelsea the next night.

One of the bandits killed at Sapulpa was from Sallisaw and was thought to be an accomplice of Floyd. The gunman killed at Chelsea was thought to have been a member of a Cookson Hills gang.

The Sapulpa shootings occurred in raids at the farm home of a man thought to be providing refuge for Aussie Elliott of Sallisaw, who was killed in the shootings, and other bandits. After word of the police chief's killing spread, a crowd of about 500 gathered at the courthouse where the farmer was held in jail. A Tulsa National Guard unit was activated to help maintain order.

Rogers County Deputy Al Powell was killed after he and a night watchman questioned two men they saw standing near a hardware store at 1:45 a.m.

The body of outlaw Eddie Clanton was found two hours later in an alley. He had been killed by fellow robber Ford Bradshaw, who kidnapped a Chelsea boy and forced him to drive him to Fort Smith.

Bradshaw warned the boy not to tell police about the trip, "for I killed a law at Chelsea last night and then I murdered my pal who was going to help me loot that hardware store." He added: "I know where you live."

While the 1,000 posse members went about their business seeking robbers and killers, Tahlequah Mayor James Thompson had another worry – the livelihood and comfort of his town's residents.

"Don't let the boys tear down any of our stills," he urged Ray. "These stills have been the means of refreshment and have furnished bread and butter to the operators all during the Depression."

Inspector Ray assured the mayor the stills would be spared "because of the quality of their product."

Dole Derby a daring, disastrous feat

Tulsa World archives

The Woolaroc won the first-place $25,000 prize in an airplane race from Oakland, Calif., to Honolulu in 1927. The plane was backed by Oklahoma oilman Frank Phillips.

Stunt pilot Arthur Goebel, who made his living flying loops for the movies, and his navigator flew from Oakland, Calif., to Honolulu to win a $25,000 prize as the first commercial pilot to make the trip.

Goebel and navigator Navy Lt. William Davis Jr. made that 1927 flight in an airplane financed by Phillips Petroleum Co. of Bartlesville as part of a race sponsored by pineapple king James Dole to promote commercial flights to the islands.

The flight was called "the greatest air feat in history" by Charles A. Lindbergh, who had flown solo from New York to Paris a few months earlier but who turned down an invitation to join the Dole Derby.

"Goebel's indomitable courage, Dole's pineapple money and Phillips' gas turned the trick," Phillips Petroleum Co. President Frank Phillips wired Dole. "Deliver the goods."

By "goods," Phillips meant the $25,000 prize. "Naturally we are delighted at having backed a winner," Phillips said. "We had a lot of faith in Goebel."

Goebel and Davis weren't the first to make the flight. Two Army pilots flew from Oakland to Oahu shortly after the Dole Derby was announced but they weren't eligible for the prize. Neither were pilots Ernie Smith and Emory Bronte, who flew from Oakland to Molokai a few weeks after the Army pilots' trip.

Lindbergh had completed his flight to Paris on May 22, 1927, and Dole announced plans for his Dole Derby three days later, offering $25,000 to the winner and $10,000 to the runner-up.

He hoped to attract Lindbergh, whose flight across the Atlantic in May he called a "forerunner of eventual Transpacific air transportation." But Lindbergh wasn't interested.

Goebel, who had been flying since 1912, used all his funds and appealed to Phillips to help him finance his flight. Phillips agreed but insisted the Travel Air plane built in Wichita be named the Woolaroc after Phillips' lodge in Osage County near Bartlesville.

Phillips and other Oklahomans also financed another Travel Air plane, the Oklahoma, in the race that began in Oakland on Aug. 16, 1927. But the Oklahoma, piloted by Bennett Griffin, had to turn back shortly after takeoff.

The race took a high toll in lives. Three men were killed en route to the Oakland airport, where they were to begin the race. Two planes carrying four men and a woman disappeared over the Pacific.

And two pilots flying a plane called Dallas Spirit disappeared over the ocean while searching for the five missing derby pilots. The Dallas Spirit had entered the race but had been forced to turn back after taking off. It later flew toward Hawaii in the search.

"We went into a tail spin – S.O.S. – we came out of it, but were sure scared," one of the Spirit pilots said in a message tapped out in Morse code. "We thought it was all off. The lights on the instrument board went out and it was so dark that Bill couldn't see the – we are in a spin – S.O.S. "

And that was the last heard from the searchers.

Smith, who had made the flight a few weeks earlier, called the Dole race a big mistake. "It is stunt flying and not practical with land planes," he said.

Secretary of the Navy Curtis Wilbur said a federal push should be made to prevent anything like the Dole disaster from happening again. Other Navy officials predicted hazardous ocean flights would be made illegal.

Goebel, who made his first visit to Oklahoma when he picked up his airplane, had wanted to make the Dole Derby flight alone to allow him to carry more fuel. But the race rules required a navigator so a fuel tank was installed between the pilot's and the navigator's compartments.

The two communicated via a clothesline pulley rigged up between the two compartments.

A few weeks later, thousands greeted Goebel and Lindbergh in Tulsa, where they were guests of the joint International Petroleum Exposition and Tulsa State Fair.

Lindbergh flew low over downtown in his Spirit of St. Louis, the plane he flew from New York to Paris, circled and made a low pass over McEntyre Airport, where thousands were waiting to greet him. Goebel had arrived earlier in his Woolaroc plane, which he flew around the Philtower before landing at McEntyre Airport.

Fairchild pioneered 'cooking with radar'

When you heat a cup of coffee in fewer than two minutes or pop a bag of popcorn in your microwave oven, you can thank former Tulsan Margaret Fairchild.

Fairchild didn't invent microwave ovens but she helped develop many of the recipes for cooking in what in the early days of its development was called a "radar range."

She explained the new contraption to a reporter during a visit to Tulsa in the early 1950s but warned they were too pricey for general use. She said the only one in this area was in Little Rock and explained that radar tubes for the ovens cost $500 and that repairs were expensive.

But she predicted the new oven would become a household necessity.

Fairchild, a home economics expert, began her microwave work in 1948 when she was at Teachers College at Columbia University and spent part of her time at Waltham, Mass., at the Raytheon Co. with electronics engineers experimenting with recipes.

"Her greatest contribution to our way of doing things was in the late 1940s and early 1950s when she helped Raytheon develop what to do with its new 'radar range,'" said her niece, former state Rep. Betty Boyd.

Boyd also was a former host of talk shows on KOTV and KTUL.

"Raytheon had this thing they were convinced would revolutionize cooking to accompany the instant lifestyle that was becoming popular," Boyd said.

But standard recipes didn't work the same in a microwave oven because everything cooked so rapidly. That meant that less water had to be used in many recipes.

"Our greatest challenge was brownies because they cook so fast," Fairchild told a reporter in a 1979 visit to Tulsa.

And cooks had to learn how to use new types of cookware because the microwaves didn't work with aluminum cookware or steel pots and pans.

Betty Boyd

Former Tulsan Margaret Fairchild pioneered microwave oven recipes.

One of her early demonstrations involved the use of a full ear of dried popcorn, which she put into a cellophane bag with a dash of salt and some butter – and in 30 seconds, she would open the oven to demonstrate a bag full of popcorn ready to eat.

Another demonstration she told about in that 1979 interview involved putting ice cream and a piece of cake in the bottom of a paper cup, topping it with fudge sauce and freezing it. A few seconds in a microwave would produce hot sauce on top of still-frozen ice cream and defrosted cake.

Fairchild came to Tulsa in 1919 when fresh out of Central Missouri State College at Warrensburg and taught at Irving and Osage elementary schools. She later opened the cafeteria at Roosevelt Elementary School and became head of food management at Central High School.

During her years in food service at the schools, she developed many recipes – chocolate pie, biscuits and bean chowder – that were used for generations and that are still sought by readers of the Tulsa World's recipe column.

Fairchild left Tulsa in the early 1940s to earn a master's degree in institutional food service at Columbia and help Raytheon develop recipes using a microwave oven in the basement. She also helped the Navy with research on the use of microwave ovens aboard submarines.

Although she was an early expert on the use of a microwave oven, Fairchild never abandoned the use of stovetop or gas oven cooking. She retired in the early 1970s and died in 1980 at the age of 82.

Fairchild was the first guest on a talk show program hosted by Boyd on KOTV in 1954, appearing as an expert on the "new and controversial" method of cooking.

During that interview, she predicted that the phrase "now you're cooking with gas" would disappear from American slang and be updated to "now you're cooking with radar."

Black aviators cross the continent

Two young Oklahoma pilots became the first black aviators to cross the continent by air when they flew from Los Angeles to New York in 1932 in an airplane put together from junkyard parts.

The trip required 41 hours and 27 minutes flying time but it was spread over 21 days because the pilots, Thomas C. Allen of Oklahoma City and J. Herman Banning of El Reno, made 25 stops to raise money during the 3,300-mile trip.

They were seeking a $1,000 prize they had heard was being offered for the first black pilot to make the trip. But the prize turned out to be fictitious – no prize sponsor was ever found.

"We were wined and dined in New York and they rebuilt the airplane for us," Allen recalled years later. But the two had to barnstorm their way back home, including putting on air shows in Pittsburgh and Chicago to earn money for the trip.

Allen, who had learned to fly as a teenager, moved to California in 1929 to work for a black airplane club but

Tulsa World archives

Thomas C. Allen is shown with his plane. In 1932, he and J. Herman Banning flew from Los Angeles to New York, stopping along the way to raise money for their trip.

"the week I arrived in California, the stock market crashed and the bank and finance company came out and took all the airplanes the club had," he told a reporter in 1981. "There we sat with nothing."

Club members scoured the junkyards and by 1932 had spent $450 on enough parts from crashed airplanes to put together a biplane that Allen, 25, and fellow club member Banning, 33, would fly in their cross-continent trip that began Sept. 19, 1932.

The two agreed to change pilots at every stop so that the flying was split evenly and also planned to split the prize money evenly.

At each landing, one or both would go into town wearing helmets and goggles and flying clothes – "we made a spectacle of ourselves," Allen recalled – to make a plea for funds at a black pool hall or a church. A collection of a few dollars was always taken up and the pilots could start on the next leg of their trip.

When they landed in Tulsa, oilman W.G. Skelly financed them as far as St. Louis, where students at an aeronautics school overhauled their 1914 Curtiss engine. The last leg of their trip was financed by Pittsburgh supporters of Franklin Delano Roosevelt who paid them to drop leaflets supporting FDR for president in the cities they flew over.

A few weeks after their cross-country flight, Banning was killed in a plane crash during an air show at San Diego. He was riding in the passenger seat of a plane piloted by a sailor who made a steep climb that caused the plane to stall and crash as an estimated 2,000 watched.

Banning was born in Oklahoma Territory in 1899 but his family moved in 1919 to Ames, Iowa, where he studied electrical engineering at Iowa State College. He learned to fly in Des Moines and became the first black person to obtain a license. He moved to Los Angeles in 1929 to become the chief pilot for the Bessie Coleman Aero Club, named for a woman who was the first black licensed pilot.

Allen fell in love with airplanes as an 11-year-old when a pilot landed on the family's farm near Quitman, Texas. The pilot asked him and other children to keep the cows away from his plane to keep them from eating the fabric off the aircraft. When the family moved to Oklahoma City, Allen traded a saxophone as a down payment and work for flying lessons – several weeks of work between each 20-minute flying lesson.

When it came time for him to solo, Allen didn't have the $500 required as a bond – in case he crashed and damaged the airplane.

But, he recalled in a 1980 interview, a white pilot told him during a hangar session that involved some home brew, "If you're the great Negro pilot you say you are, you'd just take the plane," to which Allen responded to the group of white pilots, "If you are so brave, you'll start the plane for me."

They did and he did. The owner of the plane wasn't pleased. When he saw his plane flying over Oklahoma City, he raced back to the airport – but Allen had soloed. He took a job as a mechanic at Kelly Field in San Antonio, where he slept in the hangar and ate his meals in the back of a white restaurant.

After the L.A.-New York flight, Allen made a career of aviation. He was a ferry pilot during World War II and worked as a mechanic for Douglas Aircraft Co., retiring after 30 years.

After his retirement, Allen served for several years as a lecturer at the Oklahoma Air Space Museum in Oklahoma City, often discussing the obstacles faced by early black aviators. He died in 1989.

Prosecutor too persuasive; case retried

A Tulsa woman convicted of murder in the killing of her prominent attorney husband was granted a new trial because the prosecutor's closing argument was too good.

Judge Henry Hudson said he was convinced that the jury would not have convicted Laura Reuter had it not been for the closing argument of state's attorney Pat Malloy.

"In all my experience in the criminal courts of the state, I never before heard such a convincing and analytical argument before a jury," the judge said. A large crowd in the Bartlesville courtroom, where the case had been moved on a change of venue, immediately broke into applause, which was believed to be an ovation for the Tulsa county attorney.

The judge said he also took into consideration the testimony of Tulsa attorney Harry Campbell, who said Bud Ballew, a chauffeur for another suspect, had told him that Mrs. Reuter had not taken part in the conspiracy to kill the victim. Campbell had previously represented Mrs. Reuter.

"The case is not dismissed by any means," Malloy told a reporter. "We have much newly discovered evidence and we will be prepared to prosecute the case more vigorously than ever when the new trial comes up."

But Reuter was acquitted in a retrial that ran for 19 days before it ended on Jan. 31, 1914.

The new trial ruling was announced Oct. 8, 1913, and the World published an extra edition to inform readers of the new development in what it called the state's most sensational murder case, printing details of the decision under a two-line banner headline.

Mrs. Reuter was charged with the May 5, 1912, slaying of Charles T. Reuter as he slept in a bedroom across a hall from his wife in the Reuter house in Tulsa. She told police her husband had been killed by a burglar. Neighbors, awakened by screams from Mrs. Reuter, said they had seen a man fleeing.

She testified that she awoke when someone shined a flashlight in her face and she heard her husband telling someone in his bedroom, "You have got me this time but I

Tulsa World archives

The Tulsa World front page on Oct. 4, 1913, outlines the conviction of Laura Reuter in the murder of her husband, a prominent attorney. She was acquitted in a retrial a few months later.

will get you yet, damn you." Then, she said, she heard two gunshots, heard someone fall and saw an intruder run out of the house.

The murder and subsequent trial had all the elements to make it a sensational case:

The victim was prominent.

Mrs. Reuter was an attractive woman who had been her husband's stenographer in Peoria, Ill., and she was named as a co-respondent in a divorce case filed by Reuters' first wife.

The couple quarreled frequently and slept in separate rooms.

She said he had abused her and there were rumors she had been intimate with co-defendant Guy McKenzie, whose sister was a close friend.

McKenzie and fellow co-defendant Joe Baker were convicted of murder on Nov. 1, 1912, by a Tulsa jury that required only two ballots after a 27-day trial. They were sentenced to life in prison.

Mrs. Reuter had been convicted and sentenced to life in prison in the earlier trial that had been moved to Bartlesville on a change of venue motion.

The defendant fainted in the courtroom during defense attorney J.R. Charleton's closing argument and again as the jury entered the courtroom with a verdict.

"I never heard the verdict as it was read," she told reporters later. "I dreamed last night that I was acquitted and felt confident that the jury would find me not guilty."

After the verdict, jurors visited Reuter in her apartment in a Bartlesville hotel to shake hands with her and several kissed her, she said.

In the retrial when the not guilty verdict was returned, defense attorney Bob Thompson yelped for joy, Reuter threw out her arms as she leaped up and again lapsed into unconsciousness as the crowd in the courtroom cheered until the judge restored order.

Reuter returned to Tulsa by train and told newspaper reporters in a news conference at her home that there was no truth to the rumor she planned to marry a Peoria man who came to Oklahoma to be with her during the trial. She did get married again a few months later, but to a different man.

Powerhouse club dominated foes

A group of American Indians, most from Oklahoma who got together in the early 1920s for some football scrimmaging, became a big-time professional team that developed into the powerhouse club of the Oklahoma, Kansas and Missouri area.

After the Hominy Indians players – some with experience, others with none – won 28 consecutive victories, a sportswriter called the players "the terrors of the Midwest."

It was an apt description for the players, who came from more than 20 tribes during the team's 10-year existence and traveled from coast to coast playing football against all comers, Sometimes they played in pastures with chalked yard markers and sometimes in stadiums capable of holding up to 50,000 fans.

The all-Indian pro team was organized in 1922 by Ira Hamilton, a young Osage of Hominy who bought the first uniforms, taught the players a few basic plays and served as coach until a regular coach could be hired. When the players felt ready to play a game, they competed against a team from Skiatook and won.

According to a 1967 Oklahoma Today article, the first coach of record was Pete Houser, former Carlisle and Haskell star, who guided the Indians to two winning seasons, defeating teams in Oklahoma, Missouri and Kansas.

The team had such a winning record, new opponents had to be found by 1925 to replace those who had lost earlier. That forced the Indians to travel greater distances and increased expenses. But a group of Osage tribal leaders came to the team's financial aid. Their influence helped attract boys who were graduating from Indian schools and who considered it a matter of pride to play for an all-Indian pro team.

Football players in the 1920s seldom received more than $150 per game, and they frequently received less. They also risked broken bones, torn ligaments, hospital bills and other injuries – all for the joy of playing the game they loved.

The team never owned a bus, but took road trips in a caravan of Pierce-Arrow or Buick touring cars. Touring cars were larger than standard automobiles; most were capable of holding seven passengers.

Players frequently played the entire 60 minutes of a game and often did not know what position they would play

Tulsa World archives

The Hominy Indians, coached by Tiny Roebuck, played a group of National Football League all-star players at Tulsa's McNulty Park, near 11th Street and Elgin Avenue.

until they were assigned there. Linemen played all positions on the line, and an end might be assigned to play as a fullback. They also frequently played in cold rain and used the same wet ball throughout a game.

Throughout the years, players represented Osage, Pawnee, Otoe, Creek, Seminole, Cheyenne, Arapaho, Sioux, Cherokee, Navajo, Kiowa, Seneca, Sac and Fox and Potawatomi tribes. An Eskimo from Alaska also played.

"Johnnie Martin, former pitcher for the Guthrie baseball team in the Oklahoma State League, went into the game in the fourth quarter," a Hominy News article reported about a 1924 game against Avant. "Martin skirted right end for a gain of 20 yards but Hominy was penalized 15 yards for Martin's having failed to report to the referee."

A few plays later, Martin ran from the 20-yard line for the winning touchdown.

Martin later became known as Pepper Martin, who played third base for the St. Louis Cardinals in the 1930s and became one of baseball's most celebrated players. Even after he joined the Cardinals, Martin played with the Hominy football team, to the chagrin of Cardinal officials.

The Indians' first crack at a big-name team, the New York Giants, came on the day after Christmas in 1927 at Pawhuska. Football fans from throughout the country showed up, and betting in oil-rich Pawhuska was heavy, primarily on the Giants. But the Indians won, 13-6, and again in a game in San Antonio two weeks later. It was customary for teams to place twice in a season.

A year later, the Indians, then coached by Tiny Roebuck, played a group of National Football League all-star players at Tulsa's McNulty Park, near 11th Street and Elgin Avenue, losing to the team coached by Steve Owen, 27-0. Owen later became the longtime coach of the New York Giants and was inducted into the Pro Football Hall of Fame.

Approximately 1,000 fans turned out to watch the Dec. 30, 1928, game, the only professional game played in Tulsa that season.

"The poor punting of the Indians practically contributed two touchdowns to the All Stars," according to a Tulsa World story, but it also reported the all-star backs were able to pierce the Indians' forward wall at will.

Martin was Mr. Excitement in '31 series

Pepper Martin, who rose from Oklahoma farm boy to fame as a big-league baseball player, fell in love with America's favorite pastime as a small boy when Boston Red Sox pitchers Babe Ruth and Dutch Leonard were his heroes.

His love of the game endured, continuing after Martin retired from playing baseball, became manager of several teams, coached the Tulsa Oilers, and, later, became a radio broadcaster.

He was known as the "Wild Horse of the Osage" because of a short career playing professional football with the Hominy Indians in the 1920s. In Red Smith's book on baseball, he was called, "for at least one 10-day span of his life, the most exciting ball player in human history" – the 10 days being the period of ball he played at the 1931 World Series.

While still in grammar school, Martin delivered The Daily Oklahoman in Oklahoma City – after, of course, he read the statistics of major league games under a corner streetlight at 3:30 a.m.

For the next few years, while alternately attending junior high school and working various jobs, playing ball remained on his mind.

"Oh, man, how I wanted to play ball," he told a St. Louis Post reporter in 1931.

"I played on a sandlot team and then, finally, pitched for the Second Presbyterian Church in the city league but got canned because I didn't go to Sunday school," he said. "Then I played with the National Guard team but got the gate again because I didn't want to join the Guard."

He played for company teams and for several semipro teams in Oklahoma before going to the Greenville, Texas, professional team. He finally reached the limelight with the St. Louis Cardinals in the 1931 World Series and remained with them for 13 seasons.

Martin hit .500 during 24 times at bat and stole five bases in that series, earning credit for almost single-handedly winning two of the four games that St. Louis won against the Philadelphia Athletics, which many believe was Connie Mack's greatest team.

Born John Leonard Martin on a farm near Temple, Martin changed his name legally to Pepper Martin, the name he was given while playing at Fort Smith by that team's business manager because of his pep-filled attitude and

Pepper Martin (right) is pictured with umpire Augie Guglielmo. Martin coached the minor league Miami Marlins in 1959.

excitement. He got the Wild Horse of the Osage nickname because of his speed and galloping gait while playing football with the Hominy Indians.

Martin also was noted for his head-first slides that caused his uniforms to look soiled.

When Martin died in March 1965, a Tulsa World editorial said the first instinct was to describe Martin as colorful, but pointed out "that would be like calling the giant carrier Enterprise a big ship."

He once told a reporter, "You've probably heard a lot of tales about me, and most of them are true."

When he was hired to play for the Cardinals in 1931, he showed up looking like a tramp. He had cashed in the train ticket he was given for the trip to the team's practice site at Brandenton, Fla., and instead hopped freight trains to make the trip.

It wasn't the first or last time he reasoned that it was a "waste of good money" to ride on a passenger coach instead of hopping a freight and riding free, even though he always arrived looking like a bum.

Mobbed by fans in a Philadelphia hotel, he was asked how he could account for the success of his game. "I dunno," he replied. "I'm just takin' my natural swing, and the ball is hittin' the fat part of the bat."

Another fan wanted to know where he learned to run the way he did and he replied, "Well, sir, I grew up in Oklahoma, and once you start runnin' out there, there ain't nothing to stop you."

Martin clowned around a lot off the field. One of his stunts recalled by Time magazine in 1940 was when he and a couple of other players donned white coveralls, picked up paint cans and brushes and walked into a Philadelphia hotel dining room to announce, "C'mon folks. You have to leave. We have to paint these walls for a banquet in an hour. Don't bother about paying the checks. Scram."

But he didn't joke on the baseball field. As a manager, he once was ejected from a minor league game and fined for choking the umpire.

"When you had your hands on that man's throat, what could you have been thinking?" the league president asked him later.

"I was thinking I'd like to choke him to death," Martin replied.

Bank robber said crime didn't pay

When bank robber Henry Wells was released in 1921 after serving five years in prison, the warden called him a "model prisoner."

A week later, Wells robbed the bank at Nelagony.

And he continued robbing banks until 1934, but was never convicted again, although he was tried 14 times.

He announced his retirement from the "banking business," which he said was not very profitable, in 1946. His attorneys assured him that he couldn't be prosecuted for any of his crimes because of the statute of limitations.

Wells estimated his take at $100,000, but he went on the state's old-age pension rolls when he turned 65 and lived on that plus a few dollars a day from bets on snooker games until his death in 1963 at the age of 82.

"The fact that I got away with so many bank jobs ain't any proof that it's a good business," Wells told Pawhuska Journal-Capital editor Frank Kniseley in 1946. "I had to get on the old pension rolls so I'd have enough to live on.

"The outlaws that live don't ever have anything. They either have to pay it to lawyers to keep them out of jail or else they just waste it trying to keep from getting caught."

Legends held that Wells had caches of loot hidden in various places, but he never talked about it. Several years before his death, he remembered he had hidden some cash along a creek and found $25.39. He donated the money to the Sister Kenny Foundation for infantile paralysis. He said he couldn't recall from which robbery that money came.

Wells sometimes worked with the Al Spencer gang -- including helping to plan one of the last train holdups ever. He didn't participate in it because his horse threw a shoe. He also worked with Charles A. "Pretty Boy" Floyd who, Wells said, was the "only person I ever ratted on."

He took credit for preventing Floyd from kidnapping Frank Phillips, president of the Phillips Petroleum Co., in 1934 shortly before Floyd was killed by FBI agents near East Liverpool, Ohio.

Wells told employees at Phillips' Osage County ranch

Tulsa World archives

Bank robber Henry Wells said bankers often profited more from stickups than he did.

that the kidnapping was planned, and guards were posted at all the gates the night the Floyd gang showed up at the ranch. "I told Pretty Boy I'd rather someone would kidnap my father than Frank Phillips."

He said Phillips had been "like a daddy" to him and that he had been a guest at the Phillips ranch several times.

Wells continually insisted that many bankers made more money from his crimes than he did because they exaggerated their losses to insurance agencies.

He once met one of the bankers he had robbed when he was a guest at Phillips' ranch. He said he walked up to the banker and asked "what did you do with that $22,000? You told the bank examiner I got $25,000 but I just counted $3,000."

Another time, he said, he and Spencer "cut the water off" on another banker who always reported his losses as higher than they were. "We just decided not to do any more business with that fellow. He was making more than we were by collecting more insurance than he was supposed to get."

Wells claimed that he never lied, but former Washington County Sheriff Grif Graham, who had arrested him several times, said "he just told the truth in such a way that nobody would believe it, and he let a lot people lie to provide alibis for him."

Henry had never driven a car until after robbing that bank at Nelagony a week after getting out of prison. He said he didn't get much in the robbery – "just enough to buy a new Ford and load it with canned goods and presents for the boys at Mac."

He loaded the canned goods and presents in the back and hid his .45-caliber pistol at the side of the front seat and started driving toward McAlester. But he was involved in a traffic accident because he was driving on the left side of the highway.

When a sheriff who investigated the accident learned Wells was taking gifts to his pals in the prison, he was so touched that he had Wells' car repaired and allowed him to continue on his trip.

Sands of time conceal buried treasure

You could get rich by grabbing a shovel and digging.

The key, of course, is to dig in the right place.

And it's questionable where that right place is. During the early 1930s, the Tulsa World ran a long series of articles about reports of buried treasure, none of which was ever found.

Those reports involved loot buried by bandits such as Jesse James, the Younger brothers and even Belle Starr. Other reports claimed that Spaniards buried money in the state and that pioneers hid their money in the ground. None of the reports was verified.

Some of the robbers and the pioneers went back for their treasure – but couldn't find it, according to the legends. The land had changed, and one piece of dirt looked like every other piece of dirt.

Jesse James and his gang reportedly hid $2 million of their loot near Fort Sill and cached $88,000 in the Lost City (now part of Chandler Park) area south of Sand Springs and $110,000 in a deep pit in what was known in the early days as Robbers' Canyon near Pryor.

Of course, there's a question of whether James and his gang ever had that much money, even by adding their takes from all of their robberies.

Frank James, who died in 1915, couldn't find the money in Lost City when he returned after the turn of the 20th century, so he headed to the Lawton area to search there. He bought a ranch in the Wichita Mountains and spent years in a futile search for treasure the gang had buried there before finally giving up.

When the loot was buried near Lawton, the area was a hunting ground for American Indians; but after Jesse was killed and Frank returned, the land had been homesteaded, plowed and fenced.

Cole Younger, who had been a member of the James gang, told residents of Pryor in the early part of the 20th century that he had helped hide their booty in Robbers' Canyon but the landmarks also had changed there and he couldn't find the loot.

The James-Younger gang tried to rob a bank in Northfield, Minn., where some were killed and others were injured and captured by a posse several days later. The Youngers pleaded guilty, and it was 25 years before Cole was paroled – no doubt thinking of the hidden loot during the entire period.

But Cole discovered that the landmarks near Sand

Tulsa World archives

A postcard from the 1920s shows the rocky terrain of Lost City, now part of Chandler Park, where the James gang reportedly stashed loot.

Springs also had changed when he tried to find $63,000 in gold and silver he had buried along the south bank of the Arkansas River south of Sand Springs.

He told friends he tried to retrieve the money after being released from prison but he couldn't find it, apparently because it had sunk in the soft sand of the river's bank.

Younger said he buried the gold and silver while he and his gang were being chased by a posse as they rode toward Missouri. When they came to the Arkansas River, the heavy gold and silver they had liberated from a stage coach slowed them down as they started to ford the shallow water. They jumped off their horses, dug a hole and dumped the sacks of precious metal in, planning to return for it later.

Another group of gold-laden bandits were chased in Cherokee County by a posse that killed three of the group, according to another legend. The remaining bandits hid their gold near Chimney Rock along the Illinois River before being killed by the posse, but the gold was never found.

Among the legends of Spanish treasure is that more than $30 million worth of gold and silver was buried in the 1830s near Vanoss in Pontotoc County by a group that came to Oklahoma to establish a Catholic mission.

The precious metal was to be used to finance the mission and perimeter churches, but, because there were no banks and no safe place to keep their treasure, the churchmen decided to bury it until they could begin building. They dug a tunnel, gouged out a vault at its end, lined it with pitch or asphalt and stashed their treasure.

And as they headed for Mexico, they were killed – the location of their stash lost forever.

According to a report in the Tulsa Democrat in 1905, a group of Mexicans headed by a don named Valdez were starving on the winter plains and were taken in by Osage Indians. The Mexicans noticed that the Osages left the village from time to time and returned with gold.

One of the Mexicans followed the Osage group and discovered the Indians working in a gold-filled cavern on the east side of the Grand River. Valdez and his group started filling bags with gold with plans to take it to Mexico. But the Osages discovered the plot.

While Valdez and his group were working in the cave, the Osages sealed the entrance – leaving the Mexicans and the gold inside.

Prison riot cost lives, millions

Most of Big Mac, the Oklahoma State Penitentiary at McAlester, had been seized by inmates in the biggest prison riot in the state's history.

Three convicts died at the hands of other convicts. In addition, 21 guards and inmates were injured by homemade weapons, and 12 buildings were burned. About 1,000 of the 1,750 inmates were involved in the July 27, 1973, rioting.

A prison spokesman said the trouble was started in the mess hall by five inmates "who were doped up on something" and quickly spread throughout the prison.

Tulsa World archives

Convicts at Oklahoma State Penitentiary in McAlester watch buildings burn during an uprising that began on July 27, 1973.

Twenty-five Tulsa police officers were among about 400 law enforcement personnel and Oklahoma National Guard members, equipped with riot gear, who surrounded the embattled prison.

The siege lasted for three days, with lengthy negotiations involving Gov. David Hall to free the hostages. Four high-level corrections officials were injured, although not seriously, when a can of Mace exploded.

The last of the 23 hostages held by the inmates were released by noon July 28 but the end of hostilities didn't come until early July 29.

Cost of the riot was later set at $30 million.

The riot had legal repercussions that smoldered in a class action lawsuit until 2001 and triggered a number of changes in how the Oklahoma Department of Corrections cares for today's 25,000 inmates.

The lawsuit had been filed a year before the riot but was changed to class-action status after the riot and U.S. District Judge Luther Bohannon issued injunctions requiring remedial action after finding conditions in state prisons to be unconstitutional.

Other judges handled the lawsuit later until 2001 when Judge Michael Burrage ruled that the prison's medical system was constitutional, the last issue involved.

Shortly after the riot began, the prison was described as a "nightmare world" by Dr. Rafael Cott, a prison physician who had just left the facility after treating inmates on the floor of the hospital.

Warden Park Anderson blamed a shortage of workers and funds for the outbreak.

"I testified before the Penal Affairs Committee during the last legislative session that I was short-handed and that we needed more personnel and more money and that there might be trouble here," he told reporters.

"It happened."

A prisoner's wife who was active in a group called Help Our Prisoners Exist, said, "We knew something like this would happen. We've tried to tell the governor, the board of corrections, the parole board, everyone, that the conditions there were deplorable."

She said only about 30 percent of the inmates should have been there; the others, she believed, should have been transferred to satellite prisons instead of being held in maximum security.

Some inmates helped hostages escape and some actually fought other inmates to free the guards.

Eight highway patrol troopers armed with shotguns were among the first officers to respond to a call for help and blocked the paths of inmates trying to get out.

"Those troopers," former Trooper Bennie Durant recalled years later, "stood there with their shotguns and kept the inmates from breaking out of the last gate that was holding them inside the prison.

"That's all that saved McAlester from being invaded by inmates," he said.

Durant, later a sheriff of Pittsburg County, was the executive officer in charge of the McAlester detachment of the patrol when the call came in about the uprising at the penitentiary. He immediately sent out a call for all on-duty officers and "within 30 minutes, we had a contingent of about eight troopers at the front gate."

First moon landing had Oklahoma ties

It was "just unreal . . . the miracle of the world," Tulsa Mayor Jim Hewgley said after astronauts Buzz Aldrin and Neil Armstrong became the first humans to land on the moon.

Hewgley was among four prominent Oklahomans who watched the Apollo 11 launch at Cape Kennedy July 16, 1969.

Four days later, the lunar module Eagle landed as the mother ship, Columbia, remained in moon orbit.

Half of the airframe for the Columbia, which remained in orbit flown by Mike Collins while the moon men walked on the lunar surface, was built in Tulsa, according to David Blankenship, public relations director for Tulsa's North American Rockwell plant.

Oklahomans were among the millions worldwide who watched on television as Armstrong stepped onto the dusty surface and uttered his famous quote: "That's one small step for a man, one giant leap for mankind" followed by Aldrin's "beautiful, beautiful, beautiful, a magnificent desolation" comment 20 minutes later.

Tulsa World archives

An American astronaut walks on the moon, as shown on television on July 20, 1969. Part of the airframe for the spacecraft Columbia was built in Tulsa.

They had landed on the moon's Sea of Tranquility and spent two hours collecting rocks, planting an American flag and taking pictures before returning to Columbia.

The moon trip had Tulsa connections. It was a dream that had been discussed here eight years earlier at the first National Conference on Peaceful Uses of Space which attracted more than 1,000, including rocket pioneer Werner von Braun and Abe Silverstein, director of NASA space flight programs.

The work of those who came to the Tulsa conference, 3½ years after the Soviet Union launched Sputnik I, was instrumental in ensuring Aldrin and Armstrong's historic flight and walk on the moon that millions had dreamed of for centuries.

"It's very difficult to imagine this has happened," said Paschal Twyman, president of the University of Tulsa. "If you think about how recent it is that we have even flown airplanes and how recently computers have developed, it's a whole new threshold for science and the human race.

"It kind of stretches your imagination to think of where it's all going to end."

Gov. Dewey Bartlett called the landing a "great adventure," which he said was unlike other great adventures of history because while it took daring men, "it also took a tremendous number of people from riveters to engineers" to make it happen.

Hewgley, Twyman and Bartlett watched the lift-off at Cape Kennedy along with Harry Todd, president of the Tulsa Division of North American Rockwell, who said his reaction was "sort of beyond words."

That comment probably expressed the feeling of thousands of Oklahomans who spent the day watching on television as the historic event unfolded.

Todd also was impressed with communications between the astronauts and Earth. "There were half a billion people watching on television and listening on radio and the communications between the moon and Houston and the media was unbelievable."

The moon trip seemed like science fiction to Oklahoma Attorney General G.T. Blankenship. "The impact will be realized so much quicker than similar events like the discovery of the New World by Columbus because we are here watching it happen," he said.

Although millions watched the landing on television, it was business as usual for others. The manager of a Tulsa department store said he was amazed that there was no letup in business at his store in a mall. "While history was in the making, these people were strolling around buying underwear and eating hamburgers."

However, a crowd did congregate in front of television sets in the appliance section, he said, but they made no audible response when the craft touched down on the moon.

"I remember 40 years ago when Charles Lindbergh landed in Paris – every bell, horn and siren in my hometown sounded. The reaction today was kind of a let-down."

Since that first flight, 22 other American astronauts have traveled to the moon, with 12 walking on its surface and three making the trip twice. The most excited Oklahoman, without doubt, was Tulsan Madeline Crowell, a sister of Aldrin, who watched the landing on television with other members of the family at the home of her father, a retired Air Force colonel, in Manasquan, N.J.

"We saw Buzz last Sunday and he called us Tuesday before the launch," she said. "He seemed very calm and relaxed. In fact, he was calmer than we were."

Doolins won Ingalls battle, lost war

The outlaws won the battle but lost the war in the infamous battle of Ingalls, a fight that was more intense than the better-known shootout at the O.K. Corral in Tombstone, Ariz.

Three deputy marshals, two innocent bystanders and a horse were killed, and several outlaws were injured, none fatally. One was captured.

State road maps no longer show the community of Ingalls, which at the time of the gunbattle was larger than Stillwater, the city that became the seat of Payne County. Ingalls was about halfway between Stillwater and Yale.

The battle erupted Sept. 1, 1893, just 15 days before the land run into the Cherokee Outlet, after three wagon loads of deputy marshals arrived in the town intent on capturing members of the Doolin-Dalton gang and other wanted badmen.

The marshals had learned that the bandits considered Ingalls a safe haven. The badmen behaved themselves and got along well with the residents, who tolerated them because they spent their loot freely.

It was good information, and the deputies planned their raid.

Most of the outlaws had been in town for weeks, living at the O.K. Hotel and playing poker and drinking nightly at the Ransom and Murray saloon. The group included Bill Dalton, Arkansas Tom Jones, George (Dynamite Dick) Newcomb, Tulsa Jack, Bob (Bitter Creek) Yokum and Dan (Slaughter Kids) Clifton.

The gang's leader, Bill Doolin, was there, too, but he preferred to sleep under the stars in the hills of the Cimarron River and return to Ingalls during the daytime.

The posse of 27 marshals, deputies and Indian police camped out along a creek at the edge of the town the night before they planned to strike, but they were seen by a young boy whom they discovered listening intently to their planning.

The lawmen held the boy prisoner that night, but he slipped away early the next morning and ran into town to tell Doolin: "The marshals are coming."

That gave the outlaws time to go to the livery stable to saddle their horses, but, with that chore done, they returned

Oklahoma Historical Society

In 1938, residents of the community of Ingalls in Payne County erected a stone monument in memory of three marshals killed by the Dalton-Doolin gang in 1893. The monument's original bronze plaque was stolen and was replaced by this one in the early 1990s.

to their poker game at the saloon until the three wagons – looking like a common pioneer train – drove into town about 10:30 a.m. The officers dropped out of the wagons, took cover and within minutes the battle was on.

After hundreds of bullets were exchanged, the bandits ran for the livery stable to flee the town. Doolin's horse was shot as he tried to ride out of town.

Arkansas Tom, who had waged his part of the battle from his hotel room, was the only bandit remaining. He surrendered at 2 p.m. Meanwhile, the officers had taken their wounded and dead to Stillwater as the bandits took refuge at a nearby farm.

Three officers had been killed: Dick Speed, who had fired the first shot; Tom Houston; and Lafe Shadley. A 14-year-old boy and another innocent bystander also were fatally wounded.

It appeared that the bandits had won. Five men had died but not one was a bandit.

Territorial Judge Frank Dale was infuriated and ordered his marshals to "bring them in dead. Quit trying to bring them in as prisoners."

The marshals obeyed.

Doolin was captured in 1896 in Eureka Springs, Ark., as he took mineral baths for his arthritis and was returned to Guthrie to stand trial. While he awaited his trial, someone slipped a gun to him and he escaped.

He was headed for New Mexico with his wife and baby, riding on his horse ahead of her as she drove the wagon, when he was met by a group of officers headed by Marshal Heck Thomas.

Ignoring their order to surrender, Doolin tried to draw his pistol. Two loads of buckshot in his chest ended his career.

All of the outlaws except Arkansas Tom had been killed by lawmen by 1897. He served 14 years in prison and upon his release became a peace officer – until he reverted to his former habit and was killed in Joplin, Mo., while resisting arrest for robbing a bank in nearby Asbury.

The outlaws had lost the war.

Lucille Mulhall was the first 'cowgirl'

An 18-year-old Oklahoma girl dazzled spectators when she competed against the best cowhands in a roping contest at Denison, Texas, in 1904 and beat them all.

Lucille Mulhall had lassoed and tied three steers in 3 minutes and 36 seconds – several seconds better than the best cowboys – and won a gold medal and a $10,000 prize for a world record.

"Slight of figure, refined and neat in appearance, attired in a becoming riding habit for hard riding, wearing a picturesque Mexican sombrero and holding in one hand a lariat of the finest cowhide, Lucille Mulhall comes forward to show what an 18-year-old girl can do in roping steers," The New York Times reported.

When she went to New York the next year for an appearance at Madison Square Garden, newspaper reporters referred to her as "female conqueror of beef and horn," "lassoer in lingerie," "cowboy girl" and "ranch queen."

One newspaper finally coined the term "cowgirl." It stuck.

And Lucille became known as a cowgirl.

"There was no such thing or no such word as 'cowgirl,' " humorist Will Rogers wrote in a column that was published in the Tulsa World and other newspapers throughout the country shortly after the death of Lucille's father, Col. Zack Mulhall, in 1931.

"You can tell the world that his youngest daughter, Lucille Mulhall was the first cowgirl." Rogers said she was the world's greatest rider.

President Theodore Roosevelt described her as the world's most expert horsewoman.

Riding came naturally to Lucille who told a World reporter in 1931 "I've ridden all my life. I expect my father gave me a horseback ride before I was a month old, probably took me for a 10- or 20-mile ride to show me to our nearest neighbors."

As a small child, she rode her pony over Mulhall's large ranch that had grown from the 160 acres he claimed in the 1889 run into unoccupied lands in Oklahoma Territory to 82,000 acres in what is now Logan County. And she learned to rope and tie a steer and to shoot a rifle from experts – the men who rode herd in the cattle drives of the Old West and worked for her father.

By the time she was 7, Lucille had her own herd of cattle because of an offhand remark by her father that she could

Oklahoma Historical Society

Lucille Mulhall was the world's first cowgirl. The term was invented to describe her skills.

have all the yearlings she could rope and brand herself on the Mulhall ranch. It wasn't long before he begged off his bargain – too many calves, including 20 steers, were wearing Lucille's "L.H." brand.

Lucille got her start in show business as the star of what her father called "The Congress of Rough Riders and Ropers" that he took to the 1899 St. Louis World's Fair, a show that also featured a young trick roper named "The Cherokee Kid," whom the world later came to know as Will Rogers.

After she threw and tied a steer at an El Paso roping later, the rodeo crowd went wild, swarmed onto the field and started tearing her clothes off before her brother, Charlie, went to her rescue.

"They wouldn't believe that you are really a girl," Charlie told her.

Her career got another boost a year later after Roosevelt saw the blonde teenager perform at an Independence Day Cowboy Tournament while attending a Rough Riders convention in Oklahoma and campaigning for vice president.

Roosevelt invited the Mulhalls to join him and a group of Rough Rider veterans at dinner and later stayed at the ranch where he suggested to Col. Zack that Lucille should go on the stage. Mulhall agreed and Lucille toured the country in vaudeville, with rodeo troupes and made a tour of Europe.

Lucille made a point with Roosevelt, who, while riding on the Mulhall spread, saw a wolf and expressed an interest in having its pelt. Lucille roped the wolf, killed it, had the skin mounted and sent it to the future president.

Lucille, Col. Zack and the cowboy band later led the parade at Roosevelt's inauguration in Washington.

She retired from the stage in 1917 and returned to the ranch, then reduced in size to a homestead, after a divorce from her second husband in 1922. She lived there until she was killed in an automobile-truck collision Dec. 22, 1940, two miles north of Mulhall. Another passenger also was killed, but three others in the car had only minor injuries and the truck driver was not injured.

Lucille's body was buried near the graves of her parents, a brother and two sisters on the Mulhall ranch.

A machine had killed her but horses conveyed her to her final resting place. The mud was so deep from recent heavy rain that a neighbor's plow horses had to pull the hearse from the highway to near the house.

Doughboy held his position for decades

A World War I doughboy has stood guard in Henryetta for 82 years, first at the intersection of two major downtown streets and more recently at the city library.

The Doughboy statue was a landmark for decades. People remembered Henryetta because "that's where the Doughboy is in the middle of the intersection."

The statue, titled "Spirit of the American Doughboy" by Ernest Moore "Dick" Visquesney, depicts a World War I American soldier charging out of a trench, ready to throw a grenade with his raised right hand and carrying a rifle with bayonet attached in his left.

It was one of nearly 150 similar statues, including four others in Oklahoma, erected in cities around the country in the 1920s in honor of the doughboys who fought in the war. But the location of the Henryetta statue made it unique. It was the only one that stood in the middle of a major intersection that carried the traffic of two major highways.

Almost from its unveiling on July 4, 1925, the Oklahoma Highway Department complained about the statue's location. But Henryetta residents defended their statue's location until 1969, when the City Council approved moving it two blocks away to the library at Sixth and Main streets.

U.S. 75 and U.S. 62 converged and carried heavy traffic through the intersection before Interstate 40 was completed and before the two highways were realigned to miss the city.

Local parades had problems getting past the statue. Trucks and buses usually detoured over other streets.

But Henryetta residents liked their statue where it was and resisted Highway Department efforts to have it moved. When highway officials suggested in 1950 that the statue be moved to accommodate the highways, many objected. "They will get about as far as the try in 1940," a former commander of the local VFW said.

"People all over the country say 'that's where the Doughboy is,' " another veteran said. "If we're going to have it, why hide it?"

Oklahoma Historical Society

The Doughboy statue held its ground in the center of a busy highway intersection in Henryetta for decades.

But the City Council agreed to the move in 1969 after the state Highway Commission said the statue created a traffic hazard. The commission agreed to repave the street if the statue were moved and the city prohibited angle parking on Main Street.

The Doughboy was unveiled by Mrs. George Cullen, whose son, Norman Cullen, was killed the morning of Nov. 11, 1918, one of the last Americans to die in the war. The Henryetta Veterans of Foreign Wars and the American Legion campaigned for three years to raise $1,200 to buy the statue.

The veterans held a talent show, operated a hoosegow in which residents were held until paying fines to the Doughboy fund, and sold chances on two miniature versions of the statue, according to Earl Goldsmith, a native of Henryetta whose Web site tells about the Doughboy.

The statue arrived Nov. 26, 1923, but it was another 19 months before a pedestal to hold it was financed and built.

Other Visquesney Doughboy statues stand at the Jack C. Montgomery Veterans Hospital in Muskogee and in Granite, Hobart and Cherokee. The VA statue, dedicated Sept. 5, 1925, was funded by the Five Civilized Tribes, the Bureau of Indian Affairs and others in honor of American Indians "whose record of enlistment, conduct in camp and fortitude and valor on the battlefield added luster to the triumphant victory of our country in the World War," according to the inscription on the base.

The Granite and Hobart statues, paired with two statues of sailors also by Visquesney, originally stood at each end of the Oklahoma 9 Red River bridge between Lone Wolf and Granite but were removed by the Highway Department after they were damaged by vandals who used them for target practice.

They were financed by Greer and Kiowa counties and the American Legion and were dedicated in 1929 along with the bridge as a memorial to Oklahoma's war dead.

The Granite statues now stand in a small park. The Hobart statues, and the Cherokee statue, adorn courthouse lawns.

Frankoma founder molded minds

"You're just like this piece of clay," Frankoma Pottery's founder, John Frank, used to tell youth groups as he plopped a handful of it onto a potter's wheel.

"Your character can be formed just as I'm molding this clay into an object," he would add as he started the wheel spinning and began to shape the clay into a bowl or a vase or some other object of beauty. "A person without character is just as useless as a hunk of clay."

Frank, a youth leader at First Methodist Church in Sapulpa, traveled thousands of miles at his own expense in Oklahoma and several other states, beginning in the 1950s, to speak to church groups and youth organizations, using his specially built potter's wheel for his pulpit to demonstrate what it means to be clay in the master's hands.

It was a part of Frank's devotion to God and an expression of his love for the good earth – clay – that he had turned into a pottery business, which became known internationally and attracted thousands of visitors to Sapulpa each year.

Frank was born into poverty in Chicago. He sold newspapers on street corners when he was 5, played trombone in The Salvation Army band and worked his way through the Chicago Art Institute as a museum guard and teacher's assistant. That's where he learned the art of creating beauty out of hunks of clay, the skill he used for the rest of his life.

He came to Oklahoma in 1927 shortly after his graduation and established a ceramics department at the University of Oklahoma. He left the school in 1933 to open Frank Potteries in Norman.

He renamed the business Frankoma a year later to incorporate both his surname and the last three letters of Oklahoma. The business struggled; pottery was received poorly in those Depression years and business leaders offered little help for a merchant not devoted to the college crowd.

"Norman didn't particularly want us," Frank's wife, Grace Lee Frank, told a reporter in 1983, 10 years after her husband died.

The Sapulpa Chamber of Commerce enticed Frank to move there, and the Franks set up shop in a former tavern. They built a production plant nearby on land provided by the chamber.

For years, Frank used clay found near Ada but later worked with clay found in Sapulpa.

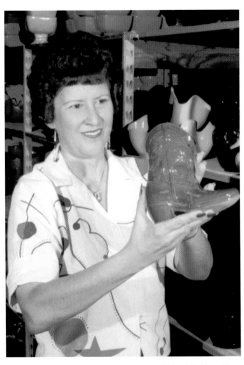

Joniece Frank Nelson, a daughter of Frankoma Pottery's founders, John and Grace Frank, holds a ceramic boot that her father molded from one she wore as a child.

The move gave Frank the support he needed for his business and provided a valuable asset for Sapulpa. Thousands of tourists driving along U.S. 66 stopped at the plant to shop for and buy pottery.

The 1942 creation of a line of Southwestern dinnerware featuring the common wagon wheel helped spread the word about the Frankoma name. That design was the company's signature line for years, and in 1947, Frank sent a set of wagon wheel dishes to every governor in the United States.

Frankoma later produced several other lines of dinnerware in many colors.

Frank was named the Oklahoma Small Businessman of the year in 1968 and 1969 and the United States Small Businessman of the Year in 1971. He also had been recognized as the outstanding board member of the International Youth for Christ organization and was the chairman of the Youth for Christ group in Tulsa.

Frank received the national award at a "John Frank Day," but he made it clear that it wasn't just his honor. "This is not John Frank Day; it's Sapulpa Day," he declared.

Frank praised Sapulpans for their support, using a couple of examples. "When I came here, I needed a car. I had no credit," he said. But a loan company employee told him: "You look good to me. I'll just take your signature."

The firm prospered, and by the mid-1950s the Franks were able to move into a house designed by the famed architect Bruce Goff. It featured Frankoma tile.

Frank retired in 1973, turning the business over to his daughter Joniece because of his health and to gain time to design a 10-plate series, "Teen-Agers of the Bible." But he died a few months later with only the first design finished. Joniece completed the series.

Another Frank daughter, Donna, detailed the involvement of her father and family in civic, religious and social causes in her book, "Clay in the Master's Hands."

Frank had been a member of the Sapulpa City Commission, the library board and the Oklahoma Bicentennial Committee. He also was an honorary chief of the Creek Nation.

Frankoma Pottery survived a fire in 1983 but was sold in 1991 and closed in early 2005.

It gained new life a few months later when it was bought by Det and Crystal Merryman. It now has 40 employees and has created Oklahoma Centennial pottery.

Dentists felt pull of Indian Territory

Early settlers in the twin territories had a lot of toothaches. But there were no dentists to ease their pain most of the time – only those who traveled from place to place periodically.

That was until Dr. J.E. Wright opened the future state's first dental office in 1885 in Savanna.

Wright came to Indian Territory to visit a friend in Caddo, planning to return to his practice in Tyler, Texas. But when it became known in Caddo that he was a dentist, he "was besieged to stay longer and do a lot of much-needed work," he was quoted later.

Wright had his equipment shipped to him from Tyler, treated the patients around Caddo, and the word spread. He was asked to go to Tishomingo, Stonewall, Pauls Valley, Mill Creek, back to Stonewall and many other places between to treat patients – a trip that lasted 10 weeks.

Although he had planned to return to Tyler, Wright settled in Savanna and opened what the book "Open Wider, Please" said was Oklahoma's first dental office in Savanna, a community with more than 300 men employed in coal mines.

Wright later practiced in McAlester until he retired in 1919 after 51 years of practice.

Ingenuity was a necessity for the early dentists in both Indian and Oklahoma territories.

The late Dr. A.L. Walters of Tulsa was quoted in the same book about his early practice in Checotah when he made house calls to patients, especially to ranches where the foreman preferred having a dentist visit than to send his hands to Checotah for treatment.

He used a rocking chair with a stick of wood under each rocker, two pillows, a stand for the instruments and a bucket for a cuspidor. The late Dr. L.M. Doss of Oklahoma City used a rocking chair tied to a big tub for his dental chair.

Another early dentist who practiced in Kingfisher told the author of "Open Wider" about treating a patient who refused to remove his gun from his holster, although Dr. J.Q. Waddell feared that stress, strain and a six-shooter were a bad combination.

"Doc, I never take this gun off, and I'm never careless with it," the patient told Waddell.

After Waddell pulled the patient's aching tooth, the pa-

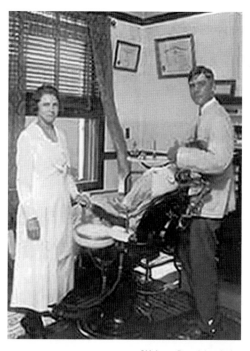

Oklahoma Dental Association

In 1885, Dr. J.E. Wright opened a dental office in Savanna, a coal-mining town south of McAlester in Indian Territory.

tient began pitching silver dollars to him to pay for the extraction, eventually giving Waddell $10, although he only expected $1.

When the dentist asked his patient's name, he was told: "I've paid you, the tooth's out, and the name doesn't matter. We're all square."

Later, Waddell learned his patient was one of the Dalton brothers who were being hunted for robberies.

Writing in the summer 1957 Chronicles of Oklahoma, Dr. F.C. Holmes of Mangum said it was not uncommon for cowboys to ride 100 miles or more to have a tooth extracted.

But sometimes people in established towns were wary of dentists setting up practices. They had experiences with some traveling practitioners who charged large fees, left town suddenly without paying bills, or failed to complete service.

When Holmes was asked how long he planned to stay in Mangum, he'd look the questioner in the eye and reply "expect to stay here for 75 years" – an answer that seemed to satisfy questioners.

Dentists and patients of today take anesthesia for granted, but it wasn't always used and many patients would suffer for years before submitting to an extraction. General anesthesia was dangerous because few dentists knew how to use it. Local anesthesia using cocaine also was imperfect and dangerous, frequently causing nausea and fainting, according to that Chronicles article.

Holmes recalled once having three patients stretched out on the floor of his office as they recovered from the effects of cocaine.

But no Oklahoma dentists ever reported a problem similar to one in New York in 1907 after a young woman was given laughing gas as an anesthetic.

A news story in the Tulsa World reported that when the gas took effect, the woman leaped from the chair, grabbed the dentist around the neck and wouldn't turn loose. The dentist's wife couldn't pry her loose and called a police officer for assistance.

Dentists in both Indian and Oklahoma territories organized associations before statehood. Dentistry was regulated by a law passed by the Oklahoma Territorial Legislature in 1891 aimed at eliminating quack practitioners.

War hero tries for first governorship

Frank Frantz, a hero of the Spanish-American war and Oklahoma Territory's last governor, was called the most popular man in the two territories in 1907.

And he probably was, to the Republicans from the two territories who met in Tulsa on Aug. 1 and 2 and picked him as their candidate to become the first governor of the new state of Oklahoma that would be born 3½ months later.

An estimated 20,000 were expected at the convention, the Tulsa World reported on July 31 as delegates began arriving, but it didn't follow up with an actual number. About 6,000 were estimated to be in the tent when Chairman J.L. Hamon called the convention to order.

Convention delegates and other visitors were greeted by a large reception committee. Flags and decorations hung from all the city's buildings.

The Republicans met in a large tent erected at Fourth Street and Boston Avenue that had a large center area for delegates and a speakers' platform, press section and four areas around the perimeter for visitors.

Two days later, the convention picked Gov. Frantz of Enid as the GOP candidate for governor and N.G. Turk of Checotah as the lieutenant governor nominee. Frantz's selection wasn't much of a surprise. There hadn't been much doubt about his nomination from the time he arrived in Tulsa for the selection by the convention.

Frantz had been named the last governor of Oklahoma Territory in January by President Theodore Roosevelt, who commanded the Rough Riders when Frantz's commanding officer was killed during the battle of San Juan Hill. First Lt. Frantz took command and led his company in the battle, earning a promotion to captain by Roosevelt.

Although there was unanimous support for Frantz, delegate J.S. McCowan of Snyder touched off a shouting match when he criticized the constitution that had been drawn up at the recent constitutional convention and spoke against statehood.

The convention also had moments of humor. Delegates from Tishomingo, in Democrat William H. Murray's home county, arrived leading a billy goat with a sign that

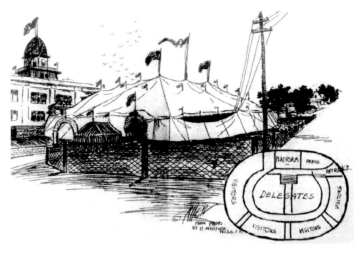

Tulsa World archives

A Tulsa World sketch by Clarence Allen shows the site of the first state Republican convention held Aug. 1-2, 1907.

said "For sale. Me to the cocklebur patches." Another delegate from there carried a long "squirrel" rifle of the type that Murray was noted for using.

Murray, known at that time as "Cocklebur Bill," later became known as "Alfalfa Bill" because he carried bales of alfalfa hay in his pickup to use for listeners to sit on while he was campaigning.

The Republican convention in the big tent was a sharp contrast to the Democratic convention in Tulsa's Brady Hotel four months earlier.

Then Charles N. Haskell of Muskogee touched off a furor by announcing that he was a candidate for the Democratic nomination for governor.

An estimated 75 percent of the delegates to that convention were believed to have been supporters of Lee Cruce, an Ardmore banker who later became Oklahoma's second governor. Candidates were not selected at that convention but at a primary election a few months later.

In his announcement, Haskell pointed out that he had been a delegate to the constitutional convention and "aided in making what is recognized as the best constitution in the United States."

"Believing that the governor of the new state should be in full sympathy with the constitution, I have consented" to be a candidate, he added. "The grafter, the trusts and the monopolies need not vote for me because I will not represent them."

Three months later, Haskell won the nomination over Cruce although the victor wasn't known for several days after the June 9 primary, and each candidate claimed victory at times during tabulation of the ballots.

Gov. Frantz set a general election for both territories for Sept. 16 to pick a new governor, ratify the new constitution and decide on the issue of prohibition. Voters gave overwhelming approval to the new state's constitution and to statewide prohibition.

But something must have happened to that popularity the Republicans claimed Frantz had. He lost by more than 25,000 votes to Haskell, who became Oklahoma's first governor.

Abernathy boys shared adventures

Two young Oklahoma boys rode their horses from Frederick to New York City in 1910 to greet former President Theodore Roosevelt when he returned from a safari in Africa and then drove a new car home.

By themselves.

It was an exciting adventure for Louis, 10, and Temple Abernathy, 6, and probably raised a few eyebrows even in that time of early self-reliance. But their Tillman County neighbors probably weren't particularly surprised.

It wasn't the first adventure for Louis, known as Bud, and Temple; and their father, U.S. Marshal John Abernathy, was famous for catching wolves bare-handed. It also wasn't their last adventure – but it was the one for which they were most famous.

"We've brought them up to take care of themselves," Abernathy told reporters in New York, where he met the boys to join in a parade welcoming Roosevelt home. "We never bother about them. Why should we?"

Abernathy told the reporters the boys had ridden to New Mexico the previous year. "They were gone over six weeks and came back better than when they started," he said.

"They've come to rely on themselves," Abernathy said. "If they haven't any money, they never ask for it. They go out and earn it."

Abernathy and his two sons became acquainted with Roosevelt when the dashing rough-riding president visited Frederick in 1905 to go coyote (or wolf) hunting. Roosevelt wanted to watch Abernathy catch the animals by riding beside them on his horse and leaping off to grab them. Roosevelt and Abernathy became close friends, and the president later named Abernathy U.S. marshal for Oklahoma Territory and gave him the nickname "Catch 'em Alive Jack."

After their mother died in 1908, the two boys developed a wanderlust, dreamed about becoming part of the adventures Abernathy had read to them – and decided to ride to Santa Fe, N.M., to visit Gov. George Curry, a friend of their father.

They planned the trip in detail and convinced their father to let them go with Temple riding Geronimo, a half Shetland pony, and Bud riding Sam Bass, his father's Arabian that he used when catching wolves.

There were experiences they hadn't planned on – such as meeting a group of outlaws, although the boys didn't know until later that they were outlaws, who escorted the

Valerie Clayton

A bronze statue of the Abernathy boys stands near the Tillman County Courthouse square in Frederick. The statue, which is the county's first piece of public art, was designed by sculptor Gary Gardner of Lawton and is dedicated to the late Frederick artist Larry Greer.

boys for many miles to ensure their safety. The outlaws later wrote to Abernathy, telling him they didn't respect him because he was a marshal. But, they wrote, they "liked what those boys were made of."

A year later, as the boys rode toward New York, they were welcomed in every city they rode through, in most cases being met by the mayors, many of whom wrote Abernathy such comments as "You certainly have a pair of boys you can be proud of." They were feted at amusement parks, at dinners, taken on automobile tours through the cities and on an aeroplane "joy ride in the air" by Wilbur Wright in Dayton, Ohio.

In Washington, after visiting President Howard Taft and being introduced to Taft's Cabinet, Bud wrote their father: "They are bully. They treated us fine. Taft is all right. He's treated us square."

Their trip to New York was pretty much without incident, except they had to buy a new horse to replace Geronimo after the animal got loose in a field of clover, nearly foundered and had to be shipped home by train. They were cheered almost as much as Roosevelt in the parade.

And then they began another adventure – driving home in a car, although they had never driven.

The boys convinced their father that they should buy a car, picked out a one-cylinder Brush runabout because it was simple and was small enough for them to start and handle, shipped their horses back home by train, practiced driving a few hours in New York and headed for Oklahoma with Bud driving and Temple as mechanic.

When they met adults, they bragged on their car, explaining if a couple of boys can handle it, any adult should be able to.

They made the trip in 23 days and, according to a 1910 news story in the Daily Oklahoman, were "petted and lionized" all the way.

Their adventures weren't over. They were challenged the next year to ride their horses from New York to San Francisco in return for $10,000 if they finished in 60 days. They made the trip but missed the deadline, finishing in 62 days, a record time but not good enough to collect the prize.

Louis later became an attorney in Wichita Falls, and Temple was in the oil and gas business in Texas.

Their adventures are described in several books, the first of which was written by Bud in 1910 and entitled "Meeting Roosevelt." A more recent book is "Bud and Me" written by Temple's wife, Alta.

Poet laureate began writing at age 10

Maggie Culver Fry didn't finish high school, but she became Oklahoma's poet laureate, wrote more than 800 articles, stories and poems and was even nominated for a Pulitzer Prize.

Fry, who died at the age of 97 in 1997, began writing poetry when she was 10.

"I was digging potatoes in the garden when it came to me that I should write these things down," she told a reporter in 1994. "God chose me and told me to write this book.

"And I did."

She continued writing until she was 94 and living in a nursing home at Claremore.

"I still write but not much," she said on her birthday that year. "There's too much gabbing."

Although prolific as a writer, she was involved in many other activities during her life -- working as the personal secretary to state Sen. Clem McSpadden for 10 years, conducting workshops on writing at high schools and colleges throughout the state. She also taught at Claremore Junior College, a Sunday school class for more than a half-century in her church and for many years on a Claremore radio station.

She also once conducted a successful letter-writing campaign to get a bill passed by Congress to allow three American Indian tribes in Oklahoma to sue the government for Arkansas River land taken by the government for the McClellan-Kerr navigation system and for land transferred to municipalities in 1909 for railroad stations.

Born near Vian, she quit high school to work in Muskogee and help support her family but continued her education by constant reading. She went back to high school in Porum while living with an aunt when she was 20 but had to quit because her health failed because of a strenuous schedule. By that time, her parents had moved to a farm near Verdigris, where she met Merritt Fry, her future husband, who lived on a nearby farm.

She became a case worker for the Claremore office of the Oklahoma Emergency Relief Administration during the Depression years of the 1930s, delivering commodities and helping people in any way they needed.

Fry created a recipe for rabbit chili that she said years later was "really good" and shared it with the people she visited.

"We also showed people how to make iceless coolers

Maggie Culver Fry, who was chosen as the state's poet laureate in 1977, is pictured on Feb. 4, 1995. She spent 87 years writing poems and stories.

with an orange crate set in a tub of water and covered with burlap bags. The water rising up through the burlap evaporated and kept food inside reasonably cool" in the years before most farm houses had electricity.

Fry never learned to drive a car and while working as a case worker hired a teenage boy for 50 cents a day to drive her through her district. It stretched from the Sequoyah community five miles north of Claremore to the Keetonville area between Claremore and Owasso.

When she worked for McSpadden at the state Capitol, she rode with the senator to and from Oklahoma City, and her husband frequently drove her to the workshops she conducted.

Not driving probably was an asset to her writing. She frequently scribbled poetry on envelopes and scraps of paper while riding in a car and later typed the poems.

Although she began writing poetry as a child, she started writing seriously after she married Fry in 1924. She worked out the rhythm for some of her first poems on the remains of an old piano that was in a chicken house.

But good rhythm didn't assure the success of a poem. She recalled sending her first nationally published poem, "Restless Angels," to 73 publications before it was finally accepted.

Fry was chosen as the state's poet laureate in 1977 after Gov. David Boren asked state schools and arts groups to choose the laureate. The next year, Boren declared a Maggie Fry Day in her honor. She was named poet laureate emeritus in 1995.

In addition to poetry, Fry wrote nonfiction, usually about noteworthy Oklahomans, and was a frequent contributor to Oklahoma Today magazine. She was nominated for a Pulitzer Prize for her book of poetry, "The Umbilical Cord," published in 1971.

Because religion played a big part in Fry's life, many of her writings have religious messages. She said she had read the Bible through 30 times and had studied biblical characters in depth.

She also loved the Cape Cod house where she and her husband lived from 1957 until Merritt Fry's death and her move to a nursing home in the early 1990s.

"I look out the window and I think 'this is the most beautiful place in the world,' " she told a reporter before moving.

Hamon death brought saucy trial

An Oklahoma oilman and political leader who helped put Warren Harding in the White House was fatally wounded by his mistress less than three weeks after Harding's landslide 1920 victory.

The victim was Jake L. Hamon, 45, who political leaders believed would be named secretary of the interior for his help in the campaign.

The trial of Hamon's lover, Clara Smith Hamon, 28, four months later was the most sensational in Carter County history and ended in an acquittal.

The case had all the elements of a detective novel – the victim was a multimillionaire oilman and political leader, and in partnership with circus magnate John Ringling had built a railroad from Lawton through Ringling to Ardmore; the defendant was a pretty younger woman who had been the oilman's private secretary and lover for 10 years and who had been married briefly to Hamon's nephew.

Hamon, the state's Republican national committeeman, had led the Oklahoma delegation to the GOP convention that year. When it became apparent that the candidate the Sooners were supporting couldn't win, he swung Oklahoma's 18 votes to Harding.

That wasn't enough votes to make a big difference but Hamon was told by a Harding aide that the Harding campaign was $18,000 in debt "and we don't know how we will pay it."

"That's easy," Hamon responded. "I'll just write you a check for it." His financing helped the Harding supporters put over their candidate at the convention, and Harding won by a landslide in the November election.

There were reports that Hamon was planning to break off his affair with Clara because Harding had told him he should bring his legitimate family to Washington and leave Clara in Ardmore. Hamon's wife and Harding's wife were cousins.

The case had its beginning in Nov. 21, 1920, at the Randol Hotel where Hamon and Clara had adjoining rooms. During the evening, Hamon was shot. He died five days later in a nearby hospital.

After being shot, Hamon walked to the hospital where he at first told a doctor that he shot himself accidentally while cleaning his .25-caliber pistol. He told the same story to other visitors.

Tulsa World archives

Oilman Jake L. Hamon was a friend to the powerful and the subject of a lurid scandal in 1920.

When the case went to trial in March 1921, the courtroom was packed tightly. Newspaper reporters from throughout the country and spectators crowded into the small room. The defendant and victim's widow were forced to sit just a few feet apart at a counsel table.

"I want to see her sent to the electric chair," Hamon's widow told reporters the first day of the trial. "Every married woman, every mother should pray for her punishment. No punishment is bad enough for her."

Contrary to Hamon's statement that he shot himself, the doctor testified at the trial that Hamon later had told him he was shot by Clara as he lay in bed.

Clara testified the shooting occurred during a violent argument. She said that as she pointed her gun at him, he switched off the light, struck her with a chair and the gun went off.

Hamon took the gun from her and put it in his coat pocket after the shooting because she wanted to kill herself with it, she testified.

"I hated him and loved him at the same time," she said, adding that love was the stronger passion.

It took just 39 minutes for the jury to return a verdict of not guilty.

After the verdict, Clara shook hands with and thanked each of the jurors and then announced that she planned to sue the Hamon estate for a share, claiming Hamon had promised her a fourth of his estate.

Clara's diaries were obtained by the Chicago Herald and Examiner after they were found in a trunk in Kansas City. They were published in serial form by the Tulsa World and other newspapers with the International News Service wire a few weeks after Hamon died.

Oklahoma City Police Chief Bill Nichols, a long-time friend of Hamon, told reporters he visited the injured oilman during his hospital stay and helped him write checks to his nurses and others. Then, he said, Hamon told him "get me a piece of paper. I want to write Warren Harding."

After writing the note, Hamon told Nichols "I want that note torn up after it is read."

Nichols later told reporters that he delivered the note to Harding and tore it up after Harding read it.

"What a wonderful fellow he was," the president-elect told Nichols. "Too bad he had that one fault – that admiration for women."

Walton's political career never dull

The big question among Oklahomans midway in Jack Walton's short, turbulent tenure as governor in 1923 was "How can we get rid of him?"

That question was published in the Tulsa World after he declared martial law in Okmulgee County and threatened to extend it to several other counties and eventually the entire state.

His tenure was also questioned because of the pardons, paroles and leaves of absence Walton had granted to prisoners, including a mass murderer. It was reported that he was issuing a pardon or parole at the rate of one a day – many reportedly for a price.

Oklahoma A & M College students and Stillwater residents showed up at the Capitol in May to protest his appointment of George Wilson, who did not have even a bachelor's degree, as A & M president.

In response, the governor threatened to declare martial law in Stillwater to "tell you when to go to bed and when to get up" if they continued opposing Wilson's appointment.

Attorneys said there was no way to get rid of him for at least two years because only the House could impeach a governor. The next regular session was nearly two years away and a special session was unlikely. Only the governor could call a special session of the Legislature, and Walton would not call a special session that would likely result in his impeachment.

When Walton put Okmulgee County under martial law on June 26, he cited three actions of the local Sheriff's Office as the reason but announced the next day that the real reason for his action was the beginning of his war against the Ku Klux Klan.

Aldrich Blake, the governor's executive secretary, said Walton was determined to put an end to mob outrages in Oklahoma and was prepared to use military force if necessary.

Blake said at least 2,500 "whipping parties" had been reported in Oklahoma during the past year.

The Okmulgee martial law lasted only a few days but in August, Walton issued another order putting Tulsa County under martial law, claiming the Klan, or Kluxers as he called members, were whipping at least one person per day.

He extended martial law to the entire state in Septem-

Tulsa World archives

Gov. Jack Walton was sworn into office, impeached and removed all in 1923, but that didn't end his political career.

ber, declaring "absolute martial law" in Oklahoma, Tulsa and Creek counties – suspending the privilege of habeas corpus and the operation of civil authorities. He also placed censors in some newspaper offices in those counties.

Meanwhile, Campbell Russell, former corporation commissioner, filed an initiative petition with the secretary of state that, if approved by the voters, would permit any member of the House to call a special session if backed by a majority of the members.

Although the governor tried to prevent a vote on the petition, it was finally approved by voters at an election on Oct. 2 that included several other unrelated issues. The Legislature was called into special session on Oct. 11 and Walton was impeached on 23 counts, convicted on 11 counts by the Senate and ousted from office.

The year after his ouster, he won the Democratic nomination for U.S. Senate but was defeated by Republican W.B. Pine. Walton moved to Houston but returned in time to make an unsuccessful run for Oklahoma City mayor in 1929. He was elected to the corporation commission in 1932.

When Walton left the corporation commission office in 1938, he told reporters he had set a record. "This is the only office I have held in which I completed my term."

He ran fourth in the Democratic primary for governor in 1938 and two years later failed in a campaign for sheriff of Oklahoma County. In 1944 he finished second in the Democratic primary race for corporation commissioner.

"There is always a fight where Jack Walton is. If not, he'll start one" was a common comment during Walton's tenure as governor and during his later political life.

Twenty-five years after his conviction, only a year before Walton died in 1949 at the age of 68, he told a reporter who asked if he harbored any ill feelings "I learned a long time ago that if you're going to be in politics, you can't murder and kill everybody who's against you. You've got to take it smiling.

"But if I were governor now and I heard threats against the people like the Ku Kluxers made then, I'd do just like I did. I'm proud of what I did and I'm glad I did it."

Pioneering teacher gave much to Tulsa

A woman who quit school as a child to care for her ill mother helped build Tulsa by teaching the children of pioneers.

And she helped in many other ways later.

That woman was Lilah D. Lindsey, who in addition to being one of the city's first teachers, held Bible classes and sometimes preached on Sundays and even conducted funerals.

Lindsey was a charter member of First Presbyterian Church, founder of a large number of civic and fraternal groups and was called the motivating force in many civic undertakings. She also gave generously to the school system and the city until her death.

She was a strong supporter of the Women's Christian Temperance Union, was responsible for the hiring in 1909 of Tulsa's first female police officer (the first in Oklahoma), campaigned for women's suffrage and raised money for charity and for World War I stamps.

Two Tulsa schools have been named in her honor – the first at 12th Street and Frisco Avenue on land she donated to the school board and the other at 2740 E. 41st Street North.

The name of the first school was changed to Riverview Elementary School because of a school board policy of not naming schools for living persons. The name later was used for the school on Tulsa's north side.

Lindsey was born in 1860 near Coweta and became a member of her mother's Creek tribe and clan, according to tribal custom, although her father was part Cherokee, and both were part Scottish. English was spoken in her house when she was a child but she used Creek most of the time.

Her father was killed in the Civil War and young Lilah later accompanied her mother on her rounds as a medicine woman. Lilah attended the Tallahassee Mission School until her mother became ill and she returned home to care for her.

After her mother's death, she attended college in Hill-

Beryl Ford collection

Lilah D. Lindsey was an early Tulsa teacher and community leader. Twice, Tulsa Public Schools have been named in her honor.

sboro, Ohio, where she graduated in 1883 and became the first Creek woman to receive a degree – a mistress of liberal arts because bachelor's or master's degrees were not issued to women.

She first came to Tulsa to teach in the Presbyterian Mission School in 1886, a year after her marriage to Lee Lindsey, a Civil War veteran from Ohio. As a contractor, Lindsey completed the stone walls and enclosure of the Creek Council House in Okmulgee that Lilah later successfully campaigned to have made into a museum.

The Lindseys left Tulsa but returned for good in 1894 and built a house near the site of the future Riverside school. The house later was sold to Tulsa's Greek community.

In 1921, she gave $2,500 to establish a community kitchen since, at that time, there was no city or county welfare office. She not only provided the money to purchase a location, the building and part of the equipment, she also personally managed the kitchen for a time.

The kitchen, organized as a project of the Women's Civic League under Lindsey's leadership, later was taken over by the city as the first local government-operated welfare agency.

Lindsey became a fundraiser during World War I, when the government was selling war savings stamps and Tulsa County's quota was $1.5 million. Under her leadership, the women of the county obtained pledges for $1,216,000.

Her success in that campaign led Tulsa civic leaders to put her in high positions when Community Fund drives began and she assisted in every campaign until shortly before her death in October 1943.

She was a member of the Frances E. Willard Home board, the Tulsa Public Health Association, the State Highway Beautification Association, was instrumental in the founding of the Humane Society and helped organize the Tulsa Indian Women's Club, which she served as first president.

She was inducted into Oklahoma's Hall of Fame in 1937.

Oklahoma celebrated peace with a bang

The day had finally arrived, and the "War to End All Wars" was over. Germany had been defeated, her dreams of conquest shattered.

And Oklahomans celebrated.

Noise and parades were standard for revelers in nearly every city and town after the Tulsa World and other newspapers reported in their Nov. 11, 1918, editions that armistice terms – dictated by the Allies – had been signed in Paris, and fighting would stop at 11 a.m. Paris time – the 11th hour of the 11th day of the 11th month of the year. That Paris time was 6 a.m. here.

The anniversary of that date was celebrated as Armistice Day until 1954 when Congress changed its name to Veterans Day. In its original manifestation, parades were held in Tulsa beginning in 1922. In other cities, veterans spoke at school assemblies and other gatherings to remind Americans of the doughboys' sacrifices before they quit shooting and came out of their trenches.

Elementary school students stood in silence for two minutes at 11 a.m. on Nov. 11 – the 11th hour of the 11th day of the 11th month – to remember the end of the war.

Silence was not one of the elements of the original Armistice Day.

Parades – some were organized with bands and impromptu floats while most were disorganized made of just residents – and noise were the primary modes of celebrating. Most paraders carried noise makers and some even fired guns into the air.

"Staid business men forgot their years and joined in. Shop girls discarded their aprons and danced into the crowd. Sober matrons left the curb and linked arms with the younger folks and paraded," the Daily Oklahoman reported.

Cowbells, alarm bells, saw blades, tin wash tubs, drums and even a disc from a plow were pressed into service to make noise.

Germany's surrender was reported in an extra edition of the World that was published shortly after 1 a.m. The World apparently got the news before that day's final home edition went to press and published it as an extra.

Newsboys circulated throughout the city, including residential districts, presumably waking up customers to make sales. Three additional extras were published that day with

Oklahoma Historical Society

Soldiers returning from World War I parade through Oklahoma City.

headlines proclaiming "DRAFT CALLS ARE REVOKED," "TERMS OF THE ARMISTICE" and "FULL TEXT OF THE TERMS."

Mayor C. H. Hubbard proclaimed a holiday and Tulsans began making plans to welcome returning soldiers, including constructing a replica of the Paris Arc de Triomphe between Third and Fourth streets on Main Street for returning soldiers to march through. It was ready for a Tulsa unit, Company D, 111th Engineers of the 16th Division, to march through when it returned on June 12, 1919.

The arch, sponsored by the newly organized American Legion, cost $3,500 and was paid for by public subscription.

Americans had developed a patriotic fervor after April 6, 1917, when the U.S. declared war on Germany. Every man in the Kendall College (now the University of Tulsa) senior class joined the Army. So did every member of Kendall's 1916 championship football team.

Reports that fighting had stopped had caused widespread celebration across the U.S. a few days earlier but apparently not in Tulsa. That report was called the "greatest hoax of recent years," but the government's denial of the reports didn't stop the celebrating and the hoax gained momentum "until it approached hysteria in many cities."

A war that was to have been over in only a few days had taken four years and the lives of millions. Modern warfare had been shown to be so horrible with poison gas, aerial bombs and rapid-fire machine guns that idealists believed there would never be another global conflict.

The cost was staggering, but the peace was fragile and the terms imposed on the defeated merely sowed the seeds of an even greater war only 21 years later.

After the shouting, screaming, whistle-tooting, gun-firing celebration over the initial announcement died down, civic groups, patriotic organizations and individuals began planning festivities to welcome our boys home.

The Daily Oklahoman provided a good description:

"The state and nation went stark, staring mad in what probably was the most noisome and boisterous celebration in history."

Tulsa's early golfers faced many hazards

Sand traps, trees and ponds weren't the only hazards for early Tulsa golfers.

They also had to keep a wary eye out for range bulls and dairy cattle and an irate woman with a Winchester rifle. Boys who played golf were concerned about being called sissy.

The game was far different from that played by Tiger Woods and others who competed at Southern Hills Country Club in the 89th PGA Championship.

Golfers in the early 20th century used balls that were larger, not as lively and didn't travel as far as today's versions; a 160-yard drive was considered mighty. Clubs were made locally from hickory limbs, and the wooden heads were fashioned from blocks of wood. The club angles were much the same as today.

"We shot in the low 90s, which was considered a good score in those days," the late Dr. W. Albert Cook, the first champion at Tulsa Country Club, told a reporter in 1956.

There were no wooden tees, but a box of moist sand was at each starting tee to allow golfers to create mounds to hold their balls off the ground.

The bulls and dairy cattle were hazards in 1908 when the Tulsa Country Club moved to a new six-hole course with sand greens on land owned by Dr. S.G. Kennedy in Osage County, where the club is today.

But shooing the cattle away from a fairway or a green was nothing compared to the hazard on the club's nine-hole first course – an irate neighbor who used a rifle to defy golfers to retrieve balls that landed in her yard.

That course was opened by the newly formed Tulsa Country Club in 1904 on an 80-acre tract at 13th Street and Utica Avenue near where Hillcrest Medical Center is today. The land was leased from Clarissa Bell, a Creek Indian who objected to wayward balls landing in her yard.

When a golfer drove a ball into her yard, she would burst outside with her Winchester rifle and dare the golfer to try to retrieve it. She reportedly had a large collection of 50-cent golf balls by the time the club moved to the Kennedy land.

Another off-course hazard existed for boys because the game was considered a sissy sport.

"I didn't tell anyone in high school that I played golf," the late James A. Kennedy told a World reporter in 1976. "A

Beryl Ford collection

Golfers enjoy a game at the Tulsa Country Club in the 1920s. Early golfers used clubs made of local hickory by the course's golf pro.

boy golfer was the object of ridicule and if caught carrying a bag of clubs off the course, he might have to defend himself."

Golf was not accepted completely until the end of World War I, he said.

Early Tulsa golfers used clubs made by the club's professional, Dan MacKay, a Scotsman who also taught them how to play the game. He made the shafts from local hickory that was considered ideal for golf clubs and even shipped some of the hickory to Scotland for the same purpose. Steel shafts came into use about 1929 and increased drives by about 20 yards.

When the Tulsa Country Club moved to its present location on land leased from the Kennedy family and later bought, a clubhouse was opened and A.W. Tillinghast, famous New York golf course architect, was hired to lay out a course.

That club house burned in 1916 and another was immediately constructed. It was used until it was sold to the Mother Tucker Ministries in 1984. It burned in 1986.

The new site was on land that Mrs. Kennedy would receive later as part of her Osage allotment. "It wasn't her allotment then but we had settled there," James A. Kennedy, son of Dr. and Mrs. Kennedy, recalled in that 1976 interview. "She couldn't give a deed so it was all by verbal agreement."

The bulls and cows were part of a herd owned by Homer Kennedy, a distant relative of Dr. Kennedy, who operated a dairy there.

"They were striking oil around Tulsa and a lot of Easterners were coming to town," James Kennedy said later. "Some of them had played golf, and Tulsa needed a place for social gatherings."

James Kennedy, who was 10 when the course was opened on the Osage tract, held the state amateur champion title from 1920 to 1924.

The standard caddy fee in those early days was 25 cents with a 10-cent tip if the golfer had a good round.

Few women played golf in those early days, but one of the first was Mrs. A.T. Allison, wife of a banker.

Holes on that first Osage course didn't have numbers; they had colorful names such as "Westward Ho," "Lone Tree" and "Profanity Creek."

Air conditioning once considered a fad

Oklahomans take the comfort of air conditioning for granted today – in their homes, their cars, at church, in theaters, at their jobs and most other places – even when the outside temperature hovers near 100 degrees or higher.

It hasn't always been that way.

Air conditioning was considered a fad dreamed up by theater owners when the first breath of cool air arrived in Tulsa in 1924 at the downtown Rialto Theater.

It was a time when many Tulsans slept on cots in their backyards or in nearby parks – a practice that extended into the 1940s – when people tried to cool off in front of electric fans and when every church had paper or cardboard fans in the book holders on the backs of pews.

Sleeping in the backyard had more benefits than just staying cool. It gave parents a chance to teach their children about the stars, the Big Dipper, the Little Dipper, Orion and others.

Tulsa's first cool air arrived at the Rialto Theater and soon was added at the Orpheum Theater, both then owned by Bill Smith. But the cool air at the Rialto was defective, leaving theater-goers more damp than cool.

When the Ritz Theater was built in 1925, owner Ralph Talbot had the latest in air conditioning equipment installed. It was supposed to provide greater cooling than at the competing Orpheum and Rialto.

But every time it was turned on, it blew electrical fuses in the theater and at nearby businesses. Talbot had the system removed and replaced with a system that worked perfectly after the first summer.

Most people considered air conditioning a fad to increase attendance. It did that and probably drew more people inside than the movies and actors.

Theaters plugged their cool air in newspaper ads and on signs on their marquees, most claiming it was 20 degrees cooler inside, a welcome respite from the searing heat outside.

Even pedestrians could get a quick, if temporary, breath of cool from the theaters' air conditioning because some of

Beryl Ford collection

A window display of the 1955 Tulsa Home Show promotes Cool Comfort electric air conditioning. Air conditioning had appeared in Tulsa long before the mid-1950s when theater owners used it in the 1920s to entice customers.

it escaped out the theater doors, many of which probably had been left open intentionally to entice people inside. People walking past could pause to read signs about upcoming movies – and enjoy a breath of cool air and the odor of freshly popped corn.

The first major building in Tulsa to be air conditioned was the National Bank of Tulsa Building, now known as the 320 S. Boston Building, followed shortly by the Philtower and the Philcade, both owned by Waite Phillips and both supplied with cool air by the same unit in the basement of the Philcade.

"The Southwest's finest and mightiest air conditioning units are now operating, literally flooding the 5,500,000 cubic feet of offices, showrooms and corridors of the Philtower and Philcade buildings with fresh, filtered, dehumidified cool air," a 1937 Tulsa World ad said.

"Do workers droop and does work lag in these modern structures?" the ad continued. "No. You'll have no 'off season' in Tulsa if you office or have your shop in the Philtower or Philcade."

And it wasn't long before air conditioning had spread to other downtown buildings.

Professor J.M. Watters, director of business education extension service of the University of Oklahoma, predicted in 1933 that homes would be air conditioned before long.

"Scientists tell us that if a person can live in a cool atmosphere at least eight hours a day, it will give him sufficient energy to carry him through the remaining 16 hours," Watters said. "Air conditioned homes will mean purer, more healthful air."

A few homes had air conditioning in the late 1930s, and window units began appearing in the early 1940s, but the beginning of World War II brought that to a halt until after the war because metal was needed for the war effort.

Tulsa architect Donald Honn wrote in the September 1957 issue of House and Home magazine that air conditioning had become standard equipment in new Tulsa houses.

The "good old days" may be gone. But they have been replaced by the "good cool days."

Civic leader's middle name was education

Alfred E. Aaronson was primarily a businessman until 1957, when he sold his business interests to his partners to devote the rest of his life to civic and cultural work.

"We (referring also to his wife, Millicent) decided we would devote ourselves to things that were crying for people to take an interest in," Aaronson said in 1962.

"To be able to serve is truly a gift of God. I hope heaven will give me the strength to continue my efforts at least until the projects I am involved in are finished," he said.

Shortly before deciding to sell his business interests, he had spearheaded a campaign that resulted in Tulsa voters approving a bond issue to acquire the Gilcrease Museum and keep it in Tulsa.

And for the next 25 or so years, Aaronson devoted himself to a wide range of civic interests – the city-county library system that he served as first chairman; the Tulsa Metropolitan Area Planning Commission; the Tulsa Psychiatric Foundation, the Tulsa County Historical Society; the Urban League; B'nai Emunah; B'nai B'rith; the Zionist Organization of America; and the Jewish Community Council.

More groups, including the University of Oklahoma, got his attention until he really retired. Then he and his wife moved into a Tulsa hospital because of their health and later moved to New York to be near their daughters just a week before he died at the age of 90.

"Working on such projects gives you a pleasure I wasn't able to get from my activities in the business world," Aaronson told a Tulsa World reporter in 1973. "I don't know of any more rewarding experience."

Aaronson was always careful not to take credit for himself for his accomplishments. "I had the most wonderful people working with me," he said. "They deserve the credit, knocking themselves out for projects that wouldn't make them a dime."

Aaronson perhaps was best known for spearheading the drive for a metropolitan library system and for serving as

Tulsa World archives

Alfred Aaronson, pictured in this undated photo, devoted himself to a wide range of Tulsa civic interests, including the city-county library system, which he served as the first chairman.

the first chairman of the City-County Library Commission. After his death, the auditorium at the downtown library was named Aaronson Auditorium.

Eulogizing Aaronson at his funeral, Rabbi Arthur Kahn said few people knew that the initial "E" in Aaronson's name stood for Enoch.

"The Hebrew equivalent of Enoch is also our word for learning," Kahn said. "One could literally say his middle name was education.

"Alfred Aaronson had a great respect for education, learning and excellent literature," Kahn reminded those at the funeral.

A native of New York City, Aaronson came to Tulsa in 1913 and was one of the founders of Mid-Co Petroleum Co. and later of Tuloma Oil Co. He built the former Court Arcade Building at Sixth Street and Boulder Avenue that housed the common pleas courts and other offices until the present courthouse was completed in 1957.

Aaronson maintained his office in the Court Arcade building while serving as vice president of Leavell Coal Co., Looboyle Inc., Consumers Oil Stations and the Commonwealth Co., a home building company, and he stayed after selling those firms.

Aaronson said he gained personal benefits from his civic work -- an appreciation of art while working on the Gilcrease project, learning the importance of books while working on the library campaign and realizing how important history is while working with the historical society.

When Aaronson's father, Lionel, a Hebrew scholar, died in 1924, he didn't leave much of an inheritance. But part of the legacy Alfred received was a book that he considered more valuable than money -- a paraphrase of the biblical book Ecclesiastes.

Included in that book was a paragraph that helped shape Alfred Aaronson's philosophy:

"The name that one leaves behind him at death is better than the good oil that he was anointed with at birth."

'Big Jim' made big difference in Tulsa

Tulsa's first traffic officer used his own funds to study traffic control in New York City and other large cities and joined civic leaders on booster trips to the East seeking industry.

He used those ideas in downtown Tulsa and took part in many civic activities.

But the biggest service to the city performed by the late James A. "Big Jim" Pilkington had nothing to do with traffic control or police.

It was water. Spavinaw water.

The campaign for a $5 million bond issue to build Spavinaw dam was under way in 1919 when a Tulsa businessman reported that Spavinaw Creek had gone dry.

He said that he had stood in the middle of the creek bed and had even picked up stones that had not been wet for months. He spread the word among Tulsa leaders that the stream engineers expected to feed the lake to provide water was dry.

"This was a hard blow to the water project," the late Glenn Condon wrote in a 1957 Tulsa World article recalling the campaign for good water for Tulsa.

But Pilkington, who was reared in Delaware County and who always dreamed of returning to the Spavinaw area, knew that the creek hadn't gone dry. The gin-clear water of that stream didn't show up on the surface for several miles, except at flood stage. He took a group of doubters on a tour to show them that the stream's natural course went underground near the Oklahoma-Arkansas state line before coming back to the surface some distance downstream.

When the water resurfaced, Pilkington knew, it came back in such great volume that a mile farther down stream, it fed a turbine-driven water mill year in and year out.

That information may have been responsible for Tulsa voters' July 10, 1919, approval of a $5 million bond issue to make Spavinaw the city's water source as promoted for more than eight years by the Tulsa World. The alternative proposal was to use Shell Creek near Sand Springs.

But that wasn't the end of the battle. The state Supreme Court ruled against the issuance of bonds because the city charter prohibited the city from acquiring property more than five miles from its city limits. The charter was changed, a new campaign was mounted and the bond issue

Jim Pilkington

James A. "Big Jim" Pilkington was well-known in Tulsa as a downtown traffic cop and as the man who helped save the Spavinaw water bond vote by disproving claims against the proposed water source for Tulsa.

was approved again.

"Big Jim" Pilkington was in the midst of the campaign, as he had been on many other civic issues.

The nickname of Big Jim for Pilkington was appropriate. He was 6 feet, 6½ inches tall. For years, beginning about 1911, he directed traffic at Third and Main streets, the city's busiest intersection in those early days, and was well known to downtown workers.

When the Commercial Club organized booster trips to seek industry for Tulsa, he always went along, wearing a uniform that he had designed for the occasion. He always carried an American flag as he led processions from the train stations to the business sections and back.

Pilkington retired in the 1930s but he didn't abandon his public service. He and his wife, Ruth, bought the remnants of the historic log cabin Powderhorn in the Spavinaw area. It had been built more than 100 years earlier as a home for Cherokee Chief Oochalata but had burned in the 1920s.

The Pilkingtons built their home on the same site, using the two fireplaces that had been built for Oochalata, and also named it Powderhorn. It became a showplace where visitors were welcome to visit, have picnics and even build fires in a stone barbecue pit with hickory wood that was provided.

Signs on a nearby highway invited travelers to visit. Busloads of garden club members came almost daily. Many clubs held meetings there.

And Pilkington's great-nephew, also named Jim Pilkington, a former Tulsa fireman who now runs a fire investigation company, has since developed another acreage into a "showplace park" that he has named Powderhorn Two.

More than 1,000 people attended a farewell party in September 1951 shortly before the Powderhorn site was inundated by the water of new Lake Eucha.

Big Jim, who died a year earlier, knew that his beloved Powderhorn would be covered by the new upper lake that would be created by a new dam on Spavinaw Creek. His widow attempted to have the new lake named Powderhorn.

But she believed Big Jim would have been happy with the name Lake Eucha.

Colorful Tinney emulated Will Rogers

Cal Tinney sang, wrote newspaper columns, acted on stage, in the movies, on radio and on television, ran businesses and developed land – always with humor.

His response to just about anything was humorous. For example, while he was running a tongue-in-cheek campaign for mayor of Tulsa as an independent candidate, he said, "If you don't think I'm independent, ask my wife. Ask her if she didn't give me permission to be independent."

Tinney's life was crammed with material suitable for story-telling, and he delighted in recalling the events in his "homespun" humor.

It was inevitable that Tinney would be compared to Will Rogers, a comparison he never resisted.

Tinney had met Rogers in the late 1920s, had begun emulating him and was writing a biography about him. Shortly before Rogers' death in 1935, a national publication misidentified Tinney as Rogers' cousin.

Rogers took a dim view of that, Tinney recalled later. But Rogers also turned it into part of his newspaper column, saying there was a fellow claiming first to be his cousin and then an uncle.

"If this keeps up," Rogers wrote, "he'll claim to be my dad."

After Rogers' death in a plane crash in Alaska, NBC hired Tinney to portray him in a radio tribute. Tinney later portrayed Rogers on Eddie Cantor's Sunday night television show.

Part of the script for that show called for Tinney to twirl a rope as Rogers had done. "At every rehearsal, I was letter perfect," Tinney recalled years later.

But between the final rehearsal and the show, Tinney had left his rope on an open window where it got wet and "I missed every damn trick." However, he softened the embarrassment by what today would be called Plan B – he started reciting some "Rogersisms."

Like Rogers, Tinney shared his humor in newspapers, radio, television and on the lecture circuit. He also entertained troops during World War II, Korea and the Vietnam War.

"America loves humor and humorists," he often said while pointing out that his favorite type of humor was the homespun kind practiced by Rogers.

He said that type of humor was strictly American. "No

Tulsa World archives
Cal Tinney's career shadowed that of Oklahoma humorist Will Rogers.

other country has it. There is no Will Rogers in Russia; no Mark Twain in Spain."

A native of Pontotoc County, Tinney often told people, "I wasn't born in a log cabin but my folks moved into one as soon as they started living indoors."

Tinney was reared in west Tulsa where his father, Dave, was a politician and policeman who sometimes was called the mayor of west Tulsa. Tulsa Tribune reporter Joe Howell, who graduated from Central High School with Tinney, recalled that Dave Tinney had a job as a policeman when his candidate was elected police commissioner and didn't when his candidate had lost.

The Tinneys lived in one house when Dave Tinney had supported a winner and in a ramshackle rooming house when he had backed a loser, Howell wrote shortly after Tinney died in 1993 at the age of 85.

When he was 18, Cal Tinney took a job on a cruise ship bound for Europe and beyond and worked his way around the world. "I peeled potatoes around the world," he often said. "I was a slow peeler."

Peeling potatoes wasn't his only job on that trip. He also worked on the Paris edition of the New York Herald-Tribune and on the North China Press, an English-language newspaper in Shanghai. When he returned to the United States he took a job as secretary to 1st District Rep. Charles O'Conner.

Tinney later enrolled at the University of Oklahoma but quit after a year because the only jobs he could find to finance his education were shining shoes and selling ties – but that year also provided additional humor.

"I didn't get into a fraternity but I lived next door to a sorority house, and I got in there once in a while," he said.

Among Tinney's endeavors was a daily Tulsa World column started in 1973 called "Will Said and Cal Says" that combined Rogers' quotes with Tinney's comments on current events. Another was Dial-A-Smile that he began in 1976 in which he recorded humorous comments about each day's news that callers could access by telephone.

In his later years, Tinney became a real estate developer and founded the town of New Tulsa near Broken Arrow.

In one of his last interviews, Tinney told a reporter "it would be hard for me to think of a regret" about his life.

Trial of judge's son grabbed spotlight

The son of a U.S. District Court judge was convicted of manslaughter in 1934 after an 11-day trial in one of Tulsa's most sensational criminal cases.

The defendant, Phil Kennamer, 19, was sentenced to 25 years in prison by District Court Judge Thurman Hurst, who said he was shocked at Kennamer's lack of concern for the misery he had inflicted on the family of the victim and his own family.

The judge noted that Kennamer sat with apparent indifference during the trial while his gray-haired father, U.S. Judge Franklin Kennamer, suffering with the anguish of a broken heart, sat beside him.

Nearly a decade later, the younger Kennamer died fighting the Nazis in France during World War II.

Kennamer was convicted of the Thanksgiving night 1934 slaying of John Gorrell Jr., 21, a dental student and son of Dr. John Gorrell, a prominent Tulsan.

Kennamer claimed that Gorrell and others planned to kidnap Virginia Wilcox, 18, a daughter of the oilman Homer Wilcox, or to extort $20,000 from Wilcox with a threat to kidnap the woman – although there was no other testimony indicating that such a plot existed.

Kennamer testified that he took part in planning the crime but claimed that he did not plan to let it proceed.

He admitted that he killed Gorrell and told the jury that he was sane, contradicting testimony by Dr. Karl Menninger of Topeka, Kan., friends and relatives, including his father.

He claimed that he shot Gorrell in self-defense at Forest Boulevard and Victor Avenue after Gorrell tried to kill him with the gun.

Kennamer said that when Gorrell pulled the trigger, the gun did not fire. Kennamer wrested it away from Gorrell during a struggle and shot him, he told the jury.

Afterward, Kennamer walked back to the area he frequented, near 18th Street and Boston Avenue.

After Judge Hurst sentenced him, Kennamer told reporters that his trial, moved to Pawnee on a change of venue, approached the semblance of a Roman holiday.

Many of the witnesses in the case were young and socially prominent. One, Sidney Born Jr., 20, committed suicide two weeks after Gorrell's death.

A Tulsa World photographer, Lee Krupnick, acted as a go-between, passing notes, some in code, between Kennamer

nstitution — OKLAHOMA STATE PENITENTIARY — Located at —

Tulsa World archives

Phil Kennamer was convicted of manslaughter in a highly publicized 1934 trial. He was paroled in 1943 to join the Army, and was killed in World War II.

and a friend while Kennamer was in the Tulsa County Jail. Krupnick decoded the notes and turned their information over to authorities.

Newspapers throughout the country printed daily detailed reports of the trial. The World assigned eight reporters and photographers to cover the trial and published many pages of almost verbatim testimony from many of the witnesses.

Kennamer's conviction and sentence were upheld on appeal, and the case became a political issue that plagued three governors.

Gov. E.W. Marland gave Kennamer a leave from prison to spend time in Arizona with his dying mother.

Gov. Leon C. Phillips refused another leave or clemency of any kind.

After an unusual parole board hearing in the chambers of the House of Representatives, Gov. Robert S. Kerr paroled Kennamer in April 1943 so he could join the Army as a paratrooper. Kennamer enlisted a few days later.

He was killed in action Aug. 15, 1944, in France.

Tulsa County Attorney Dixie Gilmer, who had prosecuted the case, objected to clemency for Kennamer.

He testified that Kennamer told him during a visit in the penitentiary that he was not sorry for killing Gorrell and would never be sorry for that.

Kennamer's unit first saw action in Italy, and then parachuted into France either just before or just after D-Day.

He and an officer, both carrying submachine guns, were killed during an attack on a German machine-gun position.

The officer began shooting, disclosing their position, and then his gun jammed, an Army statement said.

The Nazis opened fire, killing the officer and Kennamer instantly.

Gov. Kerr said of the death: "Private Kennamer has justified the confidence of the pardon and parole board. He has joined the ranks of Oklahoma sons who have given their lives that we may be free. No man can do more."

In a visit to Tulsa in November 1943, shortly before going overseas, Kennamer told a Tulsa World reporter that he had a premonition that he would be killed.

"Something just seems to tell me that I won't come back," he said.

"I hope that if I die, that those who have condemned me will hold me differently in their memories."

Summer may never be as hot as 1936

It was hot in 1980.

Old-timers like to recall the summer in 1936 as the hottest in Oklahoma's history. And, there was no air conditioning except in movie theaters and some downtown stores.

Although July 1980 was the hottest on record in Tulsa, the summer of 1936 still was warmer because the high temperatures started earlier that year. The mercury climbed above 100 on 26 days of July 1980 – one day shy of the record in July 1934. That month had had the highest-ever average monthly temperature of 91.6 compared with an average of 91 in July 1936.

The temperature fell no lower than 80 on 25 consecutive days and the low of 87 on July 16 was the highest minimum reading in Tulsa history. In addition, July 1980 was one of the driest on record with only 0.09 inch of precipitation compared with a normal of about 3 inches.

The triple-digit temperatures started in June that year and continued well into August. In the middle of July, the asphalt in Tulsa streets was reported to be melting.

By July 2, the deaths of 88 people in Oklahoma, Texas, Arkansas, Kansas and Missouri were blamed on the heat.

Gov. George Nigh declared a state of emergency, called on Oklahomans to restrict water usage and declared July 20 "a special day of prayer for rain."

In his declaration of a water emergency, Nigh said the heat wave was endangering lives, taxing water supplies, threatening firefighting capabilities and creating the potential for widespread water shortages.

Tulsans had already been ordered to curb water use by an ordinance passed in the first emergency session of the city commission in 10 years. The commission acted after Tulsans used a record 144.8 million gallons of water the previous day.

Beryl Ford collection

The hottest day in Tulsa history came on Aug. 10, 1936, when the high was 115 degrees.

The emergency ordinance set fines of up to $100 and jail terms of up to 30 days for violators of the strict rationing.

But Police Commissioner Jack Purdie said he didn't foresee many tickets being issued. "I have the feeling that most people will see the seriousness of the situation and will voluntarily cut back," he said.

No doubt July 1980 was hot. But the record highs still belong to 1936, when the mercury climbed to 115, the hottest ever, on Aug. 10; to 113 on two days in July; and to 113 once and 114 on three days in August.

Severe heat in 1923 had resulted in the deaths of at least 50 babies from what was called "summer complaint." The county health department said in mid-July the scorcher had caused "more sickness than we have experienced for more than three years." More than 250 babies were reported sick.

Dr. D.A. Beard, city health officer, blamed the babies' illness on "the sudden hot spell playing havoc with the children."

A man working in an office building downtown was overcome by the heat but revived by a doctor and taken home. Water use also was restricted that year.

The weather also seared in other years, including 1954, when farmers and ranchers reported drought conditions were second only to 1936, the most disastrous season in Oklahoma for farmers.

The only bright spot in regard to agriculture, the farmers said, was that there was more stock water – not because of rain but because hundreds of ponds had been made in the 18 years since 1936.

Ranchers reported conditions were rapidly approaching those in 1936. "We still have some water in ponds but the overall picture looks rough," a county agent said.

Tulsan produced decades of great food

Some of Oklahoma's best cooks still use recipes from a cookbook published a month after its author died in 1985.

Those recipes are still getting rave reviews.

The book was compiled by the late Cleora Butler, who began cooking when she was 10 and left home in 1923 to take a job as a cook and kitchen manager for a wealthy Tulsa family.

It was a good job and her family and friends were proud, she told a reporter a few months before her death at the age of 84 in November 1985.

She and a nephew, Dudley Thomas, compiled the book called "Cleora's Kitchens: Eight Decades of Great American Food," which contains recipes she collected through her long years as a cook for several Tulsa families. It also features stories about some of those families.

Born in Waco, Texas, Butler moved to Muskogee with her parents as a child and learned to cook at her mother's side. She recalled that she first soloed on a rainy Sunday morning while her mother took breakfast to a sick neighbor.

When her mother returned to start breakfast for her own family, Cleora told her proudly "Mother, I've already made the biscuits."

She had used a recipe from a 25-cent cookbook.

The families of George Snedden and Paul McIntyre were among those Butler cooked for before she married in 1940 and retired from full-time cooking, using her talent after that only for catering.

One of her favorite memories was a farewell dinner party the McIntyres had for Waite Phillips and his wife before they moved to California.

After dinner, she said, McIntyre brought Mrs. Phillips into the kitchen to meet the cook. "She told me that she

Tulsa World archives

Cleora Butler's recipes, published in 1985, are still in use in many kitchens.

had never tasted anything quite so good" as the coconut torte with butter sauce, Butler said.

"She told me, 'I have traveled the world but never sat down to such a beautifully prepared meal.' "

Cleora and her husband, George, obtained one of the first small-business loans in north Tulsa in 1961 to open Cleora's Pastry Shop and Catering, a shop that turned out everything from doughnuts to chili and hamburgers. She closed the shop five years later after her husband became ill. He died in 1970.

She also opened a hat shop in her home in the 1950s after she found a hat she liked in a downtown store but was not allowed to try it on. She then learned by correspondence to make hats and sold them for $50 each.

But cooking was her passion. Among her most popular recipes was one for orange nut bread that she frequently served the Sneddens – and it is included in her book.

When the book was published by Council Oaks Books, it was introduced at a Leadership Tulsa party at the Tulsa Garden Center, which had been the Sneddens' home in the 1930s when Cleora Thomas, later Butler, cooked for that family.

The menu came from her cookbook – baron of beef, rolls, spinach sauce, Mexican coleslaw, cheese spread and biscuits and the coconut torte with butter sauce that had been served at the farewell dinner for the Phillipses.

The book was introduced in Dallas the next night at a dinner co-sponsored by Neiman Marcus at the Tower Club.

The cookbook is still widely available for purchase.

"I don't know what I would do without this cookbook," she told a reporter while she was working on it.

"I wake up in the morning, stretch my legs and thank God I kept all my recipes."

Champion Black Gold inspired movie

Shortly before he died in 1917, Tulsa race horse raiser Al Hoots asked his wife to breed his favorite mare, Useeit, to a top colt in the hope the foal would win the Kentucky Derby.

According to legend, Hoots made the request on his deathbed for Useeit to be bred to a Kentucky colt named Black Toney – the sire that was used – but Hoots actually gave his wife, Rosa, a list of horses he thought could sire a winner.

Useeit produced a horse named Black Gold, who won the Golden Jubilee Kentucky Derby race in 1924, a year after the Derby was won by Zev, a horse owned by former Tulsa oilman Harry Sinclair.

Black Gold was in a tight race with Chilhowee and Beau Butler in that May 17, 1924, race at Churchill Downs, finally pulling in front to beat Chilhowee by half a length.

Hundreds of Tulsans and Osages — Mrs. Hoots was an Osage – were on hand to cheer Black Gold and jockey J.R. Mooney to victory and to collect thousands of dollars in winnings.

The story of Useeit and her foal was one of the most romantic stories of thoroughbred racing, but it didn't have a happy ending.

Black Gold won $111,503 in two years of racing before he was put out for stud for three years, but he produced only one colt, a horse that died after being struck by lightning. When Black Gold returned to the track in 1927 he won only $50 in three starts.

Although he wasn't as fast or as strong as he had been, Black Gold was entered in a race at the New Orleans Fairgrounds in 1928, still as game as when he was younger. But he broke a leg and finished the race on three legs.

Black Gold was euthanized and his body buried in the infield of the New Orleans track. Black Gold was inducted into the Hall of Fame in 1989.

A year before his death, Hoots, 59, and Useeit were banned from racing for life because he refused to sell the 9-year-old mare, which had won 34 of her starts, when a race fan tried to buy her after a claiming race at Juarez, Mexico, in which Useeit placed fifth.

Spectators were allowed to buy the horses in a claiming race, and a man named Tobey Ramsey sent his groom to

Oklahoma Historical Society

"Black Gold," the name of Oklahoma's 1924 Kentucky Derby-winning horse, was the title used for a movie starring Anthony Quinn and Katherine DeMille. It had its premiere simultaneously at Tulsa's Orpheum Theater and an Oklahoma City theater in June 1947.

buy the horse. But Hoots didn't want to part with Useeit because of his hope that one day he could breed her to a top horse and produce a Derby winner. He held off the would-be buyer's groom with a shotgun until he could load Useeit onto an Oklahoma-bound boxcar, climb in with her and head back across the border.

Although the horse and owner were barred from racing by the racing commission, they were not barred from breeding. After Hoots died, Useeit was bred to two other stallions and produced colts that won races for Rosa.

Then, in 1921, the mare was shipped to Lexington, Ky., in 1921 and bred to Black Toney, producing Black Gold.

"Black Gold" became the name of a movie starring Anthony Quinn and Katherine DeMille, which had its premiere simultaneously at Tulsa's Orpheum Theater and an Oklahoma City theater in June 1947.

But the movie was pure fiction, with no resemblance to the real story of the race horse with the exception of the name.

"It's not the story of Black Gold or any part of it," a Tulsa World reviewer wrote after a private screening before the premiere. "Tulsa is not mentioned in the picture. Oklahoma barely is referred to."

In the movie, Black Gold was a longshot and a surprise winner in the Derby. Actually, Black Gold was the 9-5 favorite of the crowd and a $2 mutuel bet paid $5.50.

The reviewer cited many differences between the fictional account of the movie and the real story it supposedly portrayed. The reviewer pointed out such technical inconsistencies as one of the characters driving a 1942 model coupe in a 1920 scene and a reference being made in the movie to the Santa Anita race track, also in a 1920 scene, although that track didn't open until 1935.

"If we hadn't been familiar with the true Black Gold story, the picture's story would have been all right," the reviewer wrote. "But most of the movie fans who see this picture came along after 1924 anyway so it won't bother them that the producers preferred a fictional Black Gold rather than the real article."

County seat dispute turned deadly

Two men were killed and a third was wounded when a dispute over the location of the McIntosh County seat erupted into gunfire in what newspapers of 1908 called the county seat war.

The argument between leaders of Checotah and Eufaula wasn't the only violent one that developed from the naming of county shires in the early days of Oklahoma, but it was the only one that involved killing.

A dispute between Jay and Grove for the right to be the Delaware County seat was won by Jay in an election in 1908. The big issue then became which Jay – New Jay or Old Jay. More than 500 shots were exchanged in 1912 between supporters of the two Jays.

The two communities were separated by a wide road with forests on each side. Buildings in either town could not be seen from the other. Rifle pits were dug on three sides of the courthouse in Old Jay. There about 75 armed men were said to be imbibing freely from liquor brought into town from nearby South West City, Mo.

Old Jay eventually won and the courthouse remains at Jay today, although fires destroyed it in 1913 and in 1941.

Although not as bitter as the McIntosh and Delaware county arguments, heated disputes also developed in Creek County between Sapulpa and Bristow; Adair County between Stilwell and Westville; Grant County between Pond Creek and Medford; Wagoner County between Wagoner and Coweta; and Seminole County between Seminole and Wewoka.

The issues didn't die immediately. Tecumseh unsuccessfully challenged Shawnee for the Pottawatomie County seat nearly 20 years later. It even suggested in 1931 seceding from the county to create its own Petroleum County.

Other disputes apparently were not as intense, although community leaders considered being named a county seat important to the growth of their towns and cities.

The leaders of many counties weren't satisfied with the choices of county seats made by the Constitutional Convention that adjourned July 6, 1907, and the state constitution provided for elections to make changes. Before Gov. C.N. Haskell's term as the state's first governor ended in 1911, elections had taken place in 72 counties on petitions to change the county seats or county boundaries.

But no changes were made, Haskell was quoted as saying in a 1936 article in the Chronicles of Oklahoma, published three years after his death. He apparently forgot about Del-

Oklahoma Historical Society

This undated image shows a postcard depicting the Pottawatomie County Courthouse in Shawnee. Tecumseh unsuccessfully challenged Shawnee to be the county seat, one of several such controversies. Disputes over county seats led to lawsuits, fights and even deaths in the state.

aware County, where the seat was moved from Grove to one of the Jays.

Many of the squabbling counties had two elections because of charges of fraud in the first balloting. Several disputes eventually were settled in court.

Sapulpa, named the seat by the convention, was picked by Creek County voters in elections in 1908 and 1912. In the second election good feeling and harmony prevailed. Sapulpa representatives at Bristow polling places on election day were treated to lunch by the Bristow committee, and the Bristow supporters in Sapulpa received similar treatment.

In a lawsuit after the first election, a referee found that "jointists" – beer tavern operators – in Kiefer favored Bristow as the county seat because it would put law enforcement farther away. Kiefer is 16 miles from Bristow but only four miles from Sapulpa.

However, Sapulpa supporters reportedly obtained the support of Kiefer jointists by threatening rigid enforcement unless the vote was cast for Sapulpa.

It didn't make much difference. All the Kiefer votes were thrown out.

The McIntosh County issue turned deadly after Checotah won a May 1908 election and a group of Checotah residents went to Eufaula on June 7, 1908, in an attempt to bodily move the county records.

During the confrontation, Eufaula City Marshal F.M. Woods and General Dunlap, a guard at the temporary courthouse, were killed and Deputy Sheriff Joe Parmenter of Checotah was wounded. Court Clerk Ed Julian, also of Checotah, was charged with murder for shooting Dunlap.

The dispute between Checotah and Eufaula began long before the Constitutional Convention. The convention's county seat committee recommended Checotah. But on the last day of the convention, W.C. Leidtke of Eufaula made an eloquent appeal and delegates ignored the committee's suggestion, choosing Eufaula.

Checotah leaders immediately sought an election to change the county seat. Voters favored Checotah over Eufaula and a third contender, Stidham, leading to the attempt to take the records.

After Eufaula leaders charged fraud, a new election was ordered, and Eufaula won. Checotah alleged that Eufaula used a big slush fund to buy votes in the second election.

Edmond man kills fellow postal employees

A former Marine methodically shot 21 of his fellow workers at the Edmond post office, leaving 14 dead and seven wounded before killing himself in the state's worst massacre up to that time.

Postman Patrick Sherrill, 44, began shooting without warning shortly after he arrived at work at 7 a.m. Aug. 20, 1986, carrying a mail sack stuffed with ammunition and three pistols.

He shot as he walked through various parts of the large building as terrified fellow workers fled the building or looked for places to hide. Many employees couldn't get out because some of the doors had been bolted from the inside by Sherrill.

"He didn't say a thing," one survivor said of the gunman who moved through the maze-like interior of the post office that had tall letter-sorting cases and room dividers.

Although he was armed with three guns, Sherrill used only two .45-caliber pistols, both the property of the Air National Guard, to fire about 50 rounds. The guns were found near his body. His .22-caliber pistol was found on a nearby shelf.

"He had enough ammunition to kill everyone in the building," a police spokesman said, adding "that apparently is what he planned to do."

Police tried to contact Sherrill by telephone during the spree but he hung up on them.

Tracy Sanchez survived by playing dead, lying among

Sherry Brown / Tulsa World

Friends and family members of people killed and injured in the 1986 Edmond post office massacre left memorial wreaths at the building afterwards.

four slain fellow workers. But about 20 percent of the work force was killed or injured.

"I don't know if I just got lucky and got out of the line of fire, or what," another survivor said. "I saw two people get hit just 30 feet from me."

The cause of the shooting will never be known, but Sherrill may have been upset because he had received a reprimand from a supervisor.

Postal officials said Sherrill had a history of discipline problems and the reprimand stemmed from customer complaints.

Rick Esser, 38, one of two supervisors who talked with Sherrill, was the first person shot to death.

Police speculated the shooting spree may have lasted only about 10 minutes but believed Sherrill sat or wandered among the corpses for 45 minutes before shooting himself. A police tactical team found Sherrill's body about 8:30 a.m. when they entered the building.

Police found additional guns the next day in a search of Sherrill's home, but there were no notes or letters that would provide any motive for the carnage or insight into Sherrill's emotional state.

An elaborate shortwave radio, copies of the magazine Soviet Life, a guidebook to Russia, and a book on how to speak Russian also were found.

Famed oil gusher out of control 11 days

Oil and gas gushed out with a deafening roar, coating houses and other buildings for five or six miles around with a black sheen and even sprinkling houses in Norman when a well being drilled in the Oklahoma City field came in unexpectedly.

The well, known as the Mary Sudik, or more popularly as "Wild Mary," ran out of control for 11 days until April 6, 1930.

The well was on a farm owned by Vincent and Mary Sudik and was named for Mrs. Sudik – who, incidentally, became a grandmother on the day the well came in.

The day after Wild Mary was brought under control, another well in the same 160-acre lease came in as a gusher, but was brought under control relatively soon.

Wild Mary was at 6,471 feet when it caught the drilling crew off guard about 6:30 a.m. March 26, 1930. First there was only gas and then the flow turned golden green until it became black.

The tired drillers had been waiting for daylight to pull tools out of the hole and hook up a new bit to drill into the sand. The drillers had failed to fill the hole with mud, which might have prevented the blowout.

Experts said later the crew may have been fatigued to a degree of carelessness or perhaps the driller did not know the top of the sand was permeated with natural gas under high pressure.

The blast twisted and threw drilling pipe and tools like toothpicks.

The oil shot 200 feet into the air and, whipped by a strong north wind, coated everything -- houses, barns, cowsheds, cows, gardens and pastures. Much of the oil was dissipated beyond recovery by the wind. A fine mist of oil was reported in Norman 12 miles south of the well.

Some residents of Purcell, more than 30 miles away, claimed they could hear the roar as the huge volume of gas, estimated at 200 million cubic feet per day, whooshed out of the well hole.

"Some of the boys lost their hearing," welder E.D. Porter, who was working on the well that day, recalled more than 25 years later. Most of the workers stuffed cotton in their ears because of the deafening noise.

"Oil was waist deep and the workers had to put on rain hats and slickers."

Traffic was stopped for miles around and the hooves of horses were wrapped in burlap to prevent their metal shoes from making a spark and setting off a massive fire.

Drillers thought they were bringing the well under control twice before they finally were able to shut off the flow.

On the sixth day, the wind shifted to the south and billows of gas headed toward Oklahoma City. The National Guard was called out to help police keep people out of the danger zone.

The flow diminished briefly on April 1 but it turned out to be just an April Fool joke – another deafening roar sent an increased flow into the sky.

About 211,500 barrels of oil were recovered from pits, tanks and streams in the area. Home owners and farmers had to be compensated for damage done by the oil showers.

Wild Mary wasted about 800,000 barrels of oil in the 11 days she was blowing, but for the next six years, she poured enormous wealth into the pockets of her owners. The well produced more than 5 million barrels of oil before being shut down in 1936.

The gushing well attracted newspaper reporters and photographers and newsreel cameramen from throughout the country.

Homer Craig, who was known as a wild well wizard, flew in from Tampico, Mexico, to help in trying to cap the well and was there when a crew of a dozen men was finally able to put a valve on the well pipe and close it.

Oklahoma Historical Society

The "Wild Mary" oil well in Oklahoma City ran wild for 11 days in 1930.

Mystery phone call led to fugitive's body

He was an Oklahoma fugitive whom the FBI had described as "an extremely dangerous badman and convicted dope peddler, burglar and auto thief who may be armed with a submachine gun and attempt to shoot it out with officers."

John Dillon's body was found in a cistern near Chelsea.

The FBI received a telephoned tip on March 2, 1964, about where to find the body from a man who tried to disguise his voice as that of a woman.

Dillon, 49, disappeared three years earlier two nights before he was scheduled for sentencing in U.S. District Court for operating a dope-peddling ring. His 14 accomplices were sentenced to a total of 246 years after Dillon, the reputed ring leader, forfeited his bond and fled. Dillon faced a possible federal sentence of 190 years in prison on 11 counts.

"I just have a feeling he's been shot," his wife, Lorine Allen Dillon, sobbed after Dillon disappeared.

His killer has not been captured but many believed when the body was found that Dillon had been tortured and killed because of a large debt he owed to "some guys in St. Louis." It was believed the killer tipped the FBI about where the body was because he needed proof that Dillon was dead to collect for the killing.

Dillon's fingers had been cut off but his body was identified by dental records. He had been knocked unconscious and tied to a piece of oil field pipe before being thrown into the 15-foot-deep cistern. An autopsy showed he drowned.

If Dillon's body had not been discovered then, it might never have been found. The cistern was in an area that was covered by the impoundment the next year of Oologah Lake.

Dillon, who used many aliases, including Matt Dillon, claimed to be a farmer and was known as a good automobile mechanic. He had operated an automobile garage in Tulsa and had operated a sawmill. He also had worked as a used car salesman and carpenter.

Dillon disappeared from his Coweta farm Feb. 15, 1961, and apparently roamed the country until December 1962, when authorities believe he was killed.

While a fugitive, Dillon worked for five months on a farm near Mineola, Kan., but he fled in November 1962 after see-

Tulsa World archives

The fugitive John Dillon was found dead in a cistern near Chelsea shortly before the area was flooded by Oologah Lake.

ing federal agents approaching.

The farmer he worked for said Dillon was a good worker but always kept a revolver strapped to the tractor when he was driving it. He told the farmer that shooting rabbits was a hobby.

He also helped the farmer's daughter with her homework, bought her a typewriter and frequently bought ice cream and candy for her and other children.

Meanwhile, Dillon's wife sold property to pay for the $35,000 bail bond that had been forfeited. Dillon also reportedly owed the St. Louis mob $56,000. His wife told a reporter that Dillon had been "awfully worried about all the money he owed – he was head-over-heels in debt."

She testified at a bond-forfeiture hearing that she and Dillon had bought an automotive garage in Tulsa and a farm at Coweta to which they had made many improvements. She also owned an apartment building in Tulsa, and Dillon owned a house when they were married.

On the night Dillon disappeared, she said, the couple was in bed when there was a knock on their door and she heard someone say "we want to talk to you."

Dillon put on his trousers and shirt, went to the door and didn't come back, she said. "I looked out the window and saw two men taking him to a car. That's the last time I saw him," she said.

Some believed that Dillon's love for his wife and his desire to see her were responsible for his killing. The Dillons had lived in a common-law marriage for two years but had a wedding a month before he fled, she testified, "so if he got time (in prison) I could take care of the property and stuff."

Dillon reportedly returned to Tulsa in October 1962, hoping to see her and at first asked a friend to call her. The friend reportedly declined, and Dillon tried to call her but wasn't successful.

Dillon was spotted in Dodge City, Kan., later but then returned to Tulsa where he was captured and killed.

The body would not have been found except for the call to the FBI in March 1964:

"Do you still want John Dillon?" a voice asked. And directions were given to the cistern near Chelsea.

Teacher walked here and left his footprint

After working his way through college in Mississippi during the early 20th century, Ellis Walker Woods saw a flier advertising the need for black teachers in Oklahoma.

And because he had no other mode of transportation, he began walking toward the Sooner state, stopping periodically along the way to work on farms in return for food and occasional lodging.

There's no record of how long it took Woods to walk the 500 miles from Memphis to Sapulpa, where he took a job teaching in a Creek County school in 1911. A year later, he became principal of a Tulsa school that was to become Booker T. Washington High School.

He kept that job until his death 35 years later at the age of 63, only a week after county commissioners awarded a $1.44 million contract for construction of a new Washington High School – thanks more to Woods than to any other person.

Woods, who was a leader in educational, civic and church affairs during his years in Tulsa, served on several committees and commissions seeking a new school building to replace the substandard and obsolete building shared by the high school and elementary school.

His efforts also helped get out the vote to pass a county bond issue.

The high school held some classes in what were called "jitney" buildings on the school grounds and other classes were held in a nearby church. Elementary and high school students used the same auditorium, gymnasium, cafeteria and grounds.

The new school, which has since been replaced by another building, opened on Sept. 3, 1950. Woods' widow, Anna, cut the ribbon to the building, which one visitor said was "fancy enough to make me want to go back to school."

Woods was born in the hills of eastern Mississippi to freed slave parents and worked hard for his education – picking cotton and hiring out as a farmhand. He even taught summer schools in Mississippi and Arkansas to finance his education at Rust College in Holly Springs, Miss.

Tulsa World archives

Ellis Walker Woods walked 500 miles from Memphis to Sapulpa, where he took a job teaching in 1911.

And then he began his trek to Oklahoma.

When Woods became principal, the high school didn't have a building of its own or even a name. It was housed in a four-room frame building that also housed the old Dunbar Elementary School, and was called the Separate School for Coloreds.

The matter of a name created a controversy – some wanted to name the new high school after W.E.B. DuBois, a civil rights activist and educator. But there was stronger support to name the school for Booker T. Washington. A former slave, he also became a civil rights leader, dedicated himself to education and became a teacher and the founder of Tuskegee Institute in Alabama.

The first unit of BTW was built in 1913 and a second unit was added five years later. There wasn't much change again until the new building opened in 1950.

The building was untouched in the 1921 race riot although every house surrounding it was destroyed. The school building became a place where the Red Cross supplied health care to the injured and temporary living quarters to refugees.

The North Tulsa Sertoma Club is leading a drive to build a memorial to Woods on the Oklahoma State University-Tulsa campus, which is in the area that was called the Black Wall Street at the time of the 1921 riot.

Woods was a former president of the Oklahoma Association of Negro Teachers, an officer of the Greenwood Chamber of Commerce, chairman of the Hutcherson branch of the YMCA for several years, served as a trustee of the Vernon A.M.E. Church and was active in the National Association for the Advancement of Colored People.

Woods was known as a motivator for his students, including attending a weekly Friday afternoon assembly for students and teachers alike. Whatever he had to say always ended with:

"You're as good as 90 percent of the people and better than the other 10 percent."

Covelle helped thousands learn trades

A $1 purchase by Oklahoma A&M College in 1946 was one of the best investments the state ever made.

That money went to the federal government for the buildings and 160 acres of land that housed the Army's Glennan General Hospital in Okmulgee.

But even that small sum wouldn't have meant much without Loyd Keith Covelle. Covelle organized Oklahoma State Tech on the site and served as its director for 17 years and later director emeritus until his death in 1976 at the age of 80.

When the school opened, it had 211 students enrolled in 11 trades. When Covelle retired, more than 18,000 people had learned a trade, business or occupation at the school.

Covelle believed in higher education, but his philosophy was that college is not for everyone and college is not the only road to success.

"There's no work anymore for the person who drops out of school," he said when the school celebrated its 15th anniversary. "He has to have some kind of training. We're here to provide it."

Students go to OST because they want to learn to press a pair of pants, half-sole a pair of shoes, bake a loaf of bread or repair an electric motor or radio set, he said.

Covelle organized the technical school as thousands of Oklahoma veterans were returning home after their lives had been interrupted by military service in Europe or in the Pacific during World War II – and needed ways to support their families.

The veterans, who composed nearly all the student body, were a mixture of high school graduates and dropouts with some college study thrown into the mix. But many didn't want to return to colleges or universities; they wanted to learn how to earn a living.

Setting up the curriculum was only part of the job Covelle had to do. He also needed to create a market for the students his school would train – a public relations job he accomplished by speaking to civic groups around the state to tell employers they would do well to hire holders of the two-year certificates from OST.

Tulsa World archives

Loyd Keith Covelle established Oklahoma State Tech at Okmulgee.

By the time he retired, job offers were more plentiful than graduating students.

"I cannot think of a greater need today than that of equipping people to earn a good living while doing necessary jobs and tasks," assistant Secretary of the Air Force Joseph Imirie said at the school's 15th anniversary and dedication of Covelle Hall, a recreational building.

"The nation needs scientists and engineers," he said. "It needs managers and executives, school teachers and lawyers, doctors and journalists.

"But it has an equal or greater need for the highly competent skilled craftsmen."

Covelle said he didn't organize the technical school by himself and gave much of the credit to the late Henry Bennett, president of Oklahoma A&M College, which became OSU. He said Bennett was responsible for obtaining the school site and guided him in setting up the school.

The site housed Glennan General Hospital for American servicemen until 1944. Then it became a hospital for treatment of German prisoners of war and was staffed primarily by POWs who had medical training. The hospital's mission reverted to a facility for American servicemen in 1945, a year before it was bought by OSU.

A native of Chicago, Covelle was a graduate of Oklahoma A&M and became a teacher at Duncan High School in 1914. He became director of engineering extension at A&M in 1917 and was connected with the college from then until organizing OST, except for five years during World War II when he served as a Navy officer.

After retirement, Covelle served as one of the original directors and as president of the Okmulgee Hospital Foundation. He was president of the Okmulgee Chamber of Commerce in 1958.

When Covelle was given credit for organizing the school, his answer was always "I didn't do it myself."

And then he would explain "the Lord assisted me in choosing some of the finest people to run the school."

Tulsa pioneer was 'father of Route 66'

Pioneer Tulsan Cyrus Avery is best remembered as the father of the mother road – U.S. Route 66 – but he also played a key role in bringing paved highways to the state and Spavinaw drinking water to Tulsa.

Add to that construction of the original Tulsa Municipal Airport, the planning of Mohawk Park and a leadership role in so many other civic activities it's difficult to list them, as was true with many of Oklahoma's pioneers.

Consider:

Avery served as a Tulsa County commissioner from 1913 to 1917. He was responsible for the county having the best roads in the state because of his development of a system for farmers using split-log drags to smooth roads after each rain in return for $1 per mile.

As president of the Eastern Oklahoma Agricultural Association in 1914, he was responsible for having farm agents placed in each county.

As president of the Albert Pike Highway Association in 1917, he was responsible for development of a highway from Hot Springs, Ark., through Oklahoma to Colorado Springs, Colo., which later became part of U.S. 64.

A state highway commissioner in 1924, he pushed through a law that created a three-man state highway commission that laid out a state highway system, organized maintenance, established a system for marking highways and had markers placed on the highways. That law also set aside a portion of the gasoline tax for highways. As the highway commissioner, he also was able to have roads paved around many cities.

Avery served in 1928 as a member of the committees that built the Tulsa airport and laid out Mohawk Park. Avery was the eastern Oklahoma district director of the Works Progress Administration from 1935 to 1937 and oversaw projects ranging from farm ponds to schools.

The list goes on, including his service twice on commissions that studied education problems in Oklahoma.

But the two things for which he is best remembered are Spavinaw water and the routing of U.S. 66 through Tulsa rather than following the old National Road from St. Louis to Kansas City and the Santa Fe Trail southwest across Kansas as some promoters wanted.

An alternate route that was proposed would have followed the old Butterfield Overland Stage coach line across southeastern Oklahoma from Fort Smith to the Sherman, Texas, area.

But Avery, who was state highway commissioner and a "consulting highway specialist" for the U.S. government, stressed that the highway had to cross the Arkansas River

Tulsa World archives

Tulsa businessman Cyrus S. Avery helped bring Spavinaw drinking water to Tulsa.

someplace and Tulsa had the best bridge on the river. It was a steel-reinforced bridge on 11th Street that had been completed in 1916 while he was a county commissioner.

That argument was key to having U.S. 66 come through Tulsa, first along Federal Avenue (now Admiral Place) and later along 11th Street.

He had taken a lot of kidding about narrow bridges, sharp curves and right-angle turns on Oklahoma highways that were built when he was chairman of the state highway commission from 1924-27. Avery told a Tulsa World reporter in 1955 they weren't mistakes or the result of poor engineering.

"Engineers were just as good then as they are now," he said. "We knew that the shortest distance between two points is a straight line. But we had to worry about money about as much as we did engineering."

Thus highways were routed around hills instead of through them, bridges were built 18 feet wide and section lines were followed in spite of the resulting right-angle turns because these things made the roads cheaper. "If the bridges had been made two feet wider," he said, "we couldn't have built as many bridges. There was never enough money."

A native of Pennsylvania, Avery came to Oklahoma as a 12-year-old with his parents in 1883 and lived along Spavinaw Creek in what became Delaware County. He fell in love with the cool, clear water of the stream that years later was dammed and became the source of drinking water for Tulsa. Avery promoted it while serving as a member of the Tulsa water board created in 1921 to bring water to Tulsa from Spavinaw.

Until his last few years, Avery made annual visits to Spavinaw Creek on his Aug. 31 birthday to wade in and drink from the stream as he had as a boy. One of his last visits there was on his 85th birthday in 1956 when he was joined by a group of friends who also had campaigned for Spavinaw water.

Avery made an unsuccessful race for governor in 1934 and served as chief right-of-way purchasing agent for a second Spavinaw pipeline in the late 1940s. At the age of 79, he took a job with Lock-Joint Pipe Co., which he held for a decade.

Avery died at the home of a daughter in Los Angeles on July 4, 1963, a few weeks before he would have been 92. His wife of 65 years, Essie, had died a few months earlier.

Tulsa landmark destroyed by fire in '52

One of Tulsa's best-known landmarks, where thousands had watched sports and entertainment events since it opened 23 years earlier, was destroyed on Sept. 20, 1952, by a fire believed caused by lightning.

Only the partially damaged walls of the Coliseum on Elgin Avenue between Fifth and Sixth streets remained standing two hours after the first alarm was turned in at 9:31 p.m.

Fire Marshal Farl Wagner said "several eye witnesses gave us information that has led us to believe a lightning bolt struck the roof."

The spectacular fire, called at the time one of the city's largest, attracted an estimated 12,000 spectators as the wooden roof burned and the brick walls collapsed.

Beryl Ford collection

Tulsa's Coliseum stands in ruins after a fire destroyed it on Sept. 20, 1952. The building near Sixth Street and Elgin Avenue was a center for sports and entertainment events.

The brick and terra cotta structure was the showplace of the Southwest in its day. It was built in 1928 at an estimated $1 million cost by Walter Whiteside, a Minnesota millionaire, and opened on New Year's Day 1929 with the first hockey game in the South.

Times were lean because of the Great Depression, and the building was taken over by the Coliseum Corp. at a sheriff's sale in 1942. Avey bought the building in 1944.

The building had been the site of many conventions and political events, and its stage had been the venue for performers such as ice skater Sonja Henie; boxer Joe Louis; orchestra leaders Rudy Vallee, Harry James, Gene Krupa and others; and singer Nat King Cole. Professional wrestling and hockey matches also were held there, as well as high school graduation exercises.

Police estimated that about 125,000 people drove past the smoldering remains the next day.

Owner Sam Avey, who was attending a housewarming party for his daughter and son-in-law, Pat and Ramon King, arrived at the building shortly after the west section of the roof had collapsed, and then he went home to watch on television.

"I've had too many happy memories in that old barn to watch it die," Avey told a reporter.

Television station KOTV, two blocks away, rigged a camera on the roof of its building and broke into its scheduled network program to broadcast periodic live shots of the fire until 10:30 p.m., when the station broadcast the fire.

A man who lived in an apartment building across the street from the Coliseum said he saw a blinding lightning flash immediately before the fire started. More than 150 firefighters from 11 companies fought the three-alarm fire, which was fanned by winds up to 35 mph.

Lightning also struck other places in the city, including a Public Service Co. substation at the fairgrounds. The storm's heavy rain flooded city streets, but the Weather Bureau measured only 0.3-inch of rain at the airport.

It was the first rain in 25 days for Tulsa.

The Coliseum loss was estimated at more than $1 million by Avey, who had owned the building since 1944 and whose KAKC radio station was located in the basement. When the fire began, the building was nearly empty except for two employees of KAKC who escaped after completing a network broadcast, and a night watchman who was not inside when the fire started.

Thousands of Tulsans learned to ice skate there. The old electric organ that pealed out the "Skatersç Waltz" for skating lovers was nothing but a shapeless ruin after rubble was scraped away. It had been installed in 1928, was rebuilt many times and originally cost between $25,000 and $30,000.

Not long after the fire, the Coliseum became a parking lot. It still is.

"It certainly is a blow," longtime building manager Eddie Quigley said in an understatement.

"The worst of it is that this looked like it was going to be our best season."

It was more than an entertainment center or sports palace for Quigley, who had spent 22 years at the Coliseum, 20 of them as manager. He often said he spent an average of 16 hours a day, seven days a week on the job.

"A little round man – Quigley – leaned against the street barricade near the front entrance of the Coliseum Sunday and viewed the ruins of his 'second home.' He held his glasses in one hand and there were tears in his eyes," a World story reported. "He was oblivious of the constant stream of cars that rolled by as thousands upon thousands viewed the rubble of what had been Tulsa's entertainment center for more than 23 years.

"Eddie's tears weren't the only ones. Thousands wept as they crowded the area to view the rubble. Their showplace was gone. And so was an era in Tulsa."

Avey helped make sure babies got milk

Thousands of Tulsans had milk to drink as babies during the Great Depression thanks to a Tulsa wrestling and entertainment promoter and philanthropist.

The Babies Milk Fund was one of Sam Avey's three favorite charities, all involving children. The other two were an annual Christmas party for needy children at his Coliseum and the state Santa Claus Commission, which provided presents for children in orphanages.

Avey didn't start the milk fund, but he became its angel – its biggest supporter – two years after it was started in 1934 by women at Boston Avenue Methodist Church. He supported the fund with an annual charity wrestling match at the Coliseum from 1936 to 1959 and frequently added money from his own pocket.

"The Community Fund took care of many situations and made life better for people in general," Mrs. Earle Porter, who was the chairwoman of the group that founded the fund, recalled in 1977. "But there was nothing for babies who needed milk, and federal aid did not extend to providing milk for babies."

The Milk Fund paid to have milk delivered by regular milkmen or to have canned or special formula milk provided to households as needed.

After the Coliseum burned in 1952, Avey moved the Milk Fund charity wrestling matches to the fairgrounds. The matches continued until 1959, when the fund's board thought it could be self-supporting. The fund supplied milk to babies until 1977, when it gave the $4,600 it had left to The Little Light House, a school for children with disabilities.

Avey's annual benefit matches brought to Tulsa the great names of the grappling game. "Many years we had three champions on the card," he told a reporter in 1959.

Most of the wrestlers took training expenses or transportation costs and nothing else, Avey said. "They took their cue from the ladies of the milk fund. Here was a charity that operated without any overhead. The ladies even paid for their own stamps."

Sometimes the milk fund received more than the gate receipts. The 1958 gate, for instance, totaled $5,200 but Avey turned over $7,100 to the fund.

Avey also suspended his rule about not taking up collections at Coliseum events to allow donations to the milk fund. He didn't like soliciting in the Coliseum because, he

Tulsa World archives

Sam Avey didn't start the Babies Milk Fund, but he became its biggest supporter two years after it was founded in 1934 by women at Boston Avenue Methodist Church.

said, spectators had paid to get in and shouldn't be expected to pay more.

Avey staged Christmas parties for needy children in the Coliseum from 1944 until 1950. The events attracted as many as 9,000 children, who sang Christmas songs, watched ice skating shows, clowns and elves and, of course, Santa. Each child received a four-pound sack of fruit, nuts and candy to take home.

Surplus sacks of goodies were delivered to local orphanages and homes.

When he died in 1962, Avey was the chairman of the Oklahoma Santa Claus Commission, the state agency that provides Christmas gifts for children in orphanages and training schools. Avey was named to the commission in 1957, succeeding the late W.G. Skelly.

Avey was born in Kingfisher. By age 15, he was on the "coal oil" theater circuit, working as a prop handler and bit actor playing juvenile leads. After six years on the stage, he joined his father in a grocery business. That didn't hold his interest and he got involved in show business of a different sort, wrestling.

He became the promoter for Ed "Strangler" Lewis, one of the big names in wrestling in the early 20th century, and came to Tulsa in 1924 to promote wrestling. He later turned over wrestling promotion to Leroy McGuirk, a wrestler who had been blinded in an automobile accident, to devote time to his other interests.

Those other interests included the Coliseum, which he bought in 1944. Under his guidance, it became a venue for many of the big entertainers of the period until it burned down in September 1952. Avey, with two partners, also started radio station KAKC in 1946 and operated it until 1955, when they sold it to an evangelist.

Avey also was a senior vice president of Farmers and Merchants State Bank.

In 1947, he received the Chamber of Commerce award for outstanding and unselfish civic achievement. That year he was the chairman of The Salvation Army building fund campaign.

But throughout the years, the milk fund remained one of Avey's favorite charities.

"I like a charity where 100 percent of the money received goes to the charity for which it was intended," Avey once told a reporter.

Best of all, he loved children.

Welcome mat rolled out for Truman

President Harry S. Truman, on a national whistle-stop campaign, had reached Tulsa, where 100,000 turned out to greet him – his largest crowd since his train left the West Coast.

Confetti and paper streamers showered the presidential parade on Sept. 28, 1948, as the cars drove along Boston Avenue from the train depot en route to Skelly Stadium.

Truman's wife, Bess, was concerned about the large downtown crowd. "There won't be a soul left to fill the stadium," she said to Tulsa World reporter Yvonne Litchfield, who rode in the car with Bess Truman and the Trumans' daughter, Margaret.

In spite of Bess Truman's fears, 15,000 were at Skelly Stadium to hear Truman's "give 'em hell" speech assailing the "Republican do-nothing 80th Congress" and GOP farm and power policies.

Retiring Sen. E.H. Moore was on hand to greet Truman as he arrived in Tulsa, although many expected Moore to be a no-show because Truman had bitterly attacked him in an earlier speech.

Truman, in a rear-platform speech in Marietta the previous day, had referred to the popular 76-year-old Oklahoma Republican senator as "Old Man Moore, he never was any good in the first place.

"I served in the Senate with him and if he ever did anything for the people, it was by accident."

The attack on Moore, 76, was considered a major blunder by many Oklahomans, but Moore turned the other cheek and announced that he still would be part of the welcoming committee at Tulsa's Union Depot.

"I want to see President Truman given a cordial reception in Oklahoma, and I urge that every courtesy be shown him," Moore said. "I personally want to welcome him to the state."

Their meeting at Union Depot was more cordial than might have been expected.

"Hello, Harry," Moore said as the two shook hands. "How are you?"

Truman replied: "Hello, Senator. It's nice to see you."

Associated Press

President Harry S. Truman shows off the inaccurate headline on the front page of the Nov. 4, 1948, Chicago Daily Tribune. Before Truman's come-from-behind win, he made a series of appearances in Oklahoma.

Stadium talk.

"I want to assure the people of Oklahoma that I shall continue my efforts in behalf of the Arkansas River development," he said.

The Pawnee High School band won a contest held at Skelly before Truman arrived. The Sand Springs band was second and Tahlequah was third in a President's Day contest sponsored by the Democratic Central Committee, which put up $600 in prize money.

Twelve bands entered and six others performed but did not compete. They were from the University of Tulsa, Tulsa Central, Will Rogers, Webster, Booker T. Washington high schools and the Oklahoma Military Academy.

During his swing through Oklahoma, Truman spoke to an estimated 400,000 people.

"Undoubtedly, more people saw the president and he spoke to more people than any man before in the history of Oklahoma," said Gov. Roy J. Turner, who accompanied the campaign train during the Oklahoma trip.

Truman's train also made stops in Oklahoma City, McAlester, Chelsea, Vinita, Ardmore and Afton.

All the experts – pollsters, political commentators, newspapers – believed Truman was waging a losing battle.

But not the voters.

Truman defeated the Republican nominee, Thomas E. Dewey. Oklahomans preferred Truman by a vote of 348,442 to 185,846.

Radio commentator Fulton Lewis, in his nationally broadcast program, talked at length about Truman's attack on Moore. Lewis reminded listeners that Moore had been a Democrat who turned Republican to defeat New Dealer Josh Lee in the 1942 Senate election. He called Moore "one of the most respected members of Congress by both Democrats and Republicans."

Waging what the "experts" said was a losing battle for election to his own term as president, Truman slashed at Republican policies on reclamation, public power, price supports and rural electrification during his Skelly

Bonds made port dreams a reality

Tulsa County voters approved a $17.5 million bond issue in August 1967 to develop the Port of Catoosa, climaxing a decades-long effort to bring river navigation to this inland area.

"There has never been a bond issue in the history of Tulsa which has meant so much to the city," Early Cass, the chairman of the City of Tulsa-Rogers County Port Authority, told a Tulsa World reporter on election night.

Few would quarrel with Cass' statement that the port bonds were important but most probably would argue that a 1921 bond issue that resulted in Spavinaw water for the city was more important.

When it was finished in December 1970, the McClellan-Kerr Arkansas River Navigation System was the largest civil project ever built by the U.S. Army Corps of Engineers, according to a corps Web site. The waterway had cost $1.2 billion when it opened, the largest amount spent up to that time by the U.S. on a water project.

Forty years later, the Tulsa Port of Catoosa – financed by that bond issue plus $2.5 million the city had spent earlier and funds from a Rogers County bond issue – is the largest and most inland port in the country and serves customers who send and receive more than 2.2 million tons of cargo each year. The 2,000-acre industrial park with 63 industrial facilities employs about 4,000 people in manufacturing, distribution and processing products.

Shipment by water has become commonplace.

The corps has had a 99 percent return on its investment, according to the port's Web site. Billions of dollars in public and private investment have occurred along the river in Arkansas and Oklahoma, including $1.5 billion at the Catoosa port and $2 billion at the Muskogee port

Navigation of the Arkansas had been a dream of Tulsa-area residents at least since 1908, but the Arkansas was used for that purpose periodically as early as 1824 when 100 recruits were brought up the river by steamboat to Fort Gibson and supplies were brought as far as Fort Smith and then shipped by keelboats and ox wagons to their destinations.

The Oklahoma Legislature passed a resolution by Tulsa Reps. Cicero Holland and Woodson Norvell and Sen. P.J. Yeager in 1908 urging Congress to restore navigation on the Arkansas. The resolution cited a Corps of Engineers report that said the Arkansas could be put in perfect condition for navigation from Tulsa to the Mississippi for $27.6

Tulsa World archives

President Richard Nixon dedicates the McClellan-Kerr Arkansas River Navigation System at the Tulsa Port of Catoosa on June 5, 1971.

million and that the cost from Tulsa to Fort Smith would be about $6.2 million for a 6-foot channel.

Businessmen in both Arkansas and Oklahoma lobbied Congress in the early 20th Century to make the whole river navigable. Clarence Byrnes, editor of the Fort Smith Southwest Times Record, wrote editorials for 40 years promoting navigation of the river, and Newton "Newt" Graham, a Tulsa businessman, also helped lead the fight.

Arkansas Sen. John McClellan said at the dedication that he and Oklahoma Sen. Robert S. Kerr, with the support of other members of the two states' congressional delegations, had worked for 14 years to have the project approved and funds appropriated.

Speaking at the dedication of the port in June 1971, President Richard Nixon credited McClellan and Kerr, whose names were put on the waterway by Congress.

"For years, the idea of an Arkansas River waterway was dismissed as a foolish dream," Nixon told about 30,000 who attended the ceremony at the port. "But there were others, men like Senators Kerr and McClellan, who held it as a bold and achievable vision. The completed project which we dedicate today has proved they were right."

Oklahoma Gov. David Hall said the project was a great challenge. "The forces of politics, economics and nature fought the dream. But the rugged Kerr-McClellan determination won. Their cause was just. The dream is a reality."

The port had been in operation for several months before Nixon's dedication. The first commercial shipment -- 650 tons of newsprint for the Tulsa World and Tulsa Tribune and several other Oklahoma newspapers -- arrived on Jan. 21. Following the pattern of most politicians speaking in Oklahoma, Nixon quoted Oklahoma humorist and philosopher Will Rogers.

"One day in 1923," Nixon said, "Will Rogers was spoofing Congress about its public works spending. He made his point by saying that with all the money being passed out that he could probably even expect to get a harbor built on the Verdigris River at Oologah.

"Well, this magnificent new port is still a few miles downstream from Oologah but it's close enough that this time the Corps of Engineers and the people of the supposedly landlocked Sooner state can have the last laugh," Nixon said.

Billy Sunday packed the house

Famous evangelist Billy Sunday was met by a "solid mass of humanity" when he arrived in Tulsa by train to begin a six-week revival in 1921.

"Never in the history of our city has any man, prince or pauper, been accorded such a welcome," a Tulsa World reporter wrote in a front page story about the evangelist's arrival from St. Louis.

There was such a jam on the train station platform that members of a reception committee couldn't get close to the colorful preacher to welcome him.

Library of Congress

Evangelist Billy Sunday received an enthusiastic welcome when he arrived in Tulsa for a six-week revival in 1921.

Sunday came to Tulsa to preach at the request of a committee headed by Cyrus Avery and made up of representatives from churches of many denominations – Methodist, Baptist, Christian, Lutheran and Presbyterian. He preached at least two sermons daily and sometimes three in a special tabernacle that would hold 6,000 and that was built for his crusade at Fourth Street and Elgin Avenue.

The revival services began on Nov. 5 and by the time Sunday left Tulsa on Dec. 17, more than 10,000 people had responded to his altar calls. The newspapers didn't report the total number who attended the services, but most had capacity crowds.

Churches dismissed their regular services on the first and last Sundays of the crusade to allow members to hear the famous evangelist at the tabernacle. But regular services were held on other Sundays during the period.

The tabernacle was filled and traffic was snarled with police turning cars away more than an hour before the scheduled beginning time for the first Sunday night service.

The Tulsa World published front page news stories about the revival every day with the full texts of Sunday's sermons printed inside. The stories were accompanied by what was called "Sundayisms," such as:

"God keeps no half-way house. It's either heaven or hell for you and me."

"Going to church doesn't make anybody a Christian any more than taking a wheelbarrow into a garage makes it an automobile."

"Why don't people go to church? Because it is too much like going to a funeral."

Six or eight of the plain-spoken preacher's Sundayisms were printed every day.

During the long revival Sunday preached against danc-

ing, movie theaters opening on Sundays, drinking, card games, smoking, cursing and many other activities. In one sermon, he said the modern church is more interested in the kitchen and pantry than the pulpit and the choir loft.

In one sermon, he told his congregation that "this is an immoral age" and criticized "that vile toddle, shimmy, the camel walk and the cheek to cheek dances with their absolutely disgusting, damnable, low, hellish, vile, brazen, sensuous appeal." Toddle, shimmy and camel walk apparently were dance steps.

During some sermons, Sunday flung flowers toward the audience, pounded his fist on a wooden stand, pulled his tie off and his collar open in his best showman stance.

During his stay in Tulsa, Sunday met stage and movie actress Theda Bara, who always played the part of a vamp and was in Tulsa to participate in a Harvest Festival at Convention Hall. The two talked briefly about mutual friends in Hollywood before the actress got into a car and was driven away from the hotel where both stayed.

Born in Iowa in 1863, Sunday had been a professional baseball player for seven years with a "crew of hard-hitting, hard-fighting, hard-drinking players."

He said he was with a group of players in 1890 when he saw a card inviting the holder to a mission. He went to that mission and heard a sermon. "I was impressed and went back again and again," he said.

After deciding to become a Christian, he said, he was worried about what the other players would say, but they all supported him. Five years later, he became an evangelist.

When he left Tulsa, Sunday received a check for $17,527, which was the total collections during his six-week revival.

"I used to get barely enough to pay my railroad fare and sometimes not that," he said, adding that he "did everything in those days – put up my own tent, led my own singin'.

"I couldn't sing, you understand, but I could wave my arms and yell to beat the band and make them think I knew a lot about it. But I didn't know a note from a horsefly."

But, he added, he could put up a tent as well as a circus hand.

He said he was happy with the amount of the check although a committee member said it wasn't as large as he would like to have made it.

State came in, liquor went out in '07 vote

The proposed Oklahoma Constitution and prohibition were approved by landslide margins in the future state's first election on Sept. 16, 1907.

Charles N. Haskell, the Democrat candidate for governor, also won by a landslide but it was two days after the election before his victory became clear. Democrats also swamped their Republican opponents in most other races.

The lone exception was Rep. Bird S. McGuire, who had served two terms in Congress from Oklahoma Territory and was elected in the 1907 voting from the 1st District, which included Tulsa. He also was elected to three successive terms.

There was no question early on about the outcome of the issue that resulted in uniting Oklahoma and Indian territories into one state and prohibiting the sale of liquor.

Haskell, of Muskogee, had defeated Oklahoma Territorial Gov. Frank Frantz, a Republican, who had been reported earlier as "the most popular man in both territories." The official returns that were announced more than a month later showed Haskell had won by nearly 30,000 votes.

Because of the uncertainty on election night, the Tulsa World of Sept. 18, 1907, told readers in a banner headline:

"RETURNS ARE AS YET INDEFINITE."

Supporters of Frantz claimed he was ahead by 15,000 votes while backers of Haskell insisted he was ahead by 30,000 votes.

There was some doubt as to the accuracy of the returns reported in that day's newspaper. The World explained "it was long after midnight before returns that could be counted on found their way to this office and in almost every message it was stated that the results were wholly based on estimates."

A Page 1 cartoon reported "We've had an election" but made it clear the results were still in doubt.

The constitution for the new state that would be born two months later had been ratified by an 80,000 majority, according to reports that were being received in Oklahoma City. Prohibition also appeared to have been approved by 30,000 votes.

President Theodore Roosevelt announced that he would approve the Oklahoma Constitution although his personal

HASKELL GETS LONG EXPECTED PACKAGE

Tulsa World archives

This Clarence Allen cartoon ran in the Sept. 20, 1907, Tulsa World following the Sept. 16, 1907, election in which Democrat Charles Haskell defeated Republican Frank Frantz.

opinion of the document "was not for publication." He said he had examined the document with the attorney general and felt the question of his approval ought not to be based on his personal opinion but on whether it complied with the terms of the enabling act.

Frantz, a Spanish-American war hero who had received a battlefield promotion to captain and who was a friend of Roosevelt, was so bitter about the outcome that on Statehood Day two months later he refused to participate in the inauguration.

Haskell and Frantz had debated each other on various issues throughout the campaign for the September election. Frantz had taken particular exception to a personal attack on him made by Haskell during a speech before 2,500 in Shawnee when he charged Frantz with drunkenness, immorality and misconduct in office.

Haskell also claimed Frantz had made similar charges against him. He said that Frantz had published statements "alleging that I have been drunk in at least seven places in the last week. You may select a committee of any three ministers and if they can find a single instance in my life when I was intoxicated, I will withdraw from the race."

In refusing to participate in the inauguration, Frantz said he was not inclined to talk for publication about his refusal. "I simply do not want to take any part whatever in the inauguration. I want to be counted out of it," he said.

During the course of the campaign, two nationally prominent figures were brought to the territories to try to elect the candidates -- Republican presidential nominee William Howard Taft campaigning for Frantz and Democratic presidential nominee William Jennings Bryan stumping for Haskell. Taft was elected.

A few days after the election the state Democratic chairman, J.B. Thompson, said he wasn't worried about a challenge to the vote.

"Should Frantz contest the election in every Democratic county in Indian Territory and succeed in having every one of those counties thrown out, Haskell and the entire Democratic ticket would still have a majority of more than 7,000 over the Republican vote," he said.

No challenge was made.

Double killing led to intense manhunt

The 2003 killing of a Depew couple and wounding of two others touched off one of Oklahoma's longest and most intense manhunts.

About 100 officers from 15 to 20 law enforcement agencies searched for more than a month in 12-hour shifts 24 hours a day for Scott James Eizember, believed to be hiding in a heavily wooded area near Bristow.

Eizember was wanted for killing A.J. and Patsy Cantrell, both 76, of Depew; wounding Tyler Montgomery, 16; and beating Karla Wright, Tyler's grandmother, with a shotgun on Oct. 18, 2003.

Wright, who was baking cakes for a Sunday school class when Eizember entered her home, probably escaped death by pretending to be dead.

"I remember thinking, 'He's going to get tired of hitting me,'" she testified at Eizember's trial. She said he had struck her four times on the back of the head and then ". . . I pretended I was dead."

Montgomery was watching television when he saw Eizember and was shot in the back as he tried to run. Montgomery told the jury that he jumped into a pickup to drive away but Eizember jumped into the bed and shot him again before the teen crashed the vehicle into a pole to try to shake his assailant.

The search for Eizember, 42, who had just been released from the Tulsa Jail after posting bail on a burglary charge, was concentrated in heavy woods near the airport after the killing of the Cantrells. Their bodies were discovered when police answered a call to a house across the street, where Wright had been beaten.

"It just blows my mind that this guy has eluded this many people for so many days," Kellyville Fire Chief Mike Kelly said at the end of October.

But, he said, "the woods are so thick and so dense this man could be 50 feet from you and you could not see him."

At one point, officers thought Eizember had moved into Tulsa County. When a deputy pulled over a vehicle on Avery Drive, the driver jumped out and fled but the fugitive wasn't found.

During the search, authorities said Eizember had no regard for human life.

But Sherri Lambart, who lived next door to Eizember in Garden City, Mich., said she was startled at the accusations against the former hockey coach and father of two. "He was a real family guy. He was always out in the yard playing with his kids," Lambart said.

Scott Eizember is escorted through the Creek County courthouse in Bristow by a deputy after a 2004 hearing.

Eizember had fled Michigan for Oklahoma due to a long list of encounters with law enforcement in Garden City, according to police. In 2002, Garden City police arrested him four times on charges of auto theft, violating a personal protection order and domestic violence against his ex-wife.

The manhunt continued in Creek County until Nov. 23, when Eizember stole a car from a Depew food bank volunteer and headed for Arkansas, where he kidnapped Dr. Samuel Peebles and his wife, Suzanne, and forced them to drive him to Texas.

He apparently had been living in the food bank that was housed in an old parsonage at the First United Methodist Church and surprised Doyce Pitre as she unlocked the door. She was so frightened she left her keys in the door and Eizember used the keys to steal her car.

Eizember had stayed at the church a year earlier when he rode up on a bicycle and asked if he could camp in the yard. Instead, he was given a place inside with hot meals.

After stealing Pitre's car, Eizember fled to Arkansas and kidnapped the Peebleses when they stopped to help after he had car trouble. He was captured near Lufkin, Texas, after being shot four times in the chest by Samuel Peebles during a struggle in Peebles' van.

Eizember was convicted of first-degree murder by a jury in El Reno after his trial was moved there from Creek County. The jury assessed the death penalty for A.J. Cantrell's killing and set a life-without-parole sentence on a second-degree murder conviction for Patsy Cantrell's death. He received 150 years for the other charges.

His appeal to the Court of Criminal Appeals failed to overturn the convictions and sentences although the court was divided 3-2 in regard to the death sentence for A.J. Cantrell's killing. Two of the judges wrote that the trial "was tainted when biased jurors who sat on his jury should have been excused."

Eizember also was found guilty in U.S. District Court in Fort Smith of kidnapping the Peebleses and was sentenced to 25 years in prison.

Linda Cantrell, 43, a daughter of the Cantrells, was killed in a murder-suicide in Oklahoma City a few days before Eizember's trial began. Police found her body and that of Fred Wheeler, 49, when they responded to a report from Wheeler's ex-wife who said Wheeler had called her to tell her he had killed his girlfriend and was preparing to kill himself.

Gruber created for big bang of WWII

The booms of big shells fired by military howitzers had replaced the puny pops of pistols and occasional submachine guns wielded by outlaws in the Cookson Hills.

This shooting sounded like WAR.

Heavy artillery was being fired for the first time on Oct. 5, 1942, at Camp Gruber near Braggs in the Cookson Hills, which had been the stomping grounds for outlaws Charles "Pretty Boy" Floyd, Matt and George Kimes and others.

War had begun in Europe three years earlier and it was obvious that the United States would be drawn into it. Congress had passed a budget for a military buildup.

By 1942, the United States was in the war and 84 new camps were under construction or planned by the War Department, including Camp Gruber.

Oklahoma was considered a good site for infantry training because of its location, climate, natural resources and large available work force. And the government already owned nearly 30,000 acres of submarginal farm land it had acquired in 1935 and 1936 for a parks and recreation project. More land was acquired through condemnation.

The camp ultimately encompassed about 109 square miles of land east of the Arkansas River in Muskogee and Cherokee counties.

After the war, Camp Gruber became a training camp for National Guard troops and was used to house survivors from Hurricane Katrina for more than a month in 2005.

Construction of Camp Gruber was begun in January 1942 by the Manhattan-Long Construction Co., which estimated it needed to build one new building every hour to meet its deadline. When completed in May 1942, the camp included 1,731 frame buildings.

The Gruber facility also used some existing buildings, including a ranch house built in 1936 that became the commanding officer's residence and the Greenleaf Lodge building constructed by the WPA in 1937. It became one of the camp's two officers' clubs.

That Oct. 5 shooting was the first time the artillery men of the 88th Infantry Division had fired live ammunition of that caliber since it was activated at Gruber on July 1. It was

Tulsa World archives

The Oct. 6, 1942, Tulsa World reported on howitzers being used for training at Camp Gruber near Braggs. One of the photos that ran with the story was censored, apparently because military authorities were concerned it would show an enemy too much about the cannon's aiming mechanism.

part of the training that would soon take the division into an actual theater of war.

"Military censorship prevents publication of the size of the howitzers," a Tulsa World story said.

"But they were big.

"And loud.

"And terrifying.

"They weren't made to merely kill. They were made to obliterate instantly human beings, tanks and fortifications," a World reporter wrote.

The story said the howitzers cost $36,000 each and their shells cost $35 to $96 apiece.

A series of photographs accompanied the story but part of one had been cut out and the word "Censored" inserted. That part of the picture apparently included a view of the howitzers' aiming mechanism, information that military authorities feared could be useful to an enemy.

Huge artillery firing ranges had been created north and east of the camp with the impact area lying in Cherokee County.

Following the 88th Division's deployment to Europe in December 1943, the 42nd Infantry Division (the Rainbow Division) trained there until being sent to Europe in November 1944. In 1945, the 86th Infantry Division (Blackhawk) was sent there for deactivation at the end of the war.

At one point, Gruber housed 3,000 German prisoners of war. Gruber was deactivated in 1947 and most of the buildings and facilities were removed or destroyed. It now serves as a training camp for National Guard troops.

Camp Gruber was named for Brig. Gen. Edmund L. Gruber, who died in May 1941. He had served in World War I as a field artillery officer and had been stationed at Fort Sill several times.

Gruber was an Army polo team champion, but his most enduring mark was in music, although he did not have a musical background.

He was the author of "The Caissons Go Rolling Along," which he wrote for the 5th Artillery Regiment in 1908 while stationed in the Philippines. The song was adopted later as the Field Artillery song and later as the Army's official anthem.

First governor attracted controversy

The election of Charles N. Haskell as Oklahoma's first governor in 1907 was a big disappointment to President Theodore Roosevelt, who thought the new state should have started with a Republican as governor.

Haskell had defeated Oklahoma Territorial Gov. Frank Frantz, who had the backing of his close friend Roosevelt, in a landslide vote in the new state's first election on Sept. 16, 1907, when voters also gave overwhelming approval to a constitution and statewide prohibition.

Regardless of his disappointment, Roosevelt signed the statehood bill admitting Oklahoma to the union as the 46th state on Nov. 16, 1907, and Haskell became governor.

It was during Haskell's term that the state capital was moved from Guthrie to Oklahoma City in a clandestine middle-of-the-night trip on June 12, 1910, after a statewide election showed Sooners preferred Oklahoma City over Shawnee and Guthrie as the capital.

Haskell had been in Muskogee, his official residence, to vote for Shawnee as his preference and had stopped in Tulsa to spend the night when he received the voting results. He organized a special train to take him and several others to Oklahoma City and called W.B. Anthony, his private secretary, with instructions to take the state seal to the Huckins Hotel by the next morning.

Haskell's feud with Roosevelt intensified and lasted until March 30, 1917, when Roosevelt apologized publicly. "I fought Haskell, and I was wrong," Roosevelt said. He also had his apology filed in the office of the Secretary of the Interior, and the two became friends.

The campaign in the presidential election of 1908 was just beginning and Haskell led the campaign in Oklahoma for William Jennings Bryan against Republican William Howard Taft and, as one reporter wrote, "whaled the tar out of the Republicans." However, it was a hollow victory; Bryan lost to Taft.

Both Bryan and Taft had been in the state before the 1907 election; Bryan campaigning for Haskell and Taft stumping for Frantz.

Roosevelt didn't take his candidate's loss in Oklahoma kindly. The smoke of the political campaign had hardly cleared when Roosevelt had the prosecution of an old criminal case against Haskell revived. In response to a letter from the president to the attorney general, a prosecutor was sent from Washington to Oklahoma to prosecute the governor.

Tulsa World archives

Charles N. Haskell, Oklahoma's first governor, moved the state capital from Guthrie to Oklahoma City and had a public feud with President Theodore Roosevelt.

"I think him one of the most corrupt blackguards in our political life," Roosevelt wrote. "If he could be put in stripes it would be an admirable thing for the cause of decent government."

Haskell and three men in the Creek Nation had been charged with conspiracy to defraud the government in 1902 in the sale of town lot sites in Muskogee. The case was dismissed because of lack of evidence, was revived and dismissed again in 1910.

The feud wasn't one-sided. Haskell called Roosevelt a "would-be dictator" and questioned the sincerity of the president "in anything except to satiate his own selfish ambitions."

After Roosevelt's apology, he and Haskell frequently dined together. Haskell was born in Ohio, became a schoolteacher and eventually an attorney. Politics seemed attractive to him and he ran for the Democratic nomination for governor in Ohio in 1896 but lost.

Later he promoted and built railroads in Ohio and in Oklahoma. He was promoting a railroad from Muskogee to Fayetteville for which several Muskogee residents donated rights of way that an attorney for the Creeks later claimed had been acquired through "dummy" purchasers.

Haskell's interest in politics continued after he came to Oklahoma and he was prominent in organizing the Sequoyah convention that sought to have Indian Territory admitted to the union as a separate state.

After leaving the governor's office, Haskell made an unsuccessful bid for the U.S. Senate in 1912 and then moved to New York where he became oilman Harry Sinclair's personal attorney. He started his own oil company, earned and lost a fortune on Wall Street.

Haskell returned to Muskogee in 1929 as head of the Municipal Gas Co. and later became president of the Sapulpa Gas Co.

After Haskell died in 1933 at the age of 73, the Tulsa World said "in general terms — it is now realized — Haskell made a good governor." The World editorial said Haskell "played politics to the limit and was always a partisan, always a fighter."

But the newspaper criticized him for the "romantic and theatrical" move of the capital to Oklahoma City and blamed that for his loss in his 1912 Senate bid.

Gov. William H. Murray said Haskell had the "keenest intellect – and the most practical – I ever knew in a man. He was not as learned as others but he quickly grasped information and solved the problems."

Soldier's sketches led to a career in art

A Pawnee Indian who began drawing pencil sketches of other soldiers to calm his nerves during lulls in World War II battles in Italy became one of Oklahoma's best-known artists after the war.

It was while his unit was fighting in Sicily that Brummett Echohawk, who left high school in Pawnee in 1940 to join Oklahoma's 45th Infantry Division, decided to become an artist.

Echohawk recalled years later that he found a large drawing board, some paper and other art supplies when he entered a house that had been shelled by the Allies. He kept the supplies and started drawing what he saw.

"After that, I drew and wrote every day," Echohawk said.

He protected the drawings in a cellophane bag but didn't intend them for anything more than his personal pleasure. That changed when he was recuperating from his second injury and a war correspondent discovered him – and his sketches – in an Army hospital.

Newspaper Enterprise Association immediately bought several of the drawings and distributed them to its client newspapers throughout the United States. Echohawk's career as an artist was launched.

Many of his sketches also were used in The Yank, the official Army newspaper.

Noting that constant fighting left little time for drawing, Echohawk said "I was the fastest pen in the West."

He frequently made two sketches of other soldiers, giving one to his model and keeping the other for himself. He once drew sketches of 35 German soldiers his unit had captured.

Echohawk wrote several articles that were published in the Tulsa World about the exploits of the all-Indian Army company from Pawnee. He once recalled that when that unit would capture a town or village, the soldiers would pull down the enemy flag and run up a wine bottle inscribed: "This village taken by Oklahoma Indians."

Echohawk was awarded three Bronze Stars and three

Tulsa World archives

American Indian artist Brummett Echohawk said his paintings portrayed spirit as much as they did photographic images.

Purple Hearts for action with the 45th Thunderbird Division in Italy and North Africa.

After the war, Echohawk studied fine arts at schools in Detroit and Chicago and was a freelance artist for a year in New York. He also worked as a commercial artist in Dallas before coming to Tulsa in 1952 as an artist for an oil company. A year later, he decided to devote his full time to being a freelance commercial artist.

Echohawk, who died in 2006 at the age of 83, also wrote several articles for the World about American Indians, and for a few years drew a weekly comic strip called "Little Chief" that was published in the World's Sunday magazine.

He was widely known for his paintings of American Indians. His landscape oil paintings were rendered in an impressionistic style with a palette knife -- and a Bowie knife.

Echohawk's paintings have hung in art museums around the world, including Tulsa's Gilcrease and Philbrook museums, and he was a former board member of the Gilcrease Museum.

One of his most significant achievements was assisting Thomas Hart Benton with the mural "Independence and the Opening of the West" for the Truman Memorial Library in Independence, Mo. He was invited by President Truman to attend the opening of the library.

Echohawk also was an actor, having performed in plays, television productions and movies.

"A painting should move you," Echohawk once said. "That's why I do impressionistic landscapes – I am painting the spirit of a picture, not a picture of a picture.

"But all some people want is something pretty. Well, if someone wants a pretty picture, they can buy a calendar."

Echohawk said his life had public meaning and impact because he was devoted to communicating facts, to authenticity and research.

"I paint the truth. And when I write, I do the same thing." he said.

Steamboats navigated the Arkansas

Steamboats regularly hauled cargo as far upstream on the Arkansas River as Muskogee – and made excursion trips between Muskogee and Fort Smith on Sundays – around the beginning of the 20th century.

Occasionally, when the water was deep enough, the boats could make it to Tulsa.

That was long before the McClellan-Kerr Navigation System was created, but river transportation was a favorite topic of the day. The 1908 Oklahoma Legislature passed a resolution urging Congress to appropriate funds to make the river navigable, and Charles N. Haskell, the state's first governor, was a big supporter. Merchandise also had been shipped between Cleveland and Tulsa when the river rose.

The Arkansas was the main form of transportation and communication for years, beginning in the 1820s when recruits were transported to the new Fort Gibson Army post and merchandise was hauled upstream routinely to Fort Smith or Fort Gibson. Thousands of American Indians were moved from their homes in the Southeast to Oklahoma by steamboat.

River travel lost favor for transportation after the railroads were extended into Indian Territory in 1871 – until residents of Muskogee bought a steamship called the Mary D and hired J.R. Dudding as its pilot in 1905 to give the river another chance as the favored mode of shipping.

The purchase of the Mary D was promoted by Haskell, who became governor two years later, in an attempt to show that the river was navigable.

"They needed $3,000 more than they had to bring the Mary D down from Indiana, so a meeting was held at the convention hall to discuss ways and means," Dudding told a Tulsa World reporter in 1931.

"Things were pretty much at a standstill when Father Joseph VanHultz, a Catholic priest, rose and said 'We need $3,000 and, in the language of the Methodists, I will now pass the hat.' And after putting $20 in his hat, he did pass it, and the money was raised."

It was on one of those Sunday excursions between Muskogee and Fort Smith that the Arkansas River Navigation Co. was organized with the intent of buying another boat to be named the City of Muskogee. Dudding recalled that the passengers on the Mary D were enjoying the scenery and the pleasure of traveling by water and were interested in expanding river travel.

A group of men held an impromptu meeting and "we sold out all the stock as we (were) drawing into Fort Smith."

Oklahoma Historical Society

The City of Muskogee steamboat was a pioneer of commercial travel on the Arkansas River.

The City of Muskogee was built in 1908 in Kokomo, Ind., and made regular trips up and down the river for several years.

After the 125-foot, 100-ton City of Muskogee had been operating for a short time with lower freight rates, the railroads began reducing their freight rates and eventually regained the business they had lost to the river boats, Dudding recalled in a 1931 interview.

Dudding also predicted in that interview that the stream would be navigable again.

The City of Muskogee operated only in daylight because there were no beacons to direct river traffic, Dudding said. The river was dangerous because of its shifting currents and sandbars, he said.

Sandbars brought the end of river transportation between Cleveland and Tulsa several years earlier. A small sternwheel steamboat, the Minnie, made semi-annual trips to deliver such things as hogs, walnut wood and farm crops to the railroad in Tulsa to be shipped to markets in the East.

"At least twice a year, we got high water," pioneer insurance man J.C. Byers of Cleveland told a Tulsa World reporter in 1935. "Then the Minnie would be steamed up and would travel to Tulsa 50 miles away by river."

The nearest railroad was in Tulsa and freight could be sent there by boat much cheaper than by team or oxen, he said.

The last trip was in 1898 when the Minnie was loaded with walnut wood to be used for making gun stocks for rifles that would be used in the Spanish-American war. The wood was to be loaded onto a train in Tulsa and shipped to the arms maker.

But the river didn't rise as expected. The flat-bottomed Minnie tried the trip anyway – the boats at that time needed only 2 or 3 feet of water – and hit a sandbar a few miles downstream. It was floated again but hit another sandbar a few miles farther downstream. The walnut wood had to be unloaded and transported by team to the railroad.

The Minnie had suffered similar problems during a previous trip, that time while loaded with hogs.

Sandbars weren't the only problem with river transportation for the Minnie. When the whistle was blown, all the steam in the boiler was released and the boat stopped in midstream.

The Minnie was sold to a group from Muskogee and was used for years for trips between Muskogee and Fort Smith. And river transportation between Cleveland and Tulsa ended.

Johnson late to Eufaula dam dedication

The giant Eufaula dam was dedicated by President Lyndon Johnson, who promised to keep the Arkansas River basin development on schedule.

"I'm here to assure you it will go on schedule," Johnson told the estimated 50,000 people who attended the dedication on Sept. 25, 1964.

"I just had to break my budget one time this year," he said. "When this bunch of Oklahomans came down and pounded that cabinet desk, it cost me $14 million but it got the Arkansas back on schedule."

The dam and the lake it created make up a key unit in the $1.2 billion Arkansas River navigation project.

Johnson recalled that President George Washington "looked at the vast possibilities of harnessing our great rivers and prayed 'would God that we may have the wisdom and the courage to improve them.' "

He said the dam and development of the Arkansas River would provide a new link between the Southwest and the industrial heartland. "It will provide relief from devastating floods and give us electricity to homes and business. It will mean new industry, new jobs and new opportunities for the people.

"It will mean a stronger Oklahoma, a more prosperous Oklahoma, a richer Oklahoma and a stronger United States.

"That development will go ahead and, as president, I am here to promise you that it will go on schedule."

Johnson's speech dealt primarily with preservation and development of natural resources. He said the lake would enrich Oklahoma earth and urged his listeners "let's work together to enrich the America we leave to our children."

Because Johnson was late arriving for the ceremony, Gov. Henry Bellmon, a Republican, started the dedication without him by telling the crowd, "The spotlight of the nation is on Oklahoma today.

"I'm not exactly sure how you welcome a president in his absence but when he gets here, we'll do it proper so he knows that we are honored to have him here," Bellmon said.

The governor also read a telegram from former President Dwight D. Eisenhower that reminded listeners that the Eufaula project was authorized during his Republican administration.

Music and drill teams kept restlessness to a minimum as the throng waited. Finally, the president's olive drab helicopter and three others appeared over the large expanse

Tulsa World archives

President Lyndon Johnson arrives in Muskogee on Sept. 25, 1964, before attending formal dedication ceremonies at the Eufaula Dam.

of water – the other three bringing the president's aides and the Washington press corps from Davis Field in Muskogee.

As the president's helicopter touched down and Johnson and his wife, Lady Bird, alighted, Henryetta High School's 104-piece band broke into "Hail to the Chief" and a thunderous cheer went up from the crowd.

Among those on the speakers' stand with Johnson were Sen. J. Howard Edmondson and Senate candidates Fred Harris and Bud Wilkinson. Harris had defeated Edmondson for the Democratic nomination and later defeated Republican Wilkinson in the general election.

A 69-year-old watchman at a lake development was taken into custody after it was noted he was armed with a shotgun and a pistol as he made his watchman's rounds. He said it had just slipped his mind that the presidential visit was that day.

An ardent Johnson fan, the watchman said he had planned to hear the president.

"But I guess I won't now," he said while waiting in the Haskell County Sheriff's Office in Stigler.

A man who had sat on a water cooler while holding his granddaughter and had waited for Johnson for four hours told a reporter, "I guess I'll stay as long as I have to.

"This is the biggest thing that I've seen in these hills in 50 years, and I don't want to miss it.

"I don't guess there has been any famous people here before, except maybe Belle Starr."

From the dam site, Johnson went to Oklahoma City, where he pleased a cheering crowd estimated at 30,000 at the Oklahoma State Fair doffing his hat as the horse he was riding cantered across the fairgrounds lawn. He had been scheduled to open the Oklahoma State Fair and help in dedicating the fair's Fourteen Flags Plaza.

His talk dealt mainly with praise for what he called the "partnership between government and people in the cause of a growing America."

Although his speech at the fair was billed as nonpolitical, he inserted some plugs for his own candidacy for re-election and made indirect references to his Republican opponent, Arizona Sen. Barry Goldwater.

He plugged his own candidacy through repeated reference to "as long as I'm president." For example, he said "as long as I am president, the government is going to continue developing its natural resources," citing the Arkansas River as an example.

Lynn Riggs inspired musical 'Oklahoma!'

Oh, what a beautiful morning . . .

Most Oklahomans recognize those words as part of the opening song in "Oklahoma!", the musical that became a Broadway sensation after Oscar Hammerstein and Richard Rodgers adapted it from Lynn Riggs' play "Green Grow the Lilacs."

The song "carries an atmosphere of peace and tenderness," Hammerstein said. "The cattle and corn and the golden haze are all there.

"My indebtedness to Riggs is obvious."

The song is based on Oklahoman Riggs' opening scene in "Lilacs," which he once described as: "a radiant summer morning – the kind which envelopes the shape of the Earth, men, cattle in the meadow, blades of young corn, streams, which makes them seem to exist now for the first time, their images giving off a visible golden emanation that is partly true and partly a trick of the imagination, focusing to keep alive a loveliness that may pass away."

"Lilacs" made its debut on Broadway in 1931 and was judged one of the 10 best plays of the year. It reappeared as the Theater Guild presentation of "Oklahoma!" in 1943 after being adapted by Rodgers and Hammerstein. In its new incarnation, it became a box-office smash, running for 2,212 performances – not counting several revivals and performances presented by touring groups and by local organizations such as that at Discoveryland near Sand Springs.

The New Yorker magazine's theater critic Wolcott Gibbs wrote in his review of "Oklahoma!" that Riggs' own drama was "a very fine and original one."

Rodgers and Hammerstein, who produced "Oklahoma!" in their first collaboration, received a special Pulitzer Prize in the category of "Special Awards and Citations – Letters" in 1944.

Hammerstein wrote in a 1943 letter to The New York Times, "I kept many of the lines of the original play without making any changes at all for the simple reason that they could not be improved on – at any rate, not by me."

Although Riggs, who died in June 1954 at age 54, was best known for "Lilacs," he had turned out a couple of volumes of poems and 21 full-length plays, more than half of which were produced or bought for production or publication. Most were set in early Oklahoma, immediately before or just after statehood.

Tulsa World archives

Lynn Riggs, pictured in New York City in this undated photo, grew up in the Claremore area and later wrote the play on which the musical "Oklahoma!" was based.

His 1926 play "The Domino Parlor" was called the best he had read in 20 years by the actor Lionel Barrymore, and the actress Bette Davis called Riggs "one of the most important contributors to the American theater."

Riggs once told a reporter that: "I didn't have to invent anything for 'Green Grow the Lilacs.' I was saturated in Oklahoma history and legend from the time I learned to walk."

Riggs was born in 1899 in the Lone Elm community in the Cooweescoowee district near Claremore. He drove a grocery wagon while attending Eastern University Preparatory School, which became Oklahoma Military Academy and later Rogers State University. He graduated in 1917 and hopped a freight train to Chicago. Two years later, he was in New York, where he swept out Wall Street offices, worked as a reporter for The Wall Street Journal and sold books at Macy's for $10 a week.

He also began writing and selling verse to New York magazines. He later worked for the Oil and Gas Journal in Tulsa, attended and later taught English at the University of Oklahoma, and worked as a movie extra and as a proofreader for the Los Angeles Times before returning to New York in 1926, hoping to crash Broadway.

Original manuscripts, pictures of events throughout his life and other belongings of Riggs are housed in the Lynn Riggs Memorial at 121 N. Weenonah in Claremore. The memorial also houses the "surrey with the fringe on top" and Laurie's wedding dress, which were used in the movie version of "Oklahoma!"

After the movie's release in 1955, a group of Oklahomans organized a sing-along in New York's Central Park to sing the songs from the movie. The event attracted about 15,000 people.

Oklahoma Gov. Raymond Gary told the Central Park crowd that the music and story from the play revealed the heart and soul of Oklahoma people. He explained that the state was proud of its farms and factories, its minerals and lakes, but it was proudest of its greatest asset – its people.

"Although it was written of days past, the same spirit is in progressive, modern Oklahoma," he said.

In his 1943 letter to the Times, Hammerstein also referred to the soul of Sooners. "Lynn Riggs and 'Green Grow the Lilacs' are the very soul of Oklahoma," he wrote.

Baseball's top lefty found home in state

Warren Spahn, the winningest left-handed pitcher in baseball history, loved baseball and just wanted to play when he got out of high school. He wasn't concerned about pay.

Spahn signed to play for the Boston Braves National League system for $80 per month – a small salary even in that pre-World War II period – right out of high school at Buffalo, N.Y., in 1940.

"I just wanted to get a chance to play ball," he told a reporter many years later. "I guess if they'd have agreed to feed me and pay my hotel bill, I'd have been ready to go for nothing."

It was a love that would last the rest of his life, although the game was relegated to second place. "My wife (LoRene) was my first love, and baseball my second," he told a Tulsa World reporter after Mrs. Spahn died in 1978.

Before his career was over, Spahn was the highest-paid player in baseball history – up to then -- with a salary of $85,000 per year, a figure that pales in comparison with today's megasalaries for the game's stars.

But Spahn invested his money wisely and eventually became wealthy, with a large ranch near Hartshorne where he and LoRene lived until she died.

Spahn made his debut in the major leagues in 1942, but his playing career was interrupted a few months later when he was drafted into the U.S. Army for World War II and was sent to Camp Gruber for training. It was the event that introduced him to his future wife and to the state that would become his home.

During one of Spahn's first visits to Tulsa while stationed at Camp Gruber, Spahn once told a reporter, he and a fellow soldier went to a little cafe and discovered they had only 13 cents between them. They told the waitress "bring us all the doughnuts 13 cents will buy.

"That waitress was really wonderful," he said. "She gave us a lot more, I am sure, than 13 cents should have bought. We used to have some wonderful times and fun here."

During another visit to Tulsa in 1943, Spahn and Roy Reimann, a fellow soldier from Buffalo, who had been the catcher on an opposing team during their high school days, attended a USO dance where Spahn met LoRene Southard, who became his wife after the war. His buddy also met his future wife at the same time.

Spahn and Reimann played on the 276th Engineer Combat Battalion's baseball team that won the Camp Gruber championship before the 276th was sent to Europe in 1943. The unit was involved in the Battle of the Bulge, in which Spahn earned a Bronze Star and received a battlefield com-

Tulsa World archives

Warren Spahn won more Major League Baseball games than any other left-handed pitcher ever. For years he also held the mark for most games won by a Tulsa Oilers manager.

mission as a second lieutenant.

The unit also was involved in the 1945 battle for the bridge at Remagen, Germany, that resulted in many of the unit's men being killed or injured. Spahn was wounded in the foot by shrapnel, an injury that he said was "only a scratch" but which earned him a Purple Heart.

After the war, Spahn credited his military service with inspiring his major league career.

"I was so thankful to get home and have a chance to play baseball, I was more dedicated than I would have been, I believe, if I had gone up earlier," he said.

In his 21-year career, he won 363 games and lost 245. He played for the Braves organization when the team was in Boston and later in Milwaukee.

Spahn was inducted into the Baseball Hall of Fame in Cooperstown, N.Y., in 1973, only the sixth player elected on the first try. He called his selection: "The greatest thing, but I'm not about to sit around now that it has happened. A man is only as good as the pride within himself and whether he accomplishes anything; he must say 'what's next?' "

Always outspoken, Spahn never hesitated to offer an opinion, once telling a reporter, "If I have strong opinions, I don't give a damn. I have the truth of my convictions."

And after being fired as the Cleveland Indians pitching coach in 1974, he said, "I would have to consider these last two years at Cleveland almost wasted."

Spahn served as manager of the Tulsa Oilers from 1967 to 1971, racking up 372 wins, making that Tulsa's all-time pro record until it was broken in 1998 by Bobby Jones. Spahn also made his final three pitching appearances for Tulsa in 1967.

Spahn, who died Nov. 25, 2003, at the age of 82, spent his latter years running his 2,800-acre cattle ranch near Hartshorne, where the sign on the water tower beamed: "Home of Warren Spahn."

A 9-foot bronze statue of Spahn in a Braves uniform in his typical pitching posture – right leg kicked high and throwing arm at his side – was unveiled in 2003 at the Osage Tribal Museum, site of the Bronze Horse Foundry, where the statue created by artist Shan Gray was cast.

Spahn attended the unveiling in a wheelchair. He was in Atlanta four days later when the statue was placed in Turner Field's Monument Grove in Atlanta.

Another casting of the statue was unveiled at Bricktown Ballpark in Oklahoma City on June 25, 2005. A third statue stands in the Oklahoma Sports Museum in Guthrie.

Teen bugler honored for WWI heroism

A young Oklahoma soldier carried several wounded doughboys to safety at an aid station and "drafted" German soldiers to help under intense enemy gunfire in World War I.

For his action on Oct. 8, 1918, Pvt. Lee Gilstrap received the Distinguished Service Cross, the country's second-highest military award.

When the medal was presented to Gilstrap in 1923, he was called its youngest recipient. Reports of the day said he was 17 on the day of the rescues. But records show he was born in 1902, which would have made him 16 during that 1918 action.

The medal was created during World War I – until then the only U.S. military award was the Medal of Honor. Gilstrap later received a Silver Star, a Bronze Star and a Purple Heart.

Gilstrap was the bugler for Company B of the 142nd Regiment of the 36th Infantry Division when the division met heavy resistance from German machine-gunners firing from dugouts along the reverse slope of a hill near St. Etienne, France.

Many U.S. soldiers were screaming in pain from being wounded by the machine-gun bullets and from mustard gas.

Gilstrap dropped his bugle and went to their rescue. On his first trip he learned that all of the regiment's litter bearers had been killed. In spite of the danger, he made several more trips into the fire zone.

A sniper's bullet knocked Gilstrap unconscious briefly, but when he came to, he aimed his rifle at the German sniper, preparing to kill him. The sniper surrendered, however, and Gilstrap put him to work helping carry the wounded Americans to an aid station.

That's when Gilstrap decided he needed more help – and he got it, in the form of several German soldiers he found in shell holes and dugouts. Persuaded by his rifle, they joined him in rescuing the injured. Two of his "drafted" helpers were killed by German gunfire. The sniper – his first draftee – died the next day from mustard gas burns he suffered while he was pulling a U.S. soldier from a gas pocket.

A native of Chandler, Gilstrap liked to lounge around

Tulsa World archives

Lee Gilstrap was a World War I hero as a private, and he held senior positions as a lieutenant colonel during World War II.

the National Guard Armory as a youth. He became a rifle marksman and joined the Guard members on hikes and encampments, always toting his load and sharing work.

When the Guard was sent to battle Pancho Villa's forces after Villa raided a New Mexico town in 1916, Gilstrap went along as the bugler but also played a role in the guerrilla warfare that was waged along the U.S.-Mexico border.

After the war, Gilstrap taught at Oklahoma Military Academy, now Rogers State University, in Claremore until he was called to active duty as a lieutenant colonel with the 45th Infantry Division in 1940 for World War II. He was transferred to the office of the European theater provost marshal as the executive officer under Lt. Gen. William S. Key of Oklahoma. He served in England and Iceland for 27 months.

Gilstrap returned to the military academy in 1946 but was fired in 1947 as its public relations director and athletics director by the school's president, Col. K.S. Perkins.

Gilstrap at first refused to talk about his dismissal, telling reporters they would have to get any comment from Perkins, who in turn told reporters that any comment would have to come from Gilstrap.

He later said the dismissal was the result of jealousy "on the hill" – the OMA campus. There were reports that a move was under way to have the popular Gilstrap replace Perkins as the president.

It was learned later that Gilstrap was fired because he didn't have a master's degree. "I have been teaching at OMA for 20 years and this is the first time my qualifications have been challenged," he said.

"It is true I do not hold a master's degree, but I have completed 213 hours of college work, and my training exceeds that of many who hold the degree."

Gilstrap said he didn't want to start a fight because "I have been associated with Oklahoma Military Academy too long, and I love it too much."

Gilstrap became a speech teacher at Oklahoma A & M College until he retired in 1965. He died in 1987 at age 85.

City cheered arrival of Spavinaw water

Spavinaw water was here, and Tulsa was ready to celebrate.

At 3 p.m. on Nov. 17, 1924, President Calvin Coolidge pressed a button in Washington, D.C., and clear mountain spring water flowed from a golden tap on a speakers' stand in Tulsa.

Gov. Martin Trapp filled a golden goblet with the sparkling mountain water, raised it to his lips – and Spavinaw water was officially welcomed. It was called the greatest event in the history of the city.

Mayor Herman Newblock, other city officials, members of the water board and thousands of citizens cheered loudly as the water gushed from the faucet.

For years, Tulsa had struggled without a reliable source of clean water. The Arkansas River was too muddy, salty and alkaline. Wells proved unreliable. By 1919, Tulsans consumed 50,000 five-gallon bottles of water a week.

Finally, Tulsa was "off the bottle."

Four miles away glinted the new city reservoir at Mohawk Park. Farther still, beyond the horizon in the Ozark foothills, lay the source of the day's excitement and Tulsa's renewed civic pride: Lake Spavinaw, five miles long and nearly a mile wide, the largest body of water in the state at the time and flowing to Tulsa through 55 miles of 60-inch concrete conduit.

From Mohawk Park, the water was pumped to the top of Oak Cliff, a steep little summit north of the end of Denver Avenue, and from there fed the city's thirsty water mains.

This day – the day water flowed from a golden spigot on Reservoir Hill – brought official parties from as far away as Kansas City and set Tulsans literally to dancing in the streets.

Although Coolidge's touch of a button signaled the official beginning of the new water system, Spavinaw water had been flowing into the city's mains for several days. But the city had warned against using it for drinking until tests determined all the river water had been flushed from the lines.

The tests began downtown where water fountains had been placed in several locations. By the day of the water ceremony, hundreds of residents told the water department they had tasted the water and that it was "pure Spavinaw."

But the next day, river water was again being pumped into the city's water mains because of a break in a high pressure line. Repairs were made and Spavinaw water distribution resumed within a couple of days – after utility officials were sure the repair would hold.

Each of the town's elementary schools performed an

D.K. Holway collection

Mohawk Reservoir was built to hold Spavinaw water before it went to Tulsa faucets.

elaborate pageant starring Tulsa as a fairy princess, Spavinaw as a wood nymph and the Arkansas River as a dragon. A parade through downtown featured bands, floats and one of Owasso's new school buses. Owasso was on the new Spavinaw water line, too.

"Oil may have built Tulsa in the past but Spavinaw water will be the product on which the future will be built," Tulsa World Publisher Eugene Lorton had said in a column about Spavinaw the previous day.

Lorton's words were prophetic. Since that statement was made, generations have credited Spavinaw water with Tulsa's growth.

Lorton had campaigned for a reliable water system since becoming editor of the World in 1911. During one period he ran memos for 1,000 consecutive days citing how long it had been since pure water had been promised by the mayor.

Voters approved a bond issue to finance Spavinaw water in 1919, but it was voided because of a provision in the city's charter. Lorton immediately began another successful battle to change the charter and a new bond issue for Spavinaw water was approved in 1921.

The Spavinaw issue touched off an acrimonious newspaper fight between the World and the Tulsa Democrat, predecessor of the Tulsa Tribune. Democrat owner Charles Page wanted the city to obtain water from Shell Creek north of Sand Springs where he owned property. The Tribune also campaigned against the Spavinaw bonds after the newspaper was sold to Richard Lloyd Jones and its name was changed.

Water Commissioner J.H. Wheatley had drilled water wells as early as 1910 or 1912 but the pumps did not operate satisfactorily to supply the city.

His successor in office had a 50-foot-diameter well dug and walled with brick and also had three other smaller diameter wells drilled. But the pumps didn't work well and the pipeline showed "alarming leakage." This line was to flow water by gravity to the pumping plant, but the whole project was abandoned within two years.

Wheatley also had considered a dam on Shell Creek but he feared that the creek would prove inadequate for Tulsa's needs.

A second lake was created with the construction of Eucha Dam in 1952 and a second flow line was added to bring raw water to Tulsa in 1954. Spavinaw has provided water for more than 80 years and Eucha for more than 50 years.

Tulsa is still "off the bottle."

Thorpe not diminished in eyes of world

An Oklahoma Sac and Fox Indian was called the "greatest athlete in the world" after the 1912 Olympic games in Stockholm, and he came home to a ticker tape parade through New York City.

"I couldn't realize how one fellow could have so many friends," Jim Thorpe said of the cheering crowd as he was driven through the city.

But a few months later, Thorpe's world blew up. The Olympic Committee stripped him of his medals and erased his records from the books. His crime was that he played semi-pro baseball to earn spending money during the summer of 1910.

Thorpe readily admitted playing for the Rocky Mount club in the Eastern Carolina league for $30 to $60 per month, but said he didn't realize it was a problem. He also pointed out that many other amateurs also played semi-pro baseball – but they all used fake names. Thorpe used his own.

Although the committee stripped Thorpe of his honors, it couldn't discount his feats or take back the words of King Gustav V, who told him in a congratulatory speech: "Sir, you are the greatest athlete in the world. It would be an honor to shake your hand."

Nor could it diminish the esteem felt by American sports writers who voted Thorpe the athlete of the half-century in 1950; nor of Oklahomans who voted Thorpe their favorite son – after Will Rogers – in a 1988 poll by the AP to pick the state's favorite son or daughter.

Thorpe also was included in the first group of athletes inducted into Pro Football's Hall of Fame in 1963. He was inducted into the Oklahoma Hall of Fame in 1950.

Thorpe had won the decathlon and pentathlon at the Olympics. With almost no specialized training, he swamped the world's best athletes, winning every event in the pentathlon except the javelin throw. He scored victories in four events of the decathlon and finished no worse than fourth in the other six.

After his medals were taken from him, the committee offered them to the runners-up, but they refused to accept the first-place prizes.

"James Thorpe won the event, not I," each said.

Replicas of the medals finally were returned to Thorpe's family in 1982 and in 1986 were donated to the state for display below Thorpe's portrait in the state Capitol rotunda. They have been at the Oklahoma Historical Society since

Tulsa World archives

Jim Thorpe was a star athlete in many sports, but gained his greatest fame for the two gold medals he won in the 1912 Olympic games.

1999 after being returned by a janitor who stole them from the Capitol.

Thorpe, who died nearly penniless in 1953 at age 73, told a Tulsa World reporter in 1950 that one of his fondest memories, aside from the Olympic games, was the Carlisle Institute football game against Army that the Indians won 27-6. Thorpe scored only one touchdown, but he had to run 195 yards to make it.

He had caught the opening kickoff on Carlisle's 5-yard line and ran all the way to score. That touchdown was called back because of a penalty, and Army kicked off again. Thorpe caught that ball on the goal line and ran the length of the field to make a score that counted.

Thorpe came to the attention of famed coach Glenn S. "Pop" Warner in 1907 when he returned to Carlisle at age 19 after an absence of a couple of years. The spring athletic season had started and Thorpe was watching high jumping practice. He asked whether he could try it after the bar was raised so high that none of the jumpers could clear it.

As the other boys snickered, Thorpe, wearing overalls and old tennis shoes, took a short run and leaped over the bar. One of the boys told Warner, who looked up Thorpe the next day.

"Do you know what you've done?" Warner asked rhetorically. "You've broken the school record for high jump. Go down to the clubhouse and trade those overalls for a track suit." Warner worked with Thorpe and he went out for football in the fall – and his athletic career had begun.

A movie about the athlete's life, "Jim Thorpe, All American," was filmed in 1950 in Muskogee with the Bacone College campus representing Carlisle. Burt Lancaster and Phyllis Thaxter played the leads with Thorpe acting as technical adviser.

He was paid $50,000 for the rights to film the picture plus other fees that totaled nearly another $50,000.

After Thorpe's death, his widow, Patricia, had his body taken to Pennsylvania where two communities, Mauch Chunk and East Mauch Chunk, merged, built a memorial to the athlete and adopted the name Jim Thorpe.

Patricia, Thorpe's third wife, said she didn't have sufficient money to build a suitable memorial in Oklahoma. The Legislature had appropriated $25,000 to build a memorial in Yale, where Thorpe lived from 1917 to 1923, but Gov. Johnston Murray did not approve the appropriation.

Hurley served city, state and country

An Oklahoman whose first job was driving a mule to haul coal out of a mine for 75 cents a day rose to international prominence and wealth in a colorful and exciting career that included serving two presidents – a Republican and a Democrat – and in two wars.

That was Patrick Jay Hurley who was a soldier, lawyer, banker, oil operator, secretary of war, diplomat and international troubleshooter. He rose from Army private in 1902 to major general in 1943.

When Hurley died at the age of 80 in 1963, former President Herbert Hoover, a Republican, called him "a devoted American and a devoted friend who lived a life dedicated to the service of our country."

He had served in Hoover's Cabinet as the secretary of war but probably was best known as the war-time ambassador to China, a job he was given in 1944 by President Franklin D. Roosevelt, a Democrat, although Hurley was a lifelong Republican. He resigned from that position at the end of World War II with a bitter blast at American policy in Asia and said a third world war was in the making.

He defended Roosevelt who had died but was being accused of having made a secret agreement at the Yalta conference that was called the blueprint for the Communist conquest of China. "I can say he is not guilty. He was a very sick man at Yalta and the secret agreement of Yalta was engineered by officials of the American State Department," Hurley said.

Hurley was born in Lehigh, Indian Territory. The town had been designated as the Coal County seat by the Constitutional Convention, but it was replaced by Coalgate.

Hurley began working in a coal mine when he was 11. Because there were no public schools, he went to a subscription school at night for $1.50 a month while working in the mine for four years and later as a cowboy.

He graduated from Indian University (now Bacone) at Muskogee, thanks to the college president who helped him finance his education. Hurley later earned a law degree in Washington. In 1908, he started law practice in Tulsa. As an attorney for the Choctaw tribe, he got his start in politics and collected his first big legal fee.

During his years of law practice, Hurley earned many big fees, including a $1 million fee from Sinclair Oil Co. to regain property nationalized by the Mexican government in the 1930s.

"I wasn't a profound lawyer, but I charged more," he told a reporter years later.

Hurley amassed a fortune in oil, real estate and uranium.

Beryl Ford collection

Oklahoma native Patrick J. Hurley rose to prominence as a businessman, diplomat, military leader and politician.

He acquired several buildings in Tulsa and served as president of a bank and on the boards of several others after World War I.

Hurley's military career began in 1902 when he enlisted as a private in the Indian Territory Militia at Muskogee. He had tried to join the Rough Riders in 1898 but was turned down because he was too young. He had risen to captain when he entered World War I and to lieutenant colonel by the end of the war.

After the war, Hurley resumed his law practice in Tulsa and used his military experience to help restore order after the June 1, 1921 race riot. He was asked by a citizens' group to assume jurisdiction. After he was deputized by the sheriff, he recruited Spanish-American War and World War I veterans to help him.

Hurley had lived in New Mexico for more than 20 years when World War II began. At the age of 54, he was called to active duty, promoted to brigadier general and assigned as Roosevelt's troubleshooter in hot spots around the world. He became a major general a few months later.

He made secret war missions and had several narrow escapes from death, including once in Darwin, Australia, when Japanese planes strafed the areas around his hotel.

Hurley had to dive into the dirt as a plane headed for him. "I was alone and in plain view," he said. Finally, an Australian appeared and showed him the way to a shelter.

He was in Darwin on his first assignment that involved buying fishing boats to run a Japanese blockade to take supplies to Gen. Douglas MacArthur's forces in the Philippine Islands. Two-thirds of those boats were sunk by the Japanese, but those that got through allowed the Americans to prolong their historic stand on Bataan.

After the war, Hurley made three races for a U.S. Senate seat from New Mexico but lost all three to Democratic nominees. After his last campaign in 1952, which he lost by fewer than 5,000 votes, Hurley charged widespread election fraud and sought to have the ballots impounded.

But a recount was impossible because the ballots in three counties had been burned, and Sen. Dennis Chaves was certified as re-elected and took his seat.

During one of those political campaigns, a rumor spread that Hurley had once killed a mule by hitting it with a fence post.

"That's not so," he responded. "Why, I've never even hit a career diplomat with a fence post."

Hurley was inducted into the Oklahoma Hall of Fame in 1938. His son, artist Wilson Hurley, was inducted into the hall in 1995.

Aunt Carrie wasn't afraid to fight

A former home economics teacher who had become a nursing home owner didn't have any idea what an "N-plant" was when she saw the term in a Tulsa World headline in 1973.

The newspaper said a proposed $450 million N-plant to produce electricity was to be built near her Rogers County farm and Carrie Dickerson was determined to find out what it was. She also wanted to know what it would mean to the family property.

During the month after Public Service Co. of Oklahoma announced plans for the nuclear facility, she spent more than $500 on telephone calls obtaining information.

"I didn't know if I was for or against the Inola plant," she told a reporter later. "All I knew was that I had to know more."

After a few months of research, she became a one-woman army to fight against PSO's plans to build the nuclear plant near Inola, a Cherokee word that means black fox.

Dickerson, known as Aunt Carrie, made her first anti-nuclear speech before the Inola City Council after PSO asked all the town councils in the area for approval of the proposed Black Fox electricity-generating facility that would have provided about $5 million per year to the Inola school district, making it the richest in the state.

After Dickerson spoke to the Inola council and passed out literature on the issue, the Inola councilmen tabled the issue and reporters began calling her to ask what group she represented.

"I couldn't admit that I didn't have a group," she told a reporter in 1982, so she formed Citizens Action for Safe Energy on the spot.

Supporters soon joined and the make-believe group grew flesh and form and teeth. Atomic Energy Commission representatives from Washington told Dickerson that projects were never stopped by local intervenors.

But PSO announced in February 1982 that plans for Black Fox had been scrapped, citing the cost of fighting local challengers.

Dickerson said the nuclear accident at Three Mile Island in Pennsylvania played a role in the PSO decision.

Tulsa World archives

Seen here in 1981, Carrie Dickerson, known as Aunt Carrie, became a one-woman army to fight against PSO's plans to build a nuclear plant near Inola.

That accident couldn't have come at a better time, she said. "Thank goodness that it wasn't a major catastrophe."

A month before she died in 2006 at age 89, Dickerson told a reporter, "People always told me that I couldn't win, that I was too small to make a difference. I always said that you can't win if you don't try."

The first time she was asked to picket PSO, Dickerson didn't think she could do it. "I kept thinking 'what if my students see me on television?'"

But picketing became easier and in 1980 she received the Community of John the 23rd award for her peaceful efforts in the David vs. Goliath fight.

She always told people she didn't do it alone and gave credit to Ilene Younghein, her co-chairwoman of CASE, attorneys Tom Dalton, Joe Farris and Louis Bullock.

And her husband . . . "my poor suffering husband," who, she said, she had left "with unwashed dishes and no lunch prepared" so many times.

The Dickersons met when she won a trip to Washington in a state 4-H essay and speech contest for girls while attending high school in Okmulgee County. Her husband won the same prize in the boys' contest. The two were married in 1938.

After her Black Fox fight, Dickerson started a retirement home, opened a health food store and began teaching quilting classes. She also wrote a book about the ordeal, "Aunt Carrie's War Against Black Fox Nuclear Plant."

For nine years, Dickerson and her group prevented PSO from moving on with the plant.

To fund the court action, Dickerson drained her savings, mortgaged her farm, sold her nursing home and sold quilts that she made. Fundraising concerts were given by musicians.

She once estimated that $550,000 was spent on the fight against Black Fox with $200,000 of that coming from her.

Left nearly destitute, she told a reporter in 2002 that the battle was worth living in poverty.

"Sometimes we're expected to do something with our lives other than what we had planned," she told a reporter.

"I think this was my purpose in life. That's the reason I can accept my condition today."

Bleacher collapsed but game played on

Major league baseball had come to Tulsa, but so had disaster.

Schools had been dismissed, Gov. Lee Cruce was here, the International Dry-Farming Congress was in full swing and the highlight of the day was to be an exhibition game between the Chicago White Sox and the New York Giants, who had just played in the 1913 World Series against the Philadelphia Athletics.

A crowd of 5,000 awaited the start of the game Oct. 27, 1913, at the South Main Street baseball park near Fifth Street when the entire right field bleachers collapsed.

"Without a moment's warning the stand crumbled into thousands of pieces," a reporter wrote. "Little noise was made by the collapse, and it came so suddenly that not even a scream was heard."

Some 700 people were buried in the debris, including a group of soldiers from Company L of the 9th U.S. Infantry of Fort Logan H. Root in Arkansas who were marching under the bleachers when they collapsed. There was only one death. Pvt. Chester Taylor, 20, of Holiday, Tenn., was dug out with serious injuries and died two hours later.

Dozens were injured, but the exact number is unknown because some left without giving their names.

The 4th Field Artillery Band from Fort Sill continued playing after the collapse and, it was believed, prevented panic. Although there was a scramble to leave the left-field bleachers, no one left the main grandstand.

The grandstand had been built more than four years earlier of light pieces of lumber and had no roof. It was reported that the lack of a roof probably prevented the death or serious injuries of many people who would have been buried under debris if a roof also had collapsed.

The left grandstand, now good only for kindling, had never been remodeled or repaired, although the main grandstand roof had been repaired several times because of damage to its roof from strong wind.

The Tulsa World and Tulsa Democrat carried a complete casualty list of the injured.

Tulsa World archives

The 64 soldiers from Arkansas had been in Tulsa for 10 days, camping in tents at the exposition ground. No explanation for their visit could be found, but they may have been assigned to help enforce security.

The game went on, starting late at 3:45 p.m., and most of the crowd stayed, including many who had come to Tulsa on six special trains.

Two of baseball's greatest pitchers starred, with pitcher Walter Johnson getting a 6-0 decision over Christy Mathewson of the Giants. However, the greatest applause seemed to go to Jim Thorpe, the great Sac and Fox Indian athlete, who was playing for the Giants.

Johnson, who lived in Coffeyville, had offered his services free to the White Sox just to get a chance to pitch against Mathewson.

A reporter wrote that Johnson's speed, his fast-breaking curves and his drop ball fooled the batters from the Giants.

"Sorrowed by the accident that preceded the game and chilled by a north wind that threatened to break into snow at any minute, the crowd greeted the big league favorites with enthusiasm but did not give the rousing welcome they had been expecting to provide."

Special trains carrying people to the Dry-Farming Congress -- and the baseball game -- began arriving at 8 a.m. that day and by noon an estimated 15,000 visitors had arrived, making it the largest crowd ever in Tulsa up to that time.

City schools were dismissed at noon for the game. "As several hundred of the students would be absent anyway on account of the ball game this afternoon we have decided to give all the privilege of seeing the world famous diamond performers in action," a school spokesman said.

Although many of the students were expected to get the price of admission, he said, it was a safe bet that many more would temporarily stop up knot holes in the fences that were more or less convenient.

Paul Harvey's father shot by bandits

Two off-duty Tulsa police officers who had been hunting rabbits east of Tulsa were shot – one fatally – by four hijackers who may have committed two other robberies a short time earlier.

The injured officers were Harry H. Aurandt, father of radio commentator Paul Harvey, and Detective Ike Wilkerson. Aurandt, 48, secretary to Police Commissioner J.H. Adkinson, died the next day, Dec. 20, 1921.

The officers said they were shooting rabbits a mile east of the city on Federal Drive (now Admiral Place) when a car containing four gunmen wearing masks drove up and the gunmen ordered them to raise their hands.

Wilkerson said his shotgun jammed when he tried to shoot at the gunmen but was able to fire at them as they drove away. The bandits shot Aurandt in the chest and leg and Wilkerson in both legs.

Although mortally wounded, Aurandt drove himself and Wilkerson a mile to the nearest farm house, where an occupant called police and an ambulance.

A manhunt was organized immediately by police, sheriff's deputies and 400 deputized citizens.

The dragnet resulted in the wounding of two young couples who had been robbed earlier and were speeding toward Tulsa.

Posse members at a roadblock shot into the car, injuring a young man and young woman, after it failed to stop when officers shined flashlights at them and held their badges up.

While the two couples were being questioned, a car containing the bandits sped past. Alvis Fears and Tom Cook were among four suspects who were arrested the next day after Wilkerson said he knew both men and could identify them in spite of the masks they wore.

He said he could not identify the others.

The suspects were moved outside the county by Sheriff W.M. McCullough to protect them from a mob of 1,000 men that congregated that night at the courthouse and was threatening to lynch them.

"These are my prisoners, and I intend to protect them,"

Identified by Wounded Police Dectective

Tulsa World archives

The Dec. 20, 1921, Tulsa World front page included a picture of three men arrested in the fatal shooting of Harry H. Aurandt, an off-duty Tulsa police officer. Aurandt's son is radio commentator Paul Harvey.

the sheriff told the mob. "They will not be taken from the jail by a mob without a fight."

Members of the mob didn't believe the suspects had been moved until a committee searched the jail to ensure they were not there. One of the committee members was the Rev. C.W. Kerr, pastor of the First Presbyterian Church, where Aurandt was a member.

Wilkerson identified Cook as the man who fired one shot and Fears as the man who had fired five shots at the officers. Fears and Cook were convicted of murder and sentenced to life in prison by a jury that deliberated for 50 hours in a trial in Pawnee County where the case was moved because of newspaper reports in Tulsa.

After a surgeon at Tulsa Hospital told Aurandt that his wounds were critical, the officer said "the dirty sons of guns shot me with both hands in the air."

He told the doctor that he knew who the shooters were but did not identify them because he was interrupted by someone else.

Cook's conviction was reversed on appeal because hearsay testimony had been allowed in the trial. Before the appellate court ruled, Fears was given a leave from prison by Gov. Jack Walton, but didn't return to prison at the end of his leave.

No information could be found on whether he eventually was captured and whether Cook was tried again.

Aurandt's survivors included his wife, a daughter, 13, and a son, Paul Harvey Aurandt, 3, now known as Paul Harvey.

Twelve members of the Ku Klux Klan added a mystery to Aurandt's funeral. The Klansmen, wearing their white robes, showed up at the cemetery although there was no indication that Aurandt had been a Klansman.

The casket had just been lowered into the grave and the minister had finished his prayer when the Klansmen walked past the open grave, each dropping a red rose onto the casket. They didn't speak during their mysterious ceremony and disappeared immediately as others stared in surprise.

No one had heard of such a ceremony previously.

Oklahoman was all-American soldier

An Oklahoma doughboy who captured 18 German soldiers without firing a shot was called one of the war's "greatest fighting machines" by Gen. John J. Pershing, the commander of U.S. forces in World War I.

Pershing used those words to describe Otis W. Leader, a Choctaw-Chickasaw who picked up two Springfield rifles from dead soldiers, slung one across his shoulder, gripped the other in his hands and dangled several grenades from his belt as he crept behind a trench containing two German machine-gun crews before yelling for them to surrender.

The machine-gunners, seeing the heavily armed sergeant and unable to turn their mounted weapons around, apparently thought more men were behind him and followed his instructions. Then Leader marched his prisoners back to his own lines. Leader went into action after his own machine-gun crew was killed during heavy fighting at Chateau-Thierry, gateway to Paris.

When he later examined the rifle he had taken from a dead doughboy and had brandished at the enemy, he discovered it held only one bullet.

Leader received a Croix de Guerre, France's highest military honor, for his action. He later received a second Croix de Guerre, a Distinguished Service Cross, a Silver Star and a Purple Heart for other actions and wounds.

Leader also was one of the 18 Choctaw code talkers who used their native language to prevent the Germans from deciphering their messages.

The Oklahoma House of Representatives called Leader the outstanding soldier of World War I in a 1955 resolution.

Leader was born in Calvin and reared in Lehigh where he played with the future major general, Patrick Hurley. He

Tewanna Edwards

A French artist chose Oklahoman Otis W. Leader to represent the typical U.S. soldier in World War I. Leader later became a war hero.

gained international attention shortly after arriving in France a year earlier not because of his bravery but because of his handsome appearance.

The 6-foot-2-inch soldier, among the first Americans to arrive in France, was being trained by the French "Blue Devils" when he was noticed by a French artist who had been commissioned by the French government to paint a picture of what he considered the ideal American soldier. The artist selected Leader as his model.

The painting was displayed in the French Hall of Fame, the British Hall of Fame and the Oklahoma Historical Society Museum and Leader became known as "Mr. American Doughboy."

Doughboy was the term commonly applied to U.S. infantrymen in World War I.

A short time later, Leader saw action with the first Americans involved in the fighting. He was standing near the first three Yanks who were killed when they were hit by an artillery shell.

Toward the end of the war, the Germans had tapped radio and telephone communications and were able to decipher all of the Allied forces' coded communications until a group of 18 Choctaws from the 36th Division, including Leader, began using their native language as a code the Germans were never able to crack.

When the war ended, Leader was in a French hospital recovering from shrapnel wounds he had received while fighting in the Argonne. He had been wounded once before and gassed twice.

Leader, who died in 1961, went to work for the Oklahoma Highway Department when he returned from service. He retired in 1948 as an auditor for the department.

High-ranking citizen-soldier lauded

When Brig.Gen. Raymond S. McLain of Oklahoma became the commander of the badly battered and demoralized 90th Infantry Division in France in July 1944, he called 2,000 of the unit's officers and noncoms together for what today would be called a pep talk.

His methods were a bit unorthodox, but that talk convinced those 2,000 that they were great soldiers who could go back to their outfits to convince the other 14,000 men of the division.

Within three weeks, the 90th had become one of the best fighting machines in the campaign through France. It killed 8,000 enemy soldiers and captured 15,000. By the end of the war, it was the only division in Gen. George Patton's 3rd Army that received a Presidential Unit Citation.

McLain's get-acquainted meeting in the woods near St. Sauveur de Lendelin violated an Army policy against having a large concentration of soldiers in such a small space. McLain slouched before them with his hands in his pockets – his frequent stance – although most high-ranking officers believed that uniforms shouldn't even have pockets and even if they did, they weren't for hands.

He told the men that he didn't care whether they saluted him or whether they shaved or stood with their hands in their pockets – unless, of course, higher brass was making an inspection. He said he'd have to spit and polish in that case and he would expect the men to do the same.

He stressed that they were in the Army to fight, not to worry about spit and polish.

The division was just about through as a fighting organization when McLain was assigned as its commander, wrote a Daily Oklahoman reporter who had been with the 90th. It had taken heavy losses on D-Day and again during the hedgerow fighting in Normandy a few days later. Many had been killed or injured. Most of the survivors were demoralized, and two previous commanders had been relieved.

Gen. Dwight D. Eisenhower considered disbanding the division and transferring the remaining soldiers to other divisions, but Patton told Eisenhower that if he could get the right general to head the division, it could become a great fighting machine.

That right general was McLain, who never saw the inside of West Point, but became the highest-ranking citizen-soldier in the Army. He hadn't gone to school past the sixth grade, but he became one of the best officers in the Army.

Promoted to major general, McLain led his division across

National Archives and Records Administration

Lt. Gen. Raymond McLain was an Oklahoman and a hero of World War II. Tulsa's McLain High School was named in his honor.

France. After that success, McLain was promoted over senior generals to lieutenant general and given command of the XIX Corps, which fought to within 35 miles of Berlin when it was stopped because of political consideration.

McLain was the first National Guard officer to reach that three-star rank.

Born in Kentucky, McLain moved to the new state of Oklahoma in 1907 and took a job in 1912 as a clerk at an Oklahoma City abstract office. From that day he never stopped studying. He learned the banking and abstract business so well that he eventually became the chairman of the board of American First Trust and Title Co.

He joined the National Guard as a private about the same time and by World War I, he was a captain commanding a machine gun company. He was one of the original members of Oklahoma's 45th Infantry Division when it was organized in 1924, and he went to Europe in 1943 as the commander of the 45th Artillery Brigade.

McLain was injured when he rode a tank destroyer ashore at Omaha Beach in Normandy and was banged against the side of the vehicle. Medics discovered three days later that he had two broken ribs, but he didn't take any time off.

McLain personally captured 12 German soldiers, probably the only general during the war to do that. He was frequently seen in his jeep with a machine gun in position. Always close to the front lines, he twice overran his troops' forward lines, getting into German roadblocks where he and his driver had to shoot their way out.

When the war ended, McLain returned to his banking job in Oklahoma City, but he was called to duty again in 1947, and he became the Army's chief information officer and comptroller in 1949. He was appointed to the National Security Training Commission in 1952, but retired after becoming ill with acute leukemia later that year. He died in 1954.

The 1955 Legislature created a memorial commission to honor McLain, but a bill appropriating $425,000 to build a memorial was killed in the 1957 Legislature by House members who said the money was needed for schools, roads and other state functions.

Rep. Lucien Spear of Hugo, who called McLain one of the greatest soldiers ever produced by Oklahoma, said McLain received many honors while he was living "and I think that's the way he wanted to receive them."

The Tulsa Board of Education named a high school at 48th Street North and Peoria Avenue in his honor.

Oologah paper oozed homestyle news

Oologah barber Bill Hoge published what he called the "world's most unusual newspaper."

That description could have been proved – if anyone had challenged it.

Hoge, who always identified himself as "an old country boy who grew up at Oologah," wasn't much concerned about fact in the articles he wrote for his Oologah Oozings.

He wrote to entertain, and his writings carried the subtle wit and imagination that at one time were found among old men sitting around a hot stove in a rural general store on a winter day.

But his stories were quoted regularly in the New York Times, New York Sun, New York Post and other newspapers around the country and in magazines such as Time and Look. His newspaper had subscribers around the country and even in England.

And after his newspaper went broke, he wrote a column for the Tulsa Sunday World for several years. Hoge had one cardinal rule: No crime news.

"But we do try to keep the folks advised on how the eggs are hatching, give them the dope on who won the latest roping contest and print instructions on how to cut the boot off a busted leg when some boy comes off second best with a buckin' hoss," he said.

"If somebody stole some chickens around here and got arrested for it, I didn't put it in the paper because I didn't want people to know we had that kind of folks in the community," he told a World reporter in 1941 after the Oologah Oozings folded because it had too much circulation and not enough advertising.

"The darned thing just wouldn't pay, and I couldn't carry it," Hoge, also the town's only barber, said.

Hoge, who learned barbering from his father at age 13, and a Tulsa humorist, Cal Tinney, started the Oozings in 1935. The editorial office was in the back of Hoge's barber shop, which was in one room of a two-room frame shack at the intersection of Coo-Wee-Scoo-Wee Avenue and Cow Trail Boulevard in the town of 244 residents – but Hoge said it was difficult to find all 244.

Tinney went to New York "for the big money," leaving Hoge to run the newspaper by himself.

In addition to not printing crime news, he didn't print scandal, rough language or raw jokes. Or political news.

"I don't like politics. I just want to run a newspaper the way I see it ought to be run," he said.

Tulsa World archives

Bill Hoge mixed wit and tall tales in his newspaper, the Oologah Oozings.

In his own newspaper and in his World column, he wrote about visits to relatives in such places as Coffeyville and Pittsburg, Kan., and attending county fairs and school reunions and other events.

Writing about a fair at Columbus, Kan., he said "there was just one quarter horse on exhibit and he looked like he was about threequarters thoroughbred and one quarter quarter horse. If we were picking out good quarter horses, we'd never pick him."

He also wrote once about his ancestors who came from Scotland and Ireland "but I didn't inherit any of the Scotch thrift nor Irish wit." He said his ancestors settled in Virginia and "reared a lot of little hogs, I mean Hoges, and here I am."

Hoge published a series of stories in 1940 about the panther of Skull Hollow, although there hadn't been a panther in the Oologah area since the last circus went through. But Hoge had the panther howling up and down the canyons at night and even organized a posse to track it to its lair.

Panther hunt updates were reported daily in newspapers throughout the country.

Hoge told a reporter that when he ran out of local news, he made up some to fill his newspaper. "I certainly amazed the town with some of the things I reported."

Time magazine cited the Oozings along with two other newspapers in small towns in Minnesota and Ohio as being typical of the small newspapers that deliver homey news to 17 million small town and rural Americans.

"Country weeklies of their kind are a big bright spot," Time said. Hoge's type of news got the Oozings circulation in 40 states and seven foreign countries at $1 per year, but Hoge couldn't make money on that circulation because he didn't have the advertising to support it.

"I could have had 5,000 more circulation if I hadn't been careful," he said. "I was losing money on circulation instead of making it."

After closing his Oologah newspaper at the end of 1940, Hoge moved to Skiatook, where he operated a barber shop. A man who remembers getting haircuts there said the haircuts should have taken 15 to 20 minutes but usually took an hour or more – because of Hoge's stories.

Hoge, who died at the age of 77 in 1971, tried politics once. He made an unsuccessful run for county commissioner in 1964.

Skelly Field has long history of change

The University of Tulsa's football team was left without a place to play after the 1929 season because a farmers' market was planned on the site where it had played for years.

But oilman-philanthropist W. G. (Bill) Skelly came to the rescue in April 1930, with a challenge donation of $125,000 for a new stadium.

The only provision attached to his gift was that it had to be matched by an equal sum in donations from others. It was just one of many gifts made by the man who became known as "Mr. Tulsa" for improvements to his city.

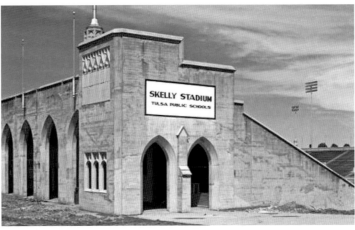

Beryl Ford collection

Skelly Stadium, shown in 1965 during expansion work, is adjacent to the University of Tulsa campus, but it hasn't always been owned by the university.

The facility, which became Chapman Stadium, Skelly Field in 2007, was involved in trades over the years that resulted in new stadiums for Webster, McLain and Memorial high schools and transferred ownership of the land on which the Philtower stands to the building owner.

Skelly told university officials before the stadium was dedicated that if a larger stadium was needed, he would make another challenge donation to help finance that.

Skelly's gift was announced on April 12, a committee was appointed and 400 members began seeking an additional $150,000 – an exact match of Skelly's gift wouldn't build the structure they wanted – to build the stadium on land between Eighth and Eleventh streets and Florence and Gary avenues.

By May 19, $135,400 of the matching funds had been raised – within $15,000 of the goal – and campaign Chairman Fred Insull assured Skelly the balance would be in hand when all the potential donors had been contacted.

During the campaign, a large sign board located on top of a drug store at Fourth and Main streets had kept Tulsans up to date on its progress. Firefighters climbed a ladder daily to paint new totals.

Even Will Rogers got involved. He couldn't come to Tulsa for a personal appearance but he sent a telegram to Tulsa World Publisher Eugene Lorton, who had asked him what terms would be necessary to get him to appear here in support of the project.

"What do you mean terms?" Rogers replied. "Wouldn't be any terms but I got to make faces at these cameras out here. Get that stadium by all means."

The stadium, named for Skelly, opened Oct. 4, 1930, with 13,000 spectators watching TU defeat the University of Arkansas 26-6.

Skelly declined to make a speech at the dedication but

earlier had said the stadium "will essentially be a university stadium, but it will also be a civic asset. It can be used by the high school and for affairs aside from athletics in which the community is interested."

Even if the McNulty Park stadium at Eleventh Street and Elgin Avenue hadn't been torn down to make way for the market that later became Warehouse Market, TU needed a new stadium.

The McNulty playing field was 10 yards shorter than regulation and kickers regularly kicked the ball into Oak Lawn Cemetery, which abutted the field.

"When a team moved the ball to the 10-yard line, officials moved the ball back to the 20 to compensate for the short field," Ed Dubie, the quarterback of the 1929-30 team, recalled in 1980 at the 50th anniversary of Skelly Stadium. "On long yardage plays, officials often had to judge whether a ball carrier would have made it to the end zone or not."

The first trade was in 1939 when TU traded the stadium to the Board of Education in return for title to the land where the Philtower stands and immediately sold the land to Waite Phillips for $231,000, enough money to pay off TU's debt and to build a $25,000 stadium for Webster.

TU also agreed to lease the stadium for at least 15 years for its home football games. The facility was to be known as Tulsa Stadium, Skelly Field but it was always called Skelly Stadium.

The Philtower land was part of a block bought by the city in 1902 for $426. All of that block except the old City Hall lot at Fourth Street and Cincinnati Avenue was deeded to the Board of Education in 1915. Within a year, the board had sold one lot for the Cosden Building, later named the Mid-Continent Building, for $50,000 and had leased for 99 years the lots on which the Atlas Life and Tulsa Club buildings stand.

The board traded Skelly in 1965 to a Stadiums Corporation Trust and mortgaged it to National Bank of Tulsa as part of a plan to upgrade the facility and to build a 10,000-seat stadium for Memorial and a 5,000-seat stadium for McLain high schools. The trust was to hold title until the debt incurred by the improvements was paid off.

But the title was transferred back to TU in 1969 although the debt had not been completely paid.

The name was changed to Chapman Stadium Skelly Field in April 2007 after an $18 million gift from the H.A. and Mary K. Chapman Foundation to renovate the facility.

Early scenes, later faces depicted in mural

You can get a glimpse of early Tulsa life from a large mural in the old City Hall building at Fourth Street and Cincinnati Avenue.

The mural is a scene from downtown Tulsa based on extensive research and attention to detail, but most of those depicted in the painting by Tulsa artist Del Jackson weren't around for the 1919 period it depicts.

Only police Sgt. J.D Pilkington, Tulsa's first traffic cop who was known as "Big Jim," is depicted in his true-to-life environment. Pilkington, who

Joe Coleman

A mural is seen inside the old City Hall building at Fourth Street and Cheyenne Avenue.

died in 1950, for many years directed traffic at Third and Main streets, then the city's busiest intersection, and was well known to downtown workers.

Jackson painted himself at the wheel of a 1915 Model T Ford that he said he chose for his 16-by-26-foot mural because he and the car were produced in the same year. Jackson's passenger in the Model T is his wife, Lucille.

Others in the painting are Waldo E. (Dode) McIntosh; oilman Julius Livingston, who died in 1990 at the age of 93; Amoco Production Co. employee Barbara Fulps, wearing a typical hairstyle of the 1919 era; and Tulsa historian Beryl Ford.

McIntosh, who served as chief of the Creek Nation from 1961 to 1971, is depicted in his World War I Army uniform that he wore in annual Veterans' Day parades until 1989 when he was 96, two years before he died. McIntosh also served as Tulsa County treasurer for several years.

Jackson, who had retired as the company illustrator for Amoco, was hired to paint the mural after the building that had been empty for five years was sold by the city in 1973 to the Coleman-Ervin & Associates architectural firm and the Kothe & Eagleton Inc. law firm to be remodeled into an office building. The mural was to depict the people and environment that prevailed in Tulsa when the building was erected in 1919.

The mural still hangs in the lobby of the old City Hall building but the building is presently occupied by the Frederic Dorwart law firm. Using recognizable people in murals wasn't new to Jackson who had painted a much larger – 13 by 56 feet – mural for the Smithsonian's Hall of Petroleum that now hangs in the center concourse of Tulsa International Airport and features 27 Tulsans.

Jackson's work had to be donated to the Smithsonian because of General Services Administration rules that required only certain artists to be used – artists who prob-

ably knew little about the oil business. But Walter Helmerich of Helmerich and Payne came to the rescue and promised financial and other support to Jackson.

Helmerich, recognizing that a mural of that size would be costly, spread the word among oil industry executives that "if you put up $5,000 you can be in the mural."

And raised the funds in one day.

The mural depicts every phase of the oil business, from exploration, through drilling, production, refining, transportation and the final distribution to the customer. Tulsa's skyline is in the background with the Texaco refinery. The Sunray refinery is in the foreground.

The mural was moved to the airport in 1998. A native of Lincoln, Neb., Jackson studied fine arts at the University of Nebraska and the University of Tulsa. He worked as a night club singer and later on radio in Tulsa where his partner was Clara Ann Fowler, the soon-to-be-famous singer known as Patti Page.

After turning to art, Jackson continued singing with barbershop quartets.

Jackson also served as a staff artist at Hillcrest Medical Center, one of only three illustrators in Oklahoma at that time. He received praise for medical illustrations, many of which were made while he was a spectator or from photographs he took while in the operating room, perhaps a natural progression since his early ambition was to be a doctor.

He prepared a series of illustrations on open heart surgery that were used by doctors who performed the surgery when they lectured and published papers on their procedures.

Jackson also made models and casts of body parts to help make artificial body parts such as eyes, hands, ears and noses.

To prepare for being a medical illustrator, Jackson attended autopsies by Dr. Leo Lowbeer, Hillcrest pathologist.

"I wanted to find out if I was temperamentally suited for the work," Jackson said.

"When the autopsies didn't make me uneasy or nauseated, I knew I was."

He also did more conventional art work – portraits, paintings of the oil industry and other subjects.

But, he said, "medical illustration is what I've always been looking for. The work serves humanity in a very real way."

McIntosh was proud of his heritage

An Oklahoman who served the country in World War I and the community in three positions also served the Creek tribe as its chief for 10 years – the fourth member of his family to hold that job.

Waldo Emerson "Dode" McIntosh was Tulsa County's tag agent, its assessor and its treasurer before being appointed as principal chief of the Creeks in 1961 and spending the next decade fighting for better education, better housing, health and sanitary facilities for the tribe.

"I was determined to make the federal government pay for violating treaties and broken promises they had made to the Creeks," McIntosh told a reporter in 1981 in reference to leading the tribe. "Our attorney was superb and we won judgment after judgment."

McIntosh, the last appointed chief of the tribe, which now elects its leaders, won $3.9 million in damages in 1964 for land taken from the Creeks by federal action in 1814 and another $1 million in 1965 for land taken in 1856. He also got an appropriation from Congress for $2.2 million for dormitories for students at a Eufaula Indian school.

He also was responsible for building health clinics and improving sanitation among Creeks' homes.

The McIntosh County Historical Society, in a paper prepared for a ceremony honoring McIntosh in 1981, said "he has a rare gift of eloquence, empathy and charisma which fitted him for sessions at the bargaining table with the highest officials in Washington."

Those same qualities were evident in his other pursuits.

McIntosh, for whose family the county was named, moved to Tulsa in 1942 from Miami, Okla., where he was the manager of a lumber yard and got his first taste of politics by serving as Ottawa County Democratic chairman for eight years.

His interest in politics continued in Tulsa, and he served as tag agent from 1951 to 1955 and later was appointed treasurer and elected to his term in 1960.

You may not have known McIntosh but you probably have seen him – if you've ever watched a Veterans Day pa-

Tulsa World archives

Waldo Emerson "Dode" McIntosh was a former Tulsa County treasurer and tag agent who fought for American Indian education and housing as chief of the Creek Nation for 10 years.

rade in Tulsa. He wore his World War I Army uniform – it still fit him through all those years – in the annual parade for many years. He started that parade by firing a rifle into the air and sat on a stool as the marchers went past.

McIntosh was born in 1893 in Tennessee but his family moved to the Checotah area in 1902 when he was 8 and he at tended school there. He met his future wife, Lulu Vance, at a Methodist Church program shortly after arriving in Checotah.

"Some day, some way, somehow, I would marry that little girl," he said he vowed. When they were 18, they eloped to Arkansas.

"She was the prettiest, sweetest and smartest ever," he said.

McIntosh was a graduate and former teacher of Checotah High School who regularly attended Checotah school reunions, which always started with his Creek war whoop. He was unable to attend the 1990 and 1991 reunions because of his health. He died the following August at age 98.

McIntosh told several times about being named for Ralph Waldo Emerson because his mother was a fan of the poet. But, he said, "as far as my father was concerned, Emerson was a damned Yankee. So he called me 'Dody' but later dropped the 'y' and substituted an 'e.'"

It was a nickname that stuck with him throughout his life.

McIntosh, part Scots, became a hit with the British press because he wore an Indian headdress when he and his daughter went to Scotland in 1964 to attend a gathering of the Clan McIntosh. He appeared on television shows as "a real live Indian from the colonies."

He was asked at one reception about America, Oklahoma and the Indians.

"Well, I knew none of them there knew the answers so I didn't have any trouble at all answering their questions," he told a reporter later.

"Later my daughter heard one of the women say 'I was really impressed by him. He has as much sense as a white man.'"

Robertson survived ouster by one vote

J.B.A. Robertson, Oklahoma's fourth governor, was saved from impeachment in 1921 by a legislator who left his sickbed and headed for the Capitol in an ambulance.

The ambulance had a wreck en route and Rep. J.T. Jenkins finished his trip in a car driven by a witness to the accident, arriving just in time to vote against the impeachment bill.

The vote by Jenkins created a 42-42 tie on a motion to approve the impeachment bill charging Robertson with corruption and gross neglect of duty.

When House Speaker George Schwabe of Nowata announced the vote and ruled the issue had failed, it touched off yelling, howling and catcalling among the spectators in the gallery and by legislators on the floor.

When the demonstrating finally ended, many legislators rushed to shake Robertson's hand.

Jenkins wasn't involved in the celebrating. He was seeking medical attention for his injuries. He died later, but apparently injuries from the ambulance wreck were not a contributing factor

Earlier, Robertson had been indicted by a grand jury in Okmulgee County in connection with the failure of the Okmulgee Bank of Commerce. The charge was dropped in February 1923, after it was determined that Robertson had never had any connection with the bank.

Robertson, a Democrat and the first governor to take office after the Capitol was built, faced a hostile Republican majority in the House – the first in state history– that year, and the impeachment bill that came late in the legislative session was seen by many as part of a Republican plot.

Robertson's term was stormy at times but also fruitful.

The day after he was inaugurated in 1919, Robertson proposed submitting a $50 million road bond issue to the public to provide better highways and jobs, especially for servicemen returning from World War I.

"It is high time for us to show that Oklahoma is the best state in the union," he told the Legislature.

The governor waged a vigorous campaign for the bonds and, as an incentive, promised that the counties with the greatest vote for the issue would be the first to have hard-surface highways. But when election day came, the issue was defeated by about 50,000 votes.

Robertson didn't give up on highways. Using deficiency certificates, he was able to obtain $9.2 million in federal funds, and by the time his term ended in 1923, the state

Oklahoma Historical Society

J.B.A. Robertson had a tumultuous term as governor, surviving an impeachment attempt by one vote.

had 1,600 miles of paved highways, compared with 50 in 1919. He also was able to build 60 major and 350 minor bridges.

He also pushed a hospital building bill through the Legislature, resulting in hospitals in Muskogee, Talihina, Clinton, Sulphur and Boley.

Among the biggest challenges he faced was a 1919 strike by 9,000 coal miners in eastern Oklahoma.

Train service and many industries were curtailed because of lack of coal.

To maintain order among the strikers, Robertson called out the entire National Guard, augmented by four troops of U.S. Army cavalry. And two years later, he called out the Guard to help restore order in Tulsa after the June 1, 1921, race riot.

Robertson was born in Iowa in 1871 as James Brooks Ayers Robertson but he used just initials after coming to Oklahoma in 1893 and settling on a rented farm near Chandler.

He was admitted to the bar in 1899, served as county attorney, as a district court judge and as a member of the Supreme Court Commission.

Robertson also battled the Ku Klux Klan, which was believed to have 75,000 members in Oklahoma in 1922, including many in the National Guard.

"There is no room for any man who owes allegiance to any power, secret organization or society that may become arrayed against the United States or the state of Oklahoma," Robertson said in an order to rid the Guard of Klansmen. "There is no compromise in this matter."

Even his inaugural night was not without drama.

He had been sworn in earlier in the day and a ball was planned that night with an orchestra and dancing.

A huge crowd attended in the Capitol Rotunda in spite of heavy rain. Suddenly, the lights went out – just as it was about to start. The National Guard ordered everyone to remain where they were.

Only a few flashlights could be found. Many used matches to provide brief light. Finally, a Guard captain announced about 11 p.m. that anyone who wished to leave could. Most so wished, but that also proved a challenge.

Taxicabs and cars were bogged down outside – there were no paved streets. And about a half-hour after most people had left, the lights came back on.

The orchestra began playing and the dance began.

There was no crowding.

Soldier sacrifices himself for comrades

A Tulsa soldier was killed during a two-man attack on more than 300 heavily armed and well-entrenched enemy soldiers in a 2½ hour battle for a Manila railroad station during World War II.

The Tulsan, Pfc. John N. Reese Jr., 22, was hit by a sniper's bullet while reloading his rifle as he and Pfc. Cleto Rodriguez were crawling back toward the American lines for more ammunition.

Reese's cousin Betty Lamarr, of Tulsa, said Rodriguez told her that Reese saved his life. "You go first because you have a family," Rodriguez said Reese told him. And Reese provided covering fire as his companion crawled away.

"The intrepid team, in 2½ hours of fierce fighting, killed more than 82 Japanese, completely disorganized their defense and paved the way for subsequent defeat of the enemy at this strong point," according to the citation awarding Reese the Medal of Honor, the nation's highest military award.

Rodriguez also received a Medal of Honor.

The battle occurred on Feb. 9, 1944, when Reese and Rodriguez decided to attempt to secure a position closer to the railroad station that was protected by soldiers in pillboxes containing machine guns flanked by dug-in riflemen. In addition, a large concrete pillbox in a building had a 37 mm gun and heavy mortars.

The station's defense, manned by a battalion of Japanese under orders to defend their position to the last, was holding up the Americans' advance until Reese and Rodriguez decided to make their attack.

According to the medal citation, the soldier's efforts aided in the advance of American troops in Manila and pro-

Tulsa World archives

Pfc. John N. Reese Jr. and another soldier each earned the Medal of Honor during a World War II battle with Japanese soldiers.

vided a lasting inspiration to all those with whom he served.

Reese attended Woodrow Wilson Junior High School before moving to Central High School but was never a member of any clubs there. He was on the track team but never won any prizes. A notation on his record card reveals he was a "quiet, sensible sort of boy."

Reese and Rodriguez were members of the 148th Infantry Regiment of the 37th Division.

The medal was presented to Reese's parents, Mr. and Mrs. John Reese Sr., on Nov. 11, 1945, in Pryor where the elder Reese worked at the Oklahoma Ordnance Works. Reese, who graduated from Central in 1941, also had worked at the OOW briefly before enlisting in December 1942.

When his body was returned, it was buried at the Fort Gibson National Cemetery.

The Army Reserve Center, 4000 E. 15th St., was named in Reese's honor, but that building now is vacant. Military units moved to Broken Arrow several years ago.

Reese's memory also was honored in 1993 when the Central High School Foundation placed a plaque in his honor in the Hall of Fame at the school at 3101 W. Edison St.

And just a year ago, a nine-mile section of Oklahoma 20 between Pryor and Salina was named the "John Reese Jr. Medal of Honor/Purple Heart Memorial Highway."

Legislation to rename the highway in honor of Reese was introduced in the House by Rep. Ben Sherrer, D-Chouteau, after the Mayes County Commission approved a resolution asking that the highway be named for Reese.

The highway has been named but the signs have not been installed, Sherrer said.

Bill Skelly always got the job done

William Grove Skelly's name was synonymous with Tulsa's progress.

Known as Mr. Tulsa among local civic leaders, friends said he detested the name. But few, if any, contributed more to the city's growth.

Known as Mr. Republican among politicians, he served his party in many capacities, promoting candidates from the courthouse to the White House, and was Oklahoma's GOP national committeeman for many years.

He was called Mr. Oklahoma by Gov. Johnston Murray in 1952 when the governor gave him a proclamation naming the 51st Street Bypass, now part of I-44, Skelly Drive.

He also might be called Mr. Broadcast because of radio station KVOO (1170 AM), Tulsa's first broadcast station, which he moved to Tulsa from Bristow in 1925; KVOO-TV, which he built in partnership with Sen. Robert S. Kerr; and KWGS, the University of Tulsa radio station which is part of the public radio system.

But whatever the title, the goal was the same: get the job done.

And Bill Skelly always got the job done. He was a hardworking, conscientious citizen behind those titles with a simple, brief philosophy: "Don't let anything get you down."

Tulsa needed a better airport to attract the Ford Reliability Tour of air shows in 1928, but there wasn't time for a vote on a bond issue before the show's proposed visit in July.

Early that year, Skelly organized a group of 47 businessmen who put up $172,000 in what was called a "stud horse note" to buy land suitable for an airport.

The Chamber of Commerce formed the Tulsa Airport Corp., and a 360-acre wheat field on the northeast corner of Apache Street and Sheridan Road was bought.

The tour had stopped briefly the previous year at McIntyre Airport, a private field west of the future airport, but Ford executives said the city would need a better airport for the tour to visit again in 1928.

That's when Skelly proposed the stud horse note.

That name came from the practice of farmers pooling their resources to buy a stud horse and paying for it with stud fees. The airport land was held in trust until the note was paid off with income from the airport – similar to a "stud horse note."

Runways were mowed, a 20-by-120-foot wooden plank building was constructed as the passenger terminal, and the air show opened on July 3. Within 18 months, the Tulsa airport was one of the busiest in the world.

Skelly's philosophy was tested first when fire destroyed his only drilling rig while he and his bride, Gertrude, were

Tulsa World archives

Mr. Tulsa? Mr. Republican? Mr. Oklahoma? He perhaps is best known as just Mr. Skelly — W.G. Skelly — Tulsa's most prominent leader for a generation.

on their honeymoon to the St. Louis World's Fair in 1904. He returned to Indiana, rebuilt the rig and soon had it pumping again.

When things got tough for him and his company during the Depression, he was undaunted. "I don't need your sympathy," he once told a visitor. "I've been knocked down before. It's only a disgrace to stay down."

In 1955, he was called "Tulsa's greatest individual asset" in state legislation introduced by the entire Tulsa County delegation and passed unanimously.

Born in 1878 near Erie, Pa., Skelly became intrigued with the oil business at an early age after listening to tales of oil-field adventure from his teamster father and friends who dropped by to say hello and reminisce about their oil-field days.

When he was 15, Skelly hopped a train to Oil City, got a job in the oil fields for $8 a week and worked there until his oil career was interrupted by the Spanish-American War. He enlisted and served in Puerto Rico.

"I entered the war as a private and came out as a private," he often related. "So I didn't gain anything or lose anything."

Skelly and his wife came to Tulsa in 1912 and he became involved in many civic activities in addition to establishing his Skelly Oil Co. in 1919. He headed the company as president until a few months before his death at the age of 78 in 1957 when he was chairman of the board.

Skelly started Spartan School of Aeronautics and Spartan Aircraft Co. in 1928, about the time of that stud horse note that bought the land for the airport.

Skelly surprised most people who knew him in 1952 by teaming with Kerr, another oilman but a Democrat, in an effort to get a Tulsa television channel that both had sought.

The political opposites forgot their differences and pooled their prestige in a joint application by a combine headed by Skelly's son-in-law, Harold C. Stuart.

Skelly's associates explained the action was strictly a business expedient to obtain another channel for Tulsa. It was successful, and KVOO-TV, channel 2, went on the air in December 1954. That station later became KJRH. The radio station is KFAQ today.

Skelly's name is still prominent in Tulsa; there's a Skelly Elementary School and Skelly Drive is still part of the highway system, but Skelly Stadium, which Skelly is responsible for, is now known as Chapman Stadium – although the playing field is Skelly Field.

"Whatever success I have had," he said in 1952, "is largely due to the type of people that I was associated with, not only in business but in these other activities."

Famous horse still keeps 'em talking

One of America's best-known horses is buried under a wild cherry tree near Tahlequah.

Maybe.

The horse, of course, of course, was Mister Ed, who talked to his owner, architect Wilbur Post, through 143 episodes of a 1960s television show that was introduced by a catchy ditty that millions probably can still sing today.

"A horse is a horse, of course, of course,

"And no one can talk to a horse, of course,

"That is, of course, unless the horse is the famous Mister Ed."

The TV show, also titled "Mister Ed," starred Alan Young as Wilbur Post, Connie Hines as Wilbur's tolerant wife and Mister Ed, of course, played by a palomino American gelding named Bamboo Harvester.

Maybe.

Some believe a different horse was used to portray Mister Ed, and there is a debate about whether the star of "Mister Ed" is buried at the site where owner Todd Carroll announced in 2007 that he wants to build 12 to 15 log houses and create a subdivision, with the entrance going past the Mister Ed monument.

After the series ended and the horse was brought to Oklahoma by Clarence Tharp, who had trained the palomino, he romped on Tharp's land until he died in February 1979, at the age of 33, and was buried under a wild cherry tree.

"He was a palomino is all I know," backhoe operator Doug Hubbard told a Tulsa World reporter in 1990. He said he was called to dig the horse's grave.

"Of course, he didn't look very good when I saw him. I assume it was him."

Him? Mister Ed, of course. Danny Snodgrass, who owned the land in 1990, said he knew "for positive it was Mister Ed."

Tahlequah veterinarian Sam Crosby, who attended to the horse a year before he died, said 33 is an unusually advanced age for a horse, roughly equal to 140 years in a hu-

A granite monument near Tahlequah claims to mark the burial spot of the famous TV horse, Mister Ed. Others dispute the claim.

man life. But another noted palomino that appeared on television – Roy Rogers' horse Trigger – also died at the age of 33.

A granite monument with a picture of Mister Ed sticking his head out of a barn door as he did on the TV show marks the graveside.

Some Internet accounts say the horse buried in Tahlequah was not Mister Ed, but one used in publicity shots after Mister Ed died in 1969. A representative of actor Young said last year that the horse that played Mister Ed died in 1970 in Burbank and his body was cremated.

There also were reports that a zebra was used, at least in some of the segments, to portray the show's star, but others claim that is a hoax. The story is, a zebra could be used because its stripes didn't show up in black and white television – color hadn't come into general use yet.

The Mister Ed series was remarkably similar to a 1950s series of seven movies about a talking mule, Francis, which also had an Oklahoma connection. The voice for Francis was that of movie actor Chill Wills, who worked in Oklahoma before becoming an actor.

As Mister Ed did in the TV series, Francis would talk only to one person. In Francis' case, it was a young soldier named Peter Stirling, played by Donald O'Connor, and he caused frequent problems for his master. Francis frequently gave Stirling advice he had overheard from generals or from discussions with other equines.

Many of those movies involved the mule's master serving in the Army – going to West Point, joining the WACs and the Navy and a few in civilian life.

Whether the horse buried near Tahlequah is Mister Ed may be debatable.

But everyone knows:

"A horse is a horse, of course, of course,

"And no one can talk to a horse, of course,

"That is, of course, unless the horse is the famous Mister Ed."

Passion for poetry set man on open road

Welborn Hope was operating a drug store in Ada when he decided to take poetry writing seriously in the late 1930s or early 1940s.

He locked the door to the store, threw away the key and took to the open road as a tramp poet.

Hope tramped through most of the country as well as Paris, London and other places, trading poems for food, for shelter, for a ride. He worked, only when necessary, at newspapers in Tulsa, St. Louis, New York, El Paso, Muskogee, wherever he stopped.

He ate what nature provided and slept under bridges, on sand bars, in fields or woods, always writing poetry.

"He is a tramp by choice, and if he were in a crowd and I was told to select the tramp, I'd pick Welborn because he looks like a tramp," Tulsa World columnist Troy Gordon wrote in 1970.

Hope refused to call anyplace home, but for more than 30 years Tulsa was his home base, primarily in the old Jefferson Hotel, the building now occupied by Guaranty Abstract Co. at 320 S. Boulder Ave. For a year before the hotel closed in 1968, he worked as its night clerk.

His first book was "Four Men Hanging," a historical recounting of a 1909 lynching in Ada, but after that he concentrated on poetry.

His first book of poems, "The Great River and Small," won the Pegasus Award as the best book of poetry in 1970. It was a collection of some of his short poems, including several that were first published in the Saturday Review of Literature.

In all, Hope wrote more than 1,700 poems.

He once said "I love America. I worry about America. I write poetry about America. It is as simple as that."

Born in 1903 in Ada, Hope was the son of a pioneer banker and graduated from East Central State Teachers College at age 18. He later received a pharmacy license and oper-

Tulsa World archives

Welborn Hope took his poetry from Oklahoma to Europe and the Ivy League.

ated a drug store in Ada until his parents' death.

One of Hope's favorite stories involved speaking at Harvard University.

"I landed in Boston approximately broke. I hadn't had a haircut in two months or a shave in two weeks," Hope told a World reporter in 1968.

"I did a little dishwashing around Skully Square and became a little greasier and a little dirtier. In fact, I looked like I had slept in a Cambridge sewer pipe.

"I showed up at Harvard and two guards gave me quite a look before they asked me where I was going. When I told them I was the speaker of the evening one of them asked 'Are you nuts?'

"I just told them to call upstairs and check. When I got up there one of the men said 'Don't you think you ought to clean up a little bit?' but I told him I was billed as a tramp poet and that's what they were going to get.

"When I walked out on stage you should have seen the astonished looks."

But Hope said the crowd realized he knew what he was talking about when he started speaking about New England poets.

After he retired as a tramp poet, Hope settled in Oklahoma City but he continued writing poetry. He died in Oklahoma City on Oct. 9, 1988.

Welborn Hope Days were held in Ada and Tulsa in 1970 to honor the tramp poet.

Hope gave a poetry reading at the University of Oklahoma's Center of Continuing Education in 1975 and was scheduled and paid $100 for another appearance several months later at a "Sense of Place" symposium. But he didn't speak because no one showed up to hear him.

"The small, disinterested crowds at the symposium were not as large as the turnout to watch the 'Messiah of the New Culture,' Steve Davis, practice football," Hope said.

"I was going to mention this in my speech, but no one showed up for my speech. They were all at the football practice."

Vet brought change to 'Little Dixie'

When Dr. John Montgomery was considering setting up his veterinary practice in Poteau, other veterinarians advised him to go elsewhere and other blacks told him that "Little Dixie" folks had strong feelings about black people.

But those opinions didn't deter Montgomery from settling in Poteau in 1951. "I took it as a challenge," he said.

It was a challenge he met. Four years later, Montgomery was responsible for Poteau schools becoming the first in Oklahoma to be integrated.

He later was appointed to various state boards by two Republican and three Democratic governors.

He also was given an honorary doctor of humane letters degree from Oklahoma State University – only the eighth person to receive such an honor. He has been inducted into the Oklahoma Hall of Fame.

He was born in 1918 in the east Texas town of Henderson, where his slave grandfather was taken by his owners before being emancipated. Montgomery received a degree in veterinary medicine from Tuskegee Institute in Alabama. He graduated magna cum laude after earlier earning an undergraduate degree from Prairie View A&M College in Texas and serving in the Army.

He picked Poteau for his practice "because I heard that 30,000 head of cattle were in LeFlore County."

When he and his wife, Doris, arrived in Poteau at dusk one day in 1951, they were welcomed by a black woman who offered them a place to spend the night and some advice:

"You all get up in the morning and leave here. You've come to the wrong place."

Montgomery said his reception from the community's white leaders was receptive and cordial. "My customers, I discovered, wanted a professional service and it didn't matter if the person providing that service was black or white."

To establish his southeast Oklahoma practice, Montgomery traveled the back roads in LeFlore and adjoining counties, making 25 to 30 "house calls" daily.

"My pickup was my office and an audience would be waiting for me at every stop," he told a Tulsa World reporter 35 years later. "They wanted to see what a black veterinarian

Tulsa World archives

Dr. John Montgomery talks about the 1955 integration of Poteau schools while sitting on the steps of the old high school in Poteau in 2005. Montgomery said he considered life in Little Dixie a challenge when he arrived in 1951 to set up his veterinary practice.

could do."

And as his practice grew, Montgomery built a clinic behind his house in Poteau and started treating house pets as well as farm animals until he retired in 1988.

For a time, he was the only veterinarian in LeFlore, Haskell and Latimer counties and also had many clients from western Arkansas.

Although those Little Dixie residents were eager for Montgomery's professional services, they weren't as eager to welcome a black family socially.

"We couldn't eat in any cafe. We couldn't use any public accommodations like the theater. We couldn't even wash our clothes in the washeteria," Montgomery recalled years later. "That's how prejudiced it was."

After the U.S. Supreme Court ruled in 1954 that separate schools were unconstitutional, Montgomery petitioned the school board to do away with segregation. The issue was on the board's agenda on June 7, 1955, and was approved with only one dissenting vote.

Gov. Raymond Gary had predicted only a week earlier that southeastern Oklahoma would lag behind in integration.

It was nearly 10 years later before the Civil Rights Act of 1964 opened all public accommodations on private property to all races – at least on paper. Montgomery and his family helped make the opening of those public accommodations reality.

Montgomery served 25 years on the board of regents for Oklahoma State University and A&M Colleges, including twice as chairman. His wife, who died of cancer in 2000, served briefly as the first woman on the state pardon and parole board.

At age 78, when he was given the honorary degree from OSU in 1996, Montgomery was called "truly a pioneer in veterinary medicine and in Oklahoma higher education" by J.W. Alexander, dean of the College of Veterinary Medicine.

Former OSU Regent Carolyn Savage said Montgomery was "a walking role model for young people of all creeds and races."

Montgomery's only comment was "I'm overwhelmed."

Train wreck culprit haunted by his deed

An angry Frisco Railroad laborer derailed a passenger train "to get even" with his foreman for firing him and created what has been called Henryetta's greatest tragedy.

Thirteen people died in the crash triggered by George Washington Darnell on Aug. 18, 1929, a mile and a half south of Henryetta.

Darnell, who served 30 years in prison for murder, said he didn't intend to hurt anyone; he just planned to derail a switch engine. But the switch engine didn't run that day and a fast-moving passenger train headed from Sherman, Texas, to Tulsa hit the open switch and was derailed.

Tulsa World archives

An Aug. 18, 1929, passenger train derailment was caused by a disgruntled railroad laborer. The wreck, near Henryetta, killed 13 people.

The switch lock had been broken and the switch was cocked open just enough to cause the train to derail but not enough to set off a warning signal.

The engineer, fireman and 11 passengers in the train's first car were scalded to death by steam from the engine.

"Language cannot convey an adequate notion of the horror," Henryetta Free-Lance editor George Hall wrote the next day. "The victims were stewed like oysters."

As the train reached the switch, the engine fell over on its side in a ditch and the boiler burst, filling the engine cockpit and the first car with live steam. But the mail car jumped over the wreckage and came to rest on its wheels on a lawn near the tracks, and the mail clerk thought it wasn't much of a wreck until he looked outside.

A passenger in the last passenger car, which remained on the tracks, said he had intended to return to Tulsa from Dallas by airplane but his wife had "objected on the grounds that it wasn't safe" so he made the trip by train.

Railroad officials believed vandals had broken the lock and opened the switch until nearly two years later when neighbors heard Darnell and his wife arguing and she threatened to tell authorities that he had caused the wreck.

One of the neighbors immediately called police and

Darnell, 36, was arrested in Parsons, Kan., and returned to Oklahoma. He told authorities he was "glad it was over" because he "could feel dead people's hands all over him."

Darnell, who went back to work for the railroad to help clear the wreckage of the train, pleaded guilty to a murder charge and was sentenced to life in prison by District Court Judge Harry Swan.

Swan said he had talked with several people who knew Darnell and decided "his mental capacities were deficient."

Besides, said the judge, "the misery in recalling again and again the tragedy would be greater punishment for Darnell than the electric chair."

Darnell told officers that his conscience had bothered him while helping to clear the wreckage. He also cried when arrested and again when he was sentenced by Judge Swan.

A prison official said Darnell was so upset about his crime that he voluntarily spent his first six years in prison cleaning septic tanks, one of the most dreaded jobs in the penitentiary.

Darnell was interviewed by the state pardon and parole board five times from 1947 until 1960 when he finally was recommended for a parole, which was approved by Gov. J. Howard Edmondson. He was 67 and had served 30 years.

Prison records showed that Darnell's only correspondence during his prison term had been with a sister who lived in Norwalk, Calif. They wrote each other regularly from 1931 until 1948, when she was killed while riding in a car that was struck by a train.

Darnell's parole was for him to work on a farm in California, where he was to receive board and room, and about $200 a month.

But he didn't want to ride a train to California, a pardon and parole officer said. He took a bus.

Fearless prosecutor successful in oil

When he stepped before a jury or made a political speech, Tulsa oilman and attorney Pat Malloy was a spellbinder.

He became known as one of the most fearless and brilliant prosecutors in the Southwest and after serving two terms as Tulsa's prosecutor, he went into the oil business.

But he probably was best known in later years because of his political activities and for a time was an assistant attorney general in Washington – until a radical idea got him into trouble with his boss.

Born in Iowa in 1885, Malloy came to Tulsa shortly after statehood in 1907, fresh out of law school at the University of Notre Dame. There he had been on the debating team and had served as president of his law class.

Malloy's forensic ability became apparent early in his career when he defeated two longtime well-known lawyers in the 1910 race for county attorney.

During the campaign, the two older lawyers arranged a series of debates between themselves and after both had their say at the first session, the crowd began to leave. Malloy got up, starting speaking and those who were mingling outside in small groups began returning inside to listen.

By the time the third meeting was held, the older lawyers had withdrawn from the debate, leaving Malloy alone with a crowded house – and he was elected.

Malloy served two terms as prosecutor and after making an unsuccessful bid for Congress in 1914 became general counsel for the Constantin Refining Co. and later president of the concern. He became a director of the Western Refiners Association and later its president for 10 years.

Malloy organized Malloy and Co. and was in El Dorado, Ark., where he had oil producing properties, when he died of a heart attack in his sleep on Jan. 31, 1934, at the age of 49.

While he was a prosecutor, Malloy offered oratory so spellbinding that Judge Henry Hudson once threw out one of his convictions because his closing argument was too

Tulsa World archives

Tulsa attorney Pat Malloy was known as a spellbinding orator.

good. The judge ruled that Malloy's eloquence had so influenced the jury that the defendant was convicted in spite of the evidence.

"In all my experience in the criminal courts of the state, I never before heard such a convincing and analytical argument before a jury," the judge said.

The ruling was in the trial of Laura Reuter, who was charged with the May 5, 1912, slaying of her husband, Charles, as he slept in a bedroom across a hall from his wife in the Reuter house in Tulsa. She told police her husband had been killed by a burglar. Neighbors, awakened by screams from Mrs. Reuter, said they had seen a man fleeing.

She testified that she awoke when someone shined a flashlight in her face, and she heard her husband telling someone in his bedroom, "You have got me this time but I will get you yet, damn you." Then, she said, she heard two gunshots, heard someone fall and saw an intruder run out of the house.

Mrs. Reuter was acquitted in a retrial.

Malloy was an early supporter of Franklin Roosevelt in his first presidential race and it was expected that he would be appointed as assistant secretary of the interior. But when he didn't get that job, Attorney General Homer Cummings named him an assistant in charge of criminal prosecutions, thanks to the personal support of FDR.

It wasn't long before Malloy's outspoken habit got him in trouble with his superiors.

Speaking at a meeting of the American Bar Association in Grand Rapids, Mich., in August 1933, Malloy proposed that every law enforcement officer in the country receive a federal commission to provide the coordination needed between local, state and federal officers in their battle against the growing number of kidnappings.

Cummings repudiated the speech after a flood of protests from lawyers and states' rights Democrats. And Malloy resigned and returned to the oil business.

General Hayes: hero of two world wars

An Oklahoma soldier won a Medal of Honor during World War I for riding horses through heavy enemy gunfire and won praise from other generals, including enemy leaders, for his division's action in the mountains of Italy during World War II.

The World War I soldier who became a three-star general was George P. Hays, who graduated from El Reno High School and Oklahoma A & M College, now Oklahoma State University.

Hays, then a first lieutenant, received the nation's highest military award for his action during the second battle of the Marne River in July 1918 after a German artillery shell destroyed telephone communications between Hays' battery and others, including a French unit.

He was talking with an artillery officer on the telephone when a German shell hit an American pit, destroying the telephone switchboard and killing two operators.

Hays immediately volunteered to carry messages to the other batteries to give them coordinates for firing at the enemy and continued for two days, riding horses through heavy enemy fire. His action was "an important factor in checking the advance of the enemy," according to the citation for his Medal of Honor.

"He used seven horses, all of which were killed," Hays' commanding officer wrote in his recommendation for the medal. "Where he found a live horse is a mystery to us all because all of ours were killed almost immediately."

Hays, who was seriously wounded while carrying those messages, received a French Croix de Guerre, a Distinguished Service Cross and a Purple Heart while still in France. He was presented the Medal of Honor two years later by Gen. John J. Pershing.

Hays remained in the Army after the armistice. When World War II began, he was a brigadier general commanding an artillery regiment before being assigned as commander of the 10th Mountain Division, and promoted to major general.

Under Hays' command, the division captured the strategic Riva Ridge, in the northern Apennine Mountains of Italy in February 1945, with minimal casualties because the Germans didn't believe any American troops could climb the ridge – day or night.

National Archives and Records Administration

George P. Hays won the Medal of Honor in World War I and wore general's stars during World War II.

Fifth Army units had failed in three previous attempts to capture Riva Ridge, which would provide a valuable observation position to allow the Yanks to see as far as the Po Valley 20 miles away.

The Germans didn't even post sentries because they thought their position was unreachable. They were wrong. They didn't know about the 10th Mountain Division, which had trained under extreme conditions in the Colorado mountains -- worse, many soldiers said, than conditions in the Apennines.

Soldiers from the 10th climbed the 1,500-foot, almost perpendicular Riva Ridge cliff at night, surprising and driving out the unprepared Germans.

It was a monumental feat by the only U.S. division trained for mountain fighting. Hays' mountain troops also captured Mount Belvedere, another key ridge, the next day but lost about 1,000 soldiers in the operation. It eventually destroyed five German divisions in Italy. Gen. Mark Clark, the commanding general of the 5th Army, called the division's action "one of the most vital and brilliant" in the Italian campaign.

German Field Marshal Albert Kesselring said the division was "outstandingly efficient." At the end of World War II, German officers believed that the 10th Division was a hand-picked elite corps, made up of physically superior soldiers and sports personalities. Two German generals insisted on surrendering only to Gen. Hays because they considered his the best American division.

Hays, born in 1892 in China to missionary parents, spent his youth in El Reno where he graduated from high school in 1912 and taught school for a year before enrolling at Oklahoma A & M. He joined the ROTC and was commissioned a second lieutenant of artillery when he graduated in 1917.

As the war wound down, Hays was promoted to lieutenant general and became the U.S. commissioner of Austria as well as commander of U.S. forces in Austria. He also was commander of the U.S. 6th Division and served as the U.S. representative for the Allied Military Government Coordinating Committee.

Hays retired from the Army in 1953 and died in September 1979 at the age of 87.

Bishop's Alley was Seminole's district of vice

The sleepy village of Seminole became the richest and rowdiest town in the world for several years after an oil well called the No. 1 Fixico came in 1926.

That well marked the beginning of production from the Greater Seminole Field that was so great a statistician wrote: "When the petroleum history of 1927 is written, it will consist largely of one word: Seminole."

It was an accurate description.

Seminole production that year was called the greatest in the history of the world, and by 1936 it was estimated the field had yielded $1 billion worth of oil — in 1936 dollars.

By 1929 the area within a seven-mile radius of Seminole that had 1,100 residents in 1926 had swelled to 65,000 with 34 cafes, 33 filling stations, 41 grocery stores, 14 drugstores, 29 doctors and three hospitals with 68 beds.

Drillers, tool dressers, roustabouts, derrick crews, pipeline layers, truck and taxi drivers and camp followers flocked to Seminole — and a place known as Bishop's Alley.

It was a hell's half-acre where, after grim 12-hour tours on shaky rigs, workers sought relaxation from the nerve-racking job of bringing oil to the surface.

"Bishop's Alley was the carnival midway of the Seminole oil boom," according to a 1967 Oklahoma Today article by David Craighead. "Most who went there knew it existed to fleece them, but in the full flush of the boom, they hardly cared."

It was a place just north of town where bootleggers and speak-easies flourished amid a row of gambling joints and shack dance halls filled with girls. The area was named for its promoter, William Bishop, a former minister who was the father of County Attorney Homer Bishop.

Until Bishop's Alley was annexed by the city in late 1929 to tame it, the only law in the red-light district was administered by Justice of the Peace Tom Heath and his deputies, who established an office in a frame shack at the top of the hill leading from Bishop's Alley.

They watched as men went to the alley sober and ar-

Oklahoma Historical Society

During the oil boom of 1926, Seminole exploded in size.

rested them for disorderly conduct as they headed back to town well-stewed.

The justice and his deputies split the fines.

There was no jail, so prisoners were chained together to await justice.

When prostitutes were arrested, they were fined $20.

But if one had only half that amount, she would be released to get the rest, according to Craighead's article.

Female whiskey peddlers such as Goldie Carter were always ready to take a driller's last dollar for a drink of washtub moonshine. But Carter would just as quickly stake a down-and-out roustabout to the price of ham and eggs.

A Daily Oklahoman reporter wrote a series of articles about Bishop's Alley after spending a few weeks there investigating it in 1928. He reported that the liquor sellers told him "there ain't nothing to be afraid of here."

"We see the law coming once or twice a week, and we know that we will have to buy a receipt for disorderly conduct and pay $20 for it." That charge apparently was used for many different offenses.

The Oklahoman's series angered Seminole businessmen, who collected as many copies of the newspaper as they could find, burned them in a bonfire and threatened to boycott the newspaper.

After Bishop's Alley was annexed, Police Chief Jake Sims — a small, soft-spoken man who seldom carried a gun but was a master of persuasion — and his officers tamed the area.

He later became chief of the Oklahoma Crime Bureau and died in 1966 at age 75.

Bishop's Alley is gone, but as long as oilmen talk about Seminole oil, it will be remembered.

It's as much a part of the city's story as the black gold that flowed from the ground.

Few of the 1920s-era oil field workers are alive. But those who are and younger workers who have heard the stories probably still talk about the alley.

Gautt broke color barrier in OU football

Fullback Prentice Gautt won a lot of honors as the fullback for the University of Oklahoma's 1957-59 football teams: All-Big Eight running back, OU's leading rusher in 1958 and 1959, most valuable player in the 1959 Orange Bowl.

He was called the "best player on the field" by the Miami Herald the morning after OU defeated Syracuse 21-6 in the Orange Bowl on Jan. 1, 1959.

In 1996, the Big 12 began a graduate scholarship named for him, and after his sudden death in March 2005 at the age of 67, Gautt was named the winner of the Outstanding Contribution to Amateur Football Award presented by the National Football Foundation and College Hall of Fame.

But his accomplishments on the playing field were less significant than those as an integration pioneer. In his refined manner, Gautt did more for integration than an army of activists.

Gautt became the first black to play football for OU when he enrolled as a freshman, thanks to financing by a group of Oklahoma City black doctors and pharmacists. He wanted to attend college as close to home as possible "because my mom was very ill – she died two years later."

By October, Coach Bud Wilkinson put Gautt on scholarship after he proved he was capable of playing. The money he had received from the OKC group was given to another black student, Wallace Johnson, who had been a classmate of Gautt and played for Wilkinson in 1961.

Integration was a delicate matter in 1956. OU had admitted some black students on a nonsegregated basis in 1950 and final restrictions on undergraduate enrollment had been lifted after the 1954-55 academic year. But there had never been a black athlete at OU.

It was the second color barrier that Gautt had broken. He had attended all-black Douglass High School in Oklahoma City and became the first black all-state football player. When he played in the all-state game in 1956, he scored twice and was named the outstanding player.

Gautt had played in the Douglass band and went out for football only because a coach told him that not many colleges offered scholarships for band members.

"I had lived a very sheltered life," Gautt told a Tulsa World reporter in 1976. "I attended an all-black school and was not prepared for what was involved. Some blacks had gone to OU the year before to play football but it was not a happy experience and they quit. But (Coach Wilkinson) tried to prepare me for what I would experience."

Tulsa World archives

Prentice Gautt integrated the University of Oklahoma football team and lived a life of quiet dignity.

While Wilkinson shielded Gautt from the hate mail and taunts to the best of his ability, discrimination could not completely be avoided. Several players quit the OU squad and Gautt was subjected to taunts and threats of physical violence. Gautt recalled that his first bad experience at OU was when he walked across campus to a drug store for a soft drink but couldn't get service.

"I was a student. I didn't think I would experience anything negative in the campus area," he said.

Another flagrant discrimination came after his freshman team's game against the University of Tulsa in Tulsa. The team had post-game reservations at Bishop's downtown restaurant. But when the team walked in, a restaurant official said the team would be welcome but not Gautt. The players and coaches walked out.

"That was the saddest feeling I ever had," Gautt said later.

But that sad feeling soon turned to joy when the team stopped at a restaurant near the Turner Turnpike gate "and they served us a great chicken dinner, and we had a great time. One second I had been extremely hurt and the next second it was the most joyful moment I'd ever known."

Gautt's roommate on road trips was white halfback Jakie Sandefer of Abilene, Texas, who once said "I didn't treat Prentice any different than I'd treat anyone else, and he didn't want any favors. He was a very special person. He was the perfect gentleman. He taught all of us something."

In introducing Gautt at his 2000 induction into the Oklahoma Sports Hall of Fame, Sandefer said "Was he different? Yeah, he had more class than the rest of us. And he was smarter than the rest of us."

During his senior year, Gautt was named to the academic All-American team and eventually earned master's and doctorate degrees in psychology.

He played professionally with the Cleveland Browns and the St. Louis Cardinals before becoming the first black football assistant coach in the Big Eight Conference at Missouri in 1968.

In 1979, he became the assistant commissioner of the Big Eight. When the conference expanded in 1996, Gautt took the job as associate commissioner of the Big 12, the position he held when he died.

OU dedicated the athletic study hall as the Dr. Prentice Gautt Academic Study Center in 1999, and he received an honorary doctorate from OU in May 2003.

Gilcrease left his mark with art

Tulsa taxpayers voted 3-1 to approve a $2.25 million bond issue in 1954 to acquire a gift worth $14 million – the Gilcrease Institute of American History and Art.

It was a bargain gift from oilman Thomas Gilcrease, who established the museum in 1942 on land near his house northwest of the city in Osage County.

He had devoted more than 35 years to collecting things that told the story of America from prehistoric times forward with special emphasis on the American Indian and the development of the western United States.

Gilcrease also donated half of the income from his East Texas oil properties for maintenance and operation of the museum in return for taxpayers' approval of the bond issue. Four years later, he gave the city the museum building and the 13½-acre tract where it stands.

The bond issue was necessary to pay off the pressing debts of the institute that was hit by financial trouble in the 1950s and was in danger of being moved out of Tulsa. There were efforts to move it to Texas, Claremore alongside the Will Rogers Memorial, North Carolina, Oklahoma City and the University of Oklahoma in Norman.

"It makes me very happy that Tulsans realized what the city has in the way of a historical collection in the museum," Gilcrease said after the election. "This collection will grow more valuable as time goes on and will attract more and more people to Tulsa."

He said adding the collection to the city's assets made him feel that "I have achieved my life's goal."

A Tulsa World editorial called the museum "a place where one may learn more of the story of the American Indian and the development of the West in a matter of hours than he could in many weeks anywhere else in the world."

Management of the museum is scheduled to be transferred July 1, 2008, to the University of Tulsa under a contract between city and TU. The city will retain ownership of the museum and its 400,000 items.

Since becoming city property, the museum has been operated by the city, the Gilcrease Museum Association and the Gilcrease Trust. A report issued in 2007 indicated that the museum's management structure was "dysfunctional" – with the potential to jeopardize the priceless collection.

Under the agreement, TU will form a Gilcrease Advisory Board to assist with fundraising and provide advice. The university would appoint the board's members.

Gilcrease bought his first painting, an oil titled "Rural Courtship," in 1912 for $1,500. An article in a 1955 national

Tulsa World archives

Thomas Gilcrease made a fortune in oil, but is best remembered for the art collection he built. That collection is the foundation for Tulsa's Gilcrease Museum.

magazine said Gilcrease "probably wouldn't look twice if a dealer showed him the painting today" but that he kept it on his living room wall out of sentiment.

But Gilcrease told a Tulsa World reporter that he admired the artist for capturing so realistically the vivid setting and poignant mood of a beautiful fall day and two young people in love.

Gilcrease went to Europe in 1925 as a diversion after building a fortune from his oil interests. He returned 14 months later because a business partner was dying. During that trip, he loaded himself down with souvenirs but few were of museum quality.

He made many more trips to Europe, collecting in earnest. After exploring other cultures, he decided to develop a museum that would preserve and display the cultural heritage of the frontier and American Indian life. By 1942, when he founded the museum, he had objects stored in Texas, California, New York, Europe and Tulsa.

The collection was put on public view in temporary quarters until the museum opened in 1949. American Indian workmen built the museum in the shape of an Indian long house. It was constructed of sandstone quarried from the nearby Osage Hills.

Born in Robilene, La., Gilcrease came to Oklahoma with his family in 1895 to take advantage of 160-acre allotments in the Creek Nation. The family settled at Twin Mounds, near Eufaula, where he attended a one-room school. In 1904, the family moved to nearby Weakala where his father operated a general store.

Gilcrease's 160-acre allotment was in the rich Glenn Pool and by 1917 the tract had 32 producing oil wells. He used his royalties to attend Bacone Indian College and Kansas Teachers College and to buy more farm land.

He soon was trading in oil leasing and drilling wells in an area southwest of Tulsa. By the mid-1920s, he was wealthy.

Shortly after returning from his European trip in 1926, he married Miss America, Norma Smallwood, whom he divorced in 1934. Gilcrease left only a small personal estate when he died May 6, 1962, at the age of 72. He had donated nearly everything and his will left his remaining assets to the Gilcrease Foundation. There was some question whether he even had enough to require probate of the will.

The donation of the museum helped Gilcrease fulfill his belief "that a man should leave some sort of track."

Gilcrease's track was his collection of rare documents, books, artifacts, paintings and sculptures.

'Red Fern' author burned manuscripts

Wilson Rawls, who became a best-selling author after he burned his manuscript and rewrote it, didn't care much for books when he was growing up on a farm on his mother's Cherokee allotment near Scraper in Cherokee County.

"We didn't even have a school house," he said in 1974. His mother taught Rawls and his five sisters the three "R's" on a small blackboard and read to them at night from books sent to the family by his grandmother who, with her husband, operated the only store in Scraper.

To improve their reading skills, the children were required to read the books back to their mother two pages at a time. But Rawls wasn't interested in what he considered "girl books." His only interests were fishing and hunting.

That attitude changed after Jack London's "Call of the Wild" arrived when Rawls was 10 and his mother read the story to him and his sisters. From that day on, he carried the book with him, reading it over and over and vowed he would be a writer.

He wanted to tell the story of a boy and his dog. And that's what he did in a book titled "Where the Red Fern Grows," a story about a country boy who finds and trains two hunting dogs. It was the most-read book for fourth through eighth grades in 1974 and was adapted as a movie in 1974 and 2003. His book was used in several universities as a model for writing children's literature.

But the road to successful author wasn't simple. Because he'd had little formal education – he went to school for a year in Tahlequah when he was 15 and for another six months in Muskogee – he decided it was more practical to follow in his father's footsteps as a carpenter.

During the Depression years of the 1930s he bummed around the country, working a few days at a time – harvesting hay or doing other farm chores. He built derricks and bunk houses for oil companies around the country and in South America.

When World War II started, he and other carpenters were pressed into service building barracks and hospitals for military units.

But he didn't forget his vow to become a writer. While he was bumming around the country and working for the

Tulsa World archives

Author Wilson Rawls, seen here in Tulsa in 1976 for an autographing party with his wife, Sophie, vowed to become a writer after reading Jack London's "Call of the Wild" as a boy. "Where the Red Fern Grows" was Rawls' first book.

government during the war, Rawls wrote on what paper he could find and later on tablets after a day's work. Sometimes he put down his words by the light of hobo town campfires or even between rides while hitchhiking around the country.

By the time he had fallen in love and decided to get married, Rawls had completed five manuscripts, including "Red Fern." He kept the manuscripts locked in a trunk at his parents' Albuquerque home. He had never shown them to anyone.

The week before the wedding, Rawls visited his family, retrieved the manuscripts and burned them all.

"My spelling was terrible and my punctuation was practically zero. I didn't want my wife to know I was that bad," he explained to a Tulsa World reporter.

Shortly after the wedding, Rawls confessed to his wife, Sophie, that his great ambition was to be a writer but that he had burned all of his manuscripts in shame.

"If you want to do it that badly," she told him, "quit work and start writing. I can spell and punctuate and type."

The first work he rewrote was the "Red Fern" book; he completed it in 1961. It was first serialized in the Saturday Evening Post and then published in hardback by Doubleday, which first promoted it as adult fiction. Rawls said he had given up on the book but suddenly it caught the public's interest and soon became a movie.

His second and final book was "The Summer of the Monkeys," about a boy who tried to catch monkeys that had escaped from a carnival. It appeared in 1976 and won the William Allen White Children's Book Award and the Oklahoma Library Association's Sequoyah Children's Book Award.

After his second book was published, Rawls, who died in 1984 at the age of 71, spent much of his time visiting schools to encourage students to read and write.

"All I ever wanted was the satisfaction of writing and having it accepted," Rawls told a reporter on one of his last visits to Tulsa. "I was never interested in fame or in more than enough money to buy a fish pole now and then.

"The only trouble is," he added, "now I don't have time to fish."

From suicide, she built chart-topper

A small photograph in a Florida newspaper of a man who had committed suicide and a remark by a former Oklahoman helped propel Elvis Presley to fame in the 1950s.

The picture in the Jacksonville Journal and the remark by Mae Boren Axton resulted in the song "Heartbreak Hotel." Written by Axton and her long-time friend Tommy Durden, it became Presley's first chart-topper.

The caption under the photo asked "Can you identify this man?" He had torn identification marks from his clothing and had left a note that said, "I walk a lonely street."

Axton said she told Durden: "Everyone has someone who cares. When someone sees this there is going to be a lot of heartbreak, so let's put a heartbreak hotel at the end of this lonely street."

And 22 minutes later, the song was on tape. She called Presley, told him she had his first million-seller and asked him to meet her in Nashville, she told a Tulsa World reporter in 1979.

Axton said she had promised Presley a few years earlier that she would write a million-selling song for him. She had met Presley in 1953, when she got the then-unknown singer, who was 18, a job on the show of Col. Tom Parker, for whom she was a promoter.

"Elvis was so sweet, and I fell in love with him, long hair and all," she said later.

Axton considered herself an Oklahoman, although she was born in 1914 in Bardwell, Texas. As a child, she lived in Lawton, Grandfield, Choctaw and Roff, where she graduated from high school. She graduated from East Central University and later took a creative writing course at the University of Oklahoma and worked on a master's degree in literature at Oklahoma A&M College (now Oklahoma State University).

She taught first through fourth grades and English and

Tulsa World archives

Mae Boren Axton, who graduated from high school in Roff, later co-wrote "Heartbreak Hotel" for Elvis Presley.

music for fifth through eighth grades as a teenager in a two-room school in southwestern Oklahoma. The job included pumping water and chopping firewood. She taught high school at Frederick before she moved on to other places – Las Vegas, Hollywood and Florida – for a variety of jobs.

She handled publicity for Dolly Parton for a year and worked for Dennis Weaver, Jerry Reed, Crystal Gayle, Kenny Rogers and other stars.

Her talents were not limited to songwriting. She spent several weeks writing for soap operas in New York City but quit because she did not want to live there. She also wrote several books, including "Country Singers As I Know Them," told in the first person and filled with photos of herself and celebrities.

One of Axton's brothers was the late Lyle Boren, who represented Oklahoma's 4th District in Congress from 1937 to 1947. She was the aunt of OU President David Boren, a former Oklahoma governor and U.S. senator.

She wrote the "Clean Sweep" campaign song that helped David Boren win election as the governor in 1974.

One of her sons was Hoyt Axton, a country music singer and songwriter who died in 1999, two years after his mother's death at age 82 in 1997.

Axton was inducted into the Songwriters Hall of Fame in New York City, where the pencil version of "Hotel" hangs. She also was inducted into the Oklahoma Women's Hall of Fame in 1985.

She wrote songs for Patsy Cline, Faron Young, Conway Twitty, Hank Snow and many other country singers. She played a part in the early careers of Parton, Willie Nelson, Mel Tills and others.

But "Heartbreak Hotel" was her greatest claim to fame. It was Presley's first single for RCA Records and was No. 1 in Billboard Magazine's list for eight weeks.

Sand Springs founder helped others

Charles Page was nearly broke when he arrived in Tulsa in 1903. He'd made fortunes and lost them a couple of times.

And now, he had invested most of his money in a piece of land where he wanted to drill an oil well but oldtimers had told him "everybody 'round here knows that tract ain't no good."

In 1889 after selling the real estate and gold and silver mining interests he had accumulated, Page began drilling for oil.

His first two wells were in Colorado, but both were dry holes. They were followed by dry holes in Michigan, in the Seminole and Chandler areas and even at Oakhurst. None of his wildcats went deep enough.

But he finally struck oil in what is known as the Taneha Field. He organized the Victor Oil and Gas Co., sold that property and turned his attention to what was known as North Glenn Pool, where several gas wells were brought in. By 1908, Page had a substantial income.

He later gained control of the famous and prolific Tommy Atkins oil lease through litigation that went to the Supreme Court, and he became one of the three richest men in Oklahoma with a fortune estimated at $20 million plus thousands of acres of land in or near the future town of Sand Springs and Tulsa.

By the time of his death in 1926 at the age of 64, it was estimated that his wealth had increased by at least $10 million. He had established the city of Sand Springs and what he termed his "partnership with God," several institutions to take care of widows and orphans as part of the Sand Springs Home Interests.

Page began the career that the world has heard of in 1908 when he had four men clear brush and briars from a hill where the Creek Indians had long maintained a campground and had a small frame house put up.

A spring under the hill threw up sand so the site became known as Sand Springs, the name given the town he founded in 1910.

The small frame building first housed a widow and her five children, the latter staying on after their mother died. The home gained residents rapidly, and then Page opened a widows' colony where widows could live in small cottages with their children.

Page believed in keeping families together in a happy home life, and he tried to do that with his orphans home

Tulsa World archives

Charles Page, who made a fortune from his oil fields in Oklahoma at the turn of the century, founded the town of Sand Springs in 1910.

and his widows' colony. He also financed college educations for any of the children who had the desire. He set up a bank, a railroad between Tulsa and Sand Springs, a dairy, a water system at Shell Creek and other interests, all aimed at taking care of the widows and orphans.

Page also tried to interest Tulsa in buying water from his Shell Creek facility and waged a newspaper battle with Tulsa World editor and publisher Eugene Lorton, who was promoting Spavinaw Lake as a source of water.

Page owned the Tulsa Democrat from 1915 until 1919 when he sold it to Richard Lloyd Jones, who changed its name to The Tulsa Tribune.

The editorial battle didn't end until Tulsans approved a bond issue to pipe water from Spavinaw, first in 1919 and again in 1921.

Never one to spend much on himself, Page maintained a plain office on the second floor of the Sand Springs State Bank that many considered inadequate for a man who transacted business involving millions. But it was all he wanted.

Page was born in Wisconsin in 1860, the seventh in a lumber mill worker's family of eight children.

His school days ended at the age of 11 after his father died and he took a job as a telegraph messenger to support his mother. In rapid succession, he became a telegraph operator, a gold miner, a timber cruiser in Colorado and Michigan, and, before he was 21, police chief of Ashland, Wis.

Page told about one night in Seattle when he was jobless, penniless, supperless and wondering where to go and what to do.

That's when he met a young woman in a Salvation Army uniform jingling a tambourine before him with an invitation to give. He told her that he had nothing, no job, no place to sleep and no supper.

"Take a dollar out of this," she told him. She directed him to a place he could get supper, bed and breakfast, and help in finding a job. Then she preached to him: "When you get a job and have a dollar to spare, put the dollar back and then tithe."

He frequently gave double or more than one-tenth.

Page was known as a person who would give for almost any worthy cause, so people who needed help often were told "Go see Charlie Page. He will help you."

Author reveals invisibility to the world

Black author Ralph Waldo Ellison, whose book "Invisible Man" is considered an American literary classic, grew up in poverty in Oklahoma City and had to hop freight trains to get to Tuskegee Institute in Alabama for an education.

His "Invisible Man," about an unnamed black man who suffers humiliation in the South and in the North, identified America as a patchwork of shifting ideologies and identities, a great debate among the invisibles. It won the National Book Award in 1953 and was voted the most distinguished novel published in the preceding 20 years in a 1965 poll of 200 authors, critics and editors.

Ellison, named after essayist Ralph Waldo Emerson, was reared in a three-room "shotgun" house in an Oklahoma City area known as Sandtown by his widowed mother who worked as a domestic after her husband died when the future author was 3.

Ellison's parents moved to Oklahoma from the Deep South, hoping the new state would be relatively untainted by segregation. His father was a self-taught man who wanted his son to be a poet and named his son after Emerson. His mother was an early activist who campaigned against racism.

Ellison's humble beginning served as a source of pride and gave him dignity he would carry for the rest of his life, said high school classmate Darlene McLeod at a memorial service for the author at the Ralph Ellison Library in northeast Oklahoma City after he died in 1994 at 80.

"His mind was on justice. His heart was cemented in compassion," said civil rights activist Clara Luper.

By the time he had finished high school, longtime friend Jimmy Stewart recalled, he was too impoverished to go to

Tulsa World archives

Ralph Ellison, author of "Invisible Man," grew up in poverty in Oklahoma City, but went on to international fame.

college. He wrote to the Tuskegee Institute about his situation and was told if he could get there, he would be admitted.

That's when cab driver Charlie Miller taught Ellison how to hobo and Ellison hopped freight trains all the way from Oklahoma City to Tuskegee where he studied music composition, Stewart said.

After leaving Tuskegee in 1936, Ellison went to New York City where he began writing short stories, articles, reviews and criticism that appeared in literary magazines and anthologies. After serving in the Merchant Marine during World War II, Ellison won a grant that helped him concentrate on the "Invisible Man."

He had nearly finished a second novel when it was destroyed in a 1967 fire. He spent the next 25 years in vain trying to re-create it.

Ellison was awarded the Presidential Medal of Freedom, the nation's highest civilian award, in 1969. He was honored by the French government with its Chevalier de l'Ordre Artes et Lettres award the same year. Ellison's life was the subject of an "American Masters" documentary on PBS in 2002, marking the 50th anniversary of his "Invisible Man."

"One of the most regrettable things that I will carry the rest of my life is the fact that Oklahoma failed to recognize Ralph Ellison," Stewart said at Ellison's memorial service.

"The fact that he was one of the few Americans who won European awards and everything else. There's been two presidents who have recognized him with presidential citations."

Ellison was inducted into the Oklahoma Hall of Fame in 2002, eight years after his death.

City bypass spawned suit, investigations

Tulsa's busiest highway, which connects the Turner and Will Rogers Turnpikes, was routed around the city as a compromise between two groups – those who wanted a Tulsa bypass and those who wanted an expressway through the city.

The bypass faction won the bitter argument, and the highway was plotted around the city as the 51st Street Bypass in 1948, before the Turner Turnpike had been funded and long before the Will Rogers Turnpike was even a line on a map.

It became known as the U.S. 66 Bypass or 51st Street Bypass – sometimes the 51st Street-U.S. 66 Bypass – and was later officially named the Skelly Bypass in honor of the oilman W.G. Skelly.

It became a segment of Interstate 44 when the U.S. interstate highway system was developed.

Today, the U.S. 66 designation is gone, little of the highway is on 51st Street and it doesn't bypass anything – it's more like an expressway through central Tulsa, but it's still part of I-44 and along Skelly Drive.

And the highway that was expected to carry about 24,000 vehicles per day is severely inadequate for its current daily traffic of more than 80,000 vehicles.

Preliminary work is under way to widen the highway from the Arkansas River to Yale Avenue. The project, which is planned for completion in 2011, will cost about $550 million.

Its proposed route resulted in a lawsuit that went to the Oklahoma Supreme Court, and its construction was investigated by a grand jury and by a congressional subcommittee in 1960, both of which dug holes in the road's surface to check its quality.

Backers of the urban expressway in the 1948 dispute argued that surveys showed that 85 percent of all vehicles crossing the Tulsa city limits were headed into the city, not around it. The bypass people believed that taking traffic off city streets would relieve congestion and be cheaper.

The dispute was a big issue in the 1948 mayoral victory of Roy Lundy, a Democrat who favored the bypass, over the incumbent, Lee Price, a Republican. Two years later, city and county voters approved bond issues to buy rights of way for the 51st Street Bridge access road and the bypass, but the project was delayed because property owners were upset by a routing change.

Beryl Ford collection

The Interstate 44 crossing of Yale Avenue, today a center of commercial activity, was pretty bare in 1959.

Those along the original alignment – from the river along 51st Street to Memorial Drive and then north to U.S. 66 at 11th Street – were upset when it was changed to the present alignment because they had expected to sell their land at a profit. Property owners along the new route were upset as well because they hadn't expected to be affected.

Some property owners filed a lawsuit that delayed the project.

The case ended in 1954 when the Oklahoma Supreme Court ruled in favor of the new routing. The highway finally opened Nov. 21, 1958, after 10 years of planning and construction that cost $15 million, a hefty sum then.

A grand jury investigated allegations that bypass contractors had used substandard material. The grand jury indicted the three principals of Layman and Sons Construction Co., which built a segment of the highway, on a charge of defrauding the state of $24,156. A court dismissed the charge against A.H. Layman Jr. on a venue issue and the state dropped the charges against his father, A.H. Layman, and brother, T.C. Layman.

Meanwhile, a state-federal task force of road experts reported that it had found no evidence of any fraud, graft, or criminality on the part of anyone in the construction of the bypass.

The state and federal governments "received their full money's worth in materials and workmanship in this bypass," the 205-page report by Oklahoma Highway Director Lee Washbourne concluded.

"The only final conclusion the committee could reach regarding this road was that the people building it and the people supervising it probably did as well as could be expected at the time and under the circumstances," the report said, noting that the road had been built in a "crash program."

About 100 core samples of the highway and its sub base were taken by an engineer for the grand jury and an additional 20 to 25 samples were taken later by federal engineers during an investigation by a House Public Works subcommittee on federal aid highway programs.

As a result of the inquiry, the Bureau of Public Roads established new procedures for inspections that states would have to pass before they could receive federal reimbursement for highway construction.

Tulsa was home to fantastic car shows

A powerful Packard automobile featuring the "finest motor ever built" was the hit of the third annual Tulsa Automobile Show in 1919 that had on display "everything in the motor car line worth while."

That Packard was powered by a 12-cylinder 450-horsepower liberty engine similar to the engine Packard had developed to power U.S. Army airplanes during World War I. It was called a great American achievement in a Tulsa World story about the show.

The Packard Motor Car Co., which built luxury cars from 1899 until 1958, had used sheet steel water jackets wrapped around its steel cylinders to cool the engines and solved for the government the problem of how to weld the thinner steel of the water jackets to the thicker steel of the cylinders. When the United States entered the war, Packard turned over all of its designs, engineering talent and production facilities to the government.

The 1919 Packard was just one of the popular automobiles that were displayed at that show at the Universal Motor Co. plant, Main and Cameron streets, that you may never have heard of – cars such as Maxwell, Franklin, Hupmobile, Velie, Reo, Essex, Chandler Six, Studebaker, Texan, Detroit Electric and the Raush & Lang Electric.

Some readers may recognize the Maxwell as the brand of car driven by comedian Jack Benny and crossword puzzle workers will recognize the Reo.

Some brands that are still sold today also were shown – Ford, Buick and Cadillac.

The Maxwell, advertised as the "World's Greatest Motor Car Value," was available for $1,200. It was a "lightweight economical car that will stand up under the most rigid conditions." It also was advertised as the car that would get the most miles per gallon and the most miles on tires.

The Franklin featured an electric primer to make starting easier in cold weather and a starting device controlled by an ignition switch. Most cars at that time were started by someone turning a crank at the front of the engine.

Oklahomans have always loved cars, and they flocked to the 1919 show as they had to the first two in 1917 and 1918,

Tulsa World archives

This Tulsa World ad for Reo automobiles ran in a special Automobile Show section on Feb. 2, 1919. Automobile shows were a regular event in Tulsa between World War I and World War II.

which were held at Convention Hall, which proved too small.

Additional car shows were held in later years and by 1937 the Tulsa World had taken over the show and moved it to the World's Magic Empire Express Building in the unit block of both North Main Street and North Boulder Avenue with entrances on both.

In opening the show, Mayor T.A. Penney recalled that when he came to Tulsa in 1906 there were only three cars in the city. And only three blocks of hard surface streets existed.

That year's car show wasn't just a chance to look at the 1938 models. Some companies showed cut-away models with engineers to explain the inner workings of the automobiles. Movies also showed visitors the insides of automobile factories as the cars moved through assembly lines.

Many of the automobile brands that had been seen in the 1919 show had disappeared, but there were new brands on display and more than 1,000 people showed up for opening day. And again, many of the brands displayed at that show are names that are not familiar to most today – Graham, Hudson, Nash, Terraplane, LaSalle, Lincoln Zepher, Willys.

Those brands were joined by Buick, Cadillac, Chevrolet, Chrysler, Dodge, Ford, Oldsmobile, Packard, Pontiac and Plymouth.

The final car show probably was in November 1940, when 1941 models were displayed. It had become more obvious that the United States would be drawn into World War II.

There probably weren't enough 1942 models to hold a show. Automobile manufacturing plants had started producing vehicles for the military services for World War II.

Government restrictions on manufacturing of consumer goods severely limited production of 1942 automobiles across the board. Manufacturers were producing parts for tanks, antiaircraft cannons and military aircraft and didn't produce new automobile models until after the war ended in August 1945.

There's no record in Tulsa World files of any automobile shows after the war.

Graham always fought for conservation

Gid Graham, a pioneer county commissioner and state senator, was Oklahoma's foremost crusader for the protection of wildlife and plant life. He even left a conservation message to be read at his funeral.

In his latter years, Graham and his wife sent 350 letters a week to newspaper editors promoting conservation of things of the forest, field and stream and criticizing high government spending.

Just before his 83rd birthday in 1950, he sent a letter to editors that he said might be his last. "I'm down with heart trouble but I'm still fighting to conserve wildlife," he wrote.

"Old age overtakes us all. It is silent and deadly. We don't appreciate life fully until we are stricken," he told a reporter. He died three weeks later on Feb. 10 while writing about conservation at his old roll-top desk at his home in Collinsville.

"My school career was very limited," he once said. "The prairies, forests and fields and creatures which lived there were my books. I read by oil lamp. I am a coal oil graduate."

But his lack of formal education didn't hamper his crusade.

As chairman of the Oklahoma Game and Fish Commission in 1932, Graham wrote most of the state's game laws, many of which are still the law in Oklahoma. He toured the state speaking to chambers of commerce and high school students about his life-long crusade to preserve wildlife.

Born Gideon W. Graham in 1867 near San Saba Peak on the Colorado River in Texas, he was married at 19. He came to Oklahoma in 1888, settling in the Grand River hills northeast of Wagoner. His only capital was his horse. He founded a ranch south of Claremore on the Verdigris River in 1900 and raised cattle, horses, hogs, Angora goats and deer.

Graham's interest in conservation came from his Cherokee heritage. The Cherokees had conservation laws when they came to this region, he once explained. It was a tribal offense to cut down pecan trees or to slaughter wild game needlessly.

Two years after Graham's wife died in 1925, he married Edith Wymer, who learned shorthand after the age of 50 so she could help Graham with his writing. Graham wrote a

Tulsa World archives

Gid Graham fought to keep nature in a pristine condition and spent many of his final days elaborately planning his own funeral.

family history as well as a book, "Animal Outlaws," and hundreds of pamphlets about wildlife.

He frequently wrote against high government spending and in opposition to damming the nation's streams to form artificial lakes. In his mind, there was no quicker way to destroy the beauties of nature than to build artificial lakes.

Graham was elected as one of Rogers County's first county commissioners in 1907 and four years later was elected to the state Senate from the Rogers-Nowata County district.

Graham had been preparing for his death since his 75th birthday in 1942. He wrote specific plans for his funeral and helped build his own casket, which he kept in the garage. He chose a grave site at the top of a limestone mound on a 15-acre plot "as my burial place and a monument to my life.

"Here is where my wife and I shall take our last long sleep," he once said. "Here is where the cattle graze, birds sing and coyotes play."

The mound, overlooking the birthplace of Will Rogers near Oologah, is about the height of a seven-story building. Tulsa's tall buildings can be seen on a clear day and the Arkansas River appears as a ribbon.

Graham supervised the blasting required to create crypts for himself and his wife in the solid rock. He recognized the difficulty in hauling the caskets up the steep mound, so he constructed a special sled attached to a winch that would be used to pull, first, his casket and later that of his wife to the top.

Many of the 1,000 mourners who attended his funeral didn't climb to the grave site because of the steepness and a heavy rain that began during the service.

Graham's hour-long funeral in the Collinsville High School auditorium ended with Supreme Court Justice N.B. Johnson reading "My Last Appeal" that the conservationist had written with instructions that it be read at his funeral. Copies were distributed to those who attended.

That message stressed the value of various birds, animals and forests and said the lives of animals and birds were ending "amid the roar of guns, the grip of talons or torn by fangs.

"I beg you to have mercy and help save them. We owe this to the children."

Coleman found her wings in France

Bessie Coleman couldn't learn to fly in America because of her color so she learned French, went to France, took flying lessons and became the first black American to earn a pilot's license.

In spite of a relatively short career, Coleman, known as "Queen Bess" or "Brave Bessie," received many posthumous honors long after her death in 1926 while preparing for her part in an air show.

A road near Chicago's O'Hare Airport was named Bessie Coleman Drive in 1990, and Chicago celebrated Bessie Coleman Day in 1992. The U.S. Postal Department issued a Bessie Coleman stamp in 1995. She was inducted into the Women's Aviation Hall of Fame in 1995 and into the Texas Aviation Hall of Fame in 2000.

She wasn't really an Oklahoman but Coleman had strong ties to the Sooner state and some of her relatives still live in Tulsa.

Born in Atlanta, Texas, in 1892, Coleman was the 10th of 13 children of a black mother and part black, Cherokee and Choctaw father. After working in Texas, her father returned to Indian Territory in 1901 because he believed he could make a better living here because of the racial barriers that existed in Texas.

But Coleman and her sisters remained in Waxahachie, Texas, with their mother, Susan. Coleman grew up picking cotton, doing laundry and attending a one-room country school.

After finishing all eight grades, she used her meager savings to pay for one term at the Oklahoma Colored Agricultural and Normal School at Langston in 1910 and that's where she first had the dream of flying after reading about the Wright Brothers and Harriet Quimby, a female pilot.

For the next few years, Coleman worked as a manicurist in Chicago while learning French at a local language school in preparation for attending a French flying school. In France, she completed a 10-month course in seven months and became the first licensed black pilot in the U.S.

Tulsa World archives

Bessie Coleman, who had strong ties to Oklahoma, was the first black American to earn a pilot's license.

She toured the country for five years, performing daredevil stunts in air shows and trying to raise money to open her own flying school. Scheduled to perform in an air show on May 1, 1926, in Jacksonville, Fla., she and her mechanic took a test flight in an airplane she had just bought.

While the mechanic was at the controls, Coleman sat in the other seat and wasn't wearing a seat belt so she could look over the cockpit edge to examine the terrain in preparation for a parachute jump the next day.

The plane suddenly went into a tailspin and flipped upside down, throwing Coleman out of the cockpit and causing her to somersault end over end until she hit the ground, breaking nearly every bone in her body. The plane crashed nearby, killing the pilot.

An investigation revealed a faulty mechanism that caused the plane's controls to jam, according to one report. But Coleman's sister and others believed the plane was sabotaged by jealous rivals. Another source said a wrench was found in the gearbox.

Former black astronaut Mae Jemison paid tribute to Coleman in an afterword to Doris Rich's 1993 book, "Queen Bess: Daredevil Aviator."

She wrote:

"I point to Bessie Coleman and say without hesitation that here is a woman, a being, who exemplifies and serves as a model to all humanity: the very definition of strength, dignity, courage, integrity and beauty. It looks like a good day for flying."

"Most African-Americans don't know her story," Coleman's grand-niece Jilda Motley of Tulsa told a Tulsa World reporter in 1993. "We are going to do everything we can to change that.

"My goal is for Aunt Bessie's story to become a part of Tulsa's and Oklahoma's educational curriculum.

"I think Aunt Bessie's story can help show our youngsters that they can do anything in life they want to if they work hard enough."

Judge survived bombing but others die

Tulsa County District Court Judge Fred S. Nelson was critically injured when a bomb exploded in his car as he was starting it to drive to his polling place Aug. 25, 1970, the day of the primary election.

The investigation of the bombing led to the murders of two witnesses who testified before a grand jury about the explosion.

The only motive ever suggested for the bombing was to get Nelson, a Republican, out of the way so Charles Pope, a Democrat, could win his judicial seat in the general election.

The slain witnesses were Cleo Epps, the "Bootleg Queen," who disappeared in November 1970, and Arles Delbert Self, who was killed in March 1971. Epps wore a disguise during her testimony and Self remained hidden in a judge's chambers until his appearance before the panel.

Albert McDonald and Tom Lester Pugh, both of Tulsa, were charged in the bombing but never tried for the crime. They were believed to be members of a loose-knit group of outlaws known as the Dixie Mafia.

Epps had told a police officer that McDonald and Pugh got dynamite for the bomb from her farm near Sapulpa.

"I never dreamed they'd do something like that," she sobbed to the detective, adding her concern that Nelson's daughter could have been in the car with him when the bomb exploded.

Pope, a former state legislator, had represented McDonald and Pugh in the past. Apparently some believed that he would be a friend on the bench if he were elected.

Nelson received 70 percent of the vote in the Republican primary election, returned to the bench six weeks after the bombing and defeated Pope in the general election.

Tulsa World archives

Fred S. Nelson: The Tulsa County district judge returned to the bench six weeks after the bombing and defeated his Democratic opponent handily in the general election.

McDonald and Pugh did not escape justice. Both died in prison while serving time for other crimes – McDonald for killing Epps, whose body was found in a septic tank at an abandoned west Tulsa farm months after she disappeared, and Pugh for killing Self.

McDonald died in 1978 after someone slashed his throat in the Oklahoma State Penitentiary at McAlester. Pugh died in December 2006 in a Department of Corrections medical ward after suffering a heart attack.

Nelson resigned in 1972 to enter private practice. He had been a judge since 1965, when he was appointed to the former Common Pleas Court. He was named a District Court judge two years later.

He said he would not run for a judgeship again until Oklahoma "raises its salaries for judges," noting that the state ranked 50th in the country in that regard.

He joined the Tulsa law firm of Hall, Estill, Hardwick, Gable, Collingsworth & Nelson. He died July 28, 1987, after suffering a heart attack at age 58, one of the firm's partners said.

Nelson was born in Tulsa, where he graduated from Rogers High School and received his bachelor's and law degrees from the University of Tulsa. He also attended the University of Oklahoma Law School.

Nelson was an Air Force veteran of the Korean War. He had been an attorney for the U.S. Interior Department and was an assistant U.S. attorney in Tulsa for four years before his appointment to the bench.

Nelson was mentioned as a possible candidate for mayor and for Congress, but he apparently had no interest in another political race.

Testimony led to 'bootleg queen's' death

Her testimony before a grand jury investigating the bombing of a Tulsa judge resulted in the death of "Bootleg Queen" Cleo Epps, whose body was found in a septic tank on an abandoned farm south of Tulsa.

Epps, who was a teacher before she began her bootlegging career, disappeared Nov. 12, 1970, a few weeks after she testified before a grand jury investigating the Aug. 25 bombing of District Court Judge Fred Nelson.

Although Epps wore a disguise, word slipped out that she had testified. Albert McDonald and Tom Lester Pugh apparently believed that she had fingered them as the bombers, using dynamite they got from her farm.

Nelson was critically injured when his car exploded as he turned the starter to drive to a polling place to vote in the primary election. He returned to the bench six weeks later.

McDonald and Pugh were never tried for that crime but both died in prison. McDonald's throat was cut while he was serving a life sentence for killing Epps, and Pugh died of a heart attack while serving a life term for killing Arles Delbert Self, another grand jury witness.

A Bryan County jury, hearing the case on a change of venue from Tulsa County, convicted McDonald of killing the 60-year-old bootlegger although the fatal shot apparently was fired by Pugh.

The two had lured Epps to a meeting at a shopping center parking lot, where she got into a car with them.

Rubie Charles Jenkins, another bootlegger who was convicted of murder in California, testified that Epps got into the front seat of the car, which McDonald was driving. Pugh, in the back seat, shot her in the head with a .22-caliber pistol as they drove near 71st Street and Union Avenue and used a towel to keep from getting blood on the car, Jenkins said.

He testified that McDonald and Pugh told him that Epps regained consciousness as they reached the area where they planned to dispose of her body, and that Pugh shot her in the head again after she told him:

"Lester, you've killed me. You didn't have to do that."

Epps had told Tulsa County District Attorney S.M. "Buddy" Fallis Jr. that if she were murdered, her "assassins would be Lester and Albert."

Epps' body was found three months later by her brother,

Tulsa World archives

Cleo Epps was known as the "bootleg queen," but she detested the nickname.

Tom Gilbert, after his son found one of Epps' shoes near the septic tank. Also in the septic tank was a towel with two small bullet holes in it.

Her funeral was attended by about 150, including U.S. Rep. Ed Edmondson, District Court Judge Bill Hayworth of Muskogee, former state Sen. Everett Collins of Sapulpa, and city and county law enforcement officials.

In spite of her reputation as a lawbreaker, she maintained a friendly relationship with several officers.

Epps was born in Arkansas. She moved in the mid-1920s to Oklahoma, where she graduated from college and taught school in Wagoner and later in Creek County.

She was married to a Tulsa lawyer but divorced him because she thought he drank too much – she never touched liquor. She later married a man who began selling liquor and joined him in the business, becoming almost legendary among Tulsa-area bootleggers and law enforcement authorities.

Most of her whiskey dealings were in wholesale lots, truckloads of booze she bought and personally drove into the state. She once told a friend, "When I invest $10,000 in a load of whiskey, I'll be doing the driving myself."

She once told a reporter: "I never sold a bottle of whiskey in my life. All I did was drive it across the state line. Everybody knows that."

The "bootleg queen" nickname that she detested was given to Epps by a reporter in the 1940s.

Another side of Epps was shown by a 1953 hunting trip with friends to Idaho, where the group became snowbound for several days in a cabin. Epps shot a moose, believing it was a deer, and told rangers that she would turn the animal over to a charitable institution.

But because of the heavy snow, she received permission to use its meat to feed snowbound hunters. At one time as many as 35 snowbound hunters were staying and eating in her cabin.

Epps' estate was valued at $740,452, according to Creek County court records. It included 13 pieces of rural real estate, totaling more than 1,500 acres and worth about $250,000, plus 34 mortgages and notes valued at $432,000.

'Hex House' didn't live up to name

A 1944 investigation by police revealed a small casket buried in the backyard of a Tulsa house and two young women who had been under hypnotic or occult control for seven years.

The probe was nicknamed the "Hex House" case because police and reporters thought it had all the spooky elements of a Halloween story – bondage, spell-casting, mesmerism, hypnotism.

But this case was real, not a Halloween tale, and led to a short prison term for Carolann Smith, 45, and freedom for the two young women, Nell Willetta Horner, 30, and Virginia Evans, 31, who had been forced to live in an unheated basement of the house at 10 E. 21st St. and to turn over their paychecks to Smith.

The young women told authorities they had been led to believe they would receive a great reward in heaven, called the "big payoff," for serving Smith, who apparently had devised a religion of her own.

Horner told police that Smith had starved and beat her under the guise of religious purification."

The investigation was touched off when Smith obtained eight World War II ration books for herself, the two young women, several fictitious names and for a daughter, Bonnie, that actually was her dog, BonBon.

Neighborhood children told Alice Allen, a teacher at Lee Elementary School, where ration books were issued, that there was no Bonnie but that Smith had a dog named Bon-Bon. They also knew that Smith and the two young women had buried a casket in the backyard in the middle of the night.

When police investigated, they discovered Horner and Evans living either in the basement or in the servant's quarters and sleeping on orange crates without blankets while Smith lived in luxury. They found 45 pairs of expensive women's shoes, many of them unworn, silverware and glassware, clothing, jewelry, expensive furniture, 18 pairs of new gloves and cash.

Meanwhile, the young women wore tattered dresses to their jobs and had no cosmetics, although Smith had "enough to stock a drug store." The hundreds of beauty items and perfumes were kept in her bedroom.

When they dug up the backyard, police first found a dog's carcass buried in a cardboard box and underneath that a small casket containing the carcass of BonBon that had been buried 5 feet deep.

Books dealing with the means of developing will power, magnetism and self-mastery of fate were found in Smith's

Tulsa World archives

The so-called Hex House at 10 E. 21st St. became a center of much speculation after a bizarre set of circumstances.

house. They also found writings by her that dealt with the means by which the human mind could be affected and about witchcraft and magic.

When the case got to court, it was something less than the sensational and lurid case observers expected, but it was still puzzling. The big question, of course, was how did Smith control the two young women?

Horner testified she always followed Smith's orders. She said she was told in 1940 to have nothing to do with her family and that from then on her last name was Sherman. She assumed that she had been adopted by Smith, who sometimes used the last name Sherman.

Evans testified that "we thought she was leading us into a good life.

"She always quoted Scriptures to bring out her point," she said. "They fitted in perfectly with what she wanted us to do."

In addition to receiving the paychecks of the two young women, Smith also received $31 a week from Evans' father for her support and extra money to pay for a nurse. She had written him that Evans was mentally ill and needed a nurse that would cost that amount.

A District Court jury found Smith guilty of suborning (inducing) perjury and sentenced her to a year in prison. She pleaded guilty in federal court to a charge of using the mail to defraud Evans' father, a wealthy Stroud merchant, and making false claims to obtain ration books. She was placed on probation for the latter crimes.

The subornation charge stemmed from a Municipal Court case in which Evans and Horner testified against a neighbor who lived in the adjoining duplex of the house. He was charged with assaulting Horner.

Horner said she and Evans were told exactly what to say in their testimony and that they were rehearsed for hours. She finally typed a script and memorized it, she said.

The "Hex House" was a favorite site for young Tulsans to visit on Halloween for years after the case was settled. But the house was torn down in 1975 and the site became the parking lot for the Akdar Shrine. The Shrine later moved to 27th Street and Sheridan Road and its old site -- where the Hex House had been -- became the site of apartments.

Police and reporters may have believed the house had the makings of a Halloween mystery at one time. But today there are no ghosts or any ties with the occult at the apartment complex.

Gushers for Slick after many dry starts

Wildcatter Tom Slick drilled a lot of dry holes before he hit a gusher that produced for the next 35 years and became the discovery well for a prolific oil field.

It was just the beginning for Slick, who drilled gusher after gusher and became known as the "King of the Wildcatters" before his death at the age of 46 in 1930, when he had a fortune valued at between $75 million and $100 million. He was the nation's largest independent oil producer.

Slick, who had what others called an uncanny ability to pick out land that possessed oil and gas prospects, was born among oil derricks in Clarion, Pa., then the center of a rich oil pool. His father was an oil-field worker and other relatives dabbled in oil.

"The first whiff of air I ever breathed was laden with the odor of oil," Slick told a Tulsa World reporter in 1929. "I came west in 1907 and decided to go into the oil game and be a millionaire."

And that's what he became.

His life story was something of a Horatio Alger story. He went to work as a child to help support his family and was sleeping on the derrick floor when he hit his first gusher.

Slick became known as "Dry Hole Slick" because he had found no oil in a large number of wells, including at least 10 he leased near Bristow for the Shaffer & Smathers Co. of Oklahoma City.

Then he moved to the Cushing area, where he and Charles Shaffer started drilling on the farm of Frank M. Wheeler in January 1912. The town of Drumright was later built on that site.

The well gushed about 4 a.m. on March 17, a Sunday, and, in spite of roping off the drilling site and posting armed guards, the news traveled fast to other leasers who, Slick knew, would try to get in on the action.

He was ready for them.

When other oilmen arrived in Cushing by train and tried to lease teams and buggies to drive around the area seeking leases, they discovered that Slick had leased all the livery stables in town, had them padlocked and guarded so that other leasers couldn't hire rigs, thus preventing them from seeking leases.

That story was told best in a report to his boss by a competing lease man, according to Petroleum Age, published by the American Oil & Gas Historical Society: "I rushed down to the livery stable to get a rig and damned if Slick hadn't already been there and hired every rig. Not only there, but every other stable in town."

That lease agent said he walked to a farm three miles

Western History Collection/ University of Oklahoma

Oilman Tom Slick made himself enormously wealthy wildcatting oil in Oklahoma.

out of town where he was able to rent a horse and headed back to town to pick up a notary public to notarize any leases he could make "and damned if Slick hadn't hired every notary in town, too."

After the Cushing field was proved, scores of operators flocked there and Slick was able to get his prices for leases he had acquired before a drop of oil was in sight.

The Cushing field wasn't Slick's only success. He was involved in drilling in Seminole, Wewoka, Tonkawa, Oklahoma City and many other fields, hitting gusher after gusher.

Throughout his business life, Slick was known as a man who never stopped working and thinking. He worked while others were asleep and made snap decisions – such as the time he asked a man on a street corner in Seminole how much he wanted for a lease on his property.

"A hundred thousand dollars," the man said. "It's a sale," Slick responded.

Another oilman once recalled that "I was talking with a man about a deal who told me 'Oh, I made a deal with Tom Slick who got me out of bed at 2:30 the other night.' "

Once while drilling a well, Slick stayed in a boarding house where the lady of the house and her daughters loved to play a piano but with more noise than skill.

After some dickering, Slick bought the piano for several times its value, wrapped a chain around it and secured the chain with a padlock. When his well was completed, he gave the key to the lock to the woman and her daughters.

After Slick sold his leases to Prairie Oil and Gas Co. in 1929 for a reported $36 million, he told a World reporter "I have just sold every barrel of production that I possess but I will wager you that in less than a year, I will have more acreage and production than I have just sold."

But before that year was up, his intensity had taken a toll on his health. The Oklahoma City field was blamed for wrecking his health, although he had always been known as the most nervous man in the oil business.

He was a heavy smoker, consuming package after package of cigarettes, and when he was working on a deal, he would pace the floor and talk, give orders and do a lot of things while considering his plans.

Slick died Aug. 16, 1930, of a cerebral hemorrhage in the Johns Hopkins Hospital in Baltimore, where he had undergone surgery.

In a touch of irony, Slick's biggest producer, in the Oklahoma City field, came in two weeks after his death at 43,500 barrels of oil a day.

Shotgun remedy led to gun museum

A shotgun used to bribe a 7-year-old boy to take his medicine led to a collection of more than 20,000 guns now housed in a state-owned museum in Claremore.

The guns were collected by John M. Davis, who housed them in his Mason Hotel in downtown Claremore until the state leased the collection for 99 years for $1, with an option to renew for another 99 years, and moved them to the museum a few blocks away at 333 N. Lynn Riggs Blvd.

Davis, born in 1887 near Calion, Ark., was given that first shotgun, a Belgium-made .410-gauge, by his father. It cost $1.50 in 1894.

From then on, Davis had the collector's bug. His interest lasted until his death at the age of 86 in 1973, four years after his collection had been valued at $7 million.

That first gun is still housed in the museum. Along with modern automatics, machine guns, a Gatling gun, Kentucky rifles, Colts, Winchesters and a 15th-century Chinese cannon are guns that were used by infamous criminals such as Pretty Boy Floyd, Bonnie Parker, Jesse James and Alvin Karpis, plus thousands of other weapons of every type.

It's believed that the Davis Museum has more firearms than any museum in the country. It has a 1,525-book reference library valued at $50,000 that was donated by Charles Suydarn, editor and author of many gun-related books and articles.

The museum also houses Davis' collection of German beer steins, swords, knives, statuary, hanging nooses and hoods, handcuffs and American Indian artifacts.

Davis moved to Claremore in 1917 from El Dorado, Ark., where he had been a property owner and building contractor. He traded 2,000 acres in Arkansas for the Mason Hotel at the main intersection of downtown Claremore and began displaying his guns in the lobby.

Eventually, his guns covered the lobby walls, the ballroom, the entrance and filled seven rooms upstairs.

"You could barely walk into those rooms," the late Lee Good, longtime director of the museum, told a Tulsa World reporter.

Good had toured Davis' collection before taking his job

Tulsa World file

This vintage postcard shows a portion of the J.M. Davis gun collection displayed in the Mason Hotel in Claremore.

with the museum, but wasn't prepared for what he found when the transfer of collection to the new museum began in 1969. Guns were stashed everywhere – under the burner of a kitchen stove, stuffed in spice drawers.

"It was unbelievable," Good said. "We took 300 muzzle-loading rifles off one wall. They averaged 9 pounds each, and their weight had sunk the floor 3½ inches."

The first attempt for the state to obtain the collection was in 1949. But it wasn't until the 1960s that necessary legislation to build a museum was passed and an agreement was reached between Davis and the state. Under the terms of the state's lease, it must provide an adequate museum building where the guns can be displayed at no cost to the public and must pay the maintenance and operating costs of the museum.

Davis transferred title to the guns to the J.M. Davis Foundation, a trust, which entered into the 99-year lease with the J.M. Davis Memorial Commission that was created by legislation written by Sen. Clem McSpadden. McSpadden was master of ceremonies at the dedication of the new museum on Davis' 82nd birthday on June 27, 1969.

The museum is governed by a five-member commission that consists of William Higgins of Claremore, whose father, Bill Higgins, operated the cafe in the Mason Hotel; Jack Mayberry of Claremore; Dr. James Marr and Chris Sutherland, both of Tulsa; and one vacancy. Gary Rohr of Claremore is the executive director of the museum that is open from 8:30 a.m. to 5 p.m. Monday through Saturday and from 1 to 5 p.m. Sundays.

And, best of all, it's still free.

Davis knew the history of nearly every piece in the collection and once demonstrated that by reaching into a stack of firearms, pulling out one at random and explaining in detail the history and background of that gun.

Shortly before the guns were moved into their new quarters, Davis told a reporter that the pieces were all in working order, at least when he put them on the hotel's walls.

"I don't collect much any more," he said. "I've already got at least one of everything I know of."

Black widow enjoyed the limelight

Nannie Doss, a friendly, grandmotherly type woman, said her husband, Samuel, "got on my nerves." So she dispatched him the same way she had three previous husbands – with a dose of rat poison.

Nannie Doss, who appeared to enjoy being in the limelight during the investigation of her husband's death and her court appearances, pleaded guilty to a murder charge and was sentenced to life in prison.

The guilty plea came as a surprise as her trial was about to begin on May 17, 1955 before Judge Elmer Adams.

Doss had been arrested several months earlier after Dr. W.D. Hidy at Hillcrest Medical Center became puzzled about the cause of Sam Doss' death in October 1954. He asked for permission to perform an autopsy on the body of the Oklahoma Highway Department worker and Nannie Doss agreed readily. The doctor had explained that an autopsy's findings might save someone else's life.

The autopsy made the cause of death clear – arsenic.

Hidy turned his findings over to police and Nannie Doss confessed that she had added small doses of rat poison to her husband's coffee earlier but because she had miscalculated, it only made him sick and he consulted Hidy.

She finally added a large dose to a bowl of prunes that she served to the man she met through a lonely hearts club.

Nannie Doss claimed that he got on her nerves and wouldn't let her have a radio or TV or read true confession magazines. Investigators discovered that when Sam Doss died, she was corresponding with another man she had contacted through a personal ad in a magazine.

She had baked and sent him a cake, but without arsenic.

Arsenic was the same method she had used to kill three previous husbands in North Carolina, Alabama and Kansas, all of whom had died mysteriously but whose bodies had been buried without autopsies. No charges were filed against her for the North Carolina and Alabama deaths, but a murder charge was filed in Emporia, Kan. She also was suspected of having poisoned her mother, Louise Hazle, in Alabama and others, including some of her children.

Born near Anniston, Ala., Nannie Doss told investigators that she poisoned her second husband, Frank Harrelson, in 1945 because he got drunk and tried to make her go to bed with him. She found his whiskey buried in her garden and spiked it with rat poison.

Tulsa World archives

Nannie Doss leaves court in June 1955 after receiving a life prison sentence in the poisoning death of her husband. She told photographers who asked her for one more smile: "Sure, I don't feel bad at all about going to McAlester."

"So I put rat poison in his rot-gut whiskey," she said. Harrelson became ill and died that night in Lexington, N.C. His last words were "it must have been the coffee."

Her first husband, Charlie Braggs, escaped because someone cautioned him about eating her food. He tiptoed out one day in 1928 and got a divorce. Braggs was located in Alabama after Nannie Doss was arrested. He told a Tulsa World reporter that one of their five children died soon after birth. Two more died when they were young.

While good-natured, Nannie Doss was described as mentally defective by attorneys, newspaper reporters and at least three psychiatrists. Her childlike good humor and calmness made her quotable to the end.

When families of Harley Lanning, her third husband, and Richard L. Morton, her fourth husband, heard about Doss they asked for an investigation of their relatives' deaths. Morton, a native of Okmulgee, died in Emporia, Kan. When his body was exhumed, the examining physician said he had enough arsenic in him to kill a horse.

Nannie Doss clearly enjoyed the attention she received, which included Life magazine buying her life story.

When Adams sentenced her to life in prison, he commented that it would "be poor precedent" to make her the first woman sentenced to death in Oklahoma. Her case sparked a drive that resulted in the Legislature passing a law requiring an examination by a medical examiner of all individuals who die without being attended by a physician.

After pleading guilty to the Tulsa murder, a smiling Nannie Doss visited with a daughter, Melvina Hedrick of Lexington, N.C. As the two parted at the jail elevator in the courthouse, Doss told her daughter: "Take it easy. And don't worry. I'm not."

When she left the courtroom, she told photographers who asked her for one more smile:

"Sure, I don't feel bad at all about going to McAlester."

She was a model prisoner and forever a jokester with a smile. Nannie Doss died of leukemia on June 2, 1965, exactly 10 years after she entered prison.

One of her last jests was when she was the second-oldest person in the prison.

"When they get shorthanded in the kitchen here, I always offer to help out," she told a visiting World reporter, "but they never do let me."

Debo made her mark in state history

Angie Debo, who came to Oklahoma as a 9-year-old in a covered wagon, spent her life researching and writing about Oklahoma and Oklahomans and became the state's foremost historian.

By the time of her death at the age of 98 in 1988, she had written 13 books but considered one far more important than all the others.

That book was "And Still the Waters Run" that she finished in 1936 but didn't get published until 1940. It tells a sordid story of fraud and graft against the Indians of Oklahoma.

"I can't think of a word bad enough to describe the things I found," she told a Tulsa World reporter in 1978. "It was a dark and evil story."

The book dealt with the liquidation of the tribal governments of the Five Civilized Tribes, exposing corruption in federal and state governments. It details kidnappings, embezzlement and murder of Indians by businessmen drawn to millions of dollars generated from the oil and gas fields.

She said she loved writing all of her books, but "you could take all of my other books and put them in a stack and together they would not be as important as 'And Still the Waters Run.' "

Joseph Brandt, the founder and head of the University of Oklahoma Press, considered the book an important contribution to the state's history and planned to publish it. But Debo withdrew it because of fears that the Legislature would stop its publication.

Others at OU had warned that publication of the book wasn't good politics because some legislators or their families or friends had benefited from the land grabs.

Brandt left OU to become director of the Princeton University Press, which finally published the book in 1940.

Debo told a reporter that Brandt, later a president of OU, wanted to go ahead with publication at OU but "I decided that the future of the OU Press was more important than its publication of my book and I withdrew it over Joe's protest."

Debo came to Oklahoma with her parents in a covered wagon from Beattie, Kan., in 1899 and was a little disappointed when she arrived— she had expected to see Indians but instead saw only white settlers. She lived the rest of her life in the small Logan county town of Marshall.

As a child, she was so impressed by the beauty of the

Tulsa World archives

Angie Debo said she loved writing all of her books, but "you could take all of my other books and put them in a stack and together they would not be as important as 'And Still the Waters Run.' "

prairie flowers that she vowed to write about them. She never wrote about wildflowers, but that is about the only aspect of the state that did not come under her pen.

Debo became a schoolteacher when she was 16 for $100 for a three-month term.

"It was a great joy and creative release for me, although I don't think I was very good," she said years later. "But I don't think I did any harm."

She had been interested in writing since learning to read at the age of 5 and, during a college vacation, she wrote two short stories. After the first was published, she spent most of the money she received on postage trying to get the second published.

Her first inclination was to become a geologist, but she discarded that idea because "it was a bad field for a girl" and settled on history. "I didn't realize that history was the worst possible field for a girl.

"The door was not only shut, it was locked for a woman who wanted to teach history."

Thirty colleges had openings for a history teacher when she was doing graduate study. "Twenty-nine said they wouldn't take a woman under any circumstances; the other said it would take a woman only if it couldn't find a man."

Debo left her books, papers and files to the Oklahoma State University library and in a letter to the librarian suggested "with one exception, I will leave it to the library to decide whether they are worth preserving."

That exception was the collection of notes she used in writing "And Still the Waters Run." She said that book deals with such explosive material that the specific facts behind the cautious generalizations lie buried in the notes; and I think those notes should be preserved for future use."

For most of her 98 years, the woman known as the first lady of Oklahoma history wrote about history made by others. But she made history of her own in 1985 when she was 95.

Her portrait by Oklahoman Charles Banks Wilson was unveiled in the state Capitol where it hangs alongside those of Sequoyah, Will Rogers, Carl Albert, Robert S. Kerr, Jim Thorpe and other great Sooners.

Debo's portrait was the first of a woman to hang in the Capitol.

State sculptor gained worldwide fame

A 14-foot bronze statue in front of the state Capitol is just one of the sculptures created by an internationally known sculptor who began life on a southwestern Oklahoma farm.

The work, titled "As Long as the Waters Flow," depicts an American Indian woman standing proudly. It is the largest sculpture done by the late Allan Houser, a native of Apache.

Houser was called "one of the few people I can unequivocally call 'great' " by Betty Price, Arts Council of Oklahoma executive director, who was instrumental in arranging for the sculpture at the Capitol. She said the statue was a tribute to cultural contributions that Indians have made in Oklahoma.

Other important Houser works can be seen in Tulsa – "Mystic Rain Arrow" at the Gilcrease Museum and "Where Friends Meet" at the University Center of Tulsa. His "Apache Family" stands in front of the Apache Tribal Headquarters at Apache, and his paintings and sculptures are displayed at the Southern Plains Museum in Anadarko.

Some of Houser's work also is part of the permanent collection of Philbrook Museum of Art.

A 9-foot Houser statue of the late Lt. Col. Ernest Childers, a World War II Medal of Honor winner, stands in a Broken Arrow park created for that purpose.

Houser didn't intend for the statue to resemble Childers – he wanted it to represent a combination war hero and native American. But after the sculptor met the Creek Indian hero, he changed his mind. He said he redid the statue four times before getting the likeness he wanted.

The Childers statue was Houser's last creation. He died on Aug. 22, 1994, a month before it was unveiled.

His works also are in private and public collections, including the United Nations, the Smithsonian Institution, the White House, the British Royal Collection, the Pompidou Museum in Paris and the Dahlem Museum of Berlin.

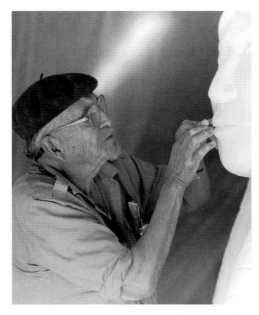

Arts Council of Oklahoma

Apache native and internationally known sculptor Allan Houser works on the plaster form for the 14-foot bronze "As Long As The Waters Flow," which was commissioned for the state Capitol.

Houser was born Allan Haozous in 1914 near Apache but changed his name early in his career. His father, Sam Haozous, was a nephew of Chiricahua Apache Chief Geronimo. The family moved to New Mexico in 1924.

As a child, Houser didn't care much for school because they "were more like jails than schools," he said in 1988. However, he showed a talent for drawing and became popular with other students by doing sketches for them.

That attitude changed when he went to the Santa Fe Indian School in 1934 to study painting. Two years later, he received an award for best artwork by a student and was commissioned to paint a mural for the 1936 World's Fair in New York. Some of his work also was displayed at the 1939 World's Fair, and others were shown on tours through Europe and South America.

Houser began sculpting in 1939 after meeting Swedish muralist Olle Nordmark, who suggested that he switch from painting. Houser's early two-dimensional work depicted traditional Indian themes. His sculpture in stone, bronze and steel ranged from realistic to abstract.

"I pretty much dropped painting because of lack of interest," he said. "I felt I had to choose one or the other, and three-dimensional work seemed to offer so many outlets."

President George H.W. Bush gave Houser the National Medal of Arts in 1992, making him the first American Indian to receive the award, for outstanding contributions to the excellence, growth, support and availability of the arts.

Among the other recipients that year were opera singer Marilyn Horne, actor James Earl Jones and country performer Minnie Pearl.

Houser was inducted into the Oklahoma Hall of Fame in 1985. In 1990, he received the American Indian Lifetime Distinguished Achievement Award by the American Indian Resource Institute in Washington.

Spooklights' source is still unknown

Floating lights that bounce up into the treetops, appear to be about the size of a basketball and frequently are seen in pairs haunting the area where Oklahoma, Kansas and Missouri converge.

The lights can be seen from a country road known as Spook Light Road many times of the year – especially at Halloween.

Sightseers in hundreds of cars drive two roads – E40 in Hornet, Mo., and E50 in Miami near Quapaw – trying to get a glimpse of the light that some say is rectangular and others claim is spherical.

Theories have been offered over the years to explain the strange phenomenon – some require a belief in the supernatural, some are more scientific and some claim that the lights are just plain hallucinations. Some, as the name implies, claim that they are ghosts – but the lights' source remains a mystery.

An Army Corps of Engineers unit from nearby Camp Crowder, Mo., studied the spooklight for several weeks during 1946 and concluded that the phenomenon was "a mysterious light of unknown origin."

Similar spooklights found in many other parts of the world have baffled observers for centuries.

Glowing in the night with an eerie, soft color, they sometimes pulse, sometimes dance about, usually near the ground or horizon. Their source is a mystery.

The phenomenon known as the Tri-State Spooklight, the Quapaw Spooklight, the Joplin Spooklight or the Hornet Spooklight caused panic in the small Missouri community of Hornet when it was first noticed by settlers in the late 1800s. Many area residents packed up and moved away.

But the Quapaw Indians reported legends about their ancestors seeing the lights in the early 1800s.

Among the earliest legends was that a handsome young American Indian man fell in love with a beautiful woman and eloped after her father refused to allow them to marry.

Fearing they would be captured, the couple committed suicide by jumping from a high bluff overlooking Spring River, known as the Devil's Promenade. According to the

Garland "Spooky" Middleton was one of a succession of people who ran a spooklight museum near the Oklahoma-Missouri border. The museum is now closed, but the spooklight phenomenon has never been fully explained.

legend, the light burns as a symbol of love between the two young lovers.

At least three early legends involve people using lanterns to search for their heads after being beheaded.

A Quapaw legend involves an old Indian looking for his head, which his wife had cut off. A similar story involves a miner who was decapitated in an accident and is using a lantern in his search.

Another early legend is about an old sergeant who was captured during a Civil War battle and was executed by using a cannon to shoot off his head, which was never found. The old sergeant's ghost somehow obtained a lantern and since then has been searching for his head.

A Joplin librarian said in 1997 said she always figured it was an accumulation of gases and you saw it when the time was right.

A Spooksville Museum was operated for several years but it has been closed for some time. It displayed photographs and a collection of stories about the light as well as a viewing platform. It also offered for sale pamphlets about the spooklight.

Some experts claimed the light is simply the glow of minerals and gases in the area. UFO experts have claimed the light is a "controlled machine from outer space – flying saucers from other worlds."

Popular Mechanics magazine sent a reporter and photographer to the area in 1965 to investigate the light and a number of theories concerning its cause.

The reporter later wrote in an article published in the September 1965 magazine that the light was produced by automobiles traveling east on U.S. 66 about 10 miles from the point where sightings of the phenomenon had been reported. The magazine said the light's unusual shimmering effect and the golden hue were caused by layers of air with varying temperature.

But area residents pointed out as soon as the magazine was published that the light was seen long before there were automobiles or highways in the area.

Coin-saving resurrects Mount Zion

Members of the Mount Zion Baptist Church in north Tulsa contributed nickels and dimes to a fund for a new building in 1909.

Twelve years later, thanks to those nickels and dimes and a $50,000 mortgage, the growing congregation moved out of a small frame building that members optimistically called a "tabernacle" into a new $95,000 structure.

The first meeting in the new structure was May 1, 1921, less than a month before much of north Tulsa, including the new church building, was burned in the Tulsa Race Riot.

After the riot that started on May 31 and lasted through the morning of June 1, the 400 Mount Zion members found there was nothing left of their red brick church building but a pile of bricks, ashes, rubbish and a $50,000 mortgage.

There were reports that fire bombs had been dropped on the church's roof because of rumors that ammunition was stored in the building.

The congregation faced a dilemma. The members could disband or declare bankruptcy and escape the $50,000 debt. Or they could pay off the mortgage and start over.

Led by the Rev. Ira Whitaker, the pastor, the members knelt in prayer. When they rose, their minds were made up. They would pay what they considered a just debt.

But it took more prayer sessions, 21 years of struggle, sometimes without a pastor after Whitaker resigned because of his health, and more donations of nickels and dimes and spare dollars in a "Joash chest" but the congregation paid off the debt in 1942.

A "Joash chest" is made of rough wood with tin bands around it for donations to the building fund and named for the Old Testament king who set up a box at the entrance to a temple to collect funds for repairs.

When the Rev. J.H. Dotson became the pastor in 1937, the congregation was meeting in the dirt-floored church basement and sitting on planks laid across sawhorses. He borrowed additional money to plaster the basement ceiling and buy 150 folding chairs and then set out to fill the chairs.

With the old mortgage paid off, the congregation renewed its dream of a new building and 10 years later moved into its present three-story structure constructed above the basement that served as the church's home for so many years.

Since that time, the church has added a family life center, which was completed and dedicated in 1986. In addition to serving the congregation, the church has been a distribution center for Meals on Wheels, a meeting place for Alcoholics Anonymous and for several community and nonprofit groups.

The church received letters from around the country – some including small donations – after its plight was reported in a Time magazine article in 1945. Most of the letters congratulated the congregation for its patience and honesty in repaying the old debt.

The church has had a couple of fires since that 1921 conflagration. But these were of the congregation's own design – one in 1942 to burn the mortgage of the original $50,000 debt and the other on the 50th anniversary in 1999 to burn the $250,000 mortgage on the family life center, now named for the Rev. G. Calvin McCutchen Sr. who succeeded Dotson as the pastor.

McCutchen was hired in 1953 to assist the ailing Dotson and succeeded Dotson as pastor in 1957. Dotson remained as pastor emeritus until his death.

McCutchen and his wife were honored on Nov. 10, 2007, for their 50 years of service to the congregation and his retirement as pastor. Events included a prayer breakfast, reception and a banquet.

Tulsa World archives

The Joash Chest of Mount Zion Baptist Church is shown by Julius Williams, deacon board chairman. Donations to pay off the church's mortgage were collected in the chest after the building was destroyed during the 1921 Tulsa Race Riot.

'Alfalfa Bill' set political benchmark

"To all my friends and the people who have supported me, I say 'God bless you.'

"To my enemies – damn you all."

That's how William H. "Alfalfa Bill" Murray ended a speech in Tishomingo, according to one of the Oklahomans who filed through the Capitol rotunda where Murray's body lay in state.

It was more than just walking past the coffin; it was a chance for hundreds of Sooners to trade stories about Murray, 86, the state's most colorful politician. Murray, who had been president of Oklahoma's Constitutional Convention, served in the Legislature, served two terms in Congress and was Oklahoma's ninth governor.

The most turbulent figure during the state's stormiest era, Murray was born a legend and just never stopped being one, the Tulsa World said in its Oct. 16, 1956, obituary for the fiery former governor.

Murray was born William Henry Davis Murray on Nov. 21, 1869, in the Toadsuck community in Grayson County, Texas, near the Red River. As he put it, "I was born in a Texas cotton patch in the midst of a snowstorm."

Murray's mother died when he was 2, and he ran away from home at the age of 12 after his father remarried. An avid reader, Murray sold books in the summer to support himself, memorized the Constitution and read history books for pleasure.

He taught school, edited a newspaper, worked as a political reporter and studied law before running for the Texas state Senate in 1898, the first of his many political defeats, and moving to Oklahoma.

During his early career, Murray became an advocate of alfalfa as a crop and picked up the tag "Alfalfa Bill" that stuck for life. Earlier he had been known as "Cocklebur Bill" because his farm near Tishomingo was covered with cockleburs after a flood.

As president of the 1906 Constitutional Convention in Guthrie, he used a heavy hand to get what he wanted. During his campaign for approval of the constitution by voters, Murray once began speaking on a street corner in Tulsa at 9 p.m. and talked for two hours, a 1907 World story reported.

At one point, the Woods County territorial court en-

Tulsa World archives

William H. "Alfalfa Bill" Murray, Oklahoma's ninth governor, came from Toadsuck in Grayson County, Texas, along the Red River, and earned a headstrong reputation in Oklahoma politics.

joined the convention from further progress toward writing a constitution, a ruling that was upheld by the Supreme Court. Some of Murray's supporters suggested he should speak kindly of the court.

"My compliments to the court," Murray said in a telegram to his supporters. "Tell them to go to hell."

After the constitution was approved, Murray was an overwhelming choice for speaker of the new state's House of Representatives. Three years later he made a race for governor but was trounced by Lee Cruce.

He was elected congressman at large, serving two terms, but was defeated when he sought a third term. In 1918 he ran again for governor but was defeated by J. B. A. Robertson.

When he became governor in 1931, Murray said "mine will not be a peaceful administration." He knew whereof he spoke.

He fired politicians; he fought the Legislature; he clashed with the state Supreme Court; he tried to reform state government and he made national headlines by calling on the National Guard whenever he really wanted to get tough.

The most notable was in 1931 when he called out the Guard to open a new free bridge to Texas across the Red River. At one point, Murray showed up at the bridge with a shotgun.

"Arrest any U.S. judges or marshals who try to interfere but be easy on the Rangers," Murray told the Guard. "Just take their guns and tobacco and give them a light kick in the pants if you have to." The bridge eventually was opened without a war between the two states.

Murray ran for president in 1932 and later lost races for governor in 1937, for congressman at large in 1940 and for the U.S. Senate in 1942.

Although the chief justice usually administers the oath of office to a governor, Alfalfa Bill administered the oath to his son, Johnston Murray, in 1951, 20 years to the day after his 98-year-old father had administered the oath to him.

Murray once said he didn't wear a hearing aid because "they're expensive and it's a pleasure to not listen to a lot of nonsense." He chained the chairs in his office to the radiator to keep visitors from pulling them too close to his desk. He was inducted into the Oklahoma Hall of Fame in 1951.

A land of leftovers and litigation

A strip of land 34 miles wide and 167 miles long is part of Oklahoma because Texas didn't want it.

That's an oversimplification, but it's a fairly accurate explanation of why the Panhandle didn't remain part of Texas when the Lone Star State was admitted to the union in 1845. There were other later factors, too, that prevented that narrow strip from being attached to another state.

The Panhandle, the only part of what now is Oklahoma that was not part of the Louisiana Purchase, was claimed by Spain, Mexico and finally by the newly independent Republic of Texas.

But when Texas, a slave state, joined the union, it had no interest in land above the 36-degree 30-minute parallel, where slavery was not legal. That parallel had been the boundary between North Carolina and Virginia since the 1600s and later was extended as the line between Tennessee and Kentucky and Arkansas and Missouri.

But the Kansas-Nebraska bill approved by Congress in 1854 identified the southern boundaries of Kansas and Colorado as the 37th parallel – 34 miles north of the slavery limit. The eastern boundary of New Mexico had been established as the 103rd meridian – leaving the strip now known as the Panhandle as the only unallocated land in the country.

That strip was a no-man's land, without laws, until 1889, when it was tacked onto Oklahoma Territory.

"It was the only spot on the American continent where civil government had no power, law no existence and courts no dominion," a 1944-45 Chronicles of Oklahoma article said.

Cattle ranchers enforced their own laws, and the only two recognized crimes were murder and cattle theft. "The latter was the worst of the two but death was the penalty for both," the Chronicles article said.

The Panhandle wasn't the only part of the Sooner State where unusual circumstances determined the boundary. The U.S. Supreme Court fixed the final boundaries by rulings in 1923 and 1930.

Texas, acting under an 1819 treaty with Spain, claimed a large area of southwestern Oklahoma that later became Jackson, Greer, Harmon and half of Beckham counties. The treaty identified part of the area that became the Republic of Texas as being west of the 100th meridian and south of the Red River.

But where was the 100th meridian?

According to the Chronicles, surveys moved that line several times after it was identified in 1818 as being a few miles east of Fort Sill; the last shift came in 1930 when the Supreme Court pegged it at 4,000 feet west of where it was believed to be in 1859. The court based its ruling on a survey it commissioned.

The Red River, another part of the boundary, should have been a simple matter, but wasn't.

The first issue was whether the treaty with Spain referred to the river's north fork or south fork. If it meant the north fork, then more than 1.5 million acres would be part of Texas; if the south fork, the land would become part of Oklahoma.

The Supreme Court ruled in 1896 that the treaty meant the south fork of the river, but that didn't end the boundary dispute between Texas and Oklahoma.

The treaty also specified the south bank of the river, an issue settled by the high court in 1923. There had been no dispute about what the south bank was until 1918, when oil was discovered in the Big Bend of the river's bed, according to the Jan. 16, 1923, Tulsa World.

No man's land
1850-1889

Boundary - 1861

North boundary - 1854 36° 30'

100th meridian - 1930

False 100th meridian - 1852

False 100th meridian - 1818

TEXAS

Oklahoma boundaries

OKLAHOMA

Tulsa

Oklahoma City

Arkansas boundary fixed by Congress in 1824 - ignored in Indian treaties. Oklahoma gained 12,000 sq. miles

Ft. Sill

Old Greer County

Source: Chronicles of Oklahoma

Tulsa World graphic

Badman never really lived his dreams

Train robber Al Jennings, sometimes described as the last of the early day badmen, once said that he wanted to be remembered as "the best governor Oklahoma ever had."

But Jennings, a lawyer before turning to crime, wasn't any more successful in politics than he had been as a bandit.

How much of a badman he was is questionable. Early day reporters who knew Jennings said his criminal career lasted only three or four months before he was captured and sent to prison and that he had never killed anyone.

However, he told an interviewer in 1957 that he killed three and wounded another in his first gun battle; but those figures don't tally. There were four men on the other side of the battle and at least two of them were alive years later. He told another interviewer a couple of years before he died in 1961 that he had killed at least 20.

Jennings used his criminal career to run for the Democratic nomination for governor in 1914, claiming in political speeches that he had been good at robbing trains and would be equally as good at governing the state.

He never got the chance to prove that claim; he came in third for the Democratic nomination behind Supreme Court Judge R.L. Williams (who was elected in the general election) and District Court Judge J.B.A. Robertson. The ex-robber claimed the nomination was stolen from him.

According to an Aug. 4, 1914, Tulsa World story, Jennings had no manager, no headquarters, no organization and no one in the big vote centers supporting him. But he attracted large crowds wherever he spoke and listeners shook his hand and promised their support.

Jennings' criminal career began in 1899 when he was serving as Canadian County attorney at El Reno and became involved in a political dispute with territorial lawyer Temple Houston, youngest son of famed Gen. Sam Houston.

Houston and a friend got into an argument with Jennings and his brothers Ed and John in a saloon at Woodward. Houston shot and killed Ed Jennings but claimed self-defense.

All of the participants, wearing guns, showed up in a courtroom for Houston's trial, which ended in an acquittal. Al and John then took a vow in blood to avenge their brother's death.

"That started me as an outlaw," he told the 1957 interviewer.

The gang's early train robberies were a bit awkward, according to a Chronicles of Oklahoma article in 1969.

In one, Jennings stood between railroad tracks attempting to flag down an approaching train and was nearly hit when it didn't even slow down; in a second, Jennings and his companions rode their horses beside the moving train, firing their guns into the air, but the engineer waved a friendly hello and kept going.

In their next attempt they piled ties on the track; the engineer merely increased the train's speed, knocking the ties away.

Jennings was captured near Onapa in 1897, two months after a train robbery near Chickasha that netted the robbers $300, a jug of whiskey and a bunch of bananas, according to a Chronicles article. He was sentenced to life in prison but was paroled in 1902 and later received a pardon from President Theodore Roosevelt. After his release, he worked variously as a lawyer, evangelist, author and technical adviser for movies.

An early author wrote that Jennings' outlaw exploits "were anything but awe inspiring; comic would be more like it. In his muddled mind, he somehow transformed himself from a bungling bandit to a much-feared outlaw."

Tulsa World archives
Al Jennings tried to rob one train by standing in the middle of the tracks to force it to stop; instead, it didn't even slow down.

Indeed, he claimed to be the fastest gun in the world and told an interviewer in 1959 that he had killed "somewhere near 20 men but I never counted."

Jennings also claimed to have known Jesse James and to have been responsible for many of the ideas in the stories William Sydney Porter wrote under the name O. Henry. He said he met Porter in an Ohio prison.

Jennings later moved to California where, one critic said, "Hollywood believed every word and made a motion picture based on his life . . . or on the life he thought he led."

Two years before Jennings died at the age of 98 in 1961, he was showing a 72-year-old friend how he used his revolver in his train-robbing days. The gun went off (Jennings thought it was unloaded) and a bullet hit the friend's elbow.

Farmer left odd political legacy

During its first century, Oklahoma has had its share (or more) of colorful politicians.

Among the most colorful was Manuel Herrick.

A Perry farmer and frequent political candidate, Herrick was elected by a fluke in 1920 to the House of Representatives in the state's former 8th District. He became the Republican nominee when incumbent Dick T. Morgan, the only other candidate, died after the filing period closed.

Herrick, who had received only three votes two years earlier when he ran as an independent, was elected in the heavily Republican district, helped by Republican Warren Harding's landslide election as president.

Calling himself the only farmer in Congress and an aerial daredevil because of his "death-defying stunts in the air" while strapped into an airplane seat, Herrick predicted he would win a second term by a landslide, according to the Aug. 1, 1922, Tulsa World.

Instead, he ran a poor third for the nomination, losing to Enid newspaper publisher M.C. Garber.

Too many of northwest Oklahoma's voters probably had read about Herrick's two years in Congress, during which he had staged a beauty contest from his Capitol office, offering himself as the prize – a contest he claimed later was designed to seek information for a bill that would ban beauty contests.

After leaving office, Herrick filed a $50,000 breach of promise lawsuit against his former stenographer. Ethlyn Chrane's refusal to marry him, he claimed, had caused him to suffer "great anguish of mind." It also prevented him from "paying court" to other eligible young women,

"why I am... I am the prize!"

Dave Carman / Tulsa World

he claimed.

Earlier, Herrick had been arrested on Miss Chrane's complaint that he was harassing her. When police searched him, they found a list of 50 names of Washington women with notations as "good," "not so good" and "bad" after each name.

He also accused Garber of unfairly influencing voters by giving away automobiles, sending free copies of his Enid News to nearly every voter in the district and giving fish and apples to others.

Several years later, after his arrest while working at a still in Maryland, Herrick told an Associated Press reporter that he may have made a mistake while in Congress by not taking some of the money that was offered him.

"When I was in Congress," he said, "I had as much as $50,000 in bills stacked on my desk – dishonest money. But I said to them, 'take it away.' Maybe I was a fool."

Barefoot, unshaven and clad in overalls, Herrick, 54, claimed he took the $15 per week job as a handyman at the still to get evidence to be turned over to prohibition officials. But a jury didn't buy his story – requiring only 10 minutes of deliberation before finding him guilty of manufacturing and possessing liquor.

He served a six-month term and complained about bad food, dirty bedding and not being allowed some of the privileges other prisoners had.

A few years later, Herrick moved to California. He disappeared during a Sierra blizzard Jan. 11, 1952, while on a trip to his mining claim. His body was found in a snowbank two miles from his cabin.

Barnard cleaned up the dungeons

Tulsa's city jail was "worse than the black hole of Calcutta," Kate Barnard told the Tulsa World after a surprise visit to the "dungeon" in 1914.

As the state's first commissioner of charities and corrections, she had visited the Tulsa jail before and had pleaded with the city commission to build a new jail or move the prisoners into the larger, cleaner and newer county jail. But the commission had taken no action.

"I found things even worse than before," she said after her surprise visit Jan. 16, 1914, and before a meeting with the commissioners, according to the World. A few hours later, Mayor Wooden ordered police to move 22 men and four women to the county jail.

Before they could be moved to the county lockup, however, the prisoners had to take showers and put on clean clothes. One of Barnard's complaints had been that the city prisoners were not allowed to use the showers in the police station's basement jail because it was reserved for police officers. She also complained that the prisoners were not furnished with clean clothes.

Her remark on the black hole of Calcutta referred to a small dungeon where Indian troops held British prisoners in the 18th century.

Tulsa's jail wasn't the first nor last lockup Barnard had visited unexpectedly – and complained about. She forced cleanups and brought needed improvements to jails and institutions that cared for orphans.

A few years earlier, she had made a surprise inspection of the Kansas penitentiary at Lansing where Oklahoma prisoners were held in territorial and early statehood days. Barnard found inmates were being tortured, including the use of "crib" and "waterhose" punishments, for failing to meet quotas in the prison's coal mine.

The crib was a coffin-like structure into which prisoners were thrown after their hands and feet were shackled and

Tulsa World archives

Prison reformer Kate Barnard became the first woman elected to statewide office as head of charities and corrections.

drawn together behind them. The waterhose was used to squirt water into the mouths and noses of bound men.

Two months later, after Barnard's complaints, the first 50 Oklahoma prisoners in Kansas were sent to McAlester where they were housed temporarily in an abandoned federal jail. Additional prisoners followed, and by the end of January 1909, all of the state's prisoners were back in Oklahoma.

Construction began a few months later on a penitentiary at McAlester on 120 acres donated by a group of residents. The prisoners built their own prison. None escaped during construction, although there were no walls, no cells and few locks.

Kate Barnard was born in Nebraska in 1875 and spent her childhood in Kerwin, Kan. She homesteaded before moving to Oklahoma City, where she graduated from high school and taught school for seven years.

Her interest in social problems began in 1904 when she attended the World's Fair in St. Louis and while there toured slums.

Barnard and other women campaigned at the Constitutional Convention in 1906 for women's suffrage. They won only their fight for child labor laws, compulsory education and the establishment of a department of charities and corrections that could be headed by a person of either gender -- the only state post that a woman could hold.

As a candidate for the corrections job in the state's first election in 1907, she polled 138 more votes than Charles N. Haskell in his race for governor and became the first woman elected to a statewide office. Four years later she was re-elected with 485 more votes than Gov. Lee Cruce received.

Her effort to win a third term failed because of a dispute with the Legislature.

Jingle helps make Edmondson governor

"E-D-M-O-N-D-S-O-N spells Edmondson.

"He's the man we need for our governor. . . ."

That little ditty, borrowed (and rewritten) from a Tulsa Press Club Gridiron show, helped propel Tulsa County Attorney J. Howard Edmondson into the Oklahoma governor's office in 1958 with a record vote.

There were important issues, too. Edmondson promised to repeal prohibition, to institute a constitutional highway commission, a nonpolitical safety commission, a merit system for state employees, a district attorney system to replace county attorneys and a permanent financing program for schools.

But the ditty got voters' attention and helped them remember Edmondson's name.

His was a campaign waged by volunteers, who gathered in the evenings in a donated storeroom to make billboards and signs to post around the state. He had no paid employees and spent only $39,000 during his primary election campaign. The limit at that time was $60,000.

At 32, his youth was regarded by many as a liability, but Edmondson frequently said: "Historically, reforms have come from young officials in government. Thomas Jefferson was 33 when he wrote the Declaration of Independence.

"I believe the people would rather have a young governor who is obligated to them than an old governor obligated to the politicians."

Most of his inner circle of supporters also were young and came to be known as "Edmondson's crew cuts" as they waged his "prairie fire" campaign, using a trailer with a loudspeaker playing "E-D-M-O-N-D-S-O-N" in visits to all areas of the state.

Before Election Day, Edmondson's "Big Red E" campaign became as well known as the Big Red football team at the University of Oklahoma.

The race for the Democratic nomination for governor that year attracted 11 candidates, including some big names. The contenders included front-runner W.P. (Bill) Atkinson, a multimillionaire builder from Midwest City, who had never sought political office but had the support of Gov. Raymond Gary; State Sen. George Miskovsky; Wil-

Tulsa World archives

J. Howard Edmondson, the first man from Tulsa County to be elected governor, is pictured around 1964.

liam O. Coe, who had been the runner-up in two races for the nomination, and William C. Doenges, who had businesses in Tulsa and Bartlesville and was known as a power in politics.

In primary voting, Edmondson not only made the runoff election but led Atkinson 108,358 to 107,616. Miskovsky came in third, followed by Coe and Doenges. The first candidate to use television effectively, Edmondson gained more support during the three weeks before the runoff primary and won the nomination by a record 200,000 plurality.

The fallout from Edmondson's runoff win resulted in a runoff victory for state Rep. George Nigh of McAlester in his campaign for lieutenant governor against the incumbent, Cowboy Pink Williams.

In November, Edmondson carried every county to win a landslide victory over the Republican candidate, Phil Ferguson of Woodward, by a vote of 367,000 to 91,000, and Nigh won by a big margin. Edmondson became the youngest man to win the governor's race and the first Tulsa County resident to be elected governor.

Edmondson had campaigned on the issues, but that "E-D-M-O-N-D-S-O-N" from the Press Club roast of officials in January drew attention. Before the campaign ended, most school children were singing it and adults recognized it immediately.

Sung to the tune of "Harrigan" by George M. Cohan, the ditty was one of two from that year's Gridiron that poked fun at the red-haired prosecutor. He borrowed the ditty, had new words written and borrowed Bill Hyden, who had played Edmondson in the Gridiron, to sing it.

A few months later, Edmondson was ushered into office with the most pomp and ceremony since William H. (Alfalfa Bill) Murray's inauguration in 1931, which included a public ball.

"We want to make it from start to finish a thing that will be remembered at the 100th anniversary of statehood," inaugural program chairman Mack Burks of Oklahoma City said.

It's 48 years later, the 100th anniversary of statehood is a year away; and that inauguration is still remembered.

Miss Alice overcame political reluctance

When Lt. Gov. Mary Fallin won her race on Tuesday, she'll be the second woman to represent Oklahoma in Congress.

But the similarities between Fallin and the late Alice Mary Robertson end with gender and the Republican Party, although Fallin's campaign slogan of "faith, family and freedom" sounds something like that of her predecessor – "I am a Christian. I am an American. I am a Republican."

It's a job Fallin, who served four years in the Oklahoma Legislature and has been lieutenant governor for 12 years, wants. Robertson, of Muskogee, didn't want to be a congresswoman until the right to vote was forced on her.

An avowed opponent of women's suffrage, she was approached about running for Congress in 1920 after women's suffrage had been ratified.

Miss Alice, as she was known throughout her district and in much of Oklahoma, was shocked but decided "since the men forced the vote on us, we'll see if they mean it." It was the only political post she ever held and she served only one term.

Fallin, of Tecumseh, raised more than $1.2 million for primary and runoff campaigns. She faces Democrat David Hunter, a doctor, and independent Matthew Horton Woodson, both of Oklahoma City, in the general election.

Miss Alice had less than $3,000 to spend on her entire campaign but devised an unusual way of campaigning by using the classified ads for her cafeteria in Muskogee's newspapers, both of which opposed her, to express her political views.

According to a 1951 Chronicles of Oklahoma article, she added campaign comments like "our campaign seems to be going well, even if we are not neglecting our customers" to the classified ads for her cafeteria that usually reported such things as "lots of hot soup today, and catfish, fried brown. Sweet potatoes getting sweeter every day."

Or "I want to go to Congress; first because a lot of men moved that I go and then because a lot of women seconded them."

A Nov. 5, 1920, Tulsa World story compared her campaign to that of President-elect Warren Harding who did most of his campaigning from his front porch, adding "but

Tulsa World archives

U.S. Rep. Alice Robertson, R-Okla., shown with U.S. Rep. J.G. Cannon, R-Ill., was the first woman to preside over a session of the House of Representatives. She presided in 1921 during a roll call vote on funding for a U.S. delegation to the centennial celebrations of Peru's independence.

instead of conducting her campaign from her front porch, it was conducted in her cafeteria."

She also sat down with new customers in her cafeteria to discuss issues.

She celebrated her victory by preparing a special menu for the next day's noon meal – some extra fruit salad and fried chicken – and shaking hands with well-wishers who went to the cafeteria to congratulate her.

Born of missionary parents, Robertson had served as Muskogee's postmaster, an appointment that came after she met President Theodore Roosevelt, and had started a boarding school in Muskogee that became Henry Kendall College and, after it moved to Tulsa, the University of Tulsa.

Robertson became Oklahoma's first congresswoman by defeating Rep. W.W. Hastings by 373 votes. But Miss Alice became the first woman to preside over the House when she was called to the chair by the acting speaker on June 20, 1921. Wild applause broke out and continued until she brought the gavel down sharply to restore order.

Earlier that year, she appeared on the platform as the charter was presented to the University of Tulsa and was given the title "mother of Kendall."

She was defeated for re-election by Hastings in 1922, possibly because of her votes against a bill that would have provided a bonus for World War I veterans and another bill that called for the government to furnish instruction to mothers of young children.

She explained her vote against the bonus bill by saying "veterans should not put a price on their patriotism." Ex-soldiers flooded her office with letters complaining that she was ignorant of veterans' needs.

Although she was a reluctant candidate in 1920, Miss Alice wanted a second term but lost to Hastings and said she had "learned that politics is a good thing for a woman to keep out of." She also said she "had been insulted." She died in 1931.

Editor's note: Republican Mary Fallin, Oklahoma's first female lieutenant governor, was sworn in Jan. 4, 2007, as a member of the new 110th Congress. Fallin, 52, became only the second woman the state has sent to Congress.

Postcards propelled Pink

A colorful name and a feud with postal officials propelled an Oklahoma Democrat into two high state offices.

The politician was Cowboy Pink Williams, who was elected lieutenant governor in 1954 and state treasurer in 1962, primarily on the basis of publicity he received from a feud over a postcard that postal officials considered obscene.

Williams wasn't the first Oklahoman with a colorful name to be elected to a state office – that claim goes to William H. "Alfalfa Bill" Murray. But Alfalfa Bill was just Murray's nickname.

When he entered politics, Williams had his name legally changed to Cowboy Pink. After all, he had been known as Pink most of his life, and he wasn't too happy with his birth name of Simeon Pinckney Williams.

Born in 1892 in South Carolina, Williams came to Oklahoma in 1900 when his family settled in Caddo, where his father became a merchant. Williams attended the old subscription schools in which traveling teachers would teach in one town for a few months and then move on to another town. He later picked cotton and rode the rails throughout Oklahoma.

Williams operated a general store in Caddo and later in Ardmore, where he also ran a loan-sharking business. He made money in the stock market, lost some in the 1929 crash and made more later. He was semi-retired on his Atoka County ranch when his feud with the Post Office Department began.

Angry at President Dwight D. Eisenhower's beef import policy, Williams had printed 100,000 postcards bearing a picture of a kicking donkey. He inscribed them with an invitation to all Democrats who voted for Eisenhower to attend a "public ass-kicking" at his ranch.

The cards mentioned that re-prints were available at the rate of 20 for $1, and he eventually sold more than 500,000.

"Orders were pouring in at the rate of $500 a day. I didn't pocket any of the money," he told a Tulsa World reporter in 1975. "I just ordered more cards. I was mailing them to officials all over the nation when the government stopped the parade."

Williams fought the ban for months and told a postal appeals board, "Where I come from, they don't consider a kick in the rear obscene."

Because he "got more publicity that year than any other man" in Oklahoma, he said, he decided to take advantage of it and run for a political office. After studying a directory of state officials, he decided to run against Lt. Gov. Jim Berry, who had been in office for 20 years.

Tulsa World archives

As lieutenant governor, Cowboy Pink Williams hitchhiked to the state Capitol until the Legislature appropriated money to buy him a car.

He ran what he called a plain folks campaign from the back of his battered farm truck. Williams and his wife would park their truck on a main street and spend hours visiting with people, eventually covering most of the state.

Williams and Berry got into a runoff and Williams immediately began telling voters "it's berry canning time."

The next January, sporting red and white cowboy boots and a Stetson hat, Williams presided over the opening session of the state Senate in a building he said he'd been in only once. "I'd only been in the statehouse once before," he said. "Showed it to my boys one day."

Because the lieutenant governor wasn't furnished a car in those days, Williams often hitchhiked to the Capitol. The Legislature finally appropriated $6,000 to buy him a car, and Williams announced he planned to buy a pink Cadillac with a picture of a kicking donkey on the side.

However, he bought a black Ford and gave back half of the money.

Williams organized his own military force while acting as governor during the chief executive's times out of state. But there were no privates or seamen – just colonels or admirals.

It was fortunate that he never tried to mobilize his militia, but those of us who were honorary officers were ready to heed his call. I might have needed a reminder about whether I was an admiral or a colonel.

One day when Gov. Raymond Gary was out of the state, Williams issued 800 commissions. Gary averaged one commission per day. It wasn't unusual for people Williams met to receive commissions the next time the governor was out of state.

Williams was defeated for re-election by George Nigh of McAlester, who later became governor. The colorful politician ran for state treasurer four years later and won, but lost in the next election to Leo Winters.

In his last years, Williams, who died in 1976 a week before his 84th birthday, boasted of his thriftiness and referred to himself as "stingy."

To prove his point, at age 81, he took a 62-day trip by bus from Oklahoma to Alaska, then to Florida, up to Maine and across the country to San Francisco, spending less than $10 a day on food and lodging.

"The other passengers would flock to the cafes when the bus stopped," he said. "I'd just amble over to the grocery store and get a half-pound of salami, some crackers and a quart of buttermilk.

"I guess my mind doesn't run to luxury."

Tent-store owner 'first citizen' of Tulsa

J.M. Hall's history was the history of Tulsa, according to his obituary in the May 25, 1935, Tulsa World.

It was a good analogy because Hall, who came to this area in 1883 to open a tent store for the benefit of railroad workers, was credited with choosing the site for what became Tulsa and remained a leader in civic projects until his death.

Hall and his brother, H.C. Hall, moved their tent store from place to place as work on the Frisco Railroad moved west toward the Arkansas River from Vinita. H.C. Hall was in charge of the payroll for the railroad workers and bought supplies for the store serving the men.

The Halls first set up their tent at about where the Frisco tracks cross Lewis Avenue, a site that had been selected for a railroad terminal and designated as the center of a new town to be established.

But they moved the store farther west into the Creek Nation, near what today is First and Main streets, to escape a problem involving non-Indians dealing with the Cherokee Nation. J.T. Archer and a few other merchants set up tent stores near that site and Tulsa's business section became a reality.

As soon as the streets were surveyed, the Halls began erecting a one-story frame building that faced east on Main Street. The 25-by-80-foot building had a 16-foot lean-to on the north and a 12-foot lean-to on the south. A second floor was added and the structure later was replaced by a brick building.

The Halls' store was soon joined by stores operated by J.C. Perryman and Hal Reed, which later was taken over by R.N. Bynum. Archer also replaced his tent store with a more substantial building.

Tulsa World archives

A group stands in front of J.M. Hall and Co. Dry Goods in early Tulsa. The store was near what today is First and Main streets. J.M. Hall, who has been credited with choosing the site for what became Tulsa, was a leader in civic projects and organized Tulsa's first Sunday school.

J.M. Hall organized Tulsa's first Sunday school -- identified as the Union Sunday School because he was a Presbyterian, one of his fellow organizers was a Baptist and the other was a Congregationalist. The Sunday school met in the organizers' homes until a mission school building was constructed.

When the First Presbyterian Church was organized, Hall became superintendent of the Sunday school, a position he held for 40 years.

Because the city had no funds to establish a public school, Hall and fellow merchants Jay Forsythe, Joe Price and R.N. Bynum bought a square block bounded by Boston and Cincinnati avenues, Third and Fourth streets, which they held until the city had funds to reimburse them. Hall served as the first president of the Tulsa school board.

Hall served as president of the Tulsa Commercial Club, now known as the Metro Chamber of Commerce, and was one of the organizers of the Tulsa Association of Pioneers, serving as that group's second president.

Hall also was involved in real estate as a partner with J.M. Gillette in developing the Gillette-Hall addition.

Born near Nashville, Hall moved to Oswego, Kan., at the age of 17. He later moved to McAlester, where he had charge of a store for coal miners, but when that store was sold, he returned to Oswego until taking charge of the railroad store at Vinita.

When Hall died, Mayor T.A. Penney ordered all city offices closed for the funeral and urged other public offices to do the same in memory "of our first citizen and the founder of the city of Tulsa who has been one of its leading and most enterprising business men, always supporting every good work."

Tulsans really loved their 'Tulsa'

Tulsans loved "Tulsa."

And they liked the movie's stars, especially actor Chill Wills, who were here for the premiere at the four major downtown movie theaters.

Wills, calling himself an Oklahoman although he was born in Texas, endeared himself to the throngs of celebrating people. He frequently climbed out of his car during a parade to talk with children, all of whom he called "cuzzin'" – the same term he used to address Gov. Roy J. Turner, Mayor Roy Lundy, oilman W.G. Skelly and others.

The term came from his character in the movie about the development

Joanne Kirlin

Cast members of the movie "Tulsa" participate in a tour of the Will Rogers Memorial in 1949. Shown are actor Robert Preston (left); his wife, Catherine Craig; actress Susan Hayward; her husband, Jess Barker; N.G. Henthorne, chairman of the Will Rogers Memorial Commission and editor of the Tulsa World; and actor Chill Wills.

The parade also featured 22 bands from Tulsa-area high schools, along with roundup club members and horse riders, one of whom was Western swing bandleader Bob Wills.

And, of course, the parade included the movie's stars – Susan Hayward, Robert Preston and Wills. Wills told Tulsans he traveled in Oklahoma as a youth with a medicine show, worked at Healdton and helped lay a water line from the Arbuckles to Ardmore, qualifying him as an Oklahoman.

When Wills' car was stopped by spectators along the parade route, he climbed out to talk with adults and children, and to trade pictures of

of the oil industry from its early days in Oklahoma and the conflict between oil promoters and cattle ranchers.

A crowd estimated at 100,000 jammed downtown Tulsa to join festivities for the premiere of the movie and to catch a glimpse of the stars. It was called the city's largest celebration, a record that still stands.

A portable oil derrick had been set up at Fourth and Main streets, and welcome banners fluttered from cables stretched across Main Street. The front page of the April 13, 1949, Tulsa World was overprinted with "Salute to Tulsa Day" in red ink. It was in keeping with Gov. Turner's "Tulsa Day in Oklahoma" proclamation that said it was the first time the motion picture industry had used the Oklahoma oil industry as a background for a feature production.

That day's newspaper also included a 32-page special section filled with stories about the oil industry, the movie and ads.

Oil equipment valued at more than $10 million rolled by in the parade, which took 2 ½ hours to pass. "Many spectators gave up and went home before the parade ended," a World story reported the next morning.

himself for kisses on the cheek from young girls.

The parade came during a day of activities that included square dancing in the streets, parties and other events. Members of the nation's media and the "Tulsa" stars also were guests at a party sponsored by the Tulsa Press Club. The party attracted about 900 guests to the mezzanine of Hotel Tulsa, which was featured in the movie.

After the premiere of the movie – shown simultaneously at the Ritz, Orpheum, Rialto and Majestic theaters downtown and attended by 6,637 people – a World reviewer summed up the reaction simply: "Tulsans loved 'Tulsa.' "

It was obvious from the crowd they did. Film critics and leaders in the oil industry said it was tops in entertainment and a true-to-life story of the oil industry.

Hayward later won an Academy Award for her role in "I Want to Live" and starred in a number of other movies. She died at 56 in 1975 of a seizure brought on by a brain tumor that had been discovered two years earlier.

Wills, who also was in "Boom Town," another movie about the oil industry, died in 1978. Preston, who later starred in "The Music Man," died in 1987.

After-war party was a blowout

The war to end all wars was over over there, and Oklahomans celebrated with parades, noise, gunshots, a goat riding on the roof of a taxi cab and even a mock hanging of German Kaiser Wilhelm.

The boisterous celebration in Tulsa began at 3 a.m. on Nov. 11, 1918, with shrieking factory whistles and continued for 24 hours. "Any way to celebrate was the proper way," the Tulsa World reported.

In a bit of exaggeration, the World said the celebration marked "the greatest event in the history of the world as no other event was ever celebrated or ever will be celebrated."

The World got the news of Germany's surrender at 1:50 a.m. and had an extra edition on the streets within a few minutes, followed by three additional extras as additional details were received.

Workers at the Cosden Refinery and at the West Tulsa railroad yard began blowing whistles after confirming the news by calling the newspaper.

They wanted confirmation because of a false report a few days earlier that the war was over – a report that touched off celebrations and later was called the greatest hoax of recent years.

Within minutes of the confirmation, Tulsans were driving through the city firing pistols and shotguns and honking car horns to celebrate the end of the World War.

Many pulled washtubs behind their cars to make noise.

Those who didn't have guns or ammunition used the backfiring of their cars to make noise.

Impromptu parades continued throughout the day, snarling traffic on Main and other downtown streets.

A taxicab drove around the city with a live goat labeled "the kaiser's goat" on its roof and carrying a casket with a sign identifying it as containing the kaiser's body.

Tulsa World archives

Tulsa welcomes home Company D, 111th Engineers of the 36th Division, a Tulsa unit, on June 12, 1919. The parade passed under an Arch of Triumph erected on Main Street, between Third and Fourth streets, at a cost of $3,500, paid for by public subscription.

Mayor Charles Hubbard proclaimed a holiday and asked all businesses to close for the day.

The World suggested a community singing be held at Fourth and Main streets the next night. Only about 3,000 showed up, but they sang all the songs made popular during the war.

Celebrations were held in other cities and towns in the state, most involving parades and noise-making and many involving guns.

Lights were shot out in Beggs and Mounds – street lights first, then lights in stores and even the parlor lamps in some of the homes. By dark, every light in town was shot out.

Three patriotic floats, each bearing a piano and a group singing patriotic songs, paraded through Sapulpa until their music was drowned out by amateur efforts of thousands of competitors. The parading continued until nearly all the spectators had joined in, leaving no one to watch.

Bristow stores, banks, gins and factories closed at 2 p.m., and whistles and bells sounded for an hour. A dummy of the kaiser was placed in a box inside a hearse drawn by two large black horses and was followed by children from the schools, making what was called the largest funeral procession in the town's history.

Another car had a dummy labeled as the kaiser on its hood that later was strung up by the neck to a wire that stretched across Main Street. As the dummy was pulled up, coal oil was poured over it and burned.

Armistice Day was celebrated annually in Oklahoma and across the nation with parades and other events but became Veterans Day in 1954 as a day to honor veterans of all wars.

Party-giver inspired musical

Perle Mesta, the Oklahoman who became the queen bee of Washington society and whose name will always be synonymous with party-giver, often expressed a wish to be remembered for her other accomplishments.

They were many – in business, politics, diplomacy and philanthropy.

But her special niche in history will be as a party-giver; as the "hostess with the mostes'," the title she got from a Broadway musical.

Mesta showed her business acumen by taking an active role in managing the vast steel and manufacturing business left to her by her millionaire husband, George Mesta, who died in 1925.

She became interested in politics as a child by eavesdropping on lobby conversations at the Skirvin Hotel, which her father, William Skirvin, opened in 1911 in Oklahoma City.

She enjoyed cordial relationships with every president (except John F. Kennedy) from Calvin Coolidge in 1923 until her death in 1975 when Gerald Ford was president.

Born Pearl Reid Skirvin in 1889 in Sturgis, Mich., she married George Mesta of Pittsburgh, who was about 20 years her senior, in 1917 and the two became active in politics when they donated $100,000 to Calvin Coolidge's campaign for president. After George died, she continued her political activities.

Mrs. Mesta switched parties and changed the spelling of her first name to Perle when Republican Wendell Wilkie lost his race for president in 1940. Four years later she was a delegate to the Democratic National Convention.

But she maintained friends in both parties and even campaigned for Republican Richard Nixon in his race for president against Kennedy in 1960.

She frequently had parties that involved guests entertaining each other. Over the years, Harry Truman played the piano; Dwight D. Eisenhower sang; former Tulsan Patrick Hurley, a diplomat, gave a Comanche war whoop; and Mrs. Cornelius Vanderbilt whistled in a duet.

She came to the rescue financially of the nearly broke Democratic Party during Truman's campaign for re-election as president in 1948 when pollsters predicted that Republican Thomas E. Dewey would win.

Truman won. And he created a diplomatic post for her as minister to Luxembourg. By the time she was recalled to the United States in 1953, she had entertained more than 25,000 servicemen at her own expense.

When she was asked how she wanted to be addressed, she replied "Call me Madam Minister." The title was shortened to "Call me Madam," which became the title of an Irving Berlin musical based on her life. It included the song "The Hostess with the Mostes'" – a nickname that stuck.

The Broadway musical was a hit with almost everyone, except the State Department. En route home for her first report, Madame Minister received a wire from Secretary of State Jim Webb who advised her to go directly to Washington and NOT to attend the musical based on her life.

Tulsa World archives

Perle Mesta was a popular Washington, D.C., hostess who went on to become U.S. minister to Luxembourg. Ethel Merman portrayed Mesta in the movie musical, "Call Me Madam."

She complied, went directly to Washington and, with the permission of the president, went to New York with Mrs. Truman and the Trumans' daughter, Margaret, and attended the Broadway show.

When show star Ethel Merman took a curtain call with a man who looked remarkably like the president, many in the theater were convinced it was Truman.

Did Madam Minister like the show?

Her reaction was lost to posterity. Secret Service agents rushed the party to a car the minute the final curtain dropped – and back to Washington.

Ex-first lady led enigmatic life

The widow of an Oklahoma governor – who also had been his niece and was once his daughter – drove her 1949 green Studebaker out of Ponca City in March 1953 and disappeared for 22 years.

Thus, Lyde Roberts Marland created one of the state's strangest mysteries that wasn't explained until the eulogy at her funeral in 1987: She left because she didn't feel accepted in Ponca City.

Lyde (pronounced and sometimes spelled Lydie) had become a recluse after the death of Ernest W. Marland, 12 years before she disappeared. She had always been terrified of being in the public eye. And she remained a public curiosity in the town that considered her husband its own father.

Finally fed up with her life, she told her maid that she wouldn't be seeing her again, loaded her car with several valuable paintings, took a supply of cash and left.

Natives of Pennsylvania, Lyde and her brother, George, had moved to Ponca City around 1910 to live with oil millionaire Marland and his first wife, Mary Virginia, a sister of the children's mother. The children's parents were nearly penniless.

About four years later, the children were adopted by the Marlands so they might have the advantages great wealth could provide. Lyde went to an Eastern finishing school and she and her brother traveled with their adoptive parents, including cruising on the Marlands' private yacht.

Two years after the first Mrs. Marland died in 1926, Marland, 54, had the adoption set aside so he could marry the 26-year-old woman who had been his niece and later his daughter.

Newspapers from coast to coast featured sensational stories about a rich playboy who was going to marry his daughter. The publicity apparently broke Lyde's health, and the wedding was postponed for several months. The wedding occurred at the home of Lyde's parents in Flourtown, Pa.

Marland lost his oil empire in the Wall Street crash of 1929 but entered politics and was elected to Congress in 1932 and as governor in 1934. As the state's first lady, Lyde avoided the public eye as much as possible.

When Marland's term as governor was over, the couple moved into a small house on the mansion property and sold the luxurious mansion Marland had built during his heyday. Lyde became almost a recluse after Marland died of cancer in 1941.

Periodic attempts to find the missing former Oklahoma first lady were never successful, but during her long absence she never failed to send money to pay her property taxes, the payments coming from various cities around the country. She always overpaid her taxes, the Kay County treasurer said.

At one point, it was learned she had lived in a motel in Independence, Mo., for several months. The motel owner's wife said Lyde had said she wanted to get away from her family.

Ponca City attorney C.D. Northcutt told those attending Lyde's funeral that he traced her whereabouts through the tax payments and after receiving a collect call from her from Washington sent her money to return to Ponca City.

When she returned she was elderly, toothless and dressed in a smock top, pantaloons and tennis shoes. She told Northcutt of living as an impoverished old woman among the street people of Washington. Lyde continued her determination to remain out of the public eye and died in 1987 at the age of 87.

A reporter who had known Lyde when she was first lady and he was covering the capital for The Tulsa Tribune described her as "an enigma to those who sought to know her, but only because she was a woman who wanted to be left alone."

Tulsa World archives

A newspaper reporter who knew Lyde Marland said she was "an enigma to those who sought to know her, but only because she was a woman who wanted to be left alone."

Kidnapping trial gave judge fame

When U.S. District Judge Edgar S. Vaught died in 1959, his obituary said he was best known for presiding at the trial of the kidnappers of the Oklahoma City oilman Charles Urschel.

Vaught gained national prominence from that trial of George "Machine Gun" Kelly and his cohorts, who kidnapped Urschel from his home and held him at a Texas farm until they received a $200,000 ransom.

Until that 1933 trial, the Oklahoma City judge had presided over primarily civil cases. The kidnapping trial, in which he found 20 defendants guilty, changed his interest from civil to criminal cases, and he was known from then on as a stern, just and fearless judge.

During the sensational trial, at which Kelly and the other defendants appeared in chains with armed guards, Vaught ignored threatening letters and ran the trials with vigilance. The FBI assigned agents to guard him around the clock. As a result, Vaught became a close friend of FBI Director J. Edgar Hoover.

"Perhaps the kidnapping case was the most important I ever tried as far as the public is concerned," he told an interviewer when he retired in 1956 after presiding over an estimated 20,000 cases.

The Kelly trial may have provided Vaught with his greatest prominence, but a 1959 Chronicles of Oklahoma story said, "His most enduring contribution to Oklahoma was his work as a member of the State Capitol Advisory Commission."

It was that commission that obtained the land, raised funds and recommended the site for the Capitol. The location, approved by the Legislature, straddles Lincoln Boulevard at Northeast 23rd Street. Vaught also served on the Capitol Building Co., where he was lauded by other members as the one who "contributed more freely than anyone."

Vaught had been among a group of men that Gov. Charles Haskell summoned June 12, 1910, to the Huckins Hotel in Oklahoma City after Haskell's secretary, W.B. Anthony, and Secretary of State Bill Cross arrived with the state seal, which they had removed from the

Tulsa World archives

U.S. Judge Edgar S. Vaught presided over the 1933 trial of George "Machine Gun" Kelly, who led the kidnapping of an Oklahoma oilman. Vaught also helped secure land for the state Capitol.

Capitol in Guthrie. It was the day after Oklahomans voted to move the state capital to Oklahoma City. The move had not been expected until 1913, but Haskell directed Anthony early June 12 to take the seal to Oklahoma City.

Born on a farm in Virginia, Vaught moved to Oklahoma City in 1901 to be the high school principal. On his first Sunday there, he attended Sunday school at St. Luke's Methodist Church. The next week, he was named the church's Sunday school superintendent, a post he held until 1909, when he organized a class that he taught for the next 50 years.

He had served the church in many capacities, including supply pastor, and was the chairman of the church's board of trustees for 25 years until his death.

During his time as the principal, he studied law at night. He was admitted to the bar in 1906.

Vaught also was active in civic affairs. He was the president of the Oklahoma City Chamber of Commerce in 1915. He was the president of the OKC Lions Club in 1921, when he attended the Lions International convention in Oakland, Calif.

A scheduled speaker at that convention did not show up, and the master of ceremonies called on Vaught to speak. He was so well-received that the Lions tried to elect him their international president ahead of the vice president in line for the job.

Vaught refused to accept the position at the 1921 convention, but he was elected a year later, ahead of the vice president who was to have moved up to the top spot.

Vaught was appointed a U.S. District Court judge in 1928 by President Calvin Coolidge. He retired in 1956 to devote his time to church work but continued to hear cases and helped clear up dockets in other jurisdictions.

Although he never held elective office, Vaught was once a member of the Republican State Central Committee and was a delegate to the national convention that nominated Coolidge in 1924.

He died Dec. 6, 1959, a month before his 87th birthday.

Tilghman died with his boots on

Famous Oklahoma lawman Bill Tilghman, who was called "the greatest of us all" by another former deputy marshal, was shot to death outside a dance hall in Cromwell by a federal prohibition enforcement officer.

Tilghman, 70, died almost instantly after the Nov. 2, 1924, shooting by Wylie Lynn of Holdenville, who surrendered to a federal magistrate.

Lynn refused to say anything that night except to admit he was the shooter but later claimed he acted in self-defense, a claim apparently believed by a jury that acquitted him of a murder charge several months later.

Lynn said that he had gone to Cromwell, known as the state's wildest town, to investigate reports that the women at Ma Murphy's dance hall were providing liquor to patrons. He said one of his guns accidentally fired and the shot attracted Police Chief Tilghman's attention.

Witnesses said Tilghman, aided by a couple of friends, struggled with the intoxicated Lynn and managed to get two of his guns but Lynn pulled a third weapon and fired three shots into Tilghman's chest. Witnesses said Lynn was armed with two .38-caliber automatic pistols and a .44-caliber revolver, but he testified later that he had only two guns.

After Lynn was acquitted in a trial at Wewoka, he was sentenced to 90 days in jail for contempt of court for carrying a pistol, which fell out of his pocket in the courtroom during the trial.

Lynn was mortally wounded in a 1932 shootout in a Madill drug store that also left the other gunman, a friend of Tilghman, and a bystander mortally wounded and a second bystander less seriously wounded. Witnesses said Lynn saw his enemy, Crockett Long, a state

Tulsa World archives

Famed lawman Bill Tilghman killed at least 20 men in shootouts in Dodge City, Kan., before becoming a U.S. deputy marshal in Oklahoma Territory.

agent, sitting in the store among about 25 customers and ordered him to put up his hands.

"I'm going to get you some time and it might as well be now," witnesses said Lynn yelled as he pointed his pistol at Long.

Long rose, pulled his own pistol and the two fired at each other until their guns were empty. Each man was hit by five bullets. Long died on an operating table a few hours later, as did one of the bystanders who was hit by a stray bullet. Lynn died the next day.

Tilghman had frequently expressed his desire to "die with his boots on" in true frontier style, Muskogee County Sheriff J.F. (Bud) Ledbetter, a former marshal, said of his old-time friend.

Tilghman's career as a law officer began as a city marshal in Dodge City, Kan., where he killed at least 20 men in shootouts before he moved to Guthrie in 1889 and became one of three U.S. deputy marshals for Oklahoma Territory.

During his career, he also had served as Oklahoma City police chief, as a state senator and as an adviser on a movie about outlaws in Oklahoma. He and former train robber Al Jennings toured the country showing the epic movie with Jennings making short talks to illustrate the doom that awaited bad men. Tilghman didn't talk but stood by for scenery, wearing his pearl handled guns and his gold badge from Dodge City.

Tilghman came out of retirement to take the marshal's job in the oil boomtown at the request of Gov. M.E. Trapp to help bring some order to the town that often was referred to as the most wicked city in the world.

After Tilghman was killed, Bat Masterson, another famous deputy marshal, described Tilghman as the "greatest of us all."

Autry changed tiny town in name only

The 227 residents of the Carter County community of Berwyn thought they had the key to growth and prosperity when the cowboy movie star Gene Autry bought a 1,360-acre ranch nearby and announced that he would move his headquarters there.

They changed the town's name to Gene Autry and staged a big celebration on Oklahoma's 34th anniversary, Nov. 16, 1941, to rechristen the town.

The gala event attracted 35,000 people, including the singing cowboy and Gov. Leon C. Phillips, who watched as the postmaster changed the sign on the post office.

As part of the celebration, Autry broadcast his weekly "Melody Ranch" radio show from the namesake town and announced that he would create a streamlined traveling rodeo that would have its headquarters at his "Flying A" ranch. He said he would spend $75,000 to $100,000 on livestock – a large sum in 1941.

The timing couldn't have been worse.

Three weeks later, the Japanese bombed Pearl Harbor and America was in World War II. Autry joined the Army Air Forces a few months later and was sent to Luke Field near Phoenix, where he took private flying lessons to become qualified for the Air Transport Command.

He spent most of the war years until his 1945 discharge making personal appearances to promote the sale of war bonds and piloting men and cargo to India, Casablanca, Iran and all over the United States.

Meanwhile, the rodeo plans were in limbo. Autry never returned to live at the ranch and made only brief visits -- if that. Some sources say he never returned to the ranch or the town. The Gene Autry Museum's Internet site claims that he made several brief visits.

The community that changed its name to honor a cowboy star is about 20 miles west of Ravia, where Autry graduated from high school.

Autry was born in 1907 in Tioga, Texas, but moved to Oklahoma with his parents as a child and to Ravia when he was 15.

As a boy, Autry sang in his nondenominational circuit-

Tulsa World archives

Before World War II interrupted, the Carter County town of Berwyn had high hopes for Gene Autry's presence there.

riding preacher father's church and got a job at 16 as a baggage handler at the local depot. In return for work, he was taught telegraphy, enabling him to get a job as a relief telegrapher for the Frisco Railroad.

While working in Sapulpa, Autry took guitar lessons on Sundays from R.P. (Bob) Ridley in Tulsa, using a guitar he had bought from a neighbor for $5. Ridley said years later that Autry's guitar playing "was just about average" but that "he sure went the farthest" of any of his students.

Autry used the guitar for his own amusement until the cowboy philosopher Will Rogers heard him singing at the Chelsea telegraph office, where Rogers had gone to send his column to his newspaper syndicate. Rogers advised Autry to continue his singing.

Autry went to New York a short time later to make a phonograph record, but was told he needed experience. He appeared at a number of places in Tulsa and landed a job singing on the Tulsa radio station KVOO as "Oklahoma's Yodeling Cowboy."

A year later, Autry recorded "That Silver-Haired Daddy of Mine," which became an immediate hit with sales that passed 1 million.

Several others of his records sold more than a million copies, too. His biggest seller was "Rudolph, the Red-Nosed Reindeer."

An associate once observed that Autry "likes to joke that the things he doesn't do very well -- play the guitar, sing and act -- have given him the success he has. He decided to be himself, and that's apparently what people like."

Autry quit acting and turned his talent to business in the mid-1950s, amassing a multimillion-dollar fortune. He owned substantial pieces of the Los Angeles Angels baseball team, the Los Angeles Rams football team, several radio and television stations, recording companies, music publishing companies and hotels, as well as cattle ranches and oil interests.

Autry, who died Oct. 2, 1998, has been inducted into both the National Cowboy Hall of Fame and the Oklahoma Hall of Fame.

Hanging turned into 'carnival'

The first person to be executed for violation of the Lindbergh kidnapping law died on a gallows in 1936 at the state penitentiary at McAlester. It was the only hanging ever at the prison.

Arthur Gooch, identified in a June 20, 1936, Tulsa World story as a kidnapper, bandit, larcenist and pervert, was executed under a 1934 law that made it a capital offense to take a kidnap victim across a state line.

He had been convicted in U.S. District Court of kidnapping two Paris, Texas, police officers and forcing them to take him into Pushmataha County, where they were released. He and five other prisoners had escaped from the Okmulgee County Jail a few days earlier.

One escapee was killed by police at the time Gooch was captured.

The Lindbergh law was enacted in the aftermath of the 1932 kidnapping of the 20-month-old son of the famed aviator. The child's body was found two months later. Bruno Richard Hauptmann, a German immigrant, was convicted of the crime and executed.

Tulsa World archives

The Tulsa World's report on the 1936 hanging of kidnapper Arthur Gooch said it had obtained "complete photographic coverage" of the execution but had elected not to publish the pictures, which were "of such a gruesome nature that it was deemed contrary to public policy and good taste to publish them."

A crowd of 350 came to the penitentiary to watch the execution of Gooch, 36, a federal prisoner, on a gallows that was constructed in the prison yard after prisoners had gone to bed. It was dismantled before they arose the next morning.

It took 15 minutes for Gooch to die, a delay that authorities said was the fault of the executioner, Rich Owen, who had electrocuted 59 persons since 1912 but had never hanged anyone.

The noose around Gooch's neck slipped, causing him to choke to death rather than die of a broken neck.

Something of a carnival atmosphere had developed at the prison.

As the witnesses began arriving in the yard for the 5:30 a.m. hanging, they were told that newspaper reporters would be allowed to stand near the gallows, but that lay witnesses would have to remain 100 feet behind.

At least 100 lay witnesses pulled out paper and pencils and claimed to be reporters. They were allowed to remain near the gallows, the World reported.

After the execution, witnesses rushed to the wooden gallows and cut off pieces for souvenirs. Some were able to cut off pieces of the rope.

Gooch's girlfriend, 20, was slipped into his cell to visit him after his mother identified the younger woman as her daughter. When the deception was discovered, the young woman said she wanted to hang with Gooch and threatened to kill herself if Gooch was hanged. He was, and she didn't.

After President Franklin D. Roosevelt denied a last-minute stay of execution, Gooch said, "I don't want to die but if I do, I will feel better after I am gone than he will."

Gooch criticized Roosevelt for his attitude: "I don't feel I should die for such a small crime as mine."

The Gooch hanging was the first legal hanging in Oklahoma since 1911, when Tulsa County Sheriff W.M. McCullough hanged Frank Henson for the murder of Deputy Sheriff Charles Stamper at Dawson five months earlier.

At that time, it was the duty of the county sheriff to perform executions, but the law was changed a year or so later to have prisoners executed by electrocution at the state penitentiary.

Actor lived Hoppy's wonderful life

Former Tulsan William Lawrence Boyd, a one-time playboy, became a "wonderful guy" to conform to the characteristics of his movie screen role as the good guy in the black hat.

Boyd modeled his personal life after his role as cowboy Hopalong Cassidy who didn't smoke, drink, swear or kiss girls and who captured villains rather than shoot them. He became a philanthropist devoted to American youth.

His role as Hopalong Cassidy became the longest-running characterization in Hollywood history. By the time of his death at 77 in 1972 of heart problems and Parkinson's disease, he had made 66 motion pictures and 52 half-hour programs for television.

Boyd also did rodeos, circuses, hospital visits and had his own Hoppyland theme park where cap guns, gunbelts, hats, lunch boxes and other items could be purchased. In 1950, Cassidy was featured on the first lunch boxes to bear an image, and Aladdin Industries sales jumped from 50,000 units to 600,000. He also had been featured in magazines such as Look and Life.

Many of the Hoppy films were shown in foreign countries, creating international fame for the actor. But Boyd never forgot his Tulsa roots and made many appearances here, frequently in support of the Tulsa Charity Horse Show. While here he always visited children in hospitals and at such places as the Tulsa Boys Home and frequently led parades.

Born in Ohio, Boyd took a job as a grocery delivery boy when he was 9. The family moved to Tulsa in Boyd's early teens and he again found a job as a grocery delivery boy, working with the late Fred Johnson, who later became president of the Fourth National Bank.

After his father was killed in an automobile accident when Boyd was 17, he went to California with his grandmother and held several jobs before moving to Flagstaff, Ariz., where he opened a general store. Two actors who met him at the store convinced Boyd he should go to Hollywood to try for a role.

Boyd was cast in romantic roles in such films as "The Volga Boatmen" and "Two Arabian Knights" and married

Tulsa World archives

Actor William Boyd, star of the popular Hopalong Cassidy motion pictures and television programs, poses at the New York Historical Society museum in 1946. Boyd lived in Tulsa as a teenager and never forgot his Tulsa roots, making many appearances here after he found worldwide fame.

and divorced four women, including three beautiful actresses. A 1958 Parade article said he had gone "completely Hollywood," had a Beverly Hills mansion, a Malibu beach house and a Ventura ranch.

The good life came to an end in 1932 because of another actor named William Boyd, who had been arrested at a drinking and gambling party. The morning newspapers used Bill Boyd's picture by error. And although the newspapers apologized, his career plunged downhill.

When the first Hopalong movie was cast in 1935, Boyd was offered the role of Buck Peters who had an ornery, limping, cussing, tobacco-spitting sidekick named Hopalong Cassidy, a character that was created in 1904 by Clarence E. Mulford. Boyd read the script, decided the Cassidy role was more colorful and got the script rewritten to make Hoppy the hero.

Movie executives said Boyd had made Hopalong too much of a gentleman. But Boyd persisted.

Boyd married his fifth wife, Grace, in 1937 and the two remained devoted to each other until Boyd's death.

The responsibility of being a children's hero transformed Boyd into a philanthropist devoted to strengthening the fiber of American youth. He founded a club called Hoppy's Troopers that had a Hopalong code of conduct and that preached loyalty, honesty, ambition, kindness and other virtues.

He also donated money to children's hospitals and homes because "the way I figure it, if it weren't for the kids, I'd be a bum today. They made my success possible. They should benefit from it."

Before he retired in 1966, Boyd traveled six to eight months a year to personally meet as many of his admirers as he could. He also rode his horse Topper in the Rose Bowl parade in Pasadena and the Macy's Thanksgiving parade in New York City.

During a 1954 visit to Tulsa, Boyd told a World reporter "when you've got kids looking up to you, and when you've got parents saying what a wonderful guy Hoppy is, you have to be a wonderful guy."

Oklahoman won 'bunion derby'

Andy Payne ran 3,424 miles in 1928 to help pay off a debt on his father's farm near Foyil.

His race in what was called the "bunion derby" also earned him an Oklahoma political job a few years later that he kept for 38 years.

The "bunion derby" was an 84-day race from Los Angeles to New York for a $25,000 prize that attracted Payne and 274 others. Only 59 completed the marathon that ended in Madison Square Garden on May 26.

Payne, the 21-year-old son of a Foyil farmer, entered the race because he wanted to help pay off a debt on the family farm. He didn't have the $25 entry fee or the $100 deposit required of a runner to assure he could get a bus ticket back to his home, but the Claremore Chamber of Commerce advanced part of the money and Payne's father borrowed the rest.

After reading in a newspaper about the cross-country derby being staged by a Chicago promoter with a $25,000 prize, Payne, a baseball and track star at Foyil High School, hitchhiked to Los Angeles to begin training.

The runners left Los Angeles and followed U.S. 66 as far as Chicago. From there to New York, the race ran wherever the promoter could get a town to pay a fee.

Thousands of Sooners cheered as the runners arrived in Oklahoma at Texola with Payne in the lead. The group later was met by Gov. Henry S. Johnston at the Capitol.

Payne was still in the lead at Bristow but his trainer ordered him to slow down, and when he reached Tulsa he was in third place -- but confident he would regain the lead and would win the race.

"Just wait; I'll finish first in Claremore," he told a World reporter. And he did.

He also expressed confidence that he would win. "I entered this race to finish first at New York City and that is what I am going to do."

Payne also told a World reporter that he ate a lot during the run. "I guess that I have to spend about $2 a day on food besides what (Charles) Pyle (the promoter) puts out.

I eat a lot of chocolate candy, ice cream, green stuff and some meat."

The road between Sapulpa and Tulsa was lined with thousands of automobiles and pedestrians eager for a glimpse of Payne. And when the runners reached Tulsa, the streets were packed. Lee Stadium, where the runners spent the night, also was packed with more than 3,000 who had paid an admission fee to see the runners.

But not everyone in Tulsa was cheering Payne. A couple of doctors warned that the runners would have permanent damage that could cut their lives by 15 to 20 years. "I'd never let a boy of mine enter such a killing race for any amount," Dr. H.C. Childs said. "The whole affair should have been prohibited," Dr. W.J. Trainer said.

Bedlam broke loose as the runners led by Payne neared Claremore, a World reporter wrote. "Hats flew into the air, crowds shrieked and automobile horns blared." A cordon of motorcycle policemen made a path for the runners into the town that then was known as the radium water town. Claremore had sent a truckload of radium water to Tulsa the previous day for Andy to bathe in.

After winning the race, Payne was flown back to Tulsa by Tulsa oilman W.G. Skelly, and he was treated much the way Charles Lindbergh had been welcomed on his return from Europe after his historic Atlantic crossing.

"I owe my success to corn bread," Payne said.

Payne later attended the University of Arkansas and Oklahoma City University School of Law. He worked as a newspaper reporter and in the oil drilling business before he found his profession in 1934.

Taking advantage of the publicity he had received in the marathon, Payne became a candidate for clerk of the Oklahoma Supreme Court and was re-elected every four years until the position became appointive and he retired in 1972. During that period, his wife, Vivian, served two years while Payne was in the Army during World War II. Payne died at the age of 70 in 1977.

Tulsa World archives

Oklahoman Andy Payne ran 3,424 miles from Los Angeles to New York in 1928 to win a marathon called the "bunion derby." He entered the race to win the $25,000 prize to help pay off a debt on his father's farm near Foyil.

Controversy nearly felled the redbud

A protest against making the redbud the state's official tree touched off a skirmish among club women and sent Oklahomans scurrying to their dictionaries, encyclopedias and Bibles in 1937.

They wanted to find out whether the redbud was connected with the suicide of Judas Iscariot after he betrayed Jesus Christ.

After a campaign by a group of women headed by Mrs. Mamie Lee Browne of Oklahoma City, the Legislature had passed a resolution designating the redbud as the official tree. Gov. E.W. Marland was about to sign the bill when he received a telegram from Mrs. Edward C. Lawson of Tulsa objecting to making the redbud the state's tree. She claimed the redbud was not appropriate for that honor because it was the tree used by Judas to hang himself.

"I think we ought to do what the women's clubs of the state want us to do – after careful consideration," Marland said and deferred signing the bill.

The controversy delayed the signing for a week with many siding with Mrs. Lawson, president of the National Federation of Women's Clubs, while the Oklahoma Garden Club Association, the D.A.R. chapters and hundreds of others backed the redbud, which also had another especially influential supporter – Mrs. Marland.

Before the issue was settled, the Tulsa Garden Club began planting redbuds at the approach to the 21st Street Bridge. Club President Mrs. Charles Haralson supported the redbud – even if it might have had a Judas suicide role.

"To glorify the tree that ended the greatest villain of all time seems to me to be quite fitting," she said.

The issue made front-page headlines in Oklahoma newspapers and was reported in other newspapers throughout the country and some in other countries. Before it was settled, a horticulturist was brought into the dispute.

"The Oklahoma redbud tree could not be the Judas tree," Dr. G. F. Gray, of Oklahoma A&M College, said, explaining it is native to Oklahoma. He said the tree used by Judas probably was a wild carob tree that belongs to a different genus of the redbud family than the Oklahoma redbud. He said that tree is native to western Asia and southern Europe and is not found in North America. The Oklahoma redbud is not found in Europe or Asia.

Gray cited a book on herbs written in the 16th century that he said states that the wild carob tree was the one used by Judas.

The fig, tamarisk, dog rose, aspen and elder all have been mentioned in folklore of various countries as the tree used by Judas, Gray said. Practically every country has a tree designated as a Judas tree in its legends, he said.

A native of Jerusalem who lived in Oklahoma City said there was no connection between Oklahoma's redbud and the Middle East's Judas tree. He said they were similar only in that both trees had the same color flowers and both bloomed early in spring.

In her protest, Mrs. Lawson argued that the elm or oak would better symbolize the pioneer spirit of the state.

The Legislature's resolution said in part "when the sturdy and hardy pioneers trekked across the rolling hills and plains, one of the first sights to greet them spread out in a glorious panorama was the redbud tree – a tree that as it arose in the spring from the verdant fields, was emblematic of the eternal renewal of all life; a tree that in its beauty renewed the worn spirit and gave hope to the tired heart of a people seeking homes in a new land.

" . . . adoption of the Redbud as the official state tree . . . would be a small, but fitting tribute, to the part it played in and the beauty it has lent to the lives of the people of this state."

"It is done," was the governor's comment as he signed the resolution nearly a week after the controversy arose. "Now I can go home in peace. Mrs. Marland has been asking me about this every day."

Mrs. G.C. Spillers, a Tulsa backer of the redbud, urged everyone to help plant redbuds "so the entire state can be a mass of pink in the spring." She said she wanted to make the state as famous for its redbuds in the spring as Washington, D.C. , is for its cherry trees.

After Gov. Marland signed the resolution, Mrs. Lawson agreed that the redbud was a beautiful tree and contributed to the Tulsa Garden Club's redbud planting program, which she said was an excellent project.

Garden Club members said the tree on which Judas hanged himself is not named in the Bible. "It's only a legend that it was a redbud," they said.

They were correct. The Bible is silent about what kind of tree, if any, Judas used to hang himself after developing remorse for betraying Jesus for 30 pieces of silver.

The New International Version, Matthew 27:55, says that "Judas threw the money into the temple and left. Then he went away and hanged himself."

Langley put the state before himself

A Pryor lawyer who helped write the Oklahoma Constitution and chose the name for Mayes County was elected to the state Supreme Court in 1930 but served less than a month before resigning.

The departure of J. Howard Langley drew praise from many–not because of a feeling that he wouldn't be a good justice, but instead because of his reason for quitting.

Langley said his health would prevent him from carrying his load on the court docket. He noted that during his campaign for the office he had promised that if elected, he would keep up his end of the work or quit.

"That was a clear instance of patriotism and common honesty," a Tulsa World editorial said when Langley died Oct. 27, 1935, more than four years later. Noting that Langley could have continued as a member of the court and would have drawn his salary until his death, the World said "he set an example of rightful conception of the importance of the court and of consideration for the state."

The World called Langley "the foremost citizen of Pryor and of Mayes County."

After his resignation, Langley spent time regaining his health until Gov. E.W. Marland appointed him as the chairman of the Grand River Dam Authority in 1935, only a few months before he died and long before the dam was built.

His answer to a questionnaire from U.S. Court of Appeals Judge R.L. Williams, a former Oklahoma governor who was trying to keep track of members of the constitutional convention, was terse and to the point:

"Elected to the Supreme Court in 1930, took office Jan. 12, 1931, so completely wrecked myself in the campaign as to render myself wholly unfit for a creditable discharge of the duties of the office and rather than half fill the office, resigned Feb. 2nd, 1931."

Langley's answer to the questionnaire was reported in a 1937 Chronicles of Oklahoma article by W.A. Kornegay of Vinita, who was named to the high court by Gov. William H. (Alfalfa Bill) Murray to replace Langley, a longtime friend.

A native of Missouri, Langley came to what is now Delaware County to help his father and brother on a farm. He returned to Missouri to complete his education, including a correspondence course in law.

Langley was admitted to the bar in 1897 at Vinita. He established a practice the following year in Pryor, where he helped with the building of a small-frame courthouse. He also was responsible for building a more substantial courthouse in 1921, a $160,000 structure that was erected without a bond issue.

The money was raised through various savings of court and county expenses.

When the U.S. entered World War I, Langley was too old for military service. He acted as a legal adviser to the Council of Defense, which earned him recognition from the War Department.

Langley was elected as a delegate to the 1906 Oklahoma constitutional convention and was responsible for naming his county Mayes, in honor of a Cherokee family that had included two tribal chiefs, including his longtime friend Samuel H. Mayes.

He also represented the city of Tulsa in hundreds of condemnation suits to obtain title for land for the Spavinaw Lake water project.

The town of Langley is named in his memory.

Tulsa World archives

J. Howard Langley, a Pryor lawyer, represented the city of Tulsa before serving briefly on the state Supreme Court.

WWII-era journalist was special

A reporter who interviewed Oklahoma war correspondent Earnest Hoberecht more than 10 years after he returned to his home town of Watonga in 1966 didn't know how to begin writing about the interview.

"It's like a gourmet diner contemplating a plate of savory spaghetti," the reporter wrote. "He doesn't know where to begin."

It hadn't become any easier after 30 years.

Hoberecht (pronounced Ho-bright) had a reputation of not taking most things seriously. Talking about a physical exam, he said his doctor had "given up on his weight problem – he's now going to teach me how to be jolly."

But he was serious when writing and talking about events during the wars and in the Far East. He helped United Press (and later United Press International) develop the reputation of providing the top news coverage of Asia.

In his serious vein, he described Gen. Douglas MacArthur as "the right man in the right place at the right time" when discussing reconstruction of Japan.

He also wrote that MacArthur was what the Japanese needed because the general knew how to behave as powerful, aloof, worthy of respect, all-knowing. "He was a white emperor," Hoberecht wrote.

Hoberecht, who went to Asia shortly after the bombing of Pearl Harbor, became one of the best known and most trusted correspondents covering the war. In 1953 he became a vice president and general manager for Asia of United Press International.

After his retirement, he wrote that one of his "great memories" was a survey conducted by the International Press Institute when he was in charge of the Asia operation that concluded UPI "had the best news coverage of Asia." He received many honors, including induction into the Oklahoma Hall of Fame and the Oklahoma Journalism Hall of Fame.

Hoberecht spent nearly a quarter of a century in Asia rubbing elbows with world leaders such as Chiang Kai-shek, the Chinese leader during World War II who later became leader of the Chinese government in exile on Taiwan; MacArthur; India's Prime Minister Jawaharlal Nehru; and South Korea's President Syngman Rhee while covering World War II, the Korean War and part of the Vietnamese War.

As a war reporter, Hoberecht accompanied MacArthur to many Pacific battlefields during World War II. He was

Tulsa World archives

Oklahoma war correspondent Earnest Hoberecht was aboard the USS Missouri when the Japanese surrendered at the end of World War II and was one of two correspondents present in a battlefield tent when the Korean armistice was signed.

aboard the battleship USS Missouri when the Japanese surrendered and was one of two correspondents present in a battlefield tent when the Korean armistice was signed.

While in the Far East, he also became a best-selling novelist with a book called "Tokyo Romance." The Japanese were eager for any information about Americans, but the MacArthur administration had banned the importation of foreign books.

Hoberecht argued successfully that the ruling did not ban books written by Americans in Japan. He hired an expert translator and dictated his soap opera-type book that immediately became a best-seller. When it was translated into English, a reviewer wrote "it is the worst novel of modern times."

"I immediately cabled the reviewer 'your statement that my book is probably the worst novel of modern times is near libelous in view of the fact that I have written worse myself,'" Hoberecht related.

Hoberecht told another reviewer the book was "no more than the Japanese deserved. They lost the war, didn't they?"

In a 1977 interview, Hoberecht recalled that he was tight-fisted when he was in charge of UPI in the Far East. He recalled that one of his reporters in New Delhi had a story from Benares about a holy man who had predicted the end of the world on a certain weekend.

A multitude of people had gathered and the reporter thought he should cover the event.

Hoberecht told the reporter to cover the event but advised "just get a one-way ticket in case he's right."

Hoberecht retired in 1966 and returned to Watonga where he lived until his death in 1999 at the age of 81. He was president of Blaine County Abstract Co. and Earnest Hoberecht Insurance Agency and chairman of Watonga Abstract Co. He also wrote a weekly humor column called Laugh With Ernie.

Hoberecht returned to Korea in 1977 with 80 former war correspondents to dedicate a memorial to the 18 newsmen killed in that war. He was the principal speaker at that event.

"Through the grace of a higher power, we are gathered here today to honor the courage, the work and the memory of brother correspondents who gave their lives in pursuit of their duties," he said.

"Each of us knows in his heart 'It could have been me.'"

Reason for double thanks

Thanksgiving Day is a day set aside to thank God for the blessings we have received because we live in America.

It's the fourth Thursday of November. Every calendar shows Nov. 23 as the holiday this year.

But that hasn't always been the case – especially in Oklahoma and several other states where the holiday was marred by confusion that caused many Sooners to observe double holidays in 1939.

That was the year when President Franklin D. Roosevelt proclaimed Nov. 23, a week earlier than usual, as Thanksgiving to accommodate retail merchants who wanted more time to sell merchandise for Christmas.

Thanksgiving would have been Nov. 30 that year under the custom of celebrating the last Thursday of November that had been followed since 1863. That would have defined the Christmas shopping period at just over three weeks because in those days, Christmas merchandise was not advertised or offered by merchants until after Thanksgiving.

But in Oklahoma, Gov. Leon C. Phillips didn't want to change the holiday and proclaimed the customary last Thursday, Nov. 30, as Thanksgiving for 1939. Governors of 21 other states also opted to celebrate the traditional date rather than what some referred to as "Franksgiving."

"It will be the last Thursday in 1939, 1940, 1941 and 1942," Phillips said. "After that, I don't care what they do about it." He would no longer be governor.

Tulsa Mayor T.A. Penney also proclaimed the traditional last Thursday as Thanksgiving. But City Attorney H.O. Bland said that both days must be observed, pointing out that state law required that. Oklahoma Attorney General Mac Q. Williamson expressed the same opinion – that both dates must be observed.

Bland quoted from a state law that "every day appointed by the president or the governor is hereby set aside as a legal holiday." The city hall, courthouse and federal building offices, except for the post office, took the easy way out.

Associated Press

A helium-inflated Superman floats over the Times Square crowd to lead the Macy's Thanksgiving Day Parade in 1940. The previous year's confusion continued in 1940 when Oklahoma was one of 16 states celebrating Thanksgiving on the traditional last Thursday of November while 32 observed it a week earlier.

They celebrated and closed both days. Many oil companies and other large employers closed both days rather than face the prospect of having to pay overtime, as required by the wage and hour law, for employees working on a holiday.

The biggest confusion was at the post office.

Because the postal service followed city custom, mail was delivered in Tulsa and the post office was open on Nov. 23 but not on rural routes where carriers followed the president's ruling. The reverse was the case a week later when city mail service was suspended and the post office was closed but mail was delivered on rural routes.

Football fans were upset because some games that traditionally had been played on Thanksgiving Day were already scheduled for what turned out to be just another Thursday in much of the country.

Several Tulsa merchants complained that, instead of the boon to business, "the result was anything but better business." They said the two holidays gave them two non-business days in November instead of the usual one.

Some Tulsans even suggested that Christmas could be scheduled in February or August, two traditionally bad business months, to improve sales. But Christmas was celebrated on Dec. 25, as usual.

The Thanksgiving confusion continued in 1940 and 1941 when Oklahoma was one of 16 states celebrating the traditional last Thursday while 32 observed the earlier date. An effort to end the confusion was already under way at Roosevelt's urging.

Legislation passed the House in October 1941 making the fourth Thursday a legal holiday, was approved by the Senate in late December 1941 and signed by Roosevelt.

Everyone in America celebrated the same day in 1942 on Nov. 26, which was both the fourth and last Thursday of November. And it has been the fourth Thursday since.

The last Thursday in November had been set by President Abraham Lincoln in 1863.

A rose in his lapel, 'Brother Robert' gave

An old man shuffling along downtown streets bundled up in a heavy wool overcoat – even in 100-degree weather – was a familiar sight to Tulsans in the 1960s.

He was Robert McBirney, a retired funeral director, philanthropist, churchman, civic worker, Boy Scout leader, patron of culture and youth supporter, who preferred to be known simply as "Brother Robert."

The old man, who died in 1968 at the age of 94, wasn't trying to keep warm, at least in the summer. He wore the coat to cushion him from falls as he walked to favorite places.

He was continuing a practice started at least four decades earlier although his pace was a little slower than his previous fast-walking gait. But he still made daily visits to hospitals, the homes of friends who were ill, to concerts, church services, art exhibits and Scout and other youth events – or just to tell his thousands of acquaintances hello.

He still wore a red or pink rose in his lapel, a flower that had replaced the carnations he wore years earlier, and was never seen wearing a hat as he went about doing what he considered his "daily bit of good."

Born in Donaghadee, Ireland, Brother Robert was a member of a pioneer Tulsa family that helped build the city. He moved to Tulsa with his family in 1904 when his father, the Rev. Hugh McBirney, retired after 30 years as a Methodist minister in Kansas.

After working for a furniture store, Brother Robert opened a funeral business in 1909 in the unit block of West Third Street where Williams Tower 1 now stands. He later moved his funeral home to Ninth and Main streets and then to 11th Street and Boulder Avenue on land now occupied by part of the First United Methodist Church, where McBirney was a life-long member.

Brother Robert told a reporter that he developed a life-long interest in religion and in helping young people because of his father's life as a minister.

That interest in religion led McBirney to pay for simple one-line reader ads on the front pages of the Tulsa World and Tulsa Tribune on Wednesdays – Prayer meeting tonight – in an era when advertisements were not printed on Page 1 of Tulsa newspapers (they're not now, either, but they had been in the 1920s and before).

Those reader ads were only a small part of Brother Rob-

Tulsa World archives
Robert Atkins McBirney, pictured here in about 1916, was a civic leader and philanthropist in Tulsa for many years. He was known as "Brother Robert."

ert's philanthropy toward religion. During his latter years, he supported at least 35 funds to help with the education of missionaries and ministers.

Earlier, he had paid expenses for thousands of Tulsa children to attend summer camps, by donating cabins to both the Boy Scout and Girl Scout camps. For many years, he visited every Tulsa school several times a year to make citizenship awards for the Civitan Club he helped organize and to give hundreds of books such as biographies of Lincoln, Jefferson, Franklin and Henry Ford and on science and nature studies to students.

When Cmdr. Richard Byrd spoke in Tulsa in 1927, a year after making the first flight over the North Pole and more than a year before flying over the South Pole, Brother Robert bought 1,000 tickets for the lecture and gave them to Boy Scouts. Although he didn't want it known who bought those tickets, the word leaked out and it became general knowledge.

It was believed that he had never missed a performance of the Central High School "Daze" until about 1965 when his condition became too frail for him to attend. A front-row seat was always reserved for him. He showed similar support for events at other schools and for University of Tulsa plays and concerts and for plays and concerts at Municipal Theater (now Brady Theater).

Never married, Brother Robert lived with his mother until her death, when he moved in with a sister and later lived in a nursing home. He once told a reporter that he wore the red or pink flower in his lapel in honor of his mother.

An avid reader, he visited the Tulsa World newsroom every night to go through piles of discarded wire stories (before the days of computers, those stories were transmitted by wire to Teletype machines that printed them on paper) that had not been selected for use in the next day's newspaper to take the culls home to read.

Brother Robert could have written a book about his philanthropies, civic work, cultural and other interests in which he participated during more than a half century. But he didn't like publicity about himself.

"I would rather not have a story about me," he told a World reporter a few years before his death.

Lucas painted stark pictures with words

"There ought to be a way to tell you about it but I don't know how. Not with words like 'frostbite.' Not with any temperate-zone words I know."

That's how Checotah native Jim G. Lucas explained to Americans the bitter cold during fighting near Wonju in central Korea, the type of description that won him a Pulitzer Prize for international reporting in 1954.

"There's no describing it," Lucas had written. "Some people call it 'frostbite.'

"Frostbite, hell. That's not the word when the flesh falls from a man's feet. Not when the toes swell and burst out of the shoes. Not when the hands turn black and the finger joints swell as big as a baby's elbow."

"His reporting, mellowed by common understanding of the sacrifices endured by the men in the line, together with unwavering journalistic integrity, has resulted in the most outstanding portrayal of the American soldier in Korea," the Pulitzer committee said of Lucas' work.

Lucas could "paint stark pictures with words," a Tulsa Tribune writer said of him in a 1983 story that recalled his coverage of World War II, the Korean and Vietnam wars. That story marked the 40th anniversary of the reporting that made Lucas famous – his reporting of the Marines' landing on Tarawa, a Japanese-held island in the Gilberts.

"Five minutes ago, we wrested this strategic Gilbert Island outpost and its all-important air strip from the Japanese who seized it from a few missionaries and natives weeks after they had attacked Pearl Harbor," Lucas wrote.

"It has been the bitterest, costliest, most sustained fighting on any front."

Lucas, a master technical sergeant in public relations, went ashore with the Marines on Tarawa for one of the fiercest battles in World War II. His story, the first report of the Tarawa fighting, was published on front pages of newspa-

Tulsa World archives

Marine Lt. Jim Lucas, a Checotah native, (below) and sitting at a typewriter (above) in Saipan on Dec. 11, 1944. Lucas won many prestigious awards for his reporting, including a Pulitzer Prize in 1954. Pictured with Lucas are John Fabian (left) of Chicago, an artist, and Capt. W. P. Cahill of Milwaukee and Pittsburgh, public relations officer for the Fourth Marine Division.

pers throughout the country. Soon after, Lucas was promoted to second lieutenant and received the Bronze Star medal.

That story won the National Headliners Award for the best combat reporting of 1943. It was the first of eight Pacific landings Lucas made with the Marines during World War II; the others included Guadalcanal and Iwo Jima.

Lucas' war reporting also won two Ernie Pyle awards as well as many other awards. Many other correspondents compared Lucas' human-interest reporting with Pyle's, and the Pulitzer citation mentioned his human-interest work during the Korean War, the cease-fire and the prisoner of war exchanges.

The library in Checotah is named in his honor.

Born in 1914, Lucas' newspaper career began with the Muskogee Phoenix. He became a Tulsa Tribune reporter in 1938 and worked for that newspaper until 1942, when he joined the Marine Corps as a private.

After World War II, Lucas joined the Scripps-Howard Newspaper Alliance as its Washington military correspondent. He covered the first atomic bomb test at Bikini and in 1947 went to the South Pole with Adm. Richard E. Byrd.

He went to Korea in 1950 at the beginning of that war and reported from there for 26 of the war's 36 months, including the end of fighting. He was in Vietnam before the big American buildup for fighting there.

Lucas briefed President Lyndon Johnson and Congress on the war in Vietnam after publication of his book, "Dateline: Viet Nam," in 1966. He later wrote a biographical book about Spiro Agnew but died of cancer in 1970 before it was published.

When he learned he had cancer, Lucas volunteered to be part of a research program aimed at finding new methods for treatment.

'Reign of terror' kills Osage family

A crime spree in the early 1920s that became known as the Osage "reign of terror" left at least seven wealthy interrelated Indians and two others dead.

The victims were killed in a plot designed to allow the plotters to collect oil money from the government on headrights held by the Brown family, a group of Osages. Some newspaper accounts from that period at times indicated as many as 21 may have been killed, but later accounts set the figure at nine.

Three men, including wealthy rancher William K. Hale, once known as the "King of the Osage Hills," his nephew and a ranch hand, were sentenced to life prison terms for their roles in the killings – one on a guilty plea and two after jury trials.

The series of mysterious deaths among wealthy Osage Indians began in May 1921 when the decomposed body of Anna Brown, holder of oil land valued at about $2 million, was found in a ravine near Greyhorse.

The body of her cousin, Henry Roan Horse, also known as Henry Roan was found frozen – a .45-caliber bullet hole in his head – in his car in a ravine between Tulsa and Fairfax in February 1923. Another victim was Charley Whitehorn, Anna's cousin, who died of a gunshot and whose body was found near Pawhuska.

Next, George Bigheart, another of Anna's relatives, became ill and was taken to an Oklahoma City hospital, where it was discovered he had been poisoned. As he neared death, Bigheart called for his attorney, Bill Vaughn of Pawhuska, to come to the hospital for a conference.

After conferring with Bigheart, Vaughn started home on a train but when the porter went to wake him in his Pullman berth the next morning, he was missing, and the berth had not been used. Vaughn's body was later found with a crushed skull, on the track near Pershing (about 5 miles south of Pawhuska). Officers later speculated that he may have learned too much from Bigheart.

Victims six, seven and eight were W. E. Smith, his wife, Rita Brown Smith, and a white servant girl who died when

Dave Carman/Tulsa World

their house at Fairfax was demolished by a nitroglycerin explosion on March 10, 1923. It was the first night the Smiths had lived in their house in Fairfax. They had moved there from a country house because they feared for their lives after Roan Horse had been killed.

Rita and Anna's mother, Lizzie Q, also died. At first it was believed that her death was caused by her age, but it later appeared to be part of the plot. Lizzie Q's death and those of the cousins left Mollie Brown Burkhart (Rita and Anna's sister and Lizzie's daughter) as the only member of the Brown family alive and gave her and, by extension, her husband control of the family's wealth. Her husband eventually admitted his role in the killings.

The murder cases remained unsolved until 1925 when federal agents entered the investigation because the killings occurred on the Osage reservation. Hale was accused of being the mastermind in the killings after Ernest Burkhart, Mollie's husband; and John Ramsey, one of Hale's ranch hands, admitted their roles and implicated Hale.

It also was discovered that Hale had a $25,000 insurance policy on Roan Horse's life, though Hale insisted that he had taken out the policy because the Indian owed him money. He maintained his innocence even after serving 20 years in prison and being paroled.

Hale said he exhausted his fortune trying to prove his innocence.

Burkhart, the first to go to trial, told the district attorney after three weeks of testimony that he was tired of lying and wanted to plead guilty to the Smith murders. He was given a life prison term for murder.

Hale received a life term after a U.S. District Court jury found him guilty of murder for Roan Horse's slaying. Ramsey was convicted after three trials in the Smith murders and received a life sentence.

All three were paroled later – Hale in 1947, Ramsey in 1948 and Burkhart in 1959. Burkhart received a pardon in 1966.

Robbery just another business for Tulsan

A Tulsa robber, who sometimes operated legitimate businesses during a long criminal career, and his three brothers helped stage what historians call the biggest train robbery in American history.

The loot in the 1924 foray by Willis Newton and seven others was $2 million, according to most sources. Some, including one of the robbers, claimed the total was $3 million.

Either figure qualified that robbery in Rondout, Ill., as the country's biggest train robbery. It became the basis for a book and a movie many years later.

The robbery may have been a perfect crime except for a gunshot fired by mistake by one of the robbers that hit Newton's brother, Willie. And, according to reporters of that era, if the Newton brothers had been a little "quicker witted."

Two other Newton brothers, Jess and Joe, joined Willis and Willie in that robbery, along with two Chicago gangsters, a Chicago racketeer and a postal inspector, who was the gang's leader and chief planner.

The postal inspector and Willis forced the train crew to stop at Rondout with the mail car across the highway and the gang demanded that certain sacks of mail be thrown out, enforcing their demands by firing bullets and tear gas into the mail car.

The robbery was going well until Willie Newton came running from the rear of the train in the dark. The gang's leader saw a running figure and fired at him, injuring Willie.

"Damn you, you've shot my brother," Willis Newton yelled at the gunman with the itchy trigger finger. As the other three Newton brothers loaded the wounded man into a car, a bystander heard one of them call him Willie.

A few days later, police got a tip that a wounded man was being cared for in a northside Chicago house. The man at first claimed his name was "John Wayne" and that he had been shot while resisting a holdup but later admitted his name was Willie. He was taken to a hospital and the other four residents of the house were taken to jail.

Police later told two other men who showed up at the house that "John Wayne" had implicated them in the robbery.

"Damn. That's the way when a guy thinks he's going to die," one said.

And Willis Newton forgot to tell his wife what alias he was using. He claimed to be H.J. Watson but his wife told police that her name was Louise Newton and that her husband, Willis Newton, was a Texas oil operator. During questioning,

Tulsa World archives

Willis Newton, former bank robber and owner of Tulsa's "Music Box" club.

Willis Newton admitted his identity and provided details of the crime.

Jesse Newton had fled to Mexico but was lured to Del Rio, Texas, to prove that he could ride a horse after police told him that it was the wildest in the world and that no one could ride it. When he mounted the beast, he was arrested.

About $450,000 of the loot was found hidden in the Tulsa house of a brother-in-law – who knew nothing about it – of train robber Brent Glasscock.

The Newtons and others all drew prison terms. Willis Newton was pardoned by President Herbert Hoover after serving half his 12-year prison term. He operated several service stations, a wholesale gasoline distributing company and several night clubs and owned real estate in Tulsa.

But his criminal career also continued. Shortly after his pardon, Newton robbed the Medford bank and was sentenced to 15 years but was released in 1942 after serving seven years.

Willis also got into various kinds of trouble with his bootlegging and gambling activities.

His last major brush with the law came in 1963 when Willis, 74, and a nephew, Noel Bruce Oglesby, were arrested after police found them driving a car containing Frank Brent in chains on the floor.

Newton was tried twice in Claremore on a kidnapping charge. The first trial resulted in a hung jury. A guilty verdict in the second trial was thrown out by the Court of Criminal Appeals for lack of testimony by the victim, who had disappeared.

"I think he's at the bottom of a lake," Sheriff Amos Ward said.

At one time there was talk of Willis Newton playing a bit part in the movie "The Newton Boys," but it was not filmed until 1998, long after Willis died in 1979 at the age of 90.

The Newton brothers, who were reared in Uvalde, Texas, robbed 87 banks and six trains during their career. According to a Uvalde Web site, they collected more loot than the Daltons, Butch Cassidy, Jesse and Frank James and other outlaw groups combined.

"We wasn't thugs like Bonnie and Clyde . . . we was just a quiet businessmen," Willis was quoted in the book "The Newton Boys" by Claude Stanush and David Middleton. "All we wanted was the money, just like doctors, lawyers and other businessmen.

"Robbing banks and trains was our way of getting it. That was our business."

'Boomer' Lillie became Pawnee Bill

Before he died in 1942, Maj. Gordon W. Lillie was the last surviving leader of the "Boomers" who helped settle Oklahoma, but he was best known as Wild West showman Pawnee Bill.

Lillie became captain of the Boomers, a group that sought to colonize Oklahoma's Unassigned Lands, after the death in 1884 of Boomer leader David L. Payne. Various Boomer groups had become a menace to peace along the Kansas border, and the Wichita Chamber of Commerce asked Lillie to organize the bands and lead them into the new territory.

He assembled about 4,000 Boomers and made plans to enter Oklahoma, but Congress passed a bill to open the state for settlement and the Boomers entered the state legally on April 22, 1889. Backed by the Arkansas City, Kan., board of trade, he also was the leader of the "Cherokee Strip Boomers" in 1893.

But the Wild West shows he produced by himself or in collaboration with Col. W.F. (Buffalo Bill) Cody brought Lillie his greatest fame and fortune.

Lillie, who was born in Wellington, Kan., in 1860, worked with a group that was killing buffalo for their hides and trapping other fur-bearing animals, primarily in western Oklahoma.

After a year as a trapper marked by a narrow escape from a small band of Comanche Indians and nearly being trampled by a stampeding herd of buffalo, Lillie went to work for the Pawnee Indian Agency at Pawnee in 1882.

During his time at the agency, Lillie learned to speak the Pawnee language and became a friend of the Indians. A year or so later he was hired by Cody to accompany a group of Pawnees who traveled with Cody's Wild West show, but Lillie left Cody after a couple of years to organize his own show.

After marrying the daughter of a Philadelphia physician, Cody taught his bride, May, how to ride and shoot, and she became noted for her trick shooting from horseback.

Tulsa World archives

Maj. Gordon Lillie (left), also known as Pawnee Bill, and Col. W.F. "Buffalo Bill Cody" both earned their fame through touring Wild West shows.

Pawnee Bill's show grew until in 1908, he and Buffalo Bill merged into "Buffalo Bill's Wild West and Pawnee Bill's Far East" show.

The show closed in 1913 in Denver when it went broke and its assets were seized, leaving Pawnee Bill only a trunk and his saddle. The Lillies retired from show business and went back to their ranch near Pawnee where Lillie had a large private herd of buffalo.

During a European trip before the two Bills merged their shows, Pawnee Bill played to primarily empty seats in Antwerp, Belgium, and went broke, he told a reporter years later. A stranger lent him enough money to continue his European tour and the show earned enough in Holland to repay the benefactor.

He told a reporter that during a Belgium tour, he saw a balloon ride advertised and got in on it. But the balloon broke away and he and the balloonist sat in the wicker basket for three days glaring at each other – neither able to speak the other's language – before they were rescued from where it had landed.

"And the stunt was a dud," Lillie added.

The Lillies celebrated their golden wedding anniversary on Aug. 31, 1936, and were injured in an automobile accident two weeks later. It happened while they were returning to Pawnee from Tulsa in a gold Oldsmobile that was given to them by five friends as an anniversary present. Lillie apparently was blinded by lights of an oncoming car and crashed head-on into it at a curve in the highway near Cleveland.

Mrs. Lillie died four days later, with her funeral conducted by the same minister who had presided when they repeated their wedding vows at their anniversary celebration.

Lillie recovered sufficiently to leave the hospital, but friends said his condition continued deteriorating until his death on Feb. 3, 1942, as friends were preparing to celebrate his 82nd birthday 11 days later.

Carry Nation's chopping sprees

Carry Nation earned fame as a hatchet-wielding woman who smashed bars and other places that served liquor.

But when she came to Tulsa in October 1905, even her hatchet couldn't get her into the dining room at the new Robinson Hotel, where liquor was being served at its opening celebration.

The Robinson banquet had been scheduled for 7:30 p.m. but was moved up 30 minutes after the hotel's owner, W.N. Robinson, heard that the saloon smasher was in town. When Nation arrived at the hotel, she found both of the dining room's doors locked, and no one answered her pounding.

Meanwhile, the 200 at the party drank a toast to her at the suggestion of George W. Mowbray Sr., the president of the Commercial Club, clinking bottles and glasses loud enough that she could hear them, the Tulsa World reported years later in a special Chamber of Commerce section March 19, 1952.

Her trip to Tulsa was one of Nation's last crusading expeditions. A short while later she moved to near Eureka Springs, Ark., where she housed widows, battered women and college girls at "Hatchet Hall."

She began smashing saloons in 1899 when she and her second husband, David Nation, lived in Medicine Lodge, Kan., where he became the pastor of a Christian Church and she helped organize the Women's Christian Temperance Union.

They had come from Seiling, Okla., where they had homesteaded a farm. David Nation, a preacher, lawyer and newspaper man, was the pastor of a church. Carry Nation earned a reputation of lecturing in schools and churches against liquor and tobacco.

She didn't begin breaking up saloons until the couple moved to Medicine Lodge, but she was known earlier for pulling pipes and cigars from men's mouths.

Nation used rocks and bricks wrapped in newspaper to

Dave Carman / Tulsa World

Carry Nation took an ax and carved herself a place in Oklahoma history.

smash several saloons before she adopted the hatchet as her symbol. She sold cheap pewter hatchet pins at speaking engagements and used the proceeds to finance her activities.

Although she had moved to Kansas, Nation didn't forget Oklahoma, making bar-smashing crusades in Oklahoma City and Guthrie and campaigning in other cities for two years before Oklahoma became a state.

She was arrested at least 30 times during her crusades.

She also fought against the Masonic Lodge and other secret societies, a hatred that probably stemmed from her first marriage to a man who she said spent too much time drinking with Masonic lodge members.

The spelling of her first name is disputed. It appears on posters announcing her crusades as "Carrie" and that apparently was the common spelling early in her life, but she later chose to be known as "Carry A. Nation" and is so listed in the Kansas Museum of History, the Encyclopaedia Britannica and Webster's New World College Dictionary.

Carry Amelia Moore was born in 1846 in Kentucky and was married in 1867 to Dr. Charles Gloyd, who had been a Civil War surgeon and was a heavy drinker. She later complained that Gloyd, who had lived with the Moore family for two years while seeking a place to establish his medical practice, was drunk on their wedding day.

She left Gloyd, who died within six months, and met and married David Nation a short time later. The Nations were divorced in 1901, when her husband lost patience with her frequent trips and told her that she would have to choose between him and her hatchet. She chose the hatchet.

Nation collapsed in January 1911 while speaking at Eureka Springs after a final public statement: "I have done what I could."

She died June 9, 1911, in Leavenworth, Kan. Those last words were chiseled onto her tombstone.

Long arm of the law held a noose

He never lived in Oklahoma and died before statehood, but Judge Isaac Parker of Fort Smith, Ark., played a major role in taming Indian Territory.

He was known as "the hanging judge."

It was a title he earned.

During 21 years on the bench, Parker sentenced 151 men and four women to be hanged, and 83 of them were executed. The others' sentences were commuted by the president, usually to life in prison.

Parker, a former Missouri judge who was completing his second term in Congress, was appointed to the federal court by President Ulysses S. Grant in 1875 to replace a judge whose tenure had been marred by corruption. The Western District of Arkansas had jurisdiction over Indian Territory, where outlaws believed laws did not apply to them.

Parker picked up the "hanging judge" nickname in 1875 after his first summer in Fort Smith. He had tried 18 men charged with murder, found 15 guilty, and sentenced eight to die. Six were executed. One was killed trying to escape, and the remaining convict's sentence was commuted because of his age.

The executions were scheduled for Sept. 3, and newspaper reporters from Little Rock, St. Louis and Kansas City flocked to Fort Smith to report on the spectacle, which attracted about 5,000 people.

The condemned men, three white, two Indian and one black, were marched from the jail to the gallows. They sat at the back of the gallows as their death warrants were read and then were asked whether they had any last words.

With the preliminaries over, the executioner, George Maledon, fitted nooses over their necks and sprang the trap doors, dropping all six to their deaths simultaneously, ac-

Tulsa World archives

Judge Isaac Parker earned his nickname — the hanging judge — by the way he wielded judicial authority over Indian Territory.

cording to a 1933 Chronicles of Oklahoma article.

Parker appointed 200 deputy marshals with instructions to arrest all the robbers, killers and thieves they could find in Indian Territory. They took him at his word, and he found most of the suspects guilty. Parker was credited as the strongest force in bringing civilization to the territory.

He was appalled at the deaths of 65 of his officers, who were killed by criminals they were trying to arrest. But the Indian Territory part of his jurisdiction was populated by thieves, killers and other criminals trying to stay out of the reach of the law.

Parker tried 13,490 cases, including 344 capital cases. He worked 10 hours a day six days a week, taking off only on Sundays and Christmas Day.

There was no right of appeal during most of Parker's tenure. When he sentenced a defendant to hang, there was a hanging unless the president issued a pardon.

That changed in 1889 and 1891, when Congress passed laws providing for Supreme Court appeals of death sentences assessed in district courts. Of 46 cases appealed to the high court, 30 were reversed.

An 1896 law gave territorial courts jurisdiction in Indian Territory, stripping Parker of his authority. He died two months later of an illness he had developed months before, but gossips claimed that he died of a broken heart because he had lost his power.

Press reports that started with the first six executions shocked people throughout the country, and Parker's court was called the "Court of the Damned."

Most local people approved of Parker's judgments, feeling that the viciousness of the crimes merited the sentences.

Bank robber done in by poultry truck

Matt Kimes, whose criminal career began in the 1920s, eluded dozens of FBI agents and hundreds of police officers in four states after robbing a bank while on leave from the Oklahoma penitentiary in 1945.

But he couldn't escape a truck loaded with poultry as he tried to cross a Little Rock street, apparently headed for a grocery store he planned to rob.

The 39-year-old convicted killer, who had been identified as the nation's Public Enemy No. 1, died of multiple injuries two weeks after being run over by the truck on Dec. 1, 1945. Police found a .38-caliber pistol, bullets and $1,625 in his pocket.

Kimes had been serving two life sentences for murder. One was for killing Sequoyah County Sheriff Perry Chuculate during a bank robbery in 1926; the other for murdering Beggs Police Chief W. J. McAnally in a double bank robbery in Beggs a year after he escaped from the jail at Sallisaw while awaiting transfer to the state prison.

A model prisoner for 18 years and a trusty who was manager of the prison canteen, Kimes was given a 60-day leave from the penitentiary in July 1945. It was extended to six months in September to give him a chance to prove he had "reformed" and to get signatures on a petition seeking clemency.

The leave was vigorously opposed by Tulsa police because he had been known to hang out in Tulsa and by the relatives of Chuculate and McAnally.

The ink was barely dry on the extension when Kimes was identified as one of three men who robbed the First State Bank at Morton, Texas. He was believed to have staged other robberies later, including the hijacking of a Tulsa grocery store.

Gov. Robert S. Kerr reluctantly admitted that he knew the case had backfired and his pardon and parole board revoked the leave, but the action was withheld from the press. It was not until after the FBI got involved in the search that Kerr's office revealed the revocation.

The produce dealer who ran over Kimes was booked into jail on a charge of reckless driving but was subsequently released and was congratulated by police.

The crime career of Kimes and his older brother, George, began when they began roaming the state as teenagers

pulling burglaries and petty thefts before Matt, George and four companions were arrested in Non, Okla., (near Coalgate) for taking $3 cash and $14.50 in merchandise from a store.

Matt, George and two of the others received three-year prison terms. Matt and George blossomed into big-time criminals when they were released from prison after 14 months.

Less than six months later, they were part of a gang that killed Sheriff Chuculate in Sallisaw during a shootout on Aug. 27, 1926. They were captured a month later and Matt was convicted of murder and given a life term. George was convicted of manslaughter and received a 25-year term. A short time later, George was given a 50-year term on a guilty plea of robbing the bank at Covington.

Matt escaped from the Sequoyah County jail while he was awaiting transfer to the penitentiary. He organized another gang and immediately made plans to pull a double bank robbery. On May 18, 1927, the gang drove into Beggs in two cars and robbed the First National and Farmers National banks.

During a shootout with McAnally, the officer was killed by gang member Roy Brandon, who was paralyzed from the waist down but who was the gang's driver and was armed with a shotgun. Matt fled to Arizona and while free boasted that he and his gang had been able to do what the earlier and equally notorious Dalton brothers gang of Coffeyville had failed to do – rob two banks simultaneously.

Matt was convicted of murder and sentenced to die in the electric chair but that sentence was commuted to life on appeal.

George escaped from the state penitentiary in 1948 by walking away while serving as a trusty. He was arrested 11 months later in Oregon.

He later was given a parole after telling the board, "I was a kid when I came in here. I am an old man now." He had spent more than 30 of his 53 years in prison. There's no record showing he was ever involved in crime again.

George Kimes was last heard from in 1958 working for a timber company in Oregon. He would be 102 if alive today.

MATT KIMES, FREED OUTLAW, HELD IN ARKANSAS HOSPITAL AFTER BEING HIT BY TRUCK

Desperado Suffers Broken Leg, Other Bruises Expected to Recover; Admits Identity but Declines to Discuss Theft Charges

LITTLE ROCK, Ark., Dec. 2 — Matthew Kimes, aged 39, the nation's No. 1 enemy sought since November 1 by dozens of FBI agents and hundreds of peace officers in four southwestern states, was a prisoner in a hospital ward here tonight, a badly battered man.

The man who successfully eluded the determined officers who wanted him as a furlough violator and for a Texas bank robbery, could not get away from an automobile truck in North Little Rock last night. Removed to the hospital in an ambulance, Kimes today admitted his identity.

Although he was badly injured, doctors said he would recover. He suffered a bad fracture of both bones below the left knee; a gouging injury to the left palm of his hand and severe scalp laceration in addition to many bruises.

His face was swollen and discolored so badly that comparison with the FBI dodger bearing his photograph was impossible. However, the profile shown on the handbill matched that of the patient in his bed.

Joe Chambley, aged 23, a North Little Rock produce dealer, driver of the truck that struck the fugitive, received the congratulations of officers here, including Police Chief J. B. Anderson of North Little Rock who explained the reckless driving charge lodged against him Saturday night was merely a formality and would be discharged this week.

B. C. Campbell, police depart-

IES PICTURED IN A HEALTHIER MOMENT

Above Matt Kimes, notorious outlaw, is pictured "sitting pretty" a horse. At present Kimes is in a Little Rock, Ark. hospital to which he was taken Saturday night after being hit by a truck while racing along the streets in North Little Rock. Kimes is described in painful condition. The above photo of Kimes was made at McAlester.

Tulsa World archives

The death of outlaw Matt Kimes was big news in the Tulsa World on Dec. 3, 1945.

State's official Santa was sometimes Scrooge

Yes, Virginia, there is a Santa Claus. Officially. At least in Oklahoma.

For the past 60 years, the Oklahoma Santa Claus Commission has been providing gifts for children in state institutions, first in a state orphanage and later in all institutions.

At one time, the Christmas presents included gifts worth $10-$20 each and included toys, wristwatches, footballs, dolls, makeup kits and other things children like. A bag of candy, gum and peanuts was included for each child. The commission frequently was guided in its shopping by the children's letters listing their wishes and some years asked each child to list his three most wanted gifts.

"...and the main clause in this Commission..."

David Carman / Tulsa World

The Oklahoma Santa Claus Commission may be a unique agency nationwide. It provides gifts for children in state institutions.

Today's gifts are more practical. Instead of toys, the children this year received stationery kits to encourage them to write to family and friends, according to Rhonda Burgess of the Oklahoma Office of Juvenile Affairs, which has supervised the agency since 1996. There will be no bags of candy.

A few years ago, the commission bought duffel bags for all the children because many arrived at the institutions with their clothes and other possessions in plastic garbage bags.

The commission's activities are funded by donations. Burgess said about $6,000 will be needed to finance this year's gift-buying for children between the ages of 12 and 19 in state institutions.

The number of children for whom gifts must be bought is determined in late November and donations are then sought. Many of the donations are not paid until January, Burgess said.

The idea for the commission came in 1935 when state budget officer R. W. Owens and his wife visited an orphanage at Helena. They were shocked – it was Christmas time, but there was no merriment. Most of the children had never heard of Santa. Only a few had ever received a Christmas gift.

Owens and his wife bought gifts for the children that Christmas and used money he collected in fruit jars and milk bottles placed around the state Capitol to buy presents for the children the following year. He persuaded Rep. Sandy Singleton of Stephens County to introduce a bill that was approved by the 1937 Legislature to create the commission with an annual appropriation of $2,500 to buy presents.

The commission's giving was expanded several years later to include children in all state institutions, including delinquents. And the state appropriation grew to about $7,500 in 1983.

Shrinking funds made the state more Scrooge-like in the late 1980s, and for several years the commission has received no state funds but has relied on donations to buy gifts.

After a state lawmaker objected to using state funds to buy gifts for children in penal institutions, Attorney General Jan Eric Cartwright issued an opinion in 1980 that the commission could not spend state money for non-orphans in state institutions because the 1937 law had specified that the Santa Claus Commission would buy gifts for orphans.

That problem was corrected a few weeks later when the Legislature approved a law to allow the purchase of gifts for children in all state institutions.

But the issue became moot with the switch to donations to finance the commission.

For Oklahoma twisters, any time will do

An out-of-season tornado that "just dropped out of the sky" cut a half-mile swath through east Tulsa on Dec. 5, 1975, disproving the belief that such storms always occur in the spring.

Although tornadoes usually are considered springtime events, they can occur at any time, according to the National Weather Service. Other out-of-season storms include four tornadoes that hit eastern Oklahoma, including Tulsa, on Dec. 23 and 24, 1982. Twenty-two December tornadoes have been documented since 1950.

A twister also struck Wilburton that night while a basketball tournament was under way at Eastern Oklahoma State College. Several game spectators were injured by flying glass, but no serious injuries were reported. Several houses and churches were damaged.

"I don't think anybody's tried to put a dollar figure on the damage," Tulsa Mayor Robert LaFortune was quoted as saying in the Dec. 6, 1975, Tulsa World. But the damage was estimated at more than $5 million two days later. The storm injured at least 34, but most had minor injuries.

Tornadoes also were reported in widely separated areas of eastern Oklahoma. The hardest-hit Tulsa area was from 11th to 27th streets along 129th East Avenue.

"It all developed over the city," chief Weather Service meteorologist Ben Barker said. "We had anticipated the system, but we were counting on it being a little farther west."

The Tulsa area had received some large hail on what had started out as a humid and unseasonably warm day, and the weather bureau had predicted the storm system would pass south of the city.

"But the funnels just dropped out of the sky," Barker said.

A dinner had been scheduled that night at the Gracemont Baptist Church. After the storm hit, the food was provided to storm victims who also were invited to spend the night at the church.

"It was to have been a dinner for missions," Pastor Jimmy Reece said. "What better mission could we have?"

A Tulsa woman said she heard a sound like a freight train or a low-flying airplane and went to a window to look out in time to see a neighbor's house explode "just like a bomb."

The witness said the funnel rose up into the clouds and "hovered and hovered and hovered for about 10 minutes. I didn't think it would ever go away."

Another unseasonable tornado hit Tulsa on Dec. 24, 1982, causing an estimated $1 million damage. A straight wind hit Ketchum 1½ hours later, demolishing 21 mobile homes and damaging several others. Several people were injured.

Although a tornado probably was present in Tulsa, Barker said, most of the damage was caused by downbursts, which are strong gusts of wind. "There was no indication of a tornado on the radar," he said, but a small one probably was present. He said the tornado never touched the ground.

Twenty-three were killed, at least 100 were injured and more than 200 houses were damaged in an out-of-season tornado that hit Bethany on Nov. 19, 1930, a storm that still ranks as one of the state's 10 deadliest.

The storm first hit the small Camel Creek School a few miles south of Bethany, killing four students and injuring the teacher and 19 other children. The storm whipped on north through the eastern side of the city.

That storm apparently was part of a system that also spawned tornadoes that hit at Hillsdale near Enid and in Topeka, Kan., where dozens were injured. Another storm also hit the same night at Ola, Ark., killing one and injuring several.

Tulsa World archives

Eastland Baptist Church was one of the buildings destroyed when an out-of-season tornado hit east Tulsa on Dec. 5, 1975. Damage from the storm was estimated at more than $5 million.

Famed lawman had secret past

"Here lies a man."

That's the epitaph that should go on Frank Canton's headstone, Oklahoma Adjutant General C.F. Barrett said when the 78-year-old Canton died in 1927. It was a tribute to Canton's years as a sheriff, a deputy U.S. marshal and as the state's first adjutant general.

But that epitaph hadn't always been appropriate for Canton. If Barrett had known of Canton's early life, he might have suggested something different.

Born in 1849 in Virginia as Joe Horner, Canton moved to Texas with his family as a teenager, became a cowboy and then a drover, moving cattle from Texas to Abilene, Kan.

He turned to bank robbing and cattle rustling after killing a soldier and wounding another in a barroom brawl in 1874 in Jacksboro, Texas. Arrested in 1877, he was sentenced to prison for bank robbery but escaped from prison and his past two years later.

Canton emerged a short time later in Wyoming, where he was hired to capture cattle rustlers by the Wyoming Stock Growers Association.

For the next few years, Canton served variously as a sheriff, a deputy U.S. marshal in Wyoming, Alaska and Oklahoma Territory, as undersheriff in Pawnee County and as an agent of the Oklahoma and Texas Cattle Raisers Association.

He first came to Oklahoma soon after the opening of the Cherokee Strip and became a deputy sheriff at Pawnee, where he lived from 1894 until 1897. Then he went to Alaska to become a U.S. marshal during the Alaska gold rush.

In Pawnee Canton had his closest shave, he related years later. He was searching for two brothers who were suspected of stealing cattle, committing robberies and killing a family they feared would testify against them in a trial for robbery.

He recalled meeting one of the brothers on a Pawnee street and said he walked up to him, looking him in the

Tulsa World archives

Frank Canton was born Joe Horner in 1849. He was arrested in Texas in 1877 and sentenced to prison for bank robbery. He escaped from prison two years later, leaving Horner behind.

eyes. Neither Canton nor the man he wanted to arrest said a word for several minutes.

Suddenly, the fugitive grabbed for his gun but it caught in his clothes. Canton drew his gun, fired, and the fugitive dropped dead with a bullet between his eyes.

Canton returned to Oklahoma in 1901 and became a deputy marshal at Perry. During Charles N. Haskell's campaign to become Oklahoma's first governor, Canton worked as Haskell's bodyguard.

After Haskell was elected, the first appointment he made was to name Canton as the state's first adjutant general, a position the former bank robber retained under Govs. Lee Cruce and Robert Williams.

As adjutant general, Canton was head of the Oklahoma National Guard with the rank of brigadier general, although he had no military experience. In the absence of a state police force, he also was in charge of enforcing the civil law, too.

He became so well-known and respected that he helped organize President William Howard Taft's inaugural parade in 1909, according to "Alias Frank Canton," a biography by Robert K. Dearment.

"No braver man ever lived than Frank Canton and no man done more than he to establish law and order," U.S. Marshal C.F. Colcord of Oklahoma City was quoted in Canton's obituary. "In my opinion, Frank Canton brought more criminals and outlaws to justice than any other peace officer in the Southwest."

Canton related many of his exploits in an autobiography, "Frontier Trails," first published in 1930 and republished in 1966. The information for that book was contained in five thick, hand-written notebooks that Edward Everett Dale organized and put together in 1930.

The autobiography didn't mention Joe Horner., Canton's real name. That part of Canton's life was detailed in Dearment's book in 1996.

Small-town guy turns crimebuster

America's best-known detective always gets his man, using high-tech devices long before their real-life invention to capture or kill strangely named bad guys.

His name is Dick Tracy, and he was created by Chester Gould, a Pawnee native. At one time, "Dick Tracy" appeared in more than 500 newspapers, including The Tulsa Tribune daily and the Tulsa World on Sundays.

Gould, who died in 1985 at 84, created the unswervingly honest detective in 1931 from ideas spawned in the crime-filled streets of Depression-era Chicago. Until his retirement in 1977, Gould led Tracy through battles against such criminals as Cutie Diamond, Flattop and Pruneface.

The strip, now drawn by Dick Locher, still appears in many newspapers, but it has evolved into the chronicling of Tracy's battles with corporate crooks, computer pirates and terrorists.

Gould's cartooning talent became apparent when he was about 14 and drew cartoons of politicians at the Pawnee County Democrat Convention. Some of the politicians were reported to be "fighting mad" at their caricatures, but others bought them.

Tulsa World archives

An Oklahoma native, Chester Gould, created the "Dick Tracy" comic strip, which he drew from 1931 to 1977.

where he worked at various times for each of the city's five newspapers while attending Northwestern University and an art institute.

For 10 years, he sent comic strips and cartoons to Joseph Patterson, the publisher of the New York News, and for 10 years received rejection slips.

Finally, Gould submitted a detective strip that the publisher liked in 1931. He bought it but suggested that the detective's name be changed from Plainclothes Tracy to Dick Tracy. The strip was the first that departed from the "funnies" approach, often showing bullets passing through bodies.

"My thought was to devise a modern Sherlock Holmes who could catch and liquidate gangsters and hoodlums," Gould said. "I try to make my stories authentic, based on real news angles brought out in our newspapers."

Over the years, Tracy battled and defeated such criminals as Big Boy, B.B. Eyes, 88 Keyes, Flattop, Mr. and Mrs. Pruneface, Itchy and Mumbles.

While Gould was still in high school, some of his sketches were used in the Oklahoma A& M College newspaper and yearbook.

His first newspaper job was at the Tulsa Democrat, the forerunner of the Tribune, within weeks of his 1919 high school graduation.

That job entailed drawing cartoons in a campaign against a proposed $5 million bond issue to develop Spavinaw Lake as Tulsa's water source. The Democrat's owner-publisher, Charles Page, was promoting Shell Creek near Sand Springs to be the city's water source.

Gould's cartoons ran on the Democrat's front page daily for six weeks but failed to sway voters, who approved the Spavinaw option, which was backed by the Tulsa World.

Gould spent two years at A & M before going to Chicago,

He also battled the Blank, a faceless man who was named Frank Redrum (murder spelled backward); and Jerome Trohs (short spelled backward). "I wanted my villains to stand out definitely so there would be no mistake who the villain was," Gould once said.

The names of Tracy's friends were no less imaginative. They included Gravel Gertie, who married B.O. Plenty, and their daughter, Sparkle Plenty; Junior Tracy, the street urchin who became a police artist after Tracy adopted him; Diet Smith, an industrialist who supplied Tracy with such things as a wrist radio and wrist TV that were invented by his son, Brilliant Smith; Vitamin Flint-heart, the pill-popping actor, and Sam Ketch-um, Tracy's partner.

Warden kept her boys in line

The inmates at the Oklahoma Reformatory in Granite were "my boys" to Warden Clara Waters, the first woman in America to head a prison for males.

She was known as "Mother Waters" by the prisoners.

Waters was warden at the reformatory for nine years after being appointed by Gov. Henry S. Johnston in 1927, when she was 37.

When Johnston sent her name to the Senate for confirmation, there was widespread lifting of political eyebrows. Senators gulped in amazement but confirmed the appointment.

She brought five years of experience with her – gained from helping her husband, Dr. George Waters, in that job earlier.

"I shall endeavor to do for these boys what should have been done for them when they were children," she promised.

She required all convicts, hard-boiled and errant youngsters alike, to attend Sunday church services. She organized Bible classes, literary societies, set up a recreation program and an education program to teach each inmate a trade.

Whatever convicts might have thought of petticoat rule, they found her an iron disciplinarian, just as her husband had been before her. She considered "rigid-discipline an essential to reformation."

"I enjoyed that work more than anything else I have ever done," Waters told a World reporter in 1976, when she was living in a nursing home in Stillwater.

Waters' association with the reformatory began in 1920 when her husband was appointed warden by Gov. J. B. A. Robertson. George Waters was a dentist and farmer from Pawnee who brought modern methods of reformatory work to the institution that previously had been considered just another prison.

At George Waters' request, Robertson directed that the institution should house only prisoners under the age of 23 who had never been incarcerated before and who were not sentenced to terms of more than 10 years. George Waters also assigned every inmate to a job, teaching them trades they could use after their terms were finished.

Assisting her husband, Clara Waters established a library and a school that all inmates who had not completed the eighth grade were required to attend. The action was unprecedented in those days but was viewed as a progressive step in prison reform.

When George Waters died in 1926, "her boys" and prison employees asked her to assume the warden's job, but Gov.

Oklahoma Department of Corrections

Clara Waters was the first woman in the United States to serve as warden of a prison that housed males. She led the Oklahoma State Reformatory for nine years, starting in 1927.

Martin Trapp didn't consider the warden's post a proper job for a woman.

A year later, Waters was appointed by Johnston, who bucked the political prejudice against women and the advice of his advisers – and drew harsh criticism for it. She reinstituted her husband's methods.

"When I first went down there, they had been having escapes and other problems, and I think the boys resented having a woman as warden but when I left they were calling me 'Mother Waters,' " she said during the 1976 interview.

She said she came to realize that "most of the boys were there because of the kind of parents they had. The parents didn't educate them and they didn't respect the law." She said she tried to make prison life as normal as possible and set down some rules that everyone was required to follow.

Waters lasted through the short term of Gov. William Holloway, who succeeded Johnston when he was impeached, and through Gov. William H. (Alfalfa Bill) Murray's term. She said during Murray's era, she lived month-to-month under the threat of being fired from the $250-a-month post. She said she met with Murray frequently and always had a letter of resignation with her in case he brought up his familiar threat.

At the end of their meetings, Murray frequently told her "well, you can stay for another month."

She was fired in 1935 by Gov. E. W. Marland two days after a guard was killed during an escape by 32 convicts. The prison break came in the wake of investigations by the State Board of Affairs and by State Commissioner of Charities and Corrections Mabel Bassett.

The investigations grew out of a prisoner who claimed his arms were broken while at the reformatory. But 519 of "her boys" signed a petition supporting Waters. "We feel it is our duty to uphold our institution and our warden against unfair or unjust accusations," the petition said. Many prisoners also testified on her behalf at a hearing.

Board of Affairs Chairman Lea M. Nichols told Marland that "I went down there (to Granite) with the preconceived idea that it was no place for a woman, and I feel that way even more strongly now."

Waters also was active in Democratic politics and after being fired as warden became state vice chairman of the Democratic Party and later director of the women's program of the National Youth Administration.

A date that still lives in infamy

The USS Shaw explodes during the Dec. 7, 1941, Japanese attack on Pearl Harbor.

Most Americans had never heard of Pearl Harbor until Dec. 7, 1941.

Even after hearing that the Japanese had made a sneak attack on Pearl Harbor, most didn't realize the significance of that cataclysmic event.

Nearly everyone today knows where it is. Equally well known is the significance of that Sunday morning 65 years ago when Japanese airplanes bombed and strafed Pearl Harbor, Hickam Field and Honolulu. It vaulted the United States into World War II.

Most people who were alive on Dec. 7, 1941, can tell you where they were and precisely what they were doing.

Veteran Tulsa newsman Jack Morris was a young radio announcer at station KOME when he heard the bells on the United Press Teletype clanging insistently on that Sunday. He recalls that he ignored the story that was sent as a flash, the highest priority for a UP story.

Morris had never heard of Pearl Harbor.

The bells continued clanging as details of the attack were reported. He finally called the station's news director, who had heard of Pearl Harbor. He rushed to the station to get on the air.

I was watching a movie when I heard about the attack and later helped my dad put out the only extra edition the Stigler News-Sentinel ever published.

The Lyric Theater in Stigler that day was showing a movie called "The Rains Came" that was based on a book by Louis Bromfield. The theater was full.

Midway through the feature film, the lights came on and the manager walked out onto the small stage in front of the screen.

"The Japanese have bombed Pearl Harbor," I recall him saying. The reaction at first was something like "so what?"

He also explained that Hickam Field and Honolulu had been hit in the attack that left thousands dead. He told us that these places were in Hawaii, an American territory in the Pacific. He also told us that President Franklin Roosevelt was expected to ask Congress for a declaration of war against Japan the next day.

I never got to see the end of that movie. Everyone left the theater numb with fear that an enemy could attack U.S. territory. They also were apprehensive about the future. Many still couldn't place in their minds where the Japanese had attacked.

I walked the two blocks to my dad's newspaper office, where he was already working on an extra edition of his weekly newspaper. The extra was made up of a new front page with stories about the attack and the location of Pearl Harbor.

It also included a new editorial page with some strongly worded opinions about what we should do to Japan and two pages picked up from the previous Thursday's edition.

My dad wrote the stories from information he heard on the radio and got from calling an editor at the Muskogee Phoenix, which had wire services. We delivered free copies of the extra to every house in Stigler that night.

It was the first word many residents of Stigler had of the bombing. Radio reception there was frequently poor and people didn't listen to radio except for specific programs.

The president was correct. Dec. 7, 1941, is a "date that lives in infamy," just as he told Congress in his request that it declare war against Japan.

Oklahoma quickly answered call to war

President Franklin D. Roosevelt asks Congress on Dec. 8, 1941, for a declaration of war after the Japanese attack on Pearl Harbor.

President Franklin Roosevelt asked Congress for a declaration of war against Japan on Dec. 8, 1941, the day after the Japanese bombed Pearl Harbor.

But he didn't have to urge Oklahomans to volunteer for military service. They were joining as fast as military recruiters could take them. One eager Tulsan even called a Navy recruiter at home on Sunday night (Dec. 7) but was told to call back the next day.

The Tulsa Army recruiter said nine men had been accepted but about 200 had sought to enlist on Dec. 8. The Navy accepted 35 from the 100 who wanted to enlist and the Marines accepted 25 on that first day of the war. Those numbers swelled by 47 more Tulsa-area men ready to fight the next day. And the numbers of volunteers continued to grow daily.

Many Oklahoma civilians were already in uniform.

They were members of the 45th Infantry Division, a National Guard unit made up of Oklahoma, New Mexico, Arizona and Colorado men. The unit was among several Guard divisions totaling 60,000 men that had been federalized in September 1940 for a year of training – a year that was extended so that the division was still on active duty when Pearl Harbor was bombed and until the end of the war in 1945.

The 45th was sent to Fort Sill but was moved later to Camp Barkeley near Abilene, Texas. After training the division was sent to Europe in June 1943 for 511 days of combat in Sicily, Naples-Foggia, Anzio, Rome-Arno, Southern France, Ardennes-Alsace, Rhineland and Central Europe.

Federalization of the Guard left Oklahoma with only the 155-member highway patrol as a statewide force. After hearing about the Pearl Harbor bombing, state Safety Commissioner Walter B. Johnson canceled all leaves of highway patrol troopers, and the officers were directed to remain in contact with their superiors when they were off duty.

The OHP officers were directed to patrol in the areas of refineries and defense facilities, such as the Douglas bomber plant in Tulsa, the gun powder plant at Chouteau and the Air Corps depot (now Tinker Air Force Base) in Oklahoma City, and to stay within a reasonable distance of them.

A few days later, Tulsa's city commission authorized the purchase of two new patrol cars and the hiring of two new officers. They joined seven officers assigned to patrol Spavinaw Lake and to make twice-daily patrols along the 70-mile water-flow line from Spavinaw to Tulsa.

Police Commissioner Russell Cobb said one of the new police cars would be stationed at the dam and would be equipped with a two-way radio capable of communicating with police in Tulsa.

Comanche code talking foiled Nazis

A World War II soldier from Oklahoma helped the Allies win the war by talking in his native tongue – something he was forbidden to do as a child.

Charles Chibitty, who died in 2005, often recalled that he had been forbidden to speak his native Comanche language while attending a government school at Fort Sill. But that language became a key element of the Allies' success in the D-Day landing on June 6, 1944.

Chibitty and other Comanches relayed critical information between commanders at the Normandy Beach landing. The Nazis were never able to break the code because they didn't know the Comanche language, which was not based on Latin and was not written down.

After the war, a Nazi general asked an American general "what was that unbreakable code the Americans used?" Chibitty recalled.

Using Indian code talkers to send messages between military officers wasn't new when Chibitty and about 20 other Comanches, all either related or close friends, joined the Army to comprise the 4th Signal Co. of the 4th Infantry Division. They spent three years training at Fort Benning, Ga., before seeing their first action on D-Day.

They later accompanied the first troops into Paris and Germany. They also helped retrieve a battalion of the 30th Infantry Division, the so-called "lost battalion," at Mortain and were instrumental in the Battle of the Bulge and in fighting near Luxembourg.

Chibitty recalled that the first message he relayed was to

Charles Chibitty

American Indian code talker Charles Chibitty used the Comanche language to encrypt messages in World War II.

another Comanche on an incoming boat on D-Day and involved the location of fierce fighting with a plea that "we need help."

In 1999, Chibitty, who had won many medals, received the Knowlton Award at a Pentagon ceremony for his outstanding intelligence work. Gov. Frank Keating declared a "Comanche Code Talker Day" in Oklahoma in honor of Chibitty.

Born in 1921 near Medicine Park, north of Lawton, Chibitty attended Haskell Indian School in Lawrence, Kan. He also attended an Indian boarding school at Fort Sill.

The boys were punished if they were caught speaking Comanche. But that didn't deter them; they used their native tongue whenever they could.

After his Army discharge, Chibitty and his family settled in Tulsa and Chibitty became a glass worker.

Chibitty became a nationally known Indian dancer and helped start an annual Indian powwow at Mohawk Park.

In 2004, Chibitty became the first member of the Tulsa City-County Library's American Indian Resource Library's "Circle of Honor." The award recognizes American Indians who enriched the lives of others.

The first use of Indian code talkers came before Chibitty was born – during World War I when Choctaw Indians were used to transmit secret messages. And Navajo Indians were used as code talkers in the Pacific Theater during World War II. Neither the World War I Germans nor the Pacific Theater Japanese were able to decipher the codes.

Orphan built department store chain

This is an ad for the grand opening of the first C.R. Anthony's store in Tulsa.

Tulsa World archives

A penniless orphan who arrived in Indian Territory in 1898 started a department store chain bearing his name that had grown to more than 300 stores before his death at 91 in 1976.

The pauper-turned-millionaire was Charles Ross Anthony, who told a Tulsa World reporter in 1973 that "I've got more pleasure out of my work than anything else I've done."

Anthony's life was a classic rags-to-riches story that earned him a Horatio Alger award in 1963. The award is based on the success stories by 19th century author Horatio Alger Jr.

Born in Tennessee to a tenant farm family, Anthony began chopping and picking cotton when he was 7. He was orphaned when he was 12, quit school and grubbed sassafras roots and split rails to earn money for food and eventually saved $25.

He used his savings to buy a ticket on a "home seekers" special train headed for Indian Territory and arrived in what now is Holdenville. There he got a job in a general store that paid him $1 a month as well as a place to sleep in a chicken pen.

For years, it was reported frequently that Anthony had only $2 in his pocket when he arrived in Holdenville but he told a World reporter in 1971 that was incorrect – "it was 2 cents" he explained with a grin.

Five years later, he bought the store with a little cash and a $5,000 bank loan that he paid off during his first year of operation. But the next year, he nearly went bankrupt because floods hit the area and wiped out farmers to whom he had extended credit.

"That was one of the bad breaks that was about the best thing that ever happened," he recalled many years later.

"I've never done credit business since. Of course, it can be done, but the customers have to pay for it through higher prices." Anthony stores' cash-and-carry policy continued until the advent of credit cards many years later.

After the flood, Anthony sold his business and moved to Wewoka where he met his wife, Lutie Mauldin, in 1910. They moved to Muskogee, to Cleveland, Okla., and later to Idaho where Anthony worked for J.C. Penney before returning to Cleveland as a partner in the small chain of J.P. Martin Dry Goods Stores, the same firm he had worked for earlier.

Anthony bought a store in Cushing from Martin in 1922, and it became the first of the C.R. Anthony's chain that had grown to 324 stores in 21 states when Anthony died.

When Anthony was honored at a ceremony in Cushing in 1973 by the Cimarron Valley Historical Society, an elderly man approached him, opened his suit jacket and showed Anthony the label.

"Bought it right here in your store 41 years ago," he told Anthony.

"That's the trouble with our merchandise," Anthony replied quickly. "It wears too dang long."

Anthony left an estate of $10 million, which went to his family, a longtime employee and charity.

Anthony was succeeded as president of the company by his son, Guy Anthony, in 1972 when C.R. Anthony retired. Guy Anthony was succeeded in 1980 by his son, Bob Anthony, who is one of Oklahoma's three corporation commissioners. Stockholders sold the chain to Stage Stores of Houston in 1997 and the Tulsa stores were closed. The other stores in the chain were renamed Stage.

'Dr. Bob' was active in more than medicine

The temperature was at least 100 degrees, and the Tulsa Downtown Lions were collecting scrap paper to raise money to finance the club's projects.

When Dr. Robert D. McCullough returned home that day, soaked in perspiration and smeared with newsprint ink, he proudly announced to his wife that he had collected 7,268 pounds – more than any other member.

The paper he had collected would bring $28, he added, prompting his wife, Bert, to suggest that it might have been easier for him to just donate $28.

"No, honey," he responded, "this way I gave a little bit of Bob McCullough."

That was typical of the man who preferred to be known simply as "Dr. Bob" and who later became the president of Lions Clubs International; served as president of the American Osteopathic Association; president of the Oklahoma Osteopathic Association and was named the association's "doctor of the year" several times; president of the Oklahoma Board of Health; and of the International Academy of Preventive Medicine.

Whatever the activity, he gave "a little bit of Bob McCullough" – although others might challenge the reference to a "little bit."

McCullough, 69, died in 1983 four days after being honored at the dedication of a new wing of Oklahoma Osteopathic Hospital (now Oklahoma State University Medical Center). There he served as chief of staff, president of the board of trustees, chairman of the building committee and as a lecturer to interns and residents. He had been named the hospital's doctor of the year multiple times.

Born in Indiana, McCullough was reared in Tulsa and was expected to become an engineer or teacher, the careers chosen by other members of his family. But he chose to attend the Kansas City College of Osteopathy and Surgery and set up a general practice in Tulsa.

McCullough later took a job as a surgeon in Muskogee, where he joined the Lions Club, but came back to Tulsa in 1943 and transferred to the Tulsa Downtown Lions.

After serving as Tulsa Downtown Lions president, McCullough became the first governor of District 3-O (northeastern Oklahoma) when the state was redistricted to accommodate the burgeoning membership. He was elected as an international director, and in 1970 became the third Oklahoman to be elected president of the international association, which by that time had 932,000 members.

As international president, he traveled the world with his wife visiting Lions organizations.

Meanwhile, he also had been giving "a bit of Bob McCullough" to the First Baptist Church, where he was a deacon and taught a Sunday school class for many years. He also served the Youth for Christ organization and the Society for the Preservation and Encouragement of Barber Shop Quartet Singing in America, which he helped organize and had served as Tulsa chapter president.

McCullough often said "religion is deeply important to me" and added that "I've anchored my life to Jesus Christ with a complete commitment to him." He had worked with the Wycliffe Bible Translators as a missionary in several countries and was on the board of the Southwestern Bible Seminary.

McCullough also loved to sing and was lead singer of a barbershop quartet called the Chord Busters, which won a 1941 national competition. He later was a member of a quartet called the Flying L Foursome, which sang at the wedding of Dale Evans and Roy Rogers and at the inauguration of President Harry S. Truman.

For several years, McCullough directed the Community Sings program on the lawn of Philbrook Museum and played cornet in the Downtown Lions Dixieland swing band.

His other activities included working on fundraisers for the United Way, the Red Cross and the YMCA, and many more.

And to all of those, he "gave a little bit of Bob McCullough."

Tulsa World archives
Dr. Robert D. "Dr. Bob" McCullough, past president of Lions Clubs International, was known for giving "a little bit of Bob McCullough" in a variety of fields.

Tree grows on designing woman

A tree grew through the roof of a house that Oklahoma's first woman architect designed for herself.

The alternative for Mary Caroline Cole would have been to cut down the large elm that was on the site where she wanted to add a combination office-living room addition to her small home at 15 E. 21st St. in 1955.

"I didn't have the heart to cut it down," the architect later told a Tulsa World reporter. "It was here first."

To accommodate the tree, Cole had holes cut in the roof for the branches to grow through, fashioned what she called "turtleneck sweaters" of clear plastic and added door springs to hold the "sweaters" tight against the branches. She put charcoal around the base of the tree to keep the soil sweet.

She also designed glass gable ends to the room to allow her to watch the moon as it moved across the sky – an idea that came to her as she lay in bed in the unfinished room. "The view was lovely, much too lovely to lose when the roof was added," she said.

The pioneering architect slept in the room even before the walls were finished, explaining that her bulldog, Honey Finn, slept on the foot of her bed and she kept a shotgun beside her.

But the nature-loving architect's efforts to save that tree failed a few years before her death in 1991 at the age of 78. A leak that couldn't be stopped developed around the tree and she had to have it removed. The house was removed a few years after she died.

Cole specialized in breaking down barriers in her profession and in designing buildings that were "friendly" to people with physical limitations.

She developed an interest in architecture in the late 1920s when her father, C.C. Cole, was chairman of the building committee at Boston Avenue Methodist Church. The building had been designed by a woman, Adah Robinson, a Central High School art teacher, she said. (Many say it was designed by Bruce Goff, who had been one of Robinson's students.)

Cole at first majored in history at Smith College but decided when she was a senior that she would rather be an architect. She received a bachelor of architecture degree in 1941 from Cornell University, the only woman in the graduating class.

She designed a house in 1949 for a child with physical limitations and began her life-long interest in helping people with disabilities. She later served on the governor's committee on the employment of the handicapped and the Tulsa mayor's commission on employment. She helped compile the barrier-free requirements for Tulsa's building codes.

She was the only Oklahoma architect delegate to the first White House conference on handicapped individuals in 1976. She also was one of the first women named a fellow of the American Institute of Architects.

Cole learned early in her career that a woman architect shouldn't inspect a project while wearing a skirt. The first time she went to a building site, she started up a ladder while wearing a skirt, causing a sudden halt to the hammering and sawing. She recalled that she climbed back down, went home, changed to slacks and returned to finish her inspection without incident.

She designed several churches, office buildings and three Tulsa fire stations.

Tulsa World archives

Tulsa architect Mary Caroline Cole was the first architect to design Tulsa fire stations with doors at both ends of the building to allow firetrucks to drive through instead of backing into the garages. The design was later adopted as standard by the city.

Sleuthing help start Midwest City

The site for a proposed huge U.S. Army Air Corps facility wasn't revealed but "it was easy for anyone with any sense at all" to figure it out.

At least that was the opinion of William P. "Bill" Atkinson, who did figure out the exact site, secretly bought adjacent land and established a community that became Midwest City adjoining what today is Tinker Air Force Base.

Atkinson, a real estate developer and former newspaper publisher and college journalism teacher, had no information about the proposed location of the Midwest Air Depot other than the formula printed in The Daily Oklahoman in February 1941.

Tulsa World archives

William P. "Bill" Atkinson (center), founder of Midwest City, gives a victory salute during an election rally with former opponents Preston Moore (left) and George Nigh. Moore and Nigh endorsed Atkinson in his 1962 Democratic runoff election with former Gov. Raymond Gary. Atkinson won the runoff, but lost the general election to Henry Bellmon.

The depot location required several thousand acres of level land within 10 miles of a major city, at least four miles from an oil well and near a railroad.

Using the First National Bank as the center, he drew a circle on a map of the area and checked for oil wells and a railroad line. "Anyone could have done it," he said later, according to a 1999 Chronicles of Oklahoma article.

Atkinson found a large plot of level land nine miles from the center of Oklahoma City near Marion Railroad Station. He found that farmers on the south side of the street weren't interested in selling their land although one said he might be willing to sell some later for $150 an acre.

The farmers on the other side of the street were willing to sell and Atkinson, using the $150 per acre price, bought two 160-acre tracts. He used the land to establish Midwest City, a community named after the original name of the proposed military facility, Midwest Air Depot.

A native of Texas, Atkinson had graduated from Texas Christian University with degrees in journalism and business administration. After marrying his high school sweetheart, he moved to Oklahoma City with his wife, where he began publishing the Oklahoma Star, a newspaper that served 22 churches.

He took an additional job of selling real estate in 1936 and later another job as a journalism professor at Oklahoma City University. He was teaching in the morning, running his newspaper in the afternoon and selling real estate at night.

With growing success in real estate, he gave up his other two jobs and became active in the Oklahoma City Chamber of Commerce. That was where he got acquainted with chamber leader Stanley Draper and Daily Oklahoman Publisher E. K. Gaylord. Atkinson became one of the "fair-haired boys" of the chamber as a member of the executive committee.

But that changed after Atkinson established his separate city near Tinker, and he and Draper and Gaylord became bitter enemies.

Trying to fulfill a longtime dream, Atkinson ran for the Democratic nomination for governor in 1958 against Tulsa County Attorney J. Howard Edmondson. Atkinson won the greatest number of votes in the primary election but didn't poll enough for a victory and lost to Edmondson in a runoff election.

He ran again in 1962 and won the Democratic primary, but lost to Republican Henry Bellmon in the general election. He was the first nominee of the Democratic Party to lose the governor's race, but that is another story.

Court denied Trapp's bid for Governor

Martin Trapp had served as the state's chief executive for nearly three years, but he never considered himself the governor.

At least that's what he claimed when he filed for governor in 1926 in the face of a constitutional provision that prohibited a governor from succeeding himself. His theory was that he had not been elected as governor, never took the oath as governor and became only acting governor when Gov. Jack Walton was impeached in November 1923.

The state Election Board agreed in a ruling that was suspect because, as one of Trapp's opponents for the Democratic nomination pointed out, Trapp appointed two members of that board and controlled the appointment of the third.

The Oklahoma Supreme Court ruled that Trapp was ineligible to seek the Democratic nomination for governor.

Trapp considered resigning from the governor's post to make himself eligible, a move the high court refused to consider.

"The person who fills the office of chief magistrate is styled the governor of Oklahoma," the court's opinion said. "He is the governor for the simple reason that he governs; he governs for the reason that the constitution expressly vests him with authority to do so; therefore he is the official governor."

"I felt I could have been elected that year had not the Supreme Court ruled against me," Trapp told a reporter

Oklahgoma Press Association

Martin Trapp acted as governor after the impeachment of Gov. Jack Walton. It took a state Supreme Court ruling to determine that that meant he actually was the governor.

several years later. Trapp made only one more political effort – as a candidate for governor in 1930. He placed fourth in the primary election for the Democratic nomination. William H. "Alfalfa Bill" Murray won the nomination and the governorship.

Trapp had succeeded in bringing harmony to many areas of the state after succeeding Walton. While serving as (acting or actual) governor, he reorganized the state Highway Department, helped build the state's first state highway system, and reorganized the state Health Department and the penitentiary. When he left office, the state treasury had a $2 million surplus.

"The success of my administration was due to the fact that I sought and secured competent men and women to fill responsible positions," he said.

Born in Robinson, Kan., Trapp came to Oklahoma in 1899 with his parents, who homesteaded in Logan County.

Trapp's first political activity was in 1904 when he was elected as county clerk of Logan County, although he was a Democrat in a Republican county. He was a spectator at the constitutional convention in Guthrie and was elected the first state auditor in 1907, a position he held until being elected lieutenant governor in 1915 and 1921.

Following his stint as governor, he became an investment securities dealer in Oklahoma City. He died in 1951.

Gable traded oil field for big screen

Rhett Butler, played by one-time Oklahoman Clark Gable, in the 1939 movie "Gone With the Wind," rescues Scarlett O'Hara, played by Vivien Leigh, during the fall of Atlanta.

"Frankly, my dear, I don't give a damn!"

That epithet spoken to Scarlett O'Hara by Rhett Butler at the end of the 1939 epic movie "Gone With the Wind" was the first time such a word had been said on a movie screen. Mild as it seems today, it was considered shocking to some.

It was Butler's response to Scarlett's plaintive "If you go, where shall I go, what shall I do?" moments before he walked off into the fog and the movie ended.

With much coarser language common in contemporary movies, few would even give such a statement a second thought.

Butler was played by Clark Gable who lived in Bigheart, Okla., and worked in the oil fields of Oklahoma as a young man; whose appearance on a movie screen during the 1930s made female hearts skip beats; and who became known as the king of the movies.

Born William Clark Gable in Cadiz, Ohio, in 1901, his mother died when he was 7 months old and he was looked after by his grandparents until his father remarried two years later.

He became hooked on acting when he saw his first stage play in Akron where he worked in a tire factory as a teen-ager.

When his stepmother died, Gable's father insisted that Clark join him in the oil field in Osage County. He later worked briefly in a Tulsa haberdashery but returned to Bigheart to join his father working in an oil field.

"My father said to me, 'Come with me to Oklahoma, and I'll make an oil man out of you,'" Gable recalled years later during an interview in Tulsa.

"It was a rough business," Gable recalled. "I would get up in the morning and in the freezing cold I'd have to go climb a rickety 85-foot wooden tower in a driving wind to oil the bearings on the rig – I also had to chop wood to keep up steam in the boilers.

"My job was to get a fire going, and after the driller heated the bit to a white heat, I'd have to swing at it with a 16-pound sledgehammer to sharpen the eating edges.

"I worked like this seven days a week eight or nine weeks at a time.

"I said to myself there must be a better way of making a living but I didn't know how to go about it."

Gable apparently found the better way when he turned 21 and his grandfather gave him $300 that allowed him to leave the oil field and head to Kansas City, where he joined a touring company known as the Jewell Players for $10 a week.

It wasn't long before he was in Hollywood where he had a series of acting jobs that included "It Happened One Night," a film for which he won an Oscar in 1934, and "Mutiny on the Bounty," which earned him an Oscar nomination in 1935.

The actor's tool-dressing days in an oil field weren't over. He starred in "Boom Town" in 1940 in a role that included dressing tools on a cable tool rig. The movie was set in Burkburnett, Texas, but also included scenes set in Tulsa and had its premier at the Orpheum Theater in Tulsa.

Gable died in 1960 at the age of 59, and his body was buried beside the third of his five wives, actress Carole Lombard.

Sooners' fate in Alcatraz escape unknown

Alcatraz, a former federal prison located in San Francisco Bay, was essentially escape-proof, but Oklahoma outlaws Theodore Cole and Ralph Roe might have gotten away alive.

Two Oklahoma badmen serving long terms may be the only prisoners to ever escape from escape-proof Alcatraz Prison – if they made it out.

That's a big if.

Federal prison officials and the FBI believed that Theodore Cole, 27, of Stroud, and Ralph Roe, 33, of Duncan died before reaching the mainland from the fog-shrouded island prison in San Francisco Bay on Dec. 16, 1937. No bodies were ever found, but the sea was rough and could have washed away their remains.

"I doubt if even the most powerful swimmer could have survived those currents," said Warden James Johnston. "And neither of the prisoners was physically powerful."

In spite of official belief that the two died trying to swim from the prison, reports of sightings of the two came from California, Peru, Chile, Kansas, Tulsa and other places for several years. But those reports didn't change the officials' minds.

A former prisoner told authorities that Cole had told him his outside contacts would arrange to have a boat pick him up in the bay on a foggy day and that he would make the break just after the noon check.

The Alcatraz warden declined to comment on that report but pointed out that "every prisoner in Alcatraz thinks of escape, and it's no news that Cole had such plans."

Among the sightings claimed was one in 1939 when a suspect in the slaying of a Kansas undersheriff told officers that he had played poker with Cole and Roe less than a week earlier.

Several Tulsans, including a drug store clerk, told police in 1940 that they had seen the two here. Two hitchhikers reported they had been given a ride by a man who boasted of escaping from Alcatraz. He told the hitchhikers that his companion was following in another car and the two were looking for a bank to rob in a small town near Tulsa.

Cole, who had once been sentenced to death by a Tulsa judge, was serving a 50-year term for kidnapping a Cushing man, and Roe was serving 144 years for robbing a Sulphur bank. Both had been transferred to Alcatraz from Leavenworth, Kan., on Oct. 3, 1936.

Cole had been a criminal since he was 11. He had shot an officer in Hot Springs, Ark., when he was 14. Roe's criminal career started when he was 19.

A Tulsa judge sentenced Cole, then 17, to die in the electric chair when he pleaded guilty in 1929 to a $415 robbery of a bottling plant. Within two months, Judge Saul Yeager had received about 3,000 letters from around the country condemning him for such a sentence.

"The boy is a potential killer and deserves such a sentence," Yeager said. But Gov. William J. Holloway heard from several women's organizations and was instrumental in getting the term reduced to 15 years.

Cole killed his prison cellmate at the state penitentiary in McAlester a few months later but was acquitted on a self-defense claim.

He also had made other escape attempts and was critically wounded by a gunshot when he tried to break out of the prison yard at McAlester. Less than two months after his recovery and return to the prison, he escaped by concealing himself in a bag of outgoing laundry.

While free, he committed several robberies and kidnapped a Cushing man and forced the man to drive him to Illinois. After his capture, he was held in the Oklahoma County jail where he tried to escape by hiding in the garbage.

That escape might have been successful if he hadn't sneezed while in the garbage can, giving officers a tip something was up.

Cole and Roe were among 34 prisoners who attempted to escape from Alcatraz during its 29 years as a federal prison. Twenty-three were captured, six were shot during their break attempt and two drowned.

Only the fate of Cole and Roe among those who tried to escape is unknown. The Bureau of Prisons Web site states they are listed officially as missing and presumed dead.

Reporter became 'Mr. Oklahoma News'

A Tulsa World reporter who was barred from legislative meetings during a 1916 special session found the perfect solution to get back into such sessions.

He ran for a seat in the House of Representatives and was elected.

That meant that pioneer newsman Glenn Condon, whose news career began in 1907 when he went to work for the Tulsa Democrat, couldn't be kicked out of future meetings.

But his legislative career didn't last long. Before his term ended, Condon resigned to join the Marine Corps and was shipped to Europe to fight in World War I.

Condon's career was "parallel with the history of Oklahoma and possibly more interesting," a speaker at a Chamber of Commerce public forum told about 300 friends of "Mr. Oklahoma News" in 1964.

It was an appropriate analogy.

Indeed, his career had been interesting. Born in Iowa, he came to Oklahoma City in 1892 as a baby and got his first newspaper job in 1907 at the Tulsa Democrat. When things were slow, he was sent to the home of the editor to rock the cradle of the editor's baby, he recalled at that 1964 forum.

Probably best remembered as the radio news reporter with a staccato delivery, his interest in a news career developed from selling newspapers on the street in Oklahoma City in 1906 about the massive earthquake that struck San Francisco. Shortly after that, he moved to Tulsa and went to work for the Democrat, forerunner of The Tulsa Tribune. He later worked for the old Tulsa Post before moving to the Tulsa World in 1911.

While working for the Post, Condon witnessed a gun-battle at an out-of-town gambling den. Believing that the Post wouldn't print such a story, he sold it to a Kansas City newspaper, which wanted more details.

"I began drawing on my imagination," Condon recalled. "Unfortunately, I overdrew."

Tulsa World archives

Glenn Condon, seen here in 1964, had been identified as the dean of Tulsa journalists and "Mr. Oklahoma News."

That story, reprinted in the Democrat, resulted in Condon being fired from the Post via a Page 1 editorial edged in a black border. "I have the distinction of being the only reporter in Tulsa history fired with a front-page editorial," he said.

The specific situation that angered the Legislature couldn't be determined, but his stories frequently rankled lawmakers. As a World reporter in 1911, Condon covered the only legal hanging in Tulsa.

In addition to his job at the Tulsa World, Condon served on the Tulsa Park Board in 1913-16 and wrote the Republican platform on which city commission candidates ran in 1916.

When he returned from service in World War I, Condon became editor and publisher of Vaudeville News and gave Walter Winchell, later to become a nationally known gossip columnist, his first job.

Condon returned to Tulsa in 1926 to manage the Ritz and Orpheum movie theaters and two years later set up the public relations department for Skelly Oil Co. He went back to news reporting in 1934 as a co-builder of radio station KOME. He later was news director of station KTUL until 1946, when he helped organize as part-owner of station KAKC (the C stands for Condon).

Condon moved to station KRMG as news director when it went on the air on Christmas Eve 1949. The next year he was named president of both the Oklahoma Associated Press Broadcasters and the Tulsa Press Club.

Condon, a popular master of ceremonies at meetings throughout the state, once introduced a public official as "the only Tulsa County commissioner who hasn't been indicted."

When the laughter died down, he added "yet."

Condon, who died in 1968, had been identified as the dean of Tulsa journalists and "Mr. Oklahoma News" because his staccato delivery was so well-known throughout the state.

Where there's a Will there's voter confusion

What's in a name?

A lot, if one happens to be named Will Rogers and lives in Oklahoma – even if not related to the famous humorist who died Aug. 15, 1935, in a plane crash in Alaska.

Moore School Superintendent Will Rogers received the most votes in the 1932 primary election for congressman-at-large, but he wasn't the person most Oklahomans probably thought they were voting for.

Rogers did practically no campaigning but led three other candidates and forced a runoff with Commissioner of Charities Mabel Bassett. His name carried him through the July 26 runoff election, when he overcame Bassett by more than 100,000 votes, and the November general election.

Rogers, who was not related to the humorist, was re-elected four times but lost a race in 1941 for the 7th District seat while still serving as congressman-at-large.

"My name's been Will for years," the dark horse candidate said after his stunning victory in the July 1932 primary election. "I was named Willie, but that's a girl's name, and I decided to use Will."

Bassett said: "I'm sure many people voted for him thinking he was the actor and humorist. I shall have to advertise that he is not Oklahoma's famous character but another fellow, a schoolteacher." She was confident that she would win the runoff, but didn't.

Election officials had been so sure that Rogers would

Oklahoma Historical Society

Will Rogers, Oklahoma's representative at large during 1932-1942, was not related to the famous Sooner of the same name.

do poorly in the primary election that they didn't even count his votes during early tabulating – until it became apparent that thousands of Sooners had voted for a household name.

Yet another Will Rogers didn't fare as well in 1974 in a campaign for labor commissioner, but he was running against Wilbur Wright, another man with a famous name.

That Will Rogers, a former Oklahoma Highway Patrol trooper, and Wright, a former labor commissioner, swamped the other five candidates in the primary election for the Democratic nomination, forcing a runoff election.

Neither Rogers nor Wright did much campaigning in the primary race, but Jim Purdy, one of the five also-rans, told voters, "The Will Rogers on the ballot is not the great Oklahoma humorist, and the Wilbur Wright is not the man who invented the airplane."

Purdy had challenged Rogers and Wright's candidacies on the ground that they were attempting to capitalize on famous names. But the state Supreme Court refused to knock the two off the ballot.

Although Wright had resigned as the labor commissioner in 1973 because of improper travel claims, he won the nomination and easily defeated the Republican nominee in the general election. He resigned again a year later because of additional improper travel claims.

Wright sought office again – his 10th time – in 1976 but lost in the runoff election for the Democratic nomination for corporation commissioner.

A&M leader also served the President

A 1951 plane crash in Iran killed an Oklahoma educator who had learned how to walk the tightrope of politics to keep his job as president of Oklahoma A & M College for 23 years.

The educator was Henry G. Bennett, who had taken a leave of absence from A & M, now Oklahoma State University, to lead President Harry S. Truman's Point Four program. Bennett's wife, Vera, and six other Americans also died in the Dec. 22 crash that killed 19.

In his State of the Union speech a few weeks later, Truman called Bennett a "great public servant who was leading an effort to bring opportunity and hope to the people of half the world."

Truman had proposed a plan for peace and freedom, the fourth point of which involved "making the benefits of our scientific advances and industrial progress available for the improvement and growth of the underdeveloped areas."

He picked Bennett to lead what became known as the Point Four program.

Bennett said the program was not designed to give anything away to foreign countries.

"It is just hard business. If we can make these countries self-supporting in a free world, we have strengthened the freedoms of all. Our aim is to increase the production of the backward areas in food, clothing and shelter."

Bennett sent technical experts to more than 30 nations to teach "how to get more per acre through better planting, better seeds or better livestock strains."

Bennett's party was en route from Baghdad, Iraq, to Tehran when it ran into a blinding snowstorm.

The pilot was told to go to Basra, Iraq, or Baghdad, but the plane crashed into a mountain north of Tehran.

Tulsa World archives

Henry G. Bennett took a leave of absence from serving as president of Oklahoma A & M College, now Oklahoma State University, to lead President Harry S. Truman's Point Four program.

It wasn't the first time Bennett had served the government. He was a 1945 delegate to the Quebec International Foods and Agricultural Organization that charted food rehabilitation for war-ravaged countries in Europe.

He served on a U.S. Army agricultural survey in U.S.-occupied Germany in 1949 and was appointed to counsel Ethiopian leaders on agriculture and education.

Bennett was granted an indefinite leave from his academic duties and was sworn in as an assistant secretary of state on Dec. 1, 1950.

Bennett, a native of Arkansas, was president of Southeastern Oklahoma State College for nine years before taking the helm at A & M in 1928.

In an era when few college presidents lasted more than one gubernatorial administration, Bennett's tenure was 23 years.

Bennett became a central figure in a tightly knit group of schoolmaster politicians.

Southern Baptist churches were considered the state's most powerful political constituency; Bennett was the son of a Baptist minister and was a leader in his church and in the denomination.

He was often mentioned as a potential candidate for governor, but he never filed.

Many advances were made at A & M under Bennett – a fire training school, a graduate school, a branch college at Okmulgee, a veterinary medicine division and many new buildings.

During World War II, A & M trained more than 40,000 people for national defense duty, operating a school for WAVES, and offering instruction in radar and Asian languages.

Magee's parking solution made cents

It was the middle of the Great Depression, but more and more Oklahomans were driving cars – and trying to find a parking place.

In an attempt to solve "one of modernity's headaches," a gadget described by the Tulsa World as "closely resembling the old-fashioned hitching post" made its debut in downtown Oklahoma City on July 16, 1935. And the rest, one might say, is history.

The World's story described the device as a nickel-in-the-slot affair: Drop your nickel and park for an hour. It also reported that after trying them for a day, some of the public liked them. Some didn't.

"All we need is time to get accustomed to it," one driver said, calling the installation of meters the "biggest thing Oklahoma City has done."

But another driver said newspapers were falling down on their job in letting "these damn foolish contraptions appear on the street."

During the first day, many found the devices good for leaning on; a child deposited a nickel in one meter expecting to get gum.

Oklahoma City had installed 150 meters downtown, alternating from one side of the street in one downtown block to the opposite side in the next block.

White lines had been painted on the pavement to indicate the parking slots governed by each meter.

The now-ubiquitous parking meter had been invented by Carl C. Magee, editor of the Oklahoma City Oklahoma News, at that time a Scripps-Howard newspaper. Magee fi-

Tulsa World archives
An attorney and a newspaper editor, Carl C. Magee went down in history as the inventor of the parking meter. His device was not immediately popular with all drivers.

nanced a contest among Oklahoma A & M College engineering students to develop a working model.

Magee, who practiced law in Tulsa in the early part of the 20th century and earned a national reputation for his investigation of what became known as the Teapot Dome oil scandals, had become interested in parking problems as chairman of the Chamber of Commerce traffic committee.

He learned Oklahoma City police were reported only 5 percent to 10 percent effective in enforcing parking limits.

Magee had made a crude model of a parking meter. But he couldn't get it to work and contacted engineering professor H. G. Thuesen at the A & M College of Engineering to suggest a contest among students.

The contest offered prizes totaling $160 for a design and $240 for a model – big prizes for those Depression years.

Some of the students used springs and other parts from old alarm clocks and received the prizes. But none had developed a satisfactory working parking meter.

Professor Thuesen then enlisted former student Gerald Hale for assistance. Three weeks later, the two had developed a working model of a parking meter.

The first meters were built by the Macnick Co. of Tulsa, a company that had a line of light automatic lathes and punch presses and whose experience included production of bomb timers used for exploding nitroglycerin in oil wells and recording meters.

Town cashed in on being scammed

Civic leaders should have been leery of smooth-talking J. Bam Morrison, a fat man wearing a checkered vest and a large gold watch chain, when he arrived in Wetumka to promote a circus in 1950.

Morrison persuaded merchants to buy thousands of hot dogs and bottles of pop, purchase hay for the elephants and to prepare space for the "biggest ever" circus. He sold advertising space on a sound truck that he said would be driven throughout the state to attract thousands of visitors to the big event in Wetumka.

The fast-talking promoter conned a local hotel into providing him free lodging and reserved an entire floor of rooms for performers. He bought advertising space in the local newspaper and ordered thousands of fliers promoting the circus.

It was to be a big celebration. But then Morrison disappeared and Wetumkans realized that they had been taken; no circus would appear.

After their fury subsided, Wetumkans had a good laugh and decided to capitalize on the incident with Sucker Day, which became an annual event until 1957, resumed 20 years later and continues today.

That first Sucker Day was covered by Time and Life magazines. A Wetumka official said a few years later that Morrison "put our town on the map."

Thousands of visitors flocked to the small Hughes County town for the first Sucker Day, which featured a parade, special prices in all the stores, a square dance, and hog-calling, husband-calling, pie-eating and bubble-blowing contests.

And the burial in effigy of J. Bam Morrison under a sign that reported: "Here lies J. Bam Morrison. He died from laughing at Wetumka Merchants."

C.A. McWilliams, then the publisher of the Wetumka Gazette and the president of the Sucker Club, said after 8,000 showed up for the next year's festival that "we're willing to forgive this guy because he did such a beautiful job on us."

A highlight of that year's Sucker Day was the presentation to McWilliams of a 20-pound sucker from the mayor of Wetumpka (spelled with a "p"), Ala. It was broken into pieces and distributed to the crowd.

Sucker Day was just one of the events used by small towns in the 1950s to attract crowds – and many are still annual events. All have similar formats – entertainment, music, food and shoppers.

The oldest such current event in Oklahoma is Rooster Days, a Broken Arrow festival that started in 1931. Typical of such events, the two-day Rooster Days now features a parade, music, arts and craft booths, food vendors, carnival rides and attractions for children.

Rooster Days began when farmers picked a Saturday in early summer to cart unwanted roosters to Broken Arrow, where they were sold and put on rail cars bound for agricultural hubs such as Kansas City. Instead of heading home afterward, farmers and their families would stick around for the day. They would eat, listen to music and participate in activities such as potato sack races.

During the Depression years, $1 bills were tied to the roosters' legs before they were released on Main Street. Whoever could catch the roosters got to keep the money.

Bixby's Green Corn Festival began in 1942 when a Bixby farmer and produce shipper decided to throw a block party for local growers and business leaders.

That festival now is sponsored by the Optimist Club to raise money for scholarships, glasses for children and uniforms for Special Olympics athletes.

The first community festival in Oklahoma took place at Locust Grove and turned into an annual event for more than 50 years. "Goose Grab Day" was organized shortly before Christmas to give residents and visitors a chance to take home a free Christmas dinner – geese, turkeys, ducks and guineas on the wing and a well-greased pig.

The birds were tossed into the air from a platform on a truck and the pig was turned loose on Main Street in annual repeats of an event started in 1912 by the town founder O.W. Gilliam. Gilliam treated unsuccessful competitors in the bird and pig grab to Christmas dinner.

Because of the large crowds in later years, the festival started two sets of goose grabs and pig chases, one in the morning and the other in the afternoon.

The event continued at least until 1965.

Most other towns have or have had events designed to attract crowds for celebrating and shopping – the Peach Festival in Porter, Pecan Festival in Okmulgee, Sorghum Day in Wewoka, Watermelon Festivals in Rush Springs and Valliant and Blackeyed Pea Festival in Hollis, among others.

But only Wetumka has an event started by a smooth-talking confidence man, wearing a checkered vest with a gold watch chain, who suckered civic leaders and merchants, a man about whom the mayor said two years later, "We owe that feller a debt of gratitude."

David Carman/ Tulsa World
The Wetumpka Sucker.

Band leader proud to be best of the worst

"Otto Gray and His Oklahoma Cowboys" toured the country from 1924 to 1936. Gray, who was a Stillwater furniture dealer, became the band's announcer.

The band leader knew only two chords on a guitar but he "played 'em real loud," and his predecessor couldn't play any instrument at all.

Nevertheless, "Otto Gray and His Oklahoma Cowboys" became one of the most popular musical groups in the Midwest and toured the country from 1924 to 1936. The band also played on Bristow radio station KFRU and KVOO after the station moved to Tulsa and its name was changed.

"I don't know what we had that appealed," Gray told an interviewer in 1958 while reminiscing about his band. "Maybe it was the novelty of it. There weren't many cowboy bands when we started.

"It wasn't the quality of our playing and singing; I know that. My slogan was 'You've heard the best – now hear the worst.'"

Gray became a part of the band by accident, as did Billy McGinty, who headed the group earlier. Gray was a furniture dealer in Stillwater. McGinty, who had been one of Teddy Roosevelt's Rough Riders, lived in Ripley, where his wife was the postmistress.

"Some of the boys at Ripley decided to get up a little band and play over at KFRU," Gray said. "They took Billy with them and decided his name was well enough known that he could give 'em a little prestige, a name anyway. So they called themselves 'Billy McGinty's Cowboy Band.'"

Gray said business was slow at his furniture store, and he was asked to go along. "They kind of made me their announcer, even if I couldn't talk worth a dern. I mispro-

nounced everything: called a pianny a pianny, you know."

The band members came from ranches in the Ripley area with the idea of bringing the music and songs of the Old West to the current generation.

"Some of the boys were fair-to-middling musicians, but when we started we were just plain terrible," Gray said.

After starting out playing his two chords on a guitar that "I thought sounded pretty good," Gray overheard some of the musicians tell McGinty that the loud chords bothered them because "I played so bad."

"So that was the end of it for me," Gray said, and he became just an announcer.

When McGinty left the band to return to his ranch, Gray and his wife took over and toured with the band, the money rolled in and they bought a fleet of Cadillacs, including some with living quarters. Billboard Magazine once headlined a story about the band: "Cowboys Here in Fancy Cars." The story noted that traffic came to a standstill as other drivers gawked at the band's fleet.

After breaking box office records at many theaters around the country, the band broke up in 1936. Gray said, "I just got tired of traveling."

Gray, a native of South Dakota, had moved to the Stillwater area with his parents in 1899. He farmed for several years before getting into the furniture business and later joining the band. The Grays moved to Springdale, Ark., where he died in 1967. His funeral procession was led by two palomino horses, symbolizing his early life.

Christmas fire brings tragedy, mystery

Fire turned a fun night of singing carols, enjoying refreshments and exchanging gifts into tragedy at a Christmas Eve celebration in 1924. It also created a mystery that wasn't solved for 32 years.

The fire in the one-room Babb Switch School near Hobart left 36 dead and many injured and also led to a new state law that was copied by all other states.

The mystery involved the one person unaccounted for – Mary Elizabeth Edens, a 3-year-old girl who had been sitting on the lap of her aunt, Alice Noah, when the fire began. Santa Claus Dow Bolding set off the blaze when he reached into the branches of the cedar Christmas tree for one of the last presents and knocked over a burning candle.

"The candle touched a little limb, and the tree was so dry that one whole side was blazing almost instantly," a witness recalled.

Noah died the next day after telling the girl's parents, Mr. and Mrs. Louis Edens, that she had handed the child to someone outside the fiery building. The parents at first thought the child might have been taken to Hobart by one of the rescuers. But no one could account for her.

The aunt's story was borne out by a count of the missing and dead. The bodies of 36 of the 37 who were missing were found, but Mary Elizabeth's body was not among them.

Mary Elizabeth's disappearance remained a mystery until 1956, when an accountant in San Bernardino, Calif., read a newspaper story about the search for the missing girl and connected it with a woman he knew as Mary Reynolds, a Barstow dress shop owner.

The accountant, a Lions Club member, wrote the Hobart Lions Club president that "I have, among my clientele, a prominent young businesswoman who does not know who her father and mother were nor has she been able to find out anything as to possible relatives."

The Hobart Lions provided information about a scar on the missing girl's foot and pictures that were compared with pictures of Reynolds when she was about the same age.

There also was information that the woman in question, as a child, had been "very fond of bacon rinds." Back in

Tulsa World archives
The Babb Switch School tragedy of 1924 led to reform legislation in the Oklahoma Legislature.

Oklahoma, her Aunt Bertha recalled snatching bacon rinds from the missing girl's hand and telling her they were bad for her.

On the night of the fire, she apparently had been handed to a vagabond couple who took her to a series of nomadic camps in Arkansas and Kansas before arriving in California, where she was abandoned. She later worked for her room and board and finally was adopted when she was 15. The woman who adopted her failed in an attempt to learn about her background.

After her identity was confirmed, the long-missing woman returned to Hobart to get acquainted with her parents and other relatives. She later wrote a book, "Mary, A Child of Tragedy," under her new married name of Grossnickle and told her story on national television.

She told her parents she had early memories of "first one family, then another."

The night of the fire, about 200 people had crammed into the small building for a typical rural Christmas Eve party. Attempts by several men to put out the fire failed.

The revelers tried to escape through the only door, the Dec. 25, 1924, Tulsa World reported. However, the door opened inwardly and the crowd trying to get out kept it from being opened wide enough for escape.

The trapped victims broke every window, but heavy screens that had been bolted over the windows to keep prowlers out kept the victims in. The broken windows also created a draft that fed the flames, farmer Andrew Jackson related after his escape. "Within three minutes the dry wood of the room was a mass of flames that licked at the heels of the frenzied, pawing mob that fought for freedom."

Gov. Martin Trapp launched a campaign immediately after the fire to require strict safety regulations in rural school buildings. As a result, the Legislature passed laws requiring that all doors swing out and banned steel netting on the windows of public buildings. The laws also required proper use of gasoline lamps and prohibited the use of candles on trees in public buildings. Buildings also were required to have more than one exit and more windows.

The new Oklahoma safety laws were copied by the legislatures in the other 47 states.

Mistletoe shares with Oklahoma Rose

The wife of a pioneer farmer died during a devastating winter in the early 1890s in what was Cheyenne Territory. Because her husband couldn't find any flowers to decorate her grave, he used mistletoe.

It was a parasite but it had blooms, was the nearest thing to a flower in that bleak winter and was found in abundance in the tops of most of the trees in what became western Oklahoma.

One of the couple's friends vowed that if Oklahoma ever became a state, he would see to it that mistletoe, considered by most as a decoration for Christmas, was made the state flower in memory of the settler's wife.

That poignant story, probably apocryphal, was included in Oklahoma history texts for public school students for decades. It was the background to explain the territorial Legislature's adoption in 1893 of a bill naming the evergreen bough as the state flower, the first state emblem named.

The bill was introduced by Rep. John Kimberly of Kingfisher and was signed into law by Territorial Gov. A.J. Seay over objections of many who maintained it was not a flower or a fitting representation of the territory.

Dan W. Peery, chairman of the Committee of the Whole in the House, later wrote that Wimberly introduced the bill at the request of a Mrs. Beason. She was an early-day settler at old Reno City, now a ghost town north of El Reno. Rep. Harper Cunningham, speaking for a group of Guthrie women, wanted to substitute another flower, but the mistletoe measure passed 16-8.

After statehood, Sen. John Golobie of Henryetta introduced a bill to retain the mistletoe. The bill was passed by the first Oklahoma Legislature but this time it was designated as the state floral emblem – although those early legislators probably thought they were naming an official flower with a fancier name.

Most Oklahomans, including newspapers, didn't consider that semantic difference and deemed mistletoe as the state's official flower. The official status of mistletoe, whether a flower or floral emblem, remained unchallenged until the term of Gov. Leon C. Phillips in 1939-43.

That's when Rep. Glade Kirkpatrick of Tulsa headed a

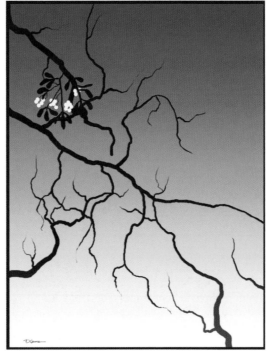

David Carman/ Tulsa World

The designation of mistletoe, a parasite, as Oklahoma's official floral emblem, has been controversial at times.

move to replace mistletoe with the Cowboy Rose, commonly known as the posy. He appeared at the Legislature one day with an armful of posies, handing one to each legislator. But his resolution to change the flower died when the House struck its calendar.

Another challenge to mistletoe came in 1961 when Rep. M. A. Diel of Clinton sponsored a move to substitute the orange and brown gaillardia, commonly known as Indian blanket flower. His bill never got off the ground.

Oklahoma gardeners weren't very excited by the Indian blanket flower even though it had been adopted by the 1910 Legislature as the official wildflower. Legislators pointed out that it would be expensive to change hundreds of textbooks and pamphlets.

The Oklahoma Rose was suggested as an appropriate state flower in 1967 in a bill by Rep. L.H. Bengston of Oklahoma City. Gov. Dewey Bartlett favored it, but it was nearly 40 years later before it received that designation.

The Oklahoma Rose was developed by Herbert Swim and O. L. Weeks of Oklahoma State University to plant in the Oklahoma exhibit at the New York World's Fair. A bed of the roses was planted near the state Capitol between the Will Rogers and Sequoyah office buildings. Most of the bushes had died because of the state's hot summers before that variety received the state flower designation.

The 2004 Legislature finally approved the Oklahoma Rose as the state's flower and Gov. Brad Henry signed the bill in April 2004. The bill had been introduced by Sen. Gilmer Capps of Snyder. It was legislation that grew out of 40 years of efforts by Dottie Weissenberger of Oklahoma City.

Those who are fond of the Oklahoma Rose say its deep crimson represents the blood shed when the Five Civilized Tribes were removed to Oklahoma.

But standing under an Oklahoma Rose doesn't evoke kissing – a tradition associated with mistletoe that dates to an ancient Greek festival called Saturnalia, when the parasite was thought to aid fertility.

And we still have mistletoe for our state floral emblem – and for kissing.

Dispute raged over church's designer

A Tulsa art teacher designed Tulsa's world-famous art deco religious edifice – the Boston Avenue United Methodist Church.

Or did she?

A dispute has continued since 1929 about whether the building at 13th Street and Boston Avenue was designed by Adah Robinson, head of the University of Tulsa's art department, or by Bruce Goff, who was Robinson's student when she taught at Central High School. He was an employee of an architectural firm when the church was built and later became a world-famous architect.

The issue developed before the congregation moved into the structure on June 9, 1929, from its previous building at Fifth Street and Boston Avenue. A Tulsa Tribune story in 1927, while the building was being constructed, credited Goff as the designer.

But when the congregation moved into the building, a Tulsa World story quoted Robinson extensively about details of the revolutionary design but did not mention Goff. Goff claimed in a 1979 interview that he had designed the building when he was a 22-year-old employee of Rush, Endacott and Rush, the architectural firm hired to oversee construction.

Boston Avenue United Methodist Church

This portrait of Adah Robinson hangs in Bishops Hall at the Boston Avenue United Methodist Church.

The legend under a bronze cast of the artist's head that was installed on a pedestal in the building in 1934 credited Robinson, "whose creative mind conceived this church, the design, significance, color, symbols; whose courage and patience carried through to completion."

Explaining the church design in a 1960 interview, she said, "We wanted something modern, something that had a strong approach to Christianity. We didn't want to copy anything because our objective was to design a church that fit Tulsa's needs and motives. It was locally inspired."

The late Tulsa architect Mary Caroline Cole, whose father, C.C. Cole, was chairman of the church's building committee, supported the art teacher in responses to news stories giving credit to Goff. She said Goff at that time was a young draftsman working for the architectural firm.

A brief history of the church on its Web site also identifies Robinson as the designer, credits Goff for the drafting and Robinson for supervising the project, working closely with church members and construction workers through the building's completion.

The Tulsa Convention and Visitors Bureau credits Goff for the design but notes that he was assisted by Robinson. The Tulsa Historical Society's Web site says "the design was a cooperative effort with iconography and color theory supplied by Robinson. The building's structural plans undoubtedly were the work of Goff."

Robinson was born in Richmond, Ind., and came to Oklahoma in 1905 with her family. She taught in Oklahoma City for four years and at the University of Oklahoma for two years before coming to Tulsa to be an art teacher at Central High School for nine years.

Goff was one of her students at Central. He designed her house that was built in 1926, working on the project until it became doubtful whether she had sufficient funds to complete the job. Another former student, Joseph Koberling Jr., supervised the construction.

Robinson left TU in 1945 to become head of the art department at Trinity University in San Antonio – in spite of a petition signed by more than 250 University of Tulsa students asking school officials to "do everything possible" to keep her in Tulsa. She retired to Tulsa 14 years later and spent her remaining years giving lectures and directing seminars on the philosophy of art.

She died at the age of 80 in 1962, and her funeral was held in the Boston Avenue Methodist Church.

Who designed the church? It was Adah Robinson.

Or Bruce Goff.

Briggs built up Phillips University

Educator Eugene S. Briggs, who was known as the "builder president" of the former Phillips University, got a practical education in Oklahoma politics early in his career.

Briggs was serving as president of Southeastern State Teachers College at Durant when he was given a "leave of absence" in 1933 to allow Gov. William H. "Alfalfa Bill" Murray to appoint another man.

Briggs' successors also learned about politics. During the next five years, the school, now Southeastern State University, had three presidents because of political appointments by Murray and his successor, Gov. E.W. Marland.

Meanwhile, Briggs earned a doctor's degree at Columbia University in New York, served as president of Christian College at Columbia, Mo., and in 1938 became the third president of Phillips University at Enid, where he remained for 23 years.

During his tenure, Phillips' enrollment doubled, campus facilities expanded with more than a dozen buildings, and its endowment increased by more than $1 million. A newspaper article about his retirement in 1960 called him the "builder president" and noted that if a campus building was beige brick, it was likely one of Briggs' projects.

Phillips was founded in 1906 by the Christian Church (Disciples of Christ) but closed in 1998 after financial problems forced it into bankruptcy.

The Phillips seminary moved to Tulsa, and a Phillips Legacy Foundation was formed with the $3 million in funds from liquidation of the university's assets. The foundation provides scholarships to undergraduate students enrolled at Disciples colleges and universities.

The former Phillips campus now houses the Enid branch of Northern Oklahoma College.

Briggs, a native of Missouri, came to Oklahoma in 1919 to be principal of Okmulgee High School and served as superintendent of Okmulgee schools from 1925 until 1928, when he was named president of Southeastern State Teachers College.

When he retired from Phillips, Briggs and his wife moved to Oklahoma City, where he became president of National Investors Life Insurance Co. They had moved back to Enid before Briggs died in April 1978.

Briggs also was active in many civic and professional organizations. He served as a member of the executive committee and board of directors of the Christian Board of Publications in St. Louis and as vice president of the International Convention of Christian Churches. He also served as president of the Great Plains Council of Boy Scouts.

He had received an honorary doctor of laws degree from Phillips, wrote many books on education, and was inducted into the Oklahoma Hall of Fame in 1951.

Briggs became a member of the Lions Clubs while at Okmulgee and served as international president in 1948-49 -- the first international president never elected.

Briggs was serving as an international director in 1945 when Oklahoma Lions proposed him for third vice president, a position usually filled at an international convention. Because of World War II, the government asked civic groups to cancel conventions and other large meetings that year.

Instead of a convention, the international directors, past presidents and governors council met for a one-day business meeting in Chicago and chose Briggs as third vice president. Selection to that office is tantamount to being elected president two years later, so Briggs became the first president never elected.

The Oklahoma Lions established a Briggs Memorial Foundation that provides 15 annual scholarships.

Tulsa World archives

Eugene S. Briggs became the third president of Phillips University at Enid in 1938 and remained at the school for 23 years. During his tenure as president, enrollment at the university doubled, and campus facilities expanded with more than a dozen buildings.

Bank robber regretted life of crime

While police were searching a five-state area for him, bank robber Henry Starr was living in Tulsa within two blocks of the sheriff and within four blocks of the mayor.

He took nightly "joy rides" in his car and frequently visited restaurants and movie theaters, he told a Tulsa World reporter in 1915.

Starr, who boasted on his deathbed six years later that he had robbed more banks than any man in the country, had used the name of R. L. Williams – Oklahoma's governor – to rent the house at 1534 E. Second St. Utilities and subscriptions to the World and the Tulsa Democrat were in the name of Laura Williams, although one utility was in the name of Wilson.

The infamous badman was being sought for a string of 14 bank robberies, which had prompted the Legislature to pass a bank robber bill and to put a $1,000 dead-or-alive bounty on Starr's head.

Starr revealed his address to Tulsa World reporter J. Burr Gibbons and gave Gibbons permission to enter the house after he was shot during a double bank robbery in Stroud on March 27, 1915. Gibbons wrote that the house appeared to be an average home – with the exception of a large amount of ammunition for .45-caliber Colts and Winchester rifles lying on a dresser.

Starr pleaded guilty to a robbery charge and was sentenced to 25 years in the state penitentiary at McAlester but was paroled four years later after he began urging young people to earn their livings instead of turning to a life of crime. "I'm 45 years old and 17 of my 45 years have been spent in prison," he told a World reporter.

It was the second time he had been released from prison early and the second time he had tried to go straight. His first release came in 1903 after President Theodore Roosevelt cut the length of his prison sentence in gratitude for Starr's help in disarming badman Crawford Goldsby. Goldsby, alias Cherokee Bill, was trying to break out of jail and later was hanged at Fort Smith.

Starr was in the Fort Smith jail serving a term on his plea

Beryl Ford collection

Henry Starr boasted on his deathbed that he had robbed more banks than any man in the country, but he admitted that crime did not pay.

of guilty of manslaughter for killing a deputy U.S. marshal for which he had twice been convicted and sentenced to hang. Both convictions were overturned by the Supreme Court.

After his second release, Starr starred in a couple of movies, including one based on the Stroud double bank robbery. He told reporters he went back to robbing banks to pay his debts – and was shot by banker J. W. Meyers during a bank robbery in Harrison, Ark., on Feb. 19, 1921. He died five days later.

It was apparent from the first that his wounds would be fatal, and Starr talked extensively with his doctor and lawmen about his life of crime. He claimed he had robbed more banks than any other man and even more than the James-Younger and the Doolin-Dalton gangs put together.

"It doesn't pay," he said, then explained, "I was in debt $2,000 and had to have money, so I turned bank robber again. I'm sorry, but the deed is done."

Starr was shot by Meyers from the bank vault into which Meyers and several other bank employees had been forced. The bullet severed Starr's spine, and his gang members started to turn their guns on Meyers. But Starr prevented them from shooting him, saying he had never killed anyone during a robbery and he didn't want his companions to break his record.

Starr's wife, son and mother were called to Harrison and remained by his bedside while he was being treated. He told them he realized he was mortally wounded. He told his wife he didn't want to be buried but preferred cremation.

However, a funeral with ground burial was scheduled. The 48-year-old bandit, a native of Fort Gibson, had told a World reporter a few months earlier that he had gone straight after being released from prison two years earlier.

"All young men should know crime is a losing game no matter who the players may be," he told the reporter. "I would not take $17 million to again face the agony I have endured."

Mix leaped into river, movie stardom

Oklahoma Historical Society

Cowboy movie star Tom Mix (left) poses with the crew that used a car to film his horseback scenes.

Cowboy movie star Tom Mix, the hero of scores of Western thrillers of the silent movie era, leaped into the nation's theaters by jumping with his horse into the flood-swollen Arkansas River.

Mix was working in a wild west show at the 101 Ranch near Ponca City in 1904 when a visiting cameraman suggested a horseback leap from a bluff over the South Fork of the Arkansas would make a good scene.

Always eager for publicity, Mix tied a handkerchief over his horse's eyes and made the jump. Stardom in Western movies followed.

Mix, at one time the highest-paid actor, and his famous horse Tony made 370 full-length silent movies, in which he and Tony performed their own stunts, from 1920 to 1928. They starred in the "Tom Mix Straight Shooters Show" on radio from 1933 until his death in a car wreck in Arizona in 1940. He made only nine sound feature films.

"The truth is hard to find" in regard to Mix's career, the Tom Mix Museum Web site notes. Some of the stories about his life were created as publicity for his studios and some were spread by Mix himself, the site says.

Even his radio program is suspect. According to Jack French, editor of Radio Recall, the Mix voice on radio was that of an actor. The program continued for 10 years after Mix's death.

But there's no doubt about Mix being America's favorite movie cowboy. Nor about his popularity among millions of youngsters who tuned in to his daily "Ralston Straight Shooters Club" radio show.

The club was complete with a secret handshake, decoder rings and patriotic messages. It sold millions of boxes of Ralston cereal that were bought to collect Tom Mix premiums. During the daily radio show, Mix (or his portrayer) always urged youngsters to "shoot straight and be honest."

According to early press releases, Mix was born in Texas, fought in the Spanish-American War and in the Chinese Boxer Rebellion, during which he was badly injured, and later served in South Africa during the Boer War.

The press agents' hype also said he served as a sheriff in Montgomery County, Kan., and Washington County, Okla., and as a U.S. marshal and was wounded several times by Oklahoma outlaws before joining the Texas Rangers.

Actually, Mix was born in Pennsylvania, not Texas, and did enlist in the Army when the Spanish-American War began in 1898 but had no service outside the U.S. He never served in the Boxer Rebellion, the Boer War or the Texas Rangers.

He was never a U.S. marshal nor a sheriff but he did work briefly as the town marshal for Dewey (in Washington County) where the Tom Mix Museum is located. During his military service, Mix failed to return to duty from a leave in 1902 but was never prosecuted.

Mix's Oklahoma years began at Guthrie where he was the drum major of the Oklahoma Territorial Cavalry band, although he was not a member of the militia nor the band. Mix was married at least five times (maybe six); his wives included two Oklahomans, Jewel Perrine of Oklahoma City and Olive Stokes of Dewey.

Although he at one time, according to the Mix Web site, had earned more than $6 million, his liabilities exceeded his estate and there were no funds to distribute after his death. He had always been a lavish spender.

Mix was killed when he lost control of his Cord sports car while driving near Florence, Ariz. He had been in Oklahoma visiting an ex-wife.

The Dewey museum is open from 10 a.m. to 4:30 p.m. Tuesday through Sunday but is closed during January.

Russian revolution turned flag blue

The Russian revolution that overthrew Tsar Nicholas II and led to the establishment of the Soviet Union sparked a move to replace Oklahoma's state flag.

Many thought the state's first flag – a bright red pennant with a white star in the center – looked too much like a symbol of the Soviets.

The simple flag also bore a blue number 46 in the star to identify that Oklahoma was the 46th state to enter the union. It had been adopted by the Legislature in 1911.

Even without its association with the Russian revolution of 1917, the state flag made many Oklahomans unhappy. Some said they didn't like to hang the flag from their porches for fear neighbors would think someone inside had scarlet fever.

The Daughters of the American Revolution announced a contest in 1924 for a new state banner.

Contest judges picked a design submitted by Louise Funk Fluke, then of Shawnee, and the Legislature adopted her design the next year.

Today's state flag is essentially the same as Mrs. Fluke's design – with only the addition of the word Oklahoma across the bottom and slightly different colors.

Fluke, who lived in Oklahoma City when she died in 1986, had studied art at Columbia University, the Audubon Tyler Art Institute and the Chicago Art Institute. She was sewing her wedding dress when the contest was announced.

Her husband-to-be, George Fluke Jr., persuaded her to enter the contest and she took three weeks off from sewing to study artifacts of the Oklahoma Historical Society. In three weeks, she had designed five entries, including the one that was adopted by the Legislature in March 1925.

Her design features an Osage warrior's shield made from buffalo hide and decorated with seven eagle feathers hanging from the edge. The shield is centered on a field of blue borrowed from the blue flag that Choctaw soldiers carried during the Civil War.

The shield is decorated with six crosses representing high ideals. And superimposed on the shield are an Indian peace pipe and an olive branch, symbols of peace from different cultures.

Oklahoma's first flag (replica at top) was unpopular because many residents thought the bright red banner looked like a Soviet symbol or a scarlet fever warning. It was replaced with a primarily blue flag nearly identical to the current one (bottom).

The 1941 Legislature added the word Oklahoma in white across the bottom of the flag and the 1988 Legislature directed that the colors of the flag be standardized because of variations among manufacturers.

"It is truly fitting that the Oklahoma flag uniting the ancient lore of the Indian and the white man and symbolizing the peace of a united people should be standardized in color as an example of the solidarity and patriotism of such people," the Legislature's 1988 resolution said.

Although Texans may brag about six flags having flown over that state, 14 flags have flown over what is now Oklahoma – although it involves a bit of fact-stretching or literary license. Some flew only briefly or only over parts of the state and some weren't exactly national emblems.

The first flag was the royal standard of Spain, brought to Oklahoma by Coronado in 1541. It was followed by the great union of Great Britain that symbolically flew over the area when Charles II gave a wide strip of America to his friends in 1663 and by the royal standard of France, brought to Oklahoma in 1719 by Bernard de la Harpe. France had claimed the entire Mississippi drainage area even earlier.

The fourth flag was the standard of the Spanish Empire in 1763 after France gave the country west of the Mississippi to Spain. Spain gave the province of Louisiana back to France in 1800 and the French Republic standard became the fifth flag over Oklahoma. Next was the U.S. flag of 1803 after the U.S. made the Louisiana purchase, and it was followed in 1818 by the U.S. flag with 13 stripes and a star for each state.

The flag of Mexico flew over part of the Panhandle from 1821 to 1836 and the flag of the Republic of Texas was flown over a section of the Panhandle from 1836 to 1839.

The Lone Star flag of Texas, which supplanted the earlier Texas flag, was next.

The 11th flag was the Choctaw tribal flag carried by Choctaw Confederate troops during the Civil War, and then came the Confederate flag.

The first Oklahoma state flag adopted in 1911 was No. 13 and the present state flag was No. 14.

Tulsa attorney rallied harmonizers

At first people just laughed.

After all, it was an unusual name for an organization: The Society for the Preservation and Encouragement of Barber Shop Quartet Singing in America.

The laughs were OK with Tulsa attorney O. C. Cash, who organized the group in 1938 with 24 other men. He watched it grow to more than 50,000 members in all parts of the country before his death in 1953. He was a man with a sense of humor who described himself as the permanent third assistant temporary vice president.

And he thought the initials SPEBSQSA, which became the group's official name, fit well among all the initials being used for programs of President Franklin Roosevelt's New Deal, which Cash detested.

Cash often said SPEBSQSA, was founded just for merriment "so let's do away with the speeches and get down to the fun – and sing."

Cash was upset at the trend against self-produced harmony because of the increased popularity of radio. So he joined with investment banker Rupert Hall in inviting 14 friends to meet for a song fest and Dutch lunch on April 11, 1938, in the roof garden of the Tulsa Club. Thirty showed up.

The invitation written by Cash and Hall said in part: "In this age of dictators and government control of everything, about the only privilege by the Bill of Rights not in some way supervised and directed, is the art of Barber Shop Quartet Singing.

"Without doubt we still have the right of 'peaceable assembly' which I am advised by competent legal authority

University of Tulsa McFarlin Library
"The Okie Four," the founding quartet of the SPEBSQSA, featured Frank Rice (left), Fred Graves, Bill Downing and O.C. Cash. Cash founded the SPEBSQSA in Tulsa.

includes quartet singing."

Chapters began springing up across the Midwest, the name was changed to the Barbershop Harmony Society and a headquarters was established in Kenosha, Wis. The group is moving its headquarters to Nashville.

Affiliate organizations are in other countries, including Canada, England, Sweden and New Zealand. Members have included singers Bing Crosby, Roy Rogers and former President Harry Truman.

A female counterpart is known as the Sweet Adelines.

Barbershop or four-part harmony developed in the early 20th century as a way of passing time for men waiting in barbershops for shaves and/or haircuts. The lead singer carries the melody, a tenor harmonizes and a baritone and a bass handle lower chords. But it was dying out when Cash and Hall organized their group.

Today, the barbershop quartet singers wear fancy clothes and have names such as the Bartlesville Barflies, the Flat Foot Four (made up of four Oklahoma City police officers) and the Chord Busters.

The organization still has two conventions a year, all featuring singing contests and, following Cash's lead, not much speaking.

Owen Clifford Cash, a tax attorney for Stanolind Oil and Gas Co., was reared in Bluejacket and graduated from Muskogee's Bacone Indian College. He passed the state bar in 1917 and came to Tulsa.

He became ill while returning from a national barbershop quartet convention in Detroit and underwent surgery for cancer. He died Aug. 15, 1953.

Patrol reduced crime, boosted safety

Oklahoma didn't need a state police force in its early days – each county had a sheriff and deputies to enforce the law, and the larger cities had their police forces.

There were few cars, and the state's primitive highways discouraged speeding.

But that need changed in the late 1920s and early 1930s with the advent of better roads, a growing highway fatality toll and faster cars used by bank robbers and other criminals who could commit a crime and flee into another county where a pursuing sheriff had no jurisdiction.

The number of cars on the highways had increased from about 6,500 in 1912 to more than 600,000 by 1929 and the traffic fatality toll had grown to about 500 per year in the late 1920s.

It was an era that spawned big-name criminals such as Bonnie Parker and Clyde Barrow, George "Machine Gun" Kelly, the Barker family, Charles "Pretty Boy" Floyd and others who took advantage of the antiquated police setup.

"In a few months of 1933-34, a series of criminal activities in the state shocked many citizens to the realization that rampant crime had indeed arrived in Oklahoma," Bob Blackburn wrote in the Chronicles of Oklahoma in 1978.

"Oklahoma had become a criminal haven in much the same fashion as it was in its days as the territories. The odds were stacked in the favor of the machine gun-toting, fast-driving outlaws of the '30s," the Oklahoma Highway Patrol's history page on the Internet points out.

And there was no state police agency to protect the state's citizens.

The Oklahoma Constitution had provided for the election of a sheriff in each county, but most of the sheriffs had no law enforcement experience or education; they were just good old boys who were popular enough in their counties to win elections.

Most sheriffs had two or three deputies, but they also lacked training and experience. One of the deputies in each county usually served as the jailer, leaving only two or three officers to enforce the law. In addition, they had to spend much of their time serving various writs for the courts and taking defendants to court.

Attempts to create a state police agency in 1929 and 1935 failed in the Legislature because of opposition from county commissioners and other groups who feared a state agency would usurp the powers of local law agencies.

Oklahoma Turnpike Authority

An Oklahoma Highway Patrol car cruises the Turner Turnpike. The agency was created in 1935.

But Oklahomans were concerned, particularly about the growing fatality toll. The first highway patrol was created in June 1935 with 12 officers in six cars, but the officers had little or no authority. They were supervised by highway safety director J. M. "Bud" Gentry of Enid. Half of the patrol members worked for the Highway Commission and half for the State Tax Commission.

Gentry said the officers were to maintain a constant patrol of state roads for law enforcement and to assist motorists.

Within a year, the small force had made 1,000 arrests and issued 500 warnings in an attempt to force motorists to obey traffic laws, proving the value of a state patrol. But the road toll continued to climb and soared to 684 in 1936, with 20,000 more seriously injured in accidents.

Finally, the 1937 Legislature approved a law creating the Oklahoma Highway Patrol and establishing a driver's license. After a three-week training school at the University of Oklahoma, 83 men began patrolling Oklahoma's highways on July 15. They were joined by 42 more troopers a few weeks later after a second training school.

The pay was $125 per month and the troopers hit the roads in black and white Fords and motorcycles. Headquarters was a borrowed house trailer that was moved from place to place, depending on where troopers were working.

The patrol cars had no radios for more than a year, and then the officers had to buy their own; even with radios, they frequently couldn't make contact with headquarters without driving to the top of a hill.

The patrol cars had no heaters, forcing the troopers to use their ingenuity to remain warm during cold, winter patrols. Some stretched old Army blankets between the dashboards and seats of their cars with holes cut for their heads. Some used kerosene lanterns and others used gasoline heaters and at least a couple set their cars on fire.

The patrol proved its value within the first year. The 1936 toll of 684 and 1937 highway death toll of 639 had been cut to 518 a year later.

Since that time, the OHP has been used for many purposes – to quell riots at the penitentiary and other places, investigate crimes, search for bank robbers and kidnappers, arrest felons and assist local officers – in addition to the OHP's basic mission of traffic control.

Lawmaker brought Boren name to fame

One of the first bills introduced by U.S. Rep. Lyle Boren when he went to Congress in 1937 would have placed an embargo on selling scrap metal to Japan.

"The iron we are now selling to Japan will come back in the bodies of American boys and break the hearts of American mothers," the representative of Oklahoma's 4th District argued prophetically. But Congress did not approve the embargo until three years later, and it was already too late: The Japanese bombed Pearl Harbor on Dec. 7, 1941.

It was just one of the important bills introduced by Boren, who served 10 years in the House but is probably better known today as the father of University of Oklahoma President David Boren, a former Oklahoma senator and governor, and grandfather of U.S. Rep. Dan Boren of the state's 2nd District.

Lyle Boren was instrumental in the passage of several landmark pieces of legislation. He was the author of the Civil Aeronautics Act of 1938, which established the first scheduled commercial airline routes; he was a co-author of legislation that created the National Cancer Research Institute, which evolved into the National Institutes of Health; and he sponsored early "truth in labeling" legislation.

He denounced John Steinbeck's novel "The Grapes of Wrath" on the House floor in 1940, calling it "a dirty, lying, filthy manuscript." He said if the vulgarity were taken out of the book "it would be a blank from cover to cover."

Steinbeck was defended by the president's wife, Eleanor Roosevelt, who praised the book. The novel also won a Pulitzer Prize, and Steinbeck later received a Nobel Prize.

The Depression-era lawmaker developed a close friendship with President Franklin D. Roosevelt, a fellow Democrat. Other friends of Boren's included President Harry Truman, with whom he played poker, and British Prime Minister Winston Churchill, with whom he shopped for cigars.

Churchill was the host of a birthday party for Boren when he visited London before the United States entered World War II. While Boren was in London, the U.S. ambassador, Joe Kennedy, assigned his son Jack to be a chauffeur for the visiting Sooner. Jack, of course, was the future President John F. Kennedy, who was elected to Congress in 1946, the same year Boren was defeated for re-election.

Boren had headed a nationwide campaign to collect scrap metal for Britain. He had written to the governors of all 48 states and to the mayors of larger cities, asking each to de-

Tulsa World archives

Lyle Boren was influential in Congressional halls.

clare an "Iron for Britain Day."

Although an avowed conservative, Boren considered FDR to be his favorite president. "I didn't have to agree with him on everything," he told a Tulsa World reporter in 1984. "The greatest men on the political horizon in my time were Roosevelt and Churchill."

He said he liked and respected Truman, but "in my opinion, Truman was just about waist-high to Roosevelt."

Outside of Congress, Boren founded the Oklahoma Cattlemen's Association and was an active Boy Scout leader. He was a co-chairman of the committee that organized the first National Boy Scout Jamboree in 1938.

David Boren said he learned from his father that public service was an honorable calling. He said his father believed deeply in the importance and dignity of all people and told him, "There's a lot you can learn from everyone you meet."

Lyle Boren, who was 82 when he died in 1992, was born in Waxahachie, Texas, and he came to Oklahoma with his family in 1917. He graduated at age 19 from East Central State University in Ada and taught at Wolf in Seminole County – where he was younger than some of his students and looked younger than many more – for four years.

When he was elected to the House of Representatives from Oklahoma's 4th District in 1936 on his second try for the post, he was a Works Progress Administration field representative distributing surplus commodities.

He had financed his race with savings from his small WPA salary and donations from friends. During a trip to Oklahoma City after he won the Democratic nomination, he revealed to a friend that he had only 50 cents and was prepared to hitchhike back to Seminole if necessary.

At 26, he was the youngest member of Congress and was barely old enough to hold the office. Because of his age and appearance, he was dubbed "the baby congressman."

The young lawmaker was criticized frequently during World War II because he was not in military service. To combat the criticism, he displayed a letter from Secretary of the Navy Frank Knox that said his request for active duty in the Navy had been denied.

Knox was acting on instructions from Roosevelt, who had decreed that members of Congress could not serve in the armed forces.

"It is my hope that members of Congress will recognize the importance of remaining in their legislative posts," the president had said.

Wildcat gang paid with wood

Don't take any wooden nickels.

You've heard that advice that dates to the early part of the 20th century when Americans began migrating from rural areas to cities and were warned about city slickers. It was good advice.

Wooden checks are another matter.

John A. Wolfe, production superintendent in charge of the well for the Prairie Oil and Gas Co., wrote a $10,000 check on a 20-inch piece of 1-inch-by-4-inch tongue-and-groove board. It was to pay for capping a gushing oil well known as the Sigmon No. 1 that was in the Oklahoma City field with the "Wild Mary" well in 1930.

Tulsa World archives

John A. Wolfe wrote a $10,000 check on a board to pay for capping a gushing oil well. His son Jim displays the check.

His son, Jim Wolfe of Collinsville, still has that unusual check and said that's how his father paid a wildcat gang that capped the gushing Sigmon well. The Mary Sudik well had been capped earlier after gushing out of control for 11 days until April 6, 1930.

John Wolfe had hired the daredevils with the understanding that they would be paid in cash "when, as and if" the Sigmon No. 1 was capped. The well was capped at 5:30 p.m. May 30 and Wolfe was called on to pay off.

But Wolfe didn't have any paper to write on and finally found a clean piece of board under other boards that were covered with oil. He used a stub pencil to write on the board "Please pay the Sinclair Daredevil Crew $10,000 for shutting in Sigmon #1."

The hard pine voucher was never presented to the Prairie accounting department for payment, but the company mailed checks to them immediately, Jim Wolfe said.

Same well, different city limit: Several Drumright readers complained about a recent Only in Oklahoma column (see page 268) that identified the Wheeler No. 1 oil well as being near Cushing.

That was the location of the well drilled by wildcatter Thomas B. Slick when oil gushed from it on March 17, 1912. It's still in the same place and is still producing.

But today, it's inside Drumright. A sprawling tent and shack town, Drumright grew up near the well to house the thousands of laborers and oilmen hoping to grab a share of the wealth.

About 80,000 people poured into the region overnight, also creating Shamrock and Oilton. Shamrock grew the most with a population of 30,000 while Drumright and Oilton had about 25,000 each.

Drumright in 2007 had a population of 3,000 while Oilton has 1,100 and Shamrock has dwindled to about 125.

The Cushing-Drumright field eventually became the largest producing field in the world. It covers about 70,000 acres in Creek and Payne counties.

The Wheeler No. 1 well and the Watchman's Cave can be visited in Drumright.

Mural on display: Visitors are also welcome to visit the old City Hall building at Fourth Street and Cincinnati Avenue to view a mural painted by Del Jackson that depicts a 1919 Tulsa scene (see page 243).

Attorney Frederic Dorwart, whose firm now owns the building, said anyone can enjoy the mural without an appointment during office hours or by appointment after office hours.

The mural is a scene from downtown Tulsa, but most of those depicted in the painting weren't around for the 1919 period it depicts.

Police Sgt. J.D Pilkington, (see page 203) Tulsa's first traffic cop who was known as "Big Jim," is depicted in his true-to-life environment. Pilkington, who died in 1950, for many years directed traffic at Third and Main streets, then the city's busiest intersection, and was well known to downtown workers.

Jackson painted himself at the wheel of a 1915 Model T Ford that he said he chose for his 16-by-26-foot mural because he and the car were produced in the same year. Jackson's passenger in the Model T is his wife, Lucille.

Others in the painting are Waldo E. (Dode) McIntosh (see page 244); oilman Julius Livingston, who died in 1990 at the age of 93; Amoco Production Co. employee Barbara Fulps, wearing a typical hairstyle of the 1919 era; and Tulsa historian Beryl Ford. Fulps and Ford are still alive.

McIntosh is depicted in his World War I Army uniform that he wore in annual Veterans' Day parades until 1989 when he was 96, two years before he died.

Stillwater woman's trial made news

Stillwater native Madeline Webb, who served nearly 25 years in prison after being convicted of murder in a sensational 1942 New York trial, spent the last 13 years of her life immersed in community affairs and serving others.

She told a reporter that during her time in prison, she had adopted as the credo for her life a statement by Cardinal Francis Spellman – "Every kind and good deed is in itself a press agent for God."

Webb, who always claimed she was innocent, died of cancer at age 67 in February 1980 in Stillwater. She had lived in Stillwater since being paroled from a life sentence in January 1967 from the Westfield State Prison for Women in Bedford Hills. She received a pardon seven years later.

Webb's two co-defendants, Eli Shonbrun, 34, her lover, and John Cullen, 45, were electrocuted in April 1943. Both claimed their innocence moments before dying in the electric chair at Ossining, N.Y.

However, Shonbrun had said at the trio's trial that he and Cullen had killed Mrs. Susan Flora Reich, a wealthy Polish refugee.

"They crucified an innocent girl and now they are about to kill an innocent man," Shonbrun said as he sat down in the electric chair.

He had made a similar claim at the trio's May 30, 1942, trial after the jury returned its verdict. "My God, my God," he screamed. "You're crucifying her – she's as innocent as my mother."

Webb pleaded "Oh, Judge Goldstein, please I did not do it," when she heard the verdict against her.

Webb and Shonbrun had made frequent outbursts during the trial. It was the kind of trial – a wealthy victim, an attractive well-educated defendant, a love angle – that attracted heavy coverage and daily front-page stories by New York and Oklahoma newspapers. Time magazine also reported extensively on the case.

Webb was accused of luring Reich to a New York City hotel room where Shonbrun and Cullen killed her in a badly bungled robbery. The victim died of suffocation from an

Tulsa World archives

Madeline Webb's trial involved a wealthy victim, an attractive well-educated defendant, a love angle and attracted heavy coverage and daily front-page stories by New York and Oklahoma newspapers.

adhesive tape gag that covered both her mouth and nose. Her diamond ring had been cut from her finger.

The suite where the body was found had been rented a couple of weeks earlier to a Mr. and Mrs. Ted Leopold, who witnesses identified as Webb and Shonbrun.

After the verdicts were read, Judge Jonah Goldstein required the three defendants to stand and answer questions about their ages, residences and occupations.

Shonbrun sneered that his home address was the city prison and "my business is murderer, just like Grumet's," referring to Assistant District Attorney Jacob grumet who had prosecuted the trial.

Webb, the daughter of wealthy parents, went to New York in 1939 to pursue an acting career but an expected part in a play failed to materialize and she never made it on Broadway. After graduating from Oklahoma A & M College in 1933, she had a brief marriage and went to California before going to New York.

She met Shonbrun in New York and the two fell in love. They professed their love for each other several times during the trial.

During her nearly 25 years in prison, Webb was called a model prisoner. Wardens and matrons wrote letters to the governor praising her and recommending clemency.

She taught illiterates in the prison school and promoted education programs for imprisoned women during her first seven years of prison life. She organized and directed the prison library during her last 17 years there.

"My one desire is that I have a wholesome, useful and happy life and the opportunity to serve my family and benefactors in a free society," she wrote in 1947.

After returning to Stillwater to live with her elderly mother, Vera Webb, she began work with the Community Action Foundation, worked with the American Civil Liberties Union, the League of Women Voters and the Stillwater Arts and Humanities Council. She also was active in the St. Francis Xavier Catholic Church and St. Elizabeth's Guild. A few months before she died, Webb wrote: "We must face the challenges as they appear in our paths."

Curtis earned his spot in history series

Editor's note: This column was written by Tulsa World senior writer and longtime friend of Gene's, Ken Neal.

—

Few features have brought the World more compliments than the "Only in Oklahoma" series that has graced the pages of the newspaper during the state Centennial year of 2007.

They have been well-selected and well-written vignettes of Oklahoma events during the past 100 years. They are the work of Gene Curtis.

Gene's byline has not appeared regularly in the World for decades, so readers might be curious about this man who writes about Oklahoma history so effortlessly.

Gene moved from reporting to newsroom management in 1961, yet he's still remembered for his reporting. Since retiring as managing editor in 1994, he has repeatedly been called upon for special assignments. When the Centennial series was conceived, Gene answered the call.

With style and grace, he wrote of fascinating Oklahomans and events that shaped and shook the state.

Gene is due a place in his own series because of his contributions to the Tulsa World and newspapering in Oklahoma for more than 65 years.

You read that right – 65 years. Gene is the son of a newspaperman. He was already working for his dad's Stigler News-Sentinel when the Japanese bombed Pearl Harbor in 1941, and he helped his dad put out a special edition of the paper. He was 12.

Why does this "Only in Oklahoma" column appear under my byline? Because I elbowed the younger World staffers aside to do it.

I won out because I am the oldest guy in the newsroom (except for Gene), and I have known him the longest.

When I showed up as a copy boy in January 1953, Gene was rejoining the staff after a stint in the Army. He stayed in the Reserve. We once got a publicity release from the Army extolling the work of Sgt. William E. Curtis of Tulsa. It took us a while to realize the release was about our Gene.

Gene got fed up with the military after a while.

"I quit," he said.

That terse comment is typical. Gene doesn't waste words.

Note that I did not use a more flowery word instead of "said." Gene taught me that "said" is the most succinct verb to use when quoting someone.

For the past 54 years, Gene and I have argued and laughed,

Tulsa World archives

Gene Curtis works in the newsroom of the Tulsa World in 1980. For years, he "put the paper to bed."

joked each other unmercifully and shared our problems with the newspaper, wives, cars and kids.

Gene is a repository of newspaper lore. He remembers nearly every staffer who worked here; he remembers the countless characters who haunted the newsroom in the old days – Brother Robert, Nurse Irene, The Tramp Poet, Tangle-Eye Williams – some of whom showed up in "Only in Oklahoma."

He knew county commissioners who were indicted; the city officials who went to the hoosegow for peddling whiskey; Nannie Doss, the killer grandmother. He knew the sheriff who announced for office from a foxhole in Korea; he knew the sheriff who was fond of quoting the "true facts."

He knew the law so well that he corrected young prosecutors at the courthouse. He knew county attorneys who became governors and Supreme Court justices.

And Gene never forgets a name. Or how to spell it.

For years, I followed Gene as he moved from one assignment to another. I succeeded him on the courthouse run; I followed him as state editor, and in both cases Gene "broke me in."

Gene's reputation for accuracy, dependability and bulldog-like pursuit could drive public officials mad.

Yet even those who dreaded to see him coming knew he would be guided by the facts, and most public officials valued him for that.

As an editor, he struck fear into the hearts of reporters and desk people who muffed a story, misspelled a name, failed to check records, or allowed the old Tulsa Tribune to beat the World to a story.

From 1963 when he became the news editor until he was named the managing editor in 1981, the last eyes to approve stories and their placement in the newspaper were those of Gene Curtis. He "put the paper to bed" in the wee hours of the morning, an awesome responsibility that he carried almost routinely.

I kid Gene that the chairman of World Publishing Co. – whom Gene also broke in as a reporter – picked Gene to do the Centennial series because Gene was around at statehood.

In fact, the assignment required someone who was a student of Oklahoma history, a bearcat of a researcher, an excellent writer and above all, one who had a great nose for news.

Gene Curtis, newspaperman.

He belongs in his own series.

Bassett had many friends - and foes

Commissioner of Charities and Corrections Mabel Bassett was a favorite with Oklahoma voters – she was elected six times, frequently getting the most votes of any candidate in any race.

But she wasn't a favorite with some of the state's elected officials.

During her 24 years in office, she fought politicians of every rank, including many governors, for what she believed was right and peeked into every orphanage, jail, prison or other institution whenever a tale of abuse or neglect was heard.

Her popularity with voters was most evident in the 1930 runoff election when she carried 76 of the state's 77 counties – the most of any candidate.

Bassett had no power; all she could do was investigate and make reports that frequently resulted in big headlines in state newspapers that politicians didn't like to see. Those headlines and news stories called attention to the deficiencies she had discovered in her inspections. But that was enough; whatever problem she had reported usually was corrected – rapidly.

Mostly, it wasn't necessary to ask Bassett to investigate an institution. All a person with a complaint had to do was threaten to write her a letter.

"Her tongue was her sword and she knew how to swing it," a political observer said in 1977.

Bassett was defeated for re-election to a seventh term in 1946 when former Highway Patrol Trooper Buck Cook won the post. Bassett, as usual, had led the field of candidates in the primary election with a vote of 122,000 to 33,000 for Cook but didn't have a clear majority. With the support of jailers and police officers who were tired of Bassett's investigations, Cook won the runoff with a vote of 175,000 to 146,000.

When Buck Cook retired after holding the office for 20 years, Rep. Jim Cook of Latimer County took advantage of the similarity of names and won the office handily. But Oklahoma voters in 1975 approved a constitutional amendment that abolished the office effective at the end of that term of office. Jim Cook resigned with two years left on his term, and Gov. David Boren appointed Hugo newspaper publisher Jack Stamper to serve the remaining two years before the office became defunct in January 1977.

Meanwhile, Bassett had made an unsuccessful race in

Tulsa World archives

Despite having no formal powers as state commissioner of charities and corrections, Mabel Bassett was able to wield great influence.

1937 for Oklahoma's at-large congressional seat, losing to famous-name candidate Will Rogers, a Moore school teacher, and tried to win the charities office back from Buck Cook in 1950 – her last political effort.

Bassett frequently raised the ire of public officials, once including Ed Lantz, superintendent of the Tulsa County farm, which she called a "public nuisance" after a 1939 inspection. She gave Tulsa County commissioners 24 hours to remove Lantz with the ultimatum that she would institute court action to have him discharged.

Lantz resigned after ouster charges were filed against him by County Attorney Dixie Gilmer.

"There are very unsanitary conditions throughout the home," Bassett said. "The kitchen is dirty, the rooms adjoining are filthy, the plumbing is in terrible condition and the odors and stench are nauseating."

All of Oklahoma's counties formerly operated "poor farms" to house indigents. Most, including Tulsa County, began selling the farms in the 1960s and providing other facilities. Part of LaFortune Park is located on the former Tulsa County poor farm site east of Yale Avenue on 51st Street.

Bassett also was the target of an investigation in 1939 when state Budget Officer R.R. Owen obtained affidavits from several hotels that she did not stay at the hotels although she filed claims with the state for compensation.

Bassett admitted filing the false claims. She said she frequently drove home at night after an investigation or stayed with friends but filed claims for staying at the hotels anyway, using the money to buy stamps for her office. She said her budget had been cut so drastically she couldn't buy postage stamps. No charges were ever filed against her for the hotel caper.

A native of Chicago, Bassett was married at 16. She and her husband, railroad conductor Joseph Bassett, came to Sapulpa, I.T., in 1902 and she got her first experience with charities and corrections there. The state's first humane society was organized in Creek County in 1910, and Bassett headed the organization.

Among her later accomplishments was a statute making wife and child desertion a felony, the establishment of a state pardon and parole board and a building for women prisoners at the Oklahoma State Penitentiary in McAlester.

Spectacular fires struck the same day

Two of Tulsa's most spectacular fires hit the city within 15 minutes of each other in bitterly cold weather that hampered firefighters' efforts to control the blazes.

The temperature was 4 degrees the morning of Dec. 19, 1945, causing water to freeze on the coats of firemen fighting the fires.

The fire at Renberg's clothing store, 311 S. Main St., was reported at 6:51 a.m., and at the Barnes-Manley laundry, 538 S. Victor Ave., at 7:06 a.m.

The bitter temperature froze all but one of the fire hydrants near the laundry, further hampering the firemen's battle there. The only injuries to firemen were facial "burns" from freezing wind and water.

Two people were hospitalized because of smoke inhalation at the laundry fire, but they were not seriously injured.

Sam Renberg, 71, the founder of the store, died a month after the fire. His death was blamed on stress from the fire and from recent surgery.

While watching the blaze, he tried to cheer up his two sons, George and Herbert Renberg, telling them, "Somehow we'll re-establish and carry on the Renberg name in the business world – even bigger and better."

Fire Chief C.C. Jennings said all the city's firefighting equipment except one company in Red Fork battled the blazes. The two fires caused what was called the city's largest single-day loss up to that time. Early estimates placed the damage at $1 million – in 1945 dollars.

Fire Marshal George Askew at first said explosions probably caused both fires – accumulated gas at the laundry and heat pressure at the clothing store. He said a heater could have been left on overnight in Renberg's, causing a heat buildup that may have broken an upstairs window and

Tulsa World archives

The Dec. 19, 1945, fire at Renberg's clothing store was one of two spectacular fires that morning.

caused a sudden rush of oxygen into the store.

Fire investigators later said the Renberg's fire originated around the gas heating system and had burned for hours before it was discovered. The flames apparently had spread through ventilation shafts in the building.

Askew said there was no explosion although many spectators "thought there was an explosion when the roof caved in."

The laundry fire was blamed on a boiler explosion.

Clarke's Clothiers, next door to Renberg's, and other nearby stores were damaged from water used to fight the blaze. Some floors of the National Bank of Commerce also had damage.

The only thing left at the laundry was a tall smokestack. The Tulsa Boys Home issued a plea for assistance because clothing for the 46 boys of the home and bedding were destroyed in the fire. The boys home had its own laundry facilities but had sent its laundry to Barnes-Manley because of illness of employees.

Renberg's rented temporary offices in the Philtower Building and opened a temporary store at 14 E. Third Street seven months after the fire – in keeping with Sam Renberg's statement to reporters the day after the fires: "The store will open as soon as possible. We do not know how or where, but we are not out of business," he said.

The store moved into a new building on its original site in August 1947.

That fire was the second at that location. An earlier blaze had destroyed the Bass Furniture store at that address in 1914.

The laundry also rebuilt and reopened 11 months after the fire, but neither firm is in business today.

Dunjee fought for racial equality

"No one is denied constitutional rights in Oklahoma," Gov. Leon C. Phillips claimed in 1941 after the newly organized Oklahoma Federation for Constitutional Rights began an investigation of discrimination.

He said the organization and its investigation were the "height of folly."

But Roscoe Dunjee, the black publisher of a newspaper in Oklahoma City, disagreed and responded with one of his fiery editorials, citing court cases and the efforts of the National Association for the Advancement of Colored People that had been fighting for racial equality for decades.

Dunjee also had personal experience that he cited: "On every train and bus in Oklahoma, this writer and all Negroes in Oklahoma are denied civil rights.

"Can the governor observe denial of Negroes to Pullman and chaircar accommodations on railroads and then, like Pontius Pilate, wash his hands, saying no one is denied constitutional rights in Oklahoma?"

It was typical of Dunjee's editorials that helped build a national reputation for the newspaper he started in 1915. At the same time, Dunjee's editorials often drew epithets of "Communist" from legislators and complaints from other blacks who feared his tactics might be damaging to the civil rights cause.

Dunjee was undaunted. He continued writing his fiery editorials and his newspaper's circulation grew to 26,000. As blacks moved from Oklahoma City to other parts of the country, they continued their subscriptions and shared their newspapers with others, who also subscribed.

He also was critical of blacks who did not vote or participate in politics. In 1920, he wrote "the most disgusting and senseless Negro that we know is the fellow who stands around and says 'Oh, I never vote; I'm not registered' and who always slurs and tells you that the Negro who is active in politics in the community is selling you out and should not be trusted."

Dunjee was born in 1883 in Harper's Ferry, W. Va., where his father, John William Dunjee, an escaped slave and a Baptist minister, published the Harper's Ferry Messenger and helped establish several black educational institutions.

When the senior Dunjee was appointed general missionary of Oklahoma by the American Baptist Home Missionary Society in 1892, the family came to Oklahoma Territory

Roscoe Dunjee, publisher of the Black Dispatch, was a key figure in Oklahoma's civil rights history.

and lived in a dugout at Choctaw. The elder Dunjee died 10 years later, leaving Roscoe to support his mother, sister and brother by raising and selling vegetables.

Roscoe Dunjee had attended a one-room country school and had finished a year at the elementary department of Oklahoma Colored Agricultural and Normal University (now Langston University) where he studied printing but otherwise was self-taught by reading extensively from the 1,500-volume library he inherited from his father.

He bought a small printing shop in Oklahoma City and in 1915 started his weekly newspaper, the Black Dispatch, to serve about 7,000 blacks in Oklahoma City. From the beginning, he wrote editorials about racism and tried to instill pride in black heritage.

The newspaper's logo was a locomotive with four passenger cars named Faith, Light, Truth and Progress and included a black angel blowing a horn labeled "Onward to the Heights."

Because of financial problems, Dunjee sold the newspaper in 1955 to a nephew who published it until 1982, when it folded.

In addition to his fiery desegregation editorials, Dunjee also was involved in many organizations. He helped organize the Oklahoma chapter of the NAACP shortly after the national organization was started in Illinois in 1910.

He joined with Clara Luper's NAACP youth group in 1958 in the nation's first sit-in and backed Ada Lois Sipuel Fisher in her integration fight at the University of Oklahoma.

You can't really talk about desegregation in Oklahoma without talking about Roscoe Dunjee, said John H.L. Thompson, a history professor at Oklahoma Christian University, in 1998.

Thompson wrote his doctoral dissertation, "The Little Caesar of Civil Rights: Roscoe Dunjee in Oklahoma City, 1915-1955," on Dunjee's life and fight for desegregation.

In his eulogy at Dunjee's funeral in 1965, Chief Justice Thurgood Marshall said "Roscoe Dunjee gave us the inspiration to get the job done. He didn't wait for anybody else."

Marshall also revealed that Dunjee paid for most of the NAACP's litigation in Oklahoma.

"Roscoe could have been the wealthiest man in the world but he never wanted anything for himself," Marshall said. "He wanted for his people."

Craftsman's masterpiece stands tall

When he retired in 1937, Ed Galloway began working on a project on his property near Foyil. The result: the world's largest totem pole.

It took him 11 years, 28 tons of cement, six tons of steel and 100 tons of sand and rock to create the 90-foot totem, which sits in a nine-acre park. Thousands of visitors have come to see it.

After completing his work, Galloway told a reporter, "It represents absolutely nothing."

Galloway's admiration of American Indians is reflected in the pole, which displays 200 carved figures, including 9-foot images of Geronimo (Apache), Sitting Bull (Sioux), Chief Joseph (Nez Perce) and a Comanche chief at the top. Also on the huge tower are faces of warriors and chiefs, thunderbirds, fish, lizards, owls and an eagle.

The pole is the most striking feature of Galloway's Totem Pole Park, on Oklahoma 28-A between old U.S. 66 and the Will Rogers Turnpike.

Galloway's main love was wood carving. He carved about 300 violins out of various woods from around the world over 40 years and built an 11-sided "fiddle house" for them. It is supported inside and out by concrete totem poles.

It also features bas-relief portraits with various kinds of inlaid wood of every U.S. president up to John F. Kennedy. To obtain different skin tones, he used different kinds of wood instead of paint.

Most of the fiddles were stolen after Galloway's death in 1962. The fiddle house now displays about 135.

The stolen violins were never recovered.

Galloway liked to make violins because they were difficult. A woman at the Totem Park said he always asked friends who were going on trips to bring him samples of wood, which he would use in his violins and other carvings.

Tulsa World archives

Totem Pole Park, featuring Ed Galloway's 90-foot totem pole, is listed on the National Register of Historic Places.

She said he also played the violin, as did his brother.

Galloway was born in Springfield, Mo. Although he had only an eighth-grade education, he earned national recognition as a folk artist.

He began wood carving after his discharge from the Army following his service in the Spanish-American War.

At first, he sold his work at a small shop in Springfield. He later worked for the railroad near Bushyhead, where he met Villie Hooten, who became his wife.

Galloway taught woodworking at the Sand Springs Home from 1911 to 1936. He made furniture for the home and taught craftsmanship to its boys. During summers, he took the boys camping on his 20 acres near Foyil, where they helped gather many of the rocks he used to build a house and the totem pole.

The pole and other parts of the park deteriorated after Galloway's death, but they were restored by the Rogers County Historical Society, which worked with the Kansas Grass Roots Art Association and the Foyil Heritage Association.

The Galloway family donated the original 1½ acres for the park, and the Rogers County Historical Society bought an additional 7½ acres.

Totem Pole Park has been featured in several books and articles on American folk art. In 1999, the park and Galloway's work were listed on the National Register of Historic Places.

The park offers tapes in which Galloway explains his sculptures to visitors walking through and looking at what have been called good examples of environmental folk art. It has a picnic area and a gift shop.

"Be sure to work on your imagination," Galloway advises on a tape his son made. "If you want to carve something, turn around and look at it this way and that way. Then carve it."

State got Capitol dome 85 years late

Oklahoma Historical Society

Oklahoma's state Capitol remained domeless for its first 85 years, as it appeared here in the 1920s. The building received its dome in 2002.

Oklahoma's Capitol was finally capped in 2002 – 85 years after the building was completed without a dome because the funds could be used better elsewhere and one of the architects said a dome would serve no useful purpose.

The state saved $200,000 during the 1914-17 construction by not putting a dome on the $1.5 million six-story building.

When a dome was added in 2002, the cost was $21 million.

There were at least a half dozen efforts to add a dome over the years, but all were doomed until 2000 when Gov. Frank Keating decided to use $5 million of a $156 million state capital improvement bond issue toward adding a dome.

Earlier proposals included such ideas as an office tower atop the building, a revolving dome with a restaurant inside and an inflatable dome. One group called DOMERS – dedicated Oklahomans Marshaling Excellence and Rallying Spirit – old granite blocks for $750 each to pave an area at the south entrance of the building with proceeds to go to a dome that the group estimated would cost $7.5 million.

Keating's plan was the first to propose the use of private funds coupled with state money, and the first to raise funds.

He said construction of a dome would make the statements that "Oklahoma is here to stay," that the state "has enormous pride" and that "the private sector is driving the project."

Keating raised more than $15 million from the private sector and the new dome was dedicated on Statehood Day 2002 to mark the beginning of the Centennial Countdown, a series of events, activities and improvements leading up to the 100th anniversary of Oklahoma on Nov. 16, 2007.

The 1998 Legislature had created the Oklahoma Centennial Act that formed the Oklahoma Capitol Complex and the Oklahoma Centennial Commission which, led by Keating, immediately began efforts to raise funds for the dome.

The dome was doomed in 1914 plans drawn by architects Solomon Layton and Wemyss Smith of Oklahoma City. Steve Douglas of Ardmore, a member of the State Capitol Commission, was an avowed opponent of a dome.

At least one member of the commission wanted a dome then.

"The dome would serve no useful purpose, its only object being to add to the majesticlike appearance of the building," the architects reported.

The architects and the Capitol commission said the money could be used "to a better advantage in some other way."

Regardless of their beliefs, the architects designed the building to accommodate a dome.

In their 1914 report to the commission, the architects wrote that they had designed a building with the "dignity required for our state and at the same time if a future legislature desires, a dome could be added without disturbing any of the internal arrangements."

Because the Capitol was designed for a dome, there was no need to strengthen the building when work began on the dome. Capitol architect Paul Meyer said structural inspections and core drilling tested the stability of the substrata and the go-ahead was given for construction.

Construction required removing a 2-million-pound saucer dome that left a 60-foot hole in the roof. A temporary building was constructed on top of the Capitol's roof to keep out water during installation of the 5-million-pound dome. The temporary building also housed construction platforms needed to build the dome.

Designers built an outer dome with an inner dome about 30 feet below it. The outer dome is strong and durable; the inner dome is decorative. Ten-foot-long rods were installed at the four corners of the building to ground the structure and the Guardian, a 22-foot tall bronze sculpture of an American Indian at the top of the dome, in case of lightning strikes.

The sculpture was made by former state Sen. Enoch Kelly Haney, who later became chief of the Seminole Nation.

A 2000 Tulsa World editorial said the dome should be a great source of state pride.

"There is something to be said for showing that as a state we can finish what we started."

Even after 85 years.

Hyechka club's work music to Tulsa's ears

Tulsa still had dirt streets in 1904 when a small group of women organized a club with a Creek Indian name "to start the cultural growth of Tulsa" along with its material growth.

They called the organization the Hyechka club, a Creek word meaning music. Now the oldest music organization in the state, it is still going strong. The club presented a free Oklahoma centennial concert in November 2007 at All Souls Unitarian Church.

The late Alice Mary Robertson, Oklahoma's first congresswoman, once said the Hyechka club was "helping to build the very soul of Tulsa," a comment that is still valid.

All of the 10 women who met in an upstairs room over the Sells Drug Store at 110 S. Main St. were musicians or music lovers. But they didn't want their club to be just a "ladies' club" whose members sipped lemonade and played for their own amusement. They wanted to have an influence on the community of about 3,500.

At that first meeting, club members elected Jane Heard Clinton, wife of Dr. Fred S. Clinton, as president and re-elected her every year until 1921 when she was named president for life. She died in 1945 at the age of 70.

Susanne Barnett Strouvelle, a Creek and the foster daughter of Alice Robertson, chose the name Hyechka.

From the beginning, Hyechka's primary goal was promoting musical activities and appreciation. But the members also supported all kinds of civic projects through the years.

They supported bond issues, beginning with one for $100,000 in 1912 to build Tulsa's Convention Hall, now known as Brady Theater. During World War I, they knitted sweaters, scarves and other garments, and made hospital gowns and surgical dressings for use by doughboys.

And during World War II, they donated 600 phonograph records and four pianos to Camp Gruber and a piano to the Naval Air Station at Norman – in addition to helping the war effort by buying war bonds. The club received a commen-

Oklahoma Historical Society

Jane Clinton was a founder and longtime president of the Hyechka club, which was formed in 1904. In the Creek language, hyechka means music.

dation because each of its 400 members bought $500 worth of bonds.

Club members were responsible for getting music added to the curriculum taught in Tulsa Public Schools.

For several decades, the club annually bought shoes for schoolchildren whose parents couldn't afford them and for many years held annual "Belles and Beaux" concerts for older people that featured music of their generations.

Throughout its first 100-plus years, Hyechka has presented musical programs featuring its members but also has brought to Tulsa great performers, such as Victor Herbert and his orchestra, violinist Fritz Kreisler, conductor Arturo Toscanini, the New York Symphony Orchestra, for six consecutive years the Chicago Civic Opera, the Von Trapp family singers and many others.

One of the early artists brought to Tulsa by Hyechka was world-renowned contralto Mme. Ernestine Schumann-Heink – although the singer was a bit reluctant to come.

Mme. Schumann-Heink was invited to perform in Tulsa in 1908 after Jane Clinton read that she was to appear in Muskogee. The famous singer responded that she doubted the little town could afford her $1,000 fee.

According to "Wherever You Go," a biography of Jane Clinton by Cecile Davis Richards, Dr. Clinton rode to Muskogee and personally gave the singer $1,000 to ensure her appearance in Tulsa.

She had such a good reception, she later referred to Tulsa as "that city beautiful," according to Richards, a grandniece of Jane Clinton.

Writing in the Tulsa World in 1941, Jane Clinton said Hyechka "has kept up the standards for the best in music and with the cooperation of members and the support of friends has brought the great for Tulsa and Oklahoma City to enjoy."

Legion post named for heroic Tulsans

Army Sgt. Joe Carson of Tulsa and two other doughboys were killed by machine gun fire as they tried to tear through a barbed wire barricade protecting a German machine gun during a World War I battle.

"It was about as hopeless as rising from a prone position into the whirling steel blades of an airplane propeller," Carson's commanding officer recalled years later.

Carson and his two fellow soldiers silenced that machine gun but fell to the murderous fire from other nearby guns.

Many may not have heard of Joseph Carson, the hero who gave his life to save his fellow soldiers in that 1918 battle that left more than 100 members of his company dead. But they have probably heard of the Carson- Wilson-Rigney-Forrester Post No. 1 of the American Legion.

That long name honors the memory of Carson and three other Tulsa heroes who died protecting America's freedom – Alexander Wilson Jr. in World War II; Keith Belvin Rigney in the Korean conflict; and Jordan Duayne Forrester in the Vietnam war.

When it was organized on May 21, 1919, it was called the Joe Carson Post. Wilson's name was added in 1947; Rigney's and Forrester's in 1983.

The group's mission in 1919 – and today – was to take care of veterans, their widows and their children.

The post offers many services, as do other American Legion posts and the national organization, for the benefit of veterans and the country.

The post sponsors Boys State, scholarship programs, a baseball program and a children's home in Ponca City that houses more than 50 children. About 60 percent of the major league baseball players started in the sport through a Legion-sponsored program.

During the Depression, the Carson Post held Christmas tree programs to give toys and candy to "every little boy or girl who might be missed by Santa." The post also provided garden spots and seeds to unemployed veterans so they could grow their own food.

The Tulsa post's headquarters, 1120 E. Eighth St., was financed by oilman-philanthropist Waite Phillips in 1927 on land donated by the city. It has since been remodeled and enlarged from the original 1,700 square feet to 10,000 square feet.

Carson, 21, was a graduate of Central High School and was an accountant before joining the Army in the fall of 1917 along with other Oklahomans who, with a group of Texans, made up the 90th Infantry Division. By the time the division landed in France in June 1918, Carson was a sergeant and had received orders to attend officers training.

Before that training was to begin, his Company D of the 358th Infantry Regiment was involved in the battle that claimed his life on Sept. 26, 1918, in the Argonne Forest. A Distinguished Service Cross was awarded to him posthumously.

Beryl Ford Collection

A vehicle participates in Tulsa's 1949 American Legion parade downtown in this image. The Tulsa Legion post, the oldest and largest in Oklahoma and the oldest continually active post in the country, is co-sponsor with the Veterans of Foreign Wars Post No. 577 of the annual Veterans Day parade.

Wilson was killed in action Nov. 27, 1944, near Aachen, Germany, by machine gun fire while attacking an enemy position. He was firing his rifle and throwing hand grenades, actions that inspired fellow soldiers. The Silver Star, Bronze Star with two Oak Leaf Clusters and the Purple Heart were awarded posthumously to Wilson, a 1940 graduate of Rogers High School.

Wilson's father, Alexander E. Wilson Sr., was a World War I veteran and was a member of the post.

Rigney, 26, served with Gen. George Patton's Third Army in Europe during World War II. He was killed just 11 days after his mother received a letter from him saying he was being sent to the battle area from Japan where he had been stationed for about a year.

"Things are getting hot over here," he wrote. "We're going to Korea for a short time."

Rigney was killed on July 14, 1950, just a few weeks after the war began on June 25, 1950, while serving with the 24th Infantry Division.

Forrester, 19, a paratrooper with the First Cavalry Division, was on a search-and-destroy mission when he encountered hostile action and was killed on Nov. 17, 1965, in Vietnam.

"He was more worried by cobras than by the Viet Cong," his mother, Mrs. Don C. Little, told a Tulsa World reporter in 1965. "God is still with me so there is nothing to worry about," he had written.

The Tulsa Legion Post, the oldest and largest in Oklahoma and the oldest continually active post in the country, is co-sponsor with the Veterans of Foreign Wars Post No. 577 of the annual Veterans Day parade in Tulsa.

It gives citizens a chance to cheer and thank a veteran for their freedom.

Oilman gave money away – secretly

The late James A. Chapman amassed a fabulous fortune in the oil, cattle and banking business that he and his wife, Leta, devoted to philanthropic activities.

Some national magazines reported that he was among the nation's wealthiest men.

When he died in September 1966, Chapman was described as a "millionaire who loved to give away money but hated to get credit for it."

In nearly all of his giving, Chapman made it clear there was to be no publicity, a policy that he was so firm about, the recipients feared they would be cut off if word leaked out. Chapman's friends and business associates were sworn to secrecy about his donations.

"I'm doing this to help people; not for publicity," Chapman frequently told his attorney, the late John Rogers, who had been associated with the philanthropist for more than 50 years when Chapman died. "He wouldn't even let me correct stories that appeared with erroneous information about him," Rogers told a World reporter.

Most Tulsans had never heard of Chapman. Many of those who had heard of him had never seen him or even a picture of him until he died. The picture used with his obituary was taken in 1958, the last photograph of him.

Chapman also was a firm believer in free enterprise and made it clear that if recipients of funds from his foundation eased being private or nonprofit or received funds from government, trustees should cease giving them funds.

A few years before he died, Chapman's wealth was estimated at $75 million by Business Week magazine. In a listing of the country's wealthiest men, Fortune magazine set his worth at between $75 million and $100 million. Others believed it was closer to $200 million.

During their lifetimes, the Chapmans had contributed at least $150 million to religious, educational and health institutions in the region. And their wills left all but small specific bequests to philanthropic foundations. The main recipients were the University of Tulsa, Trinity University at San Antonio, Oklahoma Medical Research Foundation, St. John Medical Center, Hillcrest Medical Center and John Brown University at Siloam Springs, Ark.

When Chapman's estate was being probated, Judge Whit Mauzy questioned Mrs. Chapman about whether she wanted a widow's half share of the estate. She declined.

The will had left Chapman's personal effects to her and specified that further provision was not made for her because she had her separate estate and it was their mutual desire that his estate be devoted to charitable use. Leta's

Tulsa World archives

James A. Chapman amassed an enormous fortune, and gave much of it away.

estate was added to the James A. and Leta Chapman Foundation after her death in 1974.

Chapman and his widow each left $1,000 "as a token of love and affection" to their son, H. Allen Chapman. Allen Chapman, who died in 1979 after also amassing a fortune in the oil business, and his wife, Mary K. Chapman, who died in 2002, continued his parents' pattern of giving, and set up a foundation that was valued at $90 million in a recent federal tax report.

Chapman and his partners, R.M. McFarlin and E.P. Harwell, were successful in oil producing properties in the Glenn, Cushing, Healdton and Augusta, Kan., fields.

Early in the 20th century, Chapman and McFarlin became aware that few banks would lend money for what was considered risky oil development so they and several other oilmen, including Harry Sinclair, organized the Exchange National Bank to meet the needs of the oil industry.

When Chapman died, he was the largest stockholder in the National Bank of Tulsa, successor to Exchange, which today is the Bank of Oklahoma. He also owned large blocs of Mobil, Standard of Indiana, Standard of New Jersey and Continental Oil Co. stock.

Chapman attended few social events because he was allergic to cigarette smoke. He also spent a minimum amount of time in his Tulsa office, preferring to be around one of his oil leases or on his Chapman-Barnard Ranch, which at one time encompassed 70,000 acres and that he owned jointly with H.G. Barnard, his wife's uncle.

The portion of that ranch makes up The Nature Conservancy's Tallgrass Prairie Preserve.

While on his Osage County land, Chapman frequently arose at 4 a.m. to cook flapjacks for ranch employees. It was reported that he liked to be the first one up but didn't want his employees to be far behind.

Chapman enjoyed hard work, spending long days building or repairing fences or tending to his cattle. He believed that hard work was good for people. He also believed in morality and thrift. Despite his wealth, he carried a small notebook and meticulously kept a record of his expenses in it.

In 2007, the TU football stadium, previously known as Skelly, began an $18 million renovation with half the funds contributed by the H.A. and Mary K. Chapman Foundation.

The facility was renamed Skelly Field at Chapman Stadium. Chapman funds also are being used to build a downtown park to be known as the Chapman Centennial Green.

Faith led opera singer into mission

Thousands of homeless Tulsans have had hot meals and slept in warm beds on cold nights and thousands of needy families have received baskets of food or obtained clothes because a singer quit a promising opera career in 1939 to sing for the Lord.

It was a dozen years later when Bob Geisinger arrived in Tulsa to open a mission in a former downtown fish market at 16 S. Boston Ave.

He called it the John 3:16 Mission because, he said, that verse "is the Bible in a nutshell" and "its promise is the true purpose of this mission."

The John 3:16 Mission has expanded and operates an overnight facility for men at 506 N. Cheyenne Ave. and a family and youth center at 2027 N. Cincinnati Ave. But its mission is the same: to meet the physical, spiritual and emotional needs of homeless and at-risk men, women and children.

Between its beginning in the fish market and its present locations, the mission had homes in a building at 521 N. Boulder Ave., which formerly housed the Morningside Hospital, now Hillcrest Medical Center, and later the City-County Health Department; and the old Tulsa Tribune building at Archer Street and Boston Avenue.

Its overnight facility previously was a Salvation Army citadel, and its family center building formerly housed the Cincinnati Avenue Christian Church, which became Sandusky Avenue Christian Church.

It has been the mission's custom to serve Thanksgiving meals, as will several other places.

During 2006, John 3:16 served 168,056 meals, the most in its history, according to the annual report by the Rev. Steve Whitaker, the executive director. It also provided overnight shelter for 38,535 men. It distributed 7,344 grocery baskets and distributed 10,092 articles of clothing, including 1,298 pairs of new blue jeans during a back-to-school event.

It also operates a program to prepare men to obtain jobs or to return to jobs or careers they may have had before becoming homeless.

The mission is a nonprofit organization that is supported solely through private donations and receives no government or United Way funding.

Geisinger was in training to become a singer with the

Tulsa World archives

Bob Geisinger sounds a chord and prepares to lead the singing two weeks after opening the John 3:16 Mission.

Metropolitan Opera in New York City and had sung with some small companies but not the Met when he attended an evangelist's service in 1939.

"My desire was stirred. His lecture on the second coming of Christ brought the word to me," Geisinger told a Tulsa World reporter. "I felt I had to enter the religious field."

The would-be singer told his opera coach the next day that he planned to quit to sing the gospel and was told "you'll never be as happy as with the opera."

But Geisinger said 12 years later that he never regretted the move.

His desire to open a mission began in 1942 while he was working in a mission in Philadelphia. He later worked in missions in Chicago and Kansas City and in northwestern Arkansas before he and his wife and three children arrived in Tulsa.

Geisinger took menial jobs to support his family and opened his mission "on faith" in the former fish market building that had to be scrubbed with lye soap to remove fish scales and a fishy odor.

"All we had was an empty building, a desk, two chairs and a dilapidated three-section screen," Geisinger told a reporter several years later. "But the soul-winning began there with men so drunk they couldn't kneel to pray."

The mission began by serving two meals a day, but Geisinger allowed men to sleep in the mission although there were no bunks. "They slept on benches and on the floor," he said. Several double-deck bunks were added in the basement a few years later.

Geisinger conceded that "many want a free meal or a place to sleep and nothing else," but he always required the men to attend the evening meeting "to feed them spiritually" before feeding them physically.

Geisinger, who resigned from the mission in 1963 and died in 1985, had a trademark of greeting the downtrodden at the door with a handshake. His first questions were: "How about some coffee? Are you hungry? Do you want a hot bath?"

"With a handshake, he finds someone who cares," Geisinger said. "Here is where he can come and hear that God loves him."

Daredevil turns into philanthropist

Oil was not the first love for Walter Helmerich II until after two of his close friends were killed in a plane crash near Enid at the beginning of his aerial stunt team's first performance.

Helmerich, born in Chicago in 1895, was a pilot after enlisting in the Army Signal Corps in 1917 when America entered World War I. He was so skilled that he became an instructor at Fort Sill's Post Field.

When he returned to civilian life after the war, he met and courted a young woman named Cadijah Colcord. The two eloped although her wealthy father, Charles Colcord, who had helped develop the Glenn Pool, had put her off limits to the flying daredevil.

Meanwhile, Helmerich bought three airplanes and led a barnstorming aerial stunt team until that crash during a final test flight before a scheduled performance at the Great Salt Plains west of Enid.

The concern for his safety by his wife and her parents, who finally had accepted the marriage, convinced Helmerich he should give up aerobatic flying and change careers. He went to work in the oil business for his brother-in-law, Ray Colcord.

It was the beginning of a career that resulted in formation of Helmerich & Payne that in 2007 had more than 5,600 employees and assets of $2.6 billion.

And Helmerich became known as one of Tulsa's most respected businessmen, philanthropists, civic leaders and arts patrons.

By 1920, Helmerich had saved enough money to buy a drilling rig and soon teamed up with Bill Payne, who had graduated from Oklahoma A&M College in 1915 with a degree in bacteriology and chemistry and was working as a scout for Colcord's North American Oil and Refining Co.

The science of petroleum geology was still in its infancy and Payne frequently credited success in finding oil to luck. "In the oil business, give me the luck and you can keep the brains," he once said.

Although Payne left the firm in 1936 to organize Big Chief Drilling Co. in Oklahoma City, it continued to bear the name of Helmerich & Payne.

Since the firm was organized, H&P has been one of the best-known diversified energy firms in the world while the family has become known for philanthropic endeavors through the Helmerich Foundation.

The family also has been the subject of interest be-

Tulsa World archives

Walter Helmerich II changed careers from aerobatic flying to the oil business.

cause of the marriage of Walt III to movie actress Peggy Dow in 1951 and his kidnapping in 1974 by a service station equipment supplier who held him until a $700,000 ransom was paid.

Helmerich was driving to his office in June 1974 when Freddie W. Smith, posing as a gas company employee, stopped his car and told him there was a gas leak in the area. He asked Helmerich to turn off his car's ignition to prevent a possible explosion.

When Helmerich did so, the armed kidnapper pushed him over, got in beside him and drove to Utica Square where they changed cars.

Helmerich was blindfolded and held prisoner for eight hours. The ransom was recovered the next day. Smith was arrested and was sentenced to 20 years in prison.

The elder Helmerich, who was called Walt Sr., was known as a wizard in persuading bankers to make loans at crucial times, especially during the lean years of the depression. Admirers always said his reputation for financial integrity was the company's best asset.

But he also could be tough, as witnessed by the time he stormed into the office of a lease owner who had not paid him for drilling a gas well.

The lease owner reportedly rose from his chair to greet Helmerich who reached across the desk and knocked him back to his seat with a punch to the nose.

"Now," Helmerich said, "I'm here to negotiate."

Walt III took over as president on Dec. 1, 1960. He once recalled that "Dad walked in on Dec. 1 and said 'You're president. Good luck.'"

Walt Sr. remained as chairman of the board almost until his death Dec. 19, 1981, at the age of 86. Meanwhile, Walt III became the chief architect of H&P's worldwide operations, real estate dealings and other activities.

The real estate dealings included the purchase in 1964 of Utica Square, which opened in 1952 as Tulsa's first suburban shopping center, although it now is close to the center of the metro area.

After his father died, Walt III sent a note to H&P employees explaining that Walt Sr. was more than just the founder and chairman of the company.

"It was his courage and indomitable strength that built the company; it was his honesty and integrity that became the trademark. Even after his retirement, it was really his inspirational leadership that guided us.'

Mock ceremony unites territories

The date for the "wedding" of Mr. Oklahoma and Miss Indian Territory had arrived and President Theodore Roosevelt was to sign or "shove the quill," in the vernacular of the day, on the proclamation that would make the Oklahoma and Indian territories one state at 9 a.m.

Plans had been made for a big inauguration event at Guthrie, which would be the capital of the new 46th state.

Little formality prevailed in the Cabinet room of the White House, where several Oklahomans, several senators from other states and newspaper reporters assembled as Roosevelt signed the proclamation with a large quill pen from an eagle killed in the Oklahoma Panhandle, blotted his signature and announced "Oklahoma is a state."

Roosevelt was disappointed with the results of the Sept. 16 election at which Haskell defeated Roosevelt's friend, Territorial Governor Frank Frantz. Nevertheless, Roosevelt had let it be known in late September that he would approve the constitution and statehood.

According to a Tulsa World story several years later, as the president laid the blotter aside, Albert Hammer of Enid asked whether he could have it. "I have had more requests for the pen than I have letters in my name," Roosevelt said as he handed the blotter to Hammer.

The pen and the mounted eagle from which it came were presented later to the Oklahoma Historical Society.

But a dispute arose many years later when the Scottish Rite Temple in Guthrie also claimed to have the famous feather pen on display.

The origin of the pen also was disputed – whether it came from Woodward, Osage County or near Watonga.

After Roosevelt signed the document in Washington, a mock wedding ceremony was performed at the library in Guthrie after a symbolic proposal of marriage by Mr. Oklahoma to Miss Indian Territory. A cartoon showing Mr. Oklahoma kissing Miss Indian Territory was printed on the World's Page 1 two days later.

C.J. Jones of Oklahoma City was introduced to the crowd at Guthrie by Judge Frank Dale, chairman of the executive committee of the inaugural celebration, who explained that Jones would propose marriage on behalf of Mr. Oklahoma to Miss Indian Territory.

Oklahoma Historical Society

Oklahoma celebrates statehood and the inauguration of Gov. Charles N. Haskell with a parade in Guthrie on Nov. 16, 1907.

"I have been asked to perform the agreeable duty of proposing the marriage of Oklahoma to the Indian Territory," Jones said.

The proposal was accepted on the part of the blushing bride by W.A. Durant of Durant, who told the crowd, "I present Miss Indian Territory who was reared as a political orphan, tutored by federal office-holders and controlled by an indifferent guardian a thousand miles from her habitation."

And with that, Miss Indian Territory, portrayed by Mrs. Leo Bennett of Muskogee, a Creek Indian, stepped forward. The two stood together and were united in marriage by the Rev. W.H. Dodson of Guthrie.

General celebrations throughout the day were held across the new state. The one in Tulsa began at the stroke of 9 a.m. with the ringing of the fire bell "and before the second stroke was heard, a perfect bedlam of noise broke loose.

"Two mighty engines on the Frisco tracks set forth their shrieking and joined in the clamor which was in progress. Bells of every kind, size and description joined in the din, and naught but the shrieking of whistles and resounding tones of the bells could be heard."

A new flag dotted with 13 stripes and 46 stars was hoisted on the high school's pole. Many created their own new flags by sewing extra stars on them. A crowd had gathered in downtown Tulsa and an impromptu parade began at 1:30 p.m. on Boulder Avenue between Second and Third streets, wending through downtown and ending at the opera house near Second and Frankfort. The parade included the mayor, city council members, two bands, 250 schoolchildren in carriages, labor organizations, members of the Commercial Club and others for a total of about 1,500.

Oklahoma was composed of 69,919 square miles with a population of about 1.5 million, almost double the population of 810,000 recorded in the 1890 census. It would take 75 years for the state's population to double again.

A Tulsa World Page 1 cartoon showed an American Indian looking over an outline of buildings toward the rising sun of a new day dawning. A small seven-column headline proclaimed, "While Tulsa has been 'I.T.' right along there is no reason why she should not continue to hold the same position and be 'it' on an extended scale in the new state."

PHOTO CREDITS

Thanks to the following for contributed photographs:

Andrea Gillman
Beryl Ford Collection
Betty Boyd
Boise City News
Boston Avenue Methodist Church
Broken Arrow Historical Society
Cherokee Strip Museum
Jim Pilkington
Joanne Henthorne Kirlin
Edmond Parks Foundation
Edna Graham
Frederick B. Graves
Holy City of the Wichitas
Mary Skaggs
Nancy Sevenoaks
The Metcalfe Museum
Oklahoma Dental Association
Oklahoma Historical Society
Oklahoma Forest Heritage Center
Oklahoma State Penitentiary
OSU-Okmulgee
Plains Indians and Pioneers Museum
Tewanna Edwards
Thomas Payne
Tulsa Historical Society
Tulsa World archives
University of Tulsa / McFarlin Library
USDA Soil Conservation Service
Valerie Clayton